The Prophets

The Prophets

FORTRESS COMMENTARY ON THE BIBLE
STUDY EDITION

Gale A. Yee

Hugh R. Page Jr.

Matthew J. M. Coomber

Editors

Fortress Press

Minneapolis

THE PROPHETS
Fortress Commentary on the Bible Study Edition

Unless otherwise noted, Scripture quotations are from New Revised Standard Version Bible, copyright © 1989 by the Division of Education of the National Council of Churches of Christ in the United States of America.

Excerpted from the *Fortress Commentary on the Bible: The Old Testament and Apocrypha*
(Minneapolis: Fortress Press, 2014); Gale A. Yee, Hugh R. Page Jr., and Matthew J. M. Coomber, volume editors.

Fortress Press Publication Staff:
Neil Elliott and Scott Tunseth, Project Editors
Marissa Wold, Production Manager
Laurie Ingram, Cover Design.

Copyeditor: Jeffrey A. Reimer

Typesetter: PerfecType, Nashville, TN

Proofreader: David Cottingham

Library of Congress Cataloging-in-Publication data is available

ISBN: 978-1-5064-1585-7

eISBN: 978-1-5064-1586-4

CONTENTS

PUBLISHER'S NOTE

About the Fortress Commentary on the Bible Study Editions

In 2014 Fortress Press released the two-volume *Fortress Commentary on the Bible*. See the Series Introduction (pp. 1–3) for a look inside the creation and design of the Old Testament/Apocrypha and New Testament volumes. While each comprehensive commentary volume can easily be used in classroom settings, we also recognized that dividing the larger commentaries into smaller volumes featuring key sections of Scripture may be especially helpful for use in corresponding biblical studies courses. To help facilitate such classroom use, we have broken the two-volume commentary into eight study editions.

Please note that in this study edition the page numbers match the page numbers of the larger Fortress Commentary on the Bible volume in which it first appeared. We have intentionally retained the same page numbering to facilitate use of the study editions and larger volumes side by side.

The Prophets was first published in Fortress Commentary on the Bible: The Old Testament and Apocrypha.

ABBREVIATIONS

General

AT	Alpha Text (of the Greek text of Esther)
BOI	Book of Isaiah
Chr	Chronicler
DH	Deuteronomistic History
DI	Deutero-Isaiah
Dtr	Deuteronomist
Gk.	Greek
H	Holiness Code
Heb.	Hebrew
JPS	Jewish Publication Society
LXX	The Septuagint
LXX B	Vaticanus Text of the Septuagint
MP	Mode of production
MT	Masoretic Text
NIV	New International Version
NRSV	New Revised Standard Version
OAN	Oracles against Nations (in Jeremiah)
P.	papyrus/papyri
P	Priestly source
PE	Pastoral Epistles
RSV	Revised Standard Version
TI	Trito-Isaiah

Books of the Bible (NT, OT, Apocrypha)

Old Testament/Hebrew Bible

Gen.	Genesis
Exod.	Exodus
Lev.	Leviticus
Num.	Numbers
Deut.	Deuteronomy

Josh.	Joshua
Judg.	Judges
Ruth	Ruth
1 Sam.	1 Samuel
2 Sam.	2 Samuel
1 Kgs.	1 Kings
2 Kgs.	2 Kings
1 Chron.	1 Chronicles
2 Chron.	2 Chronicles
Ezra	Ezra
Neh.	Nehemiah
Esther	Esther
Job	Job
Ps. (Pss.)	Psalms
Prov.	Proverbs
Eccles.	Ecclesiastes
Song.	Song of Songs
Isa.	Isaiah
Jer.	Jeremiah
Lam.	Lamentations
Ezek.	Ezekiel
Dan.	Daniel
Hosea	Hosea
Joel	Joel
Amos	Amos
Obad.	Obadiah
Jon.	Jonah
Mic.	Micah
Nah.	Nahum
Hab.	Habakkuk
Zeph.	Zephaniah
Hag.	Haggai
Zech.	Zechariah
Mal.	Malachi

Apocrypha

Tob.	Tobit
Jth.	Judith
Gk. Esther	Greek Additions to Esther
Sir.	Sirach (Ecclesiasticus)

Bar.	Baruch
Let. Jer.	Letter of Jeremiah
Add Dan.	Additions to Daniel
Pr. Azar.	Prayer of Azariah
Sg. Three.	Song of the Three Young Men (or Three Jews)
Sus.	Susanna
Bel	Bel and the Dragon
1 Macc.	1 Maccabees
2 Macc.	2 Maccabees
1 Esd.	1 Esdras
Pr. of Man.	Prayer of Manasseh
2 Esd.	2 Esdras
Wis.	Wisdom of Solomon
3 Macc.	3 Maccabees
4 Macc.	4 Maccabees

New Testament

Matt.	Matthew
Mark	Mark
Luke	Luke
John	John
Acts	Acts of the Apostles
Rom.	Romans
1 Cor.	1 Corinthians
2 Cor.	2 Corinthians
Gal.	Galatians
Eph.	Ephesians
Phil.	Philippians
Col.	Colossians
1 Thess.	1 Thessalonians
2 Thess.	2 Thessalonians
1 Tim.	1 Timothy
2 Tim.	2 Timothy
Titus	Titus
Philem.	Philemon
Heb.	Hebrews
James	James
1 Pet.	1 Peter
2 Pet.	2 Peter
1 John	1 John

2 John	2 John
3 John	3 John
Jude	Jude
Rev.	Revelation (Apocalypse)

Journals, Series, Reference Works

ABD	*Anchor Bible Dictionary*. Edited by David Noel Freedman. 6 vols. New York: Doubleday, 1992.
ACNT	Augsburg Commentaries on the New Testament
AJA	*American Journal of Archaeology*
AJT	*Asia Journal of Theology*
ANET	*Ancient Near Eastern Texts Relating to the Old Testament*. Edited by J. B. Pritchard. 3rd ed. Princeton: Princeton University Press, 1969.
ANF	*The Ante-Nicene Fathers*. Edited by Alexander Roberts and James Donaldson. 1885–1887. 10 vols. Repr., Peabody, MA: Hendrickson, 1994.
ANRW	*Aufstieg und Niedergang der römischen Welt: Geschichte und Kultur Roms im Spiegel der neueren Forschung*. Edited by Hildegard Temporini and Wolfgang Haase. Berlin: de Gruyter, 1972–.
ANTC	Abingdon New Testament Commentaries
AOAT	Alter Orient und Altes Testament
AbOTC	Abingdon Old Testament Commentary
AOTC	Apollos Old Testament Commentary
A(Y)B	Anchor (Yale) Bible
BA	*Biblical Archaeologist*
BAR	*Biblical Archaeology Review*
BDAG	Bauer, W., F. W. Danker, W. F. Arndt, and F. W. Gingrich. *Greek-English Lexicon of the New Testament and Other Early Christian Literature*. 3rd ed. Chicago: University of Chicago Press, 1999.
BEATAJ	Beiträge zur Erforschung des Alten Testaments und des Antiken Judentum
Bib	*Biblica*
BibInt	*Biblical Interpretation*
BJRL	*Bulletin of the John Rylands University Library of Manchester*
BJS	Brown Judaic Studies
BNTC	Black's New Testament Commentaries
BR	*Biblical Research*
BRev	*Bible Review*
BSac	*Bibliotheca sacra*
BTB	*Biblical Theology Bulletin*
BZAW	Beihefte zur Zeitschrift für die alttestamentliche Wissenschaft
CAT	Commentaire de l'Ancien Testament

CBC	Cambridge Bible Commentary
CBQMS	Catholic Biblical Quarterly Monograph Series
CC	Continental Commentaries
CH	*Church History*
CHJ	*Cambridge History of Judaism*. Edited by W. D. Davies and Louis Finkelstein. Cambridge: Cambridge University Press, 1984–.
ConBNT	Coniectanea biblica: New Testament Series
ConBOT	Coniectanea biblica: Old Testament Series
CS	Cistercian Studies
CTAED	*Canaanite Toponyms in Ancient Egyptian Documents*. S. Ahituv. Jerusalem: Magnes, 1984.
CTQ	*Concordia Theological Quarterly*
CurTM	*Currents in Theology and Mission*
ExpTim	*Expository Times*
ETL	*Ephemerides Theologicae Lovanienses*
ExAud	*Ex auditu*
FAT	Forschungen zum Alten Testament
FC	Fathers of the Church
FRLANT	Forschungen zur Religion und Literatur des Alten und Neuen Testaments
HAT	Handbuch zum Alten Testament
HBT	*Horizons in Biblical Theology*
HNTC	Harper's New Testament Commentaries
HR	*History of Religions*
HSM	Harvard Semitic Monographs
HTKAT	Herders Theologischer Kommentar zum Alten Testament
HTR	*Harvard Theological Review*
HTS	Harvard Theological Studies
HUCA	*Hebrew Union College Annual*
HUCM	Monographs of the Hebrew Union College
HUT	Hermeneutische Untersuchungen zur Theologie
IBC	Interpretation: A Bible Commentary for Teaching and Preaching
ICC	International Critical Commentary
Int	*Interpretation*
JAAR	*Journal of the American Academy of Religion*
JAOS	*Journal of the American Oriental Society*
JBL	*Journal of Biblical Literature*
JBQ	*Jewish Bible Quarterly*
JECS	*Journal of Early Christian Studies*
JJS	*Journal of Jewish Studies*
JNES	*Journal of Near Eastern Studies*

JNSL	*Journal of Northwest Semitic Languages*
JQR	*Jewish Quarterly Review*
JRS	*Journal of Roman Studies*
JSem	*Journal of Semitics*
JSJ	*Journal for the Study of Judaism in the Persian, Hellenistic, and Roman Periods*
JSNT	*Journal for the Study of the New Testament*
JSOT	*Journal for the Study of the Old Testament*
JSOTSup	Journal for the Study of the Old Testament Supplement Series
JSQ	*Jewish Studies Quarterly*
JSS	*Journal of Semitic Studies*
JTI	*Journal of Theological Interpretation*
JTS	*Journal of Theological Studies*
JTSA	*Journal of Theology for Southern Africa*
KTU	*Die keilalphabetischen Texte aus Ugarit*. Edited by M. Dietrich, O. Loretz, and J. Sanmartín. AOAT 24/1. Neukirchen-Vluyn: Neukirchener, 1976.
LCC	Loeb Classical Library
LEC	Library of Early Christianity
LHB/OTS	Library of the Hebrew Bible/Old Testament Studies
LW	*Luther's Works*. Edited by Jaroslav Pelikan and Helmut T. Lehmann. 55 vols. St. Louis: Concordia; Philadelphia: Fortress Press, 1958–1986.
NAC	New American Commentary
NCB	New Century Bible
NCBC	New Cambridge Bible Commentary
NedTT	*Nederlands theologisch tijdschrift*
Neot	*Neotestamentica*
NICNT	New International Commentary on the New Testament
NICOT	New International Commentary on the Old Testament
NIGTC	New International Greek Testament Commentary
NovT	*Novum Testamentum*
NPNF[1]	*The Nicene and Post-Nicene Fathers*, Series 1. Edited by Philip Schaff. 14 vols. 1886–1889. Repr., Grand Rapids: Eerdmans, 1956.
NTL	New Testament Library
NTS	*New Testament Studies*
OBT	Overtures to Biblical Theology
OTE	*Old Testament Essays*
OTG	Old Testament Guides
OTL	Old Testament Library
OTM	Old Testament Message
PEQ	*Palestine Exploration Quarterly*
PG	Patrologia graeca [= Patrologiae cursus completus: Series graeca]. Edited by J.-P. Migne. 162 vols. Paris, 1857–1886.

PL	John Milton, *Paradise Lost*
PL	Patrologia latina [= Patrologiae cursus completus: Series latina]. Edited by J.-P. Migne. 217 vols. Paris, 1844–1864.
PRSt	*Perspectives in Religious Studies*
QR	*Quarterly Review*
RevExp	*Review and Expositor*
RevQ	*Revue de Qumran*
SBLABS	Society of Biblical Literature Archaeology and Biblical Studies
SBLAIL	Society of Biblical Literature Ancient Israel and Its Literature
SBLDS	Society of Biblical Literature Dissertation Series
SBLEJL	Society of Biblical Literature Early Judaism and Its Literature
SBLMS	Society of Biblical Literature Monograph Series
SBLRBS	Society of Biblical Literature Resources for Biblical Study
SBLSCS	Society of Biblical Literature Septuagint and Cognate Studies
SBLSP	*Society of Biblical Literature Seminar Papers*
SBLSymS	Society of Biblical Literature Symposium Series
SBLWAW	SBL Writings from the Ancient World
SemeiaSt	Semeia Studies
SJT	*Scottish Journal of Theology*
SNTSMS	Society for New Testament Studies Monograph Series
SO	Symbolae osloenses
SR	*Studies in Religion*
ST	*Studia Theologica*
StABH	Studies in American Biblical Hermeneutics
TD	*Theology Digest*
TAD	*Textbook of Aramaic Documents from Ancient Egypt.* Vol. 1: *Letters.* Bezalel Porten and Ada Yardeni. Winona Lake, IN: Eisenbrauns, 1986.
TDOT	*Theological Dictionary of the Old Testament.* 15 vols. Edited by G. Johannes Botterweck, Helmer Ringgren, and Heinz-Josef Fabry. Translated by David E. Green and Douglas W. Stott. Grand Rapids: Eerdmans, 1974–1995.
TJT	*Toronto Journal of Theology*
TNTC	Tyndale New Testament Commentaries
TOTC	Tyndale Old Testament Commentaries
TS	*Theological Studies*
TZ	*Theologische Zeitschrift*
VE	*Vox evangelica*
VT	*Vetus Testamentum*
VTSup	Supplements to Vetus Testamentum
WBC	Word Biblical Commentary
WSA	Works of St. Augustine: A Translation for the Twenty-First Century
WUANT	Wissenschaftliche Untersuchungen zum Alten und Neuen Testament

WUNT	Wissenschaftliche Untersuchungen zum Neuen Testament
WW	*Word and World*
ZAW	*Zeitschrift für die alttestamentliche Wissenschaft*
ZBK	Zürcher Bibelkommentare
ZNW	*Zeitschrift für die neutestamentliche Wissenschaft und die Kunde der älteren Kirche*

Ancient Authors and Texts

1 Clem.	*1 Clement*
2 Clem.	*2 Clement*
1 En.	*1 Enoch*
2 Bar.	*2 Baruch*
Abot R. Nat.	*Abot de Rabbi Nathan*
Ambrose	
Paen.	*De paenitentia*
Aristotle	
Ath. Pol.	*Athēnaīn politeia*
Nic. Eth.	*Nicomachean Ethics*
Pol.	*Politics*
Rhet.	*Rhetoric*
Augustine	
FC 79	*Tractates on the Gospel of John, 11–27.* Translated by John W. Rettig. Fathers of the Church 79. Washington, DC: Catholic University of America Press, 1988.
Tract. Ev. Jo.	*In Evangelium Johannis tractatus*
Bede, Venerable	
CS 117	*Commentary on the Acts of the Apostles.* Translated by Lawrence T. Martin. Cistercian Studies 117. Kalamazoo, MI: Cistercian Publications, 1989.
Barn.	*Barnabas*
CD	Cairo Genizah copy of the Damascus Document
Cicero	
De or.	*De oratore*
Tusc.	*Tusculanae disputationes*
Clement of Alexandria	
Paed.	*Paedogogus*
Strom.	*Stromata*
Cyril of Jerusalem	
Cat. Lect.	*Catechetical Lectures*
Dio Cassius	
Hist.	*Roman History*

Dio Chrysostom
    Or.   *Orations*
Diog. Diognetus
Dionysius of Halicarnassus
    Thuc.   *De Thucydide*
Epictetus
    Diatr.   *Diatribai (Dissertationes)*
    Ench.   *Enchiridion*
Epiphanius
    Pan.   *Panarion (Adversus Haereses)*
Eusebius of Caesarea
    Hist. eccl.   *Historia ecclesiastica*
Gos. Thom.   *Gospel of Thomas*
Herodotus
    Hist.   *Historiae*
Hermas, *Shepherd*
    Mand.   *Mandates*
    Sim.   *Similitudes*
Homer
    Il.   *Iliad*
    Od.   *Odyssey*
Ignatius of Antioch
    Eph.   *To the Ephesians*
    Smyr.   *To the Smyrnaeans*
Irenaeus
    Adv. haer.   *Adversus haereses*
Jerome
    Vir. ill.   *De viris illustribus*
John Chrysostom
    Hom. 1 Cor.   *Homiliae in epistulam i ad Corinthios*
    Hom. Act.   *Homiliae in Acta apostolorum*
    Hom. Heb.   *Homiliae in epistulam ad Hebraeos*
Josephus
    Ant.   *Jewish Antiquities*
    Ag. Ap.   *Against Apion*
    J.W.   *Jewish War*
Jub.   *Jubilees*
Justin Martyr
    Dial.   *Dialogue with Trypho*
    1 Apol.   *First Apology*

L.A.E.	*Life of Adam and Eve*	
Liv. Pro.	*Lives of the Prophets*	
Lucian		
Alex.	*Alexander (Pseudomantis)*	
Phal.	*Phalaris*	
Mart. Pol.	*Martyrdom of Polycarp*	
Novatian		
Trin.	*De trinitate*	
Origen		
C. Cels.	*Contra Celsum*	
Comm. Jo.	*Commentarii in evangelium Joannis*	
De princ.	*De principiis*	
Hom. Exod.	*Homiliae in Exodum*	
Hom. Jer.	*Homiliae in Jeremiam*	
Hom. Josh.	*Homilies on Joshua*	
Pausanias		
Descr.	*Description of Greece*	
Philo		
Cher.	*De cherubim*	
Decal.	*De decalogo*	
Dreams	*On Dreams*	
Embassy	*On the Embassy to Gaius (= Legat.)*	
Fug.	*De fuga et inventione*	
Leg.	*Legum allegoriae*	
Legat.	*Legatio ad Gaium*	
Migr.	*De migratione Abrahami*	
Mos.	*De vita Mosis*	
Opif.	*De opificio mundi*	
Post.	*De posteritate Caini*	
Prob.	*Quod omnis probus liber sit*	
QE	*Quaestiones et solutiones in Exodum*	
QG	*Quaestiones et solutiones in Genesin*	
Spec. Laws	*On the Special Laws*	
Plato		
Gorg.	*Gorgias*	
Plutarch		
Mor.	*Moralia*	
Mulier. virt.	*Mulierum virtutes*	
Polycarp		
Phil.	*To the Philippians*	

Ps.-Clem. Rec.	*Pseudo-Clementine Recognitions*
Pss. Sol.	*Psalms of Solomon*
Pseudo-Philo	
L.A.B.	*Liber antiquitatum biblicarum*
Seneca	
Ben.	*De beneficiis*
Strabo	
Geog.	*Geographica*
Tatian	
Ad gr.	*Oratio ad Graecos*
Tertullian	
Praescr.	*De praescriptione haereticorum*
Prax.	*Adversus Praxean*
Bapt.	*De baptismo*
De an.	*De anima*
Pud.	*De pudicitia*
Virg.	*De virginibus velandis*
Virgil	
Aen.	*Aeneid*
Xenophon	
Oec.	*Oeconomicus*

Mishnah, Talmud, Targum

b. B. Bat.	*Babylonian Talmudic tractate Baba Batra*
b. Ber.	*Babylonian Talmudic tractate Berakhot*
b Erub.	*Babylonian Talmudic tractate Erubim*
b. Ketub.	*Babylonian Talmudic tractate Ketubbot*
b. Mak.	*Babylonian Talmudic tractate Makkot*
b. Meg.	*Babylonian Talmudic tractate Megillah*
b. Ned.	*Babylonian Talmudic tractate Nedarim*
b. Naz.	*Babylonian Talmudic tractate Nazir*
b. Sanh.	*Babylonian Talmudic tractate Sanhedrin*
b. Shab.	*Babylonian Talmudic tractate Shabbat*
b. Sotah	*Babylonian Talmudic tractate Sotah*
b. Ta'an.	*Babylonian Talmudic tractate Ta'anit*
b. Yev.	*Babylonian Talmudic tractate Yevamot*
b. Yoma	*Babylonian Talmudic tractate Yoma*
Eccl. Rab.	*Ecclesiastes Rabbah*
Exod. Rab.	*Exodus Rabbah*
Gen. Rab.	*Genesis Rabbah*

Lam. Rab.	*Lamentations Rabbah*
Lev. R(ab).	*Leviticus Rabbah*
m. Abot	*Mishnah tractate Abot*
m. Bik.	*Mishnah tractate Bikkurim*
m. Demai	*Mishnah tractate Demai*
m. 'Ed.	*Mishnah tractate 'Eduyyot*
m. Git.	*Mishnah tractate Gittin*
m. Pesah	*Mishnah tractate Pesahim*
m. Šeqal.	*Mishnah tractate Šeqalim (Shekalim)*
m. Shab.	*Mishnah tractate Shabbat*
m. Sotah	*Mishnah tractate Sotah*
m. Ta'an.	*Mishnah tractate Ta'anit*
m. Tamid	*Mishnah tractate Tamid*
m. Yad.	*Mishnah tractate Yadayim*
m. Yebam.	*Mishnah tractate Yebamot*
m. Yoma	*Mishnah tractate Yoma*
Num. Rab.	*Numbers Rabbah*
Pesiq. Rab.	*Pesiqta Rabbati*
Pesiq. Rab Kah.	*Pesiqta Rab Kahana*
S. 'Olam Rab.	*Seder 'Olam Rabbah*
Song Rab.	*Song of Songs Rabbah*
t. Hul.	*Tosefta tractate Hullin*
Tg. Onq.	*Targum Onqelos*
Tg. Jer.	*Targum Jeremiah*
y. Hag.	*Jerusalem Talmudic tractate Hagiga*
y. Pesah	*Jerusalem Talmudic tractate Pesahim*
y. Sanh.	*Jerusalem Talmudic tractate Sanhedrin*

Dead Sea Scrolls

1QapGen	*Genesis apocryphon* (Excavated frags. from cave)
1QM	*War Scroll*
1QpHab	*Pesher Habakkuk*
1QS	*Rule of the Community*
1QSb	*Rule of the Blessings* (Appendix b to 1QS)
1Q21	*T. Levi*, aramaic
4Q184	Wiles of the Wicked Woman
4Q214	Levi[d] ar (*olim* part of Levi[b])
4Q214b	Levi[f] ar (*olim* part of Levi[b])
4Q226	psJub[b] (4Q *pseudo-Jubilees*)
4Q274	Tohorot A

4Q277	Tohorot B[b] (*olim* B[c])
4Q525	*Beatitudes*
4QMMT	*Miqsat Ma'aśê ha-Torah*
4QpNah/4Q169	4Q Pesher Nahum
4Q82	*The Greek Minor Prophets Scroll*

Old Testament Pseudepigrapha

1 En.	*1 Enoch*
2 En.	*2 Enoch*
Odes Sol.	*Odes of Solomon*
Syr. Men.	*Sentences of the Syriac Menander*
T. Levi	*Testament of Levi*
T. Mos.	*Testament of Moses*
T. Sim.	*Testament of Simeon*

INTRODUCTION

The *Fortress Commentary on the Bible*, presented in two volumes, seeks to invite study and conversation about an ancient text that is both complex and compelling. As biblical scholars, we wish students of the Bible to gain a respect for the antiquity and cultural remoteness of the biblical texts and to grapple for themselves with the variety of their possible meanings; to fathom a long history of interpretation in which the Bible has been wielded for causes both beneficial and harmful; and to develop their own skills and voices as responsible interpreters, aware of their own social locations in relationships of privilege and power. With this in mind, the *Fortress Commentary on the Bible* offers general readers an informed and accessible resource for understanding the biblical writings in their ancient contexts; for recognizing how the texts have come down to us through the mediation of different interpretive traditions; and for engaging current discussion of the Bible's sometimes perplexing, sometimes ambivalent, but always influential legacy in the contemporary world. The commentary is designed not only to inform but also to invite and empower readers as active interpreters of the Bible in their own right.

The editors and contributors to these volumes are scholars and teachers who are committed to helping students engage the Bible in the classroom. Many also work as leaders, both lay and ordained, in religious communities, and wish this commentary to prove useful for informing congregational life in clear, meaningful, and respectful ways. We also understand the work of biblical interpretation as a responsibility far wider than the bounds of any religious community. In this regard, we participate in many and diverse identities and social locations, yet we all are conscious of reading, studying, and hearing the Bible today as citizens of a complex and interconnected world. We recognize in the Bible one of the most important legacies of human culture; its historical and literary interpretation is of profound interest to religious and nonreligious peoples alike.

Often, the academic interpretation of the Bible has moved from close study of the remote ancient world to the rarefied controversy of scholarly debate, with only occasional attention to the ways biblical texts are actually heard and lived out in the world around us. The commentary seeks to provide students with diverse materials on the ways in which these texts have been interpreted through the course of history, as well as helping students understand the texts' relevance for today's globalized world. It recognizes the complexities that are involved with being an engaged reader of the Bible, providing a powerful tool for exploring the Bible's multilayered meanings in both their ancient and modern contexts. The commentary seeks to address contemporary issues that are raised by biblical passages. It aspires to be keenly aware of how the contemporary world and its issues and perspectives influence the interpretation of the Bible. Many of the most important insights of contemporary biblical scholarship not only have come from expertise in the world of antiquity but have also been forged in modern struggles for dignity, for equality, for sheer survival, and out of respect for those who have died without seeing justice done. Gaining familiarity with the original contexts in which the biblical writings were produced is essential, but not sufficient, for encouraging competent and discerning interpretation of the Bible's themes today.

Inside the Commentary

Both volumes of *The Fortress Commentary on the Bible* are organized in a similar way. In the beginning of each volume, **Topical Articles** set the stage on which interpretation takes place, naming the issues and concerns that have shaped historical and theological scholarship down to the present. Articles in the *Fortress Commentary on the Old Testament* attend, for example, to the issues that arise when two different religious communities claim the same body of writings as their Scripture, though interpreting those writings quite differently. Articles in the *Fortress Commentary on the New Testament* address the consequences of Christianity's historic claim to appropriate Jewish Scripture and to supplement it with a second collection of writings, the experience of rootlessness and diaspora, and the legacy of apocalypticism. Articles in both volumes reflect on the historical intertwining of Christianity with imperial and colonial power and with indexes of racial and socioeconomic privilege.

Section Introductions in the Old Testament volume provide background to the writings included in the Torah, Historical Writings, Wisdom, Prophetic Writings, and a general introduction to the Apocrypha. The New Testament volume includes articles introducing the Gospels, Acts, the letters associated with Paul, and Hebrews, the General Epistles and Revelation. These articles will address the literary and historical matters, as well as theological themes, that the books in these collections hold in common.

Commentary Entries present accessible and judicious discussion of each biblical book, beginning with an introduction to current thinking regarding the writing's original context and its significance in different reading communities down to the present day. A three-level commentary then follows for each sense division of the book. In some cases, these follow the chapter divisions of a biblical book, but more often, contributors have discerned other outlines, depending on matters of genre, movement, or argument.

The three levels of commentary are the most distinctive organizational feature of these volumes. The first level, "The Text in Its Ancient Context," addresses relevant lexical, exegetical, and literary aspects of the text, along with cultural and archaeological information that may provide additional insight into the historical context. This level of the commentary describes consensus views where these exist in current scholarship and introduces issues of debate clearly and fairly. Our intent here is to convey some sense of the historical and cultural distance between the text's original context and the contemporary reader.

The second level, "The Text in the Interpretive Tradition," discusses themes including Jewish and Christian tradition as well as other religious, literary, and artistic traditions where the biblical texts have attracted interest. This level is shaped by our conviction that we do not apprehend these texts immediately or innocently; rather, even the plain meaning we may regard as self-evident may have been shaped by centuries of appropriation and argument to which we are heirs.

The third level, "The Text in Contemporary Discussion," follows the history of interpretation into the present, drawing brief attention to a range of issues. Our aim here is not to deliver a single answer—"what the text means"—to the contemporary reader, but to highlight unique challenges and interpretive questions. We pay special attention to occasions of dissonance: aspects of the text or of its interpretation that have become questionable, injurious, or even intolerable to some readers today. Our goal is not to provoke a referendum on the value of the text but to stimulate reflection and discussion and, in this way, to empower the reader to reach his or her own judgments about the text.

The approach of this commentary articulates a particular understanding of the work of responsible biblical interpretation. We seek through this commentary to promote intelligent and mature engagement with the Bible, in religious communities and in academic classrooms alike, among pastors, theologians, and ethicists, but also and especially among nonspecialists. Our work together has given us a new appreciation for the vocation of the biblical scholar, as custodians of a treasure of accumulated wisdom from our predecessors; as stewards at a table to which an ever-expanding circle is invited; as neighbors and fellow citizens called to common cause, regardless of our different professions of faith. If the result of our work here is increased curiosity about the Bible, new questions about its import, and new occasions for mutual understanding among its readers, our work will be a success.

Fortress Commentary on the Old Testament

Gale A. Yee
Episcopal Divinity School

Hugh R. Page Jr.
University of Notre Dame

Matthew J. M. Coomber
St. Ambrose University

Fortress Commentary on the New Testament

Margaret Aymer
Interdenominational Theological Center

Cynthia Briggs Kittredge
Seminary of the Southwest

David A. Sánchez
Loyola Marymount University

READING THE OLD TESTAMENT IN ANCIENT AND CONTEMPORARY CONTEXTS

Matthew J. M. Coomber

As students file into their desks on the first day of my "Introduction to the Old Testament" course, they are greeted with a PowerPoint slide that simply states, in bold red letters, "Caution: Dangerous Texts Ahead!" The students often respond with the mixture of chuckles and uneasy looks that I intend to provoke. To some extent, the slide is offered tongue in cheek, but not entirely. As with any wry statement, the cautionary slide holds an element of truth. The Old Testament contains powerful teachings and radical ideas that have moved the hearts and minds of both adherents and skeptics for millennia.

While the texts of the Old Testament have had a profound effect on societies and cultures for a long span of time, their texts often take a back seat to the Gospels and the Pauline Letters in popular Christian religion. Even though they constitute well over half of the content of Christian Bibles, very few of my students claim to have read much—if any—of the Old Testament or Apocrypha, despite the fact that I teach at a Roman Catholic university in which the vast majority of the students are Christian. In fact, only a handful of my students claim to have been exposed to the stories of the Old Testament outside of either Sunday school or in episodes of the popular cartoon series *Veggie Tales*. Due to this lack of exposure to the Old Testament, I feel compelled to give them fair warning about what they have gotten themselves into by signing up for what may seem like an innocuous required course. I take it as a professional responsibility to alert them to the fact that a keen examination of the ancient Near Eastern library that sits on their desks has the power to change their lives and forever alter the ways in which they experience the world.

Any collection of books containing calls to wage wars of conquest, to resist the temptation to fight while under threat, thoughts on God's role in governance, and meditations on what it means to live *the good life* has the potential to change lives and even inspire revolutions. To assume that the Bible is harmless is both foolish and irresponsible. After all, the Old Testament's contents have been used by some to support slavery and genocide while inspiring others to engage in such dangerous pursuits as enduring imprisonment, torture, and death in attempts to liberate the oppressed. And just as with using any powerful instrument, be it a car or a surgical blade, reading the Old Testament demands care, responsibility, and substantial consideration from those who put it to use.

Books that promote powerful ideas are complex tools that often belong to the readers as much as—if not more than—their authors. The level of consideration required to read, interpret, and actualize such books is magnified when approaching ancient texts such as those found in the Old Testament. These biblical books bridge multiple theological, cultural, and linguistic worlds, which demand multiple levels of understanding and interpretation. Readers must inhabit three worlds (contexts) when reading any of the books of the Old Testament or Apocrypha, from Genesis to 4 Maccabees: (1) the ancient contexts in which they were written, (2) the modern contexts into which the text is being received, and (3) all of those contexts in between wherein interpreters in each generation have shaped the reading of the texts for their own time and place. *The Fortress Commentary on the Bible: The Old Testament and Apocrypha* approaches these ancient texts with due reverence to this complexity. The purpose of this introduction is to explore a few of the many considerations that are required in reading this ancient Near Eastern scriptural library in its ancient and modern contexts.

A Few Considerations on Receiving Ancient Texts with Modern Minds

The word *context*, whether pertaining to events or a book, looks deceptively singular. A student trying to uncover the context of the US civil rights movement will find many contextual viewing points: those of African Americans who rose up against institutionalized oppression, those of segregationists who tried to maintain the status quo, those within the Johnson administration who worked to find a way forward without losing the Democrats' white voters in the South, and the list goes on.

Challenge of Finding an Ancient or Modern Context

The words *ancient context* and *modern context*, when applied to the Old Testament, also need to be considered in the plural. Considering the ancient context, the books of the Old Testament contain the theologies of diverse communities who lived, wrote, argued, and worked to understand their relationship with the divine under a wide variety of circumstances. An attempt to find a single context for the book of Isaiah, for example, is as complex as finding a single sociohistorical setting of the United States, from the colonial period to the present; it cannot be done. The same is true with the modern context. As these religious texts are received in Chicago or Mumbai, on Wall Street or on skid row, they flow into and take on very different meanings and contexts.

Differing Expectations and Intents of Ancient and Modern Histories

Readers in the age of science have certain expectations when reading a history, and these expectations inform how histories—whether written before or after this age—are received. Modern readers want to know, with scientific precision, when, why, and where events happened. Great value is placed on reconstructions of events that are backed up by reliable sources and with as little interpretive bias as possible. A *good* history of the Battle of the Bulge should include not only dates and locations but also eyewitness accounts of allied forces, Wehrmacht and SS divisions, and civilians. Expectations of accuracy and value in objectivity are a service both to the study of the past and to understanding how these events helped to shape the present. However, when dealing with the Old Testament it is easy to project our appreciation for accuracy and disdain for bias onto the ancient texts, which ultimately is not a fair way to approach these ancient texts.

Long before there was even a concept of "Bible," many of the texts of the Old Testament were passed down through oral tradition, only to be written down and finally canonized centuries later; this is evidenced in the repetitive Torah narratives, such as the creation refrain in Gen. 1:1—2:4a and the lyrical hymn of Deborah in Judges 5. To imagine the original texts as printed, bound, copyrighted, and collected works, as we hold them today, is both inaccurate and misleading. Moreover, assuming the intents and expectations of the oral historian to be akin to those of modern historians is misleading, and focusing on accuracy can limit the scope of a passage's message when the intent of the passage rests in the ideas it promotes. Cultures that employ oral tradition do not make dates, places, or accuracy a priority; rather, they are interested in the telling and retelling of a story to develop an understanding or identity that can answer the questions of the times into which they are received. Take the account of King Solomon's wealth in 2 Chron. 9:22-24, for example.

> King Solomon surpassed all the kings of the earth in wealth and wisdom. All the kings of the earth came to pay homage to Solomon and to listen to the wisdom with which God had endowed him. Each brought his tribute—silver and gold objects, robes, weapons, and spices, horses and mules—in the amount due each year (JPS).

Such an account served a purpose to the ancient author and his audience, but the account was certainly not accurate. Putting aside the issue of transoceanic travel for contemporary rulers in the Americas or the South Pacific, Israel held no such wealth in the tenth century BCE, and such superpowers as Egypt and Assyria would never have been compelled to offer tribute. While questions surrounding the reality of Solomon's wealth are not a center of contentious debate in the public sphere, questions pertaining to the creation of the universe are highly controversial; the front lines of this debate can be seen at the doors of the Creation Museum in Petersburg, Kentucky.

Founded by Ken Ham and Answers in Genesis (AiG), a Christian apologetics organization, the Creation Museum is a prime example of how scientific-age expectations are frequently placed on the ancient texts of the Old Testament. With the motto "Prepare to Believe," the museum promotes Gen. 1:1—2:4a as a scientific explanation for the creation of the cosmos, an event that is said to have occurred around 4,000 BCE, as determined through James Ussher's seventeenth-century-CE biblically based calculations. It is important to consider that the questions the Creation Museum seeks to answer do not likely match the agenda of the authors of Gen. 1:1—2:4a, which is connected to the Babylonian myth the *Enuma Elish* and/or the battle between the Canaanite god Baal and Yam, each of which centers on order's conquest of chaos. It also does not take into consideration that those who canonized the Torah followed this story with another creation story (Gen. 2:4b-25), which is juxtaposed with the first, making it unlikely that the ancient intent was to give a *scientific* account of our origins. Furthermore, the authors of the texts believed that the sky was a firmament that held back a great sky-ocean (Gen. 1:6-8), from which precipitation came when its doors were opened, and that the moon was self-illuminating (Gen. 1:14-18). A key danger in treating Old Testament books with modern historical and scientific expectations is not only receiving inaccurate messages about our past but also failing to realize the intent of the authors and the depth of meaning behind the messages they conveyed.

Projecting Modern Contexts onto the Ancient Past

The oft-repeated notion that only the winners write history is not entirely true, for readers rewrite the histories they receive by projecting their own personal and cultural perspectives onto them. The medievalist Norman Cantor stresses how individuals tend to project their own worldviews and experiences onto the past, thereby reinventing the past in their own image (156–58). Whereas Cantor dealt with issues of secular history, biblical history appears to follow suit, as found in such art pieces as Dutch painter Gerard van Honthorst's piece *King David Playing the Harp*. In the painting van Honthorst depicts the king with European-style attire and instrument. In contextually ambiguous passages, such as the land seizures in Mic. 2:1-4, we find scholars filling in the blanks with characters that make more sense in our time than in the ancient past, such as the mafia (Alfaro, 25). It is difficult for a reader not to project his or her own time and culture onto the text, for that is the reader's primary reference point; to escape doing so is likely not possible. But just as complete objectivity is not attainable, an awareness of its hazards can help readers exercise some degree of control regarding how much they project their present onto the past.

Bringing One's Ideology to the Text

Just as readers bring their notions of history to the Old Testament, so also they bring their ideologies. While attempts to view Old Testament texts through the biblical authors' eyes may be made, one's perceptions can never be entirely freed from one's own experiences, which help shape how a particular idea or story is read. This challenge is a double-edged sword. On one side of the sword, the ideology and experiences of the reader may cloud the text's original meaning and intent, causing unintended—and sometimes intentional—misreadings of a passage. When this occurs, the resulting interpretation often tells us more about the social or ideological location of the reader than the biblical characters who are being interpreted. Albert Schweitzer found that nineteenth-century biographies on the life of the "historical Jesus" turned out to be autobiographies of their authors; romantics uncovered an idealist Jesus, political radicals found a revolutionary, and so on (Schweitzer). On the other side of the sword, one finds an advantage shared by oral tradition. Reading a text through one's own experiences can breathe new life into the text and allow it to speak to current circumstances, as found in postcolonial, feminist, and queer interpretations. Since readers cannot fully remove themselves from their own ideological locations, it is important to acknowledge that a reader's ideas and biases are brought to the text and that much is to be learned by considering various interpretations.

Because ideology plays a role in interpretation, it should be noted that history—and biblical histories, in particular—do not exist in the past, but are very much alive and active in the present. YHWH's granting of land to Abraham's dependents, for example, plays a prominent role in the Israel-Palestine conflict. This is addressed by Keith Whitelam and James Crossley, who find the biblical text shaping modern perceptions of land via cartography. A post-1967 war edition of *The Macmillan Bible Atlas* contains a map of Israel with borders that look remarkably similar to the modern-day border with Gaza—despite great uncertainty surrounding ancient Israel's borders— and that is inscribed with Gen. 13:14-15: "The LORD said to Abram . . . 'Lift up your eyes, and look from the place where you are, northward and southward and eastward and westward; for all the land which you see I will give to you and to your descendants forever'" (RSV; see Whitelam 61–62; Crossley 176). Whether one sees this connection in a positive or negative light, clear political implications of the biblical past can be seen.

Differing Views on the Old Testament's History

Another factor to be considered, which is also highly political, is the lack of consensus pertaining to the historicity of biblical narratives and the state of ancient Israel, ranging from the exodus narrative to the Davidic monarchy. The degree to which these events and histories are *real histories* or *cultural memory* has been the subject of much debate and polemic within the academy. Many scholars agree that the story of the Hebrew exodus out of Egypt is cultural memory, with varying degrees of historical truth, ranging from seeing the Hebrews as an invading force to an indigenous movement within Canaan that rose up against exploitative rulers. But one of the most heated debates in the history of ancient Israel has revolved around the dating of the monarchy and the rise of Judah as a powerful state.

The traditional view, often referred to as the *maximalist* perspective, gives greater credence to the Bible's account of the monarchy's history. Scholars of this persuasion accept, to varying degrees, the Old Testament's stories of the rise of Israel beginning with King Saul and continuing on through the destruction of Israel and Judah. So-called *minimalists* give less credence to biblical accounts, relying more on archaeological and extrabiblical sources to develop their views of the monarchy and the presence of a powerful state, for which they find little evidence. While largely unnoticed outside the academy, the debate has caused great animosity within. Maximalist scholars have been accused of burdening archaeology with the task of upholding the biblical narratives (Davies), while minimalists have been accused of attempting to erase ancient Israel from world history (Halpern).

The purpose of addressing the maximalist/minimalist debate in this introduction is to emphasize that biblical scholarship contains diverse voices and points of view on the Bible's history, which will be seen in the commentaries of this volume. It is good that these different perspectives are aired. When approaching an area of history that is of such great importance to so many, yet with so little definitive information available, it is important to articulate and compare different ideas so as to produce and refine the historical possibilities of the Bible's contexts. In this way we see how differing views of biblical interpretation can work as a dance, where partners can complement each other's work, even if tempers can flare sometimes when partners step on one another's toes.

Reading the Old Testament in Its Ancient Context

It is apparent that contemplating the ancient contexts of the Old Testament requires several areas of consideration. While there is no end to the complexities involved with pursuing a greater understating of the world(s) out of which the books of the Old Testament developed, this section is intended to draw the reader's attention to some of the Old Testament's physical environments, political climates, and theological diversity.

Physical Environments of the Old Testament

The geography and ecology of ancient Palestine can easily be overlooked, but their value for understanding the Old Testament should not be underestimated. While the Old Testament represents diverse social settings that span hundreds of years, all of its authors lived in agrarian societies where land, climate, economics, and religion are inseparable. Due to agrarian societies' dire need to ensure successful and regular harvests—whether for survival or with the additional aspiration of building empire—farming practices become incorporated into religious rituals that end up dictating planting, harvesting, and land management. This strong connection between faith and farming led to rituals that served as an interface between spirituality and socioeconomic activities, effectively erasing the lines between religious and economic practice (Coomber 2013). In the end, the ritualization of agrarian economics helps shape perceptions of the deity or deities to which the rituals are connected: the Feast of Unleavened Bread (Exod. 23:14-17), the barley harvest festival incorporated in the Passover feast (Exodus 12; cf. John 19:29, the wheat-harvest Feast of Weeks, also known as Pentecost (Lev. 23:15-21; cf. Acts 2:1), and the fruit-harvest Feast of Booths (Lev. 23:33-36). Thus geography and ecology affected not only the way ancient Hebrews farmed but also how they came to understand God. Moreover, the geographical regions in which many of them farmed influenced these understandings.

Regions of Ancient Israel

Ancient Israel can be divided into a number of geographical areas, each of which presents its own unique environment. Furthest to the west is the *coastal plain*, which held great economic importance in the way of trade. This is especially visible in the development of manufacturing and shipping cities such as Ekron and Ashkelon. Due to the region's trade potential, it was usually controlled by foreign powers and is not frequently mentioned in the Old Testament (e.g., Judges 16; 2 Kings 16; Jer. 25:20; Amos 1:8; Zeph. 2:4).

The lowland *Shephelah* and the *highlands* are just east of the coastal plain, forming an important region of Israel, which is at the center of most of the Old Testament's stories. This fertile land, composed of low hills and valleys, is good for animal husbandry and the cultivation of grains, cereals, nuts, olives, and grapes. These areas were valuable for both subsistence farming and the production of trade goods, in which surrounding empires could engage. The agrarian potential of this area also made Shephelah and the highlands a target for foreign invasion. This region's political influence was heightened by the cities of Jerusalem, Samaria, and Lachish.

The *Jordan Valley*, east of the highlands, contains the lowest natural surface in the world and is part of a fault that extends into Africa. The valley follows the Jordan River from the city of Dan through the city of Hazor and the Sea of Galilee before flowing into the Dead Sea. Aside from the important role that the Jordan Valley plays in Ezekiel's vision of water flowing out of the temple to bring life to the Dead Sea (Ezekiel 47), the region is rarely mentioned.

To the east of the Jordan Valley is the *Transjordan highlands*, which is often referred to as "beyond the Jordan" (e.g., Josh. 12:1). Extending from the Dead Sea's altitude of 650-feet below sea level to the 9,230-foot peak of Mt. Hermon, this region contains a diverse range of topography and climates that allow for the cultivation of diverse agricultural goods, including grains, fruits, timber, and livestock. The agrarian potential of the area attracted a number of peoples, including the Moabites, the Ammonites, and the Edomites.

Whether valued for their sustaining, trade, or defensive capabilities, the topography of ancient Israel and its surrounding lands influenced its inhabitants' ability or inability to find sustenance and pursue their own interests. When empires such as Assyria and Babylon were on the rise, this region attracted their rulers who sought the earning potential of the land, and these events—or the cultural memories they inspired—influenced the Old Testament authors' stories of defeat and are reflected in their perceptions of God's attitudes toward them.

Climatic Challenges

While the land in and around Israel was some of the most sought after in the ancient Near East, its inhabitants endured serious meteorological challenges. The ancient Israelites lived at the crossroads of subtropical and temperate atmospheric patterns—producing rainy winter seasons and dry summers—and the effects of these patterns shaped the ways in which the Hebrews lived: the resulting erratic precipitation patterns result in a 30 percent chance of insufficient rainfall (Karmon, 27). The unpredictability of each growing season's weather pattern meant that the rainfall of a given season could play out in any number of ways, each demanding specific farming strategies for which farmers had little foresight or room for error. Subsequent failed seasons that diminished surpluses could lead to debt and the selling of family members into slavery or even the extinction of a family line.

Everything in society—from the interests of the poorest farmer to the king—depended on successful harvests and access to their crops, and the strong desire for divine assistance is reflected in Old Testament narratives that emphasize fidelity to YHWH. The seriousness placed on securing favorable rainfall and accessing harvests is clear in warnings against following other deities, such as the weather god Baal (e.g., Judg. 2:11; 2 Kings 3:2; Ps. 106:28; Hosea 9:10), God-given visions that foretell rainfall (Genesis 41), and the granting and withholding of rain as reward or punishment (Deut. 11:11-14; cf. 1 Kings 17–18). Additionally, there are strict rules to protect land access (Leviticus 25) and condemnation against abuses (1 Kings 21; Isa. 5:8-10; Mic. 2:1-4).

The physical environments of the Old Testament authors are an important consideration, because they not only affected the way the authors lived but also helped to shape their views of God and the world around them. From the development of the ancient Hebrews' religious rituals to finding either God's favor or wrath in agrarian events (see Zech. 10:1; 1 Kings 17–18), the topography and climatic environments that affected cultivation played key roles in how the biblical authors perceived and interacted with the divine.

Sociopolitical Contexts of the Old Testament

In addition to the challenges presented by Israel's geographic and climatic setting, its strategic location between the empires of Mesopotamia and northern Africa presented a recurring threat. As these empires invaded the lands of ancient Israel for military and economic reasons, the biblical authors and redactors received and transmitted these events into their religious narratives: foreign invasion was often perceived as divine punishment—with the notable exception of the Persians—and the defeat of foreign forces was perceived as a result of divine favor. Before addressing foreign influences on the Old Testament's ancient contexts, a brief overview of Israel's domestic structures should be considered.

Israel's Domestic Sociopolitical Contexts

While ancient Palestine's Mesopotamian neighbors developed cities and urban economies in the Early Bronze Age (3300–2100 BCE), Palestine largely remained a patchwork of scattered settlements that functioned as a peripheral economy, engaging in trade activity as neighboring empires made it lucrative, and receding into highland agriculture when those powers waned (Coomber 2010, 81–92). Adapting to the demands of waxing and waning empires—rather than taking significant steps toward powerful urban economies of its own—resulted in a marked reliance on subsistence strategies on into the seventh century BCE (Coote and Whitelam).

Biblical accounts of Hebrew societal structures present a patronage system that had its roots in small family units called the *bet av* ("father's house"), which together formed a *mishpahah* ("family" or "clan"), which expanded up to the tribe, or *shevet*. When the monarchy was established, the *malkut* ("kingdom") became the top rung. While the *malkut* and *shevet* held the top two tiers, the phrase "all politics is local" applies to ancient Israel: loyalty structures were strongest at the bottom.

Philip Davies and John Rogerson note that the *bet av*, "father's house," likely had a double meaning (32). While it indicated a family unit that included extended lineage and slaves—excluding daughters who left the family at marriage—it likely also denoted the descendants of a common ancestor, who may not have lived under a single roof (e.g., Gen. 24:38). While the *bet avim* grew through the births of sons and the accumulation of wives and slaves, the danger of collapse due to disease, war, and a lack of birth of sons presented a constant threat. Debt was also a threat to a *bet av*, inspiring legal texts that protected its access to arable land (Leviticus 25; Deut. 25:5). It was the patriarch's responsibility to care for the family's economic well-being, as well as to pass on traditions, the history of the nation, and the laws of God (Deut. 6:7; 11:8-9; 32:46-47). The *bet av* also had power over such judicial matters as those of marriage and slave ownership.

Mishpahah denotes a level of organization based on a recognizable kinship (Numbers 1; 26). It had territorial significance, as seen in tribal border lists of Joshua 13–19, and was responsible for dividing the land. While *mishpahah* is difficult to translate, Norman Gottwald offers the useful definition, "protective association of extended families" (Gottwald 1999, 257). If the immediate or extended families of a citizen who had to sell himself to an alien could not redeem him, the *mishpahah* became the last line of protection from perpetual servitude (Lev. 25:48-49).

Shevet refers to the largest group and unit of territorial organization, which was primarily bound together by residence. Military allegiances appear to have belonged to this level, against both foreign and domestic threats—as seen in the Benjamite battles of Judges 12 and 20–21. Gottwald sees the *shevet* as more of a geographic designation pertaining to clusters of villages and/or clans that gathered for protective purposes rather than as representative bodies within a political system (Gottwald 2001, 35).

The *malkut*, or kingdom, is a source of continued contention in the so-called minimalist/maximalist debate mentioned above. The Old Testament account claims that the kingdom of Israel was founded when Saul became king over the Israelite tribes (1 Samuel 9) and continued through the line of David, after Saul fell out of favor with God. Israel's united monarchy is reported to have spanned 1030 to 930 BCE, when King Rehoboam was rejected by the northern Israelites (1 Kgs. 12:1-20; 2 Chron. 10:1-19), leading to the period of the divided monarchy, with Israel in the north and Judah in the south. These two kingdoms existed side by side until Israel was destroyed by Assyria (734–721 BCE). Judah entered into Assyrian vassalage in the 720s and was destroyed by the Babylonians around 586 BCE. Those who give less credence to the biblical account take note that there is little extrabiblical evidence of a monarchy prior to King Omri, aside from the Tel Dan Stele, which refers to "the House of David," which may refer to a king.

While Israel's domestic organizational landscape played a major role in the development of biblical law and narrative, the biblical authors' interactions with surrounding peoples had profound effects on the stories they told. The main imperial influences, from the premonarchical period to the fall of the Hasmonean Dynasty, were Egypt, Philistine, Assyria, Babylon, Persia, the Greeks, and the Romans.

Israel's Foreign Sociopolitical Contexts

The Egyptian Empire played an important role in the development of the Torah, as seen in the stories of Abram and Sarai (Genesis 12), Joseph (Genesis 37–50), and throughout the entire exodus narrative, interwoven into many areas of the Old Testament. The authors of Exodus used the backdrop of Egypt's powerful *New Kingdom* (1549–1069 BCE) to display their faith in YHWH's power, and other books draw on this narrative as a recurring reminder of the Israelites' debt and obligations toward their god (e.g. Deut. 5:15, 24:17-22, 23:7-8; Ps. 106:21; Ezekiel 20; Amos 2:10; Mic. 6:4), and as a vehicle of praise (Psalms 78; 81; 135; 136). The Jewish holiday of Passover, which is referred to throughout the Old Testament, has its roots in this anti-Egyptian epic. A later and weaker Egypt returns to play a role in the story of Judah's lengthy downfall: King Hezekiah (d. 680s) enters into a failed anti-Assyrian alliance with Egypt (Isaiah 30–31; 36:6-9), and King Zedekiah (d. 580s) enters into a failed anti-Babylonian alliance with Pharaoh Hophra (Ezek. 17:15; Jer. 2:36).

While their point of origins are in dispute (Amos 9:7 puts their origin at Caphtor), the Philistines tried to invade Egypt in 1190 BCE, but were repelled by Ramses III, who settled them in the coastal towns of Gaza, Ashkelon, and Ashdod (Deut. 2:23). From there, they continued their incursions along the coastal plain and perhaps even drove out their Egyptian rulers, under the reign of Ramses IV (d. 1149 BCE). They play a key adversarial role in the book of Judges, as found in the stories of Shamgar (Judg. 3:31) and Samson (Judges 13–16). Their military competencies are reflected in the story of their capture of the ark of the covenant in 1 Sam. 4:1—7:2. Fear of the Philistine threat helped influence the people's decision to choose a king to unite the tribes (1 Sam. 8–9). The biblical authors continued to portray the Philistines as a threat to the Israelites, but Philistine influence in the highlands faded as the power of Assyria grew.

Assyria's fearsome power and influence in the region gave them a villain's role in the Old Testament. The biblical authors perceived Assyria's incursions into Israel and Judah as YHWH's punishment for such transgressions as idolatry and social injustice. While archaeological evidence of Philistine-Israelite interaction is scant, there is plenty of archaeological and extrabiblical evidence of Assyria's impact on Israel and Judah.

From the start of its ninth-century conquests, Assyria was feared for its ruthless force. The psychological impact of Assyria's powerful conscripted forces, iron chariots, siege engines, and public mutilations surface in the writings of the Old Testament authors. The Assyrians enforced submission through power and fear, deporting conquered rulers to prevent uprisings (2 Kings 17:6, 24, 28; 18:11). When uprisings occurred, Assyrian troops were deployed from strategically positioned garrisons to flay, impale, and burn the perpetrators, as portrayed in Assyrian palace-reliefs.

In the late eighth century, both Israel and Judah felt the full weight of Assyria's might. The northern kingdom of Israel was destroyed in 721 BCE after joining an alliance of vassals that stopped paying tribute to Assyria. At the end of the century, King Hezekiah entered Judah into a similar alliance with Egypt (Isaiah 30–31), which resulted in the invasion of his kingdom and the siege of Jerusalem. According to 2 Kgs. 18:13-16, the siege was broken when Hezekiah sent a message of repentance to the Assyrian king, Sennacherib, at Lachish, promising to resume his tribute obligations. Other texts in 2 Kings suggest that Sennacherib abandoned the siege to deal with political unrest at home (19:7, 37) or a plague (19:35-36). Despite his efforts to subvert Sennacherib's dominance of Judah, Hezekiah and his successors continued to rule as vassals.

Under the rule of King Nebuchadnezzar, the Babylonian Empire captured Nineveh in 612, destroyed the Egyptians at the battle of Carchemish in 605, and captured Jerusalem in 597, deporting many inhabitants. After a rebellion by King Zedekiah in 586, the Babylonians destroyed Jerusalem and the temple and deported a significant portion of Judah's population (2 Kings 24; 2 Chronicles 36). The prophets Ezekiel, Jeremiah, and Habakkuk saw Nebuchadnezzar's conquest as YHWH's punishment for the sins of the Judean state (Ezekiel 8–11; Jer. 25:1-14; Hab. 1:6-10). The events of the Babylonian conquest are largely supported by archaeology and extrabiblical literature (Grabbe, 210–13).

Biblical claims of the removal of all Judeans but the poorest "people of the land" (2 Kgs. 24:14-16; 25:12; Jer. 52:16, 28-30) are reflected in the archaeological record, which indicates that inhabited sites decreased by two-thirds, from 116 to 41, and surviving sites shrank from 4.4 to 1.4 hectares, suggesting a population collapse of 85 to 90 percent (Liverani, 195). Such a massive exile plays a formidable role in the Old Testament, as described in the stories of significant characters such as Ezekiel and Daniel. Rage associated with this event is found in Psalm 137, which recounts the horrors of the exile and ends with the chilling words "a blessing on him who seizes your [Babylonian] babies and dashes them against the rocks!" (137:9 JPS). The exiled Hebrews who returned to Palestine after the Persians conquered the Babylonians returned to a destroyed Jerusalem that no longer enjoyed the security of a defensive wall. Some of the returnees helped to reshape Judaism with a flourishing priesthood and the composition of scholarly works and biblical texts. While exile is portrayed in negative terms, many Jews remained in the lands to which they had been deported; this had the effect of spreading Judaism outside the confines of Palestine.

After overthrowing his grandfather King Astyages of the Medes in 553 BCE, Cyrus of Persia (d. 530) rapidly expanded his empire, moving westward into Armenia and Asia Minor and east toward India, and defeated Babylon in 539. But unlike previous conquests, the Old Testament treats Persian dominance as a time of hope. As successor to the Babylonian Empire, King Cyrus instituted a policy of allowing victims of Babylonian exile to return to their homelands, where he sponsored their local religions. To the biblical authors, this policy was met with celebration and as a sign of YHWH's love for his people. The authors of 2 Chron. 36:23 and Ezra 1:2 portray King Cyrus as crediting YHWH with his victories and with the mandate to rebuild the temple in Jerusalem; Ezra 1:7 even portrays the Persian king personally returning the vessels that Nebuchadnezzar had seized from the temple four decades before. While the Bible treats Cyrus's policy of return as inspired by YHWH, Davies and Rogerson note that the practice was neither new nor disinterested, as it served to restore the national culture of a large and culturally varied empire (59). It is important to note the great shift in how the biblical authors treated King Cyrus of Persia, as opposed to the kings of the Assyrians and Babylonians, whom they disdained. In Isaiah 40–50, Cyrus is championed as the great savior of the Judean deportees and of the rebuilding of Jerusalem. In fact, while oracles against foreign nations are a key theme in prophetic oracles, none are directed against Persia. Even when their rulers are compliant with the murder of Jews, they are portrayed as either acting against their own desires or out of ignorance (Daniel 6; Esther).

Like the exile, itself, the return from exile plays an important role in the politics and religion of the Old Testament. Accounts of these events are found in the books of Ezra and Nehemiah. While the Bible presents the return as a blessing from God and a time of joy, it does not seem to have been without its hardships. It can be deduced from Ezra and Nehemiah that resettlement involved various tensions; in Ezra 3:3, those who had remained in Judah during the exile, along with other neighboring peoples, take the Canaanites' role in the book of Joshua: "an evil influence which will, unless strenuously rejected, corrupt the 'people of God'" (Davies and Rogerson, 88). It was during the Persian period that the Jerusalem temple was rebuilt and the priesthood gained power and influence.

The long march of succeeding empires continued with the rise of Alexander the Great, who seized control of the Greek city-states in 336 BCE and conquered the Persian Empire before his death in 323. Unlike previous empires that might make their subjects worship a particular deity or relocate to a different region, the Greek ideal of *Hellenism* posed a particular cultural threat. Hellenism promoted a view in which people were not citizens of a particular region, but of the world, enabling the integration of Greek and regional cultures, thus breaking down barriers that separated local peoples from their foreign rulers. Within a hundred years, Koine Greek had become the lingua franca, and Greek philosophy, educational systems, art and attire, politics, and religion permeated the empire. The consequences of Hellenization had profound linguistic, political, and theological effects on the biblical authors who lived and wrote during this period. Jews who lived outside of Israel became more familiar with the Greek language than Hebrew. By the second century CE, Greek had become so widely spoken among the Jewish community in Alexandria, Egypt, that the Hebrew Bible was translated into Koine Greek, which came to be called the Septuagint.

Greek rule eventually led to the severe oppression of the Jewish people at the hands of the usurper king Antiochus IV (d. 164 BCE), who sought to weed out cultural diversity in the Seleucid Empire. King Antiochus, who called himself *Epiphanes* ("god made manifest"), was known for his erratic character, which manifested itself in his brutal hatred of the Jews. Even his allies referred to him by the nickname *Epimanes*—a play on Epiphanes—meaning "the crazy one." He is known for looting the Jerusalem temple to fund his battles against the Ptolemies and for forbidding the Jewish rite of circumcision and sacred dietary laws.

King Antiochus was also known for instigating treachery among the Jewish leadership, giving Jason—of the pro-Greek Onias family—the high priesthood in return for complying with Antiochus's plans to Hellenize Jerusalem by building a gymnasium and enrolling its people as citizens of Antioch (2 Macc. 4:7). Further strife erupted when Menelaus, another aspirant for the high priesthood, offered Antiochus even greater gifts for the office. The rivalry of Jason and Menelaus led to the sacking of Jerusalem, slaughtering of its citizens, and the looting of its temple (2 Macc. 5:11-23; Josephus 12.5.3 §§246–47). The horrors of life under King Antiochus IV are reflected in the horn that emerges from the fourth beast in the apocalyptic vision of Dan. 7:7-8, and is then slain by the "Ancient One" (7:11).

From stripping the temple to pay for his wars to setting up an altar for Zeus in the temple, King Antiochus IV's brutality against the Jews led to a revolt that started in the Judean village of Modein in 167 BCE and spread rapidly throughout the region—as chronicled in 1 and 2 Maccabees and in Josephus's *Antiquities of the Jews* (c. 100 CE). A guerrilla warfare campaign that was led by Judas Maccabeus eventually liberated and purified the temple—an event celebrated today in the Jewish festival of Hanukkah. The Maccabean revolt drove out the Greeks and expanded the borders to include Galilee. While the revolt was successful in ushering in a period of self-rule, the resulting Hasmonean Dynasty fell prey to the lust for power. As civil conflict broke out between two rival claims to the throne, the Roman general Pompey invaded Judea in 63 BCE, seizing control of the region for his empire. In 40 BCE, the Roman Senate appointed an Edomite convert to Judaism, *Herod the Great*, as king of Judea. Despised by his people, the puppet king had to take Jerusalem by force, from where he ruled harshly.

Each of these empires, vying for control over the Southern Levant, brought with them challenges that helped to shape the Hebrew people by influencing the ways they viewed themselves, their God, and their religious practices.

Religious Contexts of the Old Testament

Despite common perceptions of the Bible as a univocal work, the Old Testament represents diverse theologies of communities that spanned centuries and were influenced by the religious systems of their contemporaries. Babylonian and Canaanite musings over the power of order over chaos, as found in the *Enuma Elish* and Baal narratives, are present in Gen. 1:1—2:4a and referenced in Ps. 74:12-17. The authors of the Bible's Wisdom literature exchanged ideas with their foreign neighbors, as found in parallels between the Babylonian story I Will Praise the Lord of Wisdom and the book of Job, and passages from Proverbs that mirror the words of the Egyptian thinkers Ptah-Hotep and Amen-em-opet (e.g., Prov. 22:4; 22:17—24:22). Understanding the diversity of theological perspectives in the Old Testament can aid both exegesis and hermeneutics by giving the reader greater insight into the biblical authors' ideas of God and uncovering layers of meaning that might otherwise go unnoticed.

Monotheism and Henotheism

It should not be assumed that all Old Testament authors were monotheists: many were *henotheists*. Henotheism promotes a multi-god/dess universe in which the adherent gives allegiance to a supreme primary deity. Elements of this outlook appear to be found in God's decision to create humanity "in our image, after our likeness" (Gen. 1:26 RSV), and in YHWH's anxiety over the man that he created becoming "like one of us" in Gen. 3:22. YHWH also expresses his disgust in that the *sons of God* mated with human women, resulting in the birth of the nephilim (Gen. 6:2-4). In the *Song of Moses*, Moses poses the rhetorical question, "who is like you, O LORD, among the gods?" (Exod. 15:11). The writer of Ps. 95:3 proclaims, "YHWH is a great God, the king of all divine beings," while 97:9 asserts that YHWH is "exalted high above all divine beings." These examples pose a number of questions about the biblical authors' views on the divine. Two that will be briefly addressed here concern the identity of God and the role of the other deities being inferred. The supreme deity of the ancient Hebrews is given several names and titles, representing different personality traits and theological views.

Elohim

The name or title *Elohim*, which is usually translated from the Hebrew into English as "God," makes its first appearance in Genesis 1. The name Elohim is used to identify the Hebrews' supreme deity in several Old Testament texts, including those found in the books of Genesis, Exodus, Psalms, and Job. As in the Bible's priestly creation story (Gen. 1:1—2:4a), Elohim is portrayed as an all-powerful, confident, commanding, and somewhat distant deity, whose supremacy and majesty are emphasized.

YHWH

YHWH is an anthropomorphic god who exhibits tendencies toward both kindness and severity and is self-described as a jealous god who, unlike other ancient Near Eastern gods, demands the exclusive allegiance of his followers. The name YHWH, which is often translated into English as "the LORD"—from the Hebrew *adonay*—makes its first appearance in the second creation story (Gen. 2:4b). The name YHWH carries a sense of mystery. Derived from the Hebrew verb *hawah*, meaning "to be," YHWH is difficult to translate, but means something like "he who is" or "he who causes what is." Some believe that YHWH's origins can be traced to the god YHW, who was worshiped in the northwestern region of the Arabian Peninsula known as Midian: this is where Moses first encounters YHWH (Exodus 3).

YHWH has strong associations with Canaanite culture, which highlights discrepancies between biblical directions for the deity's worship and how the deity was worshiped in popular religion. Whereas the biblical authors convey strict messages that YHWH should be worshiped alone, the remains of Israelite homes reveal that other gods and goddesses, such as Asherah—whom the author(s) of Jeremiah refers to as *the queen of heaven*—were worshiped alongside YHWH (Dever, 176–89). Jeremiah 44 appears to give a glimpse into the popular polytheistic or henotheistic religion of sixth-century-BCE Judah. After YHWH threatens the people for worshiping other gods, the women say that they will not listen but will continue the traditions of their ancestors and give offerings to the queen of heaven, who protected them well (Jer. 44:16-17). Further biblical evidence of Asherah's popularity is found in the biblical authors' continual condemnation of her worship, often symbolized through the presence of pillars and poles, as they worked to direct the people toward monotheism (Deut. 7:5; Judg. 3:7-8; 1 Kgs. 14:15, 23; Jer. 17:17-18).

El

The name or title *El* appears around two hundred times in the Old Testament, with frequent use in the ancestor stories of Genesis and surfacing throughout the Old Testament. Its presence poses some interesting questions.

On one level, El is a common Semitic title for "divine being," and can be read as an appellative for "divinity," often compounded with other words such as *el-shadday* ("God Almighty" [Gen. 17:1; Exod. 6:3; Ezek. 10:5]) and *el-elyon* ("God Most High" [Gen. 14:22; Deut. 32:8-9; Ps. 78:35]). In addition to a title referring to God, El is also the name of the chief god of the Canaanite pantheon. Often portrayed as a bearded king on his throne, and referred to as the "Ancient One," El was worshiped in Canaan and Syria both before and after the emergence of Israel. The frequent use of El for God—and the Canaanite god's prominence in Israel—has led many to conclude that El developed into YHWH. Mark Smith asserts, "The original god of Israel was El. . . . Isra*el* is not a Yahwistic name with the divine element of Yahweh, but an El name" (Smith, 32; emphasis on *el* in "Israel" is mine). A cross-pollination of Canaanite and Hebrew religion is found in the use of Canaanite El imagery to describe the "Ancient One" in Dan. 7:9-10 who sits on a throne with white garments and hair as pure as wool. Furthermore, the description of "one like a human being coming with the clouds of heaven," who "came to the Ancient One and was presented before him" (Dan. 7:13), dovetails with images of the Canaanite god Baal coming before El. Whether or not the authors of Daniel 7 envisioned El, the imprint of Canaanite religion appears to have been stamped on ideas of God and passed down through the generations. While not accepted by biblical authors, popular religion in ancient Israel appears to have had a complex network of deities that fulfilled various roles in daily life. (For a helpful overview on differences between "popular" and "official" religion in ancient Israel, see Stavrakopoulou.)

The idea that El was absorbed into YHWH is also supported by the fact that the chief god of the Canaanite pantheon is never condemned in the Old Testament, but his son Baal, consort Asherah, and other gods face vicious condemnation (Num. 25:2; Deut. 4:3; Judg. 6:30; 1 Kgs. 16:31—18:40). Why would the biblical authors attack lesser Canaanite deities but leave the head god unscathed? One possible answer is that El had become synonymous with YHWH; both share a compassionate disposition toward humanity (Exod. 34:6; Ps. 86:15), use dreams to communicate (Gen. 31:24; 37:5; 1 Kgs. 3:5-15), and have healing powers (cf. *KTU* 1:16.v–vi with Gen. 20:17; Num. 12:13; Ps. 107:20 [Smith, 39]).

The Divine Council

As El served as chief of the Canaanite pantheon, YHWH was head of the *divine council*, whose members were often referred to as "the sons of gods." In Gen. 28:12; 33:1-2; Pss. 29:1 and 89:6-9, we find YHWH at the head of subordinate divine beings who are collectively referred to as the "council of LORD" (Jer. 23:18 and the "congregation of El" (Ps. 82:1). In Psalm 82, God attacks the congregants for their oppressive acts against humanity, for which they are doomed to die like mortals (vv. 5-7). In Job 1:6-7, Job's troubles begin when the divine council convenes with YHWH, and God asks "the satan" where he has been. The satan also appears on the divine council in Zechariah, where YHWH delivers judgment between two members of his entourage. The clearest depiction of the divine council's function is in 1 Kgs. 22:19-22, where YHWH seeks guidance and direction from the council, the members of which confer in open discussion before one spirit approaches YHWH with a proposal. Following a common motif in ancient Mediterranean literature, humans are sometimes transported before God and the divine council, as found in a party feasting with Elohim in Exod. 24:9-11 and Isaiah's commission as prophet in Isaiah 6 (Niditch 2010, 14–17).

Concluding Words on the Complexities of the Ancient Context

Reading the Old Testament in its ancient contexts requires a variety of considerations and an understanding that there are divergent views on these contexts. But this complexity should not discourage readers of the Bible from contemplating the origins of the Old Testament books, because a better understanding of their origins results in a broader understanding of their meanings and potential applications to our modern contexts. The authors of this volume's commentaries have worked to give the reader the best possible overview of the sociohistorical contexts that underlie the books of the Old Testament, opening its texts in new ways so that new meanings can be derived. While this section has highlighted some of the many considerations that need to be addressed when reading the "Very Dangerous Texts Ahead," the variety of contexts out of which the Old

Testament's books emerged is paralleled by the diversity of cultures, faiths, and societies into which they have been received.

Reading the Old Testament in Its Contemporary Contexts

Actively engaging the Old Testament in both its ancient and modern contexts enables readers to discover new levels of meaning that would otherwise go unnoticed. Through acknowledging an Old Testament text's historical setting, exploring how it has been interpreted through the millennia, and noticing the questions and challenges that it raises for our contemporary settings, engaged readers are better able to receive multiple levels of meaning that aid the reader in better understanding the biblical authors' intentions and discerning the passage's potential relevance to conversations that are unfolding today.

The Challenge of Bringing Ancient Context in Line with Modern Contexts

To participate in this process, however, is not a simple task. Beyond working to discern the various levels of meaning within the Old Testament, it is of paramount importance for readers to also acknowledge the preconceptions and biases they bring with them as they work to connect the ancient writings to their own world—an issue that is explored at length below.

As humorously demonstrated in A. J. Jacobs's book *The Year of Living Biblically*, it is important to remember that the texts of the Old Testament were not written for twenty-first-century audiences, but for citizens of the ancient world. As he recounts in his book, Jacobs tried to live as literally as possible according to the laws of the Hebrew Bible for one year. His experiment revealed that to live by the rules of the Hebrew Bible is to live as an outlaw in much of the modern world, whether because the Hebrew Bible calls for the execution of people who wear mixed fibers or because it mandates sacrificing animals in urban centers. This clash of ancient and modern cultures occurred in a very serious way in the tragic murder of Murray Seidman. Mr. Seidman's killer referenced Lev. 20:13 as his motivation for stoning the elderly and mentally disabled man (Masterson).

Conversely, some people, like Charlie Fuqua, assert that engaging with the Old Testament's historical contexts is not required. During the 2012 United States election, Fuqua ran for a seat on the Arkansas state legislature and released a book titled *God's Law: The Only Political Solution*. In his book, Fuqua calls for the creation of legal channels that will facilitate the execution of disobedient children, as commanded in Deut. 21:18-21 (2012, 179). While Fuqua's views represent a fringe group of theomonists that include such Christian reconstructionists as Cornelius Van Til and Rousas John Rushdoony, his example illustrates the importance of contemplating the important differences that exist between the biblical authors' societies and those into which their writings are received today. One must ask questions such as, Did the authors of Deut. 21:18-21 actually seek the execution of disobedient children, or did they pose an extreme example to illustrate a point on child rearing? Another important question to consider is, Did Deut. 21:18-21 originate at a time when resources were so scarce and the production of food so difficult that a child who didn't contribute to—but rather threatened—the common good posed a threat to the community's survival? Growing and cultivating food could certainly be a matter of life and death. Fuqua's failure to engage Deut. 21:18-21, choosing instead to blindly subscribe to the text at face value, is a very serious and dangerous matter, especially considering his aspirations for political office. But while vast differences separate the cultures and societies of the Old Testament authors and the world that we inhabit today, a surprising number of connections do exist.

Whether a Judean farmer or an American physician, we all share such aspects of the universal human experience as love, hate, trust, betrayal, fear, and hope—all of which are reflected both in the Old Testament and in our daily lives. Such themes as women working to find justice in societies that offer little, the quest for love along with its dangers and rewards, and people's struggle to understand their relationships with power, whether personal or political, are all found in the stories of the Old Testament and are still highly relevant to us today.

It should be pointed out, however, that earnestly engaging the Old Testament in its ancient and modern contexts is difficult, even hazardous. Several key considerations that help in an engaged reading of the books of the Old Testament are included here, including issues of biblical ownership, methods of interpretation, and approaches to the reception of its texts.

Whose Bible Is It, Anyway?

While the texts of the Old Testament are commonly used with an air of authority and ownership, their ownership is open to question. So, to whom do they belong? Now that their authors are long dead—and their works have passed through generations and around the world—who is the heir of these works? To which community would they turn and say, "The keys are yours"? One problem with answering this question is that the Old Testament's authors and editors did not represent a unified tradition through which a unified voice could be offered. Furthermore, the faiths and cultures of the twenty-first century CE are so far removed from the ancient authors' that they would most likely be utterly unrecognizable to them. On one level, it is a moot question. Those authors are dead, and they do not get a say regarding who uses their works, or how. Be that as it may, it is an important question to consider, for recognizing that the Old Testament has a number of spiritual heirs with divergent views of the divine underscores the vast interpretive possibilities these texts contain. While many faith traditions draw on the books of the Old Testament, the three largest—in order of appearance—are Judaism, Christianity, and Islam.

The Hebrew Bible (the *Tanakh*) of Judaism is composed of twenty-four books, which are divided into the Torah (Law), the Nebiim (Prophets), and the Ketubim (Writings). The Torah gives accounts of the creation, the establishment of the Hebrew people, and their movement out of captivity in Egypt toward the land that was promised to their ancestors. The public reading of the Torah is a religious ritual that culminates with the annual holiday of *Simchat Torah*, which celebrates its completion. Although the Tanakh forms the whole of Jewish biblical literature, it is supplemented by other interpretive collections.

The Christian *Old Testament*, sometimes referred to as the *First Testament*, sets the books of the Tanakh in a different order and serves as the first section of the *Christian Bible*, as a whole. Canonization of the Old Testament varies among different Christian traditions. Roman Catholicism,

Eastern Orthodoxy, and some Protestant groups include the seven additional books in their canon, as well as additions to the books of Esther and Daniel; these additions are called the *deuterocanon* ("second canon") or *Apocrypha* ("hidden"). Many of the books of the Old Testament are popularly seen as a precursor to the coming of Jesus and his perceived fulfillment of the law.

Islam incorporates many of the figures of the Old Testament into its sacred writings, the Holy Qur'an. Giving particular reverence to the Torah and the Psalms, the Qur'an honors Abraham, Isaac, and Moses as prophetic predecessors to the faith's final and greatest prophet, Muhammad (d. 632 CE).

While each of these traditions draws deep meaning and conviction from the Hebrew Scriptures, they also use them in different ways to reflect their own unique spiritual paths and theologies. The question of which group is the rightful heir of the biblical authors is impossible to answer definitively, since each claims to be in fact the rightful heir. The fact that such a diverse pool of people turns to these texts as sacred Scripture amplifies the many possibilities for Old Testament interpretation.

Evolving Views of the Old Testament and Its Interpretation

Whether or not it is done consciously, all readers of the Old Testament are engaged in some level of interpretation; there are no passive readers of the Bible. When people read the books of the Old Testament, they do so actively, bringing their own presuppositions, experiences, and cultural norms to a text. In essence, readers of the Old Testament bridge the ancient to the modern by way of exegesis and hermeneutics.

Exegesis looks at the texts in their ancient contexts, while hermeneutics works to discern how they relate to a modern reader's situation. Biblical scholars and readers have developed a number of methods for bringing the ancient and the modern together, often with specific objectives and theological motives in mind.

Biblical Literalism

Biblical literalism—which asserts that the Bible is the inerrant word of God, unaltered and untainted by human agency during its transmission from God to humanity—is a prevalent form of interpretation in the United States, practiced commonly within fundamentalist and some evangelical communities. The literal meanings of individual biblical texts were long considered alongside allegorical, moral, and mystical interpretations; it was not until the Reformation's second wave, in the seventeenth century, that literalism became a way to approach the Bible as a whole.

Protestant Christians who broke from the authority of Roman Catholicism found a strong sense of liberation in the idea of gaining access to God's direct word through the Scriptures. If an adherent could access God directly through a Bible, what need did they have for such individual or institutional arbitrators as priests, popes, or the Roman Church? Whereas early Reformers like Martin Luther and John Calvin viewed Scripture as being inspired by God with human involvement in its transmission, some of the second wave of Reformers, such as Amandus Polanus (d. 1610) and Abraham Calov (d. 1686), placed even greater emphasis on the Bible's inerrancy. The movement known as Protestant Scholasticism promoted the idea that any human involvement in the creation of the Bible was strictly mechanical; those who wrote the words were merely tools used by God. This was the first time that the idea of the inerrancy of Scripture as a literal interpretive approach was applied to the Bible—as a whole.

Despite the many developments in biblical interpretation that have occurred between the seventeenth and twenty-first centuries CE, many North American Christians still self-identify as biblical literalists. However, almost nobody practices biblical literalism in the strictest sense, for it would be an almost untenable position. The various contributions by the different religious communities that went into the writing of our biblical texts have resulted in contradicting versions of similar content (cf. Exod. 21:2-8 with Deut. 15:12-13). Given these challenges, how could A. J. Jacobs's experiment in living in strict accord with biblical law have any hope of being tenable, or even legal?

Historical Criticism

The influence of the Enlightenment—with its emphases on reason and searching for facts—gave rise to *the historical-critical movement*, which works to reconstruct the ancient contexts of the Bible. Baruch Spinoza (d. 1677) argued that the same scientific principles that were being applied to other areas of knowledge should be applied to the Bible as well. The results, which are still highly influential on how biblical scholarship is conducted today, have challenged such traditionally held Old Testament notions as the Genesis account(s) of the creation, Moses' composition of the Torah, and the historical validity of the Hebrew exodus out of Egypt, to name a few. Scrutinizing a particular text's origins through asking such questions as, Who wrote the text? For what purpose? and, Under what circumstances? Historical critics work to better understand what lies beneath the text.

Historical criticism's influence on biblical scholarship has shaped the way that many theologians read the Bible by adding to our understanding of the ancient contexts behind biblical texts. *Religionsgeschichte* ("history of religions") is a tool of historical criticism that reads biblical texts in their ancient religious contexts. Another historical-critical tool is *form criticism*, which has gleaned new meaning from such passages as the Song of Deborah (Judges 5) by considering their oral prehistory, reconstructing the *Sitz im Leben* ("original setting"), and analyzing their literary genres.

Social-Scientific Criticism

In the late 1970s—with the publication of Norman Gottwald's *The Tribes of Yahweh*—biblical scholars began to look at the books of the Old Testament through the lens of their sociological settings. Since then, numerous scholars have used societal patterns both to fill in many of the hidden contexts that are simply not addressed in the texts themselves and to better understand the societal motivations behind the Old Testament authors' messages.

One advantage to the social-scientific method of interpretation is its ability to inform hermeneutics (again, the application of biblical texts to modern circumstances). Social-scientific models have proven to be of particular use in shedding light on the contexts and motivations behind biblical texts while opening new ways of understanding how those texts might relate to the modern world (Chaney; Coomber 2011). A tempting misuse of social-scientific models of interpretation, however, is to treat the findings gained through social-scientific models as hard evidence that can stand on its own. Social-scientific models that deal with tribalism, urban development, religious-political interactions, or economic cycles can provide insight into how humans—and their systems—are expected to behave; they do not, however, prove how humans and systems did behave. It is for this reason that social-scientific approaches should be used in tandem with all available data, be it archaeological or literary.

Commenting on the great value of using social-scientific models in the interpretation of biblical texts, Philip Esler writes that their use "fires the social-scientific imagination to ask new questions of data, to which only the data can provide the answers" (Esler, 3). In other words, these models are useful for the interpretation of evidence, not as evidence in and of themselves. Social-scientific criticism has proven especially useful in the development of contextual readings of the Old Testament, which address issues ranging from political interpretations of the Bible to interpretations within such minority groups as LGBT (lesbian, gay, bisexual, and transgender) and disabled communities.

Contextual and Reception Readings and Criticisms

Contextual readings of the Old Testament provide excellent examples of how the ancient stories and ideas of the Old Testament can speak to the modern contexts of diverse communities. These forms of criticism, like social-scientific or literary criticism, often take on an interdisciplinary nature. While a plethora of contextual topics have been covered biblically, those that address issues of empire, gender, and race are briefly covered here.

Empire

Just as issues of empire were integral in the formation of the Old Testament, as addressed in the "Reading the Old Testament in Its Ancient Contexts" section above, Old Testament texts continue to influence the ways people approach issues of empire today. On the one hand, the imagery that celebrates conquest in the invasion of Canaan (Joshua) and the glory of Solomon's kingdom (e.g., 1 Kings 4) could be used to support the building of empire. On the other hand, those who challenge the rise or expansion of empires can draw on anti-imperial readings that condemn the conduct of royals and their exploitation of the citizenry (e.g., Micah 3), and legislation against economic injustice in the Torah, Writings, and Prophets.

Pro-imperial readings of the Old Testament can be seen in the building and expansion of US influence, such as the idea of *Manifest Destiny*, which portrays the Christian European settlement of the United States as God's divine will. Manifest destiny involved a reimagining of the Pilgrims—and later European settlers—as the new Hebrews, pushing aside the Native American peoples—who took on the role of Canaanites—in order to create a new Israel. The Rev. Josiah Strong's publication *Our Country* echoes this sentiment in its assertion that God was charging European Christianity "to dispossess the many weaker races, assimilate others, and mold the remainder" (Strong, 178). Reverberations of the Old Testament–rooted Manifest Destiny still surface in aspects of American exceptionalism, which influences the US political spectrum and can be seen in such approaches to foreign policy as "the Bush Doctrine," which works to spread American-style democracy as a path to lasting peace.

Just as the Old Testament has been used for empire building, it has also been used to challenge empire and its institutions. While the exodus narrative helped to shape the idea of Manifest Destiny, it also became a powerful abolitionist force in attacking the institutions of slavery and segregation. During the abolitionist movement, the powerful imagery of the exodus story gave hope and power to free African Americans and slaves alike. The power of the story was harnessed again in the mid-twentieth century, giving strength to those who struggled for racial equality (Coomber 2012, 123–36). Recent biblical scholarship has also turned to the Old Testament to address various issues of modern-day economic exploitation and neoimperialism (e.g., Gottwald 2011; Boer, ed.; West 2010).

A highly influential outcome of the crossing of Bible and empire has been *postcolonial interpretation*. As European empires spread throughout the world, they brought the Bible and Christianity with them. With the twentieth-century waning of European imperialism, colonized and previously colonized peoples have found their own voices in the Bible, resulting in a variety of new interpretations and new approaches to major Old Testament themes. Postcolonial interpretation has enriched the field from Mercedes García Bachmann's use of Isaiah 58 to address issues of "unwanted fasting" (105–12) to raising questions about whether the Christian canon should be reopened to include the folk stories and traditions of colonized Christian communities that feel unrepresented by the current Bible (Pui Lan).

Gender

Studies in gender have also revealed a wide range of interpretive possibilities and have come to the forefront of biblical scholarship during the past four decades. While often treated as the sex of the body, the word *gender* is a complicated term that addresses a variety of factors of embodiment, including mental and behavioral characteristics. *Masculinity* and *femininity*, for example, take on different attributes and expectations depending on the society or culture in which they exist. While gender is an area of study that is continually developing into various branches, both within and outside of biblical studies, one of its most predominant manifestations in biblical studies is found in *feminist criticism*.

Women have been longtime readers and commentators on biblical texts, even though their work has rarely been given the same consideration as their male counterparts, who have long served as the vanguard of the academy. Hildegard of Bingen (d. 1179) authored a commentary on Genesis 1–2 (Young, 262); R. Roberts (d. 1788) composed numerous sermons on a range of texts for a clergyman acquaintance (Knowles, 418–19); and abolitionist Elizabeth Cady Stanton (d. 1902) helped to publish *The Woman's Bible*. These three women serve as but a few examples of women who have made important contributions to biblical studies, though their work is unknown to many.

Feminist criticism continues to be a very effective mode for recovering women's insights, perspectives, knowledge, and the feminine principle in biblical texts, often rescuing those voices and interpretations from centuries of marginalization by patriarchal and even misogynistic interpretation. Elisabeth Schüssler Fiorenza claims that, unlike many other forms of biblical criticism, feminist biblical studies does not owe its existence to the academy but to social movements for change, and also to a desire for the ongoing pursuit of equal participation and equal rights, which have in practice been restricted to a small group of elite men (Schüssler Fiorenza, 8–9). Schüssler Fiorenza argues that since the Bible has most often been used in these struggles for either "legitimating the status quo of the kyriarchal order of domination *or* for challenging dehumanization, feminist biblical interpretation is best articulated as an integral part of wo/men's struggles for authority and self-determination" (9). Like so many forms of contextual and received readings, feminist criticism can serve as a liberating force by revealing perspectives within the Bible's texts that have otherwise gone unnoticed.

An example of recovering the woman's perspective in the Old Testament is found in feminist commentaries on such texts as Isa. 42:14, in which God says,

> For a long time I have held my peace,
>   I have kept still and restrained myself;
> now I will cry out like a woman in labor,
>   I will gasp and pant.

Patricia Tull has highlighted the way in which YHWH adopts the power of a woman in labor to emphasize God's own divine power of creation (Tull, 263). Another example of uncovering women's voices to find justice in patriarchal cultures—which work to subvert women's voices and rights—is found in Sharon Pace Jeansonne's treatment of Tamar as a woman who seizes power to find justice in a society that is set up to stop her from doing so (Jeansonne, 98–106).

Feminist criticism—as with most any other form of biblical criticism—is polyvocal, with a broad spectrum of biblical views, including those who have argued that the Bible might be best left alone (Bal, 14). Male scholars have also engaged with feminist-focused readings of Old Testament texts. Daniel Cohen's midrash on Genesis 3, for example, addresses misogynistic interpretations of the Garden of Eden story (Cohen 141–48).

Similar to some of feminist criticism's attempts to reclaim the women's voice in the Bible and address misogynistic interpretation, *queer criticism* works to uncover LGBT perspectives in the Old Testament and messages that are of importance to LGBT communities. Queer interpretation has addressed a number of such topics, including K. Renato Lings's work on homophobic critiques of the destruction of Sodom in Genesis 19—a text often used to condemn homosexuality—in which he argues that attaching homosexuality to the sin of Sodom was a later interpretive development, unrecognized by biblical authors (Lings, 183–207). Others have shed new light on the ways in which biblical texts are interpreted to affect modern-day political decisions, such as the issue of same-sex marriage (see Stahlberg).

Conclusion

To be an engaged reader of the Old Testament involves simultaneously navigating the worlds of the biblical authors and redactors, as well as all those who have interpreted its texts. It is through approaching a biblical text or idea through these multiple angles that the multilayered meanings of the Old Testament books can be unlocked, not only in regard to the authors' intentions, but also in ways that the biblical writers may have never been able to foresee. These multiple intersections with the biblical text help people to have meaningful conversation and debate on topics ranging from climate change, to same-sex marriage, to the international banking crisis, and more. Naturally, being an engaged reader requires considerable effort, but it is through deliberating on biblical texts in all of their complexity that deeper meaning can be found, and more honest—or at least informed—readings of the Bible's contents can be gleaned.

In this volume, the contributors' commentaries provide a tool through which people can develop their engagement with the books of the Old Testament and Apocrypha. Whether approaching this volume as a researcher, educator, member of the clergy, or student, it is the intent of the *Fortress Commentary on the Old Testament* to inform readers about the Old Testament books' historical contexts, interpretive histories, and the modern contexts with which they engage, while also serving as an opening through which the conversation can be expanded.

Works Cited

Alfaro, Juan I. 1989. *Justice and Loyalty: A Commentary on the Book of Micah*. Grand Rapids: Eerdmans.

Bachmann, Mercedes L. García. 2009. "True Fasting and Unwilling Hunger (Isaiah 58)." In *The Bible and the Hermeneutics of Liberation*, edited by A. F. Botta and P. R. Andiñach, 113–31. Atlanta: SBL.

Bal, Mieke. 1989. *Anti-Covenant: Counter-Reading Women's Lives in the Hebrew Bible*. Sheffield: Almond.

Boer, Roland, ed. 2013. *Postcolonialism and the Hebrew Bible: The Next Step*. SemeiaSt 70. Atlanta: SBL.

Cantor, Norman F. 1992. *Inventing the Middle Ages: The Lives, Works, and Ideas of the Great Medievalists of the Twentieth Century*. Cambridge: Lutterworth.

Chaney, Marvin L. 1999. "Whose Sour Grapes? The Addressees of Isaiah 5:1–7 in the Light of Political Economy." In *The Social World of the Hebrew Bible: Twenty-Five Years of the Social Sciences in the Academy*, edited by Ronald A. Simkins and Stephen L. Cook. *Semeia* 87:105–22.

Cohen, Daniel. 2007. "Taste and See: A Midrash on Genesis 3:6 and 3:12." In *Patriarchs, Prophets and Other Villains*, edited by Lisa Isherwood, 141–48. London: Equinox Publishing.

Coomber, Matthew J. M. 2010. *Re-Reading the Prophets through Corporate Globalization: A Cultural-Evolutionary Approach to Understanding Economic Injustice in the Hebrew Bible*. Piscataway, NJ: Gorgias.

———. 2011. "Caught in the Crossfire? Economic Injustice and Prophetic Motivation in Eighth-Century Judah." *BibInt* 19, nos. 4–5:396–432.

———. 2012. "Before Crossing the Jordan: The Telling and Retelling of the Exodus Narrative in African American History." In *Exodus and Deuteronomy: Texts @ Contexts*, edited by Athalya Brenner and Gale A. Yee, 123–36. Minneapolis: Fortress Press.

———. 2013. "Debt as Weapon: Manufacturing Poverty from Judah to Today." *Diaconia: Journal for the Study of Christian Social Practice* 4, no. 2:141–55.

Coote, Robert B., and Keith W. Whitelam. 1987. *The Emergence of Early Israel in Historical Perspective*. Sheffield: Almond.

Crossley, James G. 2008. *Jesus in an Age of Terror: Scholarly Projects for a New American Century*. London: Equinox.

Davies, Philip. 2000. "What Separates a Minimalist from a Maximalist? Not Much." *BAR* 26, no. 2:24–27, 72–73.

Davies, Philip, and John Rogerson. 2005. *The Old Testament World*. 2nd ed. Louisville: Westminster John Knox.

Dever, William G. 2008. *Did God Have a Wife? Archaeology and Folk Religion in Ancient Israel*. Grand Rapids: Eerdmans.

Esler, Philip F. 2005. "Social-Scientific Models in Biblical Interpretation." In *Ancient Israel: The Old Testament in Its Social Context*, edited by Philip Esler, 3–14. London: SCM.

Fuqua, Charles R. 2012. *God's Law: The Only Political Solution*. Salt Lake City: American Book Publishing.

Gottwald, Norman. 1999. *The Tribes of Yahweh: A Sociology of the Religion of Liberated Israel, 1250–1050* BCE. Sheffield: Sheffield Academic Press.

———. 2001. *The Politics of Ancient Israel*. Louisville: Westminster John Knox.

Grabbe, Lester L. 2007. *Ancient Israel: What Do We Know and How Do We Know It?* London: T&T Clark.

Halpern, Baruch. 1995. "Erasing History: The Minimalist Assault on Ancient Israel." *BRev* 11: 26–35, 47.

Jacobs, A. J. 2007. *The Year of Living Biblically: One Man's Humble Quest to Follow the Bible as Literally as Possible*. New York: Simon & Schuster.

Jeansonne, Sharon Pace. 1990. *The Women of Genesis: From Sarah to Potiphar's Wife*. Minneapolis: Fortress Press.

Josephus, Flavius. 1854. *The Works of Flavius Josephus: Comprising the Antiquities of the Jews, a History of the Jewish Wars, and Life of Flavius Josephus, Written by Himself*. Translated by William Whiston. Philadelphia: Jas. B. Smith.

Karmon, Yehuda. 1971. *Israel: A Regional Geography*. London: Wiley-Interscience.

Knapp, A. Bernard. 1988. "Copper Production and Eastern Mediterranean Trade: The Rise of Complex Society in Cyprus." In *State and Society: The Emergence and Development of Social Hierarchy and Political Centralization*, edited by J. Gledhill, B. Bender, and M. T. Larsen, 149–72. London: Unwin Hyman.

Knowles, Michael P. 2012. "Roberts, R. (ca. 1728–88)." In *Handbook of Women Biblical Interpreters*, edited by M. A. Taylor and A. Choi, 418–20. Grand Rapids: Baker Academic.

Kwok Pui-lan. 2003. "Discovering the Bible in the Non-Biblical World." In *Searching the Scriptures: A Feminist Introduction*, edited by Elisabeth Schüssler Fiorenza, 276–88. New York: Crossroad.

Lings, K. Renato. 2007. "Culture Clash in Sodom: Patriarchal Tales of Heroes, Villains, and Manipulation." In *Patriarchs, Prophets and Other Villains*, edited by Lisa Isherwood, 183–207. London: Equinox.

Liverani, Mario. 2007. *Israel's History and the History of Israel*. Translated by Chiara Peri and Philip Davies. London: Equinox.

Masterson, Teresa. 2011. "Man, 70, Stoned to Death for Being Gay." *NBC10 Philadelphia*. Accessed October 14, 2013. http://www.nbcphiladelphia.com/news/local/Man-70-Stoned-to-Death-for-Homosexuality-Police-118243719.html.

Niditch, Susan. 2010. "Experiencing the Divine: Heavenly Visits, Earthly Encounters and the Land of the Dead." In *Religious Diversity in Ancient Israel and Judah*, edited by Francesca Stavrakopoulou and John Barton, 11–22. London: T&T Clark.

Schüssler Fiorenza, Elisabeth. 2013. *Changing Horizons: Explorations in Feminist Interpretation*. Minneapolis: Fortress Press.

Schweitzer, Albert. 1968. *The Quest of the Historical Jesus: A Critical Study of Its Progress from Reimarus to Wrede*. New York: Macmillan.

Smith, Mark S. 2002. *The Early History of God: Yahweh and the Other Deities in Ancient Israel*. Grand Rapids: Eerdmans.

Stahlberg, Lesleigh Cushing. 2008. "Modern Day Moabites: The Bible and the Debate About Same-Sex Marriage." *BibInt* 16:422–75.

Stavrakopoulou, Francesca. 2010. "'Popular' Religion and 'Official' Religion: Practice, Perception, Portrayal." In *Religious Diversity in Ancient Israel and Judah*, edited by Francesca Stavrakopoulou and John Barton, 37–58. New York: T&T Clark.

Strong, Josiah. 1885. *Our Country: Its Possible Future and Its Present Crisis*. New York: The American Home Missionary Society.

Tull, Patricia K. 2012. "Isaiah." In *Women's Bible Commentary: Twentieth-Anniversary Edition*, edited by C. A. Newsom, S. H. Ringe, and J. E. Lapsley, 255–66. Louisville: Westminster John Knox.

West, Gerald. 2010. "The Legacy of Liberation Theologies in South Africa, with an Emphasis on Biblical Hermeneutics." *Studia Historiae Ecclesiasticae* 36, Supplement: 157–83.

Whitelam, Keith W. 2007. "Lines of Power: Mapping Ancient Israel." In *To Break Every Yoke: Essays in Honour of Marvin L. Chaney*, edited by R. B. Coote and N. K. Gottwald, 40–79. Sheffield: Sheffield Phoenix Press.

Young, Abigail. 2012. "Hildegard of Bingen (1098–1179)." In *Handbook of Women Biblical Interpreters*, edited by M. A. Taylor and A. Choi, 259–64. Grand Rapids: Baker Academic.

THE PEOPLE OF GOD AND THE PEOPLES OF THE EARTH

Hugh R. Page Jr.

The Bible Is Just the Beginning

The Bible is preeminently a book about people. That may strike some as a rather odd assertion given the stature enjoyed by the Bible as sacred text containing, in many faith traditions, everything one needs to know about God and salvation. Nonetheless, some of the more important foci of the Old and New Testaments have to do with the saga of the human family and the women and men that are dramatis personae in this unfolding drama. In the twenty-first century CE, our appreciation of how Scripture narrates that story is much more nuanced than it was perhaps a generation or two ago. We are much more aware of the processes by which traditions are shaped and preserved. We have a deeper understanding of the myriad stages through which the inspired words of prophets, poets, and sages proceed before being canonized: as well as of the place the Bible occupies in the global ecology of sacred texts. Moreover, we recognize that many of the world's sacred texts have important things to say about the human condition. Thus perspectives on what it means to be "people of God," women and men in a special relationship with a transcendent being, or members of a large and diverse human family sharing a common terrestrial abode vary widely. Moreover, in today's world, scholarship in fields such as genetics and anthropology is changing the way we think about human origins and notions of personhood.

It is because of new ideas about humanity and its origins that responsible readers of the Bible must, therefore, examine biblical conceptions of personhood, while keeping in mind the ways in which both the human family in general and those individuals called into special relationship with the God of Israel are construed. In so doing, they must also look at how such ideas have shaped, and continue to influence, notions about the world and its inhabitants today; are related to comparable ideas about personhood in other faith traditions; relate to what scientific evidence reveals about the human family; have been complicit in the exploitation of colonized peoples; and stand in relationship to those ideas about the human family articulated in documents such as the United Nations Declaration of Human Rights and the Declaration on the Rights of Indigenous Peoples. Such a task is necessary if we are to enhance the extent to which the Bible can be deployed as a resource in building a more just and equitable global community. Failure to do so may limit the extent to which members of faith communities for which the Bible is authoritative are able to join in meaningful dialogue about the future of our global community and the institutions that support it. It may also inadvertently lend credence to the idea that religious texts and traditions have no place in conversations about those ideals on which a cosmopolitan global community should be based in the future.

The Earth and Its Peoples—A View from the Ethnographic Record

Science has revealed that modern human beings are the result of a remarkable evolutionary process. We share common African ancestry, and our diversity at this point in time bears witness to an array of migratory, climatic, and genetic adaptations that span hundreds of thousands of years. Our cultural landscape is vast and remarkable in its variation. For example, the comprehensive cultural database maintained by Human Relations Area Files at Yale University (see http://www.yale.edu/hraf/collections.htm) contains information on several hundred cultures.

The *Ethnographic Atlas*, a massive project undertaken by George Peter Murdock (1969) and ultimately brought to full fruition in the 1970s, contains information on more than one thousand distinct groups. As an ethnologist, Murdock was particularly interested in both the comparative study of cultures and the identification of behavioral traits that manifest locally, regionally, and internationally (see especially Murdock 1981, 3). His work calls attention to the breadth of lifeways characteristic of peoples around the world. Scholarship continuing in the vein of Murdock's has led to the identification of some 3,500 cultures on which published data are readily available (see, e.g., Price, 10). Such studies have also resulted in the development of templates for comparing social organization, religious beliefs, and other information about the world's disparate peoples (see Ember and Ember; and Murdock et al.). Needless to say, the vision of the human family derived from this research is remarkable. Social scientists see this diverse collage of languages, customs, and religious traditions as the end result of developmental forces that have been operational for *aeons*. It is also for them a mystery to be probed using the critical tools at their disposal. Ethnographic investigations and theory testing have laid bare and will continue to reveal its undiscovered truths. However, humankind has not revealed, and is not likely to yield, the sum total of its secrets to even the most dogged of investigators. Like the stories of primordial reality we encounter in the biblical book of Genesis, such research offers a place from which to begin pondering what it means to be human.

Human life is, of course, dynamic. New social and religious groups are born constantly. The first two decades of the current millennium have even witnessed the dissolution of geopolitical boundaries, the creation of new nation states, and the birth of new religious movements. Thus notions of culture and personhood in our era are anything but static. Our human family continues to grow and with each passing day becomes more diverse and increasingly complex. Research in the social sciences has increased our understanding of how culture and identity evolve. We know more today than ever before about the ways language, physical environment, and other factors contribute to ideas about what it means to be a fully actualized self and to be in relationship with those other selves that are one's family members, friends, and neighbors. It has also shed light on the role that the collection and preservation of religious lore play in this process. Sacred traditions and texts serve as the repositories for stories about how people and the groups in which they are embedded came to be. They also function as points of reference for the nurture of persons and the communities in which they live.

The challenge we face in an era when such traditions are often read narrowly or uncritically—without an eye toward their implicit limitations—is to create charitable and inclusive approaches that allow us to engage and appropriate them. Such strategies necessitate that we become well versed in the ways that stories, both ancient and modern, shape our identities, beliefs, and relationships with one another. Whether one has in mind venerable tales such as the Babylonian *Enuma Elish* and the so-called Priestly account of creation (Gen. 1:1—2:4a), or modern cinematic myths like the *Matrix* or *Prometheus* sagas, narratives of one kind or another provide a context for understanding who we are and how we choose to live. Returning to the Bible itself, it is arguable that one of its central aims is to inform us of what it means to be finite beings that are threads in a sacred cosmic fabric woven, as it were, by a divine and ineffable artisan.

Ancient Near Eastern Lore and Conceptions of Personhood

In the late nineteenth and early twentieth centuries, scholars such as James Frazer and Stith Thompson began looking seriously at cultural practices and folklore from various parts of the world. The results were remarkable, though not without some degree of controversy. Frazer's efforts included his Victorian-era classic *The Golden Bough* (Frazer 1981) and an equally important, if less celebrated, three-volume work titled *Folk-Lore in the Old Testament* (Frazer 1918a; 1918b; 1918c); and Thompson's work on folklore motifs was pioneering insofar as it laid important groundwork for the comparison of tales from around the world. Although questions remain about the aims and theoretical presuppositions of these early works, their efforts, and those of the scholars following in their immediate footsteps, set the stage for much of the social-scientific research we have seen in the twentieth and twenty-first centuries, even in the field of biblical studies.

Among biblical scholars, the pioneers of form criticism and the so-called myth and ritual school found in this body of information—and other information gathered from ancient Near Eastern sources—a treasure trove useful for contextualizing and interpreting key portions of the Old Testament. Among form critics, Hermann Gunkel must be noted. His collection of essays in *What Remains of the Old Testament* and topical studies of literary *Gattungen* ("forms") as such pertain to the Bible in *The Legends of Genesis* and *The Folktale in the Old Testament* repay—even today—careful reading

(1928; 1964; 1987). Among myth and ritual adherents, Sigmund Mowinckel's work deserves pride of place, especially his *Psalmenstudien* (1966). These pioneers' use of ethnological resources in the study of Scripture were paralleled by those of Johannes Pedersen in his two-volume study of ancient Israelite culture (1926–1940) and extended in subsequent generations by Theodor Gaster's efforts to reclaim and expand the work of Frazer (1950; 1959; 1969); Mary Douglas's exploration of the body as social map (1966); Bruce Malina's use of a circum-Mediterranean paradigm to understand the roles of women and men in the Bible (1989); and others whose work has explored the intersections of Jewish, Christian, Mediterranean, and other cultural traditions both ancient and modern.

Several lessons can be gleaned from this body of research. The first is that people are in some ways "hardwired" to create and tell stories. These stories help in making sense of life crises such as birth, maturation, and death. They are also pivotal in defining the self and the social networks into which individual selves are embedded. A second lesson is that one particular genre, creation stories—whether they focus on the birth of deities (theogonies), the universe (cosmogonies), humanity, tribal confederations, monarchies, or all of the aforementioned—have a direct impact on the ways people understand their place in the world. Creation stories define social and ethnic boundaries, reify social and political hierarchies, and ascribe status based on age, gender, and other ontological and ascribed markers. These two factors should inform the ways information about individuals and groups embedded in poetry, rituals, royal inscriptions, and other texts is understood. A few examples from the ancient Near East are particularly illustrative.

The Mesopotamian flood tradition encountered in the Atrahasis myth has, among its more important purposes, articulation of a basic theological anthropology—one that is based on an understanding of the mutable and immutable dimensions of an, at times, capricious cosmos. Human beings are oddly situated in this power-filled and unstable environment. They are remarkable for three reasons. The first is because they are made of the flesh and blood of a divine insurgent and sacrificed because he led a rebellion against the harsh labor imposed on a subset of deities in the pantheon.

> When the gods themselves were men,
> They did the work. They endured the toil.
> The labor was onerous.
> Massive was the effort. The distress was exceedingly great. (Lambert and Millard, 42
>   [tablet 1.1.1–4], translation my own)

> Let them sacrifice the divine leader.
> Let the gods purify themselves by immersion.
> With his essence—flesh and blood—let Nintu mix the clay,
> So that divinity and humanity may be thoroughly
> Blended in the amalgam.
> For all time let us hear the drumbeat.
> In the flesh of the god let the ghost remain.
> Let her [Nintu] inform him [the slain god] of his token.
> So that there will be no forgetting,
> The spirit will remain. (Lambert and Millard, 58 [tablet 1.4.208–17], translation my own)

The human heartbeat is the "drum" reminding women and men for all time of the immortal lineage that is uniquely their own. The second reason that people are special is due to their being extended kin, as it were, of Atrahasis, the "exceedingly wise one," who managed to survive the great deluge by which all of humanity was destroyed. To them belongs the empowering, yet dangerous, model of this *liminal* ancestor. As William Moran noted more than four decades ago: "The Atrahasis Epic is an assertion of man's importance in the final order of things. It is also a strong criticism of the gods" (Moran, 59).

Humans are also special (see Moran, 60–61) for a third reason: because they are living proof of the imprudence of the gods and goddesses they serve. Created to assume the day-to-day labor deemed too difficult for immortals to bear, the din of their daily existence proved far too disruptive of their divine patrons' and matrons' sleep. Their death was decreed because they were, in a word, "noisy" (Lambert and Millard, 66 [tablet 1.7.354–59]). It is only through the quick-witted intervention of Enki, his personal god, that Atrahasis and his family are able to escape the inundation. Atrahasis is a powerful symbol of what can happen when human perseverance and divine subterfuge are allied.

The Atrahasis myth suggests that people are made of supernatural "stuff" and are heirs to a distinctive lineage. It also emphasizes that in a world filled with danger, the gods who are in control of the fates of women and men do not always have the best interest of the human family in mind. Although all mortals are in a sense beings belonging to and dependent on the gods, the implication of the sobering reality revealed in this myth is that in order to survive, women and men would do well to leverage their inner resources while at the same time relying, should all else fail, on timely divine intervention by those deities with whom they have a special relationship. Such assertions are, of course, in conversation with anthropologies articulated in other lore across a wide spectrum of genres. For example, Gilgamesh—particularly the Old Babylonian version of this Akkadian classic—focuses attention on the unique challenges confronted by one species of individual: monarchs. Of particular interest in this epic are their socialization, capacity to form friendships, quest for lasting renown, and insecurities about death. royal inscriptions, of which exemplars are too numerous to mention, continue in this vein and further define the traits of kings and those subject to their authority. Suzerainty treaties can be said to function in a comparable manner by defining the relationships of sociopolitical aggregates to one another. Sets of laws, like those found in the Code of Hammurabi, reify social status through taxonomies that identify insiders (e.g., king, free men, and those acquitted of offenses) and outsiders (e.g., criminals, widows, and orphans).

Another story, that of the travails of the god Ba'lu from the ancient city of Ugarit, offers a slightly different perspective on human life—this time from West Semitic lore. Unlike the story of Atrahasis, the Ba'lu myth is concerned primarily with how the enigmatic god of the fructifying rains—mainstays of human life—secures his place as head of the pantheon. Although the primary concern of this tale is Ba'lu's contest with rivals for ascendancy to the throne, it lifts the veil concealing the ongoing cosmic struggle between two such forces that inscribe the parameters for human existence: that is, life/fertility, represented by Ba'lu as numen of the storm, and Môtu, the embodiment of death and dissolution. At one point in this saga, he voluntarily submits himself to the authority and power of Môtu. His death, emblematic of nature's cyclic periods of aridity, leads his father 'Ilu, head of the pantheon, and his sister 'Anatu, to bewail its impact on the world. Both give voice to a lament intended, no doubt, to sum up the anguish of all affected by the storm god's departure.

> Ba'lu has died. What is to become of humanity?
> Dagan's child is no more. What will happen to earth's teeming masses? (CAT 1.5.6.23–24;
>   1.6.1.6–7)

The world and its inhabitants are part of the background landscape against which this divine drama unfolds. Nonetheless, as the narrative progresses, one realizes that each episode has a profound, if at times only partially articulated, impact on the peoples of the earth. Ba'lu returns to life, largely through the intervention of his sister 'Anatu. Eventually, he and Môtu have a fateful encounter that reveals, in no uncertain terms, that they are—and shall remain—in an interminable struggle.

> They fight each other like heroes
> Môtu is strong, as is Ba'lu
> Like raging bulls, they go head to head
> Môtu is strong, as is Ba'lu
> They bite one another like serpents
> Môtu is strong, as is Ba'lu
> Like animals, they beat each other to a pulp
> Môtu falls, Ba'lu collapses. (CAT 1.6.6.16–22)

The two battle to a virtual draw: an indication that the struggle between life and death is ongoing. The hope for "earth's teeming masses" is that the forces of life are able—at the very least—to withstand Death's furious and unrelenting onslaught. To be engaged nobly in the struggle is, therefore, to participate heroically in an age-old struggle that unites every member of the human family as kin. The warp and weft of day-to-day existence finds its ultimate significance in this ongoing cosmic battle. We see a stunning reflex of this mythology in the biblical Song of Songs, where the protagonists are anthropomorphized hypostases of Love (*'ahăbâ*) and Death (*māwet*).

> Seal me to your heart.
> Brand me on your arm.
> Love is equal to Death in its strength.
> Passion rivals Sheol in its ferocity.
> Its flames are a blazing fire.
> It is an eternal inferno. (Song of Songs 8:6, author's own translation)

Additional textual examples from Egypt and Anatolia could be cited, but the above suffice to show how implicit and explicit messaging about people—their nature, connection to one another, and relationship to the divine forces responsible for their creation and support—is conveyed in expressive culture.

The Hebrew Bible, Personhood, and Identity

Biblical references to the earth and its peoples are very much in conversation with these ancient Near Eastern traditions. The opening chapter of the Hebrew Bible contains a remarkable assertion in what scholars have traditionally designated the Priestly account of creation (Gen. 1:1—2:4a): that the world and everything in it is "good." It uses the Hebrew word *ṭôb* to describe its fundamental essence, a word whose semantic range connotes something sweet and pleasurable. Human beings are an important part of the created order. Made on the sixth day, they are distinguished only by gender: male and female. Neither ethnic nor regional markers are noted. All are made according to the divine "form" (*ṣelem*) and "pattern" (*dĕmût*)—that is, God's "image and likeness" according to the NRSV. Theirs are the tasks of reproducing and exercising control of the earth (1:26–28). The word used to describe what will be involved to reach this desired outcome (*kābaš*) connotes a process requiring forceful effort (Oswalt, 430). Also implied here is the idea that this is a laborious enterprise that is both collective and collaborative.

Following this masterful cosmogonic hymn, readers encounter in the remainder of Genesis a "mixed bag" of traditions about the earth's populace representing several sources: fragments of archaic poetry (2:23; 3:14-19; 4:23-24; 49); a descanting creation narrative (2:4b-24); etiological tales (11:1-9); ethnohistorical musings about the origins of particular peoples (4:17-22); an epic about the peregrinations of Israel's ancestors (11:31—36:43); and an extensive novella dealing with a key figure in the national saga: Joseph (37–50). While these materials can be read—as scholarly literature attests—from a variety of perspectives, one thing is very clear: together they tell the story of the God of Israel's relationship with the world and its peoples, some of whom—namely, Abraham, Sarah, and their descendants—are called to take on special responsibilities for the entirety of the human family (12:1-3). In fact, it could be argued that a significant portion of the Genesis tradition (1:1—11:32) has been intended as a creative "riff" on, or response to, Sumero-Akkadian lore (like that found in Atrahasis) about the origins of humanity.

One of the unifying threads holding together the narrative tapestry of Genesis and the remaining books of the Torah/Pentateuch is the story of how the world is affected by the shifting, strained, at times tumultuous, dynamic, and constantly evolving relationships among those who are the off-spring of the primordial family. While highlighting theological themes such as *calling* (Exod. 3:1-15); *covenant* (Exod. 6:1-8; 20:1-17); *sin and redemption* (Exod. 32:1-35); *divine immanence and transcendence* (Exod. 25:1—31:18); *holiness* (Lev. 10:3; 20:26); *significant individuals* (Exod. 2:10; 15:20; 2:21; 3:1); *groups* (Exod. 3:8; 6:19); and *events* (Exodus 15; Num. 3:14-16; 9:15-16); these books also articulate a gestalt ("general sketch") for comprehending what it means to be part of a human family. This can entail struggling both to recognize its connectedness and to honor its diversity. It can also involve wrestling with the challenge of managing intergroup crises that influence the welfare of peoples living in proximity; competing for limited resources; and dealing with those changing geopolitical realities that generate population shifts, form new social movements, and give rise to diasporas. It is for this reason that one of the foci of these books, and the sources used therein, is the establishment of social, religious, and other boundaries that determine personhood, group affiliation, and status. For example, the Priestly creation story (Gen. 1—2:4a) can be said to inscribe broad and inclusive parameters for personhood. Since all human beings bear the imprint of the creator's "form" and "pattern," they can be said to belong to a single unified group, for which gender is the only subclassification (1:26-27). The implication of this is that everyone created *by* God belongs *to* God and is therefore part of the "people of God."

Genealogical tables, such as that found in Genesis 10, offer a more nuanced view of group identity based on location, language, and kin group (e.g., 10:5). The story of the Tower of Babel goes a step further in its linkage of linguistic heterogeneity to human hubris and a divine response to quell it (Gen. 11:5-7). Although it can be read simply as an entertaining etiology accounting for the diversity and spread of languages, it does contain a polemical strain resistant to linguistic solidarity, centralized government, and the conscription of resources needed to build monumental structures and to maintain the places—that is, cities—where they are most likely to be found in antiquity. Thus the story seems to be suggesting, on one level, that diversity and difference are preferable to a homogeneity whose consequences, intended or unintended, are to transgress the boundary separating mortals from God.

The block of material inclusive of the ancestral epic and the story of Joseph's rise to Egyptian prominence offers an even more complex picture of the "people of God." On the one hand, the "yes" given by Abram/Abraham to the call of YHWH (Gen. 12:1-3), and the covenant made with him (Gen. 15:18; 17:1-27) by YHWH, serve to distinguish him and his descendants among the "people of God"—that is, as a conduit of blessing to the entirety of the human family (Gen. 12:3). On the other hand, an inversion of status—from "temporary sojourner" to "inheritor" of Canaan (17:6-8)—is also promised, one that sets the stage for what is later described in Joshua and Judges. The story of Joseph's tensions with his brothers, as well as that of the peculiar circumstances leading Jacob and his kin to go to Egypt, set the stage for further musing on several issues. The first is how the kin group through whom all of the "people of God" are to be blessed understands its internal subdivisions (Genesis 49; Deuteronomy 32–33). The second has to do with how the kin group's liberation, covenant at Sinai, sojourn in the wilderness, and occupation of Canaan (Exod. 4:1—20:21; 32:1—35:29; Num. 1:1—36:13; Joshua; and Judges) are construed, particularly in terms of how these sources present Israel's relationship to its neighbors, both as stewards of a unique revelatory experience and part of a larger family of divine offspring. The third concerns the final book of the Pentateuch—Deuteronomy—that serves as the transitional bridge to the Former Prophets. From a literary standpoint, it is a rearticulation and expansion of core precepts first articulated in Exod. 20:1-17. It inscribes very narrow parameters for Israel's self-understanding and relationship to its neighbors. "When you come into the land that the LORD your God is giving you, you must not learn to imitate the abhorrent practices of those nations" (Deut. 18:9).

The book of Deuteronomy has very strict stipulations for the centralization of worship (12:1-28), prophetic practice (18:15-22), the conduct of war (20:1-20), and the care of those without material support (24:14-15, 17-18). All of these grow out of a particular self-understanding, stated most succinctly in what Gerhard von Rad long ago identified as a short creedal statement.

A wandering Aramean was my ancestor; he went down into Egypt and lived there as an alien, few in number, and there he became a great nation, mighty and populous. When the Egyptians treated us harshly and afflicted us, by imposing hard labor on us, we cried to the LORD, the God of our ancestors; the LORD heard our voice and saw our affliction, our toil, and our oppression. The LORD brought us out of Egypt with a mighty hand and an outstretched arm, with a terrifying display of power, and with signs and wonders; and he brought us into this place and gave us this land, a land flowing with milk and honey. (Deut. 26:5-9)

Israel's identity as an "alien" subject to "hard labor" and "oppression," now liberated by YHWH, is the backdrop against which Deuteronomy's exclusive covenantal obligations are formulated. The jealousy of YHWH (Deut. 4:24) establishes impermeable cultural and ethical borders separating Israel from its neighbors. Deuteronomy and the historical narrative of the occupation of Canaan and the flowering of the monarchy are written in accordance with its principles. This so-called Deuteronomistic History (abbreviated Dtr by some scholars) consists of Joshua, Judges, the books of Samuel, and 1 and 2 Kings. It offers a far more complex, yet ultimately less inclusive, vision of the "people of God."

For example, we encounter the technical designation 'am yhwh ("YHWH's people") in the Pentateuch's oldest strata (e.g., Judg. 5:11, 13—an ancient Hebrew poem; and Num. 11:29; 16:41). Here it refers to either the members of Israel's tribal confederation (Judges) or the Israelite community on the march through the wilderness following its flight from Egypt (Numbers). It is present much more frequently in Dtr, where it denotes those faithful bound by the Deuteronomic covenant (Deut. 27:9—lĕ'am layhwh); Israel before the establishment of the monarchy (1 Sam. 2:24); the fallen military contingent that supported Jonathan and Saul (2 Sam. 1:12); and as an *ethnonym* for those under the reign of David (2 Sam. 6:21), Jehu (2 Kgs. 9:6), and Jehoida (2 Kgs. 11:17). We also find the terms 'am hā'ĕlōhîm or 'am 'ĕlōhîm ("people of God") used in reference to the Israelite tribal contingent armed for battle (Judg. 20:2) and to those under David's sovereign rule (2 Sam. 14:13). Beyond these references, we encounter the term "YHWH's people" in 2 Chron. 23:16 (paralleling 2 Kgs. 11:17). Another enigmatic reference—to "the God of Abraham's people"—is found in Ps. 47:9, a poem asserting the universal kingship of 'ĕlōhîm ("God").

Although references to "Yahweh's people" and "people of God" do not appear in the Latter Prophets (Isaiah, Jeremiah, Ezekiel, and the Book of the Twelve) or the Writings (outside of the Chronicler), we can certainly detect a keen interest in the world's peoples in many of these books. In some instances, the focus is decidedly polemical. The pointed critique of Israel's neighbors in prophetic oracles is an excellent example (e.g., Isaiah 14–19; Ezekiel 26–30). The bimodal subdivision of humanity in Proverbs (between those who heed Wisdom's voice and others who do not in Proverbs 8–9). A third case in point is the distinction made between "those who lead many to righteousness" in Dan. 12:3) and their opponents. In others, there is an affirmation of the God of Israel's keen interest in building an inclusive eschatological community (e.g., Isa. 66:18-21) and questioning a culture of entitlement and condemnatory rhetoric among Israelite prophets (Jon. 4:9-11). In Jewish apocryphal literature, we also see an interest expressed in the relationship among peoples. In the Greek Addition F to Esther, an editor has called attention to the different "lots" God has assigned to "the people of God" and to "all the nations" (10:10). The author of the Wisdom of Solomon takes a slightly different tack. While adopting a rhetoric that accentuates the difference between the "righteous" and the "ungodly" (Wisdom), it also calls attention to the common ancestry of humanity:

> there is for all one entrance into life, and one way out. (Wis. 18:9)

What we have, therefore, in the Hebrew Bible are multiple visions of what it means to be "people of God" and "peoples of the earth." Some are narrow. Others are selectively inclusive. All must be read with an eye toward genre, the setting in which the text was produced, and the social, political, and religious circumstances it seeks to address.

It goes almost without saying that biblical writers and their initial audiences were concerned with theological issues such as Israel's election and the implications such issues have on the community's holiness and distinctiveness when compared to its neighbors. In light of this special calling, as it were, boundaries—their creation, maintenance, and occasional erasure—take on particular significance. Maintenance is a sign of covenantal fidelity (Deut. 7:1-6) and purity (Lev. 10:1-3). Periodic transgression is, at least in some instances, a necessary survival strategy. Judges is an excellent case in point (see Page). We see evidence in this book of the crossing of bodily, cultural, and other borders as part of what characterizes Israelite life during that bittersweet epoch when "there was no king in Israel" and "people did what was right in their own eyes" (Judg. 21:25). Israel's identity as a people with a unique identity, mission, and teleological objective is, thus, variously articulated in the Hebrew Bible. These overlapping, competing, and complementary ideas of what it means to be a "people of God" among "the earth's peoples" require attentiveness to the religious objectives, political aims, and eschatological foci of the books in which they are found. Therefore, any attempt to fully reconcile all aspects of these disparate conceptions is likely to meet with frustration. Instead, it is perhaps better to recognize that the Hebrew Bible does not speak with a single voice on the issue of what it means to be part of the human family.

Looking beyond the Bible

One could argue that this absence of uniformity in the Hebrew Bible is an invitation not simply to read, but also to query and "talk back to" its books. Among the questions we should ask is what sources—in addition to Scripture—we ought to consult in making sense of who we are, what our relationship should be to one another, and what our place is in the universe. This process is far more involved than turning to Genesis or some other biblical book for a "proof text" (the practice of using a specific text as the final authoritative word on a given issue). Instead, it requires taking into consideration modern geopolitical realities such as globalization and what the pure, applied, and social sciences are telling us about our biological origins, diversity, and connectedness.

It also makes it incumbent on Bible readers to be aware of how documents such as the United Nations Declaration on Human Rights (1948) and the United Nations Declaration on the Rights of Indigenous Peoples (2007) influence how we think about our rights and responsibilities as people of faith and citizens of the world. For example, article 1 of the former states that "all human beings are born free and equal in dignity and rights. They are endowed with reason and conscience and should act towards one another in a spirit of brotherhood" (United Nations General Assembly 2000, 326). An affirmation of this kind shapes the way one thinks about religious texts and traditions that qualify human freedom, equality, dignity, or rights endowed at birth. Furthermore, according to article 18 of the Declaration, "Everyone has the right to freedom of thought, conscience, and religion; this right includes freedom to change his religion or belief, and freedom either alone or in community with others and in public or private, to manifest his religion or belief in teaching, practice, worship, and observance" (United Nations General Assembly 2000, 327). Such texts can't help but influence our reading and deployment of those parts of the Bible that affirm behaviors that affirm or disagree with these statements and the ideals they represent. In the case of those that run counter, a hermeneutic inclusive of exegesis and critical engagement is warranted. Article 7 section 2 of the United Nations Declaration on the Rights of Indigenous Peoples states that "indigenous peoples have the collective right to live in freedom, peace and security as distinct peoples and shall not be subjected to any act of genocide or any other act of violence, including forcibly removing children of the group to another group" (United Nations General Assembly 2007, 5). Moreover, article 8 section 1 affirms that "indigenous peoples and individuals have the right not to be subjected to forced assimilation or destruction of their culture" (United Nations General Assembly 2007, 5). The reading or deployment of biblical passages that appear to celebrate or support behaviors of this kind can be neither ignored nor interpreted in a way that treats lightly the ways they have been used to justify policies that abrogate the rights of indigenous peoples around the world.

Thus, in our current era, perhaps the Bible should be seen less as the single authoritative source from which the final word on what it means to be "people of God" and "people of the earth" is to be found, and more as one of several interlocutors—including lived experience—informing our consideration of what is an unfolding *mystery* about the larger human experience that we are invited to prayerfully ponder.

Works Cited

Douglas, Mary. 1966. *Purity and Danger*. London: ARK.

Eilberg-Schwartz, Howard. 1990. *The Savage in Judaism: Anthropology of Israelite Religion and Ancient Judaism*. Bloomington: Indiana University Press.

Ember, Melvin, and Carol R. Ember, eds. 1999. *Cultures of the World: Selections from the Ten-Volume Encyclopedia of World Cultures*. New York: Macmillan Library Reference USA.

Frazer, James. 1981. *The Golden Bough*. 1890. Reprint, New York: Grammercy.

———. 1918a. *Folk-Lore in the Old Testament*. Vol. 1. London: Macmillan.

———. 1918b. *Folk-Lore in the Old Testament*. Vol. 2. London: Macmillan.

———. 1918c. *Folk-Lore in the Old Testament*. Vol. 3. London: Macmillan.

Gaster, Theodor H. 1950. *Thespis: Ritual, Myth, and Drama in the Ancient Near East*. New York: Harper & Row.

———, ed. 1959. *The New Golden Bough*. New York: Criterion.

———. 1969. *Myth, Legend and Custom in the Old Testament*. New York: Harper & Row.

Gunkel, Hermann. 1928. *What Remains of the Old Testament and Other Essays*. Translated by A. K. Dallas. New York: Macmillan.

———. 1964. *The Legends of Genesis: The Biblical Saga and History*. Translated by W. H. Carruth. Reprint of the introduction to the author's 1901 *Commentary on Genesis*. New York: Schocken.

———. 1987. *The Folktale in the Old Testament*. Translated by M. D. Rutter. Translation of the 1917 ed. Sheffield: Almond.

Lambert, W. G., and A. R. Millard, eds. 1999. *Atra-Hasis: The Babylonian Story of the Flood*. 1969. Reprint, Winona Lake, IN: Eisenbrauns.

Malina, Bruce. 1989. "Dealing with Biblical (Mediterranean) Characters: A Guide for U.S. Consumers." *BTB* 19:127–41.

Moran, William L. 1971. "Atrahasis: The Babylonian Story of the Flood." *Bib* 52:51–61.

Mowinckel, Sigmund. 1966. *Psalmenstudien: 1921–1924*. Amsterdam: Grüner.

Murdock, George Peter. 1969. *Ethnographic Atlas*. 3rd ed. Pittsburgh: University of Pittsburgh Press.

———. 1981. *Atlas of World Cultures*. Pittsburgh: University of Pittsburgh Press.

Murdock, George Peter, C. S. Ford, A. E. Hudson, R. Kennedy, L. W. Simmons, and J. W. M. Whiting. 1987. *Outline of Cultural Materials*. 5th ed. New Haven: Human Relations Area Files.

Oswalt, J. N. 1980. "Kabash." In *Theological Wordbook of the Old Testament*, edited by R. Laird Harris, Gleason L. Archer, and Bruce K. Waltke, 1:430. Chicago: Moody Press.

Page, Hugh R., Jr. 1999. "The Marking of Social, Political, Religious, and Other Boundaries in Biblical Literature—A Case Study Using the Book of Judges." *Research in the Social Scientific Study of Religion* 10:37–55.

Pedersen, Johannes. 1926–1940. *Israel: Its Life and Culture*. 4 vols. London: Oxford University Press.

Price, David H. 2004. *Atlas of World Cultures: A Geographical Guide to Ethnographic Literature*. 1989. Reprint, Caldwell, NJ: Blackburn.

Rad, Gerhard von. 1966. *The Problem of the Hexateuch and Other Essays*. London: SCM.

Thompson, Stith. 2001. *Motif-index of Folk-Literature: A Classification of Narrative Elements in Folk-tales, Ballads, Myths, Fables, Mediaeval Romances, Exempla, Fabliaux, Jest-Books*. Rev. ed. 6 vols. Bloomington: University of Indiana Press.

United Nations General Assembly. 2000. "Universal Declaration of Human Rights (1948)." In *Sourcebook of the World's Religions: An Interfaith Guide to Religion and Spirituality*, edited by J. Beversluis, 325–28. Novato, CA: New World Library.

———. 2007. *United Nations Declaration on the Rights of Indigenous Peoples*. http://www.un.org/esa/socdev/unpfii/documents/DRIPS_en.pdf.

READING THE CHRISTIAN OLD TESTAMENT IN THE CONTEMPORARY WORLD

Daniel L. Smith-Christopher

In nineteenth-century Charleston, South Carolina, the Old Testament seemed to assure Episcopal clergyman Frederick Dalcho that slavery was consistent with Christian faith. The same Old Testament, however, particularly Josh. 6:21, just as powerfully inspired fellow Charleston resident and former slave Denmark Vesey to plan a slave revolt. Those involved in the slave revolt felt assured that God would help them "utterly destroy all in the city, both men and women, young and old, with the edge of the sword" (Edgerton 1999, 101–25). In 2010, Steven Hayward, at that time F. K. Weyerhaeuser Fellow at the American Enterprise Institute, published an essay in which he read the story of Joseph in Egypt as a dire warning against government intervention, and suggested that his reading of these texts from Genesis served as a defense of a free-market, private-property economic system. Also in 2010, John Rogerson, professor of Scripture at Sheffield University, began his book on Old Testament theology, written because he, too, believed that the "Old Testament has something to say to today's world(s)," by stating that he wrote as "an Anglican priest . . . a humanist and a socialist" (Rogerson, 11). Dr. James Edwards, of the Center for Immigration Studies, reads some of the Mosaic laws of the Old Testament as defending firm national borders, low tolerance for immigration rights, and concerns for cultural corruption by outsiders (Edwards 2009 n.p., online), while Dr. Lai Ling Elizabeth Ngan of Baylor University, an Asian American scholar, finds that the Old Testament story about God's listening to the prayers of the "foreign woman," namely Hagar, "redefines boundaries that others have inscribed for her"; the story suggests that modern Christians should uphold the dignity of all peoples and resist denigrating people because of physical or racial differences (Ngan 2006, 83).

These are six Christians, all reading their Old Testament in the contemporary world. The fact that not all of these voices are biblical scholars, however, only serves to highlight the fact that reading the Christian Old Testament in the contemporary world is a complex mixture of the scholarly as well as the popular, stereotyped traditional views as well as innovative new insights, and that reading the Old Testament often strikingly divides readers into quite seriously opposing social and political views. Does this mean that reading the Christian Bible (Old or New Testament) in the modern world is a parade example of Cole Porter's 1934 song "Anything Goes"? Is it a matter of some disappointment that we can still agree with Leo Perdue's 1994 observation that "no commanding contemporary theology has yet appeared to form a consensus" (Perdue 1994, 8)?

I would argue that there is no cause for despair. Quite to the contrary! One of the most fascinating aspects of reading the Christian Old Testament in the contemporary world is not simply that there is unprecedented enthusiasm and diversity among scholars and viewpoints in the field but also that *this diversity itself is part of an ongoing debate and discussion*. At the outset, however, we should clarify that we are interested in thinking about serious readings of the Christian Old Testament, and not merely social or political propaganda that lightly seasons its rhetoric with a few Bible verses.

Marketplaces vs. Museums

Biblical scholarship is separated from religious propaganda not only by the fact that biblical scholarship presumes a basic orientation in the relevant historical contexts of the ancient world, familiarity with a diversity of texts both ancient and modern, and the ability to recognize a good argument supported by credible evidence or reasonable suggestions. These are all essential, of course. What really separates biblical scholarship from propaganda is the fact that biblical scholarship in the contemporary world is part of an ongoing discussion—a discussion that knows *and listens* to the challenges of others and seeks to contribute one's own insights *as part of the discussion*. As in all fields of discovery and intellectual endeavor, the success of biblical scholarship is not to be measured by the achievement of some dominant unanimity, but rather is judged by the quality and results of the participation in the scholarly tasks at hand and the *shared perception* that progress is taking place. We are seeing and understanding biblical texts in ever more profound and provocative ways. However, one of the most striking aspects of the rise of simplistic or propagandist use of the Bible is precisely its refusal to engage in dialogue, self-correction, or even acknowledgment of rival views, beyond the occasional ad hominem dismissal of arguments based solely on their association with groups identified by politicized generalizations—for example, "those liberals."

What we are suggesting is that there is an essential *dialogue* in modern, serious reading of the Bible. So, if this essay on reading the Christian Old Testament is not to be a rehearsal of some of the grand theories generally agreed on, now and forever (like a quiet museum tour of accomplishments), it is time for a new guiding image. I am intrigued by suggestions of the Cuban American New Testament scholar Fernando Segovia, who celebrates diversity in dialogue over the Scriptures. Segovia has famously suggested the "marketplace of ideas," rather like Wole Soyinka's discussion of the Silk Road market town Samarkand, as an image of modern sharing and exchanging of multicultural ideas and friendships (see Segovia and Tolbert; Segovia; Soyinka). An introduction to reading the Christian Old Testament in the contemporary world does not need to provide a historical survey of the "great ideas" that led to the present. Good surveys already exist, if European-dominated ideas are one's particular interest (e.g., Ollenburger; Rogerson 1984; Hayes and Prussner). Marketplaces can be elusive, however. They exist within the totality of the lives of people from everywhere, people who set up stalls and shop. Like the night markets of Auckland, New Zealand, or Darwin, Australia, they appear at designated places, at the designated hours, but otherwise there is only quiet. In short, the image of the marketplace suggests that we need a guidebook.

Laura Pulido, Laura Barraclough, and Wendy Cheng have recently published a marvelous, politically informed tour guide titled *A People's Guide to Los Angeles* (2012). The introduction itself is worth the price of admission. In these preliminary observations, the authors reflect on guidebooks and Los Angeles itself.

> *A People's Guide to Los Angeles* is a deliberate political disruption of the way Los Angeles is commonly known and experienced. . . . Guidebooks select sites, put them on a map, and interpret them in terms of their historical and contemporary significance. All such representations are political, because they highlight some perspectives while overlooking others. Struggles over who and what counts as "historic" and worthy of a visit involve decisions about who belongs and who doesn't, who is worth remembering and who can be forgotten, who we have been and who we are becoming.

They continue,

> Mainstream guidebooks typically describe and interpret their sites through the story of one person—almost always a man, and usually the capitalist who invested in a place, or its architect or designer. In doing so, they reinforce an individualized and masculinist way of thinking about history. Meanwhile, the collectives of people who actually created, built, or used the space remain nameless.

It would be difficult to think of a better series of thoughts to begin an essay on reading the Christian Old Testament in the contemporary world, because biblical analysis is rarely, if ever, written without some contemporary concerns in mind. Modern biblical theologies, for example, now usually identify the perspective of the author in the contemporary world (e.g., Brueggemann 1997; Rogerson 2010). Thus I am quite certain that part of the reason I agree with this need for a new image is that I write as a Christian who was born into, and very self-consciously remain informed by, the Quaker tradition. I also learned a great deal of biblical history, language, and theology from my fellow Christian sectarians the Mennonites, and I was first inspired to think seriously about biblical theology in high school by reading Vernard Eller, a theologian from yet another of my sister sectarian movements, the Church of the Brethren (informally known as the Dunkers). This means that I write as a Christian raised on "counterhistories" of the Christian movement—George Fox on Pendle Hill, Margaret Fell at Swarthmore, Conrad Grebel in Zurich, and Alexander Mack in Philadelphia—in addition to the canonical events of Christian history, such as the councils, the division between Rome and the Eastern Orthodox, Calvin, Luther, Wesley, and so on. I am thus well aware that texts, like towns, are susceptible to decisions about which locations are worthy of a visit, and which locations ought to be "memorialized" as deeply important. We could visit the old, established halls memorializing conquest or power—or we can find the marketplaces where we can encounter new ideas, argue with the "stall keepers" (the authors), make offers and listen to the counteroffers. In short, Christian biblical scholarship is tolerant of a variety of particular views of biblical texts, grammar, history, or theological interpretation. It is quite properly intolerant of the refusal to participate in dialogue with others. One of the hallmarks of propagandist abuses of the Bible in the modern world is the virtual absence of dialogue with other serious students of the Bible—a refusal to appear in the marketplace where ideas are examined and challenged.

It might seem that all this "marketplace" talk runs the risk of privileging process rather than results, and thus avoiding the hard work of evaluating whether ideas are good or bad, and then promoting the good. It is a uniquely contemporary heresy, however, to privilege solitary ideas or accomplishments while overlooking the long processes that often lead to any achievements worthy of celebration. Furthermore, to celebrate dialogue in the development of Christian thought about the Bible has sometimes been thought to be a uniquely modern phenomenon. That is already a mistake. What constitutes the "Old Testament," and even whether to have one, have both been matters of serious debate in Christian history.

The Christian Old Testament as a Product of Dialogue

Let us begin with a deceptively simple question: What constitutes the Old Testament? Christians do not even agree on this! Before the early Christian movement that historians now routinely refer to as "orthodox" arose victorious, the determination of what would be the authorized and foundational writings for Christian faith was a lively debate. The so-called *Festal Letter* 39 of Athanasius, which includes the earliest authoritative "list" of a canon of the Christian Bible, is dated to (a surprisingly late) 367 CE. Before then, debates about texts clearly ranged widely, and this does not even address the interesting continued use of noncanonical lore in popular, pre-Reformation medieval theater in the streets and churches of Europe (see Muir).

Furthermore, Athanasius's fourth-century declaration did not really settle the matter. Protestant, Catholic, and Orthodox Christians have each determined to authorize slightly different Old Testaments. Catholics, staying with the collection of Jewish writings that appeared in some of the old Greek translations known as the Septuagint (LXX), have included a series of books in the Old Testament that Protestants do not recognize, which Catholics call "deuterocanonical," and the Orthodox have chosen to include even a few more of these later Jewish (but still pre-Christian) writings. Protestants usually refer to these works as "the Apocrypha." Having said this, however, the difference between Christian canons has fewer implications for biblical scholarship than one might suspect at first. This is primarily because academic biblical studies, including biblical theological work, now tends to overlook specific church doctrines regarding the categories of "canonical," "deuterocanonical," and "noncanonical" writings. In the biblical studies marketplace, no text, artifact, ancient translation, or geographical context is "off limits" to research, comment, and consideration.

Canonical works obviously get the most attention—but it is hardly exclusive—and commentaries and critical analysis of *noncanonical* writing often make significant contributions to the further understanding of the canonical work as well. But we aren't finished with dialogue in relation to the existence of the Old Testament.

In fact, Christianity was marked by diversity in dialogue from the very beginning, as any sober reading of the arguments discussed in the book of Acts clearly reveals. One reason that dialogue is such an important context for thinking about the Old Testament is the fact that *the very existence of a "Christian Old Testament" was not a matter of widespread agreement in the earliest history of Christianity*. The early Christian convert Marcion (c. 85–160) famously proposed that true Christianity ought to discard any connection whatsoever to Judaism and the Jewish tradition; he embraced only a limited number of writings to represent this clean break between Jesus and the Jewish tradition (he proposed only a version of Luke, and ten Pauline epistles). However, the reaction was furious and widespread. W. H. C. Frend argues that Marcion holds the distinction of being "one of the very few opponents of orthodoxy whom Greek and Latin theologians united in damning. For nearly a century after his death . . . he was the arch-heretic" (212). Clearly, not every idea in the marketplace survives. We can stop cynically humming Porter's "Anything Goes" now.

The first Christian centuries, therefore, bequeath a task to all subsequent generations of readers of the "Christian Old Testament," namely, to take these writings into serious consideration when determining the nature of Christian faith. Furthermore, the vast majority of modern Christian communities (Protestant, Catholic, and Orthodox) have agreed with the church fathers and mothers of the first centuries that Christianity does indeed have a "canon," and that the Hebrew writings are part of it. Is this a settled issue, then? Hardly. Before we can speak of ways the Christian Old Testament is being read in the contemporary world, it is important to acknowledge, however briefly, that there are still ways it is *not* being read, and that it is even effectively ignored, in Christian faith and practice. Marcion still haunts us.

Tourism vs. Engagement: Ignoring the Marketplace?

As Aidan Nichols has recently acknowledged for the Catholic Church (2007), and as many others have suggested for other churches (Jenkins 2006, 42–47), a serious tendency remains among many Christian traditions in the modern world to overlook the larger part of their Bible before the Gospel of Matthew begins. Effectively ignoring the witness of the Old Testament for modern Christian faith and practice has sometimes been referred to as "Neo-Marcionism" (Nichols, 81). Even though few modern Christians would explicitly admit to it, the lack of effective education or preaching in Old Testament/Hebrew Bible studies is an alarming prospect for Christian faith and practice. A Christian theology cannot be true to the historic legacy of the faith tradition if it perpetuates such a neo-Marcionite subordination of these texts. This can happen in a number of ways, but it is more typical of popular and/or propagandist readings of the Bible than in biblical scholarship. In fact, some ways of "reading the Christian Old Testament" are simply ways to avoid it!

For example, there is a huge market for "Bible prophecy" books in the United States. One of the most significant criticisms of this popular literature is not only its total neglect of serious biblical scholarship on the prophetic books of the Old Testament but also its exclusive interest in how the books of the Bible may be "decoded" so that they can be understood to refer to contemporary events—as if the eighth-century-BCE book of Amos were actually speaking about twentieth-century Russia, or second-century-BCE portions of the book of Daniel were actually speaking about the twentieth-century ayatollahs of Iran. This "decoding" process usually neglects the historical content of the Old Testament book at hand in favor of what it is "understood" to be saying about modern times. In short, the actual content is merely a code. Its decoded meaning has nothing to do with what is actually written, when it was written, or who may have written it. One effective way of entirely ignoring a biblical book, then, is to completely reconstruct it without regard to its actual content as a historical work. This may not be Marcion's original idea, but he would clearly approve. This radical transformation of the work has little to do with actual study of it, nor is this part of the serious dialogue taking place about how the books of the Old Testament ought to inform contemporary Christian faith and practice.

This case of wildly popular literature on Bible prophecy in the modern world is particularly ironic. While some Christians frequently fault biblical scholars for not accepting the "plain sense" of the biblical text, it is astounding how carefully the various approaches to Bible prophecy omit any engagement with the most straightforward, or "plain," messages of the prophets of ancient Israel, namely, God's concern for the poor and the judgment threatened against the rich and powerful, those who, in the unforgettable images of Amos and Isaiah,

> trample the head of the poor into the dust of the earth,
>   and push the afflicted out of the way (Amos 2:7)

or who

> join house to house,
>   who add field to field,
> until there is room for no one but you,
>   and you are left to live alone
>   in the midst of the land! (Isa. 5:8)

No decoding seems necessary here. Radically altering the Old Testament texts beyond any credible historical or theological contexts in the process is clearly to do violence to those texts.

Another even more problematic way to virtually ignore the Old Testament in the Christian tradition is the Christian idea that the Old Testament is "old" and therefore largely replaced by the New Testament. Jesus is thus understood to have so reformed Jewish thought, very much as in Marcion's original proposal, that very little of the Old Testament is left of any real importance for Christian theology (save, perhaps, for the Ten Commandments). The dangers of such a "de-Semiticized" Jesus are legion, beginning with the problem of failing to understand Jesus' own faith tradition. For example, the event universally known as the "cleansing of the temple" is incomprehensible apart from recognizing that Jesus cites two Hebrew prophets in the act (Jer. 7:11 and Isa. 56:7). The reactions to Jesus' famous "reading" in his home synagogue in Luke 4 are equally incomprehensible apart from carefully noting the Old Testament references therein. Such examples can be multiplied throughout the New Testament.

Finally, the Hebrew tradition in both its historic and contemporary expressions is revered by a living people. Contemporary Christian scholarship is increasingly open to dialogue with Jewish biblical scholarship. Even though all Christians share most of the books of the Jewish canon with Judaism, there has been historically a significant difference in Jewish study of the Bible as opposed to Christian study (see summaries in Sommer 2012). One of the important characteristics of modern Christian readings of the Old Testament is that Jewish, Roman Catholic, Orthodox, and Protestant Scripture scholars are all in dialogue and discussion with each other in biblical studies on levels unprecedented before the twentieth century, and these dialogues continue in a variety of academic contexts in the twenty-first century.

Exorcising the ghost of Marcion from contemporary Christian scholarship of the Old Testament properly insists that taking the Old Testament seriously for Christian faith and practice involves a consideration of what Old Testament writings can say to the Christian tradition, not vice versa; Christian tradition should not use the Old Testament to buttress predetermined doctrinal ideas derived from the New Testament. Dictating terms to the Old Testament will never allow it to speak to Christian faith and practice in new and challenging ways. That isn't the way a marketplace works, after all, and trying to fix prices and control commodities only leads to other marketplaces.

The Role of Historical Events in the Old Testament for Christian Faith and Practice

We have already determined that the adjective *Christian* in our title means that we are interested in how the Old Testament speaks to Christian faith and practice, and therefore we are interested in discussing the role of "biblical theology." Here we encounter one of the loudest sectors of our marketplace. There are contemporary scholars (see Barr) who maintain an older tradition that suggests Old Testament scholarship should never be primarily "religious" or "theological," but rather historical, examining texts and other ancient evidence and then handing the results over to the theologians. Thus some scholars believe that biblical theology seeks to identify an exclusively *historical* expression of *past* belief (e.g., What did the ancient Israelites believe?). Indeed, the famous inaugural lecture of Johann Gabler in 1787, considered by some to be the "founding document" of this understanding of biblical theology (Gabler, 497), argued quite forcefully for maintaining a clear separation between biblical theology, defined as an exclusively historical enterprise, on the one hand, and systematic ("dogmatic") theology on the other.

It should be acknowledged that many modern biblical scholars would insist on this same separation between the historical and the theological approaches to Old Testament study and firmly place themselves in the "historical questions only" camp. Some scholars, again citing the late James Barr, have no objection to doing Christian theology based on biblical ideas, but believe that the formulation of these religious ideas ought to be a separate task from the exclusively historical task of Old Testament study. There are others who have doubts about religious belief in general or about the viability or validity of the specific religious traditions that make religious use of these writings. Some biblical scholars self-identify as atheists, for example, and there are even contemporary biblical scholars who openly condemn the very notion of a viable contemporary belief informed by the Bible (e.g., Avalos).

Both versions of the "historical analysis only" argument would maintain that it is not only possible but also necessary for a scholar of biblical texts to refrain from allowing contemporary interests or commitments (religious or otherwise) to "bias" or "interfere" with the task of historical analysis. This proposed form of historical analysis is represented as an activity that seeks to emulate scientific methodology as much as possible. The goal of this approach is thus described as "objective knowledge," or at least a close approximation of objective knowledge, even if these scholars were to acknowledge that certain influences or limitations of a time period certainly apply, such as the state of historical, archaeological, and textual studies at the time. In either case, the result is similar: a form of biblical studies that would be understood entirely as an aspect of historical investigation, no different in kind from determining what Shakespeare or Isaac Newton may have "believed," on religious (or any other) questions. Thus, while some may think or hope that their work could contribute to Christian faith and practice, they would carefully leave that task to others.

Interest-Free Biblical Analysis?

Recent debates, however, forcefully challenge many of the methodological assumptions that a bias-free analysis of historical texts is even a possible, much less laudable, goal. The term *postmodernism* is normally assigned to such challenges. Especially since the work of Thomas Kuhn (who gave us the concept of a "paradigm shift," 1996) and Paul Feyerabend (who calls for an "anarchist theory of knowledge," 2010), even the notion of an "objective" *scientific* analysis (science being the purported, even if largely self-appointed, model of objective analysis for all fields of inquiry) has been largely abandoned as both claim and goal. Motivations or interests do not necessarily poison results, but in the postmodern age, we are always vigilant about their influence, and thus the tendency in postmodernism is to declare such "interests" in the work itself. Does this preclude the possibility of doing biblical theology for modern Christian faith and practice? I contend that the postmodern criticism of a "bias-free" analysis of the Bible not only allows an enterprise of biblical theology but also positively encourages it.

The endless debates about the precise meaning of postmodernism need not distract us from a useful insight associated with this term: *all knowledge is contingent.* What we "know" usually depends on what we seek to know, and thus the questions we think to ask. Furthermore, what we investigate is influenced by own concerns, and we also sort out and determine which of our results are the most important. This is all part of the dialogue of diversity and, in twenty-first-century study of the Christian Old Testament, is now a widely acknowledged working assumption. Few would deny the importance of not only the identification of one's own working interests and assumptions in thinking about how the Christian Old Testament can speak to the modern age but also the retrospective work of placing older Old Testament theological writings in important social and historical contexts in ways that deepen our appreciation of their achievements and limitations (Rogerson 1984).

Is There a "Collapse of History" in Christian Old Testament Study?

There is an interesting debate going on in another sector of the marketplace. In his recent important monographs on the problems of Old Testament biblical theology, Leo Perdue refers to a "collapse of history" in recent biblical studies. One of the ways he formulates this point is to ask: Can these predominantly religious texts really help us reconstruct historical events in ancient Israel? If not, how can it be said that Israel's experience is important for contemporary readers who are seeking to read these texts as a guide to events that inform contemporary faith and practice? Perdue alludes to an important ongoing debate that began in the late twentieth century, a debate about our ability to know much actual history from what is available to us both in the Old Testament texts and in the relevant archaeological work (both ancient texts and artifacts) that supplements the study of biblical texts.

Especially after the publication of Thomas L. Thompson's widely cited monograph *The Historicity of the Patriarchal Narratives* (1974), fiery debates ensued between scholars who were divided (often unfairly) into "camps" called "minimalists" and "maximalists." These terms referred to those who despaired of the ability to be confident about historical events at all (thus "minimalists") and those who thought there was actually a great deal more evidence for biblical history than was often acknowledged (so Dever 2001; 2003). An interesting summary view of some of the historical debates is provided by Grabbe.

However, as some contemporary scholars have pointed out (see Brueggemann), these debates about historical events and biblical narratives mask the importance of answering a previous question, namely, whether *establishing that an event happened—or precisely how it happened—automatically dictates a corresponding religious significance to that event.* Clearly, it does not. Even if I can be convinced, for example, that the measurements of the temple provided in Ezekiel 40–48 are precise, accurate dimensions of the Jerusalem temple during the first millennium BCE, this does not strike me as having monumental importance for Christian faith and practice. It may have quite fascinating historical interest, but *theological* significance? This can also apply to less obscure issues. For example, determining that the texts in the opening chapters of the book of Exodus give us a more or less "historically reliable" report of the actual events of Israelites departing from Egypt does not thereby answer the question: Of what significance is the departure from Egypt *for contemporary Christian faith and practice?* Simply agreeing on the *historical* reliability of a biblical passage leaves considerable ground to cover on questions of *significance.* Simply agreeing on the historical details of the exodus, for example, does not thereby make one a liberation theologian. In fact, precious little of the powerful writings of liberation theology, beginning with the 1968 gathering of bishops in Medellín, Colombia (CELAM), actually debated the historical details of the book of Exodus. It is not that the historical story is insignificant; but rather its historical significance, if any, needs to be *part* of the theological argument, and not the entire task.

What happens when different perspectives can no longer be united on a particular reading of biblical events, especially on the accompanying significance of those events? Dominant and influential Old Testament theologies of the past depended on accepting an assigned weight to particular passages or biblical events that were considered central or guiding concepts, and thus critically important for modern theology. For example, Walter Eichrodt proposed that the idea of God's establishing agreements or "covenants" with God's people represents the central notion of the entire Hebrew Bible (Eichrodt 1961; 1967; the original German volumes were published in 1933 and 1935). Gerhard von Rad's equally influential Old Testament theology (Rad 1962; 1965; German 1957 and 1960) argued for the central importance of certain narratives of faith that Israelites allegedly repeated (he used the term "creeds") as indications of their faith, and thus suggested that Israelites were people who identified with such narratives. There is little doubt that such theological arguments, based on readings of the Old Testament, exerted a powerful influence on Christian theological education throughout the Western world in the twentieth century.

However, what if differing perspectives on the part of modern readers of the Bible—especially influenced by differing life situations (ethnicity, gender, etc.)—suggest to some modern readers that different biblical "events" in the Old Testament (whether unquestionably historical or not) are more important than others? Examples are not difficult to cite. On the one hand, after 1968, Latin American biblical scholars (especially Roman Catholic scholars) determined that the Moses and Exodus stories had a powerful message for them in their modern-day circumstances of economic poverty. On the other hand, Native American (Osage) professor of American studies Robert Allan Warrior famously challenged biblical theologians who celebrated the exodus and the entry to a "promised land" by noting that Native Americans frankly had more in common with the beleaguered Canaanites, reminding us that indigenous peoples continue to have an ambiguous relationship with the legacy of the book of Joshua (see Warrior). Nineteenth-century African American slaves also determined that the Jonah and Daniel stories had powerful messages for them in their circumstances of oppression and suppression (Levine; Cone 1992). Finally, recent suggestions view the conquest of Jerusalem in 587 and the subsequent exile of thousands of Judeans (Albertz; Ahn) as a biblical event with serious theological implications (Brueggemann; Smith-Christopher 2002). Nineteenth-century Maori Christians in New Zealand determined that the prophets were powerful examples of a new form of pantribal leadership that had new potential to unite previously fragmented tribal peoples in opposition to growing European settlement, and some even looked to the Davidic monarchy as a model for a new and culturally unprecedented Maori king, and thus an answer to the power and authority of the British Crown (Elsmore 1985; 1989). Is all this also a "collapse of history"? Or is it really the collapse of *dominant readings* of history in the face of alternative decisions about central ideas, events, and themes?

There is little doubt that some Christian biblical scholars and theologians lament the absence of the dominant Old Testament readings. Such a view arguably represents a kind of wistfulness for the "good old days" when a dominant perspective seemed to influence writing and doing (and teaching!) Old Testament theology in Christian institutions of higher learning. Not only does this "hoped-for dominant" perspective do violence to those who were never part of the "dominant perspective" (because they were either gender or cultural minorities, e.g., women, African American,

Asian American, Latino/Latina, or theological minorities such as Anabaptists, Quakers, or Pentecostals), but it is also arguably built on a largely discredited model of intellectual progress that mimics seventeenth- to twentieth-century Western imperial politics and social values—namely, the (intellectual) goal of domination and the vanquishing of opposition.

Surely an alternative to dominance or conquest is concord, dialogue, and cooperation in common causes. If we are to read the Christian Old Testament, and consider it theologically significant, then that theological significance will have to extend to the entire world. The *emerging* Christian world is now based in the Southern Hemisphere (Jenkins 2002). Reading the Christian Old Testament is thus by necessity a global enterprise. The modern marketplace is diverse indeed, and there are a number of ways to recognize this diversity.

Contemporary Worlds in Dialogue

We have seen that Segovia's "marketplace of ideas" does not so much despair of speaking of the past at all, much less signal a "collapse of history." The issue is not whether history can be written any longer. Rather, the issue is how different histories, and different texts, can be understood to matter in differing contexts. Marketplaces can resist organization. Nevertheless, there are perhaps two general ways of sorting the diversity in view. One way is to focus on the identities of the participants themselves, especially in those cases when they consciously and explicitly draw on these identities in their reading of the Bible. The other is to focus on challenges to the human enterprise in local or global contexts. Many of these challenges will require that we marshal our collective wisdom in order to survive as a species, and there are hardly more urgent reasons for biblical scholars to make their contribution to the ideological, spiritual, and political will of people to act in positive ways.

Text and Experience: The Feminist Pioneering of New Questions

New Testament scholar Elisabeth Schüssler Fiorenza points out that it was early feminist critical studies that largely opened up critical readings of both the New and Old Testaments from a perspective informed by particular "interests" (see Schüssler Fiorenza). One of first of these interests was reviewing the long-presumed subordination of women in the narratives of the Bible. It is interesting to see how this work progressed in a variety of different directions, all inspired by gender-related questions. For some feminist readers of the Bible, restating the often unacknowledged positive and powerful roles of women in the Bible is an important corrective to assumptions about the exclusive biblical focus on men (Gafney; Meyers 1988/2013). Phyllis Trible, on the other hand, pioneered the role of an unvarnished focus on destructive texts featuring violence against women, calling them "texts of terror" and thus highlighting dangerous tendencies within historical biblical cultures themselves (see Trible). Renita Weems, similarly, opened a line of investigation on the prophetic use of violent language associated with feminized subjects and objects that also betrayed violent attitudes (e.g., "Lady Jerusalem," Weems 1995). Kathleen O'Connor, Elizabeth Boase, and Carleen Mandolfo have taken this conversation further, suggesting that there is evidence of an ongoing dialogue with "Lady Jerusalem" that began with the violent imagery noted by

Weems in Hosea and Ezekiel, but then continued to Lamentations and Deutero-Isaiah, suggesting that there is acknowledgment of and even repentance for this violence (see O'Connor; Boase; Mandolfo). There are many other directions that studies can go, many of which explicitly identify as feminist, or gender-interested, analysis (see, e.g., Yee 2003).

The feminist approach, far from being a limiting perspective, has moved methodologically from an interest in one formulation of a "minority" perspective—namely, the role of women—to a comparative interest in how this critical approach relates to other issues of "gendering" and "embodiment" in the Bible (homosexuality, prostitution, especially the vexed question of temple prostitution, foreign wives of mixed marriages, gender in relation to slavery, etc.). This approach can also move beyond questions of gender. These early feminist perspectives quite logically moved toward an interest in those who are considered "marginalized" in Hebrew texts—for example, Edomites, Egyptians, Moabites, those lumped together as "aliens" in the Mosaic laws, foreign workers—for other reasons. Interesting work indeed. But what does it have to do with Christian faith and practice?

While not all feminist analysis of the Bible is done with the hope that it will contribute to a more equitable and egalitarian Christian movement in the contemporary world, a considerable amount is.

Cultural Identities and Social Situations in the Marketplace

Feminism is not the only "contemporary interest" that has driven new questions in Christian biblical analysis. Especially those who hope biblical analysis will affect Christian faith and practice have made significant contributions. Already in narratives of freed slaves in North America, African American readers of the Bible were reflecting on their own insights, especially as a countertheology to the European preachers who constantly preached obedience and subservience (see Raboteau; Hopkins and Cummings). In fact, it is possible to trace a twentieth-century flowering of these early readings, some of which began by reexamining the role of explicitly identified Africans in biblical history (see Felder) in a manner similar to those who reexamined the Old Testament stories explicitly about women. One clear goal was to highlight African presence in the Bible that had been neglected in the face of racial prejudice in the modern world against those of African descent. However, in the wake of important calls for a more assertive black theology in the twentieth century (Cone 1970), this project then expanded in different directions in ways very similar to the expansion of gender-related questions (and often intersecting with gender questions, e.g., in "womanist" analysis; see Weems 1991). In the African American context, the appearance of the groundbreaking work *Stony the Road We Trod* (Felder) was a major contribution to the maturing of contemporary, consciously African American biblical scholarship. Included in this collection were essays that dealt not only with historical-critical analysis of the Bible from an African American perspective, but with the use of the Bible in the history of African American interpretation. Further work on African American history of interpretation (Callahan; Wimbush) continues to make important contributions to unique insights into both the later use of Scripture, but also arguments contributing to historical understanding of the texts themselves. Not only is the role of the Bible in African American history itself the subject of important analysis, but African American biblical analysis is also interested in examining texts that have been used historically to suppress both those of explicitly African descent (for example, to defend slavery) and many non-European peoples. A convergence in methods, and sometimes goals, began to emerge that sought to forge alliances across explicitly named cultural or ethnic categories.

So, even though it has followed a different trajectory than African American scholarship, Latino/Latina literature now also holds an important place in the context of the United States. For example, Justo González, Jean-Paul Ruiz, and Miguel De La Torre (2002; 2007) have published monographs and commentaries on Old Testament themes. Interestingly, however, De La Torre has taken a somewhat pessimistic attitude as to whether cross-cultural analysis of the text will influence the general discipline. De La Torre is clear—Euro-Americans are largely not to be trusted for biblical analysis, because "Euroamerican Christians, either from the fundamentalist right or the far liberal left, probably have more in common with each other and understand each other better than they do Christians on the other side of the racial and ethnic divide" (De La Torre 2007, 125). Nevertheless, serious contributions continue to challenge biblical scholars to take seriously the contributions of those who write Old Testament analysis from an openly acknowledged perspective. Gregory Lee Cuéllar, for example, compares passages of Isaiah to the Mexican and Mexican American folk music style known as the *Corrido*, not only to suggest ways that the biblical texts can be understood in contemporary Mexican American communities, but also to propose potential new readings for the book of Isaiah itself (Cuéllar 2008).

While there have been a number of important works from Asian American biblical scholars in the late twentieth century that consciously draw on Asian themes and identity, a significant milestone was the publication in 2006 of the collected volume *Ways of Being, Ways of Reading*. This volume was comparable in many ways to the impact of the 1991 work *Stony the Road We Trod* in the African American scholarly context. It includes retrospective and survey essays, even very personal reflections on academic work (e.g., Yee 2006), as well as examples of contemporary work of some of the most prominent American scholars using cross-cultural approaches.

Finally, in terms of the American context, it is notable that Randall Bailey, Tat-siong Benny Liew, and Fernando Segovia have initiated a dialogue between Latino/a American, Asian American, and African American scholarship, hoping to find common ground in "minority" analysis of the Bible (Bailey, Liew, and Segovia), suggesting the possibilities of a convergence and maturing of methods of analysis, even as they reject any sort of false consensus on similarity of cultural contexts.

Although it is fair to say that readings explicitly related to specific cultural and ethnic identities and traditions continue in the century, attention has tended to turn toward social, political, and economic locations as another significant source of issues that influence the reading of Scripture. In the last quarter of the twentieth century, a number of Old Testament scholars consciously incorporated sociological and anthropological analysis in their ancient historiography of the Bible (Gottwald; Overholt 1992, 2003), and this dialogue with social sciences certainly continues (Chalcraft). Exegetical issues of the most recent writing in Old Testament studies soon converged on a series of questions closely associated with the influence of Edward Said's classic work *Orientalism*, which further built on the early social theories and the observations of the postcolonial theorists Frantz Fanon and Albert Memmi. Once this dialogue with Said's influence was articulated powerfully in the many works of R. S. Sugirtharajah, the rise of postcolonial approaches to Scripture became a significant movement in the early twenty-first century. Sugirtharajah's now classic compendium *Voices from the Margin* signaled a new energy in "interested perspectives" in the reading of the Bible.

The Rise of Postcolonial Biblical Analysis

We have already noted that Christianity—and its Bible—is seeing profound growth in the Southern Hemisphere in the twenty-first century. Twentieth-century Christians in developing societies, especially India, South America, and Africa, began to assert their own perspectives in the analysis of the Bible. After Said's influential work, they began to identify ways in which previous European scholarship contained certain social and cultural assumptions about Western superiority. They then began readings of the Bible within their past experiences of European colonial presence. In the process of reasserting a cultural and/or national identity, however, they soon realized that a reconstruction of cultural identity in the new world could never go back to a purified "precolonial" state, but must always be in dialogue with the social, political, and philosophical realities of having been deeply affected by Western thought and practice. Although in the context of religion and the Bible, one might better speak of "post-Western-missionaryism," the discussions in biblical studies borrowed a term from social and cultural theory to identify their new reviews of the Bible in their own contexts: *postcolonialism*. Postcolonial biblical exegesis provided special tools for Christians in formerly colonized states (or among indigenous peoples in Western European settled lands, North and South America, Australia, and New Zealand). The questions whether, and to what extent, largely imported biblical scholarship was (and is) tainted by imperial goals of control and economic expansion raised serious concerns about those readings of Scripture that seemed deeply involved in that imperial process (De le Torre 2002). A prime example of attempting to counter Western domination was the Latin American assertion that the exodus is the prime event of the Old Testament—and thus liberation is the prime theological theme. However, it is important to note that these questions were being raised largely by Christian Bible scholars. Not all criticism of colonial and missionary policies rejected Christianity and the Bible as an unwanted imposition (see Roberts); sometimes it rather engaged in the more creative task of rereading the texts.

If "postcolonial" contexts include minorities living in multicultural nations, then Fernando Segovia's "Diasporic" approach to reading Scripture becomes especially suggestive. In the American context, this obviously can include African American, Asian American, and Mexican American readings of particular texts that resonate with themes, motifs, or elements of minority existence such that they lead to expositions of Old Testament texts that are suggestive for all readers of the Bible—and not only to fellow members of particular ethnic or cultural groups.

Ethnic and culturally informed readings challenge the notion that European scholarship has a privileged position in biblical scholarship generally, and in the construction of Christian theologies built from Old Testament texts particularly. What we have learned about diversity in dialogue is that the Christian reading of the Old Testament in the contemporary world will be richer, more learned, and more convincing in both textual and historical analysis only if our marketplace grows in its resemblance to the actual diversity of our worlds. What new insights into particular Old

Testament texts await the future BA, MA, or PhD theses and papers written by young Tibetan, Chinese, Navajo, Roma, or Aboriginal Australian students and scholars? What will they see that the rest of us have too quickly dismissed or completely overlooked? In the twenty-first century, we are likely to benefit from an increase of book titles like that of Senegalese American biblical scholar Aliou Niang: *Faith and Freedom in Galatia and Senegal: The Apostle Paul, Colonies, and Sending Gods.*

Let us reaffirm that diversity ought always to lead to dialogue. Agreements, shared insights, and common convictions that we are all learning from the dialogue ought to deliver even the most cynical from the simplistic hope that we Bible scholars would just please get to "the bottom line." Marketplaces don't have a bottom line! Dialogue and haggling over texts is simply the reality. The invitation, therefore, is to listen and learn. Incidentally, lest Christians think that all this is somehow radically new, those familiar with classic rabbinic dialogue and argumentation over religious texts are aware that dialogue with God and with each other is at the heart of theology.

Issues Driving Contemporary Biblical Analysis

Questions from identities and cultural experiences are not, however, the only major and significant sources of urgency in reading and rereading the Christian Old Testament. A number of contemporary global crises have inspired a renewed examination of the ways in which the Bible can be reread. The modern interest in trauma as the psychosocial reality of a world in crisis has recently gained ground in biblical analysis (see O'Connor; Janzen; Kelle). The millions of humans who flee wars and crises as international refugees have also influenced biblical analysis on ancient exile and deportation (see Ahn). The potential list of pressing issues is depressingly long, of course, but it is possible to examine a few examples to illustrate how this section of the marketplace can be organized. In fact, we can move from an example that is already very old but critically ongoing, war and peace in the Old Testament; to an issue that arguably has its roots in the twentieth century, environmentalism; and finally note the signs of a rising issue so new that it has barely begun to generate serious thought among biblical scholars: evolutionary philosophy, transhumanism, and the nature of the person.

War, Peace, and Violence and the Old Testament

Since the fourth century CE, the Christian church has been faced with direct responsibility for violence. The monarchical descendants of the Roman emperor Constantine made Christianity the official religion of the empire, leading into the Byzantine Empire. Biblical study was now intimately connected to the foreign policy of a powerful military machine, and would continue to have foreign policy implications from that time to the present. The continued relevance of the Bible to issues of war and peace is not difficult to discern in the writings of the Christian warriors and their chaplains on the one hand, and the Christian peacemakers and their communities on the other, throughout Western history especially. A clear majority in this debate has supported more violent interpretations, however regretfully they are sometimes offered.

The Jesus who said, "Love your enemies and pray for those who persecute you" (Matt. 5:44), and the Paul who exhorted, "live peaceably with all" (Rom. 12:18), were effectively trumped in Christian faith and practice very early on by an uncritical admiration for the genocidal Joshua and the conquering David (see Davies). There have been a variety of ways in which Christians have responded to the use of the Old Testament as a moral trump over the pacifist Jesus. Once again, the similarities to the methods of feminist biblical analysis are instructive.

For example, especially since the churches in twentieth-century Europe began to mobilize an opposition to the Cold War threats in their own backyards, innumerable monographs have attempted to reexamine the actual practices of Old Testament violence and warfare, either with explicit admiration (so, famously, Yadin), or appropriate levels of horror (Craigie; Niditch; Collins). In modern Old Testament study, then, one is hopefully exposed to the potential dangers of a casual and unguarded use of biblical texts that are so clearly contrary to contemporary moral judgments and international standards of justice.

Finally, similar to those who sought to lift up exemplary moments previously overlooked, there are those who seek to highlight strongly peaceful passages in the Bible that may even have been in critical dialogue with more violent episodes in the canon and thus reveal an internal dialogue or debate that reveals stronger peace voices among the canonical choir (Enz; Smith-Christopher 2007). This approach articulates how a certain form of Hebrew nonviolence would have been a logical expression of theological tendencies that had their roots in the Servant Songs of Second Isaiah and the universalism of the book of Jonah, where we find openness to the repentance of national enemies like the Assyrians, who are portrayed as repenting ". . . of the violence of their hands." Further developments can affirm the wisdom ethic of peacefulness—an ethic that frequently contrasts self-control over against brute force and earnestly recommends a sober, wise consideration of counsel and diplomacy (Prov. 16:7, 32; 17:27; 24:5-6). In fact, the Wisdom tradition may itself represent precisely a staging place for international discussion, given that wisdom values are as universal in the ancient Near East as any literary themes can be. Ancient Egyptian wisdom, Mesopotamian wisdom, and Greek wisdom all compare quite favorably to ancient Israelite forms.

Texts that reflect an Israelite "exilic" lifestyle, lived in "active nonconformity to the world" (as the famous 1955 Mennonite Church statement puts it), would also build on biblical protests against narrow ethnocentrism (e.g., the book of Ruth, Jacob's apology to Esau, Isaiah 56 and 66, and the striking affirmation in Zechariah 9 of a mixed-race people of God). In fact, there is evidence of a rising protest against violence and narrow self-centeredness (e.g., Ezekiel 40–48) that can be seen to affirm the Deuteronomic critique of the monarchy, and especially the condemnation of the monarchy in the penitential prayers of Ezra 9, Nehemiah 9, and Daniel 9. Thus the fact that there are passages where God is alleged to have called for the massacre of foreign cities does not necessarily cancel out or trump the fact that there are more hopeful passages on this subject as well, texts that openly question whether the stance of the Hebrews toward foreign peoples should be hostile and that envision a different and more peaceful reality (Isaiah 2; 19; Micah 4).

Regrettably, offering a more peaceful reading of the Old Testament will not likely bring about world peace. But if the late Colonel Harry Summers of the Army War College is correct that "it is the passions of the people that are the engines of war" (Summers, 75–76), then perhaps careful biblical analysis will remove at least one major ideological prop and provocation that has certainly been used in the past to excuse quite reprehensible behavior among those who honor the Scriptures (see Trimm).

Environmentalism

Biblical analysis that is driven by ecological concerns can be clearly dated to responses to the famous 1967 article in *Science* by Lynn White, accusing Christianity for providing the "roots" of the ecological crisis in God's injunction to the first couple in Gen. 1:28 to "subdue" and "have dominion" over nature. The late twentieth century then saw an increase of literature that highlighted ways that the Hebrew Bible/Old Testament affirmed a spirituality of care and responsibility for the earth as God's creation. Much of this work owes a great deal to the early writings of Australian biblical scholar Norman Habel (see also Hallman; so now Craven and Kaska; Deane-Drummond). The often-cited "this-worldly" emphasis of much Old Testament ethical discussion, and even the imagery of deep fascination with and appreciation of the created world (Job 38–41; Psalm 147–48), however, continues to inspire further development in pioneering biblical theologies. Genesis portrays God involving Adam in the naming of other creatures (Gen. 2:19) and further records God's intention to "re-create" the world in the Hebrew version of the flood narrative, the basic outlines of which were clearly known to the Jewish people by the time of the Babylonian captivity, and most likely borrowed from Mesopotamian traditions.

A related development is in the direction of animal rights. Concern for animal welfare is not absent from Hebrew law or narrative (Deut. 25:4; Numbers 22). The flood story, of course, involves the considerable responsibility of Noah to preserve animals. The Old Testament strikingly expresses certain visions of peace by referring to changes in the animal kingdom (Isa. 11:6: the wolf living with the lamb) and even hinting that in their first created state, humans were vegetarian (before Gen. 9:4, where eating meat is first explicitly mentioned). Psalm 148 portrays the created animals of the world praising God, and Job famously portrays God's careful attention and knowledge of the details of the animal kingdom (Job 39; on animal rights work, see Linzey 1995; 2009; Miller).

Work in environmentalism more generally, and animal rights specifically, have been parts of a move to appreciate biblical themes that buttress a more responsible care for the earth (Toly and Block). There are, however, some serious economic and even political issues at stake here. On the issue of environmentalism particularly, there has been a serious backlash from those with business interests who see strong environmentalist movements as potential threats to their expansion of industry. Not unexpectedly, then, this reaction has motivated more conservative Christian scholars to reassert a strongly pragmatic and typically short-term ethic of consumption unmitigated by strong concerns for conserving resources in the long term. Christians in this tradition, rarely biblical scholars themselves, are clearly not impressed with nuanced arguments about responsibility for species and their survival. Nor are they likely to be impressed by arguments based largely on Old Testament passages, especially if that concern is perceived as requiring economic sacrifices. An interesting example of this reaction is the work of Steven Hayward, from the conservative think tank the American Enterprise Institute. In a published essay titled "Mere Environmentalism" (the title itself is an homage to evangelical hero C. S. Lewis) and subtitled "A Biblical Perspective on Humans and the Natural World," Hayward suggests that the Genesis narratives promote the hierarchy of creation with humanity at the top. He therefore construes a biblical mandate, not for preservation of the environment, but for a "stewardship" that promotes responsible use of resources and a free-market-driven effort to conquer the "untamed wilderness," and furthermore as free of government intervention as possible. Indeed, Hayward further argues that the story of Joseph in Pharaoh's household is a warning against centralized state control, because Joseph's centralization of resources for the Pharaoh leads directly to the enslavement of the Hebrews. Environmental degradation, therefore, may be a matter calling for repentance, but definitely not for government regulation (33). Finally, Noah offers sacrifice of animals after the flood, Hayward notes, so this story provides no basis for simple preservation, and certainly suggests that animals were to be used for human benefit.

The twenty-first century is likely to see more, rather than less, of this polemical exchange in biblical scholarship. Although more propagandistic approaches have tended to avoid participation in scholarly organizations like the Society of Biblical Literature, we are likely to see more direct engagement over the use, and abuse, of Scripture on various issues of social, and especially economic, importance.

The Nature of the Person: The Rise of Evolutionary Social Science and Philosophy

Finally, it is important in the context of this essay to speculate about issues that may well emerge more fully as the twenty-first century develops. In the wake of Daniel Dennett's polemical 1996 assertion of atheist scientism, titled "Darwin's Dangerous Idea," there is a rise of perspectives represented by the following: "If you believe in a traditional concept of the soul, you should know that there is little doubt that a fuller appreciation of the implications of evolutionary theory . . . is going to destroy that concept"; and, "we must openly acknowledge . . . the collapse of a worldview that has sustained human energies for centuries" (Stanovich, 3). Will biblical studies also be challenged by evolutionary thought? If so, in what way?

In Christian theology and biblical studies, the classic beginning point for discussion of the nature of the human person is the concept of the *imago Dei*, the creation of humanity in the image and likeness of God (Gen. 1:26-27). J. Richard Middleton, for example, seeks to rethink the *imago Dei* debates in a modern context, noting that older Christian theological uses of Genesis 1 were rather strained, and usually presumed that the significance of "the image" and "likeness" of God was precisely human *reason*. Recent discussion has emphasized the royal context of these terms, suggesting that humans are portrayed as royally deputized representations of divine authority and responsibility in the world. Middleton even suggests that the *imago Dei* is, in fact, a politically sophisticated as well as theologically loaded term in Genesis, because here we find the textual staging ground for a narrative culture war against Mesopotamian hegemonic narratives of conquest and subservience. These Mesopotamian narratives were weapons in a philosophical/ideological war that accompanied the invading and conquering armies that conquered both the northern kingdom (722 BCE) and Jerusalem and Judah (597/587).

While it is quite possible to celebrate the theological importance of all humanity from an explic-itly evolutionary view of the emergence of *homo sapiens*, it is also clear that some interpretations of human evolution threaten to radically debase and reduce humanity to a mere "sack of genes," with little inherent worth, whose values, art, and faith are mere "spandrels" (that is, accidental and irrel-evant by-products) that accompany the real work of genetic reproduction. The value of life is thus no longer inherent in creation, but purely instrumental, as some humans serve as sexual slaves, soldiers, and workers for the shrinking and increasingly ruthless elite. The masses are already once again being pacified by the modern equivalent of bread and circus: ever smaller and more inexpensive sources of digital pornography, graphic violence, and (contra Kant's imperative) the view of fellow humans as means rather than ends.

In this context, religious faith (including, of course, the Bible) is strongly dismissed as "nothing but" the result of evolutionary mechanisms for survival. We perceive deities only because of our ancient and genetically honed "agency detection devices" (instincts that perceive potential threats in the environment). Others suggest that religion was merely a part of a sophisticated social "mate selection" mechanism whereby mates with trustworthy values could be quickly identified. In short, religion is a neural response pattern.

The interesting question is no longer, "Can a biblical scholar believe in evolution and teach Genesis"? Of course they can, and do. What is new is the rising insistence of a form of evolutionary social thought that would dismiss all religious speculation as irrelevant. Such a radically reduction-ist anthropology seeks to replace the "Eden myth" with an equally implausible and comprehensive "African Savannah myth" that subsumes all humanity into categories of neural survival mecha-nisms driven by reproductive genes. Does the Old Testament have anything to say in this decidedly modern discussion?

The resources of Wisdom literature and its emphasis on sober assessments of God's moral pat-terns in the created world provide a foundation beyond Genesis for seeking dialogue with naturalists and biologists. But the issues will continue to press, and will no longer be simply the leisure-time, science-fiction reading of those whose day jobs are in biblical studies. Seeking biblical guidance on the nature of the human person will become increasingly pressing in this century in the light of (1) increased emphasis in the human sciences on "transhumanism," according to which humans can be enhanced by further evolutionary merging with technology; (2) manipulation of genetic informa-tion to favor certain human traits (already taking place passively by rejecting human eggs in artificial insemination processes that bear indications of undesired genetic traits); (3) progress in artificial intelligence such that ethical questions are becoming increasingly prominent (when does turning off a machine consist of killing a living being? etc.); (4) further work in cloning; and (5) the location and identification of personhood as directly (and some would say: *only*) a function of neural brain activity, thus raising the possibility of "downloading" human persons into hardware.

Are these exclusively theological issues? Do they have any implications for biblical analysis? Will a biblical analysis arise, for example, driven in part by the prescience of the science fiction writer Philip K. Dick, who anticipated many ethical issues dealing with modern technology? It is possible that biblical scholars will simply suggest that radically new technologies are not the busi-ness of textual analysis. However, when those technologies raise serious questions about the nature and value of the human person, it is hard to resist the notion that biblical analysis has something to say to this issue.

Return to the Beginning: Does the Marketplace Matter? Are There Any Real People There?

Finally, we can pick up on a discussion that was left aside at the very beginning of this essay. What about the clashes among various readings of the Old Testament? Is biblical studies hopelessly mired in disagreements such that, in the end, an individual must simply hum along with Porter's "Anything Goes"?

Appearances, especially in the contemporary world, can be deceiving. The reality of extensive and exciting discussion and debate in biblical studies does not mean that the field is wandering aimlessly. Furthermore, the impressive level of publication and discussion does not mean that there is no consensus of methods or results among biblical scholars. Biblical scholars, like professionals in other fields such as medicine, engineering, or astronomy, certainly stay in touch with each other's work, and through international organizations (the largest being the Society of Biblical Literature) continue to pursue common interests, projects, and even enjoy continued debates and disagreements. It is hardly the case, as philosopher Alvin Plantinga somewhat sourly suggests, that biblical scholars can never agree on anything, explaining (for Plantinga, presumably) why Christians usually do not take their work seriously.

Plantinga may be surprised, however. The influence of biblical scholarship on wider Christian practices might be slow in manifesting itself, but it is absolutely clear. Plantinga should be impressed with the articulate, profound, and serious assessment of the importance of biblical analysis in the 1994 document of the Pontifical Biblical Commission titled "The Interpretation of the Bible in the Church." Calling the historical-critical method of biblical analysis "indispensable for the scientific study of the meaning of ancient texts," the document critically assesses, both positively and negatively, many current approaches to biblical analysis common in universities and biblical scholarship, and recommends much of modern biblical scholarship to the Catholic world more widely. Furthermore, the document famously refers to fundamentalist readings of Scripture as "intellectual suicide." Unimpressed with official declarations by hierarchies? One need only examine the textbooks for Catholic *high school* students, including those explicitly recommended by the bishops, to see the profound impact of biblical scholarship on questions of multiple authorship, historicity, the dangers of literalism, and so on.

Only the most conservative Christians today believe that the only way to treasure the significance of the narratives of Genesis is to take them literally, or believe that Moses wrote every word of the Pentateuch. Only the most fundamentalist Christians today would think that the book of Jonah is about surviving in the gullet of a marine animal, or that nearly one-fifth of the entire population of ancient Egypt left with Moses in the thirteenth century BCE. Furthermore, what many Christians in the church pews and Sunday schools *do* know is that a profound Christian faith can be enriched by learning that an unnamed second prophet we call "Second Isaiah" likely reapplied some of the thought of the eighth-century Isaiah of Jerusalem, but also proclaimed radically new thoughts in the late sixth-century BCE when the Persian emperor Cyrus lived. Furthermore, Christians today know much more about the horrific tragedy of the destruction of Jerusalem in 587, and how Lamentations is a powerful poetic response to that tragedy, and how Psalms contains religious poetry from long after the time of David. None of these ideas are shocking to Christians in the churches any more, and none of them are destructive of anything but the most simplistic of readings of the Old Testament.

Finally, what Christians in the churches surely know is that the Bible invites—indeed nearly demands—the careful attention of many different cultures, genders, ages, and contexts who are brought into dialogue as they listen, read, discuss, and debate the meanings and importance of these texts of the Old Testament. There is important historical information we can know, but there is so much more to ask. For those who love only quiet museum tours of "certainties" enclosed in glass cases so that the masses can be enlightened, biblical studies in the contemporary world is not for them. The marketplace is teaming, ebullient, and alive.

Works Cited

Ahn, John. 2010. *Exile as Forced Migrations: A Sociological, Literary, and Theological Approach on the Displacement and Resettlement of the Southern Kingdom of Judah.* Berlin: de Gruyter.

Albertz, Rainer. 2003. *Israel in Exile: The History and Literature of the Sixth Century B.C.E.* Atlanta: Society of Biblical Literature.

Avalos, Hector. 2007. *The End of Biblical Studies.* New York: Prometheus.

Bailey, Randall, Tat-siong Benny Liew, and Fernando F. Segovia, eds. 2009. *They Were All Together in One Place? Toward Minority Biblical Criticism.* Atlanta: Society of Biblical Literature.

Barr, James. 2000. *History and Ideology in the Old Testament: Biblical Studies at the End of a Millennium.* Oxford: Oxford University Press.

Boase, Elizabeth. 2006. *The Fulfillment of Doom? The Dialogic Interaction between the Book of Lamentations and the Pre-Exilic/Early Exilic Prophetic Literature.* London: T&T Clark.

Brueggemann, Walter. 1997. *Theology of the Old Testament: Testimony, Dispute, Advocacy.* Minneapolis: Fortress Press.

Callahan, Allen Dwight. 2006. *The Talking Book: African Americans and the Bible.* New Haven: Yale University Press.

Chalcraft, David. 2006. *Social-Scientific Old Testament Criticism.* London: T&T Clark.

Collins, John J. 2004. *Does the Bible Justify Violence?* Minneapolis: Fortress Press.

Cone, James H. 1970. *A Black Theology of Liberation.* Maryknoll, NY: Orbis.

———. 1992. *The Spirituals and the Blues: An Interpretation.* Maryknoll, NY: Orbis Books.

Craigie, Peter. 1979. *The Problem of War in the Old Testament.* Grand Rapids: Eerdmans.

Craven, Toni, and Mary Jo Kaska. 2011. "The Legacy of Creation in the Hebrew Bible and Apocryphal/Deuterocanonical Books." In *Spirit and Nature: The Study of Christian Spirituality in a Time of Ecological Urgency*, edited by Timothy Hessel-Robinson and Ray Maria McNamara, RSM, 16–48. Eugene, OR: Pickwick.

Cuellar, Gregory L. 2008. *Voices of Marginality: Exile and Return in Second Isaiah 40-55 and the Mexican Immigrant Experience.* New York: Peter Lang.

Davies, Eryl. 2010. *The Immoral Bible: Approaches to Biblical Ethics*. London: T&T Clark.

Deane-Drummond, Celia. 2008. *Eco-Theology*. London: Darton, Longman & Todd.

De La Torre, Miguel. 2002. *Reading the Bible from the Margins*. Maryknoll, NY: Orbis.

———. 2007. *Liberating Jonah: Forming an Ethic of Reconciliation*. Maryknoll, NY: Orbis.

Dennett, Daniel. 1996. *Darwin's Dangerous Idea*. New York: Simon & Schuster.

Dever, William G. 2001. *What Did the Biblical Writers Know and When Did They Know It?* Grand Rapids: Eerdmans.

———. 2003. *Who Were the Early Israelites and Where Did They Come From?* Grand Rapids: Eerdmans.

Edwards, James. 2009. *A Biblical Perspective on Immigration Policy*. Washington, DC: Center for Immigration Studies. http://www.cis.org/ImmigrationBible

Egerton, Douglas R. 1999. *He shall go out free : The lives of Denmark Vesey*. Madison, WI: Madison House, 1999

Eichrodt, Walter. 1961. *Theology of the Old Testament*. Translated by J. A. Baker. Vol. 1. London: SCM.

———. 1967. *Theology of the Old Testament*. Translated by J. A. Baker. Vol. 2. London: SCM.

Elsmore, Bronwyn. 1985. *Like Them That Dream: The Maori and the Old Testament*. Wellington, New Zealand: Tauranga Moana Press.

———. 1989. *Mana from Heaven*. Auckland: Reed.

Enz, Jacob. 2001. *The Christian and Warfare: The Roots of Pacifism in the Old Testament*. Eugene, OR: Wipf & Stock (reprint).

Fanon, Frantz. 1963. *The Wretched of the Earth*. New York: Grove.

Felder, Cain Hope, ed. 1991. *Stony the Road We Trod*. Minneapolis: Fortress Press.

Feyerabend, Paul. 2010. *Against Method*. New York: Verso.

Foskett, Mary F., and Jeffrey Kah-jin Kuan, eds. 2006. *Ways of Being, Ways of Reading: Asian American Biblical Interpretation*. St. Louis: Chalice.

Frend, W. H. C. 1984. *The Rise of Christianity*. Minneapolis: Fortress Press.

Gabler, Johann P. "An Oration on the Proper Distinction between Biblical and Dogmatic Theology and the Specific Objectives of Each." In Ollenburger, *Old Testament Theology*, 497–506.

Gafney, Wilda C. 2008. *Daughters of Miriam: Women Prophets in Ancient Israel*. Minneapolis: Fortress Press.

González, Justo L. 1996. *Santa Biblia: The Bible through Hispanic Eyes*. Nashville: Abingdon.

Gottwald, Norman. 1979. *The Tribes of Yahweh*. Maryknoll, NY: Orbis.

Grabbe, Lester. 2007. *Ancient Israel: What Do We Know and How Do We Know It?* New York: T&T Clark.

Habel, Norman. 1993. *The Land Is Mine: Six Biblical Land Ideologies*. Minneapolis: Fortress Press.

Hallman, David G. 1994. *Ecotheology: Voices from South and North*. Maryknoll, NY: Orbis.

Hayes, John H., and Frederick Prussner. 1984. *Old Testament Theology: Its History and Development*. Atlanta: John Knox.

Hopkins, Dwight N., and George C. L. Cummings, eds. 2003. *Cut Loose Your Stammering Tongue: Black Theology in the Slave Narratives*. Louisville: Westminster John Knox.

Janzen, David. 2012. *The Violent Gift: Trauma's Subversion of the Deuteronomistic History's Narrative*. LHB/OTS 561. London: T&T Clark.

Jenkins, Philip. 2002. *The Next Christendom: The Coming of Global Christianity*. New York: Oxford University Press.

———. 2006. *The New Faces of Christianity: Believing the Bible in the Global South*. New York: Oxford University Press.

Kelle, Brad. 2013. *Ezekiel*. New Beacon Bible Commentary. Kansas City: Beacon Hill.

Kuhn, Thomas. 1996. *The Structure of Scientific Revolutions*. 3rd ed. Chicago: University of Chicago Press.

Levine, Lawrence. 1977. *Black Culture and Black Consciousness.* New York: Oxford University Press.

Linzey, Andrew. 1995. *Animal Theology.* Urbana: University of Illinois Press.

———. 2009. *Creatures of the Same God.* New York: Lantern.

Mandolfo, Carleen. 2007. *Daughter Zion Talks Back to the Prophets.* Atlanta: Society of Biblical Literature.

Meyers, Carol. 1988/2013. *Rediscovering Eve: Ancient Israelite Women in Context.* Oxford: Oxford University Press.

Middleton, J. Richard. 2005. *The Liberating Image: The Imago Dei in Genesis 1.* Grand Rapids: Brazos.

Miller, David. 2011. *Animal Ethics and Theology.* New York: Routledge.

Muir, Lynette R. 1995. *The Biblical Drama of Medieval Europe.* Cambridge: Cambridge University Press.

Niang, Aliou. 2009. *Faith and Freedom in Galatia and Senegal.* Leiden: Brill.

Nichols, Aiden. 2007. *Lovely Like Jerusalem: The Fulfillment of the Old Testament in Christ and the Church.* San Francisco: Ignatius.

Niditch, Susan. 1993. *War and the Hebrew Bible: A Study in the Ethics of Violence.* Oxford: Oxford University Press.

Ngan, Lai Ling Elizabeth. 2006. "Neither Here nor There: Boundary and Identity in the Hagar Story." In Foskett and Kuan, *Ways of Being*, 70–83.

O'Connor, Kathleen. 2002. *Lamentations and the Tears of the World.* Maryknoll, NY: Orbis.

Ollenburger, Ben, ed. 2004. *Old Testament Theology: Flowering and Future, Sources for Biblical and Theological Study.* Winona Lake, IN: Eisenbrauns.

Overholt, Thomas. 1992. *Cultural Anthropology and the Old Testament.* Minneapolis: Fortress Press.

———. 2003. *Channels of Prophecy: The Social Dynamics of Prophetic Activity.* Eugene, OR: Wipf and Stock.

Perdue, Leo. 1994. *The Collapse of History: Reconstructing Old Testament Theology.* Minneapolis: Fortress Press.

Plantinga, Alvin. 2009. "Two (or More) Kings of Scripture Scholarship." In *Oxford Readings in Philosophical Theology*, vol. 2, *Providence, Scripture, and Resurrection*, ed. Michael C. Rea, 266–301. Oxford: Oxford University Press.

Pulido, Laura, Laura Barraclough, and Wendy Cheng, eds. 2012. *A People's Guide to Los Angeles.* Berkeley: University of California Press.

Raboteau, Albert J. 1978. *Slave Religion: The Invisible Institution in the Antebellum South.* New York: Oxford University Press.

Rogerson, John. 1984. *Old Testament Criticism in the Nineteenth Century: England and Germany.* London: SPCK.

———. 2010. *A Theology of the Old Testament.* Minneapolis: Fortress Press.

Roberts, Nathaniel. 2012. "Is Conversion a 'Colonization of Consciousness'?" *Anthropological Theory* 12:271–94.

Ruiz, Jean-Pierre. 2011. *Readings from the Edges: The Bible and People on the Move.* Maryknoll, NY: Orbis.

Said, Edward W. 1979. *Orientalism.* New York: Vintage.

Schüssler Fiorenza, Elisabeth. 2009. *Democratizing Biblical Studies.* Louisville: Westminster John Knox.

Segovia, Fernando F. 2000. *Decolonizing Biblical Studies: A View from the Margins.* Maryknoll, NY: Orbis.

Segovia, Fernando F., and Mary Ann Tolbert, eds. 1985. *Reading from this Place*, vol. 1, *Social Location and Biblical Interpretation in the United States.* Minneapolis: Fortress Press.

Smith-Christopher, Daniel. 2002. *A Biblical Theology of Exile.* Minneapolis: Fortress Press.

———. 2007. *Jonah, Jesus, and Other Good Coyotes: Speaking Peace to Power in the Bible.* Nashville: Abingdon.

Sommer, Benjamin, ed. 2012. *Jewish Concepts of Scripture: A Comparative Introduction.* New York: New York University Press.

Soyinka, Wole. 2003. *Samarkand and Other Markets I Have Known*. New York: Methuen.

Stanovich, Keith. 2004. *The Robot's Rebellion*. Chicago: University of Chicago Press.

Sugirtharajah, R. S., ed. 2006. *Voices from the Margin: Interpreting the Bible in the Third World*. 3rd ed. Maryknoll, NY: Orbis.

Summers, Harry G. 1984. "What Is War?" *Harper's*, May, 75–78.

Toly, Noah J., and Daniel I. Block, eds. 2010. *Keeping God's Earth: The Global Environment in Biblical Perspective*. Downers Grove, IL: IVP Academic.

Thompson, Thomas L. 1974. *The Historicity of the Patriarchal Narratives: The Quest for the Historical Abraham*. Berlin: de Gruyter.

Trible, Phyllis. 1984. *Texts of Terror: Literary-Feminist Readings of Biblical Narratives*. Minneapolis: Fortress Press.

Trimm, Charles. 2012. "Recent Research on Warfare in the Old Testament." *Currents in Biblical Research* 10:171–216.

Rad, Gerhard von. 1962. *Theology of the Old Testament*. Vol. 1. New York: Harper & Row.

———. 1965. *Theology of the Old Testament*. Vol. 2. New York: Harper & Row.

Warrior, Robert Allen. 1996. "Canaanites, Cowboys, and Indians." In *Native and Christian: Indigenous Voices on Religious Identity in the United States and Canada*, edited by James Treat, 93–104. New York: Routledge.

Weems, Renita J. 1991. "Reading Her Way through the Struggle: African American Women and the Bible." In Felder, *Stony the Road We Trod*, 57–77.

———. 1995. *Battered Love: Marriage, Sex, and Violence in the Hebrew Prophets*. Minneapolis: Fortress Press.

White, Lynn, Jr. 1967. "The Historical Roots of Our Ecological Crisis." *Science* 155:1203–7.

Wimbush, Vincent L., ed. 2000. *African Americans and the Bible: Sacred Texts and Social Textures*. New York: Continuum.

Yadin, Yigael. 1963. *The Art of Warfare in Biblical Lands*. London: Weidenfield & Nicolson.

Yee, Gale A. 2003. *Poor Banished Children of Eve: Woman as Evil in the Hebrew Bible*. Minneapolis: Fortress Press.

———. 2006. "Yin/Yang Is Not Me: An Exploration into an Asian-American Biblical Hermeneutics." In Foskett and Kuan, *Ways of Being*, 152–63.

THEMES AND PERSPECTIVES IN THE PROPHETS: TRUTH, TRAGEDY, TRAUMA

Carol J. Dempsey

Introduction

Perhaps no other collection of texts is as rich as Israelite prophetic literature, whose authors knew how to imaginatively and effectively communicate messages of woe and visions of hope. As beautiful as the prose and poetry of these texts may be, they are not without bias and oftentimes reflect the culture and thought of the day, all of which has sparked lively debates and discussions among scholars and general audiences alike. Though time-bound, Israel's prophetic literature has a timeless quality that calls listeners in new contexts to hear the message of the prophets anew. The prophets of old continue to call people of all generations to right relationship so that all life may flourish and so that the vision of the new heavens and the new earth can become realized. The following article explores the richness of Israel's prophetic literature and invites readers to consider what it means to become poets and prophets of a new day characterized by justice, righteousness, loving-kindness, and humble walks with God.

Prophetic Writings in Their Ancient and Historical Contexts

Definitions and Canon

Lush in content and form, stunning in imagery and rhetoric, Israel's prophetic literature grew out of the lived experience of its prophets. It reflects the activities of the nation's prophets as they passed judgments, provided vision, acted symbolically, and offered comfort to the people of their respective communities. Written in prose and poetry, prophetic literature describes so-called prophets who live suspended between heaven and earth. As messengers of the divine, the prophets gazed into heaven's windows and offer a picture of Israel's God seated on the throne, tending to the business of the heavenly court. As ordinary yet highly gifted human beings, the prophets presented an earthly view of reality that seems sordid and grim on the one hand but magnificent and hope-filled on the other. They had the uncanny ability to see both what was and what could be, all of which is described quite vividly in Israel's prophetic literature.

The Hebrew canon of the Bible is divided into three divisions: the Torah, the Prophets (*nebiim*), and the Writings (*ketubim*). The Prophets are further subdivided into two categories: the "Former," or Nonwriting Prophets, and the "Latter," or Writing Prophets. The literature of the former prophets includes Joshua, Judges, 1–2 Samuel, and 1–2 Kings. The latter prophets include the Major Prophets—Isaiah, Jeremiah, Ezekiel—and the Book of the Twelve: Hosea, Joel, Amos, Obadiah, Jonah, Micah, Nahum, Habakkuk, Zephaniah, Haggai, Zechariah, and Malachi.

The classification of the Former Prophets as prophetic is somewhat unusual because of the historical nature of these texts, and yet these books attest to the times in which the prophets are said to have lived and to have been active. The Deuteronomistic history attests to God's speaking to Israel through the prophets. The books of Chronicles, and most notably 1 Chron. 29:29, present the prophets as Israel's first historians.

Unlike the Hebrew canon, the Christian canon follows the divisions of the Septuagint (LXX) and has a fivefold division: the books of Law, History (containing the Former Prophets), Poetry, the Major Prophets, and the Minor Prophets. The ordering of the first six books of the Minor Prophets is also different in the Christian canon, which has Hosea, Amos, Micah, Joel, Obadiah, and Jonah coming before the other texts.

Three other books associated with the prophetic corpus but that are not part of the block of material known as the Major or Minor Prophets are the books of Baruch, Lamentations, and Daniel. The backdrop to the book of Baruch is the fall of Jerusalem and the exile in 587 BCE. This book is not part of the Hebrew or Palestinian canon of sacred texts but is found in the Greek Septuagint. Roman Catholic and Greek Orthodox regard Baruch as one of the seven deuterocanonical books. For Protestants, Baruch appears in the apocryphal texts of the Bible.

The background of the book of Lamentations is also the fall of Jerusalem in 587 BCE. The inspiration and canonicity of Lamentations has been acknowledged, but its location in the canon varies: the Hebrew tradition places the book among the Writings; the Greek and Latin traditions place Lamentations among the Prophets.

A similar situation exists for the book of Daniel. This book portrays the Judahites in exile. The two prayers in Daniel 3 and the stories of Susanna and Bel and the Dragon, chapters 10 and 14 respectively, are found in the Greek and Latin version of the text but not in the Hebrew canon. Roman Catholic tradition accepts these passages as canonical, but Protestant tradition rejects them as apocryphal. The Hebrew text places Daniel among the Writings, but the Greek, Catholic, and Protestant canons place Daniel among the Prophets.

Origins

When considering the origins of prophetic literature, no one definitive person or group can be named as author of the texts. Some texts may have been written by the prophet, others by tradents, and still others by anonymous authors and editors who preserved and added to an emerging body of texts. The words, actions, and symbolic gestures of the prophets remained alive throughout Israel's history, and generated new words and accounts that resulted in books such as Isaiah, Micah, and Obadiah.

Ancient Near Eastern Context

The earliest records of prophetic activity come from the city of Mari, located in upper Mesopotamia on the Euphrates River. In this region and specifically in the royal archives of Mari, about fifty letters have been found from the reign of Zimri-lim (around 1775–1761 BCE). Zimri-lim was the last Mari ruler before he was defeated by the Babylonian king Hammurabi. These letters were written by officials and administrators and contained communications from intermediaries delivering divine messages intended for the king. A few letters were also written to Yasmah-Addu, Zimri-lim's predecessor. In essence, a message was given from a god to an intermediary or prophet, who in turn told the message to a letter writer, who wrote it down and then gave it to the king. The intermediaries were both professional and nonprofessional men and women who received the messages in dreams and visions, often at the temple and sometimes during sacrificial rites. Interestingly, none of the Mari texts show that prophecy was associated with any one individual in particular. Most of the messages sent to the king concerned military, political, and religious matters; some even warned the king about various undertakings yet to occur. Many of the messages served to support the king in his leadership role. The Mari texts provide evidence showing that prophecy was not restricted to the Bible and is part of a much larger religious tradition. Additionally, the Mari texts show that divine communication happened through intuitive divination that took the form of a verbal message.

One other set of texts that reflect prophetic activity has been found. These less-well-known tablets, which date to the Neo-Assyrian period, roughly the eighth to seventh centuries BCE, preserve the proclamations of nine women and four men known as prophets who were contemporaneous with Isaiah and Micah.

Additionally, three Aramaic inscriptions indicate prophetic activity in the ancient Near East. First, the Deir 'Alla inscription (750–650 BCE) shows that predictive texts were known in the Transjordan, not far from Israel, in the eighth century BCE. Second, the Zakkur inscription (805–775 BCE) contains the standard "fear not" formula for salvation proclamations from both Neo-Assyrian and biblical texts. Third, the Amman Citadel inscription (late ninth century BCE) seems to show some evidence of prophetic content, but no scholarly consensus exists on this point.

For most of the twentieth century CE, scholars did not think that the socioreligious phenomenon of "prophecy" existed in Egypt. Recently, however, attempts have been made to find evidence of prophetic activity in various Egyptian texts. The only Egyptian text that may exhibit the phenomenon of prophecy, however, is *Wenamun*, a story about an Egyptian official on an adventurous journey to Byblos. His task is to acquire timber for the Amun-Re temple at Karnak. During his journey, the official encounters many obstacles and is eventually arrested. His fate changes when someone appears to him in a trance and announces that he should be set free. The official, however, is not an Egyptian; he is a Phoenician, and thus the story is better suited as a Levantine prophecy and not an Egyptian one.

Attempts have also been made to locate prophetic activity at Ugarit, Ebla, Emar, and among the Hittites. All of these attempts, however, have not yielded conclusive evidence.

Finally, research into prophetic activity in the ancient Near East has proven to be helpful to the study of prophecy in ancient Israel. The literature makes clear that prophecy was common in the ancient Near East and must not be confined to Israel. Moreover, expressions such as "thus says . . ." found in ancient Near Eastern texts and also in Israel's prophetic corpora show some similarities of prophetic activity between the ancient Near East and Israel. Unlike Israelite prophetic literature, however, ancient Near Eastern literature does not show significant cases where prophecy questioned the monarchy. Ancient Near Eastern prophecy tended to support and encourage the monarchy, which is strikingly different from Israel's prophetic literature.

Israel's Prophets: Their Diverse Roles as Seekers of Truth

Although prophecy in Israel seems to share some similarities with ancient Near Eastern prophecy, the Israelite prophetic tradition had its own distinctive character. For instance, ancient Near Eastern prophecy often made no distinction between prophet and priest, which was not the case for Israel. Some of those who were later recognized as prophets may have been priests, as in the cases of Jeremiah and Ezekiel, but others, such as Hosea and Micah, were not priests.

In Israel, various types of prophets existed: the shamanistic prophets, known for their ecstatic activity, were often itinerant and usually prophesied in groups; the cultic or temple prophets, like Jeremiah, were associated with the priesthood and were sometimes found proclaiming in the temple; the court prophets, such as Daniel, who was both a prophetic and wisdom figure, advised the king. Others were free prophets, who began their work around the mid-eighth century BCE. These prophets included Amos, Hosea, Micah, and Isaiah. For them, their primary authority was God. They often stood on the periphery of Israelite society and worked to provoke social and religious change.

Israel's prophetic literature uses three terms to characterize Israel's prophets. Appearing about four hundred times in this literature, the most important and common term is *nābî*, which is frequently used in 1–2 Samuel, 1–2 Kings, Jeremiah, and Ezekiel. The term *ḥōzeh*, usually translated as "seer," is associated with those prophets who have a vision. Three striking examples appear in Num. 24:4, 16; and Ezek. 13:16, 23. The third term is *rō'eh*, used more than a dozen times in the Hebrew Bible and usually translated as "diviner." This person could discover things that were hidden, as in the case of 1 Sam. 9:9. Saul's servant suggests that Samuel be consulted to help find missing donkeys. Related terms include "man of God," as in the cases of Samuel (1 Sam. 9:6-10) and Elisha (2 Kgs. 5:8, 14-15). In Amos 3:7, God reveals to Amos that no punishment will befall the people without their knowing the divine intentions that will be made known to the people through God's "servants the prophets." Some of Israel's prophets have also been compared to a "sentinel" (Jer. 6:17), a "watchman" (Ezek. 3:16-21; 33:1-9), a "lookout" (Isa. 21:6), and a "refiner" (Jer. 6:27-30), each implying a specific task for which the prophet was responsible.

Scholars today debate whether all of Israel's prophets were actual historical persons. Despite such historical questions, the Bible's prophetic books do offer a comprehensive picture of the "prophetic persona" and the prophets' diverse roles as seekers of truth. The Bible portrays Israel's prophets as everyday people, for the most part, but scholarly arguments based on the form and style of the prophetic texts suggest that the prophets were well educated. The prophets were the keepers of the covenant and the guardians of justice, righteousness, and loving-kindness. The prophets were unrelenting on issues concerning justice (Amos 5:21-24; 8:4-6), and they frequently challenged institutions, systems, structures, attitudes, and mind-sets that were often considered "sacred" (Isa. 1:10-20; 58:1-14; Jer. 7:1-15).

Prophecy was a charism that called Israel's prophets to remain faithful to their God, their vocation, the task to be done, and the mission to be accomplished. As divinely inspired persons, Israel's prophets were called to comfort (Isa. 40:1-2), confront (Hosea 4:1-3), offer hope (Jer. 30:31-34; Joel 2:21-29), proclaim (Mic. 1:1-16), envision (Jer. 31:31-34), energize (Isaiah 25), shed light (Amos 6:1-8), exhort (Hosea 6:1-3), intercede (Hab. 3: 1-16), announce judgment (Hosea 4:1-3), proclaim salvation (Isaiah 62), and keep alive the gift of imagination (Ezekiel 1). Hence, their mission was multifaceted.

The prophets had an ethical mission: to help liberate creation from pain and suffering, inclusive of both victims and perpetrators of injustice (see, e.g., Isa. 42:1-4; 52:13—53:12; Joel 2:21-22). They also had a theological mission: to make known that Israel's God was a God of justice and compassion (Mic. 7:18-20). Their mission was also political: they had to advise political, social, and religious leaders of the day (Jer. 38:14-28). Finally, Israel's prophets were to be forever in dialogue with God, who would reveal what needed to be said and done (Mic. 6:6-8). As keepers of the covenant, Israel's prophets were heralds of good news, calling people back to right relationship (Isa. 1:16-17).

The biblical texts suggest that the experience of the prophets was an intuitive one, as exemplified by the opening words of Jeremiah's call narrative: "The word of the Lord came to me thus . . ." (Jer. 1:4). When first called to serve as a prophet, some of the prophets were initially reluctant (see Jer. 1:4-10 and Isa. 6:1-9), but God divinely and freely bestowed the gifts needed for this vocation (Jer. 1:6-10), enabling the prophets to say, "Here am I; send me!" (Isa. 6:8).

As passionate people who felt deeply about the pressing issues of their day, the prophets experienced all sorts of emotions related to their vocation (Habakkuk 1). They felt joy, delight, fear, frustration, pain, and most notably righteous anger over the people's apostasy, idolatry, and other transgressions (Micah 3). Perhaps the best example of a passion-filled prophet can be found in the book of Jeremiah, where the prophet complains to his God (Jer. 15:10-18), expresses utter frustration, though not without a sense of confidence and hope (Jer. 20:7-18), and then prays to his God for understanding (Jer. 32:16-25). Through the person of Hosea, Israel came to know the struggle within God's heart, which vacillated between love, remembrance, frustration, fidelity, and compassion (Hosea 11:1-9). Because of an inner compulsion that often welled up inside of them, the prophets had to speak; the spirited and Spirit-filled word of God had to go forth even when the prophet would rather not proclaim it (Jer. 20:9). The prophets were in touch with God's Spirit and filled with this Spirit, the source of their proclamation and the inspiration behind their mission (e.g., Mic. 3:8).

The prophets often began their proclamations with the phrase "Thus says the LORD," a typical prophetic messenger formula and later addition lending both authority and credence to the prophets' words. Many times, the prophets delivered God's word with graphic detail (Ezekiel 21). Their message was always related to their divine mission of establishing justice in the land. For example, Micah upbraided the political, social, and religious leaders of his day because they had acted unjustly. He also addressed the priests and prophets who had corrupted their religious offices (Mic. 3:1-7, 9-12). The prophets often spoke out against idolatry (Ezek. 14:6-8; Hab. 2:18-20), a stance that not only supported torah but also firmly established the sovereignty of Israel's God over all other gods.

Although the word of the prophets was often harsh, foreboding, and reflective of the influences and mores of their times, this word was always the graced word, inviting people to change their ways (Ezek. 18:30-32) and to be transformed into the holy and godly human beings they were meant to be (Gen. 1:27; Lev. 20:26).

The prophet's word was sometimes delivered through symbolic action. The prophets would perform some sort of symbolic gesture, the meaning of which only came to light much later on in the life of the community. Micah lamented, wailed, and went barefoot and naked to draw attention to the community's sinfulness (Mic. 1:8). Jeremiah sported the yoke of oxen to symbolize to his people that they were about to go into Babylonian captivity (Jeremiah 27).

With respect to the prophet's vision, the prophetic books make clear that Israel's prophets read the signs of the time. Because they studied both their community and world events, they knew what was about to befall Israel and Judah, and they warned their communities and the surrounding nations of their fate if they did not chart a new course. They were also graced to see God's vision of unity and peace for all creation, beautifully expressed in Isa. 2:1-4; Mic. 4:1-5; and Isa. 65:17-25. The prophets heralded a vision of a new kind of leadership that would help to usher in the reign of God and a new world order (Isa. 9:1-7; 11:1-9; 32:1). One can say that they were double-visioned: they saw what was and what could be, giving both sight and insight to their listeners.

Ninth Century BCE: Elijah and Elisha

In the ninth century BCE several prophets were active: Balaam (Numbers 22–23), Samuel (1–2 Samuel), Nathan (2 Sam. 7:1-17; 12:1-15; 1 Kgs. 1:1-45), and Ahijah (1 Kgs. 11:29-39; 12:12-15; 14:1-18), among others (see also 1 Kings 12–14).

Immediately following the division of the kingdom of Israel, two strong prophetic figures emerged in the ninth century: Elijah and Elisha. The Elijah cycle of stories is found in 1 Kings 17–19, 21; 2 Kgs. 1:1—2:18. Elijah was a Yahwist prophet in the tradition of Moses, active during the reign of King Ahab. He was noted for his struggle against Baalism, which is highlighted in Elijah's confrontation with the prophets of Baal on Mount Carmel (1 Kings 18). Elijah wins the contest and establishes God's power and Baal's impotence. He also has a marvelous encounter with God at Horeb (1 Kgs. 19:9-19) and later curses King Ahab and his house for his abuses of power (1 Kgs. 21:1-29). According to the biblical text, Elijah is taken up to heaven by a whirlwind as chariots of fire appear between him and his successor Elisha (2 Kgs. 2:1-18).

Elisha's cycle of stories recount his many miracles, visionary proclamations, and his alleged legitimation of King Jehu's rule (2 Kgs. 2:1—10:35). The stories particularly reveal his concern for his marginalized followers.

Preexilic Predictions of Tragedy: From Amos to Jeremiah

During Israel's and Judah's preexilic period (922–587 BCE), some people enjoyed prosperity and peace, while others at the bottom of the economic pile suffered many hardships. The prophets tried to mitigate the unjust oppression that some suffered at the hands of others. In both kingdoms, religious apostasy and idolatry were rampant; injustices and transgressions were many. Political, social, and religious institutions were sunk in the mire of sin and corruption. Civil war raged intermittingly; nations and kingdoms made poor alliances and ineffective coalitions. On the world scene during this time, Assyria rose to its zenith of power only to be defeated by Babylon, which later succumbed to Persia.

Many of the preexilic prophets warned against alliances and coalitions, upbraided kings, large landowners, and other political and social leaders because they had become corrupt and had blatantly disregarded torah. These prophets also addressed the religious leaders of their day, many of whom had become hypocrites (see, e.g., Micah 1–3). The prophets also passed judgment on the ordinary folk who were not faithful to covenant and the law, and they addressed those nations that took advantage of Israel and other peoples (Amos 1–2; Isaiah 13–23). Despite their harsh words, these prophets saw the reign of God dawning on the horizon when all nations, all peoples, would come together in peace on God's holy mountain (Isa. 2:1-4; Mic. 4:1-5). That day, however, would not arrive until all corruption and wickedness had been rooted out. Hence, turmoil, chaos, and devastation paved the way to restoration, renewal, and transformation.

The preexilic period ended in 587 BCE, when the southern kingdom of Judah collapsed, the capital city of Jerusalem was burned, the temple was destroyed by the Babylonians, and the inhabitants of Judah were exiled to either Babylon or Egypt. These events ushered in the exilic period of prophetic activity (587–539 BCE). The books of Amos, Hosea, First Isaiah, Micah, Zephaniah, Nahum, Habakkuk, and Jeremiah describe all these events.

Exilic Promises of Comfort and Hope: From Ezekiel to Second Isaiah

The exilic years found the Israelites without land, a king and monarchy, and a temple. They wondered if their God had abandoned them completely. Life in Babylon, however, was not a terrible experience for the Israelites. In fact, when they were freed from exile, many chose to stay in Baby-lon rather than start the hard work of rebuilding and reestablishing themselves as a people and a community in Yehud. These exilic times, though, did bring a certain degree of sadness, despair, and lamentation to the Israelites. They had lost so much! The prophetic texts of this period include Obadiah, Ezekiel, and Second Isaiah. These prophets often delivered a message of comfort (see, e.g., Isa. 40:1-2; 43:1—44:28). God would redeem the people; the temple would be rebuilt; the people would be reestablished on their land; and the land and community would flourish.

When Cyrus of Persia defeated the Babylonians, he issued an edict that essentially ended the Israelites' exile. The people were now free to return to their land. Some did; some did not. This edict began the postexilic period in Israel's history (539–333 BCE).

Postexilic Return, Restoration, and New Challenges: From Haggai to Jonah

The postexilic period is also known as the restoration or Persian period. The prophetic texts of Third Isaiah, Joel, Jonah, Haggai, Zechariah, and Malachi focus on shoring up life in the community and on rebuilding the temple. The community faced many economic problems, struggled with divided opinions among themselves as to how life should be lived, and faced hostility from neighboring Samaria as to who had the right to claim the old territory of Judah. Zerubbabel's rejection of the Samaritans' offer to help rebuild the temple set in motion the enmity between the Jews and the Samaritans that continued into the next century. The people also faced the problem of religious ritualism whereby maintaining rituals took preference over one's relationship with YHWH and the living out of social justice. Thus this time was a mixture of hope and disillusionment for the people, with restoration becoming part of Israel's future and not its present lived reality.

Literary Dimensions and Perspectives of the Prophetic Writings

Israel's prophetic texts use many different forms. They include symbolic action reports (Isa. 20:1-6), commissioning reports (Jer. 1:4-10), vision reports (Amos 7:1), biographies (Jeremiah 37–44), woe proclamations (Mic. 2:1-5), dirges (Ezek. 32:17-19), laments (Amos 5:1-3), judgment speeches (Mic. 1:2-7), *rib*, or courtroom, scenes (Mic. 6:1-5; Hosea 4:1-3), parables (Isa. 5:1-7; Jer. 18:1-11), disputation speeches (Mic. 2:6-11), complaints (Hab. 1:2-17), prayers (Hab. 3:1-16), prophetic his-toriography (Isaiah 36–39; Jeremiah 52, which is basically the same as 2 Kgs. 18:13—19:37), taunt songs (Isa. 14:3-22), and legends (2 Kgs. 4:1-7), among other forms.

Written predominately in poetry, the prophetic literature uses a variety of rhetorical elements such as numerical word pairs (Amos 1–2), merisms (Jer. 46:12), imagery (Ezek. 17:1-10), rhetorical questions (Amos 3:3-8), extended metaphors (Mic. 3:1-3), similes (Hosea 9:10), anthropomor-phism, which ascribes human qualities to God (Zeph. 1:4), and personification (Ezekiel 16), among other literary techniques.

Major Themes in the Prophetic Writings

Covenant

At the heart of prophetic preaching was the Sinai covenant, which established a relationship between God and the Israelites. A myriad of images such as shepherd and flock (Isa. 56:11; Ezek. 34:8-10; Zech. 11:16-17), vine and vinedresser (Isa. 5:1-7), potter and clay (Jer. 18:1-11), and father and son (Jer. 31:9) gave expression to this relationship. Oftentimes, marital imagery captured the covenant relationship between God and the people of Israel. God was the husband; Israel was the wife (Hosea 1–2). The Deuteronomic perspective on covenant throughout the prophets emphasizes the demands of the covenant and puts those demands in the context of God's great love for the people (Deut. 4:37; 7:8; 10:15). Repeatedly, the people are called to respond with love (Deut. 6:5; 10:12).

The prophets exposed the people's violations against covenant and warned of the divine consequences that would follow these transgressions. Some of the transgressions included apostasy (Jer. 2:19), idolatry (Isa. 2:8, 20), swearing, lying, murder, stealing, adultery (Hosea 4:1-3), and profaning the Sabbath (Ezek. 20:12-13a). At times, the people even pleaded with God not to break covenant with them even though they had transgressed (Jer. 14:13-22).

Finally, the prophets proclaimed that even though Israel had broken the covenant and had suffered divine consequences, God's covenant plan remained constant (Isa. 59:21). Four prophets in particular heralded the vision of a new covenant: Second Isaiah (Isa. 42:1-9; 49:1-13; 54:9-10; 55:3-5), Jeremiah (Jer. 31:31-34), Ezekiel (Ezek. 34:23-31; 37:24-28), and Hosea (Hosea 2:16-23). Along with a new covenant, the people would be given a new heart and a new spirit that would enable them to follow God's ordinances and statutes, which would in turn allow them to live in peace and prosperity in the land.

Justice

The prophets called Israel to do good and correct oppression, to seek and execute justice (Isa. 1:7), and to wait for God continually (Hosea 12:6). Because life in Israel was essentially hierarchical, the erosion of justice on the part of some of Israel's political and religious leaders took its toll on the common good. Injustice prevailed in the land, because the Israelites themselves had forgotten God and God's ways. Various prophetic texts suggest that some of the more economically and socially powerful Israelites preyed on their own kin. These situations often went unchecked by Israel's political and religious leaders, but not by prophets (Isa. 5:8-30; Jer. 5:20-29; 9:4-11; Mic. 2:1-5, 8-9; Hab. 1:2-4; 2:6-20). Amos railed against Israel's injustices and warned the people that justice would prevail "on that day" (Amos 2:6, 16; 3:14; 5:18, 20; 6:3; 8:3, 9, 11, 13).

For the prophets, injustice would never be the people's enduring experience. The experience of darkness and utter futility characterized by the absence of justice would one day be transformed into light with the coming of God, who would clothe the people in garments of justice and salvation (Isa. 60:1-3; 61:10; 62:1). Israel's God is a God of justice (Isa. 30:18) who loves justice (Isa. 61:8) and who makes justice part of the new covenant (Hosea 2:19)

Apostasy and Idolatry

Two of Israel's main transgressions were apostasy and idolatry. Apostasy often resulted in idolatry. Apostasy consisted of acts of rebellion against God and God's laws and an abandonment of faith in God and God's covenant (Isa. 1:2-9; Jer. 5:1-17). Jeremiah denounced Judah's apostasy and infidelity and warned the people about the tragic events that would befall them because of their transgression (Jer. 5:6).

Idolatry was the worship of and trust in gods other than YHWH (Isa. 2:6-9, 12-22; Jer. 2:9-19; Ezek. 16:23-29; 23:7, 30). Idolatry was often described as sexual promiscuity, adultery, and unbridled lust. The prophets repeatedly warned the Israelite community against worshiping idols (Isa. 44:9-20; 45:16), which took the form of "the work of human hands" (Isa. 2:8; 37:19; Jer. 1:16; Mic. 5:12), molten images (Isa. 40:19; Jer. 10:14), abhorrent objects (Isa. 66:3; Jer. 4:1; Ezek. 5:11), and abominations (Isa. 44:19).

Idolatry included a wide variety of moral failures, such as oppression of the vulnerable, murder, and adultery (Jer. 7:6, 9; Ezek. 22:2-12). The most abominable form of idolatry was the kind connected with child sacrifice (Isa. 57:5; Jer. 7:31; 19:5; 32:35; Ezek. 16:20-21; 20:31; 23:39). Ezekiel, Hosea, and Micah addressed both apostasy and idolatry and made known to the people the consequences of their actions (Ezek. 6:1-7; Hosea 8:1-14; Mic. 1:2-7). Forgetfulness of God led to forgetfulness of God's ways, which resulted in political, social, economic, and religious corruption and chaos that ended in the destruction of both Israel and Judah.

The prophets proclaimed that God would reestablish Israel in right relationship marked by faithfulness and the end to idolatry (Isa. 2:17-18; 30:22; 31:7; Ezek. 11:18-20; 36:25; 37:23; Hosea 2:14-23). When idolatry would come to an end, the name of YHWH would be the only divine name on the earth (Zech. 14:9; Mal. 1:11).

Worship

Israelite prophetic literature lists a whole range of expressions of personal and communal worship: prayer (Isa. 1:15; 37:4; 56:7; Hab. 3:1-19); singing (Isa. 12:5; 26:1; 30:29; 42:10; Jer. 20:13; Amos 5:23; 8:10); lamentation and fasting (Isa. 58:3-5; Jer. 9:20; 14:12; 36:6, 9; Ezek. 32:16; Amos 8:10; Joel 1:14; 2:12, 15; Jon. 3:5; Zech. 7:5; 8:19); sacrifices and offerings (Isa. 1:11; 19:21); vows (Isa. 19:21; Jon. 1:16; Mal. 1:14); festivals (Isa. 33:20; Ezek. 36:38; Hosea 2:11; Zech. 8:19); and pilgrimages (Isa. 30:29; Ezek. 45:17; 46:11; Hosea 2:11; 9:5; Amos 5:21; Nah. 1:15; Zech. 14:16-19).

For the prophets, justice was the precondition of worship. Praxis and worship were inseparable. Israel's sacrifices and expressions of worship were useless and unacceptable to God unless the community first practiced justice (Isa. 1:10-20; 29:13-14; 58:6-14; Jer. 6:16-21; 7:21-28; Amos 4:4-5; 5:14-15, 21-28; Hosea 6:4-6; Mic. 6:6-8). Right relationship with God, with one another, and with all creation was integral to the renewal, restoration, and transformation of the community. Worship was to give expression to this right relationship.

True, False, and Corrupt Prophets

Not all who made proclamations in God's name were considered true prophets. In ancient Israel, false prophets coexisted with true prophets. The deciding factor determining a true or false prophet depended on whether the prophecy was fulfilled. For this reason, many people within the Israelite community recognized those gifted "seers" as poets, and only later on were they acknowledged as prophets. Like the true prophets, the false prophets engaged in ecstatic activities (1 Kgs. 18:19-40; 22:5-23), experienced dreams, and delivered their contents to the people, but these dreams were later condemned (Deut. 13:1-3; Jer. 23:25-38; Ezek. 13:9). Unlike the true prophets, the false prophets led the people astray, especially when they spoke in the name of Baal (1 Kgs. 18:19-40). They oftentimes gave the people a false sense of confidence (Jer. 4:10; 6:14; Ezek. 13:10) that served to undermine the message of the true prophets, thereby creating conflict. Only true prophets stood in the council of God, and only true prophets were called and sent by God (Isa. 6:1-13; Jer. 1:4-10). Jeremiah 28 describes an exchange between Jeremiah and Hananiah and provides an example of conflict and opposition that also existed among the prophets. The prophets also railed against those who were true prophets but who corrupted their prophetic office for self-serving purposes (Mic. 3:5-7).

Judgment and Suffering

Many prophetic proclamations were words of judgment. Amos inaugurated the concept of the Day of the Lord, which was a time of judgment and condemnation (5:18-20) for a people guilty of many social injustices (2:4-5, 6-8; 4:1-3; 5:7-12). Isaiah condemned worship that represented external gestures empty of any true reform of daily behavior (Isa. 1:10-17; 29:13). Israel was indicted for sins against covenant Decalogue (Hosea 4:1-2), idolatry (Hosea 2:7, 10; 4:12-13; 8:4-6), corrupt legislation (Isa. 10:1-4), oppression of the poor (Isa. 3:14-15; 10:2; Ezek. 22:29), and other social iniquities (Mic. 2:1-11; 3:1-11). Not only was Israel judged but also its enemies (Jer. 25:31). Oftentimes, the prophets depicted a courtroom scene that featured God making a case against the people (Isa. 3:13-15; Mic. 6:1-5). Divine judgment was seen as the reason why Israel and Judah were destroyed.

Not only did the people suffer under divine judgment but also the land and the natural world (Isa. 24:1-24; 33:7-9; Jer. 4:23-28; 7:16-20; 12:4; 14:1-9; 23:9-12; Hosea 4:1-3; Amos 4:6-10; 8:4-8; Zeph. 1:2-6). Because the people rejected God, God suffered (Isa. 1:2-3; 54:6; Jer. 2:1-37; 15:5-9; 18:13-15; Hosea 11:1-9; 13:4-6). The prophets also depicted God suffering with those who were suffering (Isa. 15:5; 16:9-11; Jer. 9:10, 17-18; 31:20; 48:30-36). The prophets themselves suffered because of their mission (Jer. 11:18—12:6; 15:10-21; 17:14-18; 18:18-23; 20:7-12, 14-18).

Law

Central to the preaching of the prophets was a focus on the law. Going forth from out of Zion (Isa. 2:3; Mic. 4:2), God's law was set before the people (Jer. 44:10; Ezek. 20:11), and they were called to walk in its statutes and ordinances (Ezek. 20:19). For the prophets, the torah was a way of life that safeguarded right relationship with God, self, and others. Many people, however, rejected torah (Isa. 5:24; Jer. 6:19; Ezek. 5:6; Amos 2:4), forsook it (Jer. 9:13; 16:11), forgot it (Hosea 4:6), or transgressed it (Isa. 24:5; Hosea 8:1).

The prophets taught that if people followed torah they could be transformed into a new humanity and pursue a godly life instead of a life of oppression and violence (Isa. 2:2-5). Repeatedly, the prophets put the people on notice when they broke torah (Isa. 24:5). Jeremiah proclaimed that rejection of God's commands led to expulsion from the land (Jer. 16:13; 44:23). Habakkuk preached that torah is ineffective when people commit violent acts and corrupt justice (Hab. 1:4). Zephaniah announced the judgment of God against the Israelites because of a long list of sins that included priests who did violence to torah because they had profaned what was holy (Zeph. 3:4). For Israel's prophets, torah was at the heart of ethical living; torah safeguarded covenant relationship.

Repentance

Torah created the backdrop for repentance, and the prophets continually called the people to "repent," to "return" to God (Jer. 24:7; Joel 2:12-13; Zech. 1:3; 10:9; Mal. 3:7). The prophets portrayed God as desiring a mutual relationship based on both parties' returning to each other. Even though the people had committed egregious transgressions, they were encouraged to return to God (Jer. 15:19; Zech. 1:3; Mal. 3:7). The prophets made clear, however, that repentance included amending one's ways (Jer. 26:13).

Isaiah and Zechariah called for repentance in the face of exile (Isa. 44:22; 55:7; Zech. 1:6). Jeremiah issued one of the most poignant pleas for repentance in all of prophetic literature (Jer. 3:6—4:2). He declared Judah's sinfulness, expressed God's anger, emphasized the need for the people to acknowledge their guilt, highlighted God's compassionate intercession on Judah's behalf, and proclaimed Judah's future restoration to God and the land.

If the people repented and turned back to God, then God would repent of the calamities set in motion against the people and the land. Disaster and punishment would not occur, and hope for salvation would become a reality (Isa. 45:22; 58:9-14; Joel 2:13-14).

Divine Sovereignty, Creation, Hope

The prophets depict God as Lord of heaven and earth, lord of everything (Isa. 14:26; 66:1). This God is the true God, the living God, the everlasting King (Jer. 10:10). Israel's God is above all other gods (1 Kings 18), reigns over all nations (Jer. 10:7), is the only God (Isa. 45:5-6, 14, 18, 21-22; 46:9; Joel 2:27), and is incomparable (Isa. 40:18). This God is the "Lord of hosts" (Amos 4:13) and the commander in chief who musters up armies for battle (Isa. 13:4).

To make known God's sovereignty, the prophets often used images from the natural world in their messages. In a divine indictment of the people, Isaiah and Micah featured God appealing to the earth and the heavens as witnesses (Isa. 1:2; Mic. 6:1-2). Catastrophic events in the heavens and on earth announced the coming of God (Joel 2:10; Nah. 1:5). Creation imagery and related metaphorical language became part of the prophets' poetic expression in an attempt to shake the people out of their state of lethargy, indifference, or despair. The prophets even went so far as to depict God as a wild animal—a lion (Isa. 31:4; Jer. 49:19; Hosea 11:10; Amos 3:8) and a bear (Hosea 13:8).

As the sovereign Lord over all, Israel's God had an important relationship with creation. God sustained and nurtured creation, maintained the fixed orders of the world such as day and night (Jer. 31:35-36), disrupted them (Isa. 13:10; Ezek. 32:7-8; Joel 3:15), and governed the weather patterns, giving rain for seedtime and promising a harvest in the fall (Isa. 30:23; Jer. 5:24). When God summoned creation, creation responded (Amos 1:2; 9:5-6).

The prophets described the inextricable link between human behavior and the moral order of creation. When humankind transgressed, the human community and the natural world suffered the consequences of divine chastisement. Jeremiah even linked the people's faithlessness to the well-being of creation (Jer. 4:22-26; 9:12-13) and condemned Judah's leaders for the unmaking of creation (Jer. 12:10-11).

The prophets also tied the renewal of the people's relationship with God to the restoration of creation. As humankind turned from their sinfulness and returned to their God, so they were restored to the land and the land itself was restored to its splendor. The prophets' vision of hope included the wilderness blossoming in glory, beauty, and splendor (Isa. 35:1-2; 41:18-20) and the flourishing of the mountains (Joel 3:18; Amos 9:13b). Ezekiel proclaimed that the covenant of peace included the giving of rain and the restoration of fertility (Ezek. 34:25). Hosea proclaimed a covenant that included the beast of the field (Hosea 2:18). This covenant would result in security for God's people (Hosea 2:19-22; Ezek. 34:25) as well as a full flourishing of the earth (Hosea 2:21-22). Harmony restored among the human community had a strong impact on the rest of creation (Isa. 11:6-9). The promise of salvation became reason for all creation to rejoice and celebrate (Isa. 42:10-12; 44:23). For the prophets, the natural world had a significant place in God's plan of salvation (Isa. 44:23; 45:8; 49:13).

Salvation

The concept and imagery of salvation are multifaceted and rich, particularly in the book of Isaiah, where salvation is a key term. Isaiah's vision of salvation was a universal one, extended to all (Isa. 45:22; 52:10). Salvation was eternal (Isa. 45:17; 51:6, 8) but only if the people returned to fidelity to their God (Isa. 45:22).

In the prophets, God, the source and foundation of salvation (Isa. 12:2; Jer. 3:23; Hab. 3:18), donned a helmet of salvation (Isa. 59:16-17). God's salvation was cause for joy and gladness (Isa. 25:9) because it was everlasting (Isa. 45:17). Even when the people had all gone astray, God's salvation was always a promised gift (Isa. 56:1) even when it seemed distant (Isa. 56:11). Oftentimes, salvation was for God's sake, the sake of God's holy name (Ezek. 36:22-32; cf. Isa. 42:25; Jer. 14:7-9; Dan. 9:15-19). The prophet was clothed with garments of salvation (Isa. 61:10). As righteousness rained down, so also salvation sprang up like plants (Isa. 45:8). Waters drawn from the wells of salvation would quench all thirst (Isa. 12:3). City walls were bulwarks of salvation (Isa. 26:1; Jer.1:18-19; 15:20). Many of the prophetic texts depict the prophets announcing proclamations of salvation even in the midst of their messages of judgment and doom (Mic. 2:12-13).

The key figure ushering in a time of salvation was the servant (Isa. 49:6), God's instrument and righteous branch in whose days Judah would be saved (Jer. 23:5-6). This ruler would be from Bethlehem (Mic. 5:2) and would deliver the people from the Assyrians (Mic. 5:6). This servant would establish justice, free captives from prison, and release those from the dungeon who sit in darkness (Isa. 42:7).

God

Oftentimes, Israel's prophets portrayed God as a violent God, inflicting punitive chastisements on a wayward people. This violence was reflective of the prophets' culture and times and a belief in a theology of retribution (see, e.g., Deuteronomy 28). In attempting to proclaim Israel's God as the sovereign one who was more powerful than all other gods and earthly rulers and forces at work in the culture, the prophets had to depict Israel's God in human ways as a God of unsurpassable power and might, who is larger than life and capable of leveling peoples, nations, and lands (see, e.g., Mic. 1:2-7; see also the proclamations to the nations in Isaiah 13–23; cf. Jeremiah 46–51; Amos 1:2—2:16).

The prophets depicted God as a warrior judge (Isa. 13:4-5; 42:13; Jer. 21:5; Ezek. 21:5; Amos 1:3—2:16; Joel 2:11; Zeph. 3:17; Zech. 13:7-8) who brandishes a lethal sword (Ezek. 21:1-32). God is a roaring lion in Isa. 5:8-30, an agonizing parent (Isa. 1:2-9), a teacher (Isa. 48:17-19), an artist and creator (Isa. 44:24-28), a designer and crafter of symbols (Jer. 11:11-19), a weaver of visions and maker of dreams (Amos 7:1-3), one who raises up prophets (Jer. 1:4-10), replaces stony hearts (Ezek. 36:22-36), acts as a shepherd (Ezek. 34:11-16), who is sovereign over all nations (Isa. 25:1-10), who sustains, redeems, heals, renews, restores, and transforms life (Isa. 43:1-13, 25; Hosea 14:4-9), and who desires to be one with humankind (Jer. 31:31-34; Hosea 6:4-6).

Much of the God-language in Israel's prophetic literature is predominantly male and reflects many of the roles assumed by males in their respective cultures and societies. For example, just as men are fathers, so God is described as "Father," or as an "Everlasting Father" (Isa. 9:6; 63:16; cf. Jer. 3:4, 19; Mal. 1:6). Just as men are kings, so God is named "King" (Isa. 41:21; Jer. 10:10; 51:57; Ezek. 20:33; Zeph. 3:15). Just as men are bridegrooms, so God is a bridegroom (Isa. 62:5). Just as men are husbands, so God is a husband (Isa. 54:5; Jer. 31:32). Furthermore, God the Lord is the God of hosts, the commander in chief of the heavenly and earthly powers (Isa. 1:9; 44:6; Hosea 11:5; Amos 3:13; Nah. 2:13; Zeph. 2:9; Zech. 1:3; Mal 1:4). Israel's God is the "Holy One of Israel" (Isa. 10:20; 41:16; Jer. 50:29), the "God of Israel" (Isa. 29:23; Jer. 9:15; Ezek. 8:4; Zeph. 2:9), the "Creator of Israel" (Isa. 43:15), the "Holy One of Jacob" (Isa. 29:23), the "Mighty One of Jacob" (Isa. 49:26; 60:16), the "God of Jacob" (Isa. 2:3; Mic. 4:2), the "God of David" (Isa. 38:5) and the "Lord, who redeemed Abraham" (Isa. 29:22). Julia M. O'Brien's recent study offers a rigorous critique of the God metaphors used in prophetic literature.

One point is certain: the prophets were trying to send a strong warning that one more powerful than those in power was going to establish justice by toppling over abusive, domineering, controlling, unjust leadership who had a monopoly on power. Interestingly, the biblical text and evolving history have shown that such violent and aggressive use of power has not succeeded in hastening the reign of God or ushering in peace. Violent uses of power often led to more violence, and that situation still exists today. In this way, the prophetic texts remain prophetic, beckoning people to turn their swords into plowshares and their spears into pruning hooks for the sake of a new world order. For the prophets, God was, ultimately, a God of compassion, which is the deepest expression of justice (Mic. 7:7-18). This point, however, does not preclude constructive consequences for wrongdoing.

Reception History and the Prophets

The interpretive tradition helps offer a number of interesting perspectives about the message of the prophets. These perspectives also are colored by the historical contexts in which they arose.

Perspectives from the Church Fathers

Israelite prophetic literature provided a foundation for Christian interpretation and preaching among the church fathers. Living and preaching in a time that is now considered precritical, many of the fathers read the prophets as foretelling the person of Jesus. Irenaeus identified the four faces of the living creatures in Ezekiel 1—the lion, the man, the ox, and the eagle—as representing the fourfold picture of Christ in the Gospels. For Tertullian, Ezekiel's vision of the dry bones was proof of the resurrection. Cyril of Alexandria posited that Jonah's journey in the fish was to be understood as a foreshadowing of Christ's death and resurrection. Although he saw the rebuilding of the "tent of David" as the restoration of the Jews by Cyrus, he argued that the deeper meaning of the text was to be found in Christ: the fallen tent was the fallen race suffering from death, and the restitution of the tent occurred when Jesus was resurrected and with him those who believed in him.

The church fathers believed that the "new covenant" in Jeremiah was a prophetically prefigured the Christian faith. For them, Jeremiah was a prophet under the old covenant and, as such, was heralding the gospel when he spoke of "the new covenant." The fathers viewed Isaiah as a prophet who was proclaiming the good news of Jesus to the world. For example, John Chrysostom viewed Isa. 7:14 as a prophecy that showed how Jesus was to be conceived, born, and nurtured. For Augustine, Isa. 7:14 pertained to Christ's being born as a visible man of a human virgin mother. This Christ was also a hidden God since God was Jesus' Father. For Bede, the name Immanuel signified both natures of Jesus' person. Jerome believed that Isaiah contained all the sacred mysteries of Jesus and that many of the passages from Isaiah prefigured the events of Jesus' life. For Jerome, Isaiah was an evangelist and an apostle in his proclamation of Jesus. Isaiah is the prophet quoted most in the church fathers' writings.

A few church fathers rejected the standard allegorical approach to the prophets and tried to understand the prophetic message from the historical situation as intended for the audience at the time of a particular prophet. In his commentary, Theodore of Mopsuestia (c. 350–428 CE) tried to identify the historical background of each prophet. He gave much attention to the tension that existed between how Nineveh is portrayed in Jonah and how the city is portrayed in Nahum.

Finally, Martin Luther and John Calvin took a view of the prophets similar to many of the early church fathers. Luther published interpretations of Jonah (1526), Habakkuk (1526), and Zechariah (1527). He set the prophets within their historical setting, established their historical sequence on the basis of the books' superscriptions, commented on the prophetic office, and at times offered christological readings of some texts. In his work on Ezekiel 38–48, Luther took a strong christological approach to the interpretation of the prophecy. Calvin often applied the prophets' message to Christ and his church (McKinion; Duguid, 231–32).

Perspectives from the Rabbis

Talmudic tradition does not arrange the prophetic books in chronological order. The rabbis chose a thematic or theological basis for the texts' ordering and concluded that Jeremiah should appear first among the prophets because, like the book of Kings that precedes it in the Hebrew canon, Jeremiah was concerned with destruction. Ezekiel came next because it began with destruction but concluded with consolation. Isaiah followed Ezekiel because Isaiah was concerned with consolation, one of the text's main themes. The Book of the Twelve followed Isaiah (Dempster, 75–76). This rabbinic concern with destruction and consolation represented an underlying preoccupation with several interrelated issues in the prophets: the destruction of the temple and Jerusalem, the exile of the people from the land of Israel, the restoration of the Jerusalem temple, and the return of the exiled people to the land. Talmudic tradition maintains that Jeremiah wrote the book. Rabbinic tradition questioned the canonical status of Ezekiel, since the text often conflicts with halakic statements found in the Torah.

For the rabbis, the most important prophet was Isaiah, who announced a vision of world peace for all nations (Isa. 2:2-4; Mic. 4:1-5). They viewed Isaiah as a book of comfort because it looked forward to the time when the Jews would bring torah to all peoples, and exiled Jews would return home. Isaiah was also popular because of the book's fervent loyalty to the Davidic monarchy in the first part, the prophecies of salvation and descriptions of a suffering yet vindicated figure in the second part, and the recognition of one God throughout the book as a whole.

The rabbis used midrash as their main method for interpreting the prophets. Two components determined the nature of midrashic interpretation: the text and the interpreter. Midrashic interpretation was verse-centered and philologically focused, beginning with biblical words and phrases. The rabbis saw the interrelatedness of biblical verses, and oftentimes a prophetic verse would shed light on another prophetic verse or even texts in the Torah or the Writings. For example, midrash associates Hab. 3:5 with Ps. 91:6 to describe the pestilence that overwhelms those who perpetuate deeds of darkness. Finally, the talmudic rabbis realized that the Bible's prophetic literature was only a small part of what was actually uttered. For the rabbis, the last of the biblical prophets marked the final departure of God's spirit from Israel. Thus prophecy belonged to the past. Therefore, the word of God was to be sought in the Torah and in the prophecies already delivered.

Interpreting the Prophets Anew: Contemporary Perspectives

The interpretation of the prophetic message continues today. Various perspectives address the meaning of the text and shed new light on how the prophet can be "read" with greater depth.

Feminist and Liberationist Perspectives

Two of the more controversial approaches to the biblical text have been feminist and liberationist perspectives, challenging the way people hear and read the biblical text and how they live their lives. These two approaches address patriarchy and hierarchy, two social aspects at the heart of Israel's culture and prophetic literature.

Broadly understood, patriarchy involves systems of legal, social, economic, and political relations that not only validate but also enforce the notion of male superiority and the sovereignty of males as heads of families over other dependent persons in any given household. Patriarchy violates women because it denies women the right to be autonomous. Within a patriarchal and hierarchical societal structure and household, women are denied the right to construct culture, to control property, to maintain bodily integrity, to formulate their own decisions, and to express their own views and opinions. Patriarchy restricts and prohibits women's participation in Israelite culture.

Alice L. Laffey (152) has argued that "a patriarchal culture is, by its nature, hierarchical." With respect to prophetic literature, Laffey points out that this particular kind of culture sets parameters around worship. Only the priests have charge of the temple and the altar (Ezek. 40:45-46), and the only animals fit for sacrifice to God are males without blemish (Ezek. 43:22, 23, 25; 45:18, 23; Mal. 1:14). The only appropriate wives for priests are virgins of the stock of the house of Israel (Ezek. 44:22). Other men could marry widows and divorcées, but these types of women were inappropriate for priests (Ezek. 44:22). Additionally, while all males were circumcised, women were not, and any woman who belonged to an Israelite man was subsumed under the male's circumcision.

Another topic that feminists and liberationists have addressed in prophetic literature is the marriage metaphor. Israel's lived experience of marriage influenced the biblical portrait of marriage, gender, and sexuality. Just as women are presented as sexually subordinate to men, who control their sexual reproduction, Israel is subordinate to God's control. The prophetic image of Samaria and Jerusalem as God's wife highlights this subordination.

Nancy Bowen explores the metaphorical violence of a jealous husband against his wife in prophetic literature by examining Hosea 1–3; Jeremiah 2–3; and Ezekiel 16 and 23. She points out that when relationships are hierarchically structured, the one deemed "superior" by society (the husband) often asserts control over the "subordinate" one (the wife). This assertion of control sometimes takes the form of physical violence, as in the case of Ezekiel 16. This structural situation that gives way to physical violence has also been deemed psychologically violent, as several other scholars have noted in their exploration of the book of Hosea (Pressler; Perdue et al.; Baumann).

Furthermore, because Jerusalem and Samaria are unfaithful, they deserve to be punished by God, the faithful spouse. The punishment includes a host of violent acts, such as being stripped naked (Ezek. 16:39; 23:26; Hosea 2:3), public exposure, defamation and mockery (Ezek. 16:37, 57; 23:10, 29; Hosea 2:3, 10), mutilation (Ezek. 23:25, 34), gang rape (Ezek. 16:40), stoning (Ezek. 16:40; 23:47), and death (Ezek. 16:40; 23:10, 47). Feminist interpreters often understand such imagery to be pornography, because it involves objectification, dominance, pain, and degradation.

The work of T. Drorah Setel is foundational to the discussion on prophetic pornography. Setel argues that significant congruencies exist between biblical, and especially prophetic, texts on the one hand and modern pornographic depictions of female sexuality on the other hand. She notes that in both cases objectified female sexuality is used as "a symbol of evil" (Setel, 86). Athalya Brenner points out further that even though feminist definitions of pornography vary, two claims remain constant: pornography restricts female choice to an actual act of slavery, and it serves to accentuate the nature and meaning of male power. With respect to Jeremiah 3 and Ezekiel 16, Brenner argues that "pornography preserves and asserts male social dominion through the control of female sexuality" (186).

Israel's infidelity to God is described metaphorically as harlotry. Feminist and liberationist studies have focused on this theme in Isa. 1:21; Jeremiah 2–3; Ezekiel 16; 23; Hosea 1–3; and Mic. 1:6-7. Prophetic literature presented harlotry and spiritual whoredom as violations of covenant with God. Israel sought other gods and trusted in foreign powers and often solicited protection from foreign powers instead of trusting only in God. Thus Israel was guilty of apostasy (Bellis; Setel; Weems 1989; Ortlund). According to Gale Yee, Hosea feminizes the Israelite male leadership as an adulterous woman who has broken her marital vow.

Feminist and liberationist studies have also focused on the female gender used to speak of a city, country, and people. Examples of cities include Rabbah (Amos 1:14) and her daughters (Jer. 49:3), Samaria (Ezek. 16:46; Hosea 13:16; Amos 3:9) and her daughters (Ezek. 16:53, 55), Zion (Isa. 1:27) and her daughters (Isa. 1:8; Zech. 2:10), Jerusalem (Isa. 51:17; Ezekiel 16) and her daughters (Mic. 4:8; Zeph. 3:14; Zech. 9:9), Sidon (Isa. 23:4) and her daughters (Isa. 23:12), Tyre (Isa. 23:15) and her daughters (Ezek. 26:6, 8), Sodom (Ezek. 16:46, 48-49) and her daughters (Ezek. 16:53, 55-56), daughter of Gallim (Isa. 10:30), daughter of Tarshish (Isa. 23:10), Bethlehem Ephrathah (Mic. 5:2), Gaza (Amos 1:7), Rahab (Isa. 51:9), Gebal (Ezek. 27:9), and Tehaphnehes (Ezek. 30:18).

Examples of countries that are personified as women include Moab (Isa. 16:2), Egypt (Isa. 19:14; Jer. 46:11, 24; Ezek. 23:21), Edom (Ezek. 16:57; 32:29), Elam (Ezek. 32:24), Judah (Jer. 3:7-8, 10), the land of the Philistines (Ezek. 16:27, 57), Israel (Amos 5:2; Jer. 18:13), and Babylonia (Isa. 47:1; Jer. 50:42; Ezek. 23:17; Zech. 2:7). Laffey comments, "A woman may be understood to have much in common with a city or a country: she may be more or less valuable, more or less beautiful, large or small, a greater or lesser source of nurture, faithful or unfaithful. It is a compliment to a city or a country to personify it; it is an insult to women that cities and countries are so personified!" (162).

Two striking instances where female imagery is used to cast aspersions on infidelity and wickedness of cities occur in Jeremiah and Ezekiel. Unfaithful Zion is compared to a woman dressed in crimson, decked with ornaments of gold, and eyes enlarged with paint, beautified for her lovers (Jer. 4:30). In Ezekiel, the poet uses two promiscuous sisters, Oholah and Oholibah, to describe the sordid state and wicked deeds of Jerusalem and Samaria (Ezekiel 23).

The prophets condemned Israel's enemies by means of female imagery that connotes vulnerability, powerlessness, and inferiority. For example, the Egyptians will be like women (Isa. 19:16); the Babylonians will become women (Jer. 50:37; cf. Jer. 51:30); the hearts of the warriors of Moab and Edom will be like the heart of a woman in labor (Jer. 48:41; 49:22); and the Assyrian troops have become like women (Nah. 3:13).

Last, the gendered city Daughter Zion has drawn much attention from feminist interpreters. Carleen Mandolfo builds on her earlier dialogical approach to the Psalms and brings the voice of Daughter Zion into conversation with the voices addressing or depicting Zion throughout the prophetic corpus. Mandolfo presents Daughter Zion as someone who has found her own voice. A collected volume of essays responds to Mandolfo's thought and work and offers additional insights on the Daughter Zion metaphor (Boda, Dempsey, and Snow Flesher). Christl Maier has studied the use of this metaphor and its personification in relation to feminist perspectives on the body. I have looked at the metaphor of Jerusalem/Zion in its transformative state in Isaiah 60–62 (Dempsey 2009).

Ecological Perspectives

One of the most fruitful dialogues taking place is that between Israel's prophetic writings and ecology. Norman Habel and colleagues have created a series of ecojustice principles, reading the Bible through this ecological lens. Texts and topics discussed include Isa. 24:6 and the notion of a curse destroying the earth; the vision of land in Jeremiah 32; desolation in the book of Ezekiel; prophecies against the mountains in Ezekiel 6, 35, and 36; the earth community in Hosea 2; the relation to ecojustice and anthropological justice in Isa. 65:17; and the wolf, the lamb, and the little child as transformative agents for the earth community in Isaiah 11. Guiding these studies is the notion that earth and all its communities of life are intrinsically good and can no longer be viewed from an anthropocentric, objectified perspective. The writings advocate for the voices of indigenous peoples who know how the Earth suffers from the oppression that came with colonization. They argue that these voices must be heard and listened to in light of the current ecological crisis (Habel and Wurst 2001).

A second study collection of essays of this nature edited by Norman C. Habel and Peter Trudinger introduces readers to an ecological methodology of hermeneutics. Prophetic texts studied include Lamentations 1–2; Hosea 4:1-3 and the grievance of earth; Joel and the presence of the earth community in this text; the book of Amos and the voice of the earth within this text; and the book of Jonah and the role that nonhuman characters play in this book. Each of these articles adopts a geocentric perspective for interpreting the text instead of the usual anthropocentric perspective. Texts are reread with a member of the earth community as subject. For example, in Lamentations 1–2, Jerusalem is the focus of analysis. This city, a nonhuman subject, suffers on account of humankind's behavior, is cursed because of human sin, and has its voice co-opted for human purposes. Hosea 4:1-3 is read from the perspective of the land to demonstrate that creation actively mourns the subversion of the created order, which results in the languishing and perishing of animals, birds, and fish who live in the land. This article and the others in the collected volume argue for readers to appreciate the role that earth, understood as the entire ecosystem, plays in the relationship between God and creation. They call for a radical change of posture, one that acknowledges earth as a subject in the biblical text, and specifically in the prophets. Unique to this work is the retrieval of earth's voice expressed through creative stories and poetry that conclude some of the volume's chapters. Thus a voice previously unnoticed or suppressed within the biblical text and its interpretation comes to life in ways that are prophetic and profound.

Ellen Davis works from the premise that Israel's earliest prophetic writers were distinctly agrarian and thus their voices remain prophetic for today regarding local and global issues involving food production. One section of her work focuses specifically on Amos and Hosea, two "agrarian" prophets who, as Davis argues, understood completely that the health of human lives and culture was bound up inextricably with the care of the land and the just distribution of its harvest. Davis uses the prophets' writings to expose the destructive practices and assumptions that currently dominate the global food economy. Related to Davis's work, Matthew J. M. Coomber's study looks at land and land ownership in relation to globalization and the impact that it has on the poor of the planet.

Most recently, in "Jeremiah 14:1-9: From Drought to Starvation: A National Experience, A Global Reality," I link the great drought in Jeremiah to present-day depletion of water sources, the availability of water, and global climate change. I have also written on other prophetic texts from an ecological perspective, focusing on the natural world's suffering caused by human violence, greed, abuse, and the lack of reverence for life in general. Reflecting on various texts from both the Major and Minor Prophets, I make the claim that a systemic connection exists between human sinfulness and ecological destruction. I also point out that within prophetic literature, an inherent link exists between the redemption of humankind and the restoration of the natural world. The prophets offer an eschatological vision that can provide people with a basis of hope and a paradigm for faithful, holistic living (Dempsey 1999; 2000).

Perspectives from Trauma and Disaster Studies: Encountering Jeremiah

Trauma and disaster studies, a new interdisciplinary conversation, arose in the twentieth century. These studies involve insights from cognitive psychology, counseling, sociology, literary criticism, and anthropology. Using the insights gleaned from this field of inquiry, Kathleen M. O'Connor investigates the book of Jeremiah. She shows how every passage anticipates disaster, speaks about it, and offers ways of coping with its life-changing consequences. She points out that the text addresses the victims of the Babylonian assaults in Judah in the sixth century BCE, which involved invasions, displacements, and deportations.

Looking at the metaphorical broken family in the Jeremiah text, and then moving on to Jeremiah's war poems, weeping poems, biographical stories, confessions, sermons, and the text's final chapters, O'Connor illuminates the suffering of Jeremiah and his community, the impact violence has had on them, and the wounds they have endured. She concludes that despite its elements of disaster and trauma, the book of Jeremiah is a work of hope and resilience, one that shows readers how dwelling in the midst of devastation can be a way forward to the rediscovery of life and God (O'Connor 2011).

Prophetic Literature and Communications Studies

Besides trauma and disaster studies, other interdisciplinary approaches to the Bible have developed. Another way to view the biblical text is through the lens of communication studies, which explains how people use communication to exert influence and to construct knowledge, identities, relationships, and societies. One topic that generates much discussion in prophetic literature, in communications studies, and in the lived experience of life today is conflict. Using the text of Jeremiah 37–39, Elayne Shapiro and I explore the nature of conflict from the biblical studies and communications studies lenses. We first deal with the text's biblical content that features Jeremiah's tense interaction with King Zedekiah in the final days before Judah falls to the Babylonians. Then we examine the biblical narrative from the perspective of conflict theory, which involves a struggle between at least two interdependent parties who perceive incompatible goals, scarce resources, and interference from others in achieving their goals. They focus on the dialogue between Jeremiah and Zedekiah to show how the text illustrates that Jeremiah was so concerned with the content of his message, that he ignored the impact on the receiver. As a consequence of Jeremiah's obliviousness to communication skills, his receiver becomes defensive. Defensiveness blocks Zedekiah from benefiting from the content of Jeremiah's conversation with him. Both sender and receiver contribute to the debacle. The study serves as a model of how to identify and deal effectively with conflict in daily life (Dempsey and Shapiro).

Conclusion

Truth, tragedy, and trauma are but three characteristics of Israelite prophetic literature whose poets saw things as they were and dreamed of things as they could be. The prophetic texts provide a glimpse into the world of an ancient people whose struggles, hardships, depravity, hopes, and aspirations reflect the human condition in all its beauty and shame. The world of the ancestors is not so different from contemporary times as nations jockey for position in the global arena and the prophets of today sound the alarms about climate change, globalization, life-threatening violence, hunger, growing poverty, the loss of habitat, and social, political, economic, and religious injustices. The prophets of old, however, continue to remind the listeners and readers of prophetic literature today that, despite the world's condition, all of life lives under divine promise, and the final word to be received and taken to heart is not a word of judgment or doom; rather, the final word is always a word of hope (Isa. 65:17-25; Mic. 7:18-20; Hosea 14:1-9; Joel 2:21-22).

Works Cited

Baumann, Gerlinde. 2001. "Prophetic Objections to YHWH as the Violent Husband of Israel: Reinterpretations of the Prophetic Marriage Metaphor in Second Isaiah (Isaiah 40–55)." In *Prophets and Daniel: A Companion to the Bible (Second Series)*, edited by Athalya Brenner, 88–120. Sheffield: Sheffield Academic.

Bellis, Alice Ogden. 1994. *Helpmates, Harlots, Heroes: Women's Stories in the Hebrew Bible*. Louisville: Westminster John Knox.

Boda, Mark, Carol J. Dempsey, and LeAnn Snow Flesher, eds. 2012. *Daughter Zion: Her Portrait, Her Response*. SBLAIL. Atlanta: Society of Biblical Literature.

Bowen, Nancy R. 2006. "Women, Violence, and the Bible." In *Engaging the Bible in a Gendered World*, edited by Linda Day and Carolyn Pressler, 186–99. Louisville: Westminster John Knox.

Brenner, Athalya. 1993. "On 'Jeremiah' and the Poetics of (Prophetic?) Pornography." In *On Gendering Texts: Female and Male Voices in the Hebrew Bible*, edited by A. Brenner and F. van Dijk-Hemmes, 177–93. New York: Brill.

———. 1995. "On Prophetic Propaganda and the Politics of 'Love': The Case of Jeremiah." In *A Feminist Companion to the Latter Prophets*, edited by Athalya Brenner, 256–74. Sheffield: Sheffield Academic.

Coggins, Richard, and Jin H. Han. 2011. *Six Minor Prophets through the Centuries*. Oxford: Wiley-Blackwell.

Coomber, Matthew J. M. 2010. *Re-Reading the Prophets through Corporate Globalization: A Cultural-Evolutionary Approach to Economic Justice in the Hebrew Bible*. Piscataway, NJ: Gorgias.

Davis, Ellen F. 2009. *Scripture, Culture, and Agriculture: An Agrarian Reading of the Bible.* New York: Cambridge University Press.

Day, John. 2010. "Hosea and the Baal Cult." In *Prophecy and the Prophets in Ancient Israel,* edited by John Day, 202–24. LHB/OTS 531. New York: T&T Clark.

Dempsey, Carol J. 1999. "Hope amidst Crisis: A Prophetic Vision of Cosmic Redemption." In *All Creation Is Groaning: An Interdisciplinary Vision for Life in a Sacred Universe,* edited by Carol J. Dempsey and Russell A. Butkus, 269–84. Collegeville, MN: Liturgical Press.

———. 2000. *Hope amid the Ruins: The Ethics of Israel's Prophets.* St. Louis: Chalice.

———. 2009. "From Desolation to Delight: The Transformative Vision of Isaiah 60–62." In *The Desert Will Bloom: Poetic Visions of Isaiah,* edited by Joseph Everson and Hyun Chul Paul Kim, 217–32. SBLAIL 4. Atlanta: Society of Biblical Literature.

———. 2014. "Jeremiah 14:1-9: From Drought to Starvation: A National Experience, A Global Reality." In *By Bread Alone: Approaching the Bible through a Hermeneutic of Hunger,* edited by Sheila E. McGinn, Lai Ling Ngan, and Ahida Pilarski. Minneapolis: Fortress Press.

Dempsey, Carol J., and Elayne J. Shapiro. 2011. "Jeremiah: Defensiveness and Conflict (Jeremiah 37–39)." In *Reading the Bible, Transforming Conflict,* edited by Russell A. Butkus, Anne Clifford, and Carol J. Dempsey. Theology in Dialogue. Maryknoll, NY: Orbis.

Dempster, Stephen G. 2012. "Canon, Canonization." In *Dictionary of the Old Testament Prophets,* edited by Mark J. Boda and J. Gordon McConville, 71–77. Downers Grove, IL: InterVarsity Press.

Duguid, Iain. M. 2012. "Ezekiel: History of Interpretation." In *Dictionary of the Old Testament Prophets,* edited by Mark J. Boda and J. Gordon McConville, 229–35. Downers Grove, IL: InterVarsity Press.

Dobbs-Allsopp, F. W. 2009. "Daughter Zion." In *Thus Says the Lord: Essays on the Former and Latter Prophets in Honor of Robert R. Wilson,* edited by John J. Ahn and Stephen L. Cook, 125–34. New York: T&T Clark.

Ellens, J. Harold, and Wayne. G. Rollins, eds. 2004. *Psychology and the Bible: A New Way of Reading the Scriptures.* Santa Barbara: Praeger.

Ferreiro, Alberto, ed. 2003. *The Twelve Prophets.* Ancient Christian Commentary on Scripture, Old Testament 16. Downers Grove, IL: InterVarsity Press.

Habel, Norman, and Peter Trudinger, eds. 2008. *Exploring Ecological Hermeneutics.* Atlanta: Society of Biblical Literature.

Habel, Norman C., and Shirley Wurst, eds. 2001. *The Earth Story in Psalms and Prophets.* Sheffield: Sheffield Academic.

Junior, Nyasha. 2006. "Womanist Biblical Interpretation." In *Engaging the Bible in a Gendered World,* edited by Linda Day and Carolyn Pressler, 37–46. Louisville: Westminster John Knox.

Keefe, Alice A. 2001. *Woman's Body and the Social Body of Hosea.* JSOTSup 338. Sheffield: Sheffield Academic.

Laffey, Alice L. 1988. *An Introduction to the Old Testament: A Feminist Perspective.* Philadelphia: Fortress Press.

Maier, Christl M. 2008. *Daughter Zion, Mother Zion.* Minneapolis: Fortress Press.

Mandolfo, Carleen R. 2007. *Daughter Zion Talks Back to the Prophets: A Dialogic Theology of the Book of Lamentations.* Atlanta: Society of Biblical Literature.

McKinion, Steven A., ed. 2004. *Isaiah 1–39.* Ancient Christian Commentary on Scripture, Old Testament 10. Downers Grove, IL: InterVarsity Press.

O'Brien, Julia M. 2008. *Challenging Prophetic Metaphor: Theology and Ideology in the Prophets.* Louisville: Westminster John Knox.

O'Connor, Kathleen M. 2006. "The Feminist Movement Meets the Old Testament: One Woman's Perspective." In *Engaging the Bible in a Gendered World*, edited by Linda Day and Carolyn Pressler, 3–24. Louisville: Westminster John Knox.

———. 2011. *Jeremiah: Pain and Promise*. Minneapolis: Fortress Press.

Ortlund, Raymond C., Jr. 1996. *Whoredom: God's Unfaithful Wife in Biblical Theology*. Grand Rapids: Eerdmans.

Perdue, Leo G., Joseph Blenkinsopp, John J. Collins, and Carol Meyers, eds. 1997. *Families in Ancient Israel*. The Family, Religion, and Culture. Louisville: Westminster John Knox.

Pressler, Carolyn. 2006. "The 'Biblical View' of Marriage." In *Engaging the Bible in a Gendered World*, edited by Linda Day and Carolyn Pressler, 200–211. Louisville: Westminster John Knox.

Schüssler Fiorenza, Elisabeth. 2001. *Wisdom Ways: Introducing Feminist Biblical Interpretation*. Maryknoll, NY: Orbis.

Setel, T. Drorah. 1985. "Prophets and Pornography: Female Sexual Imagery in Hosea." In *Feminist Interpretations of the Bible*, edited by Letty M. Russell, 86–95. Philadelphia: Westminster Press.

Sherwood, Yvonne. 1996. *The Prostitute and the Prophet: Reading Hosea in the Late Twentieth Century*. New York: T&T Clark.

Stienstra, Nelly. 1993. "YHWH Is the Husband of His People: The Marriage Metaphor in the Book of Hosea." In *YHWH Is the Husband of His People*, 96–126. Kampen, the Netherlands: Kok Pharos.

Streete, Gail Corrington. 1997. *The Strange Woman: Power and Sex in the Bible*. Louisville: Westminster John Knox.

Weems, Renita. 1989. "Gomer: Victim of Violence or Victim of Metaphor?" In *Interpretation for Liberation*, edited by Katie Geneva Cannon and Elisabeth Schüssler Fiorenza. *Semeia* 47 (1989): 87–104.

———. 1995. *Battered Love: Marriage, Sex, and Violence in the Hebrew Prophets*. Minneapolis: Fortress Press.

Wilken, Robert Louis, with Angela Russell Christman and Michael J. Hollerich, eds. 2007. *Isaiah Interpreted by Early Christian and Medieval Commentators*. The Church's Bible. Grand Rapids: Eerdmans.

Yee, Gale A. 2003. *Poor Banished Children of Eve: Women as Evil in the Hebrew Bible*. Minneapolis: Fortress Press.

ISAIAH 1–39

Marvin A. Sweeney

Introduction

Isaiah 1–39 is part of the larger sixty-six-chapter book of Isaiah, which is attributed to the prophet Isaiah ben Amoz, in Isa. 1:1. Isaiah was a Jerusalemite prophet who spoke during the reigns of the Judean kings Uzziah (783–742 BCE), Jotham (742–735), Ahaz (735–715), and Hezekiah (715–687/686).

The late eighth century BCE saw a number of events that had a major impact on the kingdoms of Israel and Judah. First was the Syro-Ephraimitic War in 735–732, in which Israel and Aram invaded Judah in an effort to force Judah to join their anti-Assyrian alliance. When King Ahaz of Judah appealed to Assyria for assistance, the Assyrian king Tiglath Pileser III destroyed Damascus, reduced Israel, and subjugated Judah. Second was the destruction of the northern kingdom of Israel by the Assyrians in 724–721, following its revolt against the Assyrian Empire. Third was Hezekiah's revolt against Assyria in 705–701, which saw the Assyrian king Sennacherib's invasion of Judah and siege of Jerusalem. Although the book of Isaiah claims a great victory for YHWH and Hezekiah, Assyrian records and archaeology confirm that Judah was devastated, although Jerusalem remained intact and Hezekiah remained on the throne.

Throughout this period, Isaiah advised against military confrontation with Assyria. Isaiah's theological worldview was heavily informed by the Davidic/Zion stream of ancient Judean thought, which posited an eternal covenant between YHWH, the royal house of David, and the city of Jerusalem. According to the Davidic/Zion tradition, YHWH would defend the house of David and the city of Jerusalem forever (see 2 Samuel 7). Isaiah therefore viewed political and military alliances between Judah and other nations as unnecessary and potentially dangerous. He consistently argued for reliance on YHWH as the best course for Judah's security.

Although the superscription attributes the book to the prophet Isaiah, interpreters since antiquity have recognized that major portions of the book were composed by other writers. Isaiah 40–66 appears to presuppose the conclusion of the Babylonian exile and the rise of King Cyrus of Persia in 539 BCE (see Isa. 44:28; 45:1), as well as later periods.

The Babylonian Talmud (c. 600 CE) attributes the book of Isaiah to King Hezekiah of Judah and his colleagues (*b. B. Bat.* 14b). The medieval commentator Rabbi Abraham Ibn Ezra (1089–1167 CE) hints at the possibility of a different author beginning in Isaiah 40. By the late eighteenth century, modern critical scholars recognized Isaiah 1–39 as a work based on the prophecies of Isaiah ben Amoz and Isaiah 40–66 as the work of later prophets from the exilic period and beyond. Bernhard Duhm's 1892 commentary first argued that the book of Isaiah presented the work of Isaiah ben Amoz in Isaiah 1–39, an anonymous prophet known as Deutero-Isaiah in Isaiah 40–55, and a third prophet known as Trito-Isaiah in Isaiah 56–66. Subsequent interpretation recognizes Trito-Isaiah as the work of multiple writers.

More recent scholarship focuses on reading the various components of the book of Isaiah as a literary whole. When Isaiah 1–39, 40–55, and 56–66 are read as a single work, they present the vision of Isaiah ben Amoz that spans some four to five hundred years of Judah's and Jerusalem's history and YHWH's activity in the world from the time of the Assyrian invasions in the late eighth century BCE through the anticipated recognition of YHWH as the sovereign ruler of all creation from the Jerusalem temple, the holy center for creation.

The process of the formation of the book over this period of time points to efforts in ancient Judaism to read Isaiah as a book that addresses later times as well. Second Isaiah and Trito-Isaiah both contain extensive intertextual citations of texts from Isaiah 1–39 that indicate reflection on the meaning of Isaiah's prophecies in relation to the end of the Babylonian exile and the early Persian or Second Temple period when the temple was rebuilt. Indeed, the final form of the book of Isaiah appears designed to persuade later generations of Jews that YHWH is indeed the true G-d of creation and that they should return to Jerusalem to acknowledge YHWH as the true sovereign of a restored Israel and Judah and the world at large.

The final form of the book of Isaiah is therefore designed to demonstrate YHWH's role as the true sovereign of creation and G-d of Israel/Judah. The first half of the book, in Isaiah 1–33, presents YHWH's plans to reveal worldwide sovereignty at Zion. These chapters argue that failure to recognize YHWH results in disaster, such as that realized by King Ahaz of Judah during the Assyrian invasions of Israel and Judah, whereas adherence to YHWH will result in security and restoration. The second half of the book, in Isaiah 34–66, argues that the time of restoration is at hand. Based on the model of King Hezekiah during the Assyrian siege of Jerusalem, the people need to turn to YHWH, who will return them to Jerusalem at the center of a restored creation.

The book of Isaiah is preserved in two major manuscripts from Qumran. The iconic 1QIsaᵃ, which dates to the late second century BCE, presupposes a proto-Masoretic text, although it includes many exegetical variations, including a clear division between Isaiah 33 and Isaiah 34 to mark the two halves of the book. 1QIsaᵇ, which dates to the first century BCE, preserves a proto-Masoretic text. Isaiah appears in some twenty-one other manuscripts from Qumran as well.

Jewish tradition reads the book of Isaiah as a book of comfort (*b. B. Bat.* 14b–15a) that anticipates the restoration of Jerusalem in the aftermath of disaster and exile. Selections from Isaiah are
read throughout the year in the Jewish worship service as Haftarah readings, that is, readings from
the Prophets that accompany the reading of the Torah portion at the center of the Jewish worship
service. Many of the Haftarah readings from the ninth of Av, the Jewish day of mourning for the
loss of the temple and other disasters, in the late summer through Rosh Hashanah, the Jewish Near
Year, in the early fall, are drawn from Isaiah to anticipate divine restoration and blessing at the
beginning of the New Year. According to Jewish tradition, Isaiah was put to death by Hezekiah's
evil son Manasseh, who sawed Isaiah in half after accusing him of being a false prophet (*b. Yev.* 49b;
see also the pseudepigraphical work *The Martyrdom of Isaiah*).

Christianity also views the book of Isaiah as a key text in articulating Christian theology. Isaiah is
quoted extensively throughout the New Testament, especially as a book that anticipates the coming
of Christ. Indeed, Isaiah holds out a vision of an ideal world that Christianity understands to be
realized through Jesus Christ. The reference to the birth of Immanuel in Isa. 7:14; the portrayal of
the ideal king as the "Prince of Peace" in Isa. 9:1-6; and the Suffering Servant in Isa. 52:13—53:12
all play key roles in Isaiah's anticipation of Christ in the New Testament and Christian thought. The
first part of Handel's *Messiah* (Dublin 1742) is based largely on texts from Isaiah.

Both Judaism and Christianity employ elements from Isaiah's commissioning vision in Isaiah
6, particularly the song of the Seraphim, "Holy, holy, holy, is the L-rd of Hosts, the whole earth is
filled with [G-d's] glory" (6:3), as part of their respective worship services.

In the aftermath of the Shoah (Holocaust), both Jewish and Christian interpreters have begun
to rethink the meaning of Isaiah. Isaiah's commission in Isaiah 6 to render the people blind, deaf,
and dumb without the possibility of repentance, for instance, implies that G-d deliberately punishes
innocent humans to reveal divine glory. Some maintain that Isaiah's commission calls not for acceptance of evil even when it comes from the highest authority, but instead for human beings to exercise
moral responsibility in their own right to bring about the ideal world that Isaiah holds forth.

Isaiah 1: Prologue to the Book of Isaiah: YHWH's Intention to Purify Zion

THE TEXT IN ITS ANCIENT CONTEXT

Isaiah 1 begins with the superscription for the book in 1:1. The superscription identifies the book as
"the vision of Isaiah son of Amoz," and states that his focus is on Judah and Jerusalem. It places the
prophet in the reigns of the Judean kings Uzziah (783–742 BCE), Jotham (742–735), Ahaz (735–
715), and Hezekiah (715–687/668). Major events during this period include the Syro-Ephraimitic
War (735–732), the fall of northern Israel to the Assyrian empire (722/1), and the Assyrian invasion of Judah and siege of Jerusalem (701).

Isaiah 1:2-20 constitutes the speech of the accuser in which the prophet lays out YHWH's
charges that the people of Jerusalem, Judah, and Israel act like the people of Sodom and Gomorrah

by not following divine guidance. Isaiah 1:21-31 constitutes the speech of the judge in which the prophet likens Jerusalem to unrefined ore that must be smelted to purge the city of its alleged sins. Once the process of punishment is complete, the prophet looks forward to Zion's restoration.

THE TEXT IN THE INTERPRETIVE TRADITION

Most modern scholars maintain that Isaiah 1 consists primarily of oracles by Isaiah son of Amoz, but it has been edited to serve as the prologue both to the book of Isaiah as a whole and to the first portion of the book in either Isaiah 1–39 or Isaiah 1–33 (Fohrer; Tomasino). It can function in this role because it presents an overview of the major concerns of the book, namely, YHWH's judgment against Jerusalem and Israel and the ultimate restoration of Jerusalem and Israel. Interpreters have noted its parallels with Isaiah 34, which opens the second half of the book of Isaiah, and Isaiah 66, which closes the book of Isaiah as a whole (Evans).

Christian tradition reads Isaiah 1 as a summary of the sins of Israel that calls for the coming of Jesus. Paul quotes Isa. 1:9 in Rom. 9:29 as part of his larger argument for justification by faith. Protestant Christian interpretation generally reads Isa. 1:10-17 as an indictment of temple ritual practice, although Jewish interpreters generally note that it condemns ritual practice that is not accompanied by proper moral and spiritual outlook (see Leviticus 19).

Jewish tradition reads Isa. 1:1-27 as the Haphtarah, or Prophetic Reading, for Shabbat Hazon, "the Shabbat of Vision," the first Shabbat after Tisha b'Av, "the ninth of Av," in late July or early August that commemorates the destruction of the First and Second Temples. The passage rehearses the theme of judgment that explains the destruction, but it points to restoration at the end.

THE TEXT IN CONTEMPORARY DISCUSSION

Isaiah 1 is an indictment of human wrongdoing and rejection of G-d, but it looks forward to restoration once the people have been purged by divine punishment. In the aftermath of the Shoah or Holocaust, contemporary theologians recognize such statements as a form of theodicy, that is, they defend G-d against charges of divine wickedness, absence, and impotence by asserting that human beings—and not G-d—must be responsible for evil in the world.

Isaiah 2–4: YHWH's Plan for Worldwide Sovereignty at Zion

THE TEXT IN ITS ANCIENT CONTEXT

Isaiah 2–4 begins with its own superscription in Isa. 2:1, which identifies the following material as "the word which Isaiah ben Amoz envisioned concerning Judah and Jerusalem" (author trans.). The unit presents the prophet's announcement concerning the preparation of Zion/Jerusalem for its role as the center for YHWH's worldwide sovereignty.

The Jerusalem temple was considered the holy center of creation. The portrayal of Jerusalem here as the site of the holy temple of YHWH, to which the nations would flock to learn divine instruction and bring an end to war, appears to presuppose the role that major temples played in Mesopotamian culture. During the Babylonian Akitu or New Year's festival, representatives of the nations subject to Babylonian rule would carry idols of their national gods in procession through the streets of Babylon to honor the Babylonian king. When the procession reached the temple of Marduk, the king would climb the steps to the top of the temple. There he would be granted the tablets of destiny, which gave him the right to rule the Babylonian Empire—and thus all creation—for another year on Marduk's behalf.

Following Isa. 2:2-4, the prophet presents three addresses that outline how the ideals expressed in this passage will be achieved. The first, in Isa. 2:5-9, begins with an invitation to the house of Jacob to join the nations' pilgrimage to Zion. But the passage quickly turns to accusations that the people have abandoned YHWH to follow foreign gods. As an adherent of the Davidic-Zion tradition, which maintains that YHWH alone protects the royal house of David and the city of Jerusalem, Isaiah opposed foreign alliances.

The second address, in Isa. 2:10-21, presents the prophet's announcement of the coming day of YHWH, when YHWH will punish foreign nations that threaten Israel (e.g., Isa. 13:6, 9; Joel 1:15; 2:11, 31; 3:14; Obad. 15) or those within Israel who allegedly oppose YHWH (e.g., Amos 5:18-20; Zeph. 1:7, 14; Mal. 4:5). The oracle focuses on the downfall of all who are high, mighty, and arrogant, and holds that YHWH alone will be aggrandized on the coming day of punishment.

The third address, in Isa. 2:22—4:6, focuses on the purging of Jerusalem and Judah. Following the plea in Isa. 2:22 to abandon human self-reliance, the passage turns to the punishment of the male leaders of Jerusalem and Judah in Isa. 3:1-11. The address then focuses on the leading women of Jerusalem and Judah in Isa. 3:12-4:1 who will be judged, stripped of their fine clothing, and left bereft of their husbands once the men have been killed or exiled. The passage concludes with an idyllic portrayal of a restored Jerusalem following the purge of the city.

▌ THE TEXT IN THE INTERPRETIVE TRADITION

Many modern interpreters maintain that Isa. 2:2-4 (cf. Mic. 4:1-5) dates to the Babylonian exile in the sixth century BCE, because of the analogy with the Akitu festival and the passage's many affinities with Second Isaiah. Like Second Isaiah, the passage envisions peace among the nations who will recognize YHWH as the sovereign deity of all creation and the nations of the world. Isaiah 2–4 summarizes the message of the book of Isaiah as a whole, which envisions a process in which YHWH will bring punishment upon Jerusalem as a means to purge and restore the city, thereby to reveal YHWH's role as sovereign of all creation and the nations at large.

When read as part of the prophecies of Isaiah ben Amoz, the portrayal of judgment in Isaiah 2:5—4:6 functions as Isaiah's means to explain how the Assyrian Empire will be able to overrun Israel and Judah; namely, because the king and people do not place their faith in YHWH's promises of protection, YHWH brings the Assyrians to punish them for infidelity.

In both Jewish and Christian tradition, the passage is read as an eschatological portrayal of the future restoration of Jerusalem. The New Testament presupposes Isa. 2:2-4 in defining the imagery of the city on the hill in the salt and light parable of the Sermon on the Mount in Matt. 5:13-16. The city of light is a beacon to the good works of Jesus' followers and the glory of G-d in heaven.

The reference to the city on a hill informs John Winthrop's 1630 sermon extolling the Massachusetts Bay Colonists to make their city (Boston) a shining example for the world.

Rabbinic commentators such as Abraham Ibn Ezra and David Kimhi read the passage as a portrayal of the days to come when the temple would be rebuilt and the Messiah would come. The restoration of Zion is a key theme in both biblical and modern Zionist thought. Indeed, the BILU Zionist pioneers took their name from the first letters of the Hebrew words in Isa. 2:5, "O House of Jacob, come and let us go" (*bet ya'aqov, lekhu venelkhah*).

■ THE TEXT IN CONTEMPORARY DISCUSSION

The idyllic imagery of Isa. 2:2-4, with its portrayal of the nations beating swords into plowshares and spears into pruning hooks, expresses one of the most important ideals of human life. Indeed, Isa. 2:4 serves as an unofficial motto for the United Nations. The English translation of the passage is inscribed on the Isaiah Stone, located in Ralph J. Bunche Park just across the street from the United Nations headquarters in New York City.

But Isaiah 2–4 also employs images of divine judgment against all who are high, mighty, and arrogant. Although many read such accusations as justified indictments against sinful human beings, readers must remember that Isaiah was attempting to explain the realities—whether anticipated or realized—of foreign invasion in his own time. In the aftermath of the Shoah, or Holocaust, such attempts to explain evil by accusing the victims are coming increasingly under criticism. In the end, readers must remember that the prophets faced the same problems that contemporary thinkers face, namely, how to explain evil while simultaneously positing an omnipotent and moral G-d. Our own responsibility to establish an exemplary city on a hill becomes paramount.

Isaiah 5–12

Isaiah 5–12 is a lengthy unit that focuses on the Assyrian invasions of Israel and Judah and the restoration of Jerusalem and the Davidic monarchy once YHWH defeats the Assyrians. It includes two basic subunits, the prophet's announcement of judgment against Israel and Judah in Isaiah 5 and the prophet's explanation of the significance of divine judgment in Isaiah 6–12. Isaiah 6–12 includes three basic subunits, Isaiah's vision of YHWH in Isaiah 6; the account of YHWH's judgment against Judah during the Syro-Ephraimitic War in Isaiah 7:1—8:15; and the announcement concerning the fall of Assyria and the restoration of the Davidic kingdom in Isaiah 8:16—12:6.

Isaiah 5: Announcement of Judgment against Israel and Judah

■ THE TEXT IN ITS ANCIENT CONTEXT

Isaiah 5 begins with the so-called vineyard allegory in Isa. 5:1-7, in which the prophet sings about his "friend's" unsuccessful efforts to grow good grapes in his vineyard. As the allegory progresses, it becomes evident that Isaiah's "friend" is indeed YHWH and that the vineyard with its sour grapes represents the people of Israel and Judah. A series of "woe" oracles then follows in Isa. 5:8-24, in which Isaiah, speaking on YHWH's behalf, charges the people with a series of crimes that illustrate their refusal to follow divine torah, "instruction" (5:24). The prophet's charges include illegal acquisition of land and houses (5:8-10), drunkenness and failure to heed the needs of the poor (5:9-17), impious demands for divine action (5:18-19), the confusion of good and evil (5:20-21), and the subversion of justice (5:22-23). YHWH's announcement of judgment, which portrays the approach of the Assyrian army, then concludes the subunit in Isa. 5:25-30.

▮ THE TEXT IN THE INTERPRETIVE TRADITION

Modern interpreters maintain that Isaiah 5 is the product of Isaiah, but they note its intertextual relationships with the new song of the vineyard in Isa. 27:2-13, a sixth-century text, which looks forward to the restoration of Israel and Judah once the punishment is completed. The use of the "woe" oracle is particularly important because it warns of impending danger if the nation loses sight of its obligations for justice and righteousness in the world.

▮ THE TEXT IN CONTEMPORARY DISCUSSION

The approach of an enemy army is a terrifying prospect in both the ancient and the modern world. We in the United States have been blessed in that we have not suffered a foreign invasion since the War of 1812. Nevertheless, Isaiah's warning applies to us as well, insofar as he envisions leadership that is more interested in serving its own interests rather than those of the nation at large. Gridlock in the US Congress is a case in point, as our nation suffers from the inability of our Congressional representatives to arrive at compromises that will serve the larger good.

Isaiah 6: Isaiah's Commission Vision

▮ THE TEXT IN ITS ANCIENT CONTEXT

Isaiah 6 presents the prophet's autobiographical account of his vision of YHWH in the Jerusalem temple. Interpreters are divided as to whether this is a commissioning account or a later reflection concerning the prophet's failure to convince the people to repent. The issues include the placement of the chapter after Isaiah 1–5 rather than at the beginning of the book and YHWH's commission to render the people blind, deaf, and dumb so that they are unable to repent, which seems to contradict the prophet's efforts throughout the rest of Isaiah 1–39.

The account is an example of a throne vision in which YHWH appears to a human enthroned in the earthly or heavenly temple (1 Kings 22; Ezekiel 1; Daniel 7). The vision takes place in the year of King Uzziah's death (742 BCE), before the Syro-Ephraimitic War and the Assyrian invasions of the late eighth century. It is based on the imagery of the interior of the Jerusalem temple during worship. The prophet stands by the column at the entrance to the temple, where the king stands (2 Kgs. 11:14; 23:3) so that he can see into the interior of the temple (1 Kings 7). YHWH is enthroned over the ark of the covenant, which resides in the holy of holies of the temple. The portrayal of YHWH's train or robes billowing out of the temple is based on the imagery of smoke from the thick incense generated by the ten incense burners in the great hall of the temple. The portrayal of the seraphim (fiery angelic figures) is based on the imagery of the ten menorahs or candlestands, each with seven lamps, burning within the thick incense smoke. Their hymn, "Holy, holy, holy, is YHWH of Hosts, the whole earth is full of [G-d's] glory" (author trans.), represents the song of the Levitical choir during the temple liturgy. The rumbling noise is from the heavy doors that are opened at sunrise to inaugurate the daily morning worship service. The placement of a hot coal on Isaiah's lips emulates the mouth-purification ceremonies practiced by Mesopotamian *baru* priests to prepare themselves to speak divine words. YHWH instructs Isaiah to render the people blind, deaf, and dumb so that they cannot repent and thereby save themselves. Isaiah does not object to YHWH's plans. Instead, he simply asks, "how long?" and YHWH responds with a vision of destruction (based on the Hebrew verb *sh'h*, which underlies the term Shoah) that will result in a surviving remnant of only 10 percent of the people. That remnant then constitutes "the holy seed" that will restore Jerusalem and Israel.

▐ THE TEXT IN THE INTERPRETIVE TRADITION

Modern scholars have raised questions as to whether Isaiah 6 is the work of the prophet or not. Although some maintain that it is a later composition (e.g., Kaiser, 115–21) its portrayal of coming judgment in which the people are rendered blind, deaf, and dumb is a signal that it might represent the prophet's reflection on his inability to motivate the kings and people to change. Ezra 9:2 cites "the holy seed" from Isa. 6:13 as part of Ezra's portrayal of the restoration of Jerusalem in keeping with Isaiah's prophecies.

The New Testament cites Isa. 6:9-10 frequently. In Matt. 13:14; Mark 4:12; and Luke 8:10, the quote appears to validate the disciples of Jesus who understand his words. In John 12:39 and Acts 28:25, it appears as part of larger discussion concerning the failure of Jews to recognize Jesus as the Messiah. Although such comments were generated by early Christianity's attempt to argue for its own perspective, the condemnation of Jews would have repercussions throughout the Middle Ages and the modern period, culminating in the Shoah (Holocaust). The song of the Seraphim, "Holy, Holy, Holy . . ." constitutes part of the Trisagion (thrice holy) in Christian liturgy.

Judaism reads Isa. 6:1-13, together with Isa. 7:1-6 and 9:5-6, as part of the Haftarah for Exod. 18:1—20:26, which recounts the revelation of Torah at Sinai. The Haftarah aids in helping Jews to understand G-d as the sovereign monarch who stands behind the Sinai revelation. The song of the Seraphim, "Holy, Holy, Holy . . ." constitutes part of the Kedushah (sanctification) of the morning and Musaf (additional) worship service in Judaism.

▐ THE TEXT IN CONTEMPORARY DISCUSSION

Mordecai Kaplan, the founder of Reconstructionist Judaism, finds a particularly disturbing issue is the moral character of YHWH's charge to the prophet to render the people blind, deaf, and dumb so that divine purpose might be realized (Kaplan). Such a position is an expression of teleological ethics, that is, the end result justifies the means. But the sacrifice of generations until that purpose is achieved hardly constitutes an example of ontological ethics, that is, the question of whether an act is good or evil in and of itself. Interpreters have noted that Isaiah does not challenge YHWH like

Abraham (Genesis 18), Moses (Exodus 32; Numbers 14), Job, and others do when confronted with the possibility of divine evil. Ironically, Isaiah's ideal vision of world harmony among the nations (Isa. 2:2-4) is not realized and the book ends with the portrayal of the corpses of those who would resist YHWH (Isa. 66:24). Elie Wiesel (111) states that we can say anything to G-d from within Jewish tradition. The same applies to Christianity. Perhaps we should learn from this that Isaiah should have objected, just as we must object when confronted with evil even from the highest of authorities.

Isaiah 7:1—8:15: YHWH's Judgment against Judah

■ THE TEXT IN ITS ANCIENT CONTEXT

Isaiah 7:1—8:15 presents an account of Isaiah's encounter with King Ahaz of Judah during the Syro-Ephraimitic War. Since the reign of King Jehu of Israel (842–815 BCE), the northern kingdom of Israel had been allied with the Assyrian Empire, which ensured that Israel would no longer be threatened by Aram as it was during the reigns of the Omride kings, that is, Omri (876–869 BCE), Ahab (869–850), Ahaziah (849), and Jehoram (849–842). But when King Pekah (737–732) came to the throne, he sought an alliance with Aram so that he might oppose the Assyrian Empire and bring an end to the crushing tribute that Israel had to pay. The Syro-Ephraimitic alliance therefore attempted to include all the small kingdoms of western Asia so they could present a united front against Assyria. King Jotham of Judah and his son Ahab refused to join the alliance. As Assyrian allies themselves, they knew that the Assyrians would devastate any kingdom that broke a treaty, and they likely distrusted an alliance based on two powers that had been at war with each other a century earlier. Consequently, northern Israel and Aram attacked Jerusalem in 734 BCE in an effort to force it into the Syro-Ephraimitic coalition.

The narrative portrays the fear of the house of David at the news of the Syro-Ephraimitic invasion of Judah. King Jotham apparently had passed away for reasons unknown to us, and his twenty-year-old son Ahaz was the new king. Ahaz was inspecting the water system of Jerusalem, located at the Upper Pool by the Fuller's Field ("fuller" means "one who does laundry"), which would have been located in the Kidron Valley east of Jerusalem outside the city's walls. The people of the city had access to the water through an underground tunnel, which represented a weak point in the city's defenses. Insofar as David had conquered Jerusalem by means of this tunnel (2 Sam. 5:8), Ahaz was considering how to defend the site. Isaiah's approach with his son, symbolically name Shear Jashub (Hebrew for "a remnant will return"), signaled the prophet's message that Ahaz should rely only on YHWH to defend the city, in keeping with YHWH's promise that the sons of David would sit on the throne of Israel in Jerusalem forever (2 Samuel 7). Of course, that would mean that many Judeans would die in keeping with the name of Isaiah's son, "(only) a remnant will return/survive." Ahaz preferred more practical means, however, and summoned the Assyrians to assist him as recounted in 2 Kings 16. Upon recognizing Ahaz's failure to trust in YHWH, Isaiah then proclaims that Judah will suffer as the Assyrians will invade and devastate the country, leaving

Judah to suffer under increased tribute. Although many believe Isaiah's advice to be impractical, it was based on the premise that the Assyrians would have invaded Aram and Israel anyway once their armies moved south to attack Jerusalem. The Assyrians destroyed Damascus and subjugated Israel, stripping it of its outlying territories. Pekah was assassinated. Ahaz's impetuousness did not result in an Assyrian reward; rather, it put him in Assyria's debt and resulted in heavier obligations to Assyria.

▌THE TEXT IN THE INTERPRETIVE TRADITION

Modern critics, particularly Peter Ackroyd, have noted that the Ahaz narrative in Isaiah 7:1—8:15 is formulated as a counterpoint to the presentation of Hezekiah in Isaiah 36–39. Ahaz appears to be unwilling to trust in YHWH or Isaiah, and Judah suffers invasion and subjugation to Assyria as a result. Hezekiah places his trust in YHWH and Isaiah in Isaiah 36–37, and the city of Jerusalem is delivered as a result. The two narratives thereby characterize their respective segments of the book. Isaiah 1–33 speaks especially of judgment like that experienced by Ahaz, whereas Isaiah 34–66 anticipates deliverance and restoration like that experienced by Hezekiah.

Matthew 1:23 cites the birth of Immanuel (Hebrew, "G-d is with us") in Isa. 7:14 as a prophecy that predicts the birth of Jesus. The Gospel, however, cites the Greek text of the Septuagint, which states that the boy will be born to a *parthenos*, "virgin," in keeping with Hellenistic tradition that celebrates children born to gods—for example, Zeus—and human virgins. The Hebrew text reads, *'almah*, "young woman," irrespective of her status as a virgin. Jewish interpreters understand Immanuel to be a son of Isaiah.

▌THE TEXT IN CONTEMPORARY DISCUSSION

Just as Israel was invaded by Aram (Syria) and other nations, such as Egypt, Assyria, and Babylonia, in antiquity, so modern Israel has been invaded or attacked repeatedly by Syria, Egypt, Hezbollah, Hamas, and other Arab nations in modern times, for example, in 1948, 1967, 1973, 2006, and 2012. Israel stands at a geographical crossroads in the ancient and modern Middle East, and it is therefore a tempting target. Many see the Palestinian issue as the key issue of the Middle East, but the refusal by many Arab and Muslim countries to view Israel as a legitimate state for Jews is just as crucial.

Isaiah 8:16—12:6: Announcing the Fall of Assyria and Restoration of the House of David

▌THE TEXT IN ITS ANCIENT CONTEXT

Isaiah 8:16—12:6 presents Isaiah's announcements concerning the fall of Assyria and the restoration of the Davidic kingdom. It includes two major components, namely, (1) prophetic instruction concerning YHWH's signs to Israel and the House of David in Isa. 8:16—9:6 (9:7 in NRSV) and (2) the prophet's announcement concerning the fulfillment of YHWH's signs in Isa. 9:7—12:6 (9:8—12:6 in NRSV).

Isaiah 8:16—9:6 begins with an expression of the prophet's frustration that Ahaz will not listen to him. He therefore announces his intention to "bind up the testimony and seal my instruction [torah] among my teachings" while he waits for YHWH, who is hiding the divine face from the house of Israel. He envisions the people walking in great darkness until such time as a new and righteous Davidic monarch will emerge who will be recognized as "the prince of peace."

Isaiah 9:7—12:6 announces the fulfillment of YHWH's signs. The passage begins with a lengthy sequence of oracles, all based on the formula "YHWH's hand is stretched out still," which condemn the northern kingdom of Israel in Isa. 9:7—10:4 for a variety of misdeeds. This oracular sequence constitutes the prophet's comment on the fall of the northern kingdom of Israel to the Assyrian empire in 722/721 BCE. With Israel destroyed, Isaiah then turns in Isa. 10:5—12:6 to a condemnation of the Assyrian Empire, particularly its king (presumably Sargon II), for his arrogance in threatening Jerusalem and claiming to be the true power in the world. In Isa. 10:5-34, Isaiah likens the Assyrian king to the Egyptian Pharaoh of the exodus, when he announces that the Assyrian king will fall just like a tree that has been trimmed. YHWH will grow a new, righteous Davidic monarch from the stump of Jesse. The prophet holds in Isa. 11:1-16 that the new monarch will be wise and righteous, that he will reunite Israel and Judah, and that he will swoop down on the enemies of Israel and Judah, resulting ultimately in the return of exiles from Assyria and Egypt. The concluding hymn in Isa. 12:6 draws its language from the Song of the Sea in Exodus 15, especially in verses 1-3, and various Psalms, such as 105:1 and 118:14, 21, to praise YHWH for restoring Israel and Judah.

▌ THE TEXT IN THE INTERPRETIVE TRADITION

Modern interpreters debate compositional issues in Isaiah 8:16—12:6. Although many view the royal oracle in Isa. 9:1-6 as Isaiah's anticipation of the birth of Hezekiah, they see the royal oracle of Isa. 11:1-16 as a postexilic composition. Isaiah 11 was more likely written in the time of King Josiah of Judah (640–609 BCE), who was known for his program of religious reform and national restoration. The reign of Josiah saw many editions of the narrative and prophetic books, such as Joshua–Kings, Isaiah, Amos, Hosea, and portions of Jeremiah that were edited to support the Josian reform. Isaiah 11, with its vision of a child king who would reunite Israel and Judah to bring home the exiles from Assyria and Egypt, is an example of such work. The hymn in Isa. 12:1-6 points to a liturgical setting for the performance of Isaiah, perhaps in the monarchic period as well as in the second temple of the Persian period and beyond.

Isaiah's royal oracles have been a source of constant attention in Christianity insofar as they are read as predictions of the coming of Jesus. The reference in Isaiah 8:23—9:1 (9:1-2 in NRSV) to the people who have seen a great light appears in Matt 4:15-16 as part of the evangelist's introduction to Jesus' career in the Galilee. Likewise, the phrase "a child is born" in Isa. 9:6 stands in the background of the birth of Jesus in Matt. 1:23. Isaiah 9:1-6 plays a key role in Handel's oratorio *The Messiah* (Dublin 1742), which is performed especially at Christmastime to celebrate Jesus' birth and life. Paul cites Isa. 11:1, 10, in Rom. 15:12 as part of a larger argument that the new Davidic king is a sign to the nations.

Talmudic tradition views Isa. 9:1-6 as a reference to the birth of Hezekiah. The talmudic Rabbi Bar Kappara thought that Hezekiah was supposed to be the Messiah, but the attribute of justice (*middat ha-din*) argued against this claiming that David was not made the Messiah and that Hezekiah was less worthy (*b. Sanh.* 94a). Isaiah 10:32—12:6 functions as the Haftarah reading for the eighth day of Passover because of its exodus references, its portrayal of the downfall of an oppressive king, and its vision of exiles restored to Israel and Judah from Egypt and Assyria.

THE TEXT IN CONTEMPORARY DISCUSSION

The celebration of the downfall of an oppressor expresses an important ideal in both Christianity and Judaism. In Christianity, such ideals are expressed through the coming of Christ, who brings down the oppressive powers of the world. In Judaism, such ideals are expressed especially in the celebration of Passover and the release of the people of Israel from Egyptian bondage. We may also remember the joyous celebrations at the end of World War II, when both Nazi Germany and imperial Japan surrendered. The famed picture of the sailor kissing the nurse in Times Square is a lasting reminder of the joy experienced as a result of the end of the war. At the same time, we must remember the limits of military power. The killing of Osama bin Laden, however satisfying given his crimes, did not bring the war on terrorism to an end.

Isaiah 13–27

Isaiah 13–27, concerned with the preparation of the nations for YHWH's worldwide sovereignty, constitutes a distinctive section within the book of Isaiah as a whole. It contains two basic components. The first is the announcement concerning the nations in Isaiah 13–23, including Babylon (Isaiah 13–14), Moab (Isaiah 15–16), Damascus (Isaiah 17–18), Egypt (Isaiah 19–20), the Wilderness of the Sea (Isa. 21:1-10), Dumah (Isa. 21:11-12), Arabia (Isa. 21:13-17), the Valley of Vision (Isaiah 22), and Tyre (Isaiah 23). The second concerns the restoration of Zion/Israel at the center of the nations. All of the nations mentioned were part of the Persian Empire, which indicates that the book of Isaiah associates YHWH with Persian rule.

Isaiah 13–14: The Pronouncement Concerning Babylon

THE TEXT IN ITS ANCIENT CONTEXT

Like all of the oracles against the nations in Isaiah 13–23, Isaiah 13–14 begins with a superscription that labels the following text as the *massa'*, or "pronouncement," concerning Babylon. The prophetic pronouncement functions as a means to depict YHWH's actions in the world.

Isaiah 13–14 is a lengthy oracle that anticipates the downfall of Babylon on the day of YHWH. The day of YHWH tradition is well known in the Prophets as a day when YHWH will act against enemies, including those who threaten Jerusalem, Judah, and Israel (e.g., Joel 1–2; Obadiah; Zeph. 1:2-18), and even against Jerusalem or Israel itself when viewed as acting contrary to YHWH's expectations (e.g., Isa. 2:6-21; Amos 5:18-20). King Hezekiah of Judah allied with the Babylonian prince Merodach Baladan in his attempt to revolt against the Assyrians in 705–701 BCE. The aim of the revolt was to strike Assyria from both west (Judah and its allies) and east (Babylon and its allies) and thereby divide Assyrian efforts to put down the revolt. Isaiah's opposition to this alliance is evident in Isaiah 39, where Isaiah condemns Hezekiah for receiving the Babylonian embassy in preparation for the revolt.

A short oracle against the Philistines is appended in Isa. 14:28-32 to account for one of the nations subdued by Hezekiah as he prepared for revolt.

THE TEXT IN THE INTERPRETIVE TRADITION

Most scholars recognize that Isaiah 13–14 is the product of later editing, particularly in the sixth century BCE, when the Persians conquered the Babylonian Empire and allowed exiled Jews to return to Jerusalem to rebuild the temple. Isaiah 13 in particular appears to have been composed to antici-pate the work of Second Isaiah in Isaiah 40–55, which announced the end of the exile and called on Jews to return to Jerusalem. The passage appears to have reworked an older anti-Assyrian oracle in Isaiah 14 that celebrated the battlefield death of the Assyrian monarch Sargon II in 705 BCE. His defeat was so complete that his body laid unrecovered and unburied on the battlefield (see Isa. 14:19-20). Sargon's death was an important catalyst for Hezekiah's revolt in 705 BCE. The brief anti-Assyrian oracle in Isa. 14:24-27 points to the original Assyrian referent of the oracle and demonstrates how earlier Isaian prophecies could be reread in reference to later events following the lifetime of the prophet.

Interpreters have long noted the portrayal in Isa. 14:12 of the fall of Helel son of Shachar, "the Shining One, son of the Dawn," from heaven down to Sheol (the netherworld where all of the dead go; see esp. Erlandsson). Although this was originally meant as a reference to Sargon II, later inter-preters viewed it as a description of a fallen angel from heaven who would then become the Satan figure. Thus the Vulgate translates the phrase into Latin as Lucifer, "light bearing" (in reference to the morning star, Venus), which became a name for Satan in the Christian tradition. Although the downfall of Lucifer comes to play a role in Christian eschatology, early Protestant interpreters such as Luther and Calvin denied that this text referred to Satan, preferring instead to see it as a histori-cal reference to Babylon. Jewish interpreters tended to read the name in relation to the Babylonians. Rashi saw it as a reference to Venus, the morning star, which symbolized the Babylonian goddess Ishtar, and Kimhi understood it as a reference to Nebuchadnezzar.

THE TEXT IN CONTEMPORARY DISCUSSION

Many interpreters read Isaiah 13–14 as an oracle proclaiming the downfall of Iraq during the 1991 Gulf War, especially when Saddam Hussein parked Iraqi fighter jets by the ruins of Ur, located in the territory of ancient Babylonia, in an attempt to protect them from allied forces. Saddam Hus-sein attacked Israel with Scud missiles in an attempt to draw Israel into the war and thereby prompt Arab allies of the United States such as Egypt and Syria to reconsider their participation in the US-led alliance. Iraq's Scud missiles lacked precision guidance systems, and they generally struck civilian rather than military targets. Israel was not an active member of the alliance—indeed, the United States, in an effort to attract Arab nations into the alliance, had advised Israel to stay out of the war altogether. Nevertheless, Saddam Hussein hoped to draw on the anti-Jewish sentiments of America's Arab allies by deliberately attacking Israel despite the fact that it was not directly involved.

Others see environmental concerns addressed in this text, particularly in Isa. 14:7-8 in which the trees celebrate the downfall of the King Babylon because he would no longer come to cut them down (Tucker, 161). Mesopotamian rulers were known for their expeditions to Phoenicia (modern Lebanon) to cut down cedars and other trees to decorate their imperial palaces.

Isaiah 15–16: The Pronouncement concerning Moab

▮ The Text in Its Ancient Context

Isaiah 15–16 is Isaiah's oracle concerning Moab, located east of the Jordan River and Dead Sea in modern-day Jordan. The oracle describes Moab's distress at a foreign invasion, likely the Assyrian king Tiglath Pileser III, during the Syro-Ephraimitic War (734–732 BCE). The city names indicate a flight from the region north of the Wadi Arnon, which would have been Israelite territory settled by Reuben and Gad prior to the ninth-century-BCE war between Aram and Israel. Seeing Israel's defeat by Aram, King Mesha of Moab seized Israelite territory north of the Arnon, as recorded in his famed Moabite Stone. In Isa. 16:6, the prophet recalls Moab's arrogance.

▮ The Text in the Interpretive Tradition

Although this text was likely written by Isaiah, it was reused in later contexts. It likely provided support for Josiah's interests in reestablishing Davidic rule over Moab in the late seventh century BCE. Portions of the oracle were reused in Jeremiah's oracle concerning Moab in Jer. 48:29-38.

▮ The Text in Contemporary Discussion

Isaiah 16:3-5 is frequently cited in support of causes for social justice. Gene M. Tucker, for example, understands this section to be a reference to refugees from war. He states, "The visionary poet sees the answer to the problems of refugees from war to be in a ruler descended from David, on the throne in Jerusalem. The passage is messianic in this hope for an anointed one in the future. Its vision of a time of peace under a just ruler reiterates the themes of 11:1-5" (Tucker, 169).

Isaiah 17–18: The Pronouncement concerning Damascus

▮ The Text in Its Ancient Context

Isaiah 17–18 constitutes the prophet's pronouncement against Damascus, the capital of Aram (Syria), but the reference to Ephraim and Israel in Isa. 17:3 indicates that it addresses the Syro-Ephraimitic coalition that threatened Jerusalem and Judah in 734–732 BCE. The woe oracle against

Cush (Ethiopia) in Isaiah 18 presupposes King Hosea of Israel's embassy to Cush in 724 BCE, in preparation for its ultimately fatal revolt against Assyria. Isaiah is opposed to such alliances, as they indicate a failure to put trust in YHWH.

▌ THE TEXT IN THE INTERPRETIVE TRADITION

The Aramaic *Targum Jonathan* reads the reference to Cush in Isa. 18:1 as India, which prompted medieval Jewish interpreters such as Rashi and Kimhi to read Isaiah 18 as a depiction of the eschatological war against Gog of Magog (Ezekiel 38–39).

▌ THE TEXT IN CONTEMPORARY DISCUSSION

The prophet's condemnation of Damascus raises the issue of judgment against the Assad regime of modern Syria, which is also creating for itself a heap of ruins. Hafez al-Assad was a member of the minority Alawite sect of Shia Islam who served as air force commander under the leadership of the Baathist party. He came to power by instigating two internal military coups in 1969 and 1970 to oust the leadership of his own Baathist party. Under his rule as president of Syria, Hafez al-Assad (1971–2000) was known for its belligerency against Israel, particularly the Yom Kippur War of 1973, and its suppression of dissent, particularly the killing of some twenty thousand Muslim Brotherhood supporters in Hama in 1982. Although many saw his son, Bashar al-Assad (2000–present) as a potential reformer, the outbreak of the Syrian civil war, which has now seen over one hundred thousand killed, has dashed any such hopes. Many are concerned about the future of Syria, insofar as the Syrian rebels are heavily influenced by al-Qaeda and other Islamic extremists. Assad himself is supported by Hezbollah soldiers, who are allies of Iran.

In both Isaiah 17–18 and in this modern example, we find some of the fatal consequences that come with the lust for, and desire to cling to, power. Assad's desperation to hold on to power has led to the use of chemical weapons against his own people. In one attack on August 21, 2013, over 1,400 Syrian civilians, including women and children, were killed in a gas attack apparently launched by the Syrian army. The Assad regime has responded by claiming that the attack was carried out by the Syrian rebels, but the rebels lack access to such weapons and the means to deliver them. This desperate move has now led Assad's allies to join with a United Nations resolution to strip him of his chemical arsenal, and may ultimately lead to his undoing.

Isaiah 19–20: The Pronouncement against Egypt

▌ THE TEXT IN ITS ANCIENT CONTEXT

Isaiah's pronouncements against Egypt in Isaiah 19–20 presuppose the role that Egypt played in the late eighth century in instigating revolt against the Assyrian Empire. Isaiah was opposed to military alliances between Judah and foreign powers. He points to internal struggle within Egypt during the late eighth century that eventually brought the Egyptian twenty-fifth (Ethiopian) dynasty to power as a sign of Egyptian instability. Isaiah 19:16-25 may presuppose the Assyrian conquest of Egypt in 671 and the subsequent rise of the twenty-sixth (Saite) dynasty as an Assyrian ally. Isaiah's walking about Jerusalem naked and barefoot in Isaiah 20 following the conquest of Ashdod by Sargon II in 715 BCE is a prophetic symbolic action meant to demonstrate the fate of those who would support an Egyptian and Ethiopian-inspired revolt against Assyria.

■ THE TEXT IN THE INTERPRETIVE TRADITION

Egypt ultimately became a major center for Jewish life in antiquity, prompted initially by the movement of refugees from the eighth-century Assyrian invasions and subsequent political and trade relations in the Persian, Hellenistic, and Roman periods. Although Egypt was the birthplace of the Greek Septuagint in the Hellenistic period, the emergence of antisemitism in the Roman period placed the Egyptian Jewish community at risk (see Schäfer).

■ THE TEXT IN CONTEMPORARY DISCUSSION

Although Egypt was the site of an important Jewish community from antiquity through the medieval and early modern periods, the Egyptian government expelled the bulk of its Jewish community and seized its property in the aftermath of the creation of modern Israel in 1948. President Anwar Sadat of Egypt signed a treaty with Israel in 1979 that saw the return of the Sinai to Egyptian control, but Sadat was assassinated in 1981 for his initiative and the treaty has remained rather cold to this day. The ongoing political and religious struggles between factions raise great concerns for the future of the treaty and for the Christian community in Egypt.

Isaiah 21: Pronouncements concerning the Wilderness of the Sea, Dumah, and Arabia

■ THE TEXT IN ITS ANCIENT CONTEXT

Isaiah 21 is not a single text, but it is a sequence of prophetic pronouncements concerning the Wilderness of the Sea in Isa. 21:1-10; Dumah in Isa. 21:11-12; and Arabia in Isa. 21:13-17. The reference to Babylon's fall in 21:9 indicates that the Wilderness of the Sea refers to Babylon. The term refers to the marshy area where the Tigris and Euphrates join and flow out into the Persian Gulf, that is, the modern Shatt al-Arab Waterway. Hezekiah's Babylonian ally in his revolt against Assyria (see Isaiah 39), Prince Merodach Baladan, used the area as a base to hide from the Assyrians and to conduct guerrilla operations against them. Dumah is the name of an Arabian Desert oasis conquered by the Assyrian king Sennacherib in 689. It is associated with Seir, another name for Edom. The Assyrians conducted campaigns against the Arabian tribes in the late eighth and seventh centuries. The present oracle presupposes Sennacherib's defeat at Kedar in the northern Arabian Desert in 689.

■ THE TEXT IN THE INTERPRETIVE TRADITION

A. A. MacIntosh points to the reference to Elam and Media in Isa. 21:2 as an indication that Isaiah 21 is a palimpsest, that is, a text that has been rewritten in relation to later circumstances. Babylon fell to a combination of Elamites and Medes in 539 BCE under the leadership of Cyrus. It appears that the concern with the anticipated downfall of Merodach Baladan has been updated to account for Babylon's fall to Cyrus.

Isaiah 21:9 is cited in Rev. 18:2 as part of the scenario concerning the fall of Babylon (Rome).

▌ THE TEXT IN CONTEMPORARY DISCUSSION

The reference to the watchtower in Isa. 21:8-9 inspired the title of *Watch Tower*, the publication of the Jehovah's Witnesses. The Jehovah's Witnesses believe that the destruction of the present world order through Armageddon is imminent and that the kingdom of G-d is at hand. The image of the watchtower in Isa. 21:8-9 therefore symbolizes their watchfulness in preparing for the advent of G-d's kingdom. The downfall of Babylon was symbolic of the eschatological age in Christianity when Christ would be revealed to all (Revelation 18–19).

Isaiah 22: The Pronouncement concerning the Valley of Vision

▌ THE TEXT IN ITS ANCIENT CONTEXT

Isaiah 22 is called the pronouncement concerning the Valley of Vision, but the contents of the oracle make it clear that it refers to Jerusalem after the lifting of Sennacherib's siege in 701 BCE. Although Isaiah 36–37 claims a great victory over Sennacherib, his records indicate that Hezekiah saved the city and his throne by capitulating to the Assyrians. Isaiah points out the cost of the siege, namely, Jerusalem was spared but the land of Judah was devastated.

Isaiah refers to Hezekiah's water tunnel, built in preparation for the revolt. He condemns Shebna, a major government official under Hezekiah, for building his own tomb at a time of national threat. An ancient inscription marking the tomb of Shebna has been discovered in the Kidron Valley east of biblical Jerusalem in the Arab Silwan village.

▌ THE TEXT IN THE INTERPRETIVE TRADITION

Isaiah 22:13, "let us eat and drink, for tomorrow we will die," appears in 1 Cor. 15:32 to characterize Paul's opponents who do not believe in Jesus' resurrection. The reference to the key of the house of David in Isa. 22:22 appears in Rev. 3:7 to indicate to the church in Philadelphia that the door (to Christ) is open to them.

Talmudic tradition holds that Shebna was the high priest who shot an arrow to the Assyrians with the message that all Jerusalem—except Hezekiah and Isaiah—were ready to surrender (*b. Sanh.* 26ab; see also Rashi).

▌ THE TEXT IN CONTEMPORARY DISCUSSION

Premature celebrations of victory often mask reality. Japan celebrated a premature victory over the United States at Pearl Harbor in 1941 without realizing that they had planted the seeds of their own national destruction. Likewise, although the United States was able to claim victory in Iraq, it now has little influence in Iraq. From politicians who claim victory too early to office workers who Twitter about promotions before they have been secured, this text serves as a valuable warning against the sorts of hubris that lead people to snatch defeat out of the jaws of victory.

Isaiah 23: The Pronouncement against Tyre

■ THE TEXT IN ITS ANCIENT CONTEXT

Isaiah's pronouncement concerning Tyre targets one of Hezekiah's principal allies in his revolt against the Assyrians. Tyre was the dominant Phoenician city, and it was the major sea power of the day, with a powerful navy and extensive trade relations. But when Sennacherib unexpectedly subdued the island city in 701 BCE, Hezekiah's western allies quickly abandoned him, leaving him to face the Assyrians alone.

■ THE TEXT IN THE INTERPRETIVE TRADITION

The oracle has been updated in Isa. 23:13-18 to account for Tyre's fall to the Babylonians in 588–572 BCE. Like Jerusalem, the oracle anticipates that Tyre will rise again in seventy years (cf. Jer. 25:29 on Jerusalem).

■ THE TEXT IN CONTEMPORARY DISCUSSION

The issue of being abandoned by one's allies that is raised in Isaiah 23 is still applicable in a plethora of modern contexts, whether it be betrayal on an international scale or within the family relationships. Modern Lebanon fell victim to its internal divisions between its Maronite Christian, Druze, and Muslim populations. The Palestine Liberation Organization (PLO) moved into Lebanon following its failed attempt to take over Jordan in 1971, and thereby played an important role in destabilizing the country. The Lebanese civil war of 1975–1990 saw the disintegration of Lebanon as a coherent modern state. Israel invaded Lebanon in 1982 to counteract the PLO, and later withdrew in 2000 following its failure to establish Maronite Christian control of the country. Lebanon is now dominated by Hezbollah (Party of G-d), a heavily armed Shiite Muslim militant military organization and political party backed by Iran. Lebanon never signed a peace treaty with Israel following the 1948 war of independence. Hezbollah attacked Israel from southern Lebanon in 2006, raining missiles on Haifa and other parts of the country, and Israel counterattacked with air, naval, and ground units. In the aftermath of the conflict, both the Lebanese government and the United Nations abandoned their commitments to disarm Hezbollah, leaving Israel to feel abandoned by a major governing body to which it belongs.

Isaiah 24–27: YHWH's New World Order: Salvation for Zion/Israel

■ THE TEXT IN ITS ANCIENT CONTEXT

Isaiah 24–27 concludes the oracles concerning the nations in Isaiah 13–27 with an extensive prophetic announcement concerning YHWH's new world order based in Zion. This section envisions a future withering of creation and judgment against the earth in Isa. 24:1-23 followed by a prophetic announcement of YHWH's blessing in Isaiah 25:1—27:13. This latter section includes YHWH's blessing of the earth at Zion in Isa. 25:1-12 and its results in Isa. 26:1—27:13, including an account of Judah's petition to YHWH for deliverance in Isa. 26:1-21; YHWH's defeat of Leviathan in Isa. 27:1; and an exhortation to Israel to accept YHWH's offer of reconciliation.

Isaiah 24:1-23 presents the prophet's announcement of YHWH's punishment of the earth. The portrayal of a devastated and withered land is a typical element of blessings and curses speeches, for example, Leviticus 26 and Deuteronomy 28–30, that posit natural catastrophe as a consequence of human failure to abide by the divine will. The prophets employ them constantly for the same purpose (e.g., Isa. 34:11-17; Jer. 5:6; 19:7-9; Hosea 4; 13:7-8). The imagery presupposes the period of the late summer prior to the onset of the fall rains and the New Year that inaugurates the restoration of divine rule over the world of creation. In the present instance, the withered earth presages the fall of the "city of chaos" (Isa. 24:10), that is, Babylon, and the recognition of YHWH's reign.

Isaiah 25:1-12 inaugurates the announcement of blessing with a portrayal YHWH's blessings for Zion. The imagery includes a banquet for the nations at Mt. Zion in which death will be banished forever. Such a banquet is based on the celebration of the fall festival of Sukkot, "Booths," which celebrates the completion of the summer harvest and anticipates the onset of the fall rains. In Mesopotamian cultures, the fall rains were celebrated as the time when fertility gods, such as Tammuz, were returned to life from the netherworld.

Isaiah 26:1-21 presents Judah's petition to YHWH for deliverance. The liturgical dimensions of the passage emerge here insofar as it employs an initial hymn of praise in 26:1b-6 to celebrate YHWH's deliverance of the land from the wicked city of chaos. The imagery of childbirth in 26:17-18 complements the imagery of resurrection of the dead in 26:14 and 19 to give expression to YHWH's life-giving deliverance of the people.

Isaiah 27:1 presents a brief reference to YHWH's defeat of Leviathan, the seven-headed chaos monster of the deep known also in Ugaritic/Canaanite mythology (see also Ps. 74:13-14; Isa. 11:15-16). Leviathan's defeat symbolizes YHWH's deliverance of the people from Babylonian exile.

Finally, Isa. 27:2-13 presents the new vineyard allegory in which YHWH finally gets the vineyard to produce fruit (cf. Isa. 5:1-7). The vineyard metaphor portrays Israel's taking root in the aftermath of exile to grow once again. With its restoration, the exiles of Israel will return from Assyria and Egypt.

▌THE TEXT IN THE INTERPRETIVE TRADITION

Many interpreters view these chapters as the so-called Isaiah Apocalypse, insofar as Isaiah 24–27 employs motifs of cosmic chaos and restoration, the resurrection of the dead (see Isa. 26:14, 19), and a view of the future that suggests the end of time. But these motifs are not necessarily apocalyptic. Like many prophetic writings, Isaiah 24–27 employs mythological motifs to portray divine action in the world (see, e.g., Amos 7–9; Isaiah 49–54; Habakkuk 3; Ezekiel 8–11), and the references to "in that day" in the passage are simple references to the future. Overall, the passage simply points to the downfall of an unnamed, exalted city of chaos (Isa. 24:10, 12; 25:2-3; 26:5), likely Babylon, which will precede the recognition of YHWH's sovereignty throughout the world.

The overthrow of Babylon, the restoration of good relations between Israel and the nations in these chapters (cf. Isa. 2:2-4), and the intertextual resignification of earlier prophetic texts in these chapters point to the late sixth century as the setting for composition, although Isa. 27:2-13 might be earlier. Isaiah 24–27 would then play an important role in binding together the prophecies of Isaiah ben Amoz in Isaiah 1–39 and those of the exilic prophet Deutero-Isaiah in Isaiah 40–55 to form a sixth-century edition of the book at the onset of Persian rule. This period saw the restoration of the Jerusalem temple with Persian support, thereby opening a new era for Jerusalem's relationship with foreign nations.

Paul cites Isa. 25:8 in his discussion of resurrection in 1 Cor. 15:54 and Isa. 27:9 in his discussion of forgiveness of sins in Rom. 11:27.

Rabbinic tradition views the city of chaos as Jerusalem and understands the entire block to be concerned with Jerusalem's restoration.

THE TEXT IN CONTEMPORARY DISCUSSION

The twentieth century saw two major attempts by world powers to establish an international body to which nations could turn to settle conflicts. The creation of the League of Nations was the first attempt in the aftermath of World War I, and the creation of the United Nations in the aftermath of World War II was the second. Although hardly perfect, the United Nations played important roles in the creation of the modern state of Israel in 1948 and the containment of the Cold War to regional conventional conflicts rather than all-out nuclear war. Although the United Nations is frequently politicized and rendered ineffective and irrelevant by many of its member states, it still remains an important institution for achieving peace and justice in the world.

Isaiah 28–33: YHWH's Plan for Jerusalem: Announcement of a New King

THE TEXT IN ITS ANCIENT CONTEXT

The first portion of the book of Isaiah concludes with a block of material in Isaiah 28–33 that focuses on the prophet's instruction concerning YHWH's plans for the deliverance of Jerusalem and the emergence of a new king. The oracles in this block each begin with an introductory "Woe" (Isa. 28:1; 29:1; 29:15; 30:1; 31:1; cf. 33:1), with the exception of the culminating unit in Isa. 32:1, which begins with "Behold!" This block includes five subunits, namely, Isa. 28:1-29; 29:1-24; 30:1-33; 31:1-9; and 32:1—33:24.

Isaiah 28:1-29 begins the sequence with the prophet's instruction concerning YHWH's purpose in bringing Assyrian rule. The oracle condemns the leadership of both the northern kingdom of Israel and the southern kingdom of Judah for self-indulgence, gluttony, and drunkenness, all metaphors for royal incompetence. The imagery of the covenant with death presupposes the Canaanite "marzeah" ritual, which celebrates descent into the underworld, perhaps at the outset of the dry summer season.

Isaiah is well familiar with agricultural metaphor and frequently employs it to makes his points. In order to produce dill, cumin, wheat, and so on, the produce must first be crushed.

Isaiah 29:1-24 presents the prophet's instruction concerning YHWH's purpose in assaulting Jerusalem. The term Ariel, "lion of G-d," recalls the lion as symbol of the tribe of Judah (Gen. 49:8-11) and serves as a pun on the Hebrew term, *har'el*, which designates the temple altar hearth (see Ezek. 43:15-16). The first "woe" oracle in 29:1-14 portrays YHWH's "conquest" of Jerusalem with a foreign army just as David conquered it with his own soldiers (2 Sam. 5:6-9). Isaiah 29:11-12 calls on readers to view the book of Isaiah as a sealed vision. The second "woe" oracle, in 29:15-24, focuses on the realization of YHWH's purpose for Zion so that the blind and the deaf (see Isaiah 6) will sanctify YHWH.

Isaiah 30:1-33 presents the prophet's instruction concerning YHWH's delay in delivering the people from Assyria. This oracle expresses Isaiah's dissatisfaction with Hezekiah's embassy to Egypt to enlist support for his revolt against Assyria. As in Isaiah 7, the prophet opposes military alliances as a denial of the power and sovereignty of YHWH. Consequently, YHWH will delay deliverance until the people show greater trust. In the end, a teacher will arise to guide the people to throw out their idols so that YHWH will strike down Assyria. Within the context of the final form of the book of Isaiah, this would refer to Second Isaiah and his or her successors in Isaiah 40–66.

Isaiah 31:1-9 presents the prophet's warning concerning reliance on Egyptian aid in Hezekiah's revolt against Assyria. Only YHWH will protect Jerusalem much like a lion or hovering birds protect their prey.

Isaiah 32:1—33:24 concludes the sequence with a presentation of prophetic instruction concerning the future, righteous king. The first portion of this subunit, in Isa. 32:1-20, presents the prophet's vision of the righteous king whom the blind, deaf, and dumb will see when their eyes, ears, and minds are opened to YHWH's purpose (see Isaiah 6). In keeping with Isaiah's view of YHWH as the true Creator, such recognition will result in the blooming of the wilderness and the people will be secure (see Isa. 40:1-11). The second portion of this subunit, in Isa. 33:1-24, begins with a woe oracle that introduces a liturgical presentation of the new king in conjunction with the downfall of Israel's oppressor. In the end, the people who were rendered blind, deaf, and dumb in Isaiah 6 will see the king in his beauty in 33:17 and a secure Jerusalem in 33:20, in which YHWH serves as the ultimate king.

■ THE TEXT IN THE INTERPRETIVE TRADITION

Scholars have argued that most of the material in Isaiah 28–33 was written by Isaiah ben Amoz, but some elements represent later composition. The liturgical composition in Isaiah 33 appears to be the product of the final fifth-century edition of the book, in the time of Ezra and Nehemiah. Isaiah 33 closes the first portion of the book of Isaiah with a vision of the new king and the restored Jerusalem. Its liturgical character indicates that the book could have been presented as part of a temple liturgy. Isaiah 30:19-33; 32:1-8, 15-20, which points to Josiah's restoration as the projected outcome of the prophecies of Isaiah, appears to have been composed for the Josianic edition of Isaiah in the late seventh century.

The authors of the Dead Sea Scrolls apparently saw the references to the future teachers of Israel in Isa. 30:19-33 as a reference to their own Righteous Teacher who formed the group in the early second century BCE and led them to the site of Qumran, where they awaited G-d's final apocalyptic war against the wicked of the world. Although they anticipated a restoration of Jerusalem, events did not turn out as expected and both Qumran and the Jerusalem temple were destroyed in the Zealot revolt of 66–74 CE. The Great Isaiah Scroll from Qumran (1QIsaᵃ) has a gap between Isaiah 33 and Isaiah 34, indicating that this is the main structural division of the book.

Many of these texts appear in the New Testament. The reference to speaking in tongues in Isa. 28:11 appears in 1 Cor. 14:21 as part of Paul's efforts to prompt the people to trust in prophets and not in those who speak in tongues. Nevertheless, Isa. 28:11-13 was influential in promoting such practice among Pentecostal and charismatic Christians (see Mark 16:17; Acts 19:6; 28:1-6; 1 Corinthians 12–14). The precious cornerstone of Isa. 28:16 appears in Paul's characterization of Torah in Rom. 9:33, and its reference to trust appears in his discussion of justification by faith in Rom. 10:11. It also appears in Peter's characterization of Scripture in 1 Pet. 2:6. The deep sleep of Isa. 29:10 appears as part of Paul's polemic against Israel in Rom. 11:8. The motif of vain worship in Isa. 29:13 appears in the polemics against Pharisees (rabbinic Jews) in Matt. 15:7 and Mark 7:6. The destruction of the wisdom of the wise in Isa. 29:14 factors into Paul's discussion of the demise of those who do not believe in Christ in 1 Cor. 1:19. The reference to the potter and the clay plays a key role in Paul's argument in Rom. 9:19-21 that humans cannot resist G-d.

Rashi read Isa. 30:19-33 as a reference to the days of the Messiah, but other medieval interpreters, such as Kimhi, read it as a reference to Hezekiah. Rashi, Kimhi, Ibn Ezra, and others read the righteous monarch of Isa. 32:1 as a reference to Hezekiah. The vision of the king in his beauty in Isa. 33:17 is a reference to a vision of the Shekinah, or presence of G-d, according to Rashi, although Kimhi sees it as a reference to Hezekiah once again (for comments by Rashi, Kimhi, Ibn Ezra, and others, see Rosenberg, ad loc.).

Isaiah 27:6-28:13; 29:22-23 functions as the Haftarah reading for Exod. 1:1—6:1. The Haftarah's themes of judgment leading to restoration thereby accompany the narrative of Israel's enslavement in Egypt with its initial promises of deliverance from Egyptian bondage.

THE TEXT IN CONTEMPORARY DISCUSSION

YHWH's delay in bringing about the restoration of Jerusalem following the Assyrian punishment is a major factor in the conceptualization of divine action in the book of Isaiah. It becomes a means to defend the integrity of G-d in the aftermath of the Assyrian invasions; that is, the claim that Judah and Israel deserve punishment protects YHWH from charges that the deity failed to live up to the terms of the eternal covenant with the house of David and the city of Jerusalem. Indeed, the postponement of restoration until after the Babylonian exile, again after the building of the Second Temple, and even again until after the reforms of Ezra and Nehemiah, testify to the faithful vision of G-d's power, fidelity, and integrity in the book of Isaiah over against the experience of invasion, reversal, and subjugation. Such an issue is particularly important in the aftermath of the Shoah, in which we continue to ask questions about G-d's presence, morality, and power in the face of unspeakable evil. Such questions point to continued faithfulness in G-d together with a corresponding faithfulness to truth that is inseparable from our relationship with G-d. We do not yet have all the answers, but we continue to strive to achieve them.

Isaiah 34–35: Prophetic Instruction concerning YHWH's Return of Exiles to Zion

▌ THE TEXT IN ITS ANCIENT CONTEXT

Isaiah 34–35 introduce the second half of the book of Isaiah, in chapters 34–66, with an emphasis on the judgment of the nations, here represented by Edom, and the return of the exiles to Zion, a major concern in Isaiah 40–66. Edom is condemned in biblical literature for its role in the Babylonian destruction of Jerusalem (Ps. 137:7; Jer. 49:7-22; Lam. 4:21-22; Ezek. 25:12-17; Obadiah). Isaiah 34 presents a number of parallels with Isaiah 1: the call to attention (Isa. 1:2; 34:1); YHWH's vengeance (Isa. 1:24; 34:8); unquenchable burning (Isa. 1:24; 34:10); YHWH's mouth has spoken (Isa. 1:20; 34:16); the sword of punishment (Isa. 1:20; 34:5-6); sacrificial blood and fat (Isa. 1:11-15; 34:6-7); Sodom and Gomorrah (Isa. 1:7-10; 34:9-10); and wilting leaves (Isa. 1:30; 34:4). Isaiah 35 portrays the return of the exiles to Jerusalem as a second exodus, much like Second Isaiah.

▌ THE TEXT IN THE INTERPRETIVE TRADITION

The Great Isaiah Scroll from Qumran (1QIsaiahᵃ) has a gap of several lines between Isaiah 33 and Isaiah 34, indicating the fundamental structural division of the book. Various scholars have confirmed the literary division of the book at this point.

▌ THE TEXT IN CONTEMPORARY DISCUSSION

The recollection of the exodus in Isaiah 35 points to one of the most important holidays in Judaism, the Passover, which celebrates the exodus from Egypt. The exodus is recounted each year at the Passover seder, a home dinner service that celebrates Jewish freedom from oppression and return to the land of Israel. The appearance of this motif in Isaiah 35—and indeed throughout the entire book of Isaiah—points to the importance of the Passover observance in antiquity as well as in modern times.

Isaiah 36–39: Narratives concerning YHWH's Deliverance of Jerusalem and Hezekiah

▌ THE TEXT IN ITS ANCIENT CONTEXT

The Hezekiah narratives found in Isaiah 36–39 also appear in 2 Kings 18–20, albeit it in somewhat different form. Because these chapters contain the last references to the prophet Isaiah ben Amoz in the book of Isaiah, many interpreters presume that they form an appendix to an early form of the book that focuses only on the eighth-century prophet. More recent discussion has recognized the transitional function of these chapters as the concluding reference to the Babylonian exile in Isaiah 39, which points forward to the so-called Second Isaiah, beginning in Isaiah 40. Overall, these chapters point to YHWH's deliverance of Jerusalem as a result of Hezekiah's turning to YHWH, which anticipates the calls for recognition of YHWH's deliverance at the end of the Babylonian exile in the second part of the book.

Isaiah 36–37 presents the account of YHWH's deliverance of Jerusalem during the 701-BCE siege of the city by the Assyrian monarch Sennacherib. Following the unexpected death in battle of Sargon II in 705, King Hezekiah of Judah and Prince Merodach Baladan of Babylon planned a two-pronged revolt against Assyria. Sennacherib proved able to meet the challenge, and conquered Tyre in his initial counterattack in 701. With the fall of Tyre, Hezekiah's western allies abandoned him, leaving Judah open to Assyrian attack. The Assyrian army overran Judah, destroying the city of Lachish and all other cities in Judah while laying siege to Jerusalem. When the Assyrian Rab Shakeh, chief cupbearer (a high administrative title), demanded Jerusalem's unconditional surrender, Hezekiah spread the document before YHWH in the temple and appealed for help. Isaiah answered on YHWH's behalf, indicating that YHWH would deliver Jerusalem due to Hezekiah's faithfulness. According to the account, YHWH's angel killed 185,000 Assyrian troops, and Sennacherib himself was assassinated by his own sons in the temple of his god, Nisroch. Sennacherib's records, however, claim that he forced the capitulation of Hezekiah, and returned to Assyria with many captives and much booty. He was assassinated by his sons some twenty years later, in 681 BCE. Scholars argue that Sennacherib was compelled to negotiate a settlement with Hezekiah that left Jerusalem intact and Hezekiah alive so that he could move against Merodach Baladan in Babylonia. As a result, both Hezekiah and Sennacherib claimed victory.

Isaiah 38 presents the account of Hezekiah's recovery from illness prior to the revolt. Again, the narrative stresses YHWH's response when the king turns to YHWH. The Isaian account includes Hezekiah's prayer, which is absent in the Kings narrative, to accentuate Hezekiah's faith in YHWH.

Isaiah 39 recounts the embassy of Merodach Baladan to Hezekiah in preparation for the revolt. Isaiah opposed Hezekiah's revolt and condemned Hezekiah's willingness to ally with the Babylonians, arguing that someday his sons would be carried off as captives to Babylon.

▌ THE TEXT IN THE INTERPRETIVE TRADITION

As noted above, many scholars recognize that Isaiah 36–39 serves as a transitional narrative within the book of Isaiah as a whole. The concluding reference to Babylonian exile in Isaiah 39 anticipates the return from Babylonian exile beginning in Isaiah 40. Hezekiah's faithfulness therefore serves as a model for the response of the exiles to YHWH in the second part of the book. But the Hezekiah narratives also function as a means to contrast Hezekiah with the presentation of Ahaz in Isaiah 7.

Ahaz rejects Isaiah's calls for him to trust in YHWH and sees Jerusalem subjugated to the Assyrians as a result, but Hezekiah turns to YHWH during the revolt and sees the deliverance of the city from the Assyrian siege. Interpreters note the location of Isaiah's encounter with Ahaz at the conduit of the Upper Pool by the Fuller's Field in Isaiah 7, and that the Assyrian Rab Shakeh stands at the same location when demanding the surrender of Jerusalem in Isaiah 36–37. When compared with the Hezekiah narratives in 2 Kings 18–20, differences in the text (e.g., the inclusion of the prayer of Hezekiah in Isaiah 38) indicate that Hezekiah appears far more pious and faithful in the Isaian version than in Kings, where Hezekiah immediately submits to Sennacherib at the outset of 2 Kings 18. Overall, the Isaian text presents Hezekiah as a repentant monarch who turns to YHWH in time of crisis.

■ THE TEXT IN CONTEMPORARY DISCUSSION

The Hezekiah narratives demonstrate the importance of accounting for literary and theological perspective in the interpretation of biblical literature. Although Isaiah 36–39 claims a great victory for Hezekiah, Sennacherib's records also claim a great victory for the Assyrians. Indeed, both were correct; Sennacherib forced Hezekiah's submission, and both Hezekiah and Jerusalem survived the Assyrian onslaught. Such a lesson should be borne in mind when reading biblical literature in general. When the prophets claim that Israel was punished with exile because the people sinned, does this mean that Israel actually committed sins that justified national catastrophe? Or is this a means to explain disaster as an act of G-d and thereby to defend the power, presence, and righteousness of G-d in the world when disaster strikes? In the aftermath of the Shoah (Holocaust), modern theologians continue to struggle with the notion that human suffering must be explained by human sin.

Works Cited

Blenkinsopp, Joseph. 2000. *Isaiah 1–39*. AB 19. New York: Doubleday.

Childs, Brevard S. 2001. *Isaiah: A Commentary.* OTL. Louisville: Westminster John Knox.

Erlandsson, Seth. 1970. *The Burden of Babylon: A Study of Isaiah 13:2—14:23.* ConBOT 4. Lund: Gleerup.

Evans, Craig A. 1988. "On the Unity and Parallel Structure of the Book of Isaiah," *VT* 38:129–47.

Fohrer, Georg. 1962. "Jesaja 1 als Zusammenfassung der Verkündigung Jesajas." *ZAW* 74:251–68.

Kaiser, Otto. 1983. *Isaiah 1–12: A Commentary.* OTL. Philadelphia: Westminster.

Kaplan, Mordecai. 1926. "Isaiah 6:1-11." *JBL* 45:251–59.

Rosenberg, A. J. 1982–1983. *The Book of Isaiah.* Judaica Books of the Bible. New York: Judaica.

Schäfer, Peter. 1998. *Judeophobia: Attitudes towards the Jews in the Ancient World.* Cambridge, MA: Harvard University Press.

Sweeney, Marvin A. 1996. *Isaiah 1–39, with an Introduction to Prophetic Literature.* FOTL 16. Grand Rapids: Eerdmans.

———. 2008. *Reading the Hebrew Bible after the Shoah: Engaging Holocaust Theology.* Minneapolis: Fortress Press.

Tomasino, A. J. 1993. "Isaiah 1.1—2.4 and 63-66 and the Composition of the Isaianic Corpus." *JSOT* 57:81–98.

Tucker, Gene M. 2001. "Isaiah." In *The New Interpreter's Bible*, edited by Leander E. Keck, 6:25–305. Nashville: Abingdon.

Tull, Patricia K. 2010. *Isaiah 1–39.* Smyth and Helwys Bible Commentary. Macon, GA: Smyth & Helwys.

Wiesel, Elie. 1982. *Souls on Fire: Portraits and Legends of Hasidic Masters.* New York: Vintage.

ISAIAH 40–66

Chris A. Franke

Introduction

The book of Isaiah deals with people, places, and events spanning several centuries, from 733 BCE to some time around 515 BCE. Chapters 1–39, referred to as First or Proto-Isaiah, focus on the time when Israel and Judah were under Assyrian rule. An ominous message to King Hezekiah announces the rise of the Babylonian Empire in Isaiah 39. The result is that nothing will be left of his kingdom, Judah, and his Davidic lineage will come to an end. The backdrop of the following chapters, 40–66, includes the Babylonian destruction of Judah and the exile of many of its citizens in 587 BCE; the rise of the Persian Empire under Cyrus the Great in 539 BCE; and the restoration of life in Jerusalem after Cyrus allowed all exiles to return home. While the name Isaiah never appears in 40–66, Isaiah 1–39 and 40–66 share common features, including emphasis on Jerusalem/Zion, reference to the Davidic monarchy, and common images and names of God.

Chapters 40–66 treat two different eras. Chapters 40–55 are addressed to exiles living in Babylon during the rule of Cyrus (538–515 BCE). Their liberation from Babylonian oppression is soon to come. Chapters 56–66 recount the situation in the newly formed Judah, now called Yehud, after the exiles return home and are united with those who had remained in the land after the fall of the kingdom.

Chapters 40–55 are usually identified as Second or Deutero-Isaiah and 56–66 as Third or Trito-Isaiah. Scholars disagree about the authorship of these two sections of the book of Isaiah. Some hold that they represent two different authors or prophets. The mostly hopeful messages of Deutero-Isaiah (abbreviated as DI) and its Babylonian setting are very different from the more somber and sometimes threatening tone and setting in Yehud of Trito-Isaiah (abbreviated as TI). Others see continuity between the two. The strongest defense of single authorship is the consistent literary style throughout. A geographical change does not in itself warrant asserting a new author. In this article, the book of Isaiah is abbreviated as BOI. DI indicates chapters 40–55 and TI chapters 56–66. The view here asserts a single authorial voice.

Other suggestions describing the authorship of DI include the following. Ulrich Berges proposes that cultic representatives are the authorial group responsible for the composition of 40–55 (Berges, 587–88). The people who were sent into exile after the destruction of Jerusalem surely included the priests familiar with temple worship and other cultic activities. They could also be responsible for composition of prayers and/or psalms used in worship.

Lena-Sofia Tiemeyer (26–30) proposes the possibility of female authorship of 40–55. In support of this view, she cites the many metaphors that compare God to a woman, the references to female socio-sexual roles, descriptions of tasks related to motherhood, and the absence of negative images of women.

Isaiah 40:1-31: Israel's God Is Incomparable

▌ THE TEXT IN ITS ANCIENT CONTEXT

Chapter 40 is the beginning of another major section of the BOI. It represents momentous changes of time, place, and mood from chapters 1–39, which are set in mid- to late eighth-century Jerusalem. The time and place of Isaiah 40–55 is 539 BCE, when Babylonia succumbed to Cyrus the Great of Persia. DI's message is addressed to the community of exiles living in Babylon. The chapter begins with words of comfort and reassurance and promises change for those living under Babylonian rule (40:1-2).

What is known about the exiles who lived in Babylonian territory? Some scholars describe their living conditions as relatively benign. Life continued in exile with little if any disadvantage to the exiles. However, data from sociological and psychological sciences reveal a very different view of people forcibly removed from a secure existence in their homeland. Living as minorities in a foreign country offered little if any security or civil rights. "The Judean experience of deportation . . . was a severe and traumatic personal, social, and psychological event" (Moore and Kelle, 364). Convincing people who suffered under such conditions for half a century that God was on their side would have been a difficult task. They would need constant and reliable reassurance that God is aware of their existence. DI not only acknowledges their long term of suffering but in a stunning admission also acknowledges that they "received from YHWH's hand" twice as much punishment as they deserved for their sins. Their fortunes are soon to be reversed. A way will be prepared in the wilderness, and God will lead them back home.

Isaiah 40–66 is filled with a variety of images demonstrating YHWH's power and will to save. The long poem in 40:12-31 is the first of many such demonstrations. The prominent image of God in these verses is of a powerful, all-knowing, everlasting Creator. The literary device of the rhetorical question is used here and elsewhere in DI. It often appears in connection with repetition, another technique by which DI gets the attention of the audience: "To whom then will you liken God?" (40:18) and "To whom then will you compare me?" (40:25). The intent is not to demand answers of the audience but to assert the obvious. No one can be compared to YHWH. YHWH is incomparable. The author takes an argumentative or polemical tone. The defensive aspect of the polemic is because the other side of the issue is all too obvious to the audience. They have good reason to doubt.

▪ THE TEXT IN THE INTERPRETIVE TRADITION

Anyone who has ever listened to Handel's *Messiah* will be familiar with the BOI. The libretto contains seventeen citations from the BOI (Davies, 464–84). The Messiah to whom Handel points is Jesus as described in the Synoptic Gospels. Mark's Gospel begins with an allusion to the BOI, showing John the Baptist preparing way of the Lord (Mark 1:2-3). Since the New Testament cites the BOI more times than any other Old Testament text, it is not surprising that Handel's librettist, Charles Jennens, used numerous texts from Isaiah. The librettist repeats Isa. 40:1-5 almost word for word in the first three pieces. The only phrase omitted is the troubling "double payment from the LORD for all her sins." Other citations from Isaiah 40 in the *Messiah* include 40:9, which describes the messenger who brings the good news, and 40:11, describing God the shepherd gently leading the lambs.

▪ THE TEXT IN CONTEMPORARY DISCUSSION

The frequent use of motifs and ideas from the BOI in the New Testament and later Christian interpretations has led many Christians to believe that the only way to understand Isaiah is through a christological lens. Knowledge of events in Israel's history as well as an awareness of how these texts were used well before New Testament times is crucial to a wider view of the importance of the BOI. From early on in Jewish tradition, selections from Isaiah 40–60 that recall the destruction of the temple and the exile from Judah were read in synagogues before the high holy days (Paul, 71). The message of comfort in 40:1 is the first of these readings, which mark the period of personal and national mourning for Jews. Sabbath readings in current Jewish liturgy are filled with selections from the book of Isaiah. Both Jewish and Christian traditions have appropriated texts from Second Isaiah for liturgical use.

Isaiah 41:1—44:8: The Nations and Their Gods Are Put on Trial/ God Reassures Israel

▪ THE TEXT IN ITS ANCIENT CONTEXT

DI has been called the "spider poet" because of the tangled web of connections found throughout 40–55 (Kim, 178). Chapters 41:1—44:8 illustrate this phenomenon. Motifs include the nations, the making of idols, Israel/Jacob as God's chosen, the servant, and transformation of the wilderness. Many of these motifs appear throughout the rest of 40–66. God is portrayed as warrior, attorney or judge, a woman giving birth, king, comforter. Literary genres adapted from ancient Near Eastern documents include terminology reflecting a courtroom trial, hymns used in liturgies, and rhetorical questions, all of which would be familiar to DI's audience in Babylon.

Isaiah 41 begins with a courtroom setting. God puts the nations on trial, demanding proof that they and their deities are powerful. Are they able to control events, predict the future? Do they have power enough to terrify or harm others? As evidence that it is YHWH who is able to control events, predict the future, and terrify nations, God has called up Cyrus the Persian king to defeat the Babylonian Empire in 539 BCE. The gods are unable to prove that they can control and predict the future. They remain silent and ineffectual in contrast to God's powerful acts on behalf of Jacob/Israel. A distinctive feature in this section is God speaking in the first person, emphatically asserting that "I have held my peace, I have kept still," "I will cry out," "I will lay waste mountains," "I will turn the rivers into islands," "I will lead the blind," "I will turn the darkness before them into light," "these are the things I will do," "I will not forsake them" (Isa. 42:14-16). An English translation of 41:1—44:8 reveals over 130 occurrences of first-person pronouns.

The courtroom scene in 43:9-13 brings a new and far more serious challenge to the nations. They have no witnesses who can prove that their gods exist. The nations were initially asked to show that they and their gods were powerful. YHWH now asserts that

> before me no god was formed,
>   nor will there be any after me. (43:10)

thus denying the nature or existence of the gods.

While the nations tremble with fright, YHWH comforts Jacob/Israel: "Do not fear, for I am with you" (43:5). The "fear not" formula appears throughout DI, beginning with God's opening message to the exiles (40:9). It underlies the prophet's message in 41:1—44:8. The phrase "fear not" is adapted from an ancient Near Eastern literary-theological motif used to indicate that the gods support their kings and people. Shalom Paul cites an example of the goddess Ishtar reassuring Assyrian kings that she will deliver their enemies for destruction (Paul, 166). Also familiar in these documents is the phrase "grasping the right hand," which demonstrates that a king or god supports his people. DI uses this formula in 41:10 and 13 to indicate divine support.

The hymn of praise in 42:10-12 is a familiar genre frequently used in their worship services. All are commanded to lift up their voices and sing to give glory to YHWH and declare God's praise! The hymn genre most likely originated in a cultic setting. When a group of people gathers to worship, part of their worship includes praying and singing. Motifs for these prayers include complaint, lament, and thanksgiving, which are used in Isaiah 40–66. All of these genres reflect significant events with which the audience was familiar. These features will immediately direct the audience's attention to the significance or tone of the message.

▌ THE TEXT IN THE INTERPRETIVE TRADITION

Scholars reading Isaiah 40–66 over the years have proposed a wide variety of strategies to understand its complicated features. One of the most significant contributions to understanding the literary dimensions of DI was made by James Muilenburg in his commentary in *The Interpreter's Bible*. Using the results of form-critical studies of Isaiah 40–66, he showed that the prophet used typical forms of the time but tweaked them, adding to or altering the formulas to give new depth and nuance to the message.

The cult of the Babylonian gods is described in some detail beginning in Isa. 41:6-7. DI emphasizes idolatry and especially the construction of images of Babylonian deities in chapters 40–47. The disparaging polemics against the construction and worship of statues is evidence that the exiles in Babylon were familiar with and perhaps attracted to these practices. Accentuated here is YHWH's power over nations, kings, and their deities; the idea that YHWH is "the first and the last"; and the idea that "there is no god besides me" and "no savior besides me."

Some have referred to DI as the exponent of monotheism in Israel. While one might speak of incipient monotheism in DI, it is not so much a question of how many gods there are but rather what kind of a god YHWH is. Israel's repeated attention to a single deity over the course of their history is the background of the later development of a full-fledged monotheism. See Mark Smith's discussions of this fascinating and complicated aspect of Israelite history and religion (Smith 1990; 2001).

▌ THE TEXT IN CONTEMPORARY DISCUSSION

The BOI often uses the metaphor of regeneration of land, plant life, and waters and compares these to the condition of human existence. The repeated references to life-giving water in DI and TI reflect the devastated conditions of the land reduced to a wasteland by the ravages of war. Recent interest in ecological issues has encouraged Bible scholars to address this issue.

Patricia K. Tull brings these issues to her study of Isaiah, demonstrating that Isaiah uses "plant imagery to tie human spiritual and societal health to environmental well-being" (Tull, 27). She indicates that it is sometimes impossible to tell when the text is to be understood literally or metaphorically. Referring to a group of farmers who studied Genesis 3, she cites their observation that "when humans are disconnected from God, the soil will be the first to suffer."

Isaiah 44:9-20: The Folly of Making and Worshiping Images of Deities

▌ THE TEXT IN ITS ANCIENT CONTEXT

Scattered through Isaiah 40–48 are references to features of Babylonian religion, especially the making and use of images of gods in the Babylonian pantheon. DI's perspective on images, artisans who make them, and those who worship them is consistently negative and critical. Isaiah 44:9-20 features a detailed description of the construction of *images* or *idols* (for DI the terms are synonymous), from the planting of the trees used for carvings to the iron workshop in which images are forged. The tone of this anti-idol passage is scathing sarcasm and ridicule. DI derides those who burn wood to cook their meals and warm their hands and then bow down to a statue made of the same kind of wood. Such a person is a "shepherd of ashes with a deluded mind" (44:20, author's trans.).

A recent commentary by Shalom Paul is a rich source of background information for Babylonian history, literature, religion, and culture during the time of the formation of Isaiah 40–66. Paul describes an event during the reign of Babylonian king Nabonidus, who made dramatic changes in the Babylonian cult. One of the most significant was to change the order of the gods in the pantheon. The chief god Marduk was deposed and replaced with another god. Nabonidus also canceled celebration of a religious holiday, which enraged the populace. Marduk's priests, understandably upset, published a document attacking Nabonidus's behavior, claiming that he "looks at representations [of the gods] and utters blasphemies" (Paul, 13).

DI's familiarity with the Babylonian scene is clear from the details included in the anti-idol passages. He takes for granted that his audience living under Babylonian rule for decades is familiar with these practices. Understood in light of the political situation in Babylon, it is not difficult to understand DI's polemical tone. In the words of DI, Marduk's "devotees shall be put to shame" (44:11) when their emperor deposed their chief god. Critique of the gods is critique of Babylonian politics. DI's exilic audience would relish the disarray of Babylonian's inept and divided leadership.

THE TEXT IN THE INTERPRETIVE TRADITION

DI uses satire in several poems that describe Babylonian practices and politics; for example, Isaiah 46–47. *Satire* is used to ridicule, diminish, or attack an individual, an institution, or a culture. It evokes in the audience feelings of scorn or contempt for the subject. Putting the drudgery of the artisans in elegant, poetic language heightens the level of ridicule and mockery. Some consider this literary feature to be beneath the soaring language of DI. However, reading it in light of oppressive conditions in Babylonia makes DI's satirical critique a fit way to disempower an oppressive empire.

THE TEXT IN CONTEMPORARY DISCUSSION

What significance might this satire on images of deities have for diverse religious groups? Orthodoxy has a tradition of the veneration of icons. The veneration of the Bible itself is a traditional practice for some Christians. Hindu practices include processions of images of deities as part of its tradition. Another way to reflect on this question is to ask: How is the divine made present in the world?

"Laughing at Idols" is the title of an article by George M. Soares-Prabhu (1995, 110), who critiques DI's ridiculing the Babylonian practice of making statues of their gods. He interprets Isa. 44:9-20 from his perspective of religion and politics in India, where many world religions exist "in tolerable harmony," and contrasts this with DI's "inadequate view of God." Soares-Prabhu highlights the value of pluralist Indian interpretations as a corrective to intolerance often seen in Western religions, which emphasize monotheism. Familiarity with interpretations of the Bible from the perspective of the social location of the reader opens up the richness of the biblical text for all cultures.

Isaiah 44:21—45:24: A Reminder to Israel—You Will Be Created and Freed by God

THE TEXT IN ITS ANCIENT CONTEXT

The message of hope in 44:1-6 is resumed in verse 21 after the polemic against the image makers. DI again asserts that, while they cannot predict the future, predictions made by God's messengers will be fulfilled. The ruins of Jerusalem and other cities of Judah will be rebuilt and repopulated (44:26), and the foundation of the new temple will be laid (44:28). As proof that this will happen, DI introduces Cyrus, king of Persia, who has defeated the hapless Nabonidus, ruler of Babylonia. God's purpose will be carried out by Cyrus, who YHWH calls "my shepherd" (44:28).

It must be kept in mind that the audience for these messages is the exiles living in Babylonia under Babylonian rule. They are familiar with the Babylonian scene. They know about the coming of Cyrus, the fall of Nabonidus, and would also be familiar with the form and style of official messages about Babylonian kings. The motif of rebuilding cities and their temples is often attributed to kings in Mesopotamian documents (Paul, 247). To get the attention of this audience, DI uses a variety of examples with which the exiles would be familiar.

One of the most deeply disturbing ideas for the exiles was the loss of the Davidic monarchy and the temple. God's promise of the permanence of these institutions had been broken. DI explains that God's covenant promise of an eternal Davidic line continues through Cyrus, who now takes on David's title as "the anointed one" (45:1). As a caution to those who are critical of a foreigner as the anointed one, DI makes several striking comparisons. God is a potter, and the critics are the clay pots. The potter asks if the clay can criticize its maker. In two other images, God is a father and a mother. The critics are again asked if anyone questions their parents about who they are making. No answer is needed: the critics' position is ridiculous. To dispel further objections, God announces that Cyrus "will build my city and set my exiles free" (45:13).

◼ The Text in the Interpretive Tradition

The ramifications of the assertion that God is sole creator of all things are far reaching. God can make Cyrus king and can strip other kings of their robes, signs of their power. For DI, the belief that God is one can result in only one conclusion: all nations will "follow you," "bow down to you," "come over in chains," and must admit that "God is with you alone" (45:14). This is described as a "fantasy nourished by resentment at subjection to the great powers" (Blenkinsopp, 262). Such a sentiment can be understood by any people at any time who live under the oppression of a powerful empire.

◼ The Text in Contemporary Discussion

Bible scholar Ada María Isasi-Díaz speaks of her experience living in exile from Cuba and her yearning to return home lest she forget her own country (Isasi-Díaz, 149–63). She found solace and understanding in Psalm 137, a lament of exiles yearning for their homeland. This psalm asks God to remember the fall of Jerusalem. It includes the desire for vengeance against the enemy, much like that against Babylon in Isa. 45:13-14, and expresses the wish that the babies of the enemies will be dashed against the rock. Isasi-Díaz asks: What is the theology behind this psalm?

Her personal experiences influence how she reads such texts. Seeing injustice against the poor and experiencing the effects of sexism in her church and ethnic prejudice as a Cuban living in America shaped her hermeneutical strategy. Rather than trying to read a text "objectively," that is, trying to come to the original meaning of the text, she realized the importance of clarifying her own perspective and her purpose for reading that text. She emphasizes the three-way relationship between "the reader, the writer, and the text." A reader's questions influence what the text could have meant in the past and what it means today. She describes her approach to the text as "oppression-liberation."

The language of Psalm 137 and Isa. 45:13-14 can express both personal and community grief for suffering terrible losses, including the loss of order in their world. Isasi-Díaz, while uncomfortable with the strong and vengeful sentiments, prays this psalm because it has a cathartic effect. It allows her to express a troubling feeling. She also notes that there is a great difference between words of vengeance and acts of vengeance.

Isaiah 46:1-13: Babylonian Street Scene—A Procession of Idols Carried on Beasts of Burden

■ THE TEXT IN ITS ANCIENT CONTEXT

Chapter 46 is the polar opposite of the triumphant march of the exiles returning home in Isaiah 40. Bel and Nebo, chief gods of Babylonia, are carried in an ignominious procession out of their homeland into captivity. One of the motifs in previous chapters has been the folly of making images and worshiping them. This begins in 40:18–20 and is repeated in every succeeding chapter.

This scene in 46:1–7 would have been familiar to the exiles in Babylon. On the occasion of the New Year festival, the images of Bel and Nebo were carried in a procession through the streets. Bel is a title for the god Marduk, Babylon's protector. Nebo was his son, who during the New Year celebration was to write down the fate of the cities for the coming year. A very different occasion in Mesopotamian culture was transporting images of gods out of a threatened or destroyed city. Yet another example was seizure of the statues by the conquering enemy. This was done for economic reasons, to confiscate the precious metals and stones set in the statues. It also mocked the impotency of gods of the defeated nation.

Chapter 46 describes the gods as heavy loads on weary animals. They all stoop and stumble and bow down. The phrase "bow down" can refer to obeisance to a high authority, such as a king, or an act of worship of a god. But here it highlights their utter ineffectuality and proves that they are unable to "save" or "deliver" anyone. God addresses Jacob/Israel, emphasizing that, unlike these statues, which can save no one, "*I* carried you from the beginning." "*I* made," "*I* will bear," "*I* will carry," "*I* will save" (46:3-4). Furthermore, God accuses them of being "rebels." Here, as elsewhere in these anti-idolatry passages, the offenders are rebellious Israel. God reminds them,

I am God, and there is no other;
    I am God, and there is no one like me. (46:9)

This recalls the infamous first idol-making event at the foot of Mount Sinai, when people worshiped the golden calf as their god (Exod. 32:1-14). YHWH initially threatened extermination of the community but relented from this plan.

Chapter 46 contrasts the downward spiral of Bel and Nebo and their supporters with the elevation of YHWH, who insists that "I will fulfill my intention" to a "stubborn" and perhaps unconvinced group of exiles. YHWH's word has been spoken; deliverance is at hand.

▌ THE TEXT IN THE INTERPRETIVE TRADITION

Previous scholarship approached DI (as well as other prophetic texts) with the idea that it was made up of conventional genres, short units that originated in the spoken word. In the process of writing, these shorter units were thought to have been brought together to connect similar themes or motifs. However, the poetry of DI transcends more traditional techniques and adds nuance to conventional formulas (Franke 1994, 263). An example of the literary genius of this prophet/poet is the image of procession to contrast the fate of Jacob/Israel and that of their captors. Procession for the enemies in 46:1-2 means going into captivity. In Isaiah 47, deposed Babylon falls from her throne to earth, down to the underworld. Processions for the exiles will lead them out of captivity back to their homeland in 40:3-5; 48:20-21; and 51:9—52:2. This extended image is an essential aspect of the prophet's message to the exiles; it is far more than a mere assemblage of loosely related themes.

▌ THE TEXT IN CONTEMPORARY DISCUSSION

While DI's message is often characterized as a message of comfort and consolation to those living under Babylonian rule, a crucial element in chapter 46 is the accusation against Jacob/Israel of idolatry, and warnings of the consequences. Just as Isaiah 40 begins with comfort to the disconsolate, it also includes a brief polemic against idolatry, accusing the audience of comparing God to an idol made by human hands. In many of the anti-idolatry sections in DI, the issue is not denying the existence of God. The offense is comparing God to idols or considering them equals to Israel's God. The prophet's audience is not Babylonians. It is the exiles living in Babylon who have taken on the religious practices of their captors.

Isaiah 47:1-15: The Fall of Virgin Daughter Babylon

▌ THE TEXT IN ITS ANCIENT CONTEXT

Chapter 47 is a pivot on which the main ideas and message of DI turn (Franke 1991). In the previous chapters, the disconsolate exiles lived in fear of their conquerors, doubted that God could or would come to their rescue, needed constant encouragement that they had not been forgotten, and wondered if they were still being punished for their infidelities. DI describes numerous examples of differences between the god of Jacob and the gods of the Babylonian Empire in 40–46. The critique of the Babylonian images and especially the artisans who made them pervades this section. While YHWH was powerful and carried the people, the Babylonian deities could not even move but had to be carried by those who worshiped them.

Here God speaks directly to "virgin daughter Babylon." In the ancient world, cities were often described figuratively as women needing protection of kings. In satirical language, God ridicules all of Babylon's claims. She thought: she'd be queen forever; she was secure; she'd never be widowed; and she would never lose her children. She thought she could hide her evil deeds. She thought her astrologers could predict her future or use magic to control events.

From the beginning words in 47:1, it is clear that Babylon's future will be grim. Instead of being seated on a throne, she will sit in the dust, on the ground. Even more, she will go into "darkness," intimating her passage to the underworld.

To Babylon's humiliation, she will be stripped of her garments: veil and robe will be removed, legs uncovered. In summary, her "nakedness" and "shame" will be seen by all. The latter terms indicate exposure of her genitalia. For her crimes—showing no mercy to the exiles and especially abusing the elderly—there will be no one to save her. Just as the Babylonian deities in chapter 46 bowed down and went into captivity, so Virgin Daughter Babylon will exchange her royal status for that of slavery.

This poem has features similar to satirical laments for the dead elsewhere in Isaiah (14:3-21), as well as in lamenting the death of gods in ancient Near Eastern literature (Anderson, 60–82). These laments include the hubris of the gods or nations in their belief that they will rule forever. They also fall from their thrones, sit on the ground, and descend into the underworld.

The Text in the Interpretive Tradition

The fall of Babylon has been interpreted from the perspective of anthropology as a rite of passage (Kruger). The various details of Babylon's passage—loss of status, the shame of removing her garments and exposure, doing menial work—portray her as a queen turned slave. This description is an example of a sociocultural antitype of Babylon's status as queen. It can also be read as an antitype of the status of Jerusalem/Zion. Later chapters describe the elevation of Zion's status from widow to bride, rejected and captive to redeemed, and barren to mother of many. DI uses the fall of Babylon as a contrast to the rise of Jerusalem.

The Text in Contemporary Discussion

In chapter 47, Babylon is portrayed as the object of God's punishment. She is subjected to physical abuse and punishment, which strips her of her power. She loses her husband and children and remains alone with no one to save her. How are readers today to understand this in a meaningful way? What theological problems does such a view create?

One of the most significant challenges in reading the Bible in the modern world is how to deal with the ancient Near Eastern view of women that pervades biblical texts. In the ancient world, women were viewed as the property of men. It was commonly accepted that the ideal male was powerful, able to provide his city/family with food, shelter, and protection. Sexual fidelity is not included in the list for men. The ideal female was submissive, in need of protection, faithful to her spouse. Women were the property of their male protector, husband or father or brother. They were second-class citizens at best.

In recent years, scholars have discussed this question by providing important background information to the origins of this point of view. The *Women's Bible Commentary*, now in its third edition (Newsom, Ringe, and Lapsley), provides data to support the need of a more informed view of this matter in biblical texts, both Old and New Testament.

It is no longer justifiable for interpreters to take the biblical view of women and men as acceptable views for the world today. Citing biblical views about women out of context is not sufficient evidence to draw conclusions and make rules for society today. It is not only insufficient but also damaging to both women and men. In this matter as well as many others, a contextual view of society and culture is essential to understand values and practices in the Bible.

Isaiah 48:1-22: God Warns Israel and Announces a New Exodus

■ THE TEXT IN ITS ANCIENT CONTEXT

In this chapter, several literary techniques are used by the author/editor to make connections to earlier sections, and also to segue to following material. Chapter 48 links chapters 40–47 and 49–55 by motifs or themes. These include God as Creator, Holy One of Israel, Redeemer. Cyrus, identified as "the one whom YHWH loves," is the ruler who will defeat Babylon. God declares past and future events to Jacob/Israel to demonstrate the power and reliability of the divine word over against the lifeless idols and images. However, exiles persist in their stubbornness and obstinacy.

A striking feature amid these accusations against intransigent Jacob/Israel is the depth of God's passionate reaction to their treachery. God's response is mixed. On the one hand, the people's infidelity enrages God almost to the point of exterminating them. God's reputation is at stake, only deferring from punishing them "for my name's sake," "for my own sake." God is incredulous at their behavior: "Why should my name be profaned?" (48:9-11). On the other hand, God speaks as a teacher or parent "who teaches you for your own good," observing wistfully that things would have been different if only "you had paid attention to my commandments" (48:17-19).

In the final verses (48:20-21), DI urges the audience to "go out from Babylon, flee from Chaldea" and reminds them of the exodus from Egypt. This recalls 40:1, the good news of a "highway for our God" on which they would be led through the wilderness. Øystein Lund (227–29) shows that 48:17-22 returns to several key themes in 40:12-40: YHWH's knowledge of the future and power over military and/or political events. The repetition of words or motifs at the beginning and end of a section is called an inclusio. It is a structuring device to indicate the beginning and end of a section within a text. It functions much like chapter divisions do in books today. Chapter 48 is a turning point in the direction of Isaiah 40–55. The terse statement in 48:22—"no peace for the wicked"—also points to the very end of the BOI, since it anticipates similar threatening sentiments in 57:21 and 66:24.

■ THE TEXT IN THE INTERPRETIVE TRADITION

Scholars refer to Isaiah 48 as the "problem child" of biblical criticism because of its range of motifs, grammatical peculiarities, contradictions in God's past and present actions, and excessive repetition. Some of God's actions are harsh and seemingly contradictory to the message of consolation with which DI begins. Scholars vary wildly in their assessment of this chapter. A form-critical approach fails to solve the problems. One proposal asserts that certain material was added by another writer or editor. Another eliminates repetitious features.

In a commentary that stands outside the prevailing thought of most Isaiah scholarship in the first half of the twentieth century, Charles Cutler Torrey (372–80) views Isaiah 48 as an integrated whole. It begins and ends on a note of rebuke and acknowledges that Israel, though unworthy, is the chosen people. Torrey also notes a close connection in time between the composition of Isaiah 46 and 47, as well as to motifs throughout Isaiah 40–66.

▉ THE TEXT IN CONTEMPORARY DISCUSSION

Chapter 48, more than any other chapter in the BOI, deals with Israel's relationship with God in all its permutations. It highlights the tension between Israel's dependence on God and its obduracy to God's word. Walter Brueggemann sees this originating in "the tension deep within the character of Yahweh" (Brueggemann, 100), speaking of the motifs of displacement and restoration that underlie Isaiah 48. He applies this to our own Western culture with the disappearance of certitude and the difficulties of maintaining a social infrastructure.

From one perspective, the problem is God's credibility and dependability. From another, it is the people of God. Rémi Lack describes the problem well: the only obstacle to salvation is the apathy of the people and their refusal to accept that a foreigner, Cyrus, is the instrument of that salvation (Lack, 106).

Works such as Brueggemann's and Lack's, which read the BOI as an integrated whole, are examples of canonical readings. This method of exegesis is a more recent development in biblical scholarship, which offers yet another way to read and understand complicated biblical texts.

Isaiah 49:1—52:12: Daughter Zion, the Servant, and the Role of the Nations in Judah's Future

Chapter 49 begins a new section of DI. Previous characters and places important in Isaiah 40–48—Cyrus as God's anointed, the artisans and their ineffectual statues, and Babylon—are no longer mentioned. The word pair Jacob/Israel occurs for the last time in 49:5-6 and is replaced by Jerusalem/Zion. Key figures—Zion/Jerusalem, the nations, and the servant—are intertwined in 49:1—52:12. These three figures are treated in three separate sections.

Zion/Jerusalem

▉ THE TEXT IN ITS ANCIENT CONTEXT

A major emphasis in Isaiah 49–55 is on Zion/Jerusalem. From the beginning of DI, the biggest challenge was to convince the exiles that God is not only willing to save them but also has the power to do so. The message of comfort and consolation with which DI begins (40:1) is repeated in 49:13; 51:3, 12. However, Zion remains unconvinced by these claims. YHWH has abandoned and forgotten her (49:14). The term "abandoned" is often used of a husband leaving his wife. Zion challenges God in 51:9 to "Awake, awake, put on strength!" Isaiah scholar Luis

Schökel describes 51:9—52:6 as a "bold and affectionate dialogue" between Zion and her husband (Schökel, 179).

The first words God uses to answer Zion's accusation relate to Zion as a wife and mother. The most convincing argument is the image of a mother's relationship to her child. God asks a rhetorical question, "Can a mother forget her nursing child or show no compassion for the child of her womb?" (49:15). The motifs of mother and child and wife continue through to 49:26. God promises that soon Zion will have so many children that she will need a bigger tent in which to live. God reminds Zion that "you are my people" (51:16). God responds to Zion by mirroring her previous command to "wake up" and orders her to "rouse yourself," "wake up," and "depart!" Captive Jerusalem must rise from the dust, remove the bonds from her neck, and garb herself in festive apparel. Her redemption is at hand.

▌ THE TEXT IN THE INTERPRETIVE TRADITION

It has long been clear that the Bible is filled with many images of God as male: king, warrior, husband, father. However, the increase of women scholars in biblical studies has given rise to a wider context for interpreting texts. Much of the terminology in chapters 49–54 emphasizes feminine roles to describe God's relationship to Zion. The interpretive history of DI has been expanded with the awareness of significant images and metaphors for women. Previously overlooked ideas are now highlighted and brought to the fore. Interest in feminist and gender issues, especially in the BOI, has grown within recent years. Hanne Løland in her book on gendered God language in the Bible reads three texts in DI that compare God to a woman and emphasize the bodily connections between mother and child. In 42:14, God is portrayed as a pregnant women giving birth to her child. In 46:3-4, God has carried Israel from pregnancy through birth through to old age. Last, the comparison intensifies in 49:15. God asks (rhetorically) whether a mother can forget her nursing child or have no compassion for the child of her womb. Here YHWH is compared to a mother who loves her child. Some scholars are uneasy with the idea that God would be portrayed in feminine imagery and protest that God's love is contrasted to or greater than that of a mother. However, the same protest could be raised in comparing God with a warrior, or father, or some other masculine figure.

▌ THE TEXT IN CONTEMPORARY DISCUSSION

One of the most important features of DI's emphasis on Jerusalem/Zion in recent scholarship is the recognition of the importance of feminine figures. The difficulty and beauty of moving into postmodernity is that there is not just one correct interpretation of a given text. The nature and identity of communities that read texts influences how and why interpretations vary. One rabbi explains it this way, asking, "How do donkeys read the Bible?" The answer is: they look for stories about donkeys. When reading a text, everyone brings personal experiences to their interpretation of that text. When women began studying the Bible in seminaries and universities, they brought new questions, ideas, and insights to the fore. Studies of Zion/Jerusalem in Isaiah 40–66 have increased in recent years as scholars, both women and men, incorporate the identity and role of Zion into their reading of the BOI.

Nations

▪ THE TEXT IN ITS ANCIENT CONTEXT

The term "nations" (Heb., *goyim*) appears throughout Isaiah 40–55; it is a synonym for "coastlands" and "peoples." These chapters contain several descriptions of who or what the nations are and why they are significant in DI. Richard Clifford calls chapter 49 "a press release to all the nations" (Clifford, 150). The coastlands are addressed by the servant who functions as a "light to the nations" (49:1-6). Zion/Israel, once called the slave of rulers, changes places with the nations. The message to the nations is that their rulers will work as ignominious servants, prostrating themselves and licking the dust of the feet of Zion and her children (49:22-23). The oppressors become the oppressed. A technique frequently used in DI called *inner-biblical allusion* is the citation of another biblical text to enhance meaning. The image of Zion's oppressive rulers losing their power is a foil to a text in Jer. 13:18, which portrays the opposite situation: Israel's king and queen mother lose their crowns and must take a lowly seat when Babylon destroys Judah (Willey, 203). In Isaiah 49, the tables are turned. A somewhat different view of the role of the nations is also alluded to in this section. For example, the "coastlands" wait for God and hope in God's powerful arm (51:5). In 52:10b, all nations and "the ends of the earth shall see / the salvation of our God."

▪ THE TEXT IN THE INTERPRETIVE TRADITION

An important aspect of biblical studies is textual criticism. Since there are many ancient manuscripts of the Bible in various languages, text critics study these texts to arrive at an authoritative reading of a given word or words when more than one possible reading exists. For Isaiah scholars, the discovery of the Isaiah manuscript among the Dead Sea Scrolls has given much insight into the BOI. With respect to Isa. 52:5, one of the scribes of the Dead Sea Scrolls made a change in the translation of verse 5, as did the Greek translator in the Septuagint. This may reflect ancient concerns about the meaning and/or significance of this verse. Joseph Blenkinsopp observes that attempts at "a coherent reading of 52:1-12 have not been successful" (Blenkinsopp, 340).

▪ THE TEXT IN CONTEMPORARY DISCUSSION

Past and present interpretations of the role of the nations in DI have vigorously debated the question of whether DI's prophecies were nationalistic or had a universalistic, inclusive view of the nations, including them among the redeemed. When referring to the nations, some Isaiah commentaries have used highly charged theologized perspectives that go far beyond evidence in the text. The term *goyim* has been translated as "heathens," "pagans," or "gentiles." The messenger "who brings good news" in 52:7 is called an "evangelical herald of the Gospel" in a recent Christian commentary (Lessing, 9). Yet other Christian interpreters see these texts as encouraging missionary work to convert pagans. However, the contemporary concept of conversion is not a feature of Old or New Testament religion (see "Conversion," in Anchor Bible Dictionary, Vol. 1, pp. 1131–33).

The Servant

▌THE TEXT IN ITS ANCIENT CONTEXT

The identity and role of the servant in DI is one of the most controversial issues in the BOI.

Reading the servant passages in the context of the Babylonian exile and its aftermath is essential to understanding the servant's role.

Questions asked about the servant abound: Who is the servant? Is the servant an individual, or are there many? Can the servant be identified with any individual important in Israelite history? Is it a collective term applied to all Israel? What is the role or work of the servant? Is the servant a prophet, teacher, priest, or the author of Isaiah 40–55? What is the reason for the servant's suffering?

In 49:1—53:12, the servant appears three times. In 49:1-7, he is called from birth by God to restore the survivors of Israel but laments that his work has been in vain. In 50:4-10, his role is to teach and sustain the weary community. However, he is not well received and endures persecution at their hands. The longest section devoted to the servant is Isa. 52:13—53:12. Though 52:13 begins with an announcement that the servant will prosper and be lifted up, this positive view does not continue. The servant's life is a pattern of rejection, misery, and continual violence from birth until his ignominious death. In the end, the righteous servant who intercedes on behalf of the community will see his descendants prosper, and he will be numbered among the great ones.

The role and possible identity of the servant can be more clearly understood within the sociopolitical setting of the exiles' life under Babylonian rule (Gottwald, 499–501). The prophet's ringing praises of Cyrus the Persian as liberator of the exiles (44:28—45:4) could be seen as threats to the Babylonian Empire. Some among the exiles supported the prophet's view; others feared that his words would bring retaliation against the exiles for their antigovernment stance. Alternately, a pro-Babylon position among the exiles is not hard to imagine. After living there for years, many adapted to this new life, perhaps supporting the status quo of Babylonian rule and their own social and political security. The execution of a traitor can be seen as an understandable response by the Babylonian government (Ceresko, 1–14).

▌THE TEXT IN THE INTERPRETIVE TRADITION

The identity and role of the servant is one of the most discussed issues in DI scholarship. In the late 1800s, Bernhard Duhm proposed that four sections in DI—42:1-4 or 7; 49:1-4; 50:4-9; and 52:13—53:12—were so different in composition, style, and content that they must have come from another author and were inserted into the BOI at a later time. A distinction was made between Israel/Jacob as servant and the innocent servant in these four passages, which came to be called the Suffering Servant Songs. Most scholars today consider the so-called Servant Songs consistent with the literary style and content of the rest of DI. Other occurrences of the term "servant" elsewhere in DI refer to Israel and allude to the suffering of the exiles. The sociopolitical explanations of Norman Gottwald and Anthony Ceresko relating to the servant in Isaiah 52–53 are understandable within the Babylonian context before the return to Judah. They may also shed light on the continuing challenges for community life after the return as described in Isaiah 56–66.

▌THE TEXT IN CONTEMPORARY DISCUSSION

Many Christian interpreters identify the "Suffering Servant" exclusively with Jesus and identify those who attacked the servant with Jews. Two problems arise with these views. To speak of Jesus, who lived in the first century CE, would be meaningless to exiles living in Babylonia in the sixth century BCE. In addition, this view fans the fires of antisemitism for those who hold such a misinterpretation today.

Contemporary interpretations of the Suffering Servant have been meaningful to indigenous people in countries around the world. Jorge Pixley (95–96) relates accounts of Latinas in San Salvador and Nicaragua who worked in communities to change their impoverished conditions. Offering educational opportunities and organizing groups of women resulted in the slaying of those who encouraged social action. Pixley compares the deaths of such leaders to that of the servant in Isaiah, calling them martyrs. Attempts at social transformation can and do result in persecution if the government feels threatened.

Another comparison is made between the Suffering Servant and the *minjung* of Korea. This term refers to people who are politically oppressed, economically exploited, socially alienated, religiously discriminated against, and denied education (Moon, 113). In Kwangju, capital of the poorest region in the country, protesters in 1980 demonstrated against the government, which had ignored their plight for years. Peaceful rallies were put down by military paratroopers, and in the end more than three thousand people were killed or injured. Moon compares the Suffering Servant to the *minjung* who gave their lives to liberate others.

Isaiah 54:1-17: Zion Transformed from Barren Woman and Destroyed City to Mother of Many and Rebuilt City

▌THE TEXT IN ITS ANCIENT CONTEXT

The addressee and subject of God's messages in previous chapters is Zion (Isa. 49:14—50:2, 51:2-3; 51:11—52:9). She is described as a barren woman; bride; mother; widow; divorced woman; an afraid and abandoned woman grieving the loss of her children; one who suffered devastation and destruction, famine and sword and captivity; and a destroyed and soon to be rebuilt city. In six verses (54:1-6), the prophet lists all the previously used epithets of the defeated people and then overturns them.

A tent that will be enlarged for all of Zion's children is a metaphor for the expansion of her descendants throughout the world. The dispossessed will now advance to possess and populate the nations (54:3). The shame of abandonment, widowhood, or divorce will be forgotten because God "your Maker is your husband . . . your Redeemer" (54:5).

One of the most striking declarations in this section is God's admission that

> for a brief moment I abandoned you . . .
> in overflowing wrath for a moment
>   I hid my face from you. (54:7-8)

Her husband acknowledges her terrible suffering and unjust punishments and promises to amend his ways. In terms of the marriage metaphor, it is understandable that one or both parties might admit their shortcomings. While it is not typical to hear God acknowledge fault in this or any relationship in the Bible, this sentiment was earlier expressed in Isa. 40:2 with God's admission that Jerusalem's penalty was excessive.

Another view of Zion in 54:11-17 is as a city about to be rebuilt. A new Jerusalem is described in fantastical terminology. The image of a bejeweled city recalls descriptions of Mesopotamian palaces (Paul, 427). Jerusalem's children will be taught by God and will live in great prosperity. The city will never be taken over by oppressors; no weapons will be strong enough to overtake it. No one will be able to speak against her.

▌THE TEXT IN THE INTERPRETIVE TRADITION

Does God apologize to Zion for having abandoned her, or is God's wrath against the people justified? Two commentators on Isaiah 40–66 explain God's treatment of Zion in verses 6-7. Instead of "a brief moment," Paul translates "in a fit of rage," reading the Hebrew term *rega‘* as an "antonym of love," not a measure of time. He further explains that the "Lord's rapprochement with Israel is based not on their regret but on His love" (Paul, 423). Blenkinsopp reads God's statement as a standard accusation used in Assyrian treaties as the result of breaking a treaty (Blenkinsopp, 363). It seems jarring or out of place amid the effusive language of joy to introduce such explanations or defenses of God in these passionate reassurances to Zion.

▌THE TEXT IN CONTEMPORARY DISCUSSION

One of the most basic discussions in the Bible, both Old and New Testament, relates to the questions of God's anger and why throughout history innocent people have suffered. The way scholars have interpreted Isa. 54:7-8 serves as an example of the wide range of explanations. Some consider that God's wrath is justified; people deserve punishment for their sinful acts. Others emphasize that a relationship between God and people is based not on strict rules or punitive treatment, but on a familial model that emphasizes love, acceptance, understanding, and forgiveness.

Isaiah 55:1-13: God's Word Is Reliable

▌THE TEXT IN ITS ANCIENT CONTEXT

This short chapter is a dense and complicated review of past motifs and allusions to future themes woven together by the underpinnings of the reliability of God's word. As such, it functions to link Isaiah 40–54 to 56–66. The entire BOI is connected by the assertion in 1:20, repeated in 40:5 and 58:14, that "The mouth of YHWH has spoken."

The word that goes forth from God's mouth will accomplish God's purpose for the exiles. Several images are used throughout 55:1-13 to illustrate their future. They will be given the basic sustenance of water and bread and also lavished with wine, milk, and rich food. Offers of such fare to people living in disadvantaged conditions would catch the audience's attention. God's word is compared to rain and snow falling from the heavens; just as these water the earth providing seeds for the sower and bread for the eater, God's word will provide life for the people. Similar images of renewed fertility continue in 55:12-13. A once thorny, weed-filled wilderness will be replaced by the growth of fragrant trees. Those who suffered as they were led into captivity through a hostile desert environment will return to fruitful land and an everlasting memorial that will never be "cut off." The transformation of the wilderness announced numerous times in DI will become a reality.

Another image of transformation, in 55:3-4, recalls God's covenant with David. In a radical change to the original terms of this agreement—that there would always be a Davidic descendant on the throne in Jerusalem—God alters the promise and makes an eternal covenant with the exiles, who will return to Jerusalem. The Davidic monarchy is not mentioned elsewhere in DI; it perhaps is inserted here to allude to the importance of the Davidic kingship in First Isaiah.

The Text in the Interpretive Tradition

A problem with God's promise of a permanent Davidic dynasty is that neither the dynasty nor Jerusalem survived. Here is another reason for exiles to doubt God's power and/or will to restore them. How was DI's audience to understand the arcane reference to the new "everlasting covenant" in 55:3? Many commentaries and articles have taken on these cryptic verses. Some reconceptualize the promise, referring to the "democratization" of the Davidic monarchy in which leadership resides in the entire community. Another explanation is that roles filled by individuals in the past will be taken over by a wider circle of people in the future (Clifford, 192).

The Text in Contemporary Discussion

Chapter 55 sums up motifs from previous chapters. It also functions as a connection with the following chapters. In Isaiah 56–66, the issue of leadership in Jerusalem in the postexilic period continues to be problematic. Reference to the "memorial" and "everlasting sign" of the regeneration of the land is considered by some to be a garden or park that memorializes the return home. Others view it as a metaphor for the renewal of creation. Jewish tradition has interpreted the "memorial, / for an everlasting sign" that will never be cut off (55:13) as a reference to the Sabbath. This refers to the importance of keeping the Sabbath in 56:4-7, as well as the promise to the foreigner and eunuch that they will not be cut off from the community in Jerusalem. It does not, however, resolve the underlying issue—the continuing problem of fulfillment of God's promises to the exiles.

Isaiah 56:1—59:21: Problems after the Return—Relationship between the Returnees and Those Who Remained in Judah

The Text in Its Ancient Context

Chapters 56–66 (TI) are set in Yehud (a term for Judah as a Persian province) after the exiles return to begin life in what remained of their ravaged homeland. The returnees, the Diaspora, include those who left Babylonia as well others who were exiled elsewhere after the destruction of Jerusalem. They joined people who remained in the land after 587 and eked out an existence with no infrastructure: no economic security, no food, and no governing bodies.

Chapters 56–66 continue in a literary style similar to that of 40–55. The same themes and motifs appear with variations. Two major sections in TI (Isa. 56:1—59:21 and 63:1—66:24.) reflect the current troubled realities of life in Yehud. Chapters 60–62, however, focus on hopes for the future in a restored Jerusalem and temple.

In this mixed community, disagreements reach a high pitch. Factions argue about who is in charge, what is considered evidence of faith, what rules govern worship, and who is allowed to participate in this new community. One group emphasizes an inclusive viewpoint, accepting participation by all regardless of ethnicity or background. Another is more exclusive in perspective, especially with respect to foreigners and the indigenous populace.

Chapters 56–59 describe bitter conflicts in the newly constituted Yehud. Issues in Isaiah 56 include proper observation of the Sabbath, rules about sacrificial offerings, and the role of foreigners and eunuchs in worship. The latter are assured that if they keep the Sabbath and the covenant they will not be separated from the community. God will gather outcasts because "my house shall be called a house of prayer / for all peoples" (56:7).

Another issue is misuse of authority by leaders. The shepherds and sentinels who are supposed to protect their community are compared to wild animals and dogs with voracious appetites for food and drink (56:9-12). Leaders are referred to as offspring of a sorceress and are accused of slaughtering their children (57:3-5). Their adulterous mother, the sorceress, is the focus of the attack in 57:6-13. Her sexual behavior is explicitly described in what can be called the most violent, lurid polemic in the Bible. Imagery relating to adultery committed by a woman is found in other prophetic literature. In the book of Hosea, the prophet's wife Gomer is accused of being unfaithful. However, it is not found elsewhere in Isaiah 40–66.

Chapters 58–59 return to the theme of the divided community and inadequate ritual behaviors. The issue in 58:1-9 is the efficacy of fasting. People protest that, while they fast and humble themselves, God does not acknowledge their acts. However, their behaviors belie the significance of fasting: they oppress their workers, quarrel with one another, and engage in acts of violence. An air of sarcasm and impatience underlies God's accusations that they fast only for show. God redefines fasting as acts of social justice: freeing the oppressed; sharing food with the hungry, homes with the homeless, clothes with the naked; and satisfying needs of the afflicted (58:6-7, 10). The grievous nature of the people's offenses intensifies in 59:1-4. Their hands are filled with blood, and they speak lying words; they have corrupted the court system. God's defense is that their own sins prevent them from seeing God's face and hearing God's word.

Chapters 58–59 have a homiletic tone. People claiming to seek God's presence indulge in unacceptable behaviors. If they change these behaviors, they will dwell in the light of God's presence. Conditions that guarantee God's guidance and sustenance are laid out in 58:10-14. People respond with a lament in which they admit their sins and take responsibility for the divisions within the community (59:9-15). In fact, their offenses have contributed to the continuing chaotic conditions.

God grows increasingly indignant at their vile behavior and asks: "Shall I be appeased for these things?" (57:6); "Have I not kept silent and closed my eyes and so you did not fear me?" (57:11); and

"Do you call this a fast, a day acceptable to the LORD?" (58:5). Specific references to God's wrath continue in 57:16-17. A finale to all this bloodshed and violence is a spectacular theophany of God as an angry warrior (59:15a-19). God, appalled at the lack of justice, puts on garments of vengeance and a mantle of fury. God's wrath will punish all adversaries and enemies; they will be repaid according to their deeds.

▌ THE TEXT IN THE INTERPRETIVE TRADITION

The eunuch laments that he has no children to carry on his name (56:5). But God promises that, if he observes the covenant, he will not be forgotten, and will be given an everlasting "monument and a name" (Heb., *yād vāshēm*). Yad Vashem is the name of a holocaust memorial complex in Jerusalem that preserves the memory of the six million people killed during World War II. Names, photos, films, and other artifacts of those killed ensure that they will have an "everlasting name that will not be cut off."

▌ THE TEXT IN CONTEMPORARY DISCUSSION

The BOI begins with a blistering critique of people who bring sacrifices and burnt offerings while oppressing the poor in their community (Isa. 1:10-20). God refuses to acknowledge their prayers and warns that they will be devoured by the sword unless they defend the *widow and the orphan*. This phrase is used throughout the Bible; it refers to the neediest in society, who have no means of supporting themselves. Isaiah 58:13 repeats the accusation from Isa. 1:12 that people are "trampling the Sabbath," and redefines the meaning of fasting and Sabbath observation as restoring justice, freeing the oppressed, feeding the hungry, sheltering the homeless, and clothing the naked.

Of all the passages in the Bible cited as a command to the faithful, the one most often repeated is the command to care for the widow and the orphan. Unfortunately, all too many well-intentioned believers direct their attention to other offenses. As a result, the oppressed and needy continue to be ignored, not seen or heard. Society often overlooks the existence of the poor. Data from the National Coalition for the Homeless shows 3.5 million people (1.35 million of them children) experience homelessness in a given year (DeYoung et al., 875).

Isaiah 60:1—62:12: Restoration of Jerusalem and Its Inhabitants

▌ THE TEXT IN ITS ANCIENT CONTEXT

An issue continuing throughout Isaiah 40–66 is the deferment of God's promise of comfort and deliverance. From the very beginning (Isaiah 40), the disconsolate exiles protested that their

> way is hidden from the LORD,
> > and [their] right is disregarded by [their] God. (40:17)

When the exiles returned to their homeland, hopes of a new and improved life failed to materialize. Life in a fractured and fractious community as described in Isaiah 56–59 brought different problems.

Chapters 60–62 form a stark contrast to the surrounding sections, 56–59 and 63:1—65:16, which portray difficulties, intrigues, and rancorous disagreements among groups in Yehud. From beginning to end, chapters 60–62 emphasize the glorious future of the once devastated Jerusalem. It will be restored to include Zion's children, and also kings and peoples of other nations. Numerous images describe the return of fertility to land and people, the radiance of rebuilt Jerusalem, and the shining beauty of the city and its inhabitants, all of which demonstrate the reversal of Zion's fortune.

One of the most notable features of 60–62 is the reappearance of feminine images of Zion. These include the feminine forms of address, as well as references to Zion as a wife, bride, and mother, as in 49, 52, and 54. Chapter 60 swarms with feminine grammatical forms. Recalling 49:15-21, Zion is again directly addressed by God in 60:1-22 (Wells, 198–202). A key image of the city's restoration in chapter 60 is that of light. Zion will be radiant as nations are drawn to her. God's everlasting glory will replace the light of sun and moon. Also repeated from DI is God's apology (60:10). Because people received a double portion of shame, they will now possess a double portion of everlasting joy (61:7).

Much of Isaiah 60–62 uses motifs and language from 40–55, often showing how the situation of Zion/Jerusalem is renewed and transformed. The people begin a new life in Yehud with a mixed group that includes returnees, those who had stayed in the remains of a destroyed Jerusalem, as well as foreigners with no national or ethnic connections to the original Jacob/Israel community.

▋ THE TEXT IN THE INTERPRETIVE TRADITION

The relationship of the nations/foreigners to the returnees is introduced in two ways. Striking images describe the reversal of status among foreigners, kings, nations, and the renewed Zion. Foreigners will build the city walls; kings will bow down to Zion and bring their wealth to her (60:10-12). They will also do the work of shepherding and farming while the once oppressed will serve as priests and ministers of God (61:5-6). Are foreigners accepted or rejected in this new community? One view is that 60:2-7 portrays a tolerance, even acceptance, of gentiles whose offerings God regards as "acceptable on my altar" (Smith-Christopher, 126–27). Reading the same verses, another view is that in Isaiah 60–63, foreigners are viewed in a negative light because of their ancestry, ethnicity, and/or national identity. One explanation for these differing views is that in a later period a *redactor* (editor) of TI acknowledged that foreigners were eventually incorporated into the community.

▋ THE TEXT IN CONTEMPORARY DISCUSSION

It could be said that cognitive dissonance is a consistent feature of the audiences' mind-set throughout Isaiah 40–66. They hold in tension a belief in God's promise of comfort and extravagant prosperity alongside an experience of continuously deferred hope. Some interpreters have characterized views of the future in TI as *eschatological* or *apocalyptic*. The term *eschatology* refers to an end time or climax of history. The term *apocalyptic* is applied to types of literature that arose in the Hellenistic and Roman period around 333 BCE, several centuries after the destruction of Babylon. Works such as the books of *Enoch* and Daniel anticipated catastrophic and imminent upheavals: earthquakes, massacres, world war against unholy nations, and the like. Referring to DI or TI as eschatological or apocalyptic is misleading and vague. When people in any age imagine a better future in positive and exaggerated terms, it does not necessarily indicate that they are thinking of the end time, or the last days. It can be a sign of hope for what is to come.

Isaiah 63:1—66:24: The People Lament God's Unfulfilled Promises and Community Divisions Continue

▌ THE TEXT IN ITS ANCIENT CONTEXT

Chapters 60–62 describe the restoration of Jerusalem and its inhabitants. Jerusalem's radiant light replaces sun and moon. Daughter Zion's fortunes are reversed. Violence ceases. Absent from this idyllic picture is any note of the bitter divisions among the community that marked chapters 56–59. The last chapters of the BOI (63–66) return to the somber view of the state of affairs in Yehud with an additional feature. A contrast is drawn between the fates of two groups within the community. Those engaging in illegitimate ritual practices are "destined to the sword," while God's servants will rejoice in Jerusalem.

Chapter 63 begins with the appearance of a mysterious figure whose garments are splattered with the blood of Edom. God is portrayed here as a warrior who has taken vengeance against Edom, a longtime enemy of Israel. A number of commentators, offended by the violent image, deny that the wrathful warrior could be God. However, the motif of God's wrath throughout Isaiah 57–59, and the warrior image elsewhere in TI (in 59:15b-19 and 66:14b-16), are consistent with God as an angry warrior. A major difference between these passages is that in chapter 59 God's anger is directed against injustices within the Jerusalem community; in chapter 63, it is aimed at Israel's enemies.

The remaining chapters consist of a lament in which people bemoan the loss of God's help (63:7—64:12), and God's response to their desperate pleas (65:1-15). Jerusalem's destiny is portrayed in chapter 66 in surprising and graphic images of reward for the faithful and punishment for the intransigent reprobates.

In the lament, people again remind God of unfulfilled promises. The tone of their complaints reaches a desperate pitch. They ask: Where is the one who led Moses through the sea? Where is your zeal and your might, your compassion? They blame God for hardening their hearts and causing them to sin. Still suffering from the loss of their nation and their temple, they ask, "Will you keep silent, and punish us so severely?" (64:12). God speaks in self-defense, asserting that though "I held out my hands all day long" (65:2), rebellious people angered God with idolatrous rituals. God warns them that they will receive full payment for their actions and promises to destine them to slaughter (65:1-15).

Not all will be destroyed in the fiery blast of God's anger. A group within the community, the servants who did not forsake God, will inherit blessings. The contrasting destinies of these two groups are listed in 65:13-15. The chosen, God's servants who have followed God's commands, will live and rejoice in a glorious new Jerusalem. God is about to create a new heaven and earth where all ills will be forgotten. Descriptive language for this new state of life in chapter 65 is taken from earlier Isaiah texts, including the peaceable community, where predatory animals and their prey will eat together (11:6-9), and from the blossoming wilderness of Isaiah 35.

The last chapter alludes to previous motifs from chapters 60–62. One of the most striking is the recurrence of Jerusalem as a mother and wife. In 66:7-13, Zion/Jerusalem is portrayed as a woman giving birth after a speedy labor, nursing the child from her glorious bosom, carrying the baby in her arms, and dandling the baby on her knees. God is also compared to a mother and to a midwife who assists in the delivery of the child. These images emphasize physical features of a mother giving birth and caring for her child. Her birth pains last for only a moment. Her womb is opened: 66:9 literally translated is "breaking" (the membrane). She nurses the child from her "consoling breast" and "glorious nipple" (Franke 2009).

These images are complicated. Zion/Jerusalem and God are portrayed as mother. In previous chapters, these same images appear in similar combinations. God is a woman gasping in labor pains (42:13-14); God is compared to both a father and to a mother in labor (45:10), and to a nursing mother who has compassion for the child of her womb (49:5). Some scholars disagree that God is portrayed here or anywhere as a woman and read these passages as a contrast, saying that God's love is greater than that of a mother. It is difficult to defend such a position in view of the passages cited above. Images of Zion as a bride, a once barren woman, a mother who has lost her children, a woman once captive now dressed in beautiful garments, a widow, a divorced woman, a wife rejected and then taken back by God are recapitulated in glowing portrayals of God and Jerusalem/Zion in Isaiah 60–62 and 65–66.

The BOI contains a pastiche of ideas and forms. Ritual offenses are contrasted with emphasis on appropriate offerings and Sabbath observance. Many nations will be called to Jerusalem to bring offerings to God on Mount Zion. The last verse, 66:24, describes a ghastly scene: the bodies of all who have rebelled against God burn in unquenchable fire. However, in Jewish tradition, books of the Bible should end with a positive perspective. Therefore, verse 24 is sometimes followed by the repetition of verse 23:

> From new moon to new moon,
>   And from Sabbath to Sabbath,
> All flesh shall come to worship before me
> All flesh will come to worship before God.

◼ THE TEXT IN THE INTERPRETIVE TRADITION

While the violence of the Divine Warrior image is shocking, it has been used from New Testament times to the present. The bloodied warrior appears in Revelation 14, describing the fall of Babylon. The son of man and others wield sharp sickles, harvesting the earth of evil. The "wine press of God's wrath" yields vast quantities of blood. It has also been used to illustrate and justify war in US history in the name of truth and justice. The Divine Warrior inspired Julia Ward Howe to compose a Civil War song still sung today in many contexts. Recall the first verse of this song.

> Mine eyes have seen the glory of the coming of the Lord,
> He is trampling out the vintage where the grapes of wrath are stored,
> He hath loosed the fateful lightning of his terrible swift sword;
> His truth is marching on. Glory, Glory, Halleluiah.

Another use of Isaiah 66 is found in Brahms's *Eine Deutsches Requiem*. Grieving mourners long for the one who has died, but they are reassured: "I will again behold you, and your heart will be joyful. . . . Look at me. . . . I have found comfort at last. I will give you comfort, as one whom his own mother comforts."

Selections from the BOI have caused difficulties for some Roman Catholic authorities that have recently made changes in the liturgy. The document *Liturgiam Authenticum* aims at using transcendent language and warns against Isaiah texts because they often portray God as too human. However, use of images taken from human life and experience in the BOI is what makes it such an important text in Judeo-Christian tradition. The Bible is *the primary* source of "sacred vocabulary." Problematic texts should be used, explored, read, and discussed. Texts that make a divine-human connection and cause problems for readers are precisely those texts that advance the development of theological and religious thinking.

▮THE TEXT IN CONTEMPORARY DISCUSSION

After the destruction of the Twin Towers on 9/11, the world was forever changed. Scholars responded to this event, realizing the need to address directly questions of vengeance and violence in the Bible, both Old and New Testaments. At the annual meeting of the Society of Biblical Literature that followed 9/11, many research and study groups changed their direction and began to focus on these issues in the Bible, in religion, in churches, and in other religious bodies. This topic now forms a major body of study in areas of scholarship (Franke and O'Brien). Religious groups—Jews, Christians, and Muslims—also make this issue part of interfaith discussions.

Works Cited

Anderson, Gary A. 1991. *A Time to Mourn, a Time to Dance: The Expression of Grief and Joy in Israelite Religion*. University Park: Pennsylvania State University Press.

Berges, Ulrich. 2010. "Farewell to Deutero-Isaiah or Prophecy without a Prophet." In *Congress Volume Ljubljana 2007*, edited by André Lemaire, 575–95. VTSup 133. Leiden: Brill.

Blenkinsopp, Joseph. 2002. *Isaiah 40–55*. AB. New York: Doubleday.

Brueggemann, Walter. 1998. *Isaiah 40–66*. Westminster Bible Commentary. Louisville: Westminster John Knox.

Ceresko, Anthony R. 2002. *Prophets and Proverbs: More Studies in Old Testament Poetry and Biblical Religion*. Quezon City, Philippines: Claretian.

Clifford, Richard J. 1984. *Fair Spoken and Persuading: An Interpretation of Second Isaiah*. New York: Paulist.

Davies, Andrew. 2007. "Oratorio as Exegesis: The Use of the Book of Isaiah in Handel's *Messiah*." *BibInt* 15:464–84.

DeYoung, Curtiss Paul, Wilda C. Gafney, Leticia Guardiola-Saenz, George E. Tinker, and Frank M. Yamada, eds. 2009. *The Peoples' Bible*. Minneapolis: Fortress Press.

Franke, Chris A. 1991. "The Function of the Satiric Lament over Babylon in Second Isaiah (xlvii)." *VT* 41:408–18.

———. 1994. *Isaiah 46, 47, and 48: A New Literary-Critical Reading*. Biblical and Judaic Studies 3. Winona Lake, IN.: Eisenbrauns.

———. 2009. "'Like a Mother I Have Comforted You:' The Function of Figurative Language in Isaiah 1:7-26 and 66:7-14." In *The Desert Will Bloom: Poetic Visions in Isaiah, Ancient Israel and Its Literature*, edited by A. Joseph Everson and Hyun Chul Paul Kim, 35–55. Atlanta: Society of Biblical Literature.

Franke, Chris, and Julia M. O'Brien, eds. 2010. *Aesthetics of Violence in the Prophets*. New York: T&T Clark.

Gottwald, Norman K. 1985. *The Hebrew Bible: A Socio-Literary Introduction*. Philadelphia: Fortress Press.

Isasi-Díaz, Ada María. 1995. "By the Rivers of Babylon: Exile as a Way of Life." In *Reading from This Place*. Vol. 1, *Social Location and Biblical Interpretation in the United States*, edited by Fernando F. Segovia and Mary Ann Tolbert, 149–63. Minneapolis: Fortress Press.

Kim, Hyun Chul Paul. 2009. "The Spider Poet: Signs and Symbols in Isaiah 41." In *The Desert Will Bloom: Poetic Visions in Isaiah*, edited by A. Joseph Everson and Hyun Chul Paul Kim, 159–80. SBLAIL. Atlanta: Society of Biblical Literature.

Kruger, Paul A. 1997. "The Slave Status of the Virgin Daughter Babylon in Isaiah 47:2: A Perspective from Anthropology." *JNSL* 23:143–51.

Lack, Rémi. 1973. *La symbolique de livre d'Isaïe: Essaie sur l'image littéraire comme élément de structuration*. AnBib. Rome: Pontifical Biblical Institute.

Lessing, R. Reed. 2011. *Isaiah 40–55: A Theological Exposition of Sacred Scripture*. St Louis: Concordia.

Løland, Hanne. 2008. *Silent or Salient Gender? The Interpretation of Gendered God-Language in the Hebrew Bible, Exemplified in Isaiah 42, 46 and 49*. Tübingen: Mohr Siebeck.

Lund, Øystein. 2007. *Way Metaphors and Way Topics in Isaiah 40–55*. FAT. Tübingen: Mohr Siebeck.

Moon, Cyris Heesuk. 1999. "Isaiah 52:13—53:12: An Asian Perspective." In *Return to Babel: Global Perspectives on the Bible*, edited by John R. Levison and Priscilla Pope-Levison, 107–13. Louisville: Westminster John Knox.

Moore, Megan Bishop, and Brad E. Kelle. 2011. *Biblical History and Israel's Past: The Changing Study of the Bible and History*. Grand Rapids: Eerdmans.

Muilenburg, James. 1956. "The Book of Isaiah: Chapters 40–66." In *Interpreter's Bible*. Vol. 5, *Ecclesiastes, the Song of Songs, Isaiah, Jeremiah*, edited by George A. Buttrick, 381–773. New York: Abingdon.

Newsom, Carol A., Sharon H. Ringe, and Jacqueline E. Lapsley, eds. 2012. *Women's Bible Commentary*. 3rd ed. Louisville: Westminster John Knox.

Paul, Shalom M. 2012. *Isaiah 40–66: Translation and Commentary*. Eerdmans Critical Commentary. Grand Rapids: Eerdmans.

Pixley, Jorge. 1999. "Isaiah 52:13–53:12: A Latin American Perspective." In *Return to Babel: Global perspectives on the Bible*, edited by John R. Levison and Priscilla Pope-Levison, 95–100. Louisville: Westminster John Knox.

Schökel, Luis Alonso. 1987. "Isaiah." In *The Literary Guide to the Bible*, edited by Robert Alter and Frank Kermode, 165–84. Cambridge, MA: Belknap Press of Harvard University Press.

Smith, Mark. 1990. *The Early History of God: Yahweh and the Other Deities in Ancient Israel*. San Francisco: Harper & Row.

———. 2001. *The Origins of Biblical Monotheism: Israel's Polytheistic Background and the Ugaritic Texts*. Oxford: Oxford University Press.

Smith-Christopher, Daniel L. 2002. *A Biblical Theology of Exile*. Minneapolis: Fortress Press.

Soares-Prabhu, George M. 1995. "Laughing at Idols: The Dark Side of Biblical Monotheism (an Indian Reading of Isaiah 44:9-20." In *Reading from This Place*. Vol. 1, *Social Location and Biblical Interpretation in the United States*, edited by Fernando F. Segovia and Mary Ann Tolbert, 149–63. Minneapolis: Fortress Press.

Tiemeyer, Lena-Soria. 2011. *For the Comfort of Zion: The Geographical and Theological Location of Isaiah 40-55*. Leiden: Brill.

Torrey, Charles Cutler. 1928. *The Second Isaiah: A New Interpretation*. Edinburgh: T&T Clark.

Tull, Patricia K. 2009. "Persistent Vegetative States: People and Plants and Plants as People in Isaiah." In *The Desert Will Bloom: Poetic Visions in Isaiah*, edited by A. Joseph Everson and Hyun Chul Paul Kim, 17–35. SBLAIL. Atlanta: Society of Biblical Literature.

Wells, Roy D. 2009. "'They All Gather, They Come to You': History, Utopia, and the Reading of Isaiah 49:18-16 and 60:4-16." In *The Desert Will Bloom: Poetic Visions in Isaiah*, edited by A. Joseph Everson and Hyun Chul Paul Kim, 187–216. SBLAIL. Atlanta: Society of Biblical Literature.

Willey, Patricia Tull. 1997. *Remember the Former Things: The Recollection of Previous Texts in Second Isaiah*. SBLDS. Atlanta: Scholars Press.

JEREMIAH

Kelly J. Murphy

Introduction

The name Jeremiah likely derives from the Hebrew "YHWH exalts," but the prophet is better known as the "weeping prophet" because of the grief-filled words that constitute the book of Jeremiah. In fact, the English word *jeremiad* stems from Jeremiah's name, designating a genre of literature in which an author laments the current state of affairs in his or her society, customarily predicting looming disaster (see Carroll 2008, 229). Accordingly, the biblical book of Lamentations is traditionally ascribed to the prophet because of its mournful tone. Jeremiah has long been a favorite of artists and theologians: Michelangelo painted the prophet on the ceiling of the Sistine Chapel, where Jeremiah holds his chin in his hands and appears deeply troubled, and a Romanesque sculpture often identified as a reflective Jeremiah is located at the Church of St. Pierre, Moissac in southern France. Martin Luther King Jr. once wrote, "[Jeremiah's] life and character are full of surprises that stimulate thought on great moral and religious problems" (King 1992, 181), and Dietrich Bonhoeffer drew on Jeremiah while imprisoned by the Nazis. Yet for contemporary readers, entering the textual world of the book of Jeremiah can be disorienting and disturbing. Somewhat famously, John Bright once called the book a "hopeless hodgepodge" (Bright 1986, lvi). There is no clear chronological order to the events described in the book, the pages brim with violent, disquieting imagery, and the world of ancient Israel can seem far too different from our own.

The book itself is initially set in the period of Josiah, an era marked by a series of both religious and political reforms in ancient Israel that might have held a promise of hope for the tiny nation of Judah, surrounded by the dominant empires of Assyria, Egypt, and Babylon, as they struggled to survive amidst the political turmoil that rocked the ancient Near East during and following Josiah's reign. Yet from the outset of the book, readers know Judah's fate: Jerusalem will fall to the Babylonians in 587 BCE, and the people will be exiled from the land. In short, the book is placed in one of the most troubling, and theologically and politically important, periods for the composition of the Hebrew Bible: the events leading up to the Babylonian exile, the beginning of the exile itself, and its aftermath.

Composition, Structure, Literary Elements

As Bright's "hopeless hodgepodge" comment suggests, the book of Jeremiah displays no clear order and is combined of a mix of poetry and prose. In the past, many biblical scholars assumed that the poetic oracles derived from the "historical" Jeremiah, while his scribe Baruch was responsible for the biographical material, and a later writer/editor (perhaps influenced by the so-called Deuteronomists, with their Deuteronomy-inspired theology) wrote the additional prose sermons. According to the superscription in Jeremiah 1:1-3, the prophet is the son of Hilkiah, a member of a priestly family and from the city of Anathoth (see 11:18-21). More recent scholarship proposes that not all of the poetic oracles can be attributed to the historical Jeremiah, about whom not much can be known with any certainty, and that the book overall is the result of a long history of composition and the work of many authors/editors. In its final form, the book is likely the result of an exilic or postexilic community. The complex redactional history of the book is perhaps most clearly evident when the Masoretic text (Hebrew) and the Septuagint (Greek) versions are compared; the Septuagint is considerably shorter and appears to preserve an earlier form of the book.

Various genres are embedded in the pages of Jeremiah, which, combined with the lack of a chronological narrative, makes it is difficult to delineate the structure of the book clearly. Generally, scholars divide the book into two major parts: Jeremiah 1–25 (before the fall of Jerusalem) and Jeremiah 26–52 (the fall of Jerusalem and its aftermath). Despite—or because of—its complicated redactional history, the book demonstrates substantial familiarity with other biblical texts, alluding to stories from Genesis, Exodus, the books of Joshua–2 Kings, the book of Hosea, the book of Job, and the Psalms.

Key Themes

Several key themes and words span the book. First, the book emphasizes that YHWH is sovereign, powerful, and the creator of all (e.g., 10:10-13). Israel/Judah belongs to him (e.g., 2:3; 10:16; 51:19), but consistent throughout is the idea that an enemy from the north is descending on the land. Although at times Jeremiah blames the oncoming disaster on the people's moral and ethical failures, the major concern of the book is that the people "go after [hālak]" other gods and have not remained faithful to YHWH. Thus any disaster that comes is the fault of the people. Yet the book also repeatedly calls on the people to šûb, or "to return/repent." In this way, while destruction is assured, there also remain occasional moments of hope. Nevertheless, the realities of war, loss, and trauma overflow from the pages and resonate in the voices of its characters.

Like many biblical prophetic books, the book of Jeremiah is largely centered on men: the two major characters are YHWH, principally depicted as a vengeful, warrior god ("YHWH of hosts"), and Jeremiah, the reluctant and sometimes bitter prophet. Though there are occasional positive images of women, females primarily function as stock characters intended to shame Israel/Judah as a whole or the men of Israel/Judah in particular. When women appear, they are usually the familiar figures of the adulterous wife or the unfaithful daughter.

As is often noted, a plethora of voices appear in the book: YHWH, the people, the kings, Jeremiah, the other prophets, the land itself, and occasionally even the women speak. At times, the polyvocal nature of the text makes it difficult to determine the speaker; such ambiguity literarily represents the chaos of the period the book depicts. Yet in spite of the many divine speeches, YHWH's silence also marks the book: in the final laments voiced by the prophet, the deity fails to respond and God is strikingly absent from many of the events surrounding life in Judah after the fall.

Jeremiah 1:1-19: Introduction and Call Narrative

▌ THE TEXT IN ITS ANCIENT CONTEXT

The opening of the book of Jeremiah consists of two parts: a superscription, which places the prophet in a specific historical context (1:1-3), and a call narrative, which includes two visions (1:4-19). Together 1:1-3 and 1:4-19 serve as a prelude, launching the reader into the devastating period of ancient Israelite history that followed the fall of the Assyrian Empire and the rise of the Babylonian Empire, ultimately resulting in the destruction of Judah and the ensuing exile.

The book begins Jeremiah's prophetic activity in the thirteenth year of the reign of King Josiah (627 BCE), and claims that it ends with the captivity of Jerusalem in 587 BCE (1:1-3). However, other Jeremianic texts suggest that the prophet continued to be active after the destruction of Jerusalem (see 40:1; 42:7; 43:8; 44:1, 24-25). According to this timeline, Jeremiah lived through the reign of five Judahite kings: Josiah, Jehoahaz, Jehoiakim, Jehoiachin, and Zedekiah. Yet the book does not proceed chronologically through their reigns, but rather jumps between events in different periods with no clear timeline; O'Connor notes that the "messy date-line conveys the interruption of time that accompanies trauma and disaster" (O'Connor 2012a, 132). Overall, the text claims that Jeremiah had a prophetic career of forty years, recalling the forty years Moses wandered in the wilderness. For later readers who are aware of how the events that take place during the reign of these kings will progress, the superscription casts a portentous tone over the book. Though the book begins with the phrase "the words of Jeremiah," 1:2 quickly identifies the source of these words: YHWH. Divine speech plays a central role in the book, which includes over one hundred uses of the formulaic phrase "Thus says YHWH" (parallel language is found throughout the ancient Near East, including at Mari, where the phrase "Thus spoke Annunitum" [a deity] appears in a prophetic text; see Petersen 2002, 16), as well as numerous instances of "the word of YHWH came to me." Thus the superscription establishes from the outset the close relationship between the deity and the prophet, while also underscoring that Jeremiah speaks for YHWH, granting divine authority to both the prophet's words and the book overall.

Jeremiah 1:4-19 opens by emphasizing the divine word: "Now the word of YHWH came to me" (1:4). Form critically, 1:4-10 is a call narrative, and as such it aligns with the call narratives of other key figures in the Hebrew Bible (e.g., Moses [Exod. 3:11; 4:10-11] and Gideon [Judg. 6:11-24]).

Such call narratives typically follow a prescribed order: the deity addresses the appointed person and gives a task (1:4-5), the appointed individual objects by citing inadequacy for such an undertaking (1:6), the deity offers assurances that he will be with the person (1:7-8), and then the deity provides a sign as proof (1:9-10). In particular, 1:10 will serve as an important verse as the book unfolds, for after putting "his words" in Jeremiah's mouth, YHWH proclaims,

> See, today I appoint you over nations and over kingdoms,
> to pluck up [*nātaš*] and to pull down [*nātas*],
> to destroy [*'ābad*] and to overthrow [*hāras*],
> to build [*bānâ*] and to plant [*nāṭaʿ*].

Like the superscription, the call narrative also contains parallels with the figure of Moses. Both Jeremiah and Moses claim problems with speech (Jer. 1:6; cf. Exod. 4:10-12), and the deity promises to give them both the means to speak (Jer. 1:9; cf. Exod. 4:10-12). The final editors of the book portray Jeremiah as the "prophet like Moses" foreshadowed in Deut. 18:15-22. Despite the similarities, there are also noteworthy differences. The text recounts Jeremiah's call from the first person, and Jeremiah, alone out of all of the prophetic figures in the Hebrew Bible, is appointed as a prophet before his birth (1:5). Like Jer. 1:1-3, 1:4-10 functions as a prelude, introducing themes that will run like threads throughout the following pages: Jeremiah is a "prophet to the nations" (1:5, 10), the disaster will come from the north (1:13), and while destruction looms, there is also language of rebuilding and hope (1:10).

Jeremiah 1:11-19 consists of two visions. In the first, Jeremiah sees "a branch of an almond [*šāqēd*] tree" (1:11). YHWH then interprets the vision: "You have seen well, for I am watching [*šōqēd*] over my word to perform it" (1:12). The wordplay in Hebrew serves as a reminder to the reader: YHWH is with Jeremiah and will do what he promises. The second vision is of a "boiling pot, tilted away from the north" (1:13). Again, YHWH interprets the vision: disaster from the north approaches Jerusalem and Judah, a direct result of the misdeeds of the people, who have been worshiping other gods (1:14-16). Jeremiah 1:15 emphasizes the idea that all nations are under YHWH's control. Although later readers often immediately associate the "disaster from the north" with Babylon, it is not until 20:4-6 that the text names Babylon as the enemy chosen by God to punish Judah for its offenses. Though many scholars have attempted to identify a precise location for this "boiling pot from the north" (see Holladay 1986, 42–43), it seems more likely that this is metaphorical language that draws on mythological and cosmic images (see O'Connor 2001, 490; Clements 1988, 21).

The visions end with YHWH's directive that Jeremiah "gird up his loins" and proclaim to the people of Judah everything the deity commands him (1:17). While the preceding visions focused on the ominous threat approaching Judah, 1:17-19 focuses on the prophet himself. The attention on Jeremiah introduces several more themes that will follow in the book. First, Jeremiah will have enemies among the established leaders of Judah, including the kings and priests, as well as the people of the land (1:18). Additionally, the passage reiterates that YHWH will be with Jeremiah to deliver him from his enemies, and that the deity has outfitted him appropriately: he is "a fortified city, an iron pillar, and a bronze wall" (1:19), invoking warfare imagery. While Jeremiah will be protected as a "fortified city," Jerusalem itself—YHWH's own city—is doomed. As the first sense unit of the book ends, the reader is left with an uneasy feeling: Jeremiah, in true prophetic fashion, will stand with only God on his side, and an (as yet unidentified) enemy is set to destroy the people of Judah, sent by their own God.

▌THE TEXT IN THE INTERPRETIVE TRADITION

That Jeremiah is informed of his prophetic mission "in the womb" sets him apart from other prophets. Accordingly, in rabbinic tradition, Jeremiah is described as one of four men whom YHWH created directly (along with Adam, Jacob, and Isaiah); the rabbis use Jer. 1:5, which reads "before I formed [i.e., "created"] you in the womb, I knew you" to draw this conclusion (*Pesiq. Rab.* 26:1). Additionally, rabbinic commentary focused on the introductory material that sets the stage for Jeremiah as a prophet like Moses. For the rabbis, the line "one of the priests of Anatoth" (1:1), which connected Jeremiah to a priestly line associated with wrongdoing (cf. 1 Kgs. 2:26-27), leads to the interpretation that Jeremiah lamented, "Among the priests my name is deprived of the respect due it" (*Pesiq. Rab Kah.* 13:13). What follows is a comparison between the fates of Moses and Jeremiah, where Jeremiah laments all the good that happened to Moses and contrasts it with all the bad that befell him: for example, Moses is blessed (Num. 6:24), while Jeremiah is cursed (Jer. 29:22). In other rabbinic texts, however, the comparison between Moses and Jeremiah concentrates on their similarities: both were prophets for forty years, both prophesied concerning Judah and Israel, the people revolted against them, one was cast into water and the other into a pit, both were saved by a slave, and both spoke words of reprimand (*Pesiq. Rab Kah.* 13:6). Another midrash reports that Moses had the voice of a boy from birth (*Exod. Rab.* 1:24), a parallel with Jer. 1:6.

In Christian tradition, Tertullian and Irenaeus both based arguments for human life in the womb based on Jer. 1:5, while Maximus of Turin and Jerome compare the stories of Jeremiah and John the Baptist in the womb to illustrate that even before birth God consecrated these men (Wenthe, 3-4). Additionally, Jer. 1:5 was used by Ambrose to argue for the twofold nature of Christ: the divine aspects of the Christian savior came from the deity, while the human characteristics came from his human mother without negatively affecting his divinity (Wenthe, 4). Finally, both Athanasius and Ambrose invoked the passage in arguments against the Arians, claiming that while some, like Jeremiah, are created, Christ was begotten but not created and, per Athanasius, "he is the Father's image and eternal word, never having not existed" (Wenthe, 4).

▌THE TEXT IN CONTEMPORARY DISCUSSION

The opening chapter of the book continues to speak today, transcending the boundaries of both temporal and cultural differences. The first words of Jeremiah are marked by both despair and hope and are set in a period of historical trauma and disaster; accordingly many scholars and theologians argue that the book is especially pertinent in addressing the fears and concerns of contemporary trauma and disaster survivors (see O'Connor 2012a, 2012b; Weems 2004). Jeremiah's words have been used to grapple with events ranging from the Nazi Holocaust, terrorism, war, colonization, to wanton violence and natural disasters. One contemporary message of the book—even if the following pages may be far from universally uplifting—is that it is possible for disaster survivors to move from having been "pluck[ed] up" to "rebuild[ing]" (1:10); in other words, from disaster to recovery.

Although the introduction to the book problematically blames the victims for the looming disaster, O'Connor notes that such a direct cause-and-effect correlation, while nevertheless insufficient, does "make space for recovery to begin" (2012a, 72). Similarly, Stulman and Kim suggest that 1:10 provides "hope in crisis" (2010, 100) and may help victims toward a "reestablishment of agency" (104). Accordingly, the book of Jeremiah can be a useful, if also challenging, resource for trauma survivors.

Additionally, Jer. 1:5 has played a significant role in the ongoing debate about abortion. On the one hand, opponents of abortion frequently cite the passage as proof that the fetus is a human being from conception. On the other hand, since 1:5 is poetry, others suggest that it is "difficult . . . to know if this passage is meant literally or metaphorically" (Friedman and Dolansky 2011, 48). Drawing any certain conclusions about what the ancient poetry means is challenging at best.

2:1—4:4: Divine Pleas and Indictments

■ THE TEXT IN ITS ANCIENT CONTEXT

Jeremiah 2:1—4:4 begins with the "word of YHWH" coming to Jeremiah (2:1). O'Connor calls this section a "drama of the broken family" rather than the more commonly used "broken marriage metaphor" (O'Connor 2012a, 35; also see 145n1). It is not simply the married couple that is affected by the charge YHWH levels against Judah and Israel; rather, YHWH indicts the couple's offspring as well (2:9). Israel and God are a "broken family" (O'Connor 2012a, 35).

In Jer. 2:1—3:5, the deity relates his intention to divorce Judah for its apostasy, particularly citing Judah's devotion to Baal, a Canaanite god, rather than to YHWH. Intriguingly, the reference to Jerusalem in 2:1 is missing from the Septuagint; the remainder of the passage is directed to Israel (the northern kingdom) and thus may reflect an original composition intended to entice the northern kingdom to reunite with Judah as a part of Josiah's reforms (see 1 Kings 1–11; Holladay 1986, 62–63). Later redactors appear to have added Jerusalem and Judah to the oracle. As is often noted, the following passages draw heavily from the imagery found in Hosea: Jer. 2:1-3 romanticizes the postexodus wilderness period (see Hosea 2:14-20), and YHWH describes Israel as his wife, recalling the "devotion of [her] youth" (2:2; see Hosea 2:15). But according to this oracle, things quickly went amiss once the Israelites entered the promised land. In particular, "the prophets prophesied by Baal, and went after [*hālak*] things that do not profit [*lō'-yô'ilû*]" (2:8). The verb for "to profit" in Hebrew comes from the root *ya'al*, which can also mean "to help or "to be of use." The Hebrew wordplay between the name of Baal and the verb underscores the futility of worshiping Baal, who cannot help or be of use. The indictment is to the point: YHWH's designated officials and people have failed to perform their roles and have worshiped worthless deities (see Hosea 2:8-17).

Ambiguity runs rife throughout the passage: at times, it seems that Israel (the northern kingdom) is male, while Judah (the southern kingdom) is depicted as the unfaithful wife—O'Connor suggests that they are blended together in 3:20 (see O'Connor 2012a, 36–37). Moreover, at times Israel seems to refer only to the northern kingdom, while in other passages it seems to refer to the two kingdoms together. Yet the predominant theme is the unfaithfulness of *both* Israel and Judah, which is expressed through the use of the marriage metaphor commonly found throughout the prophetic books of the Hebrew Bible (e.g., Hosea 1–3; Isaiah 40–55; Ezekiel 16): YHWH, the loyal husband, has been abandoned by Israel/Judah, the faithless wife. Here and throughout Jeremiah, the text draws on the widespread ancient Near Eastern depiction of cities as female, and this gendered imagery is (largely) employed negatively. The text describes Israel/Judah-the-woman as shameful and degraded (e.g., 2:22-24; 2:29—3:5). Any Israelite male is thus also shamed and degraded, forced to understand himself as female according to the textual metaphor (see O'Connor 2001, 492; Claassens 2013, 126; Weems 2005, 216).

Form critically, 2:9-14 is often called a "prophetic lawsuit," where YHWH formally accuses Israel of wrongdoing and makes it explicit that the fault sits with the people, who "changed its gods . . . for something that does not profit [ya'al]," again invoking Baal (2:11). The result is that the "land is a waste" (2:15), foreshadowing the oncoming exile. The mention of Egypt and Assyria implicates the people for making treaties with these foreign powers and thus not relying on YHWH alone (2:18; 2:36). Jeremiah 2:29—3:5 reiterates the image of Israel as adulterous wife, and sets the stage for the question posed in 3:1. The text of Deut. 24:1-4 lurks behind the passage: a man cannot remarry a woman who has married another man. Left unanswered is the question: If a human man cannot take back a wife who has gone astray, can YHWH? Jeremiah 3:6 continues the marriage metaphor and purports to relate an exchange between YHWH and the prophet during the reign of Josiah. In contrast with the preceding verses, there is a clear contrast between the northern kingdom, who abandoned YHWH first, "and yet her false sister Judah did not fear" (3:8). Though YHWH thought Judah would not go astray after seeing how Israel was "cast off" (3:8), nevertheless Judah strayed, only insincerely repenting. For this reason, 3:11 states that Israel is less guilty than Judah, and 3:12 calls for Israel to šûb, to return/repent.

The metaphor then switches from that of an adulterous wife to a parent-child relationship between God and Israel/Judah: "Return [šûb], O faithless children" (3:14). The following verses paint a picture of a compassionate God allowing his errant children to return to their homeland, a time when "all nations" shall assemble in Jerusalem (3:17) and both Israel and Judah will "come from the land of the north to the land that I gave your ancestors for a heritage" (3:18). In 3:22b, the speaker shifts from YHWH to the children, who admit their wrongdoing and seek to return (3:22-25). YHWH speaks again in 4:1-4. In 4:1, the Hebrew 'im, "if," is repeated three times: if the Israelites return (šûb), if they remove (šûb) the abominations from before YHWH, and if they swear to worship YHWH in "truth, justice, and righteousness," then the other nations of the world shall be blessed and praised through them (4:2). The text echoes with the promise to Abraham in Gen. 12:2-3 (through Israel all nations will be blessed). The passage ends by calling for the people to both break up fallow ground and to stop sowing among thorns, as well as to circumcise themselves to YHWH and remove the foreskins of their hearts (4:4; see Deut. 10:6): the repetition of "removing" throughout the verse implies the need to begin again and suggests that the foreign gods are the problem (Allen 2008, 62). However, the passage ends with an ominous warning,

> or else my wrath will go forth like fire,
>   and burn with no one to quench it,
> because of the evil of your doings. (4:4)

■ THE TEXT IN THE INTERPRETIVE TRADITION

Despite the divine indictments, some early Jewish interpretations focused on the theme of hope for repentance. For example, one rabbinic interpretation explains the Hebrew letters in Jeremiah's name (*yrmyh*) as composed of the Hebrew words *yôd* ("ten"), *rm* ("to journey up"), and *yh* ("the Presence [of the deity]") (*Pesiq. Rab Kah.* 13:11). Accordingly to the story, "in ten stages the Presence journeyed up and away" from the temple, descending and remaining on Mount of Olives for three and half years, where three times a day he repeated the words of Jer. 3:22 in the hopes of getting his people to repent (*Pesiq. Rab Kah.* 13:11).

In the New Testament, the author of the Gospel of John invokes the depiction of God as the "fountain of living waters" from Jer. 2:13 and applies it to Jesus (John 4:10-11). Early Christian interpretation also focused on the "fountain of living water" as well as the "broken cistern": Theodoret of Cyrus claims that the mystery of the Trinity is revealed in the phrase "fountain of living water," while Augustine asserts that Christ was the fountain of living waters, and those who do not believe in Christ rely on the broken cisterns (Wenthe, 17). Drawing on the harvest imagery of the choice vine gone wild in Jer. 2:21, Origen describes how the church has replaced Israel (Wenthe, 24–25). Finally, based on 4:4, many early Christian interpreters noted that spiritual circumcision replaced physical circumcision (Wenthe, 41–43).

Carl Rakosi's poem "Israel" draws from the KJV's rendering of Jer. 3:6: "Hast thou seen that which backsliding Israel hath done?"

■ THE TEXT IN CONTEMPORARY DISCUSSION

From the beginning, there are two troubling aspects of the book for contemporary readers: the negative depiction of women and how the book blames the victims of the expanding Babylonian Empire for what befalls them.

The negative depiction of women throughout Jeremiah—and especially how violently they are treated throughout the book—can isolate even readers who are able to place the book within its historically patriarchal confines. Yet as Renita Weems notes, if "women readers can hold their disgust at bay long enough to stay with the poetry and press certain questions" (218), then female (and male) readers can decide to "face the language of sexuality in Jeremiah" and "to speak up about the ways in which religious texts distort reality, re-inscribe sexual abuse, force connections where there are none, and hide behind language about authority to maintain the status quo" (219; see also O'Connor 2012a, 2012b). As readers, we can ignore the realities of gendered language in Jeremiah—or we can fight against and challenge them.

While for the author(s) of Jeremiah, placing the blame on the victims is clearly a theological explanation for the sociopolitical events that surrounded the fall of both Israel and Judah, for contemporary victims of violence, natural disasters, illness, and the like, it can be difficult to find much to redeem in 2:1—4:4. However, placing the blame on the people, while problematic, also hands victims some power over their situations; in other words, they can do something in the future to change what happens to them and thus "gain a sense of control" (O'Connor 2012a, 44). Even if such blame-the-victim language is ultimately unsatisfying, it is nevertheless an "effort to make meaning" in an uncertain, traumatized world (2012, 44). Thus, for modern readers, this is a text that provides "vital, explosive speech that both reveals and heals wounds" (O'Connor 2012a, 45). In short, the book helps illustrate to victims how to speak again in the face of tragedy.

Jeremiah 4:5—6:30; 8:4—10:25: The Foe from the North

■ THE TEXT IN ITS ANCIENT CONTEXT

The largely poetic material found in 4:5—6:30 and 8:4—10:25 is united by a common theme: the approach of an unnamed enemy from the north and the predicted devastating results, which YHWH confirms through the repeated prophetic messenger formula, "Thus says YHWH" (Jer. 4:27; 5:14; 6:6, 9, 16, 21-22; 7:3, 20-21; 8:4; 9:7, 15, 17, 22-23; 10:2, 18). Despite the focus on the enemy, it is never identified specifically; rather, enemy is often described as a wild animal as in Jer. 4:7 and 5:6 (cf. Ezek. 5:17) and overall depicts the disaster as cosmic in scope (see Jer. 4:23-28). Although it is difficult to date the oracles with any precision and many of the prose narratives may have been edited or added later, there are indications that the warnings are addressed to both the northern and southern kingdoms, and some material may stem from before the invasion of 587 BCE (see Holladay 1986, 132–38).

From a literary perspective, the text is marked by polyvocality. A number of voices speak in this unit, including those of "YHWH, Jeremiah, a narrator, the people, the northern kingdom, daughter Zion, and the foe" (O'Connor 2001, 493). As is often noted, the clamor of voices makes it difficult to determine the speaker. Yet the reality of the war and destruction is pervasive amid the din: 4:7-8 underscores the futility of the situation, as a lion—often depicted in the Hebrew Bible, along with other wild animals, as Israel's enemy and a sign of danger and terror—is coming. There is nothing the people can do to stop it, and so they are implored to put on sackcloth and lament,

> The fierce anger of YHWH
> has not turned [*šûb*] away from us. (4:8)

While the book often uses the verb *šûb* to call the people to repent, here the verb casts a dark shadow over whether YHWH's anger will turn from the people.

The narrator blames various leaders in Jer. 4:9—the kings, officials, priests, and prophets. Jeremiah 4:10 returns to the prophet: "Ah, YHWH God, how utterly you have deceived this people and Jerusalem, saying, 'It shall be well with you,' even while the sword is at the throat!" Although the NRSV reads, "I said," presumably intending the first-person speaker to be understood as Jeremiah, other texts preserve, "they said," perhaps indicating the prophets from 4:9 (Carroll 1986, 161). As Carroll notes, this places the blame not on the prophets but on YHWH, who misled them by giving them prophecies of peace rather than destruction ("it shall be well with you"; 4:10; 14:13-16, 23:17; see also Mic. 3:5). The support of prophets other than Jeremiah differs from the largely critical attitude toward the prophetic office that weaves throughout the book (Carroll 1986, 161; see 14:13-16; 23:9-40; 27–28; 29:21-23). The protest is strikingly bold: YHWH allowed the prophets to make false prophecies of peace. There is no divine response to this claim; rather, 4:11-18 reiterates that the impending disaster is Jerusalem's own fault, though here the metaphor shifts from that of a lion to an oncoming wind that will punish rather than "winnow" or "cleanse" (4:11). In Jer. 4:19, an unknown speaker, sometimes identified as Jeremiah and sometimes identified as the land personified, speaks again, momentarily letting the reader witness the torment felt by those facing the destruction of the people and city.

> My anguish, my anguish! I writhe in pain!
>> Oh, the walls of my heart!
> My heart is beating wildly;
>> I cannot keep silent;
> for I hear the sound of the trumpet,
>> the alarm of war.

From a feministic perspective, Bauer translates 4:19 as "My belly! My Belly! I-writhe-in-labor," reading "labor" with the Septuagint and Vulgate instead of "wail" with the Hebrew MT (Bauer 1999, 63–66). In this interpretation, the prophet himself takes on the female metaphor applied to the city, and so "Female Israel (earlier identified as 'Daughter My People') and the prophet Jeremiah have merged to cry out in light of the impending devastation" (Bauer, 64). Next, the phrase "I looked" is repeated four times in 4:23-26. What the speaker sees is destruction: quaking mountains and hills, an absence of people, a sky without birds, the land turned to desert, and the cities destroyed. A moment of hope is found in 4:27, "yet I will not make a full end," but 4:28 reiterates that YHWH will not "turn back [*šûb*]" from the oncoming devastation. Daughter Zion is addressed in 4:29-31 as both a whore and a mother giving birth amid the destruction and chaos, and the chapter ends with the haunting image of the woman "gasping for breath" and "fainting before killers" (4:31).

Jeremiah 5:1-13 restates the divine hesitation at bringing about the disaster, while also providing a kind of "theodicy" to justify YHWH's actions (Carroll 1986, 174). The first six verses of the chapter recall the story of Abraham and Sodom in Gen. 18:23-32. If Jeremiah can find just one person who "acts justly and seeks truth," then YHWH will forgive and the disaster can be averted. First, Jeremiah searches among the poor, but they refuse to turn (*šûb*) from their ways; next, Jeremiah seeks a just person among the rich, but there too he fails to find even one (5:3-5). The result is death by wild animals: lion, wolf, and leopard (5:6). Jeremiah 5:7-11 reiterates the adulterous ways of YHWH's people. Since the people failed to heed the prophets, YHWH puts fire into the mouth of Jeremiah and vows to bring a nation from "far away" (5:15). This nation will "eat up" the harvest, the children, the flocks, and the fig trees, and will destroy the fortified cities in which the people naively put their trust (5:16-17). Though 5:18 looks forward to "those days," the days of the exile, promising an incomplete end, the following verses enumerate the reasons the people deserve their fate, and the passage ends by again indicting the failure of the leaders, both the priests and, especially, the prophets, pointedly stating that YHWH's people "love to have it so" (5:30-31).

Daughter Zion appears again in 6:1-30, and a number of voices merge, including the voice of YHWH, the enemy, Jeremiah, and the people. Perhaps most powerfully, though YHWH calls on the people to repent, any repentance is pointless (6:26). Jeremiah is working with "rejected silver"

(6:30) that cannot be used; the people have failed. There is no escaping the army that comes rushing like the "roaring sea" (6:23).

When the poetic oracles resume in 8:4, the text returns to the theme of Israel's disobedience and the approaching disaster. The passage opens with a fivefold repetition of *šûb*: to return (8:4 [2×], 5 [2×], 6). Why, asks YHWH, do the people refuse to "turn back"? Drawing on the notion from Proverbs that wisdom is discovered by observing the natural world (e.g., "Look to the ant!" in Prov. 6:6), YHWH compares the people with storks, turtledoves, swifts, and cranes, which know their place (8:7), while his own people claim to be "wise" but do not know theirs.

In the first-person lament in 8:18—9:3, it is difficult to discern the speaker: is it Jeremiah who wishes "O that my head were a spring of water, and my eyes a fountain of tears, so that I might weep day and night for the slain of my poor people!" (9:1)? Or is it YHWH? Scholarly opinion is divided (for different explanations, see Allen, 111; Carroll 1986, 235–36). O'Connor attributes the words to YHWH, and suggests that in this way the text holds a "promise of healing," for "it puts aside punishment, eschews questions of causality, and understands God in radically different terms from much of the rest of the book" (O'Connor 2001, 497). Jeremiah 8:21-22 reads—from either Jeremiah, the city, or YHWH's perspective—

> For the hurt of my poor people I am hurt,
>   I mourn, and dismay has taken hold of me.
> Is there no balm in Gilead?
>   Is there no physician there?
> Why then has the health of my poor people
>   not been restored?

Gilead, located in Deut. 3:16 east of the Jordan River, is associated here with balm and healing, yet the section that stretches from 8:4—10:40 offers little hope.

Jeremiah 9 articulates the divine wish to leave Israel in the desert "for they are all adulterers" (9:2; see Exodus 32–34; Numbers 14), ending with yet another divine promise to "turn Jerusalem into rubble" (9:10) because Israel abandoned the torah and followed other gods (9:12). Funeral imagery dominates 9:17-21: death has entered Jerusalem because of the people's unwillingness to devote themselves to YHWH, and while God delights in "kindness, justice, and equity," Israel remains "uncircumcised in heart," unwilling to realize that ritual actions alone (like physical circumcision) will not save them.

In Jeremiah 10, the MT is arranged differently than the Septuagint, lacking 10:6-8, 10. Additionally, verse 11 is in Aramaic and not Hebrew. The Septuagint is likely older than the MT, and the Aramaic is likely a later addition to the MT; in short, 10:6-8, 10, praises YHWH as a God like no other and ascribes a kind of monotheism to the text that is not otherwise seen in the Septuagint, while the Aramaic of 10:11 claims that any gods who did not "make the heavens and the earth" shall perish (see Petersen, 100–102). As Brueggemann notes, the gods described in 10:1-6 are "characterized by a series of negatives": they cannot move, speak, walk, do evil, do good, nor make (Brueggemann 1998, 103). In contrast, in 10:10-16, YHWH makes, establishes, stretches out, utters, makes rise, brings out, and forms (Brueggemann, 103). Many scholars wish to place these verses in an exilic context, since "idolatry was a particular temptation for the assimilating community in Babylon" (O'Connor 2001, 498). However, since YHWH is the one who "formed all things" and Israel is his (10:16), there remains some hope: surely the creator God can return his people to their land.

Jeremiah 10:17-25 changes the overall thrust of the chapter. YHWH speaks, "I am going to sling out the inhabitants of the land" (10:18). The concluding words portray Mother Zion without her children, standing amid ravaged tents (10:20). Again, the speaker remains ambiguous in this passage: Is it Jeremiah or the personified city? Nevertheless, 10:23-25 ends by acknowledging YHWH's power while also imploring the deity for both mercy (10:24) and justice (10:25). The final plea for divine wrath to punish the "nations" quotes Ps. 79:6-7, and overall, 10:17-25 may be a passage written in an exilic context (see Carroll 1986, 263–65).

◼ THE TEXT IN THE INTERPRETIVE TRADITION

In rabbinic tradition, Jeremiah's anguished cries "My anguish! My anguish! I writhe in pain!" (4:19) are connected to his birth; following these words, he opened his mouth and accused his mother of being faithless. When his mother asks, "What makes this infant speak thus? Surely on no account of mine!," the text reports that Jeremiah spoke not of his birth mother, but from the womb knew Jerusalem would be destroyed because of her unfaithfulness (*Pesiq. Rab.* 26.1/2).

In Christian tradition, Jerome identifies "the lion who seeks to destroy" (4:7) as Nebuchadnezzar in the historical sense, but also as the devil (Wenthe, 44). Both Origen and Theodoret of Cyrus invoke Jer. 9:25-26 to illustrate that spiritual circumcision is more important than physical circumcision (Wenthe, 87).

In more contemporary reuses, the "Battle Hymn of the Republic" draws on Jer. 6:9-15: "My eyes have seen the coming of the glory of the Lord; He is trampling out the vintage where the grapes of wrath are stored." Holocaust survivor Elie Wiesel would remember Jer. 10:25 ("and all the birds of the air had fled") when he returned to Auschwitz, writing, "Then and only then did I remember that, during the tempest of fire and silence, there were no birds to be seen on the horizon; they had fled the skies above all the death-camps. I stood in Birkenau and remembered Jeremiah" (Wiesel, 126; cited in Carroll 1986, 170).

◼ THE TEXT IN CONTEMPORARY DISCUSSION

The violence, despair, and war-filled oracles that focus on the cosmic battle coming from the north are often troubling for contemporary readers. In a modern world that is still ravaged by war—and both the physical and sexual violence that often accompany it—these verses can be overwhelming, especially because they clearly illustrate that the oncoming disaster comes directly from the deity. For that reason, the question posed in Jer. 5:19 is especially timeless, "Why has YHWH our God done these things to us?" The question of theodicy, while unanswerable, remains vital to contemporary theological discussions among people of all faiths.

Despite this, positive images can also be found in the otherwise terror-filled depictions contained in these oracles. While the largely male-centered text of Jeremiah often uses the image of a woman in labor negatively, birth also has a "powerful, life-giving nature" (Claassens, 122). If readers see the anguished cries of 8:18—9:3 as Jeremiah's, then such a reading might help them to contest "traditional gender roles," and "to grasp something of the notion of gender as performative" (Claassens, 127). Such an interpretation enables us to understand that dichotomies like "masculine" and "feminine" are largely constructed by societies and opens a window into healthy dialogue about other possible understandings of gender. Similarly, if it is God who speaks in anguish in 8:18—9:3, the text provides an opportunity for thinking constructively about images of the divine in the Hebrew Bible that are not exclusively male and violent (O'Connor 2012b, 277). Finally, Jer. 4:23-28 reminds readers that human actions have an effect on the natural world, while giving the earth itself a voice to mourn (O'Connor 2012b, 277).

7:1-15; 7:16—8:3; 26:1-24: The Temple Sermon and Related Material

▌ THE TEXT IN ITS ANCIENT CONTEXT

The material in Jer. 7:1-15, often called the "Temple Sermon," interrupts the poetic material found in 4:5—6:30 and 8:4—10:25, and is followed by another prose passage in 7:16—8:3 that, although closely related to the Temple Sermon material, many scholars suggest is a secondary addition. Jeremiah 26:1-23 also retells the Temple Sermon, though with some differences. According to 26:1, Jeremiah preached the sermon in the year 609 BCE, when King Jehoiakim ascended to the throne following Josiah's death in the battle against Neco II at Megiddo. Prior to Jehoiakim's ascension, Josiah's son Jehoahaz ruled for a brief three months before Neco II deported him to Egypt, replacing him with Jehoiakim. Despite the claim that the sermon took place in 609 BCE, it is likely that these texts are either exilic or postexilic compositions, although they may contain kernels of the "historical" Jeremiah's own views about the corruption of the temple and its personnel.

Jeremiah 7:1 begins, not surprisingly, with "the word that came to Jeremiah from YHWH." The prophet is commanded to stand at the gates of the temple and to implore the people to listen to YHWH's warning: "Amend your ways and your doings, and let me dwell with you in this place" (7:3). However, the Hebrew can be read in two ways: either YHWH is to dwell *with* Judah in the temple, or, alternatively, the text reads "I will *let you* dwell in this place" (see Holladay 1986, 236–37). In the second case, the meaning is clear: if the people repent and reform, they will be spared the punishment of exile. The Judahites are then warned that they should not fool themselves into thinking that YHWH will not let his temple be destroyed: "Do not trust in these deceptive words: 'This is the temple of YHWH, the temple of YHWH, the temple of YHWH'" (7:4). Literarily, the threefold repetition emphasizes how naive the authors of the sermon believed the Judahites to be; despite Jeremiah's warnings, no one understood that God would let the temple be destroyed (see 4:10; 14:13-16; 23:17 on the prophets who falsely prophesied peace). What YHWH wants from his people is not empty words in a building that they believe to be important, but rather ethical and moral behavior based on the covenant (7:5-15). If the Judahites wish to avoid exile, they must repent. The language evokes the book of Deuteronomy: act justly, protect the marginalized, refrain from murder, and remain faithful to YHWH alone (7:5-7). In exchange for these actions, YHWH promises to dwell in the temple.

Despite the possibility of a reprieve offered in Jer. 7:5-7, 7:8-11 casts a dark shadow over YHWH's previous words: the people stand in the temple and claim, "We are safe!" Jeremiah 7:9 implicates the Judahites as transgressing five of the Ten Commandments (see Exod. 20:1-17; Deut. 5:6-21): stealing, murdering, committing adultery, swearing falsely, and going after (*hālak*) other gods. The temple has become nothing more than a "den of robbers" (Jer. 7:11). Next, the text shifts the reader's attention both geographically and temporally as YHWH reminds the Judahites of his former dwelling place in Shiloh, a shrine to YHWH in the northern kingdom where he no longer dwells (see Josh. 21:1-2; 1 Sam. 1:3, 9). Like the "offspring of Ephraim," symbolizing the northern Israelites, who according to the theology of the books of Joshua through 2 Kings disobeyed YHWH and subsequently fell to the Assyrians in 721 BCE, YHWH will also cast the Judahites out of his sight (15:15).

In Jer. 7:16-20, YHWH forbids Jeremiah to intercede on behalf of the people, while 7:21-28 suggests that sacrifices are not necessary, again moving away from an emphasis on ritual action: "For in the day that I brought your ancestors out of the land of Egypt, I did not speak to them or command them concerning burnt offerings and sacrifices" (7:22). Jeremiah 7:29—8:3 details Judah's ultimate destiny and the fate of the dead—including a lack of burial. Perhaps most interestingly, this exilic or postexilic passage recalls the writer(s)' memories of Judah's religious practices, which are quite distinct from the "YHWH-alone" religion that later develops as the norm. In particular, the text records how the people felt compelled to stay faithful to the "Queen of Heaven," as well as the practice of sacrificing the firstborn child. Scholarly identification of the "Queen of Heaven" varies, from Ishtar, a Mesopotamian goddess identified with the planet Venus, to Astarte, a Canaanite goddess of fertility and war and beyond (see below on Jeremiah 44; Cohn 2004; Ellis 2009). Likewise, the extent of child sacrifice in ancient Israel remains a matter of scholarly dispute.

Jeremiah 26 begins what scholars generally recognize as the second half of the book, largely repeating the Temple Sermon from 7:15-22. Like in 7:15-22, Jeremiah is commanded to warn the errant Judahites that their ways could lead to the same end that befell Shiloh. The difference is what follows in 26:7-24, which records Jeremiah's run-in with the priests and the prophets and the trial for his life. Accusing Jeremiah of treason, the authorities call for Jeremiah to be put to death. However, a new character is introduced: Ahikam the son of Shaphan, who is later identified as the father of Gedeliah, saves Jeremiah (see 2 Kgs. 22:12, 14).

■ THE TEXT IN THE INTERPRETIVE TRADITION

The Aramaic Targum of Jeremiah radically changes 7:4, reading, "Do not trust in the words *of the prophets of* falsehood *who say*, '*In front of* the Lord's temple *you are worshiping*; *in front of* the Lord's temple *you are sacrificing*; *in front of* the Lord's temple *you are paying homage: three times in the year you appear before him*'" (*Tg. Jer.* 7:4). In accordance with the rabbinic idea that repetition in scriptural texts holds an unlocked meaning, the Targum thus connects the threefold repetition of "YHWH's temple" to the three annual pilgrimages in ancient Israel (see Exod. 23:14; 34:23; Deut. 16:16; see

Hayward 1987, 26). In the Talmud, Jer. 7:4 is understood as a prediction of the destruction of both the First and Second temples (*b. Naz.* 32b). In a discussion that ends with a citation of Jer. 7:24, a midrash notes that Jeremiah was one of three prophets of his time: the other two included Huldah, who prophesied to the women, Zephaniah, who prophesized in the temple, and Jeremiah, who was sent to the city squares (*Pesiq. Rab.* 26:2).

In the New Testament, the phrase "den of robbers" appears in Jesus' words at the temple in Matt. 21:13. Additionally, like the Temple Sermon text, the interpretive tradition warns against placing too much emphasis on structures and buildings rather than on ethics and actions. For example, Jerome notes of the church "we are not to put our faith in the splendor of its buildings" (Wenthe, 65).

THE TEXT IN CONTEMPORARY DISCUSSION

For contemporary readers, the Temple Sermon might seem no longer applicable: it represents the problems and wrongdoings of the ancient Israelites, not our own. Yet for the author(s) of these passages, it seems clear that being faithful to God is not enough; people must act justly, shun violence toward their neighbors, and care for the destitute. Buildings and material goods are not important, but behaviors and actions are. Such a message speaks especially to the privileged members of the Western world, where material goods such as large houses or fancy cars are often seen as indicators of prosperity and divine blessing, whereas being poor or underprivileged is often attributed to some "bad" action of the affected individual or group. Thus the Temple Sermon can speak to modern people that focus primarily on their own well-being (spiritually or materially) while ignoring responsibility toward the greater community.

Jeremiah 11:1-17: The Broken Covenant

THE TEXT IN ITS ANCIENT CONTEXT

Jeremiah 11:1-17 begins a prose narrative that focuses on how Israel and Judah broke the covenant with YHWH. Jeremiah 11:6-8 invokes the memory of Israel's ancestors in Egypt and God's deliverance, while also proclaiming that they "walked in the stubbornness of an evil will" (11:8). Jeremiah 11:9 returns to the present and calls for the people to turn back (*šûb*) from their ways. The following section specifically lists the "house of Israel," the northern kingdom, as also implicated in the deity's accusations (11:10). The accusation is that both Israel and, in particular, Judah are no longer serving YHWH, but rather are serving many gods (11:13).

In 11:14-17, the focus shifts from YHWH's accusing the Judahites through Jeremiah to YHWH's directly addressing the prophet himself, again commanding that Jeremiah not pray for the people (see 7:16; 14:11; also Exod. 32:30-35). Jeremiah 11:15 personifies Judah as YHWH's beloved, who has done "vile deeds" that cannot be erased with vows or sacrifices (see 6:20; 7:21-22). The speaker appears to change in 11:16, stating "YHWH once called you," referencing a green olive tree (see Hosea 14:7; Ps. 52:10). Jeremiah 11:17 reminds readers that YHWH of hosts "planted" Israel, recalling the language of "to plant" and "to pluck up" in 1:10. The phrase translated into

English as "YHWH of hosts" literally means "YHWH of armies," and conjures the image of God as masculine warrior (11:17). The decision appears final: destruction is coming.

▌ THE TEXT IN THE INTERPRETIVE TRADITION

Jeremiah 11:6, which places Jeremiah's prophecies in the towns of Judah and streets of Jerusalem, reflect the midrashic idea that he was assigned to the city squares while Huldah preached to the women and Zephaniah preached at the temple (*Pesiq. Rab.* 26:2).

In his *Homilies on Jeremiah*, Origen argues that "the word that came to Jeremiah" in 11:1 means Christ was with and spoke through Jeremiah, noting the use of the "Word" in John 1:1, and stating, "And I could say that Christ was with Moses, with Jeremiah, with Isaiah, with each of the righteous" (Wenthe, 94).

▌ THE TEXT IN CONTEMPORARY DISCUSSION

A clear set of rules governs the world depicted in 11:1-16: good things will come to those who follow the rules of the covenant, while those who disobey the stipulations set forth will be punished. Yet as both ancient and contemporary audiences know all too well, life is rarely so neatly ordered. Good people suffer, innocent people die, and the wicked all too often go unpunished. As such, the Temple Sermon can be less satisfying than other theodicy-oriented protests, such as those found in the book of Job or in the following laments of the prophet and the people in the book of Jeremiah.

Jeremiah 11:18—20:18: Laments and Symbolic Actions

▌ THE TEXT IN ITS ANCIENT CONTEXT

The material found in 11:18—20:18 is both bracketed and punctuated throughout by Jeremiah's personal laments (11:18-23; 12:1-6; 15:10-21; 17:14-18; 18:18-23; 20:7-13; 20:14-18), while also containing laments by the people (14:1-10, 19-22) and the deity (12:7-13; 14:17-18; 15:5-9). The language is reminiscent of both the lament Psalms (e.g., Psalm 3; 4; 7; 28; 31) and the book of Lamentations. Dispersed throughout these chapters is also a series of what scholars name "symbolic action reports"; these narratives report "prophetic behavior that is designed to convey a message" (Petersen, 20) and are found throughout the book of Jeremiah (13:1-11; 16:1-4; 19:1-2, 10-11; 25:15-29; 27:1-3, 12; 28:10-11; 32:1-15; 43:8-13; 51:59-64). Although some scholars have attempted to attribute the laments and symbolic actions to the historical Jeremiah, overall the sense unit located in 11:18—20:18 appears to be the result of later reworking, providing both a way to understand the events of 587 BCE and following, and giving later exilic readers a means to mourn their current situation (see Allen, 144–45; Carroll 1986, 277–78).

Even if only as a literary character, within these verses Jeremiah as an individual begins to emerge: he is a lonely, suffering, tormented prophet who faithfully carries out the actions prescribed to him by the deity but also laments his own situation and role in the unfolding events. For example, in 11:18-20 Jeremiah bewails how, as a prophet announcing to his fellow Judahites their wrongdoings, he has been like a "gentle lamb led to the slaughter" and the people "devised schemes" against him; thus, he asks that YHWH punish them. Though the ending of Jeremiah 7 was ambiguous about the fate of the prophet, the short prose narrative in 11:21-23 indicate that the people of Jeremiah's own hometown of Anathoth sought the death penalty against him (see 1:1; 7:12). The oracle is grim: YHWH will punish Anathoth, and the young men will die by the sword and the sons and daughters by famine. The promise of death by sword and famine reveals the realities of warfare: children die and people starve. In both the face and aftermath of the Babylonian invasion, such realities would have been familiar to any survivors (19:9; see 2 Kgs. 6:24-29). Jeremiah 12:1 returns to a second lament by the prophet, in which he "lay[s] charges" against YHWH (from the Hebrew verb *rîb*, meaning "to dispute" or "to conduct a lawsuit"). The idea of bringing charges against the deity invokes biblical courtroom language found elsewhere (see, e.g., Job 21) and emphasizes the question of divine justice. The questions of "Why?" and "How long?" from 12:1, 4, illustrate how Jeremiah's laments continue to escalate: "God becomes the object of Jeremiah's complaint" (Petersen, 111). Overall, Jer. 12:1-4 raises the question of theodicy (see Hab. 1:13; Job 21:7). In this lament, the book departs from the traditional language of the books of Joshua through 2 Kings or the book of Proverbs, with their rigid notion of cause and effect for human suffering, to a demand for a more satisfying answer.

In Jer. 12:5-13, YHWH answers, and like Jeremiah's words, the deity's words are filled with sorrow. However, as commentators often point out, the deity fails to respond to Jeremiah's question of theodicy (Brueggemann, 120). Poignantly, the deity states that he has

> . . . given the beloved of my heart
> into the hands of her enemies. (12:7)

The shepherds, who symbolize Israel and Judah's kings, have destroyed God's vineyard (12:10-11; see Isa. 5:1-7). Personified in 12:11, the land mourns for the deity. In 12:9, it was the wild beasts that "devoured," yet by 12:12 it is "the sword of YHWH" that devours. The passage ends in a short prose section that is likely the addition of a later editor (12:14-17). While the preceding material was mournful in tone, these verses offer a word of hope. Though YHWH "plucks up" Judah (see 1:10), he will later have compassion on the people and restore them to the land. Jeremiah 12:17 threatens that any nation that does not listen will be "uprooted and destroyed," recalling the prelude (1:10). Nevertheless, "there is hope, if [the other nations] learn to swear by YHWH's name" (O'Connor 2001, 500). Here Jeremiah truly is a "prophet to the nations" as foretold in the opening chapters of the book (see Carroll 1986, 292).

Jeremiah 13:1-11 introduces the first symbolic action performed by the prophet: YHWH commands him to buy a linen loincloth, wear it, and then hide it near a rock by the Euphrates (13:1-5). "After many days," YHWH tells Jeremiah to find the loincloth, which is now *šāḥat*—ruined (13:6-7). YHWH then explains the strange action: just as the loincloth is ruined, so too will the deity ruin Judah and Jerusalem, which like the loincloth will be "good for nothing" (13:8-9). As Brueggemann explains, "The proper use of a loincloth is to be worn by a man. It is to be worn, not hidden and buried. Thus Israel's proper use is to cleave to Yahweh, not to be autonomous, stubborn, or committed to other gods" (Brueggemann, 128). The loincloth, which "clings" to the person wearing it (13:11), is now ruined, as is the close relationship between YHWH and Israel.

In Jer. 13:12-14, YHWH dictates that Jeremiah tell the people that "every wine-jar should be filled with wine" (13:12); when the people question this action, Jeremiah is to tell them that YHWH is about to make all the inhabitants of Jerusalem drunk, and will "dash them one against another, parents and children together. . . . I will not pity or spare or have compassion when I destroy them" (13:13-14). The verb translated as "destroy" (*šāḥat*) derives from the same Hebrew root as "ruin" in the loincloth story (13:9). The remainder of Jeremiah 13 is composed of a series of oracles that implore the Judeans to listen and turn away from arrogance (see 13:15, 17), ending with a decree from YHWH that he himself will shame Israel for its iniquities (13:22-27). Jeremiah 13:22 contains some of the most disturbing gendered imagery in the book: Judah's "skirts will be lifted"— an act intended to cause shame and associated with sexual assault—and she will be violated. As O'Connor bluntly states, "God rapes her; Judah is destroyed" (O'Connor 2012a, 54).

Jeremiah 14:1—15:21 contains oracles concerned with drought and war, marked by lament language voiced by the people as they ask YHWH to help them despite knowing that they have acted in the wrong (14:7-9). Their cry for aid is sternly refused in 14:10. YHWH again tells the prophet that he is not to intercede on their behalf (see 7:16; 11:14; 14:11). The repetition of "sword, famine, and pestilence" (see 14:12, 13, 15, 16) describes what awaits the people and their lying prophets, who are promising peace to the people (14:13). The following verses, spoken by YHWH, reiterate the coming sword and famine (14:17-19). Another lament voiced by the people ensues, as they confess their sin and profess their faith in YHWH (14:20-22).

Despite the prominence of hope in the people's laments, Jeremiah 15 indicates the hopelessness of the situation: even if Moses or Samuel, famous for their appeals to YHWH on behalf of the people, stood before him, YHWH would not save those addressed here (15:1). These people are destined for four things: pestilence, sword, famine, and captivity (15:2), which the text connects with four kinds of destroyers, including "swords to kill, dogs to drag away, and the birds of the air and the wild animals of the earth to devour and destroy [*šāḥat*]" (15:3). Jeremiah 15:4 places the responsibility for the forthcoming destruction on Manasseh, who ruled from 698 to 642 BCE and is blamed throughout the book of Kings for Judah's demise (see 2 Kgs. 23:26-27). Yet in the book of Jeremiah, where the people are regularly regarded as bringing about their own fate by their failure to return, the mention of Manasseh seems to clearly indicate a later addition. Jeremiah 15:5-9 includes a lament by the deity himself, followed by another of Jeremiah's laments in 15:10-21. Famously, Jeremiah complains that he was ever born: "Woe is me, my mother, that you ever bore me, a man of strife and contention to the whole land!" (15:10; cf. Job 3:2-12). By stating that he has neither "lent" nor "borrowed," Jeremiah establishes his innocence—and yet the people curse him (see Carroll 1986, 327). Though many English translations of the passage continue in 15:11 with "YHWH said," the Septuagint reads, "So be it YHWH," placing the words in Jeremiah's mouth (see Carroll 1986, 325). Jeremiah 15:15-18 also continues in the lament of an individual to the deity, with Jeremiah stressing his innocence and challenging the deity even more than he did previously (Petersen, 113). Each lament grows in agitation and anguish. YHWH's response is located in 15:19-21, where the repetition of *šûb* ("return") is featured, and once again the response, while assuring, fails to address the specific complaints voiced throughout 15:15-18, yet again drawing another parallel with the response Job receives from the deity in Job 38–41 (see Carroll 1986, 333). Jeremiah is reminded of his prophetic duty (15:20); this is the last time the deity will respond to a lament.

In Jer. 16:1-4, YHWH instructs Jeremiah not to take a wife or to have children—any children born shall "die of deadly diseases," and there will be no one to mourn them or bury them (16:4). Likely, this passage is a symbolic action that works as a literary device rather than a biographical account of the historical Jeremiah's marital status. The passage continues by forbidding a variety of mourning practices (16:5-9), for YHWH promises "to banish from this place, in your days and before your eyes, the voice of mirth and the voices of gladness, the voice of the bridegroom and the voice of the bride" (see 7:34; 25:10; 33:11). Again, the text reiterates that the forthcoming disaster is because of the sins of both Judah's ancestors and the current generation (16:10-13), and though YHWH claims he will not show mercy (16:13), the following verses offer yet another occasion for hope: the saying "As YHWH lives who brought the people of Israel up out of the land of Egypt" shall become "As YHWH lives who brought the people of Israel out of the land of the north and out of all the lands where he had driven them," returning them to their own land (16:15). Jeremiah 16:16-18 turns again to the language of divine judgment and wrath: "carcasses of their detestable idols" have polluted the land, and so Judah will pay double for their iniquity (16:18; see Lev. 11:10-12). The chapter ends with a hymn of praise (16:19-20) and a divine promise that all the nations will know YHWH (16:21; see Jer. 10:5, 8, 14-15; Isa. 2:2; 60:3; Mic. 4:2).

Jeremiah 17 begins with further polemic against those who rely on idols rather than YHWH. Drawing again on drought language, 17:5-8 illustrates that those who trust in idols made by human hands shall "live in parched places in the wilderness" (17:6), while those who rely on YHWH will be like a "tree planted by the water" (17:8). Jeremiah 17:12-13 returns to the idea of YHWH as hope (see 14:8), reminding the reader that YHWH is the "fountain of living waters" (see 2:13). Jeremiah 17:14-18 contains another of Jeremiah's personal laments, beginning, "Heal me, O YHWH, and I shall be healed" (17:14); the passage continues with Jeremiah imploring the deity to shame his persecutors, but to protect Jeremiah himself, even as Jeremiah urges YHWH to "bring on the day of disaster" (17:18). There is no divine response to the lament.

The chapter ends with YHWH instructing Jeremiah to stand in the "People's Gate," and to remind those who pass through to honor the Sabbath; if they do not, YHWH will "kindle a fire" in the gates of Jerusalem, a fire that "cannot be quenched" (17:27). Fire that destroys the city—tied here to a failure to observe the Sabbath—connects the verses found in 15:14 and 17:4 (see Carroll 1986, 367). The text is clear: failure to stay faithful to YHWH brings disaster on the city.

In yet another symbolic action, which draws on the language of "plucking up" and "breaking down" from 1:10, YHWH commands Jeremiah to visit a potter's house, where he witnesses a potter reshaping a new pot out of clay from a previously spoiled attempt (18:1-4). In 18:6, YHWH then compares the potter's action with his own abilities; surely he too can rework the flawed pot that is Israel ("Can I not do with you, O house of Israel, just as this potter has done?"). Should a nation turn from its evil, YHWH can turn from his plan to "pluck up and break down and destroy it" (18:7-8). Similarly, if YHWH is "build[ing] and plant[ing]" a nation but it turns toward evil, he can likewise change his mind (18:9-10). Jeremiah 18:11-12 reports that YHWH implores the people to turn from their ways since he is a "potter shaping evil against you," but the people refuse. In 18:13-17, YHWH laments their ways, ending with his decision to

> . . . show them my back, not my face,
>   in the day of their calamity.

Jeremiah's lament in 18:18-23 finds the prophet bitterly complaining about his enemies and asking YHWH to "deal with them while you are angry" (18:23). YHWH does not respond.

Jeremiah 19 continues the theme of potter, pots, and divine judgment with another symbolic action. YHWH commands Jeremiah to buy a potter's jug and to take the elders of the people and the senior priests to the Potsherd Gate, located in the "valley of the son of Hinnom," also called Topheth, a place associated with the sacrifice of children to Baal and Molech in biblical tradition (see Deut. 18:10; 2 Kgs. 16:3; 21:6; Isa. 20:33; Jer. 7:31). Repeating the warning of a forthcoming disaster (19:1-9), Jeremiah is to break the jug before the people and say, "Thus says YHWH of hosts: So will I break this people and this city, as one breaks a potter's vessel, so that it can never be mended" (19:10-11). The story of the shattered pot is embedded in a longer sermon against the practices associated with Topheth, and as such "it incorporate[s] the kings, people, and houses of Jerusalem" into the condemnation of those religious observances (Carroll 1986, 386). The passage ends with Jeremiah returning to the temple's court and again announcing that the disaster is coming because the people have refused to listen (19:14-15).

Jeremiah 20 includes a short pericope that describes how Pashhur, the "chief officer" at the temple, arrests the prophet and places him in the stocks (20:1-2). Upon his release, Jeremiah says to him, "YHWH has named you not Pashhur but 'Terror-all-around'" (20:3). Pashhur's act will result in all of his family and friends dying in Babylon (20:6). Jeremiah 20:7-18 contains the last of Jeremiah's personal laments, in which he claims to have been tricked by the deity (20:7), noting that no one will listen to him and he is weary of his prophetic role (20:9). Again, he curses the day of his birth (20:14-18). The sense unit ends on a personal note of misery, anguish, and despair. The deity does not respond; Petersen notes that while traditionally lament language is hopeful because it anticipates a response, Jeremiah's laments "make clear that a response—at least the hoped-for response—was not, finally, forthcoming" (Petersen 116).

▮ THE TEXT IN THE INTERPRETIVE TRADITION

Both the Jewish and Christian traditions customarily credit Jeremiah with writing Lamentations because of the prevalence of lament language in the book of Jeremiah. Early Jewish interpreters often depicted the reasons for Jeremiah's laments, including that he was born knowing of Jerusalem's eventual destruction (*Pesiq. Rab.* 26:1/2).

Rembrandt's *Jeremiah Lamenting the Destruction of Jerusalem* captures the anguish of the prophet, while Igor Stravinsky, Ernst Krenek, and Leonard Bernstein (among others) have written modern compositions of the laments, often borrowing from the book of Lamentations. Gerard Manley Hopkins's "Thou Are Indeed Just, Lord" is inspired by the question of theodicy posed in Jeremiah's laments (cf. Jer. 12:1).

More than any other texts from the book of Jeremiah, it is Jeremiah's laments and weeping that stand out in contemporary discussion; these are the sections of the text that make the prophet appear both human and relatable. For modern readers who face traumatic situations, Jeremiah's weeping can be a window into recovery once they have moved past the stage of numbness that follows (see O'Connor 2012a, 2012b). Moreover, Jeremiah's laments in particular are a clarion call that reminds readers that it is difficult to be a prophet and to speak truth. Any number of modern-day "prophets" attest to this, from Malcolm X to Martin Luther King Jr., from Simone Weil and Dietrich Bonhoeffer to Oscar Romero. Perhaps most importantly, Jeremiah's laments provide a means by which contemporary people can invoke age-old questions of theodicy, can call God to court and ask for answers, and can voice their experiences of present-day sufferings. Yet the text is also increasingly marked by YHWH's silence and his failure to respond to the prophet's cries. Such divine silence is disturbing, but philosophers and theologians such as Simone Weil and Gustavo Gutiérrez, in their different ways, find in such silence and mystery a means by which the experiences of human suffering and violence can be wrestled with rather than ignored (see Nava 2001).

Jeremiah 21:1—23:40: The Fall of Jerusalem and the Question of Hope

■ THE TEXT IN ITS ANCIENT CONTEXT

Jeremiah 21 begins with a prose narrative that professes to take place during the reign of Zedekiah (597–587/586 BCE), one of Josiah's sons and a descendant of David, who was placed on the throne by the Babylonian king Nebuchadrezzar following the initial Babylonian conquest of Jerusalem in 597 BCE. According to the text, Jeremiah repeatedly warned Zedekiah to accept Babylonian rule and not to rebel. In Jeremiah 21, the familiar "word of YHWH" comes to Jeremiah and he is instructed to tell Zedekiah that YHWH has given them into the hands of the Babylonians (21:4-7). Jeremiah 21:8 includes a speech addressed to the people of the land rather than to the monarch, and it follows a covenant formula from the book of Deuteronomy: "I am setting before you the way of life and the way of death" (see similar language in Deut. 15:19, 30). In Jeremiah, ironically, the people are advised to surrender to the Chaldeans (i.e., the Babylonians) rather than fight against them in order to follow "the way of life." Those who do not will "die by the sword, famine, and pestilence" (21:9). To faithfully follow YHWH is to let the Babylonians—YHWH's chosen instrument of punishment—attack and take the city.

The prose narrative ends and once again the book returns to both poetic oracles and smaller prose units throughout Jeremiah 21:11—23:40. This section of text is largely concerned with the fate of the Davidic monarchy. Zedekiah's pleas for divine help are chillingly refused; YHWH himself will fight against the city (21:5). Jeremiah 22:6 recalls 8:22, citing Gilead.

> You are like Gilead to me
>   like the summit of Lebanon;

though it ends direly,

> but I swear that I will make you a desert,
>   an uninhabited city.

The brief section in 23:1-8 looks forward to the restoration of the monarchy following the Babylonian exile, but overall the poetry and prose in 21:11—23:40 are marked by a critique and distrust of the institutions of Jeremiah's day—the kings (21:11—22:30) and the priests and the prophets (23:9-40).

At the end, the passage turns from a critique of the monarchy to a critique of prophecy. The fulcrum of this section is that Jeremiah is a true prophet; according to Jeremiah, the people tragically listened only to the false prophets. If a new branch of David is to sit on the throne in Jerusalem, then the audience of the book of Jeremiah must accept that Jeremiah's words carry authoritative, divine weight.

▌THE TEXT IN THE INTERPRETIVE TRADITION

In rabbinic tradition, the association between Gilead and Lebanon in Jer. 22:6 leads the rabbis to claim that YHWH showed Moses the temple (*Mekilta de-Rabbi Ishmael, Amalek* 2:87). Among the early Christian interpreters, Ambrose uses 22:13 to caution against extravagant homes, writing, "The person who builds with justice builds not on earth but in heaven" (Wenthe, 165). Theodoret argued that the "righteous branch" of 23:5 foreshadowed Christ (Wenthe, 166), while Ephrem the Syrian and Origen used Jeremiah's words about false prophets to caution against listening to them (Wenthe, 180).

References to Gilead abound in popular culture; sometimes these are positive and align with the idea of comfort and healing found in Gen. 27:25 and Jer. 8:22, as exemplified by the African American hymn "There Is a Balm in Gilead." At other times, references cast aspersions on Gilead and seem to conform to the more negative images of Gilead and its ruin such as in Jer. 22:6 (see also 46:11). For instance, Margaret Atwood's *The Handmaid's Tale* takes place in a totalitarian nation called the "Republic of Gilead," where the character Moira calls the hymn "There Is a Bomb in Gilead" (Atwood 1998, 218).

▌THE TEXT IN CONTEMPORARY DISCUSSION

Jeremiah 21–23 focuses on the fall of Jerusalem and the failure of the kings, priests, and prophets during a time of national crisis. Such a text reminds readers that ancient peoples also looked to their leaders during moments of uncertainty; like other prophetic books, this passage places responsibility in the hands of the people themselves (Jer. 21:8). If the people want to save themselves, they must abandon the divine city and accept their fate; if they wish to remain and fight the Babylonians, they will die abandoned by YHWH. The passage is a stark warning that what seems like the right or the easiest course of action is not always the correct course. In the contemporary world, when we often want to blame political leaders for their actions, we also frequently fail to take into account our own inactions. We too are responsible for "choosing life," for taking care of the ecological well-being of the earth, the health and welfare of others, and political crises both near and far.

Jeremiah 24:1—25:38; 27:1—29:32: Prophets, Prophecies, Power, and Politics

■ THE TEXT IN ITS ANCIENT CONTEXT

Jeremiah 24:1-10; 25:1-38; 27:1-22; 28:1-17; 29:1-32 largely focus on the relationship between prophets, prophecies, politics, and power, particularly the overarching theme that all power ultimately comes from YHWH. These chapters are united in their depiction of Babylon as YHWH's tool for punishing the errant Judahites, of Jeremiah as a true prophet, and a prophet to the nations. While Jeremiah 24 introduces the metaphor of those who remain in Jerusalem as "bad figs," Jeremiah 27 concludes with a reference to what will happen to those "bad figs" that did not go to Babylon as commanded.

Prophets in ancient Israel (and in the context of the larger ancient Near East) are often described as communicating with their god(s) in a variety of ways: through symbolic actions, judgment oracles, woe oracles, lawsuits, laments, and hymns (see Petersen, 28–30). Often, prophets report visions, such as in Isaiah 6 or Ezekiel 1–3. While visions play a prominent role in many prophetic books, the book of Jeremiah contains only a few. In 24:1-10, Jeremiah receives a vision of two baskets of figs: one is full of ripe, good figs, and the other is full of bad figs that could not be eaten. The surprising divine revelation is that the good figs represent the exiles: those who go to Babylon (Jer. 24:4-5; see Ezek. 11:14-15). In biblical writings, figs are associated with security and economic prosperity (see 1 Kgs. 4:25; 2 Kgs. 18:31; Isa. 36:16). Recalling the words of Jer. 1:10, those who go to Babylon will build (*bānâ*) and plant (*nātāʾ*); those who stay in the land will be overthrown (*hāras*) and uprooted (*nātaš*). The text also invokes the covenant formula, "they shall be my people and I will be their God," found in 7:23; 11:4; 30:22; 31:1, 33; 32:38. Additionally, YHWH promises that he will give these exiles a "heart to know me" (24:7; see 31:33-34), while 24:8 explicates that King Zedekiah, his officials, the remnant of Jerusalemites who remain in the land, and the exiles who fled to Egypt are the "bad figs," whom YHWH will "make a horror, an evil thing" to "all the kingdoms of the earth." Such a description starkly contrasts the promise to Abraham in Genesis 12, which is alluded to in Jer. 4:2; rather than becoming a blessing, Israel/Judah will become a "horror." The "bad figs" are destined for "sword, famine, and pestilence," and will be "utterly destroyed" (24:10).

Literarily, the passage is set during the rule of Zedekiah, following the deportation of Jehoiachin to Babylon in 597 BCE (see 2 Kgs. 24:8—25:30; 2 Chron. 36:9-21). The book of Jeremiah portrays Zedekiah and his supporters negatively, if at times ambiguously (see 22:27; 29:17; 2 Kgs. 24:10-17; see Applegate 1998). The passage reflects the three major geographical areas of interest during this tumultuous period: Babylon, where many were exiled beginning in 597; Judea, where a remnant remain; and Egypt, where others had already and would continue to go into exile (see Jeremiah 43). Although some scholars see this as an example of an actual vision Jeremiah had while at the temple (see Bright, 194; Allen, 275–76), others posit that the chapter is a later addition to the book (see Carroll 1986, 482–88). Carroll sees this later addition as a "propaganda" piece for those who returned to Jerusalem after the exile but traced their lineage to the first exiles who left with Jehoiachin in 597 BCE; the image thus supports through a divine revelation the returnees' claim to leadership positions in Jerusalem following their absence from the land (Carroll 1986, 482–88; see Brueggemann, 212). In short, the text clearly identifies with the exiles; those who remained or who fled to Egypt are left without hope.

Jeremiah 25 then goes back in time to the reign of Jehoiakim and the first year of Nebuchadrezzar's reign (25:1). Jeremiah complains to the people of Judah and Jerusalem that he has been speaking to them for twenty-three years, but they fail to listen, and he notes that he is part of a long line of prophets, whom "YHWH persistently sent you," and, like those who came before him, the people did not listen to those prophets either (25:4-7). Accordingly, enemies from the north—including King Nebuchadrezzar of Babylon—will attack, and YHWH will make the people "an object of horror and of hissing, and an everlasting disgrace" (25:8-9). Despite the use of "everlasting," 25:11 specifies the period of the exile as seventy years (25:11). In 25:12, YHWH promises, "after seventy years . . . I will punish the king of Babylon and that nation" (see Jeremiah 50–51). The addition of seventy might be the result of "the actual end of the exile and the return of deportees to the homeland" (Brueggemann, 222).

In another symbolic action report, YHWH commands Jeremiah to take a cup filled with "the wine of wrath," and sends Jeremiah to a list of nations who must drink from it (25:15). The result is madness and the coming sword (25:16). The list of nations is long (25:19-26) and concludes with "the king of Sheshach shall drink." Sheshach is a code word for Babylon, "a cryptographic device whereby letters of the alphabet in reverse order are substituted for letters in the proper order" (Carroll 1986, 500). In English, the letters *a-b-c* would become *z-y-x*; in Hebrew, the root *b-b-l* becomes *s-s-q*. The chapter ends with war imagery: YHWH of hosts is "summoning a sword" (25:29), he will "roar from on high" (25:30), "clamor will resound to the ends of the earth" (25:31), and the dead "shall not be lamented, or gathered, or buried; they shall become dung on the surface of the ground" (25:33). The deity, like a lion, will destroy the land "because of his fierce anger" (25:38).

Jeremiah 27:1 returns to the reign of Zedekiah. The passage is marked by a symbolic action: Jeremiah is to make a yoke of straps and bars and put them on his neck (27:2), and then he is to send word to the kings of a number of nations who have sent envoys to Jerusalem in the hopes of making a treaty against Babylon with Zedekiah (27:3). The yoke, used agriculturally with oxen, represents "political subjection" (Allen, 306). The message is this: YHWH has given Nebuchadrezzar his "servant" all of their lands. Any nation that refuses to "put its neck under the yoke of the king of Babylon" will experience the deity's divine wrath: famine, pestilence, and destruction (27:1-8). Such symbolic actions reiterate that prophets were speaking to their immediate contexts rather than predicting far-off events; even more so, Jeremiah's symbolic wearing of the yoke illustrates the strange behaviors associated with biblical prophets. Jeremiah's message clearly outlines that any earthly political power comes not through the hand of the king but rather through the will and strength of the Israelite deity.

Next, YHWH announces that the people "must not listen to your prophets, your diviners, your dreamers, your soothsayers, or your sorcerers" when they speak against serving Babylon (27:9). The only way to be saved and to keep their own lands is to obey YHWH (27:10-11), and Zedekiah should ignore the Judahite prophets who encourage him to rebel against Babylon; these prophets are "prophesying a lie" and were not sent by YHWH (27:14-15). Jeremiah implores the priests and the people not to listen to the prophets who claim that the stolen vessels from the temple will soon be returned to Judah (27:16). Rather, "serve the king of Babylon and live" (27:17), for a time is approaching when the remaining vessels will also be carried off to Babylon (27:21-22). Yet 27:22 ends on a note of hope: one day YHWH will return these stolen items to the temple.

Jeremiah 28 illustrates the interplay of power, politics, and prophecy in a scene that places Jeremiah into direct contest with another prophet: Hananiah, who challenges Jeremiah in the temple before priests and "all the people" (28:1), claiming that YHWH has told him that he broke the yoke of the king of Babylon, and that within two years the exiled king, people, and stolen property will be returned (28:2-4). The prophetic showdown continues as Jeremiah responds, at first by saying, "May YHWH do so!" (28:6). But he follows this with a reminder of the prophets who preceded them: it is only when the word of a prophet comes true that it can be known that YHWH sent that prophet (28:8-9; see Deut. 18:20). In response, Hananiah takes the yoke from Jeremiah's neck and breaks it (28:10). YHWH responds through Jeremiah by explaining that Hananiah has only succeeded in certifying the oncoming disaster; as a punishment, Hananiah will be dead within a year (28:16). Jeremiah's prophecy is then shown to be true: "In that same year, in the seventh month, the prophet Hananiah died" (28:17).

Next, Jeremiah sends a letter to the priests, prophets, and people in exile in Babylon. Within the letter is the prophetic messenger formula, "Thus says YHWH of hosts" (29:3). The command is surprising: live and prosper in the land of Babylon. The people are commanded to build houses, plant gardens, take wives, have children, and to marry their daughters so they too might "multiply there" (29:5-6). Moreover, they are to pray to YHWH on *behalf* of Babylon, for "in its welfare you will find your welfare" (29:7). The chapter continues to focus on the prophets and their power plays: the prophets among the exiles should not be allowed to deceive them because YHWH did not send them (29:8-9). Jeremiah 29:16-20 is absent from the Septuagint. Those who remained in Judah will suffer YHWH's wrath, and he will make them "like rotten figs that are so bad they cannot be eaten" (29:17). The letter concludes by addressing three specific prophets in Babylon: Ahab son of Kolaiah, Zedekiah son of Maaseiah, and Shemaiah of Nehelam, who will die as a result of their lies (29:21; 29:31-32).

▌ THE TEXT IN THE INTERPRETIVE TRADITION

In a rabbinic tradition, Jer. 24:6 is used in conjunction with Amos 9:15 to claim that once the Israelites are again "planted" in the land, they will not again be plucked up again (*Mek. R. Ish, Shirata* 10:10). A story in the Talmud relates that the prophets Ahab and Zedekiah from Jeremiah 29 were put to death because they asserted that YHWH commanded them to sleep with Nebuchadrezzar's daughter—connected to the captivity of Hananiah, Mishael, and Azariah from the book of Daniel, these two prophets were proven false when they were also thrown into the furnace but did not survive (*b. Sanh.* 93a).

In early Christian interpretation, the "bad figs" became a symbol for the synagogue, while the "good figs" symbolized the church (Wenthe, 181). Jerome emphasized that it is right to "seek the peace of the city or the land" where a person lives based on 29:7; similarly, Augustine urges people to pray for their kings, saying that Jeremiah gave the exiles "the divine command to go obediently . . . counseled them also to pray for Babylonia" (Wenthe, 198–99).

THE TEXT IN CONTEMPORARY DISCUSSION

For contemporary readers, questions of power and politics remain especially pertinent. The vision of the good and bad figs is one of God's merciless judgment, and one in which the deity is depicted as ultimately unforgiving. Such a black-and-white view of human morality can be comforting if we want those who do wrong to be punished, but such a categorical vision of the world is difficult to maintain. Surely not everyone who remained behind in Jerusalem and Judah were "bad figs." After all, as the text claims, many of those who stayed behind did not have the privilege of leaving because they were not among the elite of Jerusalem. Accordingly, this passage challenges contemporary readers to think behind the final form of the text and to examine the motives and contexts of the writers (see Weems, 119). Today the text dares readers to think about how we might address those who are left in frightening situations, in war zones and in occupied territories, or in the aftermath of natural disasters. Do we blame them for "bringing it on themselves," such as certain conservative Christian leaders blamed Hurricane Katrina on American "sinfulness"? If read with the victims and with those left behind, such a dichotomous text encourages readers to recoil from too easily accepting that there is always a "good guy" and a "bad guy" in any given situation, but rather to acknowledge that real life is often far more complicated than such easy oppositions. Moreover, it is a powerful reminder that such simple dichotomies often come at the expense of those who, materially, have the least.

Additionally, these passages with their emphasis on power and politics call on those in power to act conscientiously (see Masenya 2010, 148–49). These passages also call on people—both privileged and marginalized—to attempt to discern "true" prophets from "false" ones; as Weems notes, "Despite appearances, when it comes to prophets and their preaching, it is never easy to tell true ones from false ones—not back then and not now" (Weems, 23). Only history—per Deuteronomy—can tell the difference between a true and a false prophet.

Jeremiah 30–33: The Book of Consolation

THE TEXT IN ITS ANCIENT CONTEXT

Jeremiah 30–31 is frequently called "the Book of Consolation" or "the Little Book of Comfort," though an overarching hopeful theme unifies all of Jeremiah 30–33. Set amid so much lamentation, war imagery, and violence, "readers are simply not prepared for the explosive beauty of the 'little book of consolation'" (O'Connor 2012a, 103). Some scholars argue that this material may have originally been written for the northern kingdom, while others suggest an exilic writer later redacted the chapters (Stulman 2005, 258–59). R. E. Clements calls these chapters "the pivotal center for the entire book" (Clements, 8).

The Book of Consolation opens with YHWH instructing the prophet to "write in a book all the words that I have spoken to you" (Jer. 30:1). Since the unit opens with the divine instructions for Jeremiah to write "in a book/scroll" the words dictated to him, it is possible that parts of Jeremiah 30–31 were once part of an individual "book" (see Holladay 1989, 155–67). In Jeremiah 30–31, the phrase "the days are coming" frames the chapters, reiterating that these passages look to the future rather than the present (30:3; 31:27, 31, 38). The repeated use of the prophetic messenger formula, "Thus says YHWH," delineates the separate oracles (Jer. 30:2, 5, 12, 18; 31:2, 7, 15-16, 23, 35, 37; 32:3, 14-15, 28, 36, 42).

The oracle in Jer. 30:5-11 sets the stage for many of the important themes and metaphors that run throughout the Book of Consolation. The current situation is one of "terror without relief" (30:5); this is a topsy-turvy world where life is so calamitous that men are suffering pain "like a woman in labor" (30:6). Unusual for the book of Jeremiah is a somewhat positive depiction of a woman in labor, for here labor equals new life (Claassens, 122). Invoking both the exodus tradition and the promise of an eternal Davidic king (30:8), the passage ends on a note of hope: though YHWH will punish Israel/Judah (also reiterated in the oracle in 30:12-17), he will not make an end of them (see 30:11). The oracle in 30:18—31:1 focuses on rebuilding Jerusalem, while 30:22 invokes the covenant formula, "And you shall be my people, and I will be your God," indicating a future time when the relationship between YHWH and the people will be repaired. Yet 30:24 is a reminder that this restoration is in the future: "in the *latter days* you will understand this." Jeremiah 31:2-6 and 7-14 likewise invoke the exodus and wilderness traditions; in particular, 31:4 recalls Miriam with her tambourine (see Exod. 15:20-21; Stulman, 269). Jeremiah 30:5-6 may contain clues that this oracle once spoke to the northern kingdom. For example, the divine promise to "bring them [i.e., the survivors or remnant] from the land of the north" (31:8) elicits Jeremiah's initial predictions of an oncoming enemy from the north in Jeremiah 2–6, but may also be left over from Jeremiah's attempts at Josiah's behest to bring to Jerusalem some of the people who survived the Assyrian destruction of the northern kingdom in 721 BCE. In any case, "the text offers hope" to anyone living in exile or uncertainty; thus the audience might have originally been the "Judean exiles residing in Babylon during the sixth century" (Stulman, 258).

The short oracle in Jer. 31:15-22 is perhaps one of the most famous of the book of Jeremiah: Rachel weeps for her exiled children, and the text promises that her children shall be restored. Jeremiah 31:22 ends with gender reversal: a woman who courts a man (see 30:6), stressing the curious idea of YHWH forgiving his faithless wife and restoring her to the land—but also perhaps imagining a "changed order of relationships" in the gendered world of ancient Israel (O'Connor 2012b, 276). Jeremiah 31:23-34 emphasizes that with the return shall also come a new/renewed covenant: "And just as I have watched over them to pluck up and break down, to overthrow, destroy, and bring evil, so I will watch over them to build and to plant, says YHWH" (31:28; see 1:10). The focus, however, is still on the future: YHWH *will* watch over them to build and to plant. In this future period, children will be responsible for their own sins (cf. Ezek. 18:1-32, from which Jeremiah appears to draw, but which places such individual responsibility in Ezekiel's own period). Jeremiah's world remains ambiguous, trauma-filled, and uncertain. Nevertheless, in the future, the covenant will be rewritten into their hearts, from the "least of them to the greatest" (31:34).

Chronology falls apart in Jeremiah 32, which is set just prior to the siege of Jerusalem, when Zedekiah reigns and Jeremiah is imprisoned. Zedekiah approaches Jeremiah and implores him for help, but the prophet remains silent and Zedekiah merely repeats Jeremiah's prophecies about the city's fall to him (32: 3-5). When Jeremiah finally speaks, it is about an entirely different matter and seems to have happened before his imprisonment; the word of YHWH came to him and predicted that his cousin would arrive and ask Jeremiah to purchase a plot of family land (32:7-8). Jeremiah does so and then has Baruch take the deed of purchase and bury it in a jar (32:14). The symbolic action that Jeremiah recounts is one of hope: "houses and fields and vineyards shall again be bought in this land" (32:15). The land Jeremiah purchases becomes symbolic for all of the land of Israel.

Scholars regularly divide Jeremiah 33 into two sections: 33:1-13 and 33:14-26. The first section depicts the coming devastation with utter brutality, but closes by imaging Jerusalem once again filled with "the voice of mirth and the voice of gladness, the voice of the bridegroom and the voice of the bride, the voices of those who sing, as they bring thank offerings to the house of YHWH" (33:11), an about-face of 7:34; 16:9; and 25:10, which promised to bring an end to these things. Jeremiah 33:14-26 is missing from the Septuagint and is likely a late addition to the MT, which focuses on the restoration of the house of David: there remains a future for Israel (a message that would certainly have been good news to the exiles in Babylon). In short, the Greek and Hebrew texts of Jeremiah illustrate how later interpretive communities used (and sometimes added to) the textual tradition to address their own concerns and needs—and the presence of 33:14-26, often dated to as late as the Persian period, attests to the ongoing legacy of Jeremiah and his words.

■ THE TEXT IN THE INTERPRETIVE TRADITION

The image of Rachel weeping over her children in Jeremiah 31:15 draws on the story from Genesis 35, which records the death of Rachel. There the text reports how she named her last son Ben-oni, "son of my sorrow" (Gen. 35:18). Though Genesis is silent on the precise location of Rachel's burial, the book of Samuel locates her grave in Ramah (see 1 Sam. 10:2). The Jeremiah text appears to combine known traditions and is an excellent example of intertextuality in the Hebrew Bible.

Targum Jeremiah also illustrates interpretive differences. Instead of a "voice heard in Ramah," the *Tg. Jer.* reads "the height of the world": the Hebrew root *rmh* ("height") evokes "the highest heaven where God's throne is" (Hayward, 133 n. 13). Similarly, Rachel is no longer the one weeping; rather, "the house of Israel" weeps. The Targum draws on the idea that Jeremiah was at Ramah with the exiles before they left for Babylon (Jeremiah 40); Israel weeps because Jeremiah did not choose to go with them (Hayward, 131 n. 13).

The New Testament employs the image of a "new covenant" from the Book of Consolation (see Matt. 26:27-28; Mark 23–24; Luke 22:20; 1 Cor. 11:25; 2 Cor. 3:6), while Matt. 2:17-18 cites Jer. 31:15 in one of the fulfillment prophecies; namely, Herod's slaughtering of the children is understood as a fulfillment of the Jeremianic prophecy "foretold" by Rachel's weeping over her own children. Similarly, many early Christian interpreters drew on the image of Rachel weeping. For example, Ephrem the Syrian wrote that the passage was fulfilled in a "historical sense" when the sons of Judah and Benjamin where first sent to Ramah and then exiled to Babylon (see Jer. 40:1) and fulfilled in a "spiritual" sense when Herod slaughtered the innocent children (Wenthe, 208). Jeremiah 31:29-30, along with the "new covenant" in 31:31-32, would also be important for early Christian interpreters, since it claims individual responsibility for wrongdoing rather than inherited guilt from the wrongdoings of an individual's parent. Augustine wrote, "In this new covenant through the blood of the Mediator, the paternal decree having been cancelled, humankind by rebirth begins to be no longer subject to the paternal debts that bind them at birth" (Wenthe, 211). Numerous interpreters also used 31:31 as proof that the New Testament replaced the Old Testament, including Augustine, Irenaeus, John Chrysostom, and Theodoret of Cyrus (Wenthe, 212–13).

Beyond early Jewish and Christian interpretations, the Book of Consolation continues to be used in contemporary interpretations of the book of Jeremiah. For instance, Verdi's *Nabucco* (i.e., Nebuchadrezzar) is an Italian opera that in act 2 draws on Jeremiah 30 (the other three acts use Jeremiah 21; 50). In poetry, William Cowper's "Ephraim Repenting" draws on Jer. 31:18-21. Additionally, the image of Rachel weeping for her children often appears in art, including in a sculpture by Linda Gissen that was commissioned by a Roman Catholic bishop in the diocese of Richmond, Virginia, to teach about and honor those who died in the Nazi Holocaust.

▮ THE TEXT IN CONTEMPORARY DISCUSSION

The image of Rachel weeping for her children continues to speak across the ages, "for all the lost ones are the same to this mother, regardless of their generation" (Brueggemann, 287). The text has been invoked in discussions of the Nazi Holocaust, when examining the prevalence of gun violence in the United States and the frequent related death of young children, to other instances of violence against children, such as the kidnapping of young Nigerian girls in 2014. Rachel refuses to be consoled, and, similarly, contemporary readers can refuse consolation as they fuel both their outrage and social action in the face of senseless violence. The promise of return also offers hope to those who grieve.

In a book that otherwise often presents troubling images of women for contemporary readers, Jeremiah 30–33 provides positive descriptions of women who are "symbols" for the rebuilt life imagined by the text (O'Connor 2012b, 275). Here childbirth equals life (31:8), the voice of the bride will be heard (33:11), and the text depicts a different kind of relationship between men and women (31:22). Similarly, Jeremiah 30–33 delivers an opportunity to imagine God as healer, mother, and justice-seeker, images often associated with women (O'Connor 2012b, 277; see Jer. 30:17; 31:20, 33-34; 33:6). Broadly speaking, Jeremiah 30–33 functions as an integral part of "survival" literature for people clinging to hope in what might seem to be otherwise hopeless situations (see Weems, 123). Set in the middle of the book, it can speak to those people who are *still* suffering and *still* attempting to survive in the face of what may seem like hopeless situations.

34:1—36:32: Two Groups, Two Scrolls

▮ THE TEXT IN ITS ANCIENT CONTEXT

Jeremiah 34 again returns the book to the past; namely, Nebuchadrezzar's siege against Jerusalem and Judah. While Jeremiah predicts Zedekiah's own exile, he also promises that the king will "die in peace," and his death will be accompanied by all of the appropriate funeral rites known to ancient Israel, including spices and laments (34:3-5; see 52:8-11). Jeremiah 34:8-10 reports that Zedekiah made a covenant with the people in Jerusalem and allowed all Hebrew slaves to go free. Historically, this may have been done to help prepare the city for the Babylonian attack, especially in order to provide more people to fight. Many scholars suggest that this may reflect the period when Babylon temporarily stopped their march toward Jerusalem to deal with Egypt (see 37:3-15). However, 34:11 records an abrupt reversal of Zedekiah's proclamation of freedom.

The remainder of the passage outlines the ongoing problem of Israel's unfaithfulness. First, YHWH invokes the exodus tradition and the injunction to set free Hebrew slaves every seventh year (34:12-14). Citing the Judahites "turn[ing] [*šûb*] around" and taking back the slaves after their manumission, YHWH says, "You have not obeyed me by granting a release to your neighbors and friends; I am going to grant a release to you, says YHWH—a release to the sword, to pestilence, and to famine. I will make you a horror to all the kingdoms of the earth" (34:17). The covenant with Abraham is now void; the corpses of the Judahites will become food for animals (34:20). Gone are the promises of the appropriate funeral rites. Instead, YHWH promises to bring the Babylonians back to the city, where they take it and "burn it with fire" (34:22). Words of comfort are absent; the towns of Judah will become "a desolation without inhabitant" (34:22).

While Jeremiah 34 reiterates that Zedekiah and his officials stand in a long line of those disloyal to YHWH, Jeremiah 35 focuses instead on a group that is capable of maintaining righteousness. Again, the time period is set before the exile, although now the text returns to the days of Jehoiakim, sending the reader even further back into the history of Judah; such a temporal shift exemplifies that Judah's wrongdoing long precedes the reign of Zedekiah. Jeremiah is commanded to visit a group called the Rechabites (see Exod. 3:1; 18:1; 2 Kgs. 10:15-28; 1 Chron. 2:55; Neh. 3:14). The Rechabites lived according to a series of strict regulations: drinking no wine, building no houses, neither planting nor owning fields or vineyards, and living in tents (35:6-7). In short, the Jeremiah text depicts the Rechabites as nomadic tent-dwellers. Their unusual presence in Jerusalem is the result of the oncoming Babylonian army (35:11). When Jeremiah takes the Rechabites to the temple and offers them wine, they steadfastly refuse, citing the above-mentioned precepts (35:8-10). As is often noted, the Rechabites become the perfect counterexample to the people of Judah and, especially, to Zedekiah's actions in the preceding chapter. In contrast with Jeremiah 34, Jeremiah 35 ends with a promise of hope rather than devastation: for their faithfulness, the Rechabite descendants will continue to thrive for "all time" (34:19).

Jeremiah 36 returns to the fourth year of King Jehoiakim. Jeremiah is instructed to write YHWH's words on a scroll, summarizing all the words the deity spoke to Jeremiah since the days of Josiah "until today" (36:2), in the hopes that when Judah hears of the forthcoming disasters, they may "turn" (*šûb*) from their evil ways (36:3). Jeremiah dictates these words to Baruch, his scribe, and orders him to go and read the words on a fast day before all the people in the hopes that they might "turn" (*šûb*) (36:5-7). Next, the narrative moves forward into the fifth year of Jehoiakim during a fast, when Baruch reads the scroll in the hearing of Gemariah the secretary; Jeremiah's message is subsequently reported to the officials (36:9-13), who summon Baruch to bring the scroll and read it to them. Upon hearing it, the officials decide to tell the king (36:14-16), but they first instruct Baruch to go into hiding with Jeremiah (36:17-19). Following this, the scroll is read before the king (36:20-21), who, piece by piece, burns the scroll in a fire. The arrogant act appears to symbolize an attempt to nullify Jeremiah's words (for an alternative explanation, see Carroll 1996, 31–42). The king ignores the officials' warnings to heed the words of the scroll and instead orders that Baruch and Jeremiah be arrested; however, YHWH hides them (36:23-26). The final scene returns to another divine message from YHWH, in which the prophet is instructed to write the words again on a second scroll (36:27-28). Jehoiakim's fate is spelled out: his descendants will not sit on the throne, his body will not receive proper burial, and his children, servants, and all the people of Jerusalem and Judah will suffer "all the disasters with which I have threatened them" (36:31-32). The passage blames the king for the oncoming disaster, while the second scroll reiterates the divine origin of the prophecy, which cannot be ignored.

Although some scholars have attempted to find an original, historical book of Jeremiah behind this scene (see Holladay 1989, 253), Carroll suggests that the chapter is a fictional story based on 2 Kgs. 22:8-13 (Carroll 1986, 662–68). While the chapter may not reflect historical reality, it nevertheless contains important symbolic value: the chapter establishes Baruch as an authority, sent by Jeremiah and divinely commissioned to continue Jeremiah's prophetic mission. For Carroll, "Chapter 36 belongs more to Baruch's story than it belongs to Jeremiah's" (1996, 33). Additionally, Jeremiah 36 is an important chapter in the book, because it is one example of how "the book starts reflecting on itself" (Carroll 1996, 33). Scroll after scroll is recorded in the upside-down chronological world of Jeremiah, but the book continues to live long past the disaster the prophet predicted.

▌THE TEXT IN THE INTERPRETIVE TRADITION

The Mishnah records the existence of the Rechabites during the Second Temple, when a particular day was provided for them to make offerings (*m. Ta'an.* 4:5), while a midrash explains that the covenant made with Jonadab was greater than that made with David; Jonadab's covenant, based on Jer. 35:19, was unconditional, while the covenant made with David was conditional, citing Ps. 132:12 and 89:33 (*Mek. R. Ish., Amalek* 4:131). Often, the Rechabites are held in high regard in rabbinic literature (e.g., *Mek. R. Ish., Amalek* 4:120).

Similarly, early Christian readers also elevated the Rechabites as worthy of emulation, including Jerome: based on a comparison of the Rechabites, who lived outside in tents, to Moses who wandered in the desert, and to the followers of Christ who were first simply fishermen, Jerome claimed that "solitude [is] paradise," while Theodoret of Cyrus praised the Rechabites but also imagined "what sort of people . . . they would have been if they had heard the law of the gospel" (Wenthe, 230–31).

An apocryphal work titled *The Story of Zosimus* or *The History of the Rechabites* includes an expanded version of Jeremiah 35 (see Charlesworth 1985, 443–62).

▌THE TEXT IN CONTEMPORARY DISCUSSION

Unlike other places in the book of Jeremiah where all of the people are guilty, the story of the Rechabites provides readers with an alternate case. While the Rechabites are not Israelites, and so are in some way the "Other," they are nevertheless lifted up as an example of a faithful group blessed by the deity. The book of Jeremiah overall pays little attention to this group; nevertheless, they can be an example of resistance to cultural norms and imperial policies even as the text depicts them as "Other" and exotic (see Davidson, 189–207).

Additionally, the act of the king burning the scroll because it contains words that he is uncomfortable with is not an unfamiliar action in the modern world. Carroll writes, "In the twentieth-century book burning has become an art form" (1996, 39). From the burning of Jewish books by the Nazis, the banning of certain books in school libraries, to burnings of the Qur'an in the United States, the "art" of book burning continues to be a way that people express their discomfort over what might seem "other," strange, or dangerous to them. Yet what makes us uncomfortable can also teach us, challenge us, and offer us an opportunity for healing.

Jeremiah 37:1—45:5: The Baruch Account

■ THE TEXT IN ITS ANCIENT CONTEXT

In 45:1, the text names Baruch as the narrator of the preceding material, reiterating that Baruch was the scribe who wrote down the messages Jeremiah received from YHWH (36:32); Jer. 37:1—45:5 is often called the "Baruch account" and consists largely of third-person narratives about Jeremiah. O'Connor compares the Book of Consolation with the Baruch account, writing, "Whereas the little book of consolation promise that future life will be radiantly idyllic, the Baruch document focuses on immediate problems of brute survival" (O'Connor 2001, 518). Gone is the time for predictions and dire warnings; the siege and its aftermath unfold.

Jeremiah 37–38 focuses on Jeremiah's imprisonment during the reign of Zedekiah, once again radically shifting the chronological timeline. Again the book returns to the brief lull in the Babylonian invasion of Jerusalem as they dealt with the approaching Egyptian army (32:1, 3). Zedekiah implores Jeremiah to pray for him and the people (37:3). However, the deity's response is dire; Jeremiah is to tell the king that the Babylonians will return—and even their wounded men alone could destroy the city (37:10). Jeremiah 37:11-16 describes Jeremiah's arrest—charged with attempting to desert to the Babylonians—and imprisonment in the house of the secretary Jonathan, where he is placed in a cistern, likely a former repository for water storage. In 37:17-21, Jeremiah is brought before Zedekiah, who asks if there has been any reply from YHWH; Jeremiah answers in the affirmative, "You shall be handed over to the king of Babylon" (37:17). Zedekiah moves Jeremiah to the "court of the guard," which would have been located in Zedekiah's own house (37:21). In a haunting reminder of the realities of war, the text reports "a loaf of bread was given him daily from the bakers' street, until all the bread of the city was gone" (37:21).

Jeremiah 38 gives a slightly different version of this same story. As in the previous chapter, Jeremiah preaches that the city will fall at the hands of the Babylonians (38:2-3). Here the officials complain to the king that Jeremiah is "discouraging" both the soldiers and the people left in the city (38:4; see 21:8-10; 32:3-5; 34:2-5). Zedekiah allows Jeremiah to be imprisoned, but in this version of the story he is thrown into a cistern in "the court of the guard" (38:6). Lowered into the cistern by ropes, Jeremiah sinks into the mud (38:6), which may indicate a period close to 587/586 BCE and the ultimate destruction of Jerusalem when the cistern waters were beginning to dry up. Jeremiah

38:7-13 tells the story of Jeremiah's rescue from the cistern by a man named Ebed-melech, meaning "servant of the king," who is identified as a Cushite (often translated as Ethiopian) and a eunuch in the king's house. Notably, it is not Jeremiah's native supporters who rescue him, but rather a stranger and an Egyptian. In 38:14-28, the king again asks the prophet for divine support for his revolt, but Jeremiah declines to give him any reassurance, only repeating that surrender is the only way to ensure survival (see 20:1-16; 21:4-10; 27:1-11). Zedekiah fears for his life if he surrenders to the Babylonians, but Jeremiah assures him that he and his house will survive (38:20). However, if he continues to rebel, Jerusalem will burn, and Jeremiah reports a vision in which the women remaining in Zedekiah's house taunt him as they are led out, recalling Jeremiah's own previous imprisonment in the muddy cistern,

> Your trusted friends have seduced you
>> and have overcome you;
> Now that your feet are stuck in the mud,
>> they desert you. (38:22)

Zedekiah swears Jeremiah to secrecy about their conversation and moves Jeremiah from the cistern to house arrest (37:28).

Jeremiah 39 reiterates that Jeremiah's prophecies have been true all along. Zedekiah flees, but is captured by the Babylonians in the plains of Jericho, and brought before Nebuchadrezzar (39:3-6; see Jeremiah 52; 2 Kgs. 25). The results are gruesome: Zedekiah's sons are slaughtered "before his eyes," along with the nobles of Judah, and Nebuchadrezzar then "put out the eyes of Zedekiah" (a common practice in ancient Near Eastern warfare; see Judg. 16:21; 2 Kgs. 24:18—25:7), binding him in chains and taking him to Babylon (39:6-7). The king's house, the houses of the city, and the walls of Jerusalem are destroyed, and the "rest of the people" of the city are exiled to Babylon (39:8-9), although "some of the poor people who owned nothing" are left behind and given vineyards and fields to work (39:10). The Babylonian king then commands that Jeremiah be looked after but not harmed, and he is given to Gedaliah, one of Jeremiah's allies (39:11-14; see 26:24). The chapter closes with "the word of YHWH" that comes to Jeremiah: Ebed-melech will not be harmed because he trusted in YHWH, though Jerusalem is doomed (38:15-18).

The next two chapters describe life in Judah following the Babylonian invasion, when Gedaliah, a descendant of the Shaphan family who seems to have supported the Babylonians and warned against rebelling, functions as a Babylonian appointed governor (40:7). Jeremiah 40:1 places the prophet in Ramah, where he is offered release by the captain of the guard and the chance to accompany the captives being exiled to Babylon. However, Jeremiah is also given the opportunity to return to Gedaliah and to stay with the people, or to "go wherever you think it right to go" (40:5). Surprisingly, Jeremiah returns to Gedaliah rather than accompanying the exiles to Babylon (40:6). Mizpah, which means "watchtower" or "lookout" in Hebrew, is established as the capital following the destruction of Jerusalem (2 Kgs. 25:24-25). When the surviving remnants of Judah come to Gedaliah at Mizpah, he instructs them to serve the Babylonian king and to gather food (40:7-12).

The following material reports the assassination of Gedaliah at the hands of Ishmael son of Nethaniah (40:14-15; 41:1-3). The day following Gedaliah's assassination, a group of eighty men from Shechem, Shiloh, and Samaria arrive in traditional mourning attire to make offerings: their beards shaved, clothes torn, and bodies gashed (41:5). Ishmael meets them as they enter Mizpah and slaughters all but ten, throwing them into a cistern (41:6-7, 9) and taking the remaining people before setting out to the Ammonites (41:10; on the strange story of Ishmael, see Carroll 1986, 710–12). Upon hearing of this, Johanan son of Kareah, who had initially warned Gedaliah of the assassination plan, follows after Ishmael and his captives, meeting them at the pool of Gibeon (40:12). The captives with Ishmael join Johanan's forces (41:13-14), while Ishmael escapes to the Ammonites (41:15). The chapter ends by reporting that Johanan, the leaders of the forces, and the remaining people, including soldiers, women, children, and eunuchs, set out with the intention of fleeing to Egypt, fearing the Babylonians on account of Gedaliah's assassination (41:16-18).

Jeremiah 42:1 begins with Johanan and all of the remaining people approaching Jeremiah to ask for divine instruction (42:1-3). Jeremiah agrees to intercede with the deity on their behalf, and they agree to do as YHWH commands them (42:4-6). Ten days later, YHWH answers: remain in the land and YHWH will "plant you, and not pluck you up; for I am sorry for the disaster that I have brought upon you" (42:10; see 1:10). However, if the people are determined to go to Egypt, then "there you shall die" (42:16). There will be no remnant or survivors (42:17). Jeremiah 42 reports that the various leaders, including Johanan, accuse Jeremiah of lying and Baruch of inciting Jeremiah against them (43:2-3). As a result, the people go to Egypt, settling at Tahpanhes (43:4-7). Jeremiah and Baruch go with them to Egypt (43:6), where the word of YHWH again comes to the prophet, instructing him to perform yet another symbolic action (42:8-13). Jeremiah is to take large stones, bury them in the clay pavement before the Pharaoh's house in Tahpanhes and in the presence of the Judeans, and say to them, "Thus says YHWH of hosts, the God of Israel: I am going to send and take my servant King Nebuchadrezzar of Babylon, and he will set his throne above these stones that I have buried, and he will spread his royal canopy over them" (43:10). What will follow is, predictably, disaster: Nebuchadrezzar will ravage Egypt and destroy their gods; and pestilence, captivity, and the sword will come to all who are destined for them (42:11-13).

YHWH next reminds the exiles that they have seen the "disaster that I have brought on Jerusalem and the towns of Judah," especially because they made offerings to other deities (44:2-3). Moreover, the deity repeats that he continually sent prophets to warn them but that the people "did not listen or incline their ear" (44:5). Then YHWH accuses the people of continuing to make offerings to other gods while in Egypt (44:8), blaming their ancestors and their wives, their own crimes, but especially the offenses "of your wives, which they committed in the land of Judah and in the streets of Jerusalem" (44:9). The people reply in 44:15-19, stating that they will continue to make "offerings to the Queen of Heaven," claiming that when they did so in the past they prospered, but when they stopped, their lives took a turn for the worse (44:18). Jeremiah 44:20-30 reiterates the fate of these people: they shall all perish by sword and by famine, and Egypt will fall to its enemies just as Judah fell to Babylon.

The final section explains that when the words of YHWH came to Jeremiah, Baruch wrote the words in a scroll (45:1). The passage returns the story to the fourth year of Jehoiakim's reign, addressing YHWH's words to Baruch, and recalling Jer. 1:10 once again: "breaking down" what was built and "plucking up" of what was planted will happen (45:4). While Baruch's future is bleak, he will survive: a "prize of war" in the oncoming disaster (45:5).

▌ THE TEXT IN THE INTERPRETIVE TRADITION

While Baruch is mentioned only a few times in the book of Jeremiah, he lives on in both the Jewish and Christian interpretive traditions. A talmudic passage notes that both Jeremiah and Baruch were descendants of Rahab, a prostitute (*b. Meg.* 14b; see *Pesiq. Rab Kah.* 13:5). Another rabbinic discussion revolves around whether Baruch is also a prophet; one story recounts how Baruch complained that he was not, but was reminded by YHWH that after the exile there was no longer a need for prophecy because "there is no flock, what need is there of a shepherd?" (*Mek. R. Ish, Pisha* 1:148–66). Baruch is counted among the prophets in the Talmud (see *b. Meg.* 14b–15a).

In Christian tradition, Baruch is attributed with writing the deuterocanonical work Baruch, as well as the Syriac *Apocalypse of Baruch*, the Greek *Apocalypse of Baruch*, and a work referred to as *The Rest of the Words of Baruch* (*4 Baruch*). In the Eastern Orthodox Church, Baruch is considered a saint, and both Peter Paul Rubens and Henry Miller Block depicted the image of Jeremiah dictating to Baruch in paintings. Dietrich Bonhoeffer, when imprisoned by the Nazis after speaking out against the injustices he witnessed, wrote to a friend and fellow prisoner, "we shall have to repeat Jer. 45.5 to ourselves every day" (Bonhoeffer 1997, 279).

One notable component of Jeremiah 44 is the vilification of the Israelite's worship of the "Queen of Heaven." Despite the book's negative imagery, the text here (and in Jer. 7:18) may give contemporary readers a glimpse into what might have been the realities of ancient Israelite religion before it became more masculinized in the writings of later editors and redactors; in other words, it is possible that ancient Israelite women (and men) worshiped a female deity called the Queen of Heaven (see Jeremiah 44). As O'Connor notes, the women who worshiped the Queen of Heaven are "resourceful, independent women" who "become religious agents, taking worship into their own hands, as are many women today" (O'Connor 2012b, 273). In the contemporary world, such texts can encourage women to take up leadership roles within their own religious and nonreligious communities and can offer a counter-reading to the otherwise problematic gendered language of Jeremiah. Kathleen Norris's poem "Cakes for the Queen of Heaven" invokes Jeremiah 44 and reflects on gender relations in the book of Jeremiah and beyond.

▌ THE TEXT IN CONTEMPORARY DISCUSSION

On the one hand, the narrative in the Baruch account attests to the possibility of human choice; though Zedekiah repeatedly asks for Jeremiah's advice, he also repeatedly misses opportunities to "turn" from his ways and reform. Similarly, those who end up in exile in Egypt also miss their opportunity to listen to the divine command and do as they have been told. Yet the narrative also includes the story of Ebed-melech, which exemplifies both how one individual can save another's life and illustrates that it is possible to take an alternate position from the status quo. In more contemporary examples, it is possible to lift up the figures of Dietrich Bonhoeffer or Martin Luther King Jr. as those who were willing to call for reform and to exemplify such reform in their own lives.

On the other hand, it is important for contemporary readers to remember that exile is not always a matter of choice—and the results of resistance can be brutal.

The murder of Gedaliah offers a different problem for modern readers, where the question of theodicy resurfaces, and again God is entirely silent. Though Gedaliah remained in the land, a "good fig," he did not live; rather, he was brutally murdered. The deity is absent from these events, and the divine silence is troubling. Yet this silence is also "essential"; it allows the voices of the victims "to be heard" (Stulman, 328) rather than subsumed under divine explanation. In the face of unspeakable tragedy, perhaps divine silence is more appropriate and more akin to human experience.

Jeremiah 46:1—51:64: Oracles against the Nations

■ THE TEXT IN ITS ANCIENT CONTEXT

Jeremiah 46–51 consists of a series of "oracles against the nations" (OAN), a scholarly designation for a genre of literature commonly found in the prophetic material. Literarily, the oracles often begin by denouncing the enemy nations and then move on to a condemnation of Israel itself (see the book of Amos). Remarkably, despite the fact that Jeremiah was designated as a "prophet to the nations" in 1:10, there are only six chapters devoted to the OAN, while much longer sections consisting of prophecies concerning foreign nations are found in Isaiah 13–23 and Ezekiel 25–32 (see Petersen, 110). Outside of the Major Prophets, Obadiah and Nahum consist almost entirely of OAN.

The placement and order of the OAN in Jeremiah are different in the Septuagint and the Hebrew MT, the latter of which is found in contemporary English-language Bibles. In the Septuagint, the OAN begin in Jer. 25:14 (49:34 in the MT) and continue through Jeremiah 32. In the Septuagint ordering, the OAN follow the divine claim that the exile will last for seventy years, after which the deity will punish the nation from the north that he has first sent on Judah (Jer. 25:11-13). The Septuagint begins with Elam and concludes with Moab. The Hebrew MT, however, begins with Egypt and ends with Babylon.

Jeremiah 50–51 of the MT, written in both poetry and prose, is largely devoted to the fate of Babylon. For most of Jeremiah, the Babylonian invasion is depicted as appropriate; it is the will of YHWH and a just sentence for the people's inability to stay faithful to their God. However, in these passages, Babylon is depicted negatively: "Babylon must fall for the slain of Israel" (51:49). While some of the material may stem from the prophet himself, scholars suggests that because of the mix of poetry and prose, the blend of military (Jeremiah 50) and hymnic (Jeremiah 51) material, and the abrupt about-face concerning the role and fate of Babylon, the final two chapters are likely a collection of oracles from exilic and/or postexilic writers who are hoping for a return to the land (see Petersen, 127–28; also Isaiah 5–12; 13–14; 36–37; Jer. 15:17-18).

The OAN are united by a number of literary themes and metaphors. Perhaps most predominately, these oracles feature significant warfare imagery: Egypt's defeat is linked to the "Day of YHWH," when the deity would intervene in history to ultimately destroy Israel's enemies (e.g., Joel 2; Amos 5). Moreover, these texts frequently invoke "YHWH of hosts"—or, more literally,

"YHWH of armies" (Jer. 46:10, 18, 25; 48:1, 15; 49:5, 7, 26, 35; 50:18, 25, 31, 33, 34; 51:5, 14, 19, 33, 57, 58). The Hebrew *ḥereb* ("sword") appears repeatedly, accompanied by terrifying imagery and usually wielded by the deity. For example,

> A sword against the Chaldeans, says YHWH,
>> and against the inhabitants of Babylon,
>> and against her officials and her sages!
> A sword against the diviners,
>> so that they may become fools!
> A sword against her warriors,
>> so that they may be destroyed!
> A sword against her horses and against her chariots,
>> and against all the foreign troops in her midst,
>> so that they may become women!
> A sword against all her treasures,
>> that they may be plundered! (Jer. 50:35-37; see also 46:10; 49:37)

Frequently, the text depicts the warriors of the foreign nations mockingly—as beaten and fleeing (46:5), as compared to women (48:41; 49:22; 51:30), and as captured (51:56). The deities of the other nations are also discredited: YHWH defeats the Egyptian bull god Apis (46:15); Chemosh, the god of Moab, will be exiled and his people ashamed of him (48:7, 13); the Babylonian gods Bel and Marduk are "shamed" and "dismayed" (50:2), while 51:44 recounts how YHWH will

> . . . punish Bel in Babylon,
>> and make him disgorge what he has swallowed.
> The nations shall no longer stream to him;
>> the wall of Babylon has fallen,

reversing the image of 55:34 (Carroll 1986, 848).

The section concludes with a final symbolic action report in Jer. 51:59-64. According to this short narrative, Baruch's brother Seraiah (Jer. 32:12) accompanied Zedekiah to Babylon, and Jeremiah sent a scroll with him that included "all the disasters that would come on Babylon" (51:60). Jeremiah commanded Seraiah to read the scroll in Babylon, and then to tie a stone to it and throw it into the Euphrates River, saying, "Thus shall Babylon sink, to rise no more, because of the disasters that I am bringing on her" (51:64). The sense unit ends with the words "Thus far are the words of Jeremiah," a conclusion that leads many to suggest that Jeremiah 52 is a later addition.

Despite the terrifying war imagery and violence depicted in the OAN, there remains an element of hope that runs throughout the OAN—not just for Israel but also for the very nations that the oracles are prophesying against (see 46:26; 48:47; 49:6; 49:11; 49:39). With the exception of Babylon, each nation is promised a restoration (see 46:26; 48:47; 49:6; 49:11; 48:39). Babylon, however, will fall: ironically, it will fall to an "enemy from the north," recalling especially Jeremiah 1–4, where the "enemy from the north" approached, threatening Israel (also see 50:3, 9, 41; 51:48). The fact that Babylon will fall at the hand of an "enemy from the north" reinforces the cosmic and mythological nature of the threat throughout the book; it was always bigger and more terrifying than even the mighty Babylonian Empire. The people are urged to flee Babylon and to return home (51:46, 50). In the future when Israel is restored to the land, the "iniquity of Israel shall be sought, and there shall be none; and the sins of Judah, and none shall be found; for I will pardon the remnant that I have spared" (Jer. 50:20).

▌ THE TEXT IN THE INTERPRETIVE TRADITION

In contemporary Judaism, Jer. 46:13-28 is the *haftorah* (the reading from the Prophets) for the *parashah* (the reading from the Torah) of Exod. 10:1—13:16, and "counterposes the theme of Israelite servitude in Egypt in the *parashah* with a promise of Egypt's eventual destruction (Jer. 46:14-24)" (Fishbane 2002, 97).

In the Christian tradition, Jerome calls on believers to listen to Jeremiah's command to flee from Babylon in 51:6, connecting this passage with Rev. 18:2, to illustrate the seductive allure of "Babylon" while reminding his readers that nevertheless, "heathenism has been trodden down, the name of Christ daily exalted higher and higher" (Wenthe, 269).

In contemporary poetry, verses from Jeremiah 51 inspired both Edna St. Vincent Millay's "Make Bright the Arrows," and Thomas Hardy's "In Time of 'The Breaking of Nations.'" Jeremiah 51:7 is depicted in Simeon Solomon's 1859 drawing *Babylon Hath Been Given a Golden Cup.*

▌ THE TEXT IN CONTEMPORARY DISCUSSION

The vivid descriptions of violence, disturbing images of divine retribution, and bloody images of God as divine warrior in the OAN are difficult texts and not usually what one associates with "sacred" Scripture. YHWH is both vengeful and a god who flippantly uses and discards nations for his own purpose. At first, Babylon is YHWH's instrument in punishing Israel, but later God decides to take retributive actions against Babylon for performing the very actions that the text of Jeremiah claims God impelled Babylon to do. On the one hand, it is easy to dismiss these chapters as examples of the "unsophisticated" thought of ancient Israel, a time and a place far removed from our own. On the other hand—difficult though it may be—the OAN also provide an opportunity for contemporary readers to wonder about our own internal depictions of the deity: Do we imagine that God hates those whom we ourselves hate, those who seem "other" and foreign? Do we picture our God as loving and kind to us, but as a warrior to those who stand in our way? Moreover, in what ways do the realities of war depicted in the OAN continue to the present—including and especially against women and the marginalized (see Jeremiah 46)?

If contemporary readers of the OAN can move beyond the disturbing language, there are elements that may continue to be useful rather than simply disturbing. For example, with Stulman, if these texts emerged out of the "*world of worship and not warfare*, their weapons are rhetoric and imagination"—and therefore can be of use for people "who find themselves on the margins of society without power, temple, land, or hope," where "the only power they wield is the power of theater, which reimagines and reframes social reality" (Stulman, 384–85). Again, the book of Jeremiah gives voice to those who have suffered and may find themselves afraid to speak. Additionally, the occasional moments of hope and restoration for the enemy nations throughout the book of Jeremiah indicate that God can forgive. Examples such as Jer. 49:11 serve as stark textual prompts amid difficult language that God cares for the orphans and widows, even of his enemies.

Such a divine example can impel modern readers to move toward forgiveness—or at least, some form of reconciliation—for their own enemies after the appropriate healing has occurred. Perhaps this is the point of the vengeful, violence-filled OAN (or the imprecatory psalms, such as Psalm 137): there are "psychological benefits" to venting, honestly expressing feelings of rage and hurt (see Strawn 2013, 412). Such violence—especially when it is written and not acted out physically—becomes the space for recovery from trauma and disaster, returns agency and voice to survivors, the colonized, and the marginalized (see Strawn; O'Connor 2012a, 2012b; Weems).

Jeremiah 52:1-34: Historical Appendix

▋ THE TEXT IN ITS ANCIENT CONTEXT

As noted throughout, the book of Jeremiah renders both its characters and its timeline ambiguous at various points. The present form of the book now contains what scholars often deem a "historical appendix" (Jeremiah 52). In short, this chapter reiterates the story of Zedekiah's reign, the fall of Jerusalem, the series of deportations, and the release of Jehoiachin (Jer. 52:31-34; see 2 Kgs. 25:27-30). As is often observed, the chapter is a nearly word-for-word repetition of 2 Kgs. 24:18—25:21, 27-30, while 52:4-16 occurs in Jer. 39:1-2, 4-10. Overall, the addition of Jeremiah 52 appears to serve as proof that Jeremiah's prophecies were fulfilled (similarly, see Isaiah 36–39).

Jeremiah 52:4-6 indicates that the Babylonian siege lasted two years, ending only in the eleventh year of King Nebuchadrezzar (587/586 BCE). The enduring siege resulted in famine (52:6), and the text repeats the story of Zedekiah's flight and capture. Jeremiah 52:13 reports the devastating reality of the loss of the temple. In 52:15, the text records that some of the poorest people, along with others left in the city, are deported to Babylon; this is in contrast with the earlier deportation in 597 BCE, which largely included only the elite of the city. However, 52:16 also notes that some of the poorest people remained, "to be vinedressers and tillers of the soil." The remaining people will be a source of conflict in the Persian period of return (see Ezra-Nehemiah). The chapter continues with a lengthy list of all that was removed from the temple (52:17-23), a regular practice of conquering armies in the ancient world. Jeremiah 52:24 includes that "the chief priest Seraiah" was also deported (see 1 Chron. 5:40; Ezra 7:1).

The book concludes with the release of Jehoiachin from his Babylonian imprisonment, though he must remain in Babylon. The addition may have been a later editorial attempt to end Jeremiah in an encouraging way: a descendant of the Davidic line still lives and may yet return. Yet, as is fitting for Jeremiah, it is also ambiguous and open-ended: the former king is not returned to his land.

▋ THE TEXT IN THE INTERPRETIVE TRADITION

One of the issues resulting from Jeremiah 52 in Jewish tradition is that the dates do not correspond with those provided in the book of Kings. One talmudic passage explains the two different biblical dates listed for when Nebzaradan entered the temple (the 7th of Av in 2 Kgs. 25:8-9, but the 10th of Av in Jer. 52:12), by noting that the enemy entered the temple on the 7th of Av, vandalized it on that day and the 8th, kindled a fire in it on the 9th, but the major damage was done on the 10th of Av; nevertheless, the priority goes to when the catastrophes begin (*b. Ta'an.* 29a).

In Christian tradition, Chrysostom used Jer. 52:14-16 and the fact that only a small number of people remained in Jerusalem and Judah to argue, in a homily on Romans, that God saves people through "much kindness" and "faith"—but not because of their "own resources" (Wenthe, 271).

▌THE TEXT IN CONTEMPORARY DISCUSSION

Jeremiah ends with the fall of Jerusalem and Judah in 587 BCE, returning to the tragedy about which the prophet so drastically forewarned his contemporaries. For the readers of the final form of the book, this ending is not a surprise—the destruction of Jerusalem had already been foretold, told, and retold throughout the book. Furthermore, the original audience may have been those who survived the disaster itself. While the ending might be read as one that offers hope—a Judahite king is still alive, being treated with some kindness in Babylonian captivity, and thus hope for return and a new Davidic king is not entirely lost—the reappearance of the central tragedy of the book reminds readers of how the book of Jeremiah might function, as many scholars have suggested, as "survival" or "trauma" literature. The polyvocal text—with its jumble of poetry and prose, its displaced chronology, its violence and its hope, the speech *and* the silence of its characters—is ultimately a work that gives voice to readers' human experiences, both comforting and catastrophic. The book allows readers to imagine themselves in different places: as invaders and as exiles, as Babylon and as Jerusalem, as the powerful and the marginalized, as male and female, as divine and as human, and, perhaps most importantly, as a prophet who can give voice to the sometimes harsh reality of human experience and the catharsis of lament, as well as to the knowledge of divine presence *and* divine silence.

Works Cited

Allen, Leslie C. 2008. *Jeremiah: A Commentary.* OTL. Louisville: Westminster John Knox.

Applegate, John. 1998. "The Fate of Zedekiah: Redactional Debate in the Book of Jeremiah." *VT* 48, no. 3:301–8.

Atwood, Margaret. 1998. *The Handmaid's Tale.* New York: Anchor Books.

Bauer-Levesque, Angela. 1999. *Gender in the Book of Jeremiah: A Feminist-Literary Reading.* New York: Lang.

Bonhoeffer, Dietrich. 1997. *Letters and Papers from Prison.* Edited by Eberhard Bethge. Rev. ed. New York: Simon & Schuster.

Braude, William G. 1978. *Pešikta dě-Rab Kahaňa: R. Kahana's Compilation of Discourses for Sabbaths and Festal Days.* Philadelphia: Jewish Publ. Society of America.

———. 1968. *Pesikta Rabbati: Discourses for Feasts, Fasts, and Special Sabbaths.* New Haven: Yale University Press.

Bright, John. 1986. *Jeremiah: A New Translation with Introduction and Commentary.* AB. New York: Doubleday.

Brueggemann, Walter. 1998. *A Commentary on Jeremiah: Exile and Homecoming.* Grand Rapids: Eerdmans.

Carroll, Robert P. 1986. *Jeremiah: A Commentary.* OTL. Philadelphia: Westminster Press.

———. 1996. "Manuscripts Don't Burn: Inscribing the Prophetic Tradition; Reflections on Jeremiah 36." In *Dort ziehen Schiffe dahin*, edited by M. Augustin et al., 31–42. Frankfurt am Main: Peter Lang.

———. 2008. "Century's End: Jeremiah Studies at the Beginning of the Third Millennium." In *Recent Research on the Major Prophets*, edited by A. Hauser et al., 217–31. Sheffield: Sheffield Phoenix.

Charlesworth, James H. 1985. *Expansions of the "Old Testament" and Legends, Wisdom and Philosophical Litera-ture, Prayers, Psalms, and Odes, Fragments of Lost Judeo-Hellenistic Works*. New York: Doubleday.

Claassens, L. Julianna. 2013. "'Like a Woman in Labor': Gender, Postcolonial, Queer and Trauma Perspec-tives on the Book of Jeremiah." In *Prophecy and Power: Jeremiah in Feminist and Postcolonial Perspective*, edited by C. Maier and Carolyn J. Sharp, 117–32. London: Bloomsbury.

Clements, R. E. 1988. *Jeremiah*. IBC. Atlanta: John Knox Press.

Cohn, Herbert. 2004. "Is the 'Queen of Heaven' in Jeremiah the Goddess Anat?" *JBQ* 32, no. 1:55–57.

Davidson, Steel. 2013. "'Exoticizing the Otter': The Curious Case of the Rechabites in Jeremiah 35." In *Prophecy and Power: Jeremiah in Feminist and Postcolonial Perspective*, edited by C. Maier and Carolyn J. Sharp, 117–32. London: Bloomsbury.

Ellis, Teresa Ann. 2009. "Jeremiah 44: What If 'The Queen of Heaven' Is YHWH?" *JSOT* 33, no. 4:465–88.

Epstein, Isidore. 1961. The Babylonian Talmud. London: Soncino Press.

Fishbane, Michael A. 2002. *Haftarot: The Traditional Hebrew Text with the New JPS Translation*. Philadelphia: Jewish Publication Society.

Freedman, H., and Maurice Simon. 1983. *Midrash Rabbah*. London: Soncino Press.

Friedman, Richard Elliott, and Shawna Dolansky. 2011. *The Bible Now*. New York: Oxford University Press.

Hayward, Robert. 1987. *The Targum of Jeremiah: Translated, with a Critical Introduction, Apparatus, and Notes*. Wilmington, DE: Michael Glazier.

King, Martin Luther, Clayborne Carson, Ralph E. Luker, and Penny A. Russel. 1992. *The Papers of Martin Luther King, Jr. January 1929–June 1951 Volume 1*. Berkeley: University of California Press.

Holladay, William Lee. 1986. *Jeremiah 1: A Commentary on the Book of the Prophet Jeremiah, Chapters 1–25*. Hermeneia. Philadelphia: Fortress Press.

———. 1989. *Jeremiah 2: A Commentary on the Book of the Prophet Jeremiah, Chapters 26–52*. Hermeneia. Min-neapolis: Fortress Press.

Lauterbach, Jacob Zallel. 1976. *Mekhilta de-Rabbi Ishmael*. Philadelphia: Jewish Publication Society of America.

Masenya, Madipoane. 2010. "Jeremiah." In *Africa Bible Commentary*, edited by Tokunboh Adeyemo et al., 147–56. 2nd ed. Nairobi, Kenya: WorldAlive; Grand Rapids: Zondervan.

Nava, Alexander. 2001. *The Mystical and Prophetic Thought of Simone Weil and Gustavo Gutiérrez: Reflections on the Mystery and Hiddenness of God*. Albany: State University of New York Press.

Norris, Kathleen. 1989. "Cakes for the Queen of Heaven: A Poem in Praise of Darkness." *Journal of Feminist Studies in Religion* 5, no. 2:79–82.

O'Connor, Kathleen M. 2001. "Jeremiah." In *The Oxford Bible Commentary*, edited by John Barton and John Muddiman, 487–527. Oxford: Oxford University Press.

———. 2012a. *Jeremiah: Pain and Promise*. Minneapolis: Fortress Press.

———. 2012b. "Jeremiah." In *Women's Bible Commentary*, edited by Carol A. Newsom, Sharon H. Ringe, and Jacqueline E. Lapsley, 267–77. 3rd ed. Louisville: Westminster John Knox.

Petersen, David L. 2002. *The Prophetic Literature: An Introduction*. Louisville: Westminster John Knox.

Strawn, Brent A. 2013. "Sanctified and Commercially Successful Curses: On Gangsta Rap and the Canoni-zation of the Imprecatory Psalms." *Theology Today* 69, no. 4:403–17.

Stulman, Louis. 2005. *Jeremiah*. Nashville: Abingdon.

Stulman, Louis, and Hyun Chul Paul Kim. 2010. *You Are My People: An Introduction to Prophetic Literature*. Nashville: Abingdon.

Weems, Renita J. 2004. "Jeremiah." In *Global Bible Commentary*, edited by Daniel Patte, 212–25. Nashville: Abingdon.

Wenthe, Dean O., ed. 2009. *Jeremiah, Lamentations*. Ancient Christian Commentary on Scripture, Old Testament 12. Downers Grove, IL: InterVarsity Press.

Wiesel, Elie. 1981. *Five Biblical Portraits*. Notre Dame: University of Notre Dame Press.

LAMENTATIONS

Wilma Ann Bailey

Introduction

The book of Lamentations consists of a collection of five poems generally believed to have been composed subsequent to the conquest of Jerusalem by a Neo-Babylonian military force in 587/586 BCE. Most of the poems appear to be a response to that conquest or a similar event. They are focused on the plight of those who survived the carnage of war and remain in Jerusalem, a destroyed and depopulated city, whether by choice or happenstance after the elite and ruling families were carried away into exile. The authors of the poems are unknown, though tradition ascribes them to the prophet Jeremiah, which is why the book appears after Jeremiah in Christian Bibles. In Jewish Bibles, it appears in the collection known as the "Writings," following the book of Qohelet (Ecclesiastes). The Hebrew title for the collection is taken from the first word, 'ĕkâ, which is usually translated into English as a cry of distress, "How?" or "Alas!"

Laments are poems that express sorrow or grief and secondarily other emotions that are outcomes of pain and loss such as anger and bewilderment. The Hebrew word qînâ (plural qînôt) is sometimes translated "lament" and sometimes "dirge" in English Bibles. The two genres are similar. But unlike dirges, which are usually described as funeral songs, laments tend to have a hopeful element expressed, for example, in the form of an appeal to God for relief. Oddly, the word qinah itself is not used in the book of Lamentations, though it is used in other books such as Jeremiah, Ezekiel, Samuel, 2 Chronicles, and Amos. It may be that the ancient Israelites classified these poems differently. That is, they may not have thought of them as qînôt. Sigmund Mowinckel, a Norwegian scholar working in the first half of the twentieth century and using form-critical categories, identified two types of Laments in the Bible: national and personal. "Communal" rather than "national" may better describe the laments in the book of Lamentations because there is no nation, certainly not in the modern sense, in the aftermath of the fall of Jerusalem.

This article, which relies heavily on the author's research and writing for a commentary on Lamentations in the Believers Church Bible Commentary series (in process, Herald Press), will use Mowinckel's classifications because his work—in Western scholarly circles—is considered central in illuminating the genre. He points out that the "I" language found in many laments, though appearing to be an individual's voice, may in fact be a communal voice. According to Mowinckel, characteristics of the national lament include an invocation, a statement of complaint, a request for help, motivations for the request, a promise of sacrifice, expressions of thanksgiving, and a statement of assurance that the prayer has been heard (Mowinckel, 229–30). Few biblical laments actually exhibit all of these characteristics, though most have several. The sine qua non identifying mark is the statement of loss or complaint. Something has gone terribly wrong, and the lamenter is giving voice to it. Laments are a common biblical genre, and they appear outside of the book of Lamentations. According to Toni Craven, 40 percent of the psalms are laments (Craven, 26). It is believed that biblical laments were originally set to music and therefore sung. The sounds, tones, and rhythms are as significant as the meaning of the words. Nevertheless, they can stand by themselves because the pathos comes through.

Lamentations 1:1—5:22: We Have Known Grief

■ THE TEXT IN ITS ANCIENT CONTEXT

Four of the five poems in the book of Lamentations are structured as alphabetic acrostics, each line of poetry starting with a subsequent letter of the Hebrew alphabet in order. The Hebrew alphabet has twenty-two letters, yielding twenty-two verses in each chapter. The third poem is a triple acrostic. Each letter is repeated three times at the beginning of three lines in a row. The last poem, chapter 5, is the only one not structured as an acrostic, which may be a testimony to its independent origin. The acrostic structure may have been chosen as a mnemonic device or for aesthetic reasons. It has also been suggested that meaning is attached to the structure, in that it reflects the idea that grief must be fully expressed and then brought to an end. Life must go on.

The conquest of Jerusalem destroyed not just human lives, walls, and buildings but also political, social, and economic structures of southern Israelite life. It also caused a theological crisis. Zion and Davidic theologies, to which many in the southern tribe of Judah adhered, believed in the inviolability of Jerusalem and that there would always be a Davidic descendant on the throne of Israel. Now there was no throne, no independent Israelite state. Surviving Davidic descendants were imprisoned in Babylon. Something was needed to replace the weakened Davidic theology, but it had not yet emerged. Furthermore, one school of Israelite thought blamed disaster, whether personal or communal, on sin. Sin, it argued, caused God to either withdraw divine protection or directly use an enemy to punish. The poems in Lamentations express this conventional theology (a theology that is still dominant in the twenty-first century CE), but they also challenge it. The voices in the poems, for example, confess that they have sinned, but they seem to be at a loss as to what those sins were. They seem to not know what they could have done to merit such punishment. There is no listing of sins in the book or confessions of specific sins. One finds only vague allusions to rebellion or transgression. Moreover, the close juxtaposition of phrases describing the suffering of children to the confessions is a statement of protest, implying that the children, at least, had not done anything to merit the suffering they are experiencing. Therefore, it cannot possibly be just. A theology that always connects suffering to sin must confront the question of the justice of God. A just God would not cause the suffering of innocent children. The remnant is clearly struggling with how to understand God's role in the disaster. Through the lament form, the writers describe their situation in using both descriptive and metaphorical language. They express their feelings about it and their hopes for change or revenge. This essentially is the function of biblical lament.

■ THE TEXT IN THE INTERPRETIVE TRADITION

The primary way in which the book of Lamentations is used in the synagogue and church is as a lectionary reading in the liturgy. In the Jewish tradition, it is chanted in its entirety on the ninth of Ab, a summer (in Israel) fast day that mourns the Babylonian destruction of Jerusalem in 587/586 BCE, by the Romans in 70 CE, and other tragedies that have befallen the Jewish people. In Christian liturgical traditions, it is read in part or whole during Holy Week, most often on Good Friday, thereby associating it with the passion of Christ.

Outside of its function in the liturgy, the best-known part of the book is the middle section of chapter 3, which contains words of comfort, hope, and reassurance. The New Revised Standard Version (NRSV) translates them this way:

> The steadfast love of the Lord never ceases,
>> his mercies never come to an end;
> they are new every morning;
>> great is your faithfulness. (3:22-23)

Readers have tended to give primacy to this part of the book because it is consistent with common theological understandings about the nature of God. God is good and compassionate. It is also used as an interpretive pivot for the rest of the book. Chapter 3 begins with a complaint uttered by a person who is described as a *geber*, a word usually translated as "strong man." In the interpretive tradition, as articulated by Delbert Hillers, it has been assumed that this person is to be understood in one of three ways: as "everyman," an actual historical individual, or Israel, collectively (Hillers, 109, 122). However, *geber* is not used to describe an ordinary person elsewhere in the Bible. It describes an outstanding man, a militarily competent man, or prominent person. In Lamentations, it is a *geber* who feels that he is under attack by God. The point is, If such a man can be defeated, what hope is there for the ordinary person, whether male or female? Conventional statements about God's mercy and compassion in the middle of the chapter are interpreted to counteract the statements of despair uttered by the *geber*. But that is not enough to make the central section of chapter 3 the prevailing theology of the book. The additional content and complaints in the chapter and chapters 4 and 5, suggest that the *geber* and the lofty statements of chapter 3 must play an important but perhaps more limited role in the interpretation of Lamentations in the thought of the ancient redactors.

Traditionally, Lamentations has been read as a reflection on sin and deserved punishment. That assessment has been changing because of a greater willingness to confront the theological

difficulties that emerge when the question of innocent suffering is raised. The Zion figure prominent in chapters 1 and 2 has drawn the attention of scholars and other readers of the text and lead
them to a different way of interpreting it. Tod Linafelt, who has studied Lamentations alongside
other contemporary examples of "literature of survival," sees the Zion figure rather than the *geber*
as the interpretive key (Linafelt, 20–25). Survival literature is a witness that the catastrophe did not
exterminate a people. There are survivors, and life will continue. He points out that God is thought
to be the cause of the suffering in Lamentations but also the one to whom one appeals for relief,
revenge, or an explanation as to why the suffering has occurred. This creates a theological and ethical problem, particularly because Zion, like most places in the Hebrew Bible, is feminine in grammatical gender and personified in female imagery. Zion, Linafelt writes, is like an abused woman.
She must accept the abuse and confess that she deserves it. Texts in the Bible (though probably
not Lamentations because it is more a read than studied text) have been used inappropriately to
counsel abused women, insisting that they must have done something wrong to incur the wrath of
the abuser.

However, the Zion figure along with other female imagery in Lamentations may be interpreted
in another way, as being there to engender sympathy and protest against interpretations that blame
Zion and therefore the Jewish people for its own destruction. In chapters 1 and 2, Zion is imaged in
multiple female roles: a princess, a widow, a lover, an abandoned woman, a refugee, a woman forced
into servitude, a mother who has lost her children, a wanton woman, and a virgin daughter of Judah.
Many of these images envision Zion as a victim who deserves sympathy. Her former lovers have
deserted her. Her friends have betrayed her. She has suffered. She has lost her home, her place, her
status. In some of the images, but clearly not all, Zion is given agency and therefore held culpable
for the things that have befallen her.

Carleen Mandolfo constructs a theory about Lamentations which places it in dialogue with
prophetic books that also use the Zion imagery. In the prophetic books, Zion is silent in the face of
critique, but in Lamentations, she points out, Zion speaks. Zion's speaking in Mandolfo's interpretation is not just to the context of the book of Lamentations but to the prophets as well (Mandolfo,
59). She points out that the power dynamics in the dialogue between God and Zion must be taken
into consideration. God has more power, but that does not mean Zion does not have a credible
theological voice (Mandolfo, 85).

God in Lamentations is a literary character who reflects one theological point of view, and
Zion is a literary character (or set of characters) that reflect other theological points of view, and
then there is the distinct voice of the narrator who also has a theological point of view. When the
narrator blames Zion for having sinned, Zion does not respond to the narrator's charge; rather, she
appeals to God to notice her suffering. She blames her lovers (generally understood to be political
allies) for having deceived her. The pattern of the shifting of blame is similar to that of the man and
woman in the garden in Genesis 3. Zion's appeals suggest a theological position that even when one
bears some responsibility in a wrong, God's compassion can mitigate the punishment.

In Lamentations, God is spoken about, but God speaks only once, in a recollection of the com-
poser of the third poem. There, in 3:35, the poet confesses that God did respond when called on. The
message that God brought was "Do not be afraid" (author's translation). This standard formulaic

phrase is found in many places in the Bible. Usually, the context is a theophany. Typically, either God or a divine messenger appears and says, "Do not be afraid," before providing further instructions. In Lamentations, the phrase is followed not by further words from God but by the poet affirming that God has redeemed him, has seen his affliction, and will bring about justice. In Lamentations, the narrator describes what he (or she) understands to be God's role in the suffering, as does Zion and the *geber*. God never agrees or disagrees with the role assigned by the narrator, Zion, or the *geber*, but God does speak a word of comfort and hope. In four of the five poems, however, God is silent.

Chapter 4 contains a poignant description of the aftermath of war. Starvation and a collapse of the social structures are highlighted. The poet draws attention to the persons who in the poet's estimation have suffered the most: the children who are starving and abandoned, and the elite who have been debased. This poem focuses on the religious elite, the prophets and priests. They are blamed for having brought on the crisis by "pouring out the blood of the righteous" (Lam. 4:13 author's translation). This idea is consistent with Jeremiah 35, where it is the elite, the shepherds, who are to be blamed for the disaster, not the ordinary folk. The chapter ends with a call for vengeance against Edom. Edom did not attack Jerusalem, but it took advantage of it after the Babylonian army completed their work, leaving the city open and vulnerable according to the book of Obadiah.

The fifth chapter of Lamentations is different from the others, not just in that it lacks the acrostic structure, but in its character. More so even than chapter 4, it highlights socioeconomic differences in ancient Israelite society and the differences between the way in which the conquest affected the wealthy and the poor. The chapter, like the others, is primarily complaint, but it is the complaint not of all Israelite society but only the elite. The elite now live as the poor do every day. The complaint is that this is not right. The social order has been turned upside down. The elite in the normal order are those who rule. But in the aftermath of the war, "servants [or slaves]" are ruling over them. The rich complain that they have been reduced to grinding and gathering wood and other chores that the lower class normally performs for them every day. The elite used to own the resources, but now they have to pay for them, like the poor do. They are outraged by the injustice of it all. But they seem incapable of realizing that what they are now experiencing is the everyday lot of their former servants, the poor, and the ordinary people in ancient Israelite society.

▌THE TEXT IN CONTEMPORARY DISCUSSION

Lamentations raises a number of issues that merit discussion in contemporary times. One is the question of sin and its relationship to suffering. In both Jewish and Christian traditions, sin is thought to be a cause of suffering. This leads to the next step, where the sufferer is said to be the cause of his or her own suffering or alternatively that God is punishing the sufferer because of sins that he or she committed. In Lamentations, Zion assumes that she must have committed some grievous sin to merit the suffering that she is experiencing, but she is at a loss to know what the sin is. To be sure, sometimes individuals do suffer as a result of their bad behavior, but too often this line of thinking leads to blaming victims both as individuals and as religio-ethnic groups such as the Jews or a socioeconomic group such as the poor for their own oppression. Blaming the victim diverts attention from structures, powers, and policies that sin against individuals and communities causing suffering and scapegoating. When God is thought to be punishing persons or groups for sins, oppressors or those who stand by can justify their actions or inactions as being complicit with God's justice. This theology also suggests that if the individual or group stops sinning, the suffering that is a result of punishment meted out by God may be mitigated. God is merciful and will forgive if confession is made or repentance ensues.

The notion that sin and suffering are related can have a positive impact in that suffering created by humans can be corrected by humans. If the sin is one's own, one can stop sinning and the suffering will come to an end. If someone else or some institution is causing the suffering, the institution can be forced to change its ways. Justice can be brought to unjust situations. These things are not outside the control of the human community because they are not just a matter of fate or happenstance. This theology of sin has justified evil but also spawned great works of justice and charity. Both Jewish and Christian traditions also recognize that some suffering is not attached to sin. This is more difficult to understand and more difficult to correct. The book of Job deals with that issue, as do portions of Lamentations (e.g., 2:11-12; 4:2-4). They do not provide answers to this difficult question, but they do recognize it is there and pose a challenge to conventional theologies that posit God as all good, all just, and all-powerful. Harold Kushner struggles with this issue in his well-known book, *When Bad Things Happen to Good People* (see the 2004 reprint of this classic).

Another issue raised by Lamentations is the hiddenness of the real culprits in disaster. Is it the tornado or flood, or is it a weakening climatic system caused by human intervention, or is it caused by unseen divine forces? The book raises the issue of the role of God in disaster and how the role of God is to be interpreted in Scripture. God speaks only once, and then a word of comfort, yet several of the voices in the book including Zion, the *geber*, and the narrator blame God for the disaster. Jerusalem was destroyed by an armed Babylonian force, not God, but God is blamed. The theological notion in play is that God is the cause of all that happens, both good and bad. The Babylonian fighting force was simply a tool for God. The images that we create of God in circular fashion shape our images of God as they get passed from generation to generation. We might ask ourselves, What are our images God, Where did they come from, and, Why do they continue? Why do we blame God when humans have clearly created a disaster? Is God the scapegoat for humans, or are humans the scapegoat for the actions of God?

Calls for vengeance, which are not rare in biblical poems of lament, are discomforting for modern readers. Contemporary theologies teach that vengeance is never an appropriate response to experienced evil. Most modern readers dismiss the calls for vengeance as a reflection of a more primitive mind-set. This, too, is a way to claim superiority over other people without attempting to understand the function of these calls for vengeance in the ritual of ancient Israel. The question is, Is a call for vengeance to be equated with taking vengeance, or is it a way to express how one feels? If one is granted permission to emote, does that mitigate the need to act on one's feelings? What is the function of the calls for vengeance, and what did it mean in its ancient literary context? Is there a place in the liturgy or spiritual practice for calls of vengeance today?

Lamentations is essentially a tool to help people and groups move through the grieving process. It is not meant to be used alone. It is one part of the liturgy, one part of acts of mourning such as tearing one's clothing and putting ashes on one's head. It accompanies the visits by families and friends and the wailing of the professional mourning women. The book in effect gives permission to mourn and grieve losses in a way that is emotive and at times disturbing. One is freed to say exactly what one thinks at the moment. Some Western communities have moved away from rituals of mourning altogether. Even after a death, rituals celebrating a person's life have taken their place. Is this a move in a healthier direction, or is this a way to distance one's self from the pain of the loss?

The structure of Lamentations suggests that mourning should be expressed fully and emotively, and then mourning should be brought to an end. It is inappropriate to be like Jacob, who upon being led to believe that his son Joseph had been torn apart by a wild animal said that he will "go down to Sheol to my son, mourning" (Gen. 37:35). A time for mourning must give way to a time for dancing according to Eccles. 3:4. That is the way of the world. The community cannot afford to lose the input and productivity of one of its own to perpetual mourning. One must get on with life not only for one's own sake, but also for the sake of the living community.

Works Cited

Craven, Toni. 1992. *The Book of Psalms*. Collegeville, MN: Liturgical Press.

Hillers, Delbert. 1992. *Lamentations,* revised edition. Anchor Bible. New York: Doubleday.

Kushner, Harold S. 2004. *When Bad Things Happen to Good People*. New York: Knopf Doubleday.

Linafelt, Tod. 2000. *Surviving Lamentations: Catastrophe, Lament, and Protest in the Afterlife of a Biblical Book.* Chicago: University of Chicago Press.

Mandolfo, Carleen R. 2007. *Daughter Zion Talks Back to the Prophets*. Atlanta: Society of Biblical Literature.

Mowinckel, Sigmund. 1979. *The Psalms in Israel's Worship*. 2 vols. Translated by D. R. AP-Thomas. Nashville: Abingdon.

EZEKIEL

Corrine L. Carvalho

Introduction

The book of Ezekiel is set against the backdrop of the fall of Jerusalem. The book contains several dates that cover a twenty-year span, from July 593 BCE to March 573. For the original audience, these dates were ominous. As the book opens, Judah is a colony of Babylon. The king Jehoiachin and his staff have been exiled to Babylon in 597, and a puppet king, Zedekiah, rules in his stead. But after a rebellion by Zedekiah, the Babylonians besiege Jerusalem, destroying the city in 587, and exiling a significant number of its elite citizens. Judah ceases to exist as an independent state, and the religious identity of its citizens is seriously compromised. Even by 573, there is no indication that the nation would be restored.

The prologue of the book (1:1-3) introduces its main character, Ezekiel, a priest who was exiled in the first deportation of 597 BCE. This opening marks Ezekiel as part of the elite class, whose work supported the royal ideology of the time. The oracles in the book express the experience of destruction and exile from this specific social location. Ezekiel represents the male elite of the preexilic period who lost status, prestige, and honor in the fall of their city.

The book is clearly written from the perspective of male urban elites. For them, Judah's identity is threatened by their loss of land ownership, the destruction of the temple, and the treatment of the Davidic monarchy. The book views the ideal society as one based on male patriarchal privilege, and both disaster and restoration are defined in terms of male landowners.

The elite perspective is also found in more subtle elements of the book, such as the literary quality of the book. The oracles display a profound familiarity with various literary and intellectual traditions not just in Judah but also in the wider context of the ancient Near East. The author deliberately uses earlier traditions to create new and startling images. The oracles are detailed and intricate, while the book is more organized than most prophetic texts, including Jeremiah and Isaiah.

The preservation of Ezekiel's oracles in written form is a deliberate part of this text. The prophet is depicted as made mute by God in chapter 3 and told to eat a scroll, indicating that the written version of the oracles is more important than their oral form.

A priestly perspective permeates the book as well. Ezekiel is not an elite male who happened to be a priest. Rather, the depictions of sin and restoration both are told in priestly terms. Sin leads to urban defilement. Defilement prompts God to abandon the temple, and that divine abandonment results in the fall of a city bereft of its divine warrior. The image of God on a throne borne by cherubim, an image tied to God's presence in the temple, provides structure to the book. Ezekiel has a vision of this enthroned God within the temple in chapter 1. God leaves the city in chapters 8–11 and returns as a mark of restoration in chapter 43. The book ends with a nine-chapter vision of a restored Israel, at whose center stands an ideal temple inhabited by God on this throne.

The book is told from a male perspective. Women are hardly mentioned, and when they are, they serve male concerns. Two chapters (16 and 23) personify the city as a woman in a way that indicates the presumption that female behavior is only important for the way it affects male honor. Human women appear most prominently in the condemnation of female prophets in 13:17-23 and the death of the prophet's wife in 24:15-18, but these also reflect male concerns. Unlike the book of Lamentations, for example, there are no poems that describe the fall of the city from the experience of wives and mothers.

In this patriarchal culture, male honor becomes the uppermost social value. Shame only exists insofar as honor is possible. Much of the book's rhetoric flows from the shame the male elite experienced in the fall of their city and their new status as forced laborers in exile. But in a surprising twist, the book does this by encouraging the male elite to embrace their experience of shame. It accomplishes this by the way it depicts God. The book aims to preserve the honor of YHWH by casting God as the ultimate male head of household. This rhetorical strategy makes the human male elites inferior to this divine head of household; the book uses the notion of shame to recast them as underlings of this sovereign Lord. The purpose of the shameful defeat of the male elite was to reveal to them their true status as low-class persons with no rights in comparison to their patriarchal divine head.

The book insists that God's actions, whether in Israel's glorious past, in their present state of shame, or in their future restoration, are all predicated on the preservation of divine honor. Two repeated phrases drive this idea home. First, the text repeatedly states that God acts for the sake of the divine name or reputation. Second, God constantly asserts that "I am YHWH." Both statements are assertions of divine honor and prerogative. God does not act out of love; "he" acts only to assert his divine right.

These social assumptions make it difficult for contemporary audiences to appreciate the book. In fact, some contemporary scholars have wondered whether its author suffered from mental illness. The book presents vivid images of a God actively destroying the city, shaming its citizens, constantly reminding them that they deserve nothing. Readers expecting a loving, nurturing God will not find it here. The rhetoric of the book is meant to shock and aggravate its audience, so that they question their own assumptions about human election and divine power.

Contemporary readers often want to reject the view of God the book projects. Interestingly, the book hints that the ancient audience had a similar reaction. Ezekiel 33:32-33 states that the people came to hear Ezekiel, not because they believed he was a prophet, but because they considered him an entertainer. They too wanted to distance themselves from the theology he presented.

The book of Ezekiel insists, however, that its audience needs to face what tragedy and loss reveal about the nature of God and humanity. Its setting urges its readers to hear the voices of people like Ezekiel, those marked by tragedy and unspeakable loss. It reminds its audience that even today war refugees suffer not just economic hardship but also shame, especially when they undergo a significant loss of status. The book calls on today's elite to recognize that an elite status is just an illusion, one that draws faith communities away from God. Those who truly understand God's power are those for whom "exile" becomes part of their innate identity.

Ezekiel 1–3: The Opening Vision

▌ THE TEXT IN ITS ANCIENT CONTEXT

The first three chapters, sometimes referred to as the call of Ezekiel, describe Ezekiel's first prophetic experience and set out the book's view of the prophetic office. They also introduce the three main characters in the book: the measly mortal Ezekiel, the kingly God, and the rebellious people. The first three verses introduce Ezekiel as an elite priest who now lives in Babylon as an exile.

Ezekiel's call begins with a vision of God in the temple of Jerusalem before the fall of the city. Most prophetic visions were short; Amos sees a basket of fruit (8:2), and Micaiah is shown a battlefield (1 Kgs. 22:17). Ezekiel's vision of a portable throne is striking for the level of detail that it utilizes. Similar to Isaiah's vision of God enthroned above the seraphim in Isaiah 6, Ezekiel 1 describes heavenly beings that support the throne (identified as cherubim in 9:3), the appearance of the throne, the sounds of the wings, and the clothing of God. The vision progresses from bottom to top, and as it gets closer to describing God, the language begins to fail.

God does not speak until the second chapter, where the prophet is given an overview of what he is being called to do. The speech characterizes the people of Israel as rebellious. This term, often used in the Pentateuch to describe the people when they sinned, is applied in a variety of ways in Ezekiel. Sometimes their rebellion takes the form of violating God's laws (Ezekiel 20). Other times, it refers to political rebellion (17:12-15). Ezekiel 2:7-9 describes them as hard as a stone, meaning that they are unrepentant and stubborn in their rebellion.

God defines Ezekiel's role as prophet. Chapter 3 describes the prophet as a sentinel on a city's walls whose job it was to warn the inhabitants of an advancing enemy. This book views the prophet as someone who warns Israel of its fate unless they take immediate steps to prevent it. But the book has already noted that they will not be warned, foreshadowing their refusal to recognize him as a prophet. They are stubborn, unwilling to change, so that Ezekiel's message contains words of "lamentation and mourning and woe" (2:10).

These chapters make clear that Ezekiel has no agency in what will follow. He is dragged to Jerusalem in a vision in chapter 1 and returned to Babylon, stunned, in 3:15. God addresses him throughout the book, not as a "man of God" (the title for prophets in the historical books), but as a "mere mortal" (literally "son of man"). Ezekiel is simply God's mouthpiece. This point is driven home at the end of the call narrative, when God makes the prophet mute except when pronouncing an oracle (3:24-27). Since Ezekiel cannot speak on his own, the things he says in the rest of book are to be viewed as God's own words.

▌ THE TEXT IN THE INTERPRETIVE TRADITION

The opening vision of the book of Ezekiel, which is repeated in chapters 8–11 and 40–48, became a prominent image in both the Jewish and Christian traditions. Ezekiel's text became the springboard for descriptions of other heavenly journeys found in later Jewish apocalyptic texts. In postbiblical Judaism, it became the basis for a stream of Jewish mysticism called "Merkabah mysticism" (*merkabah* is the Hebrew word for "chariot"), which viewed the chariot as an allegory for heaven itself (see Sweeney).

A different allegorical tendency is seen in Christian exegesis, which viewed the four faces of the cherubim as allegories for Christian Scripture. On the one hand, they represented the four parts of the Christian Old Testament (Law, History, Wisdom, Prophets) mirrored by the four parts of the New Testament (Gospels, Acts, Epistles, Revelation). On the other hand, they foreshadowed the four evangelists, where each of the four evangelists is represented by one of the four animals in the vision. The wheel within the wheel became a standard metaphor for the relationship of the Old and New Testaments: the New was hidden within the Old (Stevenson and Glerup, 11). These interpretations are prominent up through the Reformation period, when they began to wane. Reformers identified the enthroned figure in this vision as Christ (Beckwith, xlvi and 16–20).

▌ THE TEXT IN CONTEMPORARY DISCUSSION

One of the biggest challenges for contemporary readers of the book is to recognize the social location of the original audience of the book. The book's rhetoric is aimed at justifying the fall of Jerusalem as an act of God. In order to do this, it portrays its citizens as fully deserving of such violence. Contemporary readers often want to identify with the character of God, and thus rush to judge these ancient people as sinful and rebellious.

Contemporary discussions of the book, however, assume a different starting point. The book reached its final form after the destruction of the city. Death, violence, degradation, and displacement were everyday realities for the book's original audience. That reality undercut every pillar on which Israelite identity depended: gone were its political, religious, and social institutions. No longer were they Israelites whose nation was founded on a covenant with YHWH. They were forced laborers in Mesopotamia, displaced refugees in Egypt, and colonized farmers in a land occupied by a foreign army.

Daniel Smith-Christopher applies the insights of refugee studies to the exilic literature of ancient Israel. He notes that one of the most prominent results of such a tragedy is an overwhelming feeling of loss of control. If the event(s) is viewed as capricious or unprovoked, then a community has more difficulty overcoming feelings of dread and foreboding. Individuals and communities who fare best after trauma are those who take some responsibility for their fate, which restores a sense of control. Kathleen O'Connor's (2002; 2012) analysis of Jeremiah and Lamentations couples this perspective with the insight that the other prominent result of trauma is loss of language, especially when the trauma overwhelms the person or community. Literature of trauma attempts to provide language for overwhelmingly tragic experiences.

What distinguishes an exilic text like Lamentations from that of Ezekiel is that, while Lamentations describes the fall of the city from the perspective of its human inhabitants, the book of Ezekiel puts the description of the disaster into the mouth of God. These descriptions then become folded into a rhetoric of castigation. As a result, the same events that the book of Ezekiel describes seem to be exalted rather than mourned. It hides the fact that both texts affirm the breadth of the disaster that the people of Judah experienced. Neither book backs away from how horrible those events were; they do not minimize them, ignore them, or belittle them. The honesty with which Ezekiel speaks of the city's horrors alone gave their suffering purpose or meaning.

Ezekiel embodies how war feels to former elites rendered helpless. Since he is portrayed as a righteous sufferer, the prophet's portrayal tempers the book's overt rhetoric that the punishment was deserved. His fate shows that not all sufferers had been evil sinners, and that tragedy strikes all alike.

Ezekiel 4–7: Oracles before God Leaves

▌ THE TEXT IN ITS ANCIENT CONTEXT

Ezekiel's prophetic activity begins in earnest in chapter 4. The first oracles take the form of symbolic acts, a form the book inherits from the Israelite prophetic tradition. For example, Isaiah walks around naked for three years as a sign that Israel will be left with nothing once God's punishment comes (20:2-4). Ezekiel does three complicated symbolic acts. First, he acts out the sieges of Samaria and Jerusalem (4:1-17), then he shows the various ways people will die when the city falls (5:1-12), and last, he prophesies against mountains (6:1-7). Each of these is followed by an explanation of the symbolic public performance.

Behind these texts is the reality of siege warfare that shaped so much of the cultural memory of the ancient world. Throughout the ancient Near East, literature can be found that describes cultural fears of sieges. Many of them contain similar descriptions of death through violence, disease, and even cannibalism. Ezekiel 4:9-17 focuses on the realities of gradual communal starvation. Chapter 5 reflects the varieties of ways people die in times of ancient war; even those who survive the war itself (represented by the hair in the prophet's hem in v. 3) are still vulnerable to violent deaths in exile.

While similar events are described in the book of Lamentations, the insistence that this fate is deserved makes Ezekiel's versions more difficult to appreciate. Chapter 6, in particular, blames ritual sins as the cause for the destruction. In keeping with the book as a whole, the chapter characterizes sin as defilement. God promises to destroy the religious institutions of Judah, symbolized by the destruction of altars, because their worship has become idolatrous. While this may be a reference to worship of other gods, the same language is also used for any ritual irregularity even in the worship of YHWH.

This section introduces other major themes that will permeate the book. First, the detail of God's command that Ezekiel cook his food on human dung (4:12) reinforces the uneven power structure that is at the heart of Ezekiel's relationship to God. Second, the reader will experience the siege, fall, and destruction of the city through the character of Ezekiel. Since the book depicts the prophet as fully controlled by God, even when that experience horrifies him, it represents the reality that the Judeans' fate was also forced on them.

Ezekiel 6:7 contains the first of many repetitions of the phrase, "then you shall know that I am the Lord." This phrase, which punctuates the book, sums up the reason for the horrible events it describes: to reveal God to the world. What is shocking about Ezekiel's version of divine self-disclosure is that God is revealed not through acts of mercy and kindness but rather through violence and destruction. Even chapter 7, which contains the first oracles in the book in a poetic form, seems to relish the violence that it describes. Here the audience encounters multiple vibrant pictures of the realities of siege warfare, which unrelentingly blame the victim for its violent fate.

▌ THE TEXT IN THE INTERPRETIVE TRADITION

Pre-Enlightenment texts rarely commented on how the prophet is depicted in the first six chapters of the book. That focus has shifted in the modern period. With the rise of psychoanalysis in the nineteenth century, many scholars began to ask whether the prophet suffered from some sort of psychosis. The most recent example is David Halperin's conclusion that Ezekiel had been molested as a child and blamed his mother. While these interpretations flow out of the odd language of the book, they fail to deal directly with the book's own testimony that Ezekiel's "trauma" was the fall of the city. By assigning the "real" meaning of these disturbing oracles to the author's personal psychosis, interpreters distance themselves from the horrors that the text describes.

Another way scholars have distanced themselves from the text's overt meaning has been the recent trend to view exilic texts like Ezekiel that describe the horrors of the war and its aftermath as propaganda by the former ruling elite to project themselves as the true Israel. Hans Barstad states that texts that describe the land as empty or the whole country as devastated were myths designed to assert the exiles as the "true" Israel. He concludes that the fall of the nation did not disrupt most people's lives, only the lives of the elite.

Such approaches to exilic literature distance contemporary readers from the texts' explicit content. The images of devastation in the book of Ezekiel must have resonated enough with the post-fall community for it to be preserved even though the texts are so shocking. This history of interpretation demonstrates common approaches to disturbing biblical texts: they are either ignored, trivialized, or resisted.

▌ THE TEXT IN CONTEMPORARY DISCUSSION

Contemporary witnesses to war remind us that the tragedies of war are experienced at every level of society. The book aptly describes the multiple ramifications of a war-torn society. Although the most obvious deaths come from enemy fire (swords in the ancient world), death takes many forms as a nation-state crumbles. In fact, it is telling that the book pays less attention to death in armed combat and more to the tragedy of a lingering death through disease and famine. During a siege, when a city is cut off from its food and water supplies, food rations become insufficient to keep the population healthy. Those weakened through starvation are more vulnerable to illness, and, as food supplies rot or water becomes contaminated, those sickened by food-borne illnesses are more likely to die.

Contemporary readers who use a variety of stances to distance themselves from the shocking language of the book can fail to recognize that what it describes is the reality of many people even in today's world. War destroys communities, not just with bombs or guns, but through the destruction of reliable sources of clean water and food. Even today, those who have escaped war-torn countries find themselves in refugee camps, where they are still vulnerable to violence and lacking adequate food and clean water.

This section of Ezekiel begins and ends with the twin companions to death by the sword: death through starvation and disease. It represents the reality of those who have lived through war only to find that their safety is still precarious. To hear Ezekiel is to hear the fate of too many in our world today.

Ezekiel 8–11: God Leaves the City

▌ THE TEXT IN ITS ANCIENT CONTEXT

The opening oracles of Ezekiel are followed by another vision report, which describes the prophet's second visionary journey to Jerusalem about three years before its siege. Here the prophet sees the chariot throne described in chapter 1 leave the temple and its city because of the defiling sins of the urban elite.

Chapter 8 has a clear ritual focus. The sins that it describes are ritual sins, and their effect is ritual defilement. In the ancient world, the rituals associated with temples were designed to keep this divine residence protected from contact with the profane world. Courtyards that surrounded temples formed circles of protection from anything ritually unclean. Priests were charged with ensuring this security.

Although the exact nature of the rituals that the prophet describes in chapter 8 is unclear, they are obviously not producing the effects the worshipers hoped for. Instead of guaranteeing their security, they cause the city's only divine resident, YHWH, to leave. In the ancient world, cities were under the protection of a patron deity; once that deity left, the unprotected city was vulnerable to enemy attacks. These chapters follow this motif of divine abandonment. They linger over descriptions of God's chariot throne and detail God's slow progression outside of the city. YHWH is first transported to the door of the sanctuary building (9:3, repeated in 10:18). From there it flies up to the east gate of the inner courtyard (10:19), and finally leaves the city in 11:23. At this point, the reader knows that the city is doomed.

The passage also describes a variety of heavenly beings that carry out God's decrees. The creatures that bear God's throne are explicitly identified as cherubim (9:3), multiformed creatures that served as divine guardians throughout the ancient Near East. It also introduces six heavenly executioners who slay sinners (9:1-2). Finally, there is a recorder who marks those whom the executioners should spare (9:3-4). We are never told how many, if any, the recorder marks for survival. Instead, the passage focuses on the widespread death wrought by the executioners (9:5-6).

In the midst of chapter 11 is a brief oracle of hope. Verses 17-20 look for the return of the exiles and the restoration of Israel, even though the city has not yet been destroyed. As with all of the oracles of restoration in the book, this one will not be motivated by the people's behavior: they do not repent and are no better than when God sent them away. The remedy to this problem is a heart transplant (replacing a dead heart [stone] with one that is alive) and the infusion of a new spirit. The result will be a community that will keep God's commandments, thus not defiling the land again.

▌ THE TEXT IN THE INTERPRETIVE TRADITION

The Christian tradition was fascinated by the marking of the righteous. Christians noted that this angel marked the people with the Hebrew letter *tau*, which was shaped like a cross. Therefore, Origen states that the mark prefigures the rite of baptism, which includes marking the baptized with the sign of the cross on their forehead (Stevenson and Glerup, 34–35). This interpretation persists even into the Reformation period, where the divine figure is identified as Christ.

One of the difficulties of this passage is that, although the angel seems to mark some people as righteous, the chapter describes the destruction of the whole city. Steven Shawn Tuell (185–202) compares how this passage is treated in both rabbinic writing and in Calvin. While the rabbis state that the righteous are punished for not preventing their neighbors from sinning, Calvin distinguishes between the physical death felt by everyone in the city and the spiritual salvation of the righteous through the gift of eternal life.

▌ THE TEXT IN CONTEMPORARY DISCUSSION

While on the surface these chapters seem to address only ancient assumptions about divine activity, beneath them is a more troubling question that has plagued many communities of faith. Where is God when disaster strikes? If God is powerful, how can tragedy happen? Images of divine abandonment were one way ancient peoples negotiated the tension created by their assertions of divine beings who are powerful and can control the world over against their experience of communal tragedy. The motif of divine abandonment protects the belief in a powerful God. Israelite texts that use the images of abandonment also strive to maintain God's justice. This is not a capricious and untrustworthy god, but rather one who acts according to principles of justice. It is fascinating to see how much blame this community was willing to accept in order to maintain that their God is both powerful and just, despite the fall of the city.

This is not just an ancient problem, though. Even today, people who have experienced great tragedy often describe their suffering as God's will. Some fundamentalists like Pat Robertson have claimed that natural disasters, such as Hurricane Katrina, are punishments from God for the legalization of abortion. To many other American Christians, such claims are not only untrue but also offensive. Using human tragedy as an opportunity to make a political statement seems like the basest abuse of religious authority. As a result, many American Christians are reluctant to say that national calamity is God's judgment for sinful behavior. Yet even with this reluctance, many of them still find comfort in the belief that God has a purpose in their suffering even if that purpose is not clear in the midst of the tragedy.

Ezekiel 12–13: True and False Prophets

▊ THE TEXT IN ITS ANCIENT CONTEXT

These two chapters focus on the role played by prophets in the years leading up to the fall of the city. These oracles are dated to three years before the siege of Jerusalem, while Zedekiah, the king appointed by the Babylonians, was on the throne. Although the city had been enjoying peace for seven years, these chapters depict this time as Judah's last chance to listen to its prophets.

Although there are many accounts of prophets preserved in the Bible, the fact is that there were many more prophets who existed at any given time in Israel. The biblical texts preserve glimpses of the controversies that arose when prophets disagreed. In these two chapters, it is clear that inhabitants of Jerusalem either don't believe prophets like Ezekiel who warn that the city will fall or they believe that these warnings pertain to some distant future. Ezekiel calls their complacency "rebellion" (12:2).

The two chapters condemn both the prophets who give false hope and the people who do not believe the prophets who warn of disaster. Chapter 13:17-23 includes an indictment of female prophets. Although this passage is our only evidence of a professional class of female prophets in Judah, the details of their activities accords well with what we know of female prophets in Mesopotamia. Female prophets tended to work in groups, have less prestige than male counterparts, and use divination as an accepted vehicle for prophetic statements. It is important to notice that Ezekiel's criticism of them is not based on gender; all prophets who prophesy "out of their own imagination" (13:1 and 17), whether they are male or female, are condemned.

In contrast to these false prophets, chapter 12 characterizes Ezekiel as a true prophet. In this symbolic act, performed in Babylon, Ezekiel's metaphoric flight closely mirrors the final fate of Zedekiah, as related in 2 Kgs. 25:4-7. Although the passage may have been revised or added after the fall of the city, the rhetorical effect of this detailed account marks Ezekiel as an unusually accurate prophet.

That characterization is reinforced in 12:6 and 11, two of the three times in the book when Ezekiel himself serves as a prophetic sign (the other is in 24:24). Ezekiel embodies the prophetic message. In both passages where he serves as a sign, the text states that what happens to him will happen to the whole community. Ezekiel is not only a priest of the temple but also the embodiment of the perfect prophet and its message.

▊ THE TEXT IN THE INTERPRETIVE TRADITION

These chapters in Ezekiel also do not garner as much attention as the visionary material in the book. Like many Old Testament passages that deal with false prophets, the description of false prophets in chapter 13 becomes an occasion for Christian exegetes to talk about heretics in their own day, as is found in Jerome's commentary on Ezekiel (Stevenson and Glerup, 45–50).

THE TEXT IN CONTEMPORARY DISCUSSION

While this passage focuses on the failure of the prophets in a time of crisis, Ezek. 7:26 castigates other religious leaders as well. The ancient Israelites, like people today, turned to their religious leaders for guidance in times of crisis. Notice, however, that this passage does not place all of the blame on the religious leadership's failure to discern the situation properly. It also condemns the people who hear only what they want to hear. Although it may be easy to understand why they would have ignored a prophet who was not even in the city, the text makes clear that the real problem is the people's unwillingness to confront their own responsibility for their nation's fate. The book of Ezekiel reminds its readers that not only are political and religious leaders responsible for communal ethics but responsibility also rests equally with those who hear the message but choose not to listen.

Today's world is not that different. Perhaps a stark example is found in the media treatment of the sermons of President Obama's pastor, Rev. Jeremiah Wright. During Obama's first run for the presidency, Wright's review of America's history of colonial expansion and racist policies, including how these attitudes should temper responses to the events of 9/11, were often used to present him as a false and even dangerous prophetic voice. Yet, when his sermons are heard within the context of African American liberation theology, he demonstrated the connections between white treatment of indigenous peoples, race-based slavery, and contemporary politics. It remains a message many people do not want to hear.

Ezekiel 14 and 18: Moral Responsibility

THE TEXT IN ITS ANCIENT CONTEXT

In any disaster, people immediately begin to wonder who is to blame. These two chapters demonstrate that the ancient world was little different from our own. Both of these chapters, however, virulently deny that the blame for the fall of the city could be displaced either onto an earlier generation or onto some small segment of the population. Ezekiel does not let anyone in his own generation off the hook.

Chapter 14 seems to be responding to the assertion that the prophets had not adequately warned the people, and are to blame for the city's fall. The chapter assumes the three major activities of ancient prophets: people could ask them to get an oracle from God on their behalf; they could deliver oracles that had been revealed to them for the whole community; and they could intercede to God on behalf of the people. Ezekiel 14 asserts that these prophetic functions have all been in place, so the true prophets are not to blame.

Chapter 14 keeps the blame on the people in three ways. It denies oracles of salvation to those who are sinners (vv. 7-8), and it promises punishment for false prophets (vv. 9-11). More prominently, however, it deals with the question of intercession. In 14:12-20, the longest section of the chapter, the oracle asserts that Israel's sins are so great, God will respond to no one's intercessions on their behalf, not even three legendary righteous heroes from Israel's past: Noah, Daniel, and Job. All three of these figures were blameless individuals who suffered in spite of their righteousness. Because this chapter is about the responsibility of the prophetic voice in the national crisis, the chapter is really about Ezekiel's inability to avert the disaster that befell Jerusalem. By using the characters of Noah, Daniel, and Job, the chapter projects Ezekiel as another innocent sufferer whose pleas for the people God rejects.

Chapter 18 deals with a different issue: the question of intergenerational punishment. There are many biblical texts which assert that God punishes later generations for the sins of an earlier generation. The Ten Commandments, for example, state that God will punish "children for the iniquity of parents, to the third and the fourth generation" (Exod. 20:5). Ezekiel's lengthy chapter goes through various scenarios of parents and children committing sins, each time stating that the sinner alone deserves punishment. This was clearly a hotly debated topic at that time. The proverb that is quoted in 18:2 is also quoted and denied in Jer. 31:29-30. The denials of this view in both Ezekiel and Jeremiah make sure the generation that experienced the fall of the city would recognize that they alone were responsible for its fall.

Last, it must be recognized that chapter 18 is not about individual responsibility; it is about intergenerational punishment (Joyce). The book of Ezekiel is more ambiguous about individual responsibility. While it asserts that God holds individuals responsible for their sins, it also knows that many innocent people suffered in the various deportations by the Babylonians and in the destruction of the city. Chapter 14's portrayal of innocent sufferers suggests that Ezekiel was one of those whose suffering was not the result of his sinful behavior. In addition, ancient texts tend to focus on the suffering of landowners and their individual responsibility without questioning that the result of their punishment is often meted out on their whole households (wives, children, servants, and slaves), regardless of their personal behavior.

▌THE TEXT IN THE INTERPRETIVE TRADITION

With both of these chapters, patristic writers focused on the efficacy of repentance for the forgiveness of sins. John Chrysostom uses 14:12-23 to argue that the righteousness of a person's ancestors will not save a person; they only serve as a model of righteous behavior (Stevenson and Glerup, 54). Augustine and Ambrose, among others, apply a similar message to chapter 18. Repentance brings life, which, for these Christian exegetes, means eternal life (Stevenson and Glerup, 76–85).

In the Reformation, these chapters became the basis for discussions about repentance and grace. The discussion of repentance in chapter 14 led William Greenhill, for example, to note that repentance is the work of the Spirit, while Calvin tempers Ezekiel's statement that Noah, Job, and Daniel were saved by their righteousness (Beckwith, 72–80). Similarly, the discussion of salvation in chapter 18 led Reformers to discuss the efficacy of adherence to the law, the question of double predestination, and whether one who has been saved can turn back to sin (Beckwith, 98–108).

Another passage that draws comment is the statement in 18:23 and 32, repeated in 33:11, that God takes "no pleasure in the death of the wicked." John Sawyer notes that, although Luther does not pay much attention to the book of Ezekiel throughout his writings, he quotes this verse some sixteen times in a variety of settings (2011, 4).

◼ THE TEXT IN CONTEMPORARY DISCUSSION

American culture valorizes rugged individualism to such a degree that it often masks communal interdependency. Yet, even with the rhetoric of the individual, there are ways that questions of intergenerational and intercommunal responsibility leak out. Statistics show that a higher percentage of those incarcerated suffered from child abuse than is found in the general population. Those abused as children experience increased rates of substance abuse, mental illness, and symptoms of post-traumatic stress disorder. On a communal level, it is also clear that one generation's misuse of natural and financial resources is felt more by later generations than by those who wrought the damage. Later generations do, in fact, suffer for the acts of earlier generations.

Communities suffer the effects of the sins of individuals, especially when those individuals have a leadership role. Workers often pay an undue price for fiscal mismanagement of a company's resources. Families can be torn apart when a parent abuses alcohol or becomes violent. Here is where it is important to remember the book's social location. Ezekiel 14 and 18 do not deny that much suffering is undeserved, but these chapters attempt to make those in leadership positions recognize that their own elite status does not release them from liability. They have sinned, and God holds them accountable.

Ezekiel 15, 17, and 19: Parables, Allegories, and Laments

◼ THE TEXT IN ITS ANCIENT CONTEXT

These three chapters use literary genres found more often in nonprophetic texts. Chapters 15 and 17 are extended allegories, a category associated with proverbial literature. Chapter 19 is a dirge, or funeral song. The use of vines, plants, and lions to represent the nation and its leaders is found in both the literary record and Judean iconography. Prophetic texts such as Isa. 5:3; Hosea 10:1; and Jer. 2:21 liken Israel to a vine. The king is a plant in Isa. 11:1, while the nation is an olive tree in Jer. 11:16-17. Royal seals from Judah show that the symbol for the Davidic monarchy was a lion. While chapter 15 uses the vine to represent the fate of the city as a whole, chapters 17 and 19 focus on the role the final kings of Judah played in these turbulent times. The details of the allegories are complicated, and scholars disagree about what each element of the symbols means, but even with this ambiguity, certain things are clear.

First, the poems maintain the focus of blame on the inhabitants of Jerusalem. Nowhere is Babylon condemned for its attacks on Judah. In chapter 19, the nation is consumed in an act of self-immolation (19:12-14). Second, Ezekiel objects to Zedekiah's rebellion against Nebuchadnezzar (17:11-21; see also 2 Kgs. 24:20—25:1). When royals made treaties, they swore by their patron gods to uphold the treaties. Ezekiel uses this to cast Zedekiah's rebellion against Babylon as a rebellion against God.

Last, these poems are the work of a literary master. The author creatively uses poetic forms that fit different situations to deliver damning indictments against the nation and its leadership. Chapter

19's use of the dirge is especially delicious: it is a funeral song delivered while the king is still alive, a bit like running the obituary for a sitting president. The artistry is found in the creative ways the author uses traditional forms and motifs to deliver detailed oracles about the international politics of his day.

◼ THE TEXT IN THE INTERPRETIVE TRADITION

In the Christian tradition, chapter 17 receives far more attention than either chapter 15 or 19. In part, this is because Jesus' speech in John 15 that he is the vine and believers are the branches shares more vocabulary with Ezekiel 17 than with similar images in either Isaiah or Jeremiah (Manning, 36–40). While Jerome picks up on this idea and identifies the vine as Christ, Origen focuses more on the branches, interpreting the image as the church (Stevenson and Glerup, 75–76).

◼ THE TEXT IN CONTEMPORARY DISCUSSION

Sometimes a political cartoon can capture outrage better than words; these chapters are verbal cartoons. They remind readers that, although much of the rhetoric in the book seems to address individuals, the book is really a critique of the international policies that led to the nation's fall. In today's world, criticism of American policies during periods of disaster is often labeled unpatriotic. These poems challenge contemporary communities of faith not to confuse patriotism with naiveté or, worse, self-righteousness.

In post-9/11 America, criticism of American policies, especially in the Middle East, is often deemed anti-American. Yet Ezekiel's assertions that Judah's quest for aid from Egypt was a root cause for the fall of the city, especially in a time when Egypt was Judah's only ally, is a far more radical statement than contemporary critiques of America's policies throughout the Middle East. What Ezekiel proposes means either total capitulation to Babylon or full destruction of the city, yet he bases these claims on a sense of Judah's true identity as completely under God's control. Patriotism is not blind acquiescence to political powers, but stems rather from a broader sense of a nation's ethical identity. Sometimes the most patriotic thing a person or group can do is protest.

In the 1960s, feminists often noted that the personal is political. These poems put a different spin on this adage: the spiritual is political. The focus on international politics as the arena for faith-based decisions adds a different lens for our current debates about religion and politics. While the media often casts disagreements over personal decisions such as abortion and marriage equality as religious issues, faith-based critiques of war or foreign policies are often ignored. The biblical text insists that faith-based groups should ponder the relationship between international relations and religiously informed ethical principles.

Ezekiel 16 and 23: City Leaders as God's Wives

◼ THE TEXT IN ITS ANCIENT CONTEXT

These two chapters, so troubling to contemporary readers, take another common metaphor found in Israelite prophetic literature, that the city is like God's wife. Ezekiel's version develops it in creative and disturbing ways. That creativity is designed to provoke outrage in the readers, a task it still accomplishes today.

The personification of capital cities as women is found in Jeremiah and Hosea in particular. The metaphor works because of the ancient understanding of marriage. In Israel, husbands and wives were not equals; men had legal control over their wives. As was true for any subservient person within the household, the male head of household was allowed to beat his wife (and slaves and children) as punishment for their wrongdoings. Wives who were caught in adultery could be stoned to death, while those suspected of adultery had to undergo a ritual ordeal to prove their innocence. Male honor was preserved through the behaviors of his dependents. Women's actions were evaluated by whether they brought honor or shame to their male partners.

Jerusalem and Samaria were like wives, because they were dependent on God for all they had. They owed complete allegiance to God, who could punish them for any challenge to his male-defined authority. Worshiping other gods was tantamount to adultery, punishable by death. One of the goals in both chapters is to get the male audience to accept their shameful, dependent status in relationship to God.

In these two chapters, Ezekiel's use of the metaphor is far more graphic than what is found in other prophetic books. In fact, many modern translations of the texts tone down the sexually explicit language of the Hebrew text. Both chapters review Israel's history, describing the founding of the nation and its subsequent history. In both historical reviews, the wives are completely undeserving of God's notice of them. Neither text states that the marriage was based on love. The details in the chapters distinguish the two versions of the metaphor. Chapter 16 deals with the history of Israel's religious practices, practices cast as idolatrous and therefore deserving of capital punishment. Chapter 23, on the other hand, again deals with international relations. The lovers are allies of Judah, and the courting of those allies is depicted as "whoring" after illicit lovers.

The graphic rhetoric makes it all too easy to forget that these female figures are metaphors and are not descriptions of real Judean women at the time. In fact, the wicked women actually personify the male elite of these cities. These chapters require the male audience to identify with the sexually uncontrolled female figure, although they might rather identify with the male husband. Rhetorically, these passages feminize their male audience.

Feminization was one way to shame a man. It casts the man as someone who was controlled and subservient. In ancient Near Eastern literature, the defeat of soldiers is likened to rape and the labor pains of a woman who dies in childbirth. Prisoners of war were stripped, mutilated, and sometimes castrated in order to shame them. These chapters pick up on the rhetoric of shaming but make the one doing the shaming not the Babylonians but rather God. In Ezekiel, God's masculinized honor is maintained through the shaming of his dependents, turning them into women.

THE TEXT IN THE INTERPRETIVE TRADITION

Within the commentary tradition, these chapters were rarely used to substantiate the subjugation of women. In the patristic period, two trajectories of interpretation can be found. First, God's washing of the infant in 16:9 becomes a foreshadowing of Christian baptism (Stevenson and Glerup,

57–59). Second, the passage was also used to condemn contemporaneous opponents; for Jerome, these were heretics, while for Calvin, they were papists. Andrew Mein (159–83) notes that these later authors accept Ezekiel's gender hierarchy, and thus use female metaphors as insults.

Since the rise of second-wave feminism, the gendered assumptions that undergird these texts have been challenged. Drorah Setel was the first to compare texts like these to pornography because they turn the audience into voyeurs of female sexual activity and sexual assault. Feminist scholars have noted that the texts have too easily been used to substantiate domestic violence, sexual assault as "punishment," and the natural sinfulness of women (Weems).

Feminists have employed a counter-reading to the texts, one that deconstructs the rhetoric of legitimate male control. They note the ways the texts actually encapsulate male fear of women. Others have noted that Ezekiel itself is supposed to be a counter-reading of the prevailing male rhetoric (Patton).

THE TEXT IN CONTEMPORARY DISCUSSION

Although this text is not about real women, it inadvertently hints at the fate of women and children during wartime. In the ancient world, since male honor was demonstrated by the fate of their households, women and children were pawns used to demonstrate defeat. In ancient iconography, this was accomplished by showing the conquering king as the one who protects women and children (Chapman), but the literature attests to a much different fate. Women were raped or forced to become slaves in the households of the conquerors. As slaves, they were sexually available to the men of the household. Men and children were put on the front lines of the conqueror's army without armor, so that they would be killed while exhausting the weaponry of the opponent.

The fate of women and children in war is not much different in the modern world. Still today, more women and children die in armed conflict than do combatants (see Indra). Rape is still used as a military tactic; in the former Yugoslavia, women were systematically raped and impregnated as an element of ethnic cleansing. In the Republic of Congo, the rape of women and children reinforced the army's destruction of male opponents (see Kristof and WuDunn).

Given that Ezekiel's audience would have been one that had seen such acts of war, it invites today's readers to think about what these metaphors sound like to contemporary audiences who have undergone similar fates. Are they heard as substantiating such activity, or do they in fact undercut the claim by any human in power to have the right to perform such actions? Do these texts substantiate sexual assault, or do they undercut the power claims that are constituent of such crimes?

Ezekiel 20: A History of Sin

THE TEXT IN ITS ANCIENT CONTEXT

Chapter 20 is the longest review of Israel's history in the book. It focuses on the wilderness period, when God revealed the law to the Israelites. The passage focuses on the people's response, throughout characterizing them as sinful and disobedient. Earlier prophets also focused on the wilderness period as the time that was constitutive of the Israelite community. Hosea, for instance, depicts it as a honeymoon period, when God had first taken Israel as a bride, and she was still faithful to him (2:15). As in chapters 16 and 23, Ezekiel depicts the Israelites as never deserving God's favor, opening with the charge that they committed idolatry while still slaves in Egypt (20:7). Because Israel is so weak, undeserving, and unexceptional, all of God's actions on behalf of Israel have been and will be done for one reason alone: to enhance YHWH's international reputation.

The chapter uses irony in its radical theology. In this review, God reveals laws three times to the people (18:11-12, 19-20, 25-26). The first two times, the laws, which are characterized by observation of the Sabbath, are life-giving, meaning that if the Israelites had obeyed them, they would have prospered, but the people reject these laws. The third time, God decides to punish them for their disobedience by giving them laws that, when they follow them, actually cause them to sin (vv. 25-26). The irony is that these are the only laws the Israelites follow. Once defiled, Israel's punishment by God is justified.

The passage ends with an oracle of restoration in 20:40-44. This restoration, however, is not a reversal of the earlier assessment of Israel's worthiness. It only occurs to reinforce to the world that YHWH is powerful. The key to the success of the restoration will be Israel's acceptance of its unworthiness. Once they "loathe" themselves (v. 43), restoration can proceed.

■ THE TEXT IN THE INTERPRETIVE TRADITION

In 20:25, the laws revealed to the Israelites are called "statutes that were not good." This reference to divinely revealed evil laws has led to a long history of interpretation. In the patristic period, Christians identified the "bad laws" as Jewish torah. Early Christians like Augustine and Chrysostom, following Paul's view of the law, viewed these laws as ultimately unable to save a sinner (Stevenson and Glerup, 86–87). In the Middle Ages, Christians used this tradition in their polemical writings against Jews. To counter this trend, Jewish interpreters like Rashi and Kara viewed the sinfulness of that particular generation to have been so great that it undercut any good that came from observing torah (Harris, 79–83). Reformers like Calvin, on the other hand, used the passage to discuss the relationship between faith and observing the sacraments, as well as keeping the Sabbath (Beckwith, 113–15).

■ THE TEXT IN CONTEMPORARY DISCUSSION

Although Ezekiel 20 is a review of Israel's history, it is clearly told with an ideological focus in mind. The history is meant to characterize the people as unworthy and depict God as all powerful. This chapter offers particular challenges to people of faith. First, the events it recalls are those usually used either to illustrate the goodness of God or to exalt heroes like Moses. Ezekiel's twist on the tradition is as surprising to contemporary audiences as it was to the ancient one.

The chapter also offers the tantalizing possibility that laws touted as religiously binding might in fact lead people to sin. Prior to the nineteenth century, the biblical slave laws were used as justification for Christian slavery, yet today Christians view these as "not good" laws, ones that do not affirm life, but rather led people to sin. Today, many Christians use biblical laws about sexuality to limit access to marriage for members of contemporary society. Ezekiel 20 invites readers to question whether these also might be laws that do not affirm life, but rather lead to sin and injustice. It undercuts the equation that a law that is divinely revealed must be good, by stating that God can reveal laws that are meant to be disobeyed.

Ezekiel 21-22 and 24: The End Is Near

▌THE TEXT IN ITS ANCIENT CONTEXT

Chapters 21–24 are the final oracles before the report of the fall of Jerusalem reaches the prophet. Chapters 24 and 33, which bookend the oracles against foreign nations, deal explicitly with the final destruction of Jerusalem. In the chapters under consideration here, the condemnation of the city intensifies the motifs found in earlier chapters of the book, as they paint an inevitable portrait of Jerusalem's doom.

Chapter 21 contains various oracles that center on the image of the sword. City walls were breached so that soldiers could enter the city and slay its inhabitants. Neo-Assyrian reliefs that depict siege warfare in this period show that swords were used not just to kill people but also to dismember and behead them. The clipped nature of the language in these poems conveys the sense of panic as the walls were breached.

Chapters 22 and 24 focus on the filth of the slaughter through its images of blood and defilement. These disturbing images would have been all too familiar to survivors of the devastation. There must have been pools of blood and human waste where the slaughtering occurred. The sights and smells would have assaulted any human sensibility. The depiction of the walled city as an iron pot in which body parts float in 24:6-13 re-creates the horror of the city's fall. These poems masterfully capture the reality of warfare through flashes of images that encapsulate that destruction. They are also disturbing in their attribution of that destruction to God. Although usually it is the victors who write history, here we have the historical witness of the defeated Judeans. In a kind of photographic negative of the Assyrian reliefs, it is as if those dismembered bodies rose up to tell their story.

The final verses of chapter 24 mark a turning point in the book. For the book of Ezekiel, the destruction of the temple in Jerusalem is Judah's final punishment. The passage once again uses the character of Ezekiel to personalize the experience of national collapse. The death of his wife, who was his "delight," symbolizes the destruction of the temple, the delightful possession of the Judeans. But the sign that the chapter focuses on is not the loss of wife and temple, but rather on God's command that these losses cannot be mourned. Mourning was an important ritual in the ancient world. It was a public act that both provided communal support for the mourner and paid honor to the dead. The inability to mourn the dead is the final horror endured by the survivors, leaving them alone and shamed.

▌THE TEXT IN THE INTERPRETIVE TRADITION

The Ancient Christian Commentary on Scripture lists no patristic commentary on these chapters, and contemporary research into the history of interpretation of the book of Ezekiel has done little to fill this gap. The silence, however, is deafening. It demonstrates a common interpretive move made when biblical texts contain disturbing images: dismissing them through silence. It also helps explain why the heart of Ezekiel's message has failed to inform the Christian tradition in a significant way. While contemporary Christians may be familiar with Ezekiel's visions or his image of the dry bones (Ezekiel 37, see below), they are often completely unfamiliar with the violent images that permeate the book.

Recent biblical scholarship has sought to redress this lapse by wrestling with the interpretation of violent texts. A volume devoted to violent images in the prophets, for example, looks at the aesthetic function of violent images (Franke and O'Brien). These studies challenge contemporary readers to consider the role that violent images in film, art, and music play today, and how that function relates to contemporary theologies.

▌ THE TEXT IN CONTEMPORARY DISCUSSION

The close of this section in Ezekiel reminds readers that death is not the worst of war's horrors. Those who survive often face a perennially interrupted life. The modern world is not so different. Ezekiel's use of mourning rituals to signify major social disruption resonates with the experiences of refugees today. Ezekiel 24 uses mourning to signify the disruption to basic social practices within refugee populations. Jeremiah 16 similarly talks about the interruption to both mourning and marriage rituals. Gregory Lee Cuéllar, who reads Isaiah 40–55 through the lens of Mexican immigrant experience, notes similar themes of disruption. Simple family-based rituals become political statements when a community has minority status. Ezekiel 24 depicts mourning as a basic human right whose denial is an ultimate horror for those who could not mourn Judah's dead or bury the mutilated bodies of loved ones, let alone weep at family gravesites.

Although these texts address the experience of the defeated, they also invite readers to ponder what such violence does to its perpetrators. Here, God personifies the stance of the perpetrator, and it is not a very pleasant portrayal. Readers are struck by the text's attempt to justify violence, the smug self-assurance that might makes right. The victims in the passages are not individuals but a faceless mass, eventually reduced to dangling body parts. Yet the reader's sympathy remains with the victims and not the perpetrator. YHWH seems more monster than hero.

Is this chapter really about God? Or is it about how perpetrators of violence turn themselves into God in order to commit acts that horrify normal human sensibilities? Trauma literature gives voice to those whose experiences have left them without words; like the book of Lamentations (O'Connor 2002), these chapters in Ezekiel provide language for those traumatized by national defeat.

Ezekiel 25–32 and 35: Oracles against Foreign Nations

▌ THE TEXT IN ITS ANCIENT CONTEXT

Many prophetic collections contain a section of oracles condemning nations other than Israel and Judah. Chapters 25–32 in Ezekiel show signs of conscious editing, which indicate that they play an important rhetorical function in the book. For example, seven nations are condemned, and the last nation, Egypt, is denounced seven times. The oracles are placed just after the notice of the fall of Jerusalem and mark the book's turn toward oracles of restoration.

Although this section, along with a recapitulation in chapter 35, contains oracles against some of the minor nations that surrounded Israel, the bulk of the material focuses on Tyre to the north and Egypt to the south, both economic titans at the time. Surprisingly, there are no oracles against Judah's military enemy Babylon. Instead, the focus is on the two neighbors of Israel that Babylon was unable to defeat. The poems that make up these oracles use metaphoric and mythic language to create vivid pictures of these two nations. These poems reflect a Judean perspective on the unique culture of each nation.

The oracles against Tyre (26:1—28:19), the capital of the Phoenicians, focus on its relative security from enemy attacks (chapter 26, which describes the city's location) and its economic prosperity (chapter 27, which depicts Tyre as a merchant ship). Phoenicia was one of the few nations in the Levant with natural ports, which afforded it a bustling trade on the Mediterranean. As a result, its wealth was not solely dependent on the unreliable rains on which the agricultural economy of the rest of the Levant depended. The geography of its main city, Tyre, also accorded it protection against siege. Built on an island that was connected to the mainland only at low tide, the siege works of the Babylonian army were ineffective against it. In Ezek. 29:18-20, Ezekiel sounds almost sorry for the unsuccessful effort of the Babylonians, stating that God will reward Babylon's thirteen-year effort by giving them Egypt instead.

The oracles against Egypt (29:1—32:32) use language that engages Egyptian religious iconography in order to subvert its claims to power. Although it may seem odd to find such vitriol against an ally of Judah who did in fact come to Judah's aid (albeit unsuccessfully), Ezekiel blames Egypt for presenting itself as a nation on which Judah could have relied. These oracles are framed by two condemnations of the Pharaoh, who is depicted as a reptilian creature whom God fishes out of the Nile, which Pharaoh claims to have created. At the end of the oracles, Egypt and its warriors have their proper reign, enthroned in the depths of the land of the dead surrounded by the dead armies of Judah's other enemies (32:17-32; see also 31:15-18).

Both sets of oracles castigate the foreign kings for their hubris, and both do so in part by engaging Israel's traditions about Eden. Although most contemporary readers of the Bible are familiar with Eden from the story of the creation of Adam, for the Israelites Eden was simply God's garden, a lavish place filled with every good tree, marvelous gems, and springs that watered the earth. In 28:2-19, Tyre's king is mocked for claiming to be a god, responsible for his own wealth, rather than a creature of God banned from Eden. In 31:2-18, both Assyria and Egypt are ridiculed for likening themselves to the loftiest tree in Eden; as punishment, God chops them down, felling all of their allies in the process.

The strong language in the oracles against Tyre and Egypt reveal that for this author, the real threat to Judah was not military defeat but rather cultural colonization. Both of these nations were attractive to Judeans, because their economic dominance seemed to protect them against invasion. In addition, Egypt housed Judean refugees after the fall of the city. This section of Ezekiel reveals the author's fear of the loss of Judah's cultural identity that would result from both appeasing these neighbors and settling in their lands.

■ THE TEXT IN THE INTERPRETIVE TRADITION

Although much of this material receives little comment in the Christian tradition, the interpretation of the prince of Tyre in chapter 28 has a long history within both Judaism and Christianity. The passage describes a person created with every kind of wisdom and glory who then falls from his exalted position because of his own pride. Although very early Jewish texts identified this figure as Adam before being driven out of Eden, later sources say that he is Hiram, who supplied the Israelites with material for the temple (Patmore, 59–69).

Christian tradition, on the other hand, linked this story to the creation and fall of Satan. Although the Bible contains no clear story of the fall of Satan, it was a popular legend, dating back to at least the Hellenistic period. Christians looked for evidence of this tradition in the Bible, offering various texts as evidence for the tradition. The language of exalted creation and fall due to sin suit this purpose handily (Stevenson and Glerup, 90–97).

■ THE TEXT IN CONTEMPORARY DISCUSSION

A major threat to the identity of a colonized nation is cultural hegemony. In our postcolonial world, the effects of European colonization around the globe are felt today not just in terms of economics but also through its effects on culture. The triad of Babylon, Tyre, and Egypt in Ezekiel represents three different types of colonization that were at play both in the ancient world and today: military, economic, and political. For Ezekiel, it is the allure of those nations, which are economically and politically attractive, that makes them so dangerous.

In our postcolonial world, the same holds true. While there is far less military occupation of the Southern Hemisphere by the North, cultural hegemony continues through a global economy that depends on maintaining economic disparity, and through the promise of military "aid" that uses the rhetoric of alliance to mask the reality of dependence. Egypt's horses are today's US fighter planes.

This section of the book also hints at the kind of cultural annihilation that refugee populations experience. While Egypt did provide a safe haven for Judean refugees, this section of the book invites contemporary US readers to recognize the struggle that refugees from Somalia, Liberia, and Southeast Asia face in their attempts to maintain vestiges of their cultural identity. These texts ask if this lifeline is really a noose that will destroy the very identity of those seeking aid. These chapters warn Judah of the allure of dominant cultures, even when the other choice may be military collapse.

Ezekiel 33: The Fall of Jerusalem

■ THE TEXT IN ITS ANCIENT CONTEXT

Chapter 33 closes off the oracles condemning Judah; placed after oracles against Judah's neighbors, it recapitulates themes found in chapters 1–24. It does this in a way that relieves Ezekiel of any responsibility for the nation's destruction. First, it reiterates the image of the prophet as a sentinel, found in 3:16-21. Second, it reviews the discussion of individual sin and salvation found in chapter 18. Most importantly, though, the second half of the chapter focuses explicitly on Ezekiel. His mouth is opened to speak freely (cf. 3:25-27) just as news of the fall of the city comes to the exiles. This loosening of his mouth marks the end of his function as sentinel; the prophesied events have now come to pass.

The passage ends with a summary characterization of the people. In the beginning of the book, they are characterized as rebellious and unwilling to listen. Even after the notice of the fall of the city, they still fail to believe Ezekiel. They assert that, although God has destroyed those living in Judah, the exiles must be blessed since God seems to be giving the land to them (33:24). Even after Ezekiel announces that they are mistaken, they dismiss him as a mere entertainer (33:30-33). Ezekiel, and subsequently God, have done all that they could do.

◼ THE TEXT IN THE INTERPRETIVE TRADITION

Christian exegetes use the two passages about the prophet as sentinel to talk about the office of the bishop. In Greek, the word for "bishop" (*episkopos*) means "overseer" or "watchman." In the patristic period, both this chapter, along with 3:16-21, are used as a paradigm for the role of the bishop. While everyone must speak when they see wrong happening, this is especially true for bishops (Stevenson and Glerup, 25–29, 98–103).

◼ THE TEXT IN CONTEMPORARY DISCUSSION

The depiction of a people only willing to hear what they want to hear is eerily familiar. Even today, for example, many people dismiss warnings about how our choices direly affect the environment. Although this chapter seems to be about Ezekiel, it is really about the justice of God. In fact, by making every speech by Ezekiel a direct oracle from God, the book asserts that God sent warning after warning to the people as disaster loomed. In one of the most striking verses in the book, YHWH states, "I have no pleasure in the death of [even] the wicked" (33:11, "even" added for emphasis). Disaster is not God's will; change is.

Since natural disasters happen all of the time, it is easy to dismiss them as meaningless, not reflecting anything about the nature of God or the effects of human sin. But abdicating all responsibility for the extent of natural disasters is even more morally blind. Why is it that the poor and marginalized suffer the effects more than the rich? How do we define safe and adequate housing? What do we count as a disaster? Who benefits from practices that continue the polluting of the atmosphere, and why is there so little will to enact programmatic change? This passage in Ezekiel states that disasters are not God's will; facing communal responsibility for natural disasters and their aftermath is. But, like the ancient Israelites, sometimes it is easier to blame God than it is to change a group's way of life.

Ezekiel 34 and 36: Hope for the Future

◼ THE TEXT IN ITS ANCIENT CONTEXT

Chapters 34 and 36 contain the first lengthy oracles of restoration in the book. Chapter 34 focuses on political restoration, while chapter 36 discusses the restoration of the land. Both chapters start with a summary of what had gone wrong in the past; kings had failed the people, and the land had been laid waste. Both chapters symbolize restoration as the flourishing of nature. In an agriculture-based economy, this is tantamount to a booming stock market.

The oracles in chapter 34 play with shepherding images. In the ancient world, it was common to depict the king as a shepherd of the people, who are the flock. In the ancient world, shepherds did not own the flock; they worked for the flock's owner. In 34:31, God is the owner of the flock, and the kings, who work for God, keep that flock safe. The restoration of the Davidic monarchy is mentioned only twice in the book, here and in chapter 37. What is important to notice in this chapter, however, is that it deals less with human agents of restoration and instead focuses on God. It is God who seeks out the flock, YHWH who restores them. This results in a "covenant of peace" (v. 25), that is, a restoration of all nature.

The oracles of restoration in chapter 36 can be divided into two parts. Verses 1-12 depict the restoration of the land itself, which had been devastated as the Babylonian army advanced southward. Verses 13-21 contain the surprising conclusion that the worst result of the fall of Jerusalem is how it damaged YHWH's reputation among other nations. God defends this reputation first by asserting that the punishment of Judah was deserved, and, second, that the restoration of Israel will occur to prove God's "sanctity" or power.

Verses 22-36 provide a brief outline of Ezekiel's program of restoration. First, God will gather the people from every place they have been scattered. God will first purify them and then give them a new heart along with a new divine spirit. Only then will the people be returned to the land. Once there, nature will respond with bounty. Finally, everyone will recognize that YHWH is the agent of this restoration: Israel will feel shame both for their earlier sins and in recognition of the greatness of God, and the other nations will finally recognize the holiness and power of Israel's God.

The oracles throughout the chapter are couched in ritual imagery. The land that is restored will be the "mountains," a veiled reference to the restoration of the temple on its holy mountain. The sins of the people are compared to the defilement of a menstruating woman (vv. 17-19), and the restoration of the people includes a divine purification ritual (v. 25). God's reputation is equated with sanctity and holiness, while the inhabited cities will teem with people, like the temple teems with flocks on festival days (vv. 37-38).

▌ THE TEXT IN THE INTERPRETIVE TRADITION

Early Jewish literature used the image of the good shepherd as a messianic designation. *First Enoch* 85–90 seems to identify this figure as Judas Maccabaeus, while *Psalms of Solomon* 17 applies it to the restoration of the Davidic monarchy. The Gospel traditions engaged this same imagery, applying it to God and Jesus. The passage with the most explicit connection to Ezekiel 37 is John 10 (Manning, 27–36). Because of these New Testament references, far more attention has been paid to 34:11-31 than to any other part of the book of Ezekiel. The good shepherd was also applied to Christian leaders, especially bishops and abbots, who were charged with caring for their "flock" (Stevenson and Glerup, 104–15).

■ THE TEXT IN CONTEMPORARY DISCUSSION

Tragedy challenges belief in God. It is difficult to believe in a powerful, just, and loving God in the face of innocent suffering. God either seems cruel or ineffective. Ancient peoples faced similar challenges. Ezekiel abandons the notion of a loving God; the word is never used in the book. But the author holds on to two essential divine elements: divine justice and power. Jerusalem's fall was deserved, but its restoration, though undeserved, will demonstrate God's power.

This is not the solution favored by the elite in today's world: people want God to love them and do not want to admit how little control they have over the world writ large. Often people would rather have a loving God who is willing to forgo justified punishments or who is no match for the evil humans do, than one who directly causes disasters in the world.

Twelve-step programs, like Alcoholics Anonymous, view the admission of one's lack of control over addictions and the acceptance of a higher power as an important step in recovery. One of its slogans, "Let go and let God," embodies this surrender to divine power. Although addiction is not the same tragedy as wartime devastation, it does provide a model for equating the acceptance of personal responsibility with the recognition of where human power ends and divine power begins.

Acceptance of divine control is also an important element in Protestant views of divine grace. Luther states that what freed him from worrying about his salvation was his recognition that he would never deserve it. Calvin's view of human depravity especially after the fall shares with Ezekiel the ideas that humans are damaged, unable to do good on their own, but infinitely salvageable because of God's choice to save them. The image is one of profound hope, because its surety stems from God and does not depend on fallible human effort. And reliability is what humans most desire when they feel profoundly their own inability to control the world.

Ezekiel 37: The Valley of the Dry Bones

■ THE TEXT IN ITS ANCIENT CONTEXT

Both chapters 36 and 37 depict restoration as a return from death. In 36:26-27, the heart of stone represents death. While the heart transplant means the body lives, it is the infusion of divine breath or spirit that really represents human life, as is seen in Gen. 2:7. In 37:1-14, the prophet has a vision of a battlefield strewn with dead bodies. Assyrian reliefs indicate that bodies were often left to rot unburied where carrion birds and the ravages of weather would strip them of all flesh. Ezekiel's vision of a valley filled with bones is an image of these desiccated carcasses.

God calls on the prophet to revivify these skeletal remains. The prophet's answer that only God knows if they can be revived (v. 3) shows the hopelessness of dreams of restoration. Yet through the prophetic proclamations, what God promises comes true. The bodies that rise up from field and grave are a metaphor for the restoration of the living, breathing nation (vv. 11-13).

The parallel vision of restoration in verses 15-23 reinforces this metaphoric meaning. In this section, two dry sticks are grafted together representing not just the restoration of Judah but also the future restoration of all twelve tribes of Israel. The northern kingdom, composed of ten tribes, had been exiled by the Assyrians more than a century before the fall of Jerusalem. Those exiles had been scattered throughout Mesopotamia. Yet, within Israel's prophetic tradition, there always remained a hope that all twelve tribes would one day be restored and reunited.

This chapter reiterates the pattern of restoration seen in earlier oracles. First, restoration includes divine purification of the restored community (v. 23; see 36:25). Second, the passage repeats the hope for the restoration of a Davidic king (v. 24; see 34:23-24). Last, it refers to this restoration as a "covenant of peace" (v. 26; see 34:25-29). It also anticipates the final vision of the restoration of the temple in chapters 40–48, first by the insistence on the restoration of all twelve tribes (see esp. 47:21—48:7), and finally by the notice that God will once again restore the temple (37:27-28).

▌▐ THE TEXT IN THE INTERPRETIVE TRADITION

Ezekiel 37:1-14 has often been seen as an image of bodily resurrection. In fact, patristic writers asserted that these verses accurately describe the way bodies would be resurrected after the second coming of Christ (Stevenson and Glerup, 12–24). This became the text's standard interpretation, seen in places as wide ranging as wall paintings in the ancient Jewish synagogue of Dura Europos (Manning, 40–43), to nineteenth-century African American spirituals (Callender).

The Reformers expanded the interpretation of the passage in two ways. First, they focused on the fact that the bones are brought together by prophetic speech. For William Greenhill, this passage is about the efficacy of God's Word; even if it falls on something dead, it can bring it to life. Second, they paid more attention to the image of the two sticks, but for them these did not represent the two nations of Judah and Israel, but rather the division of Jews and gentiles. The question remained whether the oracle was fulfilled with the rise of Christianity that brought together Jews and gentiles, or whether it referred to an unfulfilled oracle about the ultimate conversion of all of the Jews (Beckwith, 179–87).

In modern commentaries, attention has turned to the placement of this chapter within the book as a whole. Recently discovered ancient Greek manuscripts, which agree with Old Latin versions, place this chapter right before chapter 40, which starts the vision of the restored temple (see Lust). The placement of this chapter affects the interpretation of the Gog material that follows. Is it a vision of God's defeat of another human enemy (indicated by its placement in the ancient Greek texts), or is it a vision of God's future cosmic battle (implied by its current placement)?

▌▐ THE TEXT IN CONTEMPORARY DISCUSSION

The images in chapter 37 face squarely the feelings of despair felt by those displaced by war. Although the image of a field of dead bodies may seem rather gruesome, it effectively depicts the experience of war refugees who have had to leave the gravesites of loved ones who have died. The art installation *One Million Bones* (onemillionbones.org) in Washington, DC, has a similar task: to provide a visual reminder of the extent of genocide in the modern world and to raise awareness of the survivors. Similarly, Ezekiel 37 should remind us that refugees in our communities, even those grateful for a sense of safety, still yearn for what may seem impossible: a return not to what life was but to the best of what life could be in their land of origin.

Ezekiel 37 does not deny the sense of hopelessness. It does not offer a false sense that the refugee community can change their situation or that the restoration will come easily. What it does do is encourage the community to dream big. But those dreams are not based on human effort, which is not up for the task; they are based on God, for whom all things are possible.

This trust in God is not a way to pacify a disgruntled community. It is not a denial of their communal tragedy. In fact, it is the opposite. It validates the community's sense that their own visions of a better world are not silly, insignificant pipe dreams. Ezekiel 37 states they are what God had wanted all along. This chapter calls on communities of faith to support refugee communities and to experience their visions of a better world as a prophetic voice.

Ezekiel 38–39: God's Role in Israel's Future

◼ THE TEXT IN ITS ANCIENT CONTEXT

Right before the final vision of the book, Ezekiel 38–39 contains a vision of a future attack on the restored nation by a mythic enemy. The enemy in this passage is an unidentified king, Gog, who hails from a mythic land, Magog. He gathers an army from every corner of the globe and marches against people living in unwalled villages. The text states that he does this simply to gather more plunder.

Gog is defeated handily by God; in fact, the battle is not even described, insinuating that it was literally "no contest." Instead, the passage focuses on three postbattle scenes: the gathering of the spoils of war by the Israelites, the burial of the corpses, and the postbattle sacrifice of the enemy. In the first two of these scenes, the details stress the enormous size of this army. It takes seven years to burn all of the spoils, while the pile of bodies becomes a monument. In the third postbattle scene, God feeds the corpses to carrion birds and other beasts in what the text terms a "sacrifice," thus inverting the usual offering made to God at the end of a battle.

The passage ends with the longest recognition formula of the book. It not only states that this will happen so that "they will know that I am YHWH," but also goes on to note that with this battle everyone will recognize that the Babylonian exile occurred because Israel had sinned. In other words, God's defeat of the greatest human enemy anyone could imagine proves that Babylon's defeat of Judah was not the result of God's weakness but rather the result of God's choice to let Babylon win.

◼ THE TEXT IN THE INTERPRETIVE TRADITION

The vision of Gog and Magog has had a significant interpretive history. From as early as Zechariah, the text has served as fodder for later apocalyptic images. Sverre Bøe traces the way that Revelation, especially chapters 19–20, reuses imagery from these chapters in creative ways.

Because Gog cannot be identified with any historic enemy of Judah, this literary figure became a trope for any evil enemy of God's chosen people. Gog represents all that is evil, and Israel becomes the innocent victim whom God vindicates. Jerome views Gog as the antichrist, a view found into the Middle Ages. Reformers, who also identified Gog as Satan, looked to the Jewish community in their own day as the subject of these chapters. Disturbingly, they believed that these chapters dealt with how God would bring about the conversion of all Jews, who currently suffered because they lacked faith in Christ (Beckwith, 190–93).

Today, Christian millennialist groups continue to use the term "Gog" for any archenemy of Christianity. During the Cold War era, for example, some American Christian churches viewed Russia as the new Gog. Today, some Messianic Christians, who view the re-creation of the nation of Israel as a harbinger for the second coming of Christ, identify Arab Islam as the new "Gog."

▌ THE TEXT IN CONTEMPORARY DISCUSSION

The celebration of violence in the Gog pericope has often been problematic for Christians living in colonizing countries, such as England, Germany, and the United States, but when the chapters are read from the perspective of the colonized, a vision in which God annihilates evil incarnate makes poetic sense. The chapters tell the story of a people who view themselves as utterly defenseless, whose only hope of survival lies in an otherworldly power.

The victim in this passage is never the aggressor. The attack by Gog is unprovoked and gratuitous, just as the colonization of economically depressed areas of the globe by nations of relative wealth and privilege is also gratuitous, unprovoked, and motivated by the basest of human instincts: greed. The passage unravels the ideology of the colonizer. Not only are the boasts of Gog vain, but they are laughable in light of the source of true power—God. The details of the text serve to highlight this uneven power distribution: as numerous and as well-equipped as the army is, God dispatches them in a moment.

The passage also uses details from nature to undercut the ideology of the colonizer. The passage notes that all of nature recognizes God's power, trembling at the warrior's entrance onto the battle scene. The text mentions "creeping things," for example, worms, bugs, lizards, and locusts, that recognize God's power. Even trees benefit from God's duties as warriors; they avoid being cut down as firewood for seven years, while the Israelites use the spoils of war as fuel for cooking, heating, and light. Gog and his armies are rendered less than geckos and ginkgoes, a beautiful fantasy indeed.

Ezekiel 40:1—44:4: Visions of the Temple

▌ THE TEXT IN ITS ANCIENT CONTEXT

The book of Ezekiel ends with a nine-chapter vision of the restoration of the nation of Israel. That restoration begins and ends at the restored temple of Jerusalem. The rest of the vision radiates out from this liturgical center. The vision is told through the eyes of Ezekiel, who is led on a visionary tour by an unidentified heavenly tour guide. These chapters contain no prophetic speeches, except the command to observe the vision and write it down (40:4; 43:10-11).

The opening section of the vision contains the prophet's tour of the temple complex, starting in its outer courtyard (40:5-27), proceeding to the inner courtyard (40:28-47), then into the outer parts of the sanctuary building (40:48—41:26). The tour then proceeds back outside to the inner court, the arena for priestly rituals (42:1-20).

In chapter 43, Ezekiel once again sees God on the portable throne, this time flying back into the temple complex, a vision that ties the restoration to the oracles of condemnation in the first part of the book. The image marks the restoration as the reversal of the problems that led to national defeat. Twice the passage states that God will dwell in this temple "forever" (43:7, 9). This idea is reinforced when the gate through which God traveled is permanently shut (44:2).

God's move back into the temple is followed by a number of items found in other biblical texts that describe the founding of a temple. First, God's presence in the temple requires the restoration of daily sacrifices, seen in the restoration of the altar and the priesthood in 43:13-27. Second, God's indwelling requires the reestablishment of ritual laws (43:11-12) spelled out in the next section. Last, the reality of God's presence in the temple is symbolized by the divine "glory" that emanates from the temple (44:4).

THE TEXT IN THE INTERPRETIVE TRADITION

Although Christians today often pay little attention to these final chapters of the book, it was fertile ground for patristic and medieval interpretation. The details were often interpreted allegorically: the temple was the church, and each detail represented some aspect of Christian belief. This trend lasted into the Reformation period, where it was coupled with a focus on Christ as the center of the vision (Tooman, 215–20; Beckwith, xlvi, 205–13).

Ezekiel's temple came to prefigure Mary in the Christian tradition (Sawyer, 7–9), a view that persisted in Catholicism, but not among Reformers. First, just as a temple housed the real presence of God, Mary's pregnant body "housed" the divine Christ. If Mary were to be a dwelling place for God, then like the temple, this "house" had to be pure, free from any defilement. The typology that Mary's body was a temple for Christ led to the tradition that Mary herself had to be pure, and for Christians this meant free from original sin. The doctrine of Mary's "immaculate conception" expresses this belief that she had to have been conceived without the stain of original sin in order for her to function as a pure vessel for Christ.

The doctrine is really about the nature of Jesus, as true God even before Mary's impregnation whose "house" had to be prepared prior to his incarnation within her body. Catholic tradition also looks to the image of the locked gate as an allegory for Mary's permanent virginity. Her purified body is protected from any subsequent defilement or impregnation. If her body is God's temple, then it cannot house anything else.

THE TEXT IN CONTEMPORARY DISCUSSION

These chapters in Ezekiel are not often read in the church; their focus on detailed measurements of walls and spaces does not seem to be the stuff of spiritual nourishment. But the chapters do invite contemporary Christian communities to consider what it really means to proclaim that Christ is among them. Ezekiel suggests that such a statement should result in concrete changes in how societies are organized, worship is ordered, and people relate to God and each other. The details themselves are not as important as the fact that faith results in concrete changes that are communally visible.

While the Christian tradition often looks down on the practice of sacrifices as something "pagans" do, the fact is, the active sacrificial liturgies in other religions, such as Islam, the shamanistic sacrifices in Hmong communities, and the sacrifices of Hindu religion provide a living witness to the fact that all liturgy is really an acting out of metaphors about the divine reality. If God is among the people, then rituals of feeding provide a way for that community to express that the divine presence should be nurtured, honored, and cared for through ritual hosting and festive feeding. Recognizing how important those rituals are in the biblical tradition helps foster interreligious dialogue with those who still practice forms of sacrifice.

Ezekiel 44:5—48:35: The Blossoming of a World Made Right

▌ THE TEXT IN ITS ANCIENT CONTEXT

The final five chapters in the book finish the vision of the restored nation begun in chapter 40. They extend the effects of God's presence in the temple to the nation as a whole. Ezekiel 44:5—46:24 contains the book's ideal laws for this visionary restored community. While the laws in the Pentateuch reflect life in a settled economy, these laws focus on cultic matters, an indication of the book's priestly perspective. Although these laws may seem more practical than visionary, their utopian quality should not be ignored.

The final chapters of the book bring the utopian nature of the vision back to the fore. In the ancient Near East, temples were often touted as a ritual paradise, the site from which all creation bursts forth. In arid lands, this was most often symbolized by an abundance of fresh water; this idea is the basis of the four rivers in Gen. 2:10-14. Ezekiel 47 paints a picture of a fructifying river flowing out from beneath the temple itself and watering the land. The image of the Dead Sea teeming with freshwater fish encapsulates this paradise.

Another idyllic detail is the distribution of land among the twelve tribes of Israel. Each strip of land is equitable, especially since the vision imagines a land of universal fertility. Although some tribes are closer to the nation's center, which might suggest a privileged position, the nation's new geography makes clear that nothing profane can reach God in the temple. Here, the temple is not located inside the capital city, but rather is surrounded by land given to the priests. It is literally set in a ring of holiness. The capital city, with its restored monarchy, is adjacent to this holy area.

In addition to the changes in geography, this utopian vision also changes city and society. The leading monarch is not called a "king" but rather a "prince." The vision makes clear that the monarchy serves primarily a ritual function as leader of lay worship. Second, the king is never identified as Davidic, nor is the capital city ever called Jerusalem. This is new space. The book ends with the renaming of the city. Naming the city "YHWH is there" reinforces the main message of these chapters, that restoration is equated with God taking up residence again in Israel's national temple.

▌ THE TEXT IN THE INTERPRETIVE TRADITION

While Jewish tradition focused on the laws in Ezekiel that did not match similar precepts in the Pentateuch (Sweeney, 13–16), Christian exegetes looked at the figure of the king, who, as first among the worshipers, came alternatively to symbolize Christ as well as the priests. In addition, the life-giving waters of Ezekiel 47 became fertile ground for interpretation. Jerome, who saw the temple tour as an allegory for the mystical ascent to heaven (Stevenson and Glerup, 125–47), likened the river to the teachings of the church, while the *Epistle of Barnabas* says that it represents baptism (Stevenson and Glerup, 125–47). The Reformers viewed the river as the proclamation of the gospel (Beckwith, 225–29).

▌THE TEXT IN CONTEMPORARY DISCUSSION

What does paradise look like? In a world where drought destroyed whole communities, where water supplies were scarce and often vulnerable to contamination, paradise could be symbolized by flowing fresh water. But this world does not exist only in the past. Today drought threatens thousands of people daily. In the 1960s, drought in what was then called Biafra resulted in images of starving children. These droughts are exacerbated today by climate change, so that even places that do get rain have been left barren because the timing of those rains can no longer be predicted. For other people, like those in Haiti and Egypt, the need for fresh water has left many people displaced when dams are built to harness that water.

Reading Ezekiel 47 through the lens of these experiences shows that in an ideal world, there would be no need to fight for water or for the crops that result from that water. Utopia is marked by equal and easy access to natural resources. If people all had what they needed, this vision suggests, then wars over land possession would also cease. Society could set up equitable portions of land. It suggests that there would be no need of big government, and communities could look for leaders who primarily led them in praising God. It is not the utopia of big business or corporate greed, but it is a vision of a world set right.

Works Cited

Barstad, Hans M. 1996. *The Myth of the Empty Land: A Study in the History and Archaeology of Judah during the "Exilic" Period.* SO 28. Oslo: Scandinavian University Press.

Beckwith, Carl L., ed. 2012. *Ezekiel, Daniel.* Reformation Commentary on Scripture, Old Testament 12. Downers Grove, IL: IVP Academic.

Bog, Sverre. 2001. *Gog and Magog: Ezekiel 38–39 as Pre-Text for Revelation 19, 17-21 and 20, 7-10.* WUNT 2/135. Tübingen: Mohr Siebeck.

Callender, Dexter E., Jr. 2010. "Ezekiel." In *The Africana Bible: Reading Israel's Scriptures from Africa and the African Diaspora*, edited by Hugh R. Page Jr., 157–63. Minneapolis: Fortress Press.

Chapman, Cynthia R. 2004. *The Gendered Language of Warfare in the Israelite-Assyrian Encounter.* HSM 62. Winona Lake, IN: Eisenbrauns.

Cuéllar, Gregory Lee. 2008. *Voices of Marginality: Exile and Return in Second Isaiah 40–55 and the Mexican Immigrant Experience.* American University Studies 7. Theology and Religion 271. New York: Lang.

Franke, Chris, and Julia M. O'Brien, eds. 2010. *Aesthetics of Violence in the Prophets.* LHB/OTS 517. New York: T&T Clark.

Halperin, David J. 1993. *Seeking Ezekiel: Text and Psychology.* University Park: Pennsylvania State University Press.

Harris, Robert A. 2011. "The Reception of Ezekiel among Twelfth-Century Northern French Rabbinic Exegetes." In *After Ezekiel: Essays on the Reception of a Difficult Prophet*, edited by Andrew Mein and Paul M. Joyce, 71–88. LHB/OTS 535. New York: T&T Clark.

Indra, Doreen, ed. 1999. *Engendering Forced Migration: Theory and Practice*. New York: Berghahn.

Joyce, Paul M. 1989. *Divine Initiative and Human Response in Ezekiel*. JSOTSup 51. Sheffield: JSOT Press.

Kristof, Nicholas D., and Sheryl WuDunn. *Half the Sky: Turning Oppression into Opportunity for Women Worldwide*. New York: Vintage, 2010.

Lust, Johann. 1981. "Ezekiel 36–40 in the Oldest Greek Manuscript." *CBQ* 43:517–33.

Manning, Gary T., Jr. 2011. "Shepherd, Vine and Bones: The Use of Ezekiel in the Gospel of John." In *After Ezekiel: Essays on the Reception of a Difficult Prophet*, edited by Andrew Mein and Paul M. Joyce, 25–44. LHB/OTS 535. New York: T&T Clark.

Mein, Andrew. 2011. "Ezekiel's Women in Christian Interpretation: The Case of Ezekiel 16." In *After Ezekiel: Essays on the Reception of a Difficult Prophet*, edited by Andrew Mein and Paul M. Joyce, 159–83. LHB/OTS 535. New York: T&T Clark.

O'Connor, Kathleen M. 2002. *Lamentations and the Tears of the World*. Maryknoll, NY: Orbis.

———. 2012. *Jeremiah: Pain and Promise*. Philadelphia: Fortress Press.

Patmore, Hector M. "Adam or Satan? The Identity of the King of Tyre in Late Antiquity." In *After Ezekiel: Essays on the Reception of a Difficult Prophet*, edited by Andrew Mein and Paul M. Joyce, 59–69. LHB/OTS 535. New York: T&T Clark.

Patton, Corrine L. 2000. "'Should Our Sister Be Treated Like a Whore?' A Response to Feminist Critiques of Ezekiel 23." In *The Book of Ezekiel: Theological and Anthropological Perspectives*, edited by Margaret S. Odell and John T. Strong, 221–38. SBLSymS 9. Atlanta: Society of Biblical Literature.

Sawyer, John F. A. 2011. "Ezekiel in the History of Christianity." In *After Ezekiel: Essays on the Reception of a Difficult Prophet*, edited by Andrew Mein and Paul M. Joyce, 1–9. LHB/OTS 535. New York: T&T Clark.

Setel, Drorah T. 1985. "Prophets and Pornography: Female Sexual Imagery in Hosea." In *Feminist Interpretation of the Bible*, edited by Letty Russell, 86–95. Philadelphia: Westminster.

Smith-Christopher, Daniel. 2002. *A Biblical Theology of Exile*. OBT. Minneapolis: Fortress Press.

Stevenson, Kenneth, and Michael Glerup, eds. 2008. *Ezekiel, Daniel*. Ancient Christian Commentary on Scripture, Old Testament 13. Downers Grove, IL: InterVarsity.

Sweeney, Marvin A. 2011. "The Problem of Ezekiel in Talmudic Literature." In *After Ezekiel: Essays on the Reception of a Difficult Prophet*, edited by Andrew Mein and Paul M. Joyce, 11–23. LHB/OTS 535. New York: T&T Clark.

Tooman, William A. 2011. "Of Puritans and Prophets: Cotton Mather's Interpretation of Ezekiel in the *Biblia Americana*." In *After Ezekiel: Essays on the Reception of a Difficult Prophet*, edited by Andrew Mein and Paul M. Joyce, 203–27. LHB/OTS 535. New York: T&T Clark.

Tuell, Steven Shawn. 2011. "The Meaning of the Mark: New Light on Ezekiel 9 from the History of Interpretation." In *After Ezekiel: Essays on the Reception of a Difficult Prophet*, edited by Andrew Mein and Paul M. Joyce, 185–202. LHB/OTS 535. New York: T&T Clark.

Weems, Renita. 1995. *Battered Love: Marriage, Sex, and Violence in the Hebrew Prophets*. OBT. Minneapolis: Fortress Press.

DANIEL

Anathea Portier-Young

Introduction

Daniel combines story, prayer, vision, and interpretation in a creative and hope-filled response to domination, state terror, and persecution. One of the earliest exemplars of the literary genre of apocalypse, it makes visible the hidden workings of empire and God. More specifically, Daniel is a *historical* apocalypse. It interprets events and circumstances of the past, present, and future and helps God's people claim their history and identity in a time of unspeakable trauma.

The text of Daniel that is the foundation for this commentary consists of twelve chapters that alternate between Hebrew and Aramaic, with 1:1—2:4a in Hebrew, 2:4b—7:28 in Aramaic, and 8:1–12:13 in Hebrew. This bilingual structure is part of the book's artistry: just as sacred language frames imperial language, so religious identity, belief, and praxis is the ground for all interactions with foreign empires.

The first six chapters contain the stories of four Judean children—their Hebrew names are Daniel, Hananiah, Azariah, and Mishael—who are led captive from their homeland during Babylonia's conquest of Jerusalem. They soon rise to power in the courts of four kings: Nebuchadnezzar, king of Babylon (1:1), his son Belshazzar (5:1), Darius the Mede (5:31), and Cyrus the Persian (6:28). Some of these stories may have originated in a Diaspora setting, perhaps among Jews in Babylonia during the Persian period (between 539–333 BCE), a time when political domination also made space for negotiation and collaboration. The stories appear to have been crafted into a written collection of court tales that provided the basis and beginning for the longer book of Daniel that took shape in Judea in the second century BCE.

The stories coalesce around the figure of Daniel, wise and prayerful youth, interpreter of dreams, bold in speech. They are hero stories: Daniel and his friends provide readers with models of courage, faithfulness, and success against odds. Though prisoners, they have opportunities for education and personal advancement within the foreign government. At the same time, they confront jealousy, conspiracy, and execution. Their stories highlight challenges of negotiating Jewish identity and maintaining faithful praxis in the context of foreign domination.

The court tales in Daniel 1–6 also incorporate diverse literary forms, including prayer, dream report, dream interpretation, divine decree, and royal letter. These forms play a key role in the book's treatment of sovereignty, power, and knowledge. Daniel receives wisdom and insight to interpret dreams as well as divine writing. His interpretations clarify the relationship between human kingdoms and divine kingship. Even while God's people are in exile, God reigns over time and history, appointing kings, humbling them, and bringing kingdoms to an end.

These stories provided a group of visionary scribes with a model for their own nonviolent witness in the face of imperial exploitation and violence. In the year 167 BCE, Judea was a province within the Seleucid Empire. Seleucid king Antiochus IV Epiphanes aimed at the re-creation of his empire through reconquest of Judea, undertaking a campaign of state terror that culminated in religious persecution of Jews as well as plunder and captivity. The apocalyptic visions and discourse in Daniel 7–12 were crafted by scribes who resisted persecution and terror through their teaching, writing, prayer, and martyrdom. They composed the Hebrew and Aramaic book of Daniel as a gift of understanding and hope for the many.

The dream of the statue in chapter 2 provided a model for Daniel 7's vision of a succession of four kingdoms, now imaged as monstrous and predatory beasts, followed by an eternal kingdom granted to one like a human. At the vision's heart is an Ancient of Days seated on a fiery throne. The vision thus shifts attention away from the glamour of earthly imperial armies to focus on divine sovereignty and justice. A second vision in chapter 8 portrays Antiochus's assault on God's sanctuary and provides a timeline for the cessation of sacrifice. Despite the touch and assurances of the man Gabriel, Daniel remains devastated and confused by what he has seen. In Daniel 9, Daniel turns to the scroll of Jeremiah for understanding. He also fasts and prays. He has a vision of a man clothed in linen, then is touched once more by Gabriel, who unfolds for him a future history from the time of the kings of Persia through the wars of the Hellenistic kings, to the time of persecution in Judea and finally the intervention of Michael, protector of Daniel's people (Daniel 10–12). This final discourse culminates with the promise of resurrection and the command to Daniel to go his way and rest.

The biblical book of Daniel may more properly be called books of Daniel: ancient versions witness to a vibrant set of scriptural traditions in Hebrew and Aramaic, on one hand, and Greek, on the other. The ancient Greek texts of Daniel also exhibit multiplicity, so that we have not one ancient Greek version but two. The Hebrew and Aramaic text of Daniel examined here holds the status of sacred Scripture for Jews and Protestant Christians. For Catholics and Orthodox Christians, one or both Greek texts also hold the status of sacred Scripture. These Greek versions are longer, containing the stories of Susanna, Bel and the Dragon as well as additional narrative and two hymns within the story of the three young men in the furnace. Collectively, these stories foreground religious experience, including worship of the one God; they also mark a literary shift from apocalypse to short novel and saint's life.

Daniel 1:1-21: Wisdom in Captivity

▌The Text in Its Ancient Context

The setting in Babylon highlights themes of exile, captivity, and alienation. For readers in second-century-BCE Judea, this story setting invited a novel interpretation of their own experience as colonial subjects. Foreign rule created a set of competing demands and loyalties. Would it be possible to remain faithful to God while serving the empire? Would God equip the faithful with the wisdom and strength to speak to ruled and ruler alike the words of truth that would lead to righteousness and life?

Daniel and his friends are given new names in a language that is not their own and that invoke the names of gods they do not worship (Dan. 1:7). They are trained in the literature and lore of a foreign culture that prides itself on reading the future in stars, entrails, and even dreams (1:4-5). Yet Daniel and his friends draw a line at eating the king's food, recognizing in this royal nourishment an act of patronage that demands allegiance and claims the power to sustain and shape human life (1:8). Confident that *God* will sustain and shape them, they ask instead to be given water to drink and parts of plants to eat (1:12). Subsequently, God grants them far more extensive knowledge and wisdom than that of their Chaldean captors. To Daniel, moreover, God grants understanding of visions and dreams (1:17). For the ancient audience of Daniel, this story establishes the source of the book's visionary authority and roots the book's wisdom and promises for the future in the traditions of Judah's past.

▌The Text in the Interpretive Tradition

Early Jewish and Christian interpretations of Daniel survive in Josephus's *Jewish Antiquities*, various rabbinic midrashim, and commentaries by Jerome and Theodoret of Cyrus, among others. Their treatments of Daniel 1 combine legend, intrabiblical interpretation, allegory, and theological reflection.

Theodoret of Cyrus's reading of Daniel 1 emphasizes the relationship between human free will and divine care. Daniel's choice to abstain from the king's food was simultaneously a choice to follow God's commands. This choice enabled him to enjoy divine mercy, protection, and providential care. This interpretation resonates with modern Christian spiritual disciplines based on Daniel 1, commonly known as "Daniel fasts," entailing a diet of water and plant-derived foods. Those who practice such fasting aim at sanctification and nearness to God while simultaneously expecting greater prosperity in matters of health and even finances (Gregory).

▌The Text in Contemporary Discussion

Recent scholarly treatments of Daniel 1 have focused on identity, bodily boundaries, and colonialism. Mary Mills links imagery of food and table and the spaces that contain them with social identity. In the border crossing from homeland to exile, bodily boundaries map the limits of competing sovereignties. In Daniel 1, the king's table contrasts with God's; the latter is invoked by the transfer of Jerusalem's sacred vessels to Babylon; Daniel is also a vessel. By abstaining from the king's food, he maintains his bodily purity, rooting his identity in divinely granted nourishment and wisdom rather than in royal provision and courtly education.

Philip Chia argues that by refusing to eat from the king's table, Daniel and his friends resist colonization. By contrast, Danna Nolan Fewell challenges readings of Daniel 1 as resistance narrative, arguing that the text portrays accommodation and emphasizes the vulnerability of Daniel and his friends as children in exile.

Daniel 1 thus offers a rich resource for youths in particular, who must negotiate identity in complex social spaces, imperial and otherwise. In what ways will they be countercultural? In what ways will they conform to the culture they inhabit? Food, language, education, and naming are central elements in this negotiation.

Daniel 2:1-49: Dreaming and Speaking Empire's End

■ THE TEXT IN ITS ANCIENT CONTEXT

Daniel 2 is most widely known for Nebuchadnezzar's dream of a giant statue made of metals and clay (2:31-35). The centrality of the dream and its interpretation in this chapter mirrors its Babylonian setting, in which "visions of the night" were believed to convey messages from the gods. Babylonian dreamers and diviners wanted to know first of all whether a dream was favorable or unfavorable (Rochberg 2004). Over time, a more detailed system of interpretation developed. Dream interpreters in Sumer, Babylon, Susa, and elsewhere in ancient Mesopotamia kept records of dreams and the fortunes that followed, handing these on through generations. Interpreters drew on this divinatory tradition to understand symbols within a dream. The audience of Daniel would have connected Daniel's interpretation of Nebuchadnezzar's dreams in Daniel 2 and 4, as well as his confusion concerning his own visions in later chapters, with this Babylonian art of dream interpretation.

The idea of a revealed sequence of kingdoms is found in the diviner's manual *Enuma Anu Enlil*. The surviving tablets of this compendium date to around 650 BCE. Ancient readers might have imagined that this compilation, like the *Ziqīqu* tablets, formed part of the training Daniel and his friends received in the language and literature of the Chaldeans. Here is part of an oracle from this collection (Tablet 20, §11, line 7, Recension A; Rochberg 1988, 211).

> The prediction is given for Babylon: The destruction of Babylon is near. The scattering of the scattered land is near (?). . . . The king to whom they said, "yes." . . . His reign will end. In the m[outh of the god]s (?) his destruction is near. Ur will take away the rule of Babylon. Ur will take supremacy over Babylon.

The book of Daniel is informed by and interacts with biblical as well as Mesopotamian and Hellenistic traditions. In this chapter, we see the seeds of apocalyptic literature taking root within a rich and diverse cultural matrix (see J. J. Collins 1998, 26–37).

The earliest Jewish readers of Daniel 2 understood themselves to be in the time of the fourth kingdom of iron and clay (2:33). They expected God to establish the stone (2:34), that is, the enduring kingdom (2:40-43), in the near future, and they understood that kingdom to be their own. Throughout the later history of interpretation, readers have similarly located themselves at this turning point between kingdoms.

By the first century CE, the fourth kingdom was understood to be Rome. For Christian interpreters in the medieval and Reformation periods, the fourth kingdom was still "Rome," but not the Rome of antiquity. It might be the Holy Roman Empire, the Roman Catholic Church, or another major power. In the seventeenth century, Portuguese Jesuit António Vieira interpreted Daniel 2 in conjunction with Revelation as a prediction of Portuguese independence and imperial expansion in America (Valdez).

■ THE TEXT IN CONTEMPORARY DISCUSSION

Daniel is a bilingual book, switching from Hebrew to Aramaic in 2:4b, continuing in Aramaic through the end of chapter 7, then switching back to Hebrew for the remainder of the book. For Jews, Hebrew was the language of sacred Scripture and of liturgy. It invoked the demands and promises of their covenant with God. Aramaic was a Mesopotamian language that became the lingua franca of the Persian Empire.

In the time of Daniel's composition, Aramaic was the language spoken by the people of Judea; it also remained a language of international commerce and imperial administration. The linguistic structure of the book provides a normative frame around Jewish life and their interaction with the empires that ruled them. Their allegiance was owed finally not to Nebuchadnezzar nor, later, to the Seleucid king Antiochus IV Epiphanes, but to God. The bilingual character of this biblical book alerts us to the languages and registers in which we speak. What do they convey about power, identity, rights, and obligations? What claims do our political rhetoric and our language about God make on us?

Daniel 3:1-30: Into the Furnace

■ THE TEXT IN ITS ANCIENT CONTEXT

The portrait in Daniel 3 of royal folly satirizes the pretensions and preoccupations of empire. In the face of such imperial arrogance, the actions and words of Shadrach, Meshach, and Abednego model courage and fidelity. The narrative of miraculous deliverance confirms the power of God and relative powerlessness of the Babylonian king.

Within the narrative, repetition creates a liturgical rhythm that mimics the king's attempt to command universal worship. At the narrative's beginning, the statue commands attention (3:1-5). Repeated references to the statue are then interwoven with references to the furnace (3:6-18), until the furnace takes the place of the statue as the heart of the narrative (3:19-26). This shift highlights the king's failure: the three young men willingly enter the fire rather than worship the statue (3:18).

The statue is characterized by its material—gold—and its dimensions of sixty cubits high and six cubits wide. Paired with repeated lists of administrative officials, this extravagant display of wealth evokes imperial patterns of economic exploitation such as taxation, tribute, and plunder (see 2 Kgs. 16:8; 18:14; 23:33-35; 24:13). Gold is brilliant, but not strong. The dimensions, while visually impressive, suggest instability. The rapacity of empire produces an unsustainable economic and social system.

By contrast with the Genesis creation story (1:26-27), here the king, not God, creates an image to represent to the world his own power and dominion. The king mimics God but can create only an inert object. Shadrach, Meshach, and Abednego reject the confusion between king and God that the statue represents, and in so doing refuse complicity in the economic and ideological structures of empire.

■ The Text in the Interpretive Tradition

The Greek Old Testament, or Septuagint, preserves a longer form of Daniel 3 that is canonical for Catholics and many Orthodox Christians. It includes two hymns, the Prayer of Azariah and the Song of the Three Young Men, as well as narrative sections that introduce the songs and create a bridge between them (3:24-90 LXX; see the entry for "Azariah and the Song of the Three Jews," below)). The Greek text answers Nebuchadnezzar's farcical liturgy with a truly universal counter-liturgy of confession and praise. Through worship, the flames are transformed into a locus of divine presence, anticipating the fiery throne of the Ancient of Days (Dan. 7:9-10).

■ The Text in Contemporary Discussion

Elements of satire in Daniel 3 remind readers that humor has its place in the most serious of moments and in our most sacred texts (Avalos; Valeta; Chan, 16). Satire can be a powerful tool for critique, challenge, and change. Like Daniel's friends, we are immersed in media that market to us habits and systems of exploitation and consumption that are unstable and unsustainable. Advertisements and "reality" shows summon us to worship soulless images that are at best a parody of the image of God. Satire can reveal their absurdity and prompt us to reclaim our faculties of judgment and dedicate our bodies and whole selves to witness for the welfare of humankind and all creation.

Daniel 4:1-37: Royal Madness

■ The Text in Its Ancient Context

Ancient sources suggest that Daniel 4 draws on oral traditions about Babylon's last king, Nabonidus, who ruled from 556 to 539 (Henze, 69). Criticism of Nabonidus's behavior and beliefs had blossomed into a portrait of royal derangement. The account of Nebuchadnezzar's humiliation in Daniel 4 adapted oral traditions about Nabonidus, substituting Judah's conqueror for his successor as the story's main character.

Nebuchadnezzar II was an avid builder. In one inscription, he proclaimed, "the defenses of Esagila and Babylon I strengthened and secured for my reign an enduring name" (Sack, 66). Yet Daniel 4 cautions against mistaking royal work of empire- and city-building for divine power to order and create.

To drive home this point, Daniel makes creative use of the Mesopotamian mythological trope of the "wild man." Its best-known exemplar is the figure of Enkidu in the Gilgamesh Epic. The wild man Enkidu accepts the rule of the king and is thereby transformed into a "civilized" human being, symbolizing transformation of disorder into order and uncharted territory into city and kingdom. Daniel utilizes this trope in its animalization of the king, who has failed to understand the governing order that has established his own kingship and built up his kingdom (Henze, 93–99). He can become human again only when he recognizes the divine sovereign power that orders all things.

THE TEXT IN THE INTERPRETIVE TRADITION

In the late eighteenth century, Daniel 4 inspired English poet and artist William Blake's portrait of a debased king in his illuminated *Marriage of Heaven and Hell*. Blake's king is naked, on all fours, mouth gaping, and beard hanging to the earth. Uncomprehending eyes sink beneath a furrowed brow that betrays anxiety even as the swollen orbits suggest age and exhaustion. The king wears a four-pointed crown atop his head of long, thick hair; his drooping face and helpless expression contradict a body thick with muscle. The image satirizes monarchy. At the same time, its caption, "One Law for the Lion and Ox Is Oppression," critiques a liberal democracy, market economy, and industrial revolution that render humans interchangeable with one another (Makdisi).

THE TEXT IN CONTEMPORARY DISCUSSION

Daniel 4 and the artistic traditions it inspired trade heavily on the trope of madness. They raise questions about what it means to be human in an age of empires, industrialization, technology, and global capitalism. Empire markets exploitation, destruction, and degradation of human beings and natural resources alike as normal, reasonable, and inevitable. For example, in the modern industrial world, transnational corporations advertise to young consumers that fashion and electronics are keys to identity, self-expression, and social success. Low retail prices and ever-changing selections persuade consumers that these goods are disposable. While corporations profit, their laborers and the earth pay the greatest cost. This madness is often hidden from view. How might readers of Daniel today use the arts to help others see the destructive logic and practices of the systems that dehumanize us and degrade creation for what they are? What does Nebuchadnezzar's story teach about human vocation?

Daniel 5:1-30: Writing on the Wall

THE TEXT IN ITS ANCIENT CONTEXT

Daniel 5 opens with a new king in Babylon, Nebuchadnezzar's son Belshazzar. Historically, Belshazzar was the son not of Nebuchadnezzar, but of Nabonidus. Belshazzar acted as regent in Babylon during his father's ten-year absence from the capital. This detail reminds us that the Daniel stories do not aim at simple historical reportage. Rather, the composers of the stories play with history, deploying familiar motifs and traditions to evoke their associations in popular imagination while at the same time articulating truths about God and empire that cut through time and space.

One such truth is the relationship between empire and idolatry. As Belshazzar and his company drink from the vessels plundered from the Jerusalem temple, they praise gods that are not gods, but are rather the inert materials: "gold and silver, bronze, iron, wood, and stone" (5:4). In the Hebrew Scriptures, the pair "wood and stone" commonly refers to gods made by human hands (Deut. 4:28; 2 Kgs. 19:18; Isa. 37:19). Deuteronomy 29:17 adds to the pair "silver and gold," while Hab. 2:19 parodies the idols of wood and stone that are ornamented with these precious metals. The longer list in Daniel 5 adds two metals, bronze and iron, not found in the other lists (5:4, 23). Together with gold and silver, they are the four metals from which the statue of Daniel 2 was composed (2:32-33). Joined with stone and wood, they suggest that Belshazzar has conscripted his princes, wives, and concubines in idolatrous worship of empire itself.

▌ THE TEXT IN THE INTERPRETIVE TRADITION

The writing on the wall in Daniel 5 and the divine will it encoded provided Galileo Galilei (d. 1642) with a metaphor that would prove enormously influential in the philosophy of science. Just as the writing on the wall was inscrutable to all but Daniel, so too nature requires a specialist to decode its language of geometry and proportion (Reeves).

Although Galileo is often conscripted into a modern narrative of warfare between science and religion, he did not conceive of his own work in this way. Galileo found in Scripture a metaphor for his scientific study of nature. They were not opposed to one another, but complementary, as he wrote in 1613: "Holy Scripture and nature proceed alike from the divine Word—Scripture as dictated by the Holy Spirit, and nature as the faithful executor of God's commands" (Galilei, 56).

▌ THE TEXT IN CONTEMPORARY DISCUSSION

While Belshazzar stages his feast "for his lords" (5:1), in attendance are also "his wives, and his concubines" (5:2). The repeated possessive pronoun identifies them as belonging to him and subject to his command. After fulfilling his command, the wives and concubines disappear from the story.

A second supporting role is played by the queen (5:10-12). She offers personal counsel and reassurance, recounts history, and names key relationships. She places special value on insight, interpretation, and revelation from the heavenly realm. Belshazzar obeys her command; her prediction proves true. Yet the queen disappears from the story as well. In some respects, she provides a model for breaking out of scripted roles of subservience. In other respects, she reinforces the narrative's gendered hierarchy. How are women's roles scripted in the movies, television shows, and commercials we watch or in the books, magazines, and newspapers we read? How are women's roles defined and performed in our churches, families, and places of work? In what ways do women in authority reinforce, challenge, or displace patriarchal norms? The Geena Davis Institute on Gender in Media (www.seejane.org) provides resources for discussions about women and gender in media. Paired with study of Daniel 5 and other biblical texts, these tools provide a point of entry for discussions of women's roles in church and society.

Daniel 6:1-28: The Lion's Den

■ THE TEXT IN ITS ANCIENT CONTEXT

In earlier chapters, Daniel has repeatedly outperformed his fellow courtiers; by the end of Daniel 5, he has been promoted to high administrative rank. Now in Daniel 6, his success inspires jealousy and conspiracy. Jealousy and conspiracy among courtiers are well-known tropes in ancient Mesopotamian and early Jewish literature, including the Akkadian wisdom poem *Ludlul bēl Nēmeqi*, the Aramaic tale of Ahiqar, and the book of Esther. Karel van der Toorn has argued that the Daniel stories adapted earlier Mesopotamian narrative models to portray Daniel's success at court as well as the opposition he faced.

In addition to adapting a familiar plot, Daniel 6 also borrows the image of the lion's den from Mesopotamian scribes as a metaphor for the scribe's fall from royal favor: the one who previously received a lion's share of honor and material reward (including food) was now to be the lion's meal (see Toorn). By literalizing the metaphor, the storyteller opens wide the doors of imagination and gives new life and meaning to familiar tropes. In the process, literal settings take on new symbolic meanings (Goatly).

■ THE TEXT IN THE INTERPRETIVE TRADITION

Hippolytus of Rome's *Commentary on Daniel* (c. 202–211 CE) is considered the earliest extant Christian commentary on a biblical book. In his allegorical reading, Babylon is the world and the den of lions is Hades. By imitating Daniel's courage and steadfastness, his reader will be brought living out of the den and "found as a sharer of the resurrection" (Hippolytus, 3.31.2–3). The association between Daniel's deliverance from the lions' den and resurrection made this scene popular in early Christian and late antique funerary art (Jensen; Sörries).

■ THE TEXT IN CONTEMPORARY DISCUSSION

Michelle Alexander documents the effects of racial profiling and the War on Drugs in the United States, including mass incarceration and disenfranchisement of a stunning percentage of African American men. Analysis of who benefits and who is harmed reveals a disconnect between stated and actual motives driving these policies and practices. Daniel 6 and other biblical texts that portray incarceration and the manipulation of justice systems can help readers perceive systemic abuse and reclaim the power to reform and transform legislative, judicial, and carceral systems.

The imagery of Daniel 6 also conveys the dynamics and consequences of bullying. Psychologists studying the effects of adult bullying have noted that its victims "feel like slaves and animals, prisoners, children, and heartbroken lovers"; these similes highlight feelings of confinement, objectification, debasement, isolation, vulnerability, betrayal, and loss (Tracy, Lutgen-Sandvik, and Alberts).

Daniel's imagery acknowledges victims' pain, offers models of courage and a source of hope, and underscores the need for strong leadership to prevent bullying.

Daniel 7:1-28: Beastly and Humane Rule

■ THE TEXT IN ITS ANCIENT CONTEXT

In Daniel 2 and 4, Nebuchadnezzar dreams and Daniel interprets. Now, in chapter 7, Daniel dreams and angels interpret. In the biblical canon, an angelic interpreter first appears in the book of Zechariah (e.g., Zech. 1:9, 13-14, 19-21). Over time, revealing angels became a characteristic feature of Jewish apocalyptic literature. As residents of heaven with special access to the divine court, the angels were also believed to possess divine knowledge. They could travel freely between heaven and earth and mediated between humans and God in roles analogous to priest, prophet, and ruler. Daniel 7 accents each of these roles.

Another key feature of apocalyptic literature is its novel combination of familiar and fantastic imagery, which directs the imagination to see reality in a new light. The symbolism of Daniel's dream in chapter 7 has roots in the biblical books of Genesis, Hosea, and Ezekiel, as well as Canaanite and Mesopotamian mythology and Hellenistic royal iconography (Eggler). Each myth and symbol is refracted through a distinctively Jewish theological lens and given new meaning.

The contrast between the four beasts and the one like a human develops further a dichotomy explored already in Daniel 4. The beasts are monstrous, defying created categories of order. Daniel first sees a beast like a lion with eagle's wings, which appears to represent the Babylonian Empire. Echoing Nebuchadnezzar's debasement and restoration of reason in Daniel 4, its wings are removed and it receives a human heart (7:4). The second beast, like a bear, may represent the Median kingdom; it is portrayed with ribs between its teeth and receives the command to feast on flesh (7:5). The third beast, representing the Persian Empire, is like a leopard with four wings and four heads; its mobility and gaze thus extend toward the four corners of the earth (7:6). The fourth beast, representing the Hellenistic Empires, is mutated more than all the beasts before it; with iron teeth, it eats and crushes; its feet smash what remains (7:7). Its ten horns embody the might and treachery of its kings; it has a mouth for boasting and eyes like a human's (7:8). In each case, form mirrors ontology: predatory and mixed forms convey the violence of imperial rule, while quasi-human faculties of reason, sight, and speech call attention to empire's distorting logic. After the body of the fourth beast is destroyed, sovereignty is given to one like a human. This human form gives bodily expression to the humane rule of the kingdom of the people of the holy ones of the Most High and links that rule with the angels, who, throughout the latter half of Daniel, are also described as sharing visible likeness to humankind.

■ THE TEXT IN THE INTERPRETIVE TRADITION

In the Gospel of Mark, Jesus alludes to Daniel 7 in his discourse from the Mount of Olives (Mark 13:26). Later, Jesus' self-identification with the figure who comes with the clouds is linked to his divine Sonship and future glorious advent (Mark 14:62). The Gospels of Matthew and Luke add further emphases on the kingdom of the son of man and his future role as judge and advocate (A. Y. Collins, 98–100).

THE TEXT IN CONTEMPORARY DISCUSSION

The book of Revelation adapts Daniel's descriptions of the beastly kingdoms in its portrayal of Rome (13:1-2, 11-14). For the writers of Daniel, the Seleucid Empire seduced, devoured, and exploited its subjects. For the seer of Revelation, it was Rome. In looking for the modern-day analogue to these ancient empires, American scholars have often pointed to the United States (Horsley). Yet political philosophers Michael Hardt and Antonio Negri contend that the role of empire no longer belongs to colonizing or occupying nation-states. In today's global economy, transnational corporations and the economic systems that support their practices of exploitation and segmentation are the new empire.

Readers of Daniel 7 in the twenty-first century must analyze not only ancient text but also modern context. What is the nature of the political and economic systems in which we participate? Do they destroy and devour, seduce, and exploit, or do they enact justice for humankind and for the earth?

Daniel 8:1-27: A Limit to Desolation

THE TEXT IN ITS ANCIENT CONTEXT

At the conclusion of the vision in Daniel 8, Daniel hears a holy one ask how long the assaults on the heavenly sanctuary and host will last (8:13). The response is measured by the number of evening and morning sacrifices: 2,300 evenings and mornings (8:14). This great number of mornings and evenings are not the only measure in Daniel for the cessation of the temple offerings. Later, the angel Gabriel describes the same period as "a half-week" (9:27), that is, three and a half years. The man clothed in linen will similarly declare its duration "a time, two times, and half a time" (12:7; cf. 7:25). These numbers are partly symbolic: they are one-half of seven years. Seven was the number of days of creation, and so symbolized divine order and providence as well as totality, completion, perfection, and sanctity. Half seven symbolized Antiochus's assault on holiness, his failure to undo God's order, and his inability to create and sustain on his own. The 2,300 mornings and evenings are also a source of hope: God has set a limit to the time of desolation.

THE TEXT IN THE INTERPRETIVE TRADITION

The interpretation of Dan. 8:14 was a cornerstone in the premillennial historicist calculations of American Protestant William Miller (d. 1849). Miller interpreted the 2,300 evenings and mornings as years. The desolated sanctuary was the entire earth, and the years of desolation were the pope's rule. At their conclusion, in 1843 (later revised to 1844), Christ would return (Newport). By 1844, Christ's return was not evident. Followers of Miller dealt with this "Great Disappointment" in different ways. Hiram Edson concluded that Christ *had* come—to "the second apartment" of the *heavenly* sanctuary (Newport).

■ THE TEXT IN CONTEMPORARY DISCUSSION

The book of Daniel continues to figure prominently in modern-day calculations of the "end times." The data in Daniel suggest that this effort is misguided. At the same time, the impulse to reinterpret biblical prophecy for the present day is very much in keeping with methods practiced in the book itself, as we see further in Daniel 9.

Daniel provided perspective on current events by placing them within a broader narrative and historical framework and interpreting them in relation to God's work in history and plan for the future. The activity of the horn and the period of desolation in Daniel 8 described events and circumstances in the audience's present. The vision and its interpretation helped them to understand their plight in terms not just political but also theological. It also helped them to perceive an end, not to history, but to foreign domination.

Daniel 9:1-27: Study, Fasting, and Prayer

■ THE TEXT IN ITS ANCIENT CONTEXT

Daniel's study of Jeremiah's scroll offers insight into the interpretation of Scripture in early Judaism. Daniel approaches interpretation as a sacred and even mystical endeavor. He fasts and humbles his body with sackcloth and ashes, enacting heightened awareness of human mortality and dependence on God. In response to what he has read and seen, he also prays, confessing his people's sins and shame and begging God to hear, see, and forgive, to pay attention and act for the sake of God's city and people. In response to Daniel's pleading, Gabriel comes to him and interprets Jeremiah's scroll. The time of exile has not ended: seventy years are seventy weeks of years (Dan. 9:2, 24-27).

Similar prophetic periodization of history is found in the Apocalypse of Weeks (*1 En.* 93:1-10; 91:11-17), a Jewish historical apocalypse contemporary with the book of Daniel. In this apocalypse, history is divided into ten weeks. Reading Daniel 9 in the context of other early Jewish apocalypses reveals a shared view of time and history. As in the Apocalypse of Weeks, so in Daniel 9 the division of history into weeks of years invokes time's created, sabbatical structure and calls to mind the Jubilee of Lev. 25:8-22. Jubilee was a time of liberation, restoration, and justice and was closely linked with the Day of Atonement. Accordingly, Gabriel declares that the seventy weeks have been appointed to atone for guilt and bring justice (Dan. 9:24).

■ THE TEXT IN THE INTERPRETIVE TRADITION

An exegetical text from Qumran known as 11QMelchizedek (11Q13; mid-first century BCE) may preserve one of the oldest extant references to Dan. 9:25-26 (Campbell). Melchizedek is the central figure in this eschatological text. His role is similar to that of Michael in Daniel: the people are his inheritance, he is a leader among the "sons of God," or angels, and he will be an instrument of God's judgment and will liberate his people in "the last days." Like Daniel and the Apocalypse of Weeks, this text envisions history measured in heptads. Its quotations of Lev. 25:9 and 13 and Deut. 15:2 explicitly link Daniel's discourse with jubilary traditions of justice and restoration.

■ THE TEXT IN CONTEMPORARY DISCUSSION

The apocalyptic timetables in Daniel 9 and the Apocalypse of Weeks are often characterized as expressing a deterministic view of history. Yet this understanding of providence does not negate the emphasis on teaching and justice in both works. Moreover, the prayer in Daniel 9 shifts the focus from the crimes of empire to the community's relationship with God. It offers an avenue from failure to renewal through responsibility and forgiveness. Gabriel's discourse places this understanding of sin and reconciliation within an apocalyptic framework. Even in the midst of appointed times, God remains responsive to petition and confession. Here and throughout the book, Daniel's actions and prayer provide a model for his audience to follow. In the same way, Gabriel's words to Daniel provide the book's readers with wisdom, understanding, and the assurance, "you are greatly loved" (9:23).

Daniel 10:1-21: Vision, Understanding, and Strength

■ THE TEXT IN ITS ANCIENT CONTEXT

Daniel spends three weeks in mourning. During this time, he abstains from meat, wine, and delicacies and refrains from anointing his body. Gavin Flood argues that ascetic practices are a means of transforming subjectivity. They root the self in tradition but also provide a way to transcend the limits of body, culture, cosmology, and individual desire. They create a "new" body able simultaneously to push back against these boundaries and to open itself to the will of God (Flood).

Daniel's abstention precipitates a vision as he stands by the bank of the Tigris River (Dan. 10:3-5), one of the four rivers that flow from the Garden of Eden (Gen. 2:14). The banks of flowing waterways mark a boundary between heaven and earth (Genesis 1), eras (Genesis 6–9), life and death (Exodus 14–15; Carlsson), promise and fulfillment (Josh. 1:2-3). For Daniel, like Ezekiel before him (Ezek. 1:1.3), the riverbank is a space of revelation. At the water's edge, he will learn of his people's future in their own land, the end of empire, and the passage from death to life. In Daniel 12, the detail is added that the man in linen stands above the waters of the stream, while two others stand on each side (12:5-6). The angels who appear to Daniel occupy heaven and earth; they stand in past and future; they are witnesses to death and to the promise of life eternal. The man in linen bridges these divisions to bring understanding and strength to Daniel.

■ THE TEXT IN THE INTERPRETIVE TRADITION

The Jewish apocalypse *4 Ezra* (c. 100 CE) draws on Daniel's portrayal of visionary praxis, including mourning, fasting, and dietary abstinence (*4 Ezra* 6:35; Dan. 9:3; 10:2-3). *Fourth Ezra* also adds a new element. Toward the book's conclusion, the Most High provides Ezra with a cup to drink. Its fiery liquid imparts understanding and wisdom, allowing him to dictate his revelations to the five men who are with him (14:39-48). The Most High declares that seventy of the books they have written contain "the river of knowledge" (14:47). Abstinence has prepared the seer to receive a different kind of substance and sustenance. Moreover, the act of writing places the river within the text, making it possible for others to receive revelation by consulting the books.

◼ THE TEXT IN CONTEMPORARY DISCUSSION

Scholars have debated whether visionary texts such as Daniel or *4 Ezra* reflect genuine religious experience or literary convention (Stone). Apocalypses are richly allusive, drawing heavily on earlier prophetic and apocalyptic tropes, images, and symbols. They attribute visionary experience to a figure from the past, creating a fictional narrative to frame their reports of revelation. Does this mean that they do not reflect actual visionary experiences on the part of their authors and their faith communities?

Increasingly, we are learning that ancient visionary praxis relied heavily on reading and interpreting sacred Scriptures (Rowland with Gibbons and Dobroruka). An earlier text like Ezekiel or Daniel could provide a later visionary with an example of mystical asceticism as well as imagery and language to describe her or his vision of God's throne, angels, and divine glory. The sacred text itself was also a gateway to mystical transformation and divine encounter (DeConick).

Daniel 11:1-45: War, Betrayal, and Persecution

◼ THE TEXT IN ITS ANCIENT CONTEXT

The angel's discourse in Daniel 11 reveals to Daniel events that will unfold from his time through the death of Antiochus IV Epiphanes. Yet the discourse does not simply foretell events to come; it interprets them. While names and dates can help modern readers establish context for interpreting the chapter, the style of the angel's discourse suggests that more important than the names and dates of particular individuals, battles, negotiations, and betrayals are their character. Kings of the North (Seleucids) and South (Ptolemies) seem almost interchangeable; at times, even these designations are abandoned for pronouns that leave the reader unable to distinguish one actor from another (e.g., 11:11-12). The kings are alike in war making, pride, deception, and weakness. And they do not last.

The discourse highlights themes of sovereignty, wealth, and warfare. A notice at the chapter's beginning suggests that empire's greed will be its undoing: the final Persian king "will heap up greater wealth than all who have gone before, relying on his wealth as his strength" (author's own translation); in so doing, he will wake the kingdom of Greece and so bring about his own downfall (11:2). In later verses, violence, exploitation, and idolatry characterize the rule of Antiochus IV (11:24, 28, 36). The discourse employs critique as a mode of resistance to the military, economic, and religious ideology and practices of empire.

In the year 167 BCE, Antiochus IV undertook a persecution of Jews in Judea. Daniel 11 describes a group of "wise teachers" among the Judeans who will help many of their people to understand the events that are happening, what God asks of them, and what God will do (11:33). Their nonviolent witness and martyrdom (11:33) provide a further example of resistance for the audience to follow.

◼ THE TEXT IN THE INTERPRETIVE TRADITION

For the writers of Daniel, the description of the king of the North who "shall exalt himself and consider himself greater than any god, and shall speak horrendous things against the God of gods"

(Dan. 11:36) referred to Antiochus IV Epiphanes. In the first century CE, this verse inspired the portrait of the "lawless one" (literally "human of lawlessness") in 2 Thess. 2:1-8. Among early Christian interpreters, this "lawless one" became further identified with *antichristos*, a term used in 1 and 2 John (1 John 2:22, 4:3; 2 John 7). The label "antichrist" was used to help members of the writers' community discern between teachings and spirits that were of God and those that were not of God and to identify as untrustworthy teachers of false doctrine (Fuller). Over time, *antichristos* evolved from adjective to title, coalescing into a composite portrait of the Antichrist assembled from key passages in Daniel, 2 Thessalonians, 1 and 2 John, and Revelation (e.g., Rev. 13:1-4; Fuller).

THE TEXT IN CONTEMPORARY DISCUSSION

In her essay "Queering the Beast: The Antichrists' Gay Wedding," biblical scholar and cultural critic Erin Runions calls attention to interpretations of Dan. 11:37 among culturally conservative Christians in the United States that identify the Antichrist as a gay male. In this stream of interpretation, Runions detects an "apocalyptic logic" driving much political opposition to gay marriage (Runions, 80).

In her 1928 novel *The Well of Loneliness*, lesbian writer Radclyffe Hall reads Daniel differently (Madden). Hearing the words of a spiritual—"Didn't my Lord deliver Daniel, then why not every man?"—leads Stephen, the novel's protagonist, to pose another question that draws on Dan. 8:13 and 12:6: "Yes, but how long, O Lord, how long?" (Hall, 330). Later in the novel, Stephen asks more pointedly: "How long was this persecution to continue? How long would God sit still and endure this insult offered to . . . creation? How long tolerate the preposterous statement that inversion was not a part of nature? For since it existed what else could it be? All things that existed were part of nature!" (Hall, 368).

Same-sex love, "gender-inversion," and "congenital sexual inversion" had been medically pathologized and socially stigmatized. Nor were same-sex unions blessed by the church, though Stephen and others long for this blessing (Hall, 369). Ed Madden has argued that Hall's appropriation of Daniel and other biblical texts simultaneously writes a "reverse discourse" of legitimation and voices a hope of future acceptance.

Daniel 12:1-13: The End of Days

THE TEXT IN ITS ANCIENT CONTEXT

The angel's discourse culminates in a prediction of salvation, freedom, life, and knowledge for Daniel's people. The angel also foretells resurrection followed by judgment and reward or punishment for some of those who have died (12:2-3). Daniel draws on earlier traditions even as it articulates a new vision for life after death (Nickelsburg).

The prophet Hosea voiced the hope of some among his people that after two days God would restore their health and after three days raise them up to live in God's presence (Hosea 6:2). Hosea appears to have had in view the continuation of life through healing from sickness, not resurrection from death, yet later interpreters would associate the two (Macintosh, 222).

In Ezekiel's vision of dry bones, God instructs the prophet to declare to the bones that they will live (Ezek. 37:4). God explains that the bones are all Israel (37:11) and God will open their graves and bring them up from their graves (37:12-13) and they will live in their land (37:14). Like Daniel 12, Ezekiel 37 simultaneously envisions bodies raised from the earth and a nation's new beginning and restoration.

Isaiah 24–27 contain a vision of cosmic upheaval, destruction, judgment, and renewal. These chapters foretell the end of death: God will destroy the shroud and swallow death for all time (25:7-8). Daniel 12:2 shares with Isaiah 26:19 imagery of waking from the dust from death to life.

■ THE TEXT IN THE INTERPRETIVE TRADITION

The portrait of Michael as angelic warrior in Daniel 10 and deliverer who would liberate God's people in Daniel 12 influenced later imperial ideology. In the Carolingian Empire, beginning in the eighth century CE, liturgical acclamations called *laudes regiae* were sung at coronations and on festival days. The centerpiece of the *laudes* invoked for the king the protections of Mary and the archangels, with Michael listed as the first of these (Kantorowicz). In a similar vein, Charlemagne's military standards depicted Michael with the legend "Patron and Prince of the Empire of the Gauls" (Johnson). Michael, a figure associated in Daniel with the end of empire, is thus transformed in the Byzantine era into a symbol of empire's divine aid and military might.

■ THE TEXT IN CONTEMPORARY DISCUSSION

For Barbara Leung Lai, the differing portraits of Daniel in Daniel 1–6 and 7–12 represent Daniel's public and private selves. In public, Daniel displays confidence and God-given understanding. In private, Daniel is terrified and confused by his experience. His body manifests his distress. Yet the angel has lifted him to his feet and given him strength and partial understanding. Daniel's story can help pastoral-care providers acknowledge and cope with the dissonance between their public and private experiences and with the psychic and physiological effects of fear and confusion. The predictions and promise to Daniel at the book's end offer hope and assurance not just to Daniel but also to pastors.

The final commands to Daniel also offer practical instruction. Some interpret the commands "go your way, and rest" (12:13), with reference to Daniel's death (e.g., Pace 2008, 343). Yet the word "rest" (*nûaḥ*) does not typically refer to death. Here it may more closely correspond to Sabbath (cf. Exod. 20:11; 23:12). In the face of suffering, despair, weakness, and confusion and in response to God's own work of creation, salvation, and liberation, the reader, like Daniel, is reminded that rest provides a path to renewal and life (cf. Exod. 31:16-17; Deut. 5:15).

Works Cited

Alexander, Michelle. 2010. *The New Jim Crow: Mass Incarceration in the Age of Colorblindness*. New York: New Press.

Avalos, Hector. 1991. "The Comedic Function of the Enumerations of Officials and Instruments in Daniel 3." *CBQ* 53, no. 4:580–88.

Bull, Malcolm, and Keith Lockhart. 2007. *Seeking a Sanctuary: Seventh-day Adventism and the American Dream*. 2nd ed. Bloomington: Indiana University Press.

Campbell, Jonathan G. 2007. *The Exegetical Texts*. Companion to the Qumran Scrolls. London: T&T Clark.

Carlsson, Leif. 2004. *Round Trips to Heaven: Otherworldly Travelers in Early Judaism and Christianity.* Lund: Lund University.

Chan, Michael. 2013. "Ira Regis: Comedic Inflections of Royal Rage in Jewish Court Tales." *JQR* 103, no. 1:1–25.

Charlesworth, James H. 2007. "Can We Discern the Composition Date of the Parables of Enoch?" In *Enoch and the Messiah Son of Man: Revisiting the Book of Parables*, edited by Gabriele Boccaccini, 450–68. Grand Rapids: Eerdmans.

Chia, Philip. 2006. "On Naming the Subject: Postcolonial Reading of Daniel 1." In *The Postcolonial Biblical Reader*, edited by Rasiah S. Sugirtharajah, 171–84. Oxford: Blackwell.

Collins, Adela Yarbro. 1993. "The Influence of Daniel on the New Testament." In John J. Collins. *Daniel: A Commentary on the Book of Daniel*. Hermeneia. Minneapolis: Fortress Press.

Collins, John. J. 1993. *Daniel: A Commentary on the Book of Daniel*. Hermeneia. Minneapolis: Fortress Press.

———. 1998. *The Apocalyptic Imagination: An Introduction to Jewish Apocalyptic Literature*. 2nd ed. Grand Rapids: Eerdmans.

DeConick, April D. 2006. "What Is Early Jewish and Christian Mysticism?" In *Paradise Now: Essays on Early Jewish and Christian Mysticism*, edited by April D. DeConick, 1–24. Atlanta: Society of Biblical Literature.

Eggler, Jürg. 2000. *Influences and Traditions Underlying the Vision of Daniel 7:2-14: The Research History from the End of the 19th Century to the Present*. Göttingen: Vandenhoeck & Ruprecht.

Erdman, David V. 1977. *Blake: Prophet against Empire: A Poet's Interpretation of the History of His Own Times*. 3rd ed. Princeton: Princeton University Press.

Fewell, Danna Nolan. 2003. *The Children of Israel: Reading the Bible for the Sake of Our Children.* Nashville: Abingdon.

Flood, Gavin. 2004. *The Ascetic Self: Subjectivity, Memory and Tradition*. Cambridge: Cambridge University Press.

Fuller, R. C. 1995. *Naming the Antichrist: The History of an American Obsession*. Oxford: Oxford University Press.

Galilei, Galileo. 2012. *Selected Writings*. Translated by William R. Shea and Mark Davie. Oxford: Oxford University Press.

Goatly, Andrew. 1997. *The Language of Metaphors*. New York: Routledge.

Gregory, Susan. 2010. *The Daniel Fast: Feed Your Soul, Strengthen Your Spirit, and Renew Your Body*. Tyndale Momentum.

Hall, Radclyffe. 2005. *The Well of Loneliness.* Hertfordshire: Wordsworth.

Hardt, Michael, and Antonio Negri. 2000. *Empire*. Cambridge, MA: Harvard University Press.

Henze, Matthias. 1999. *The Madness of King Nebuchadnezzar: The Ancient Near Eastern Origins and Early History of Interpretation of Daniel 4*. Leiden: Brill.

Hippolytus of Rome. 2010. *Commentary on Daniel*. Translated and edited by Tom C. Schmidt. CreateSpace. www.chronicon.net. Accessed August 4, 2013.

Horsley, Richard A., ed. 2008. *In the Shadow of Empire: Reclaiming the Bible as a History of Faithful Resistance.* Louisville: Westminster John Knox.

Jensen, Robin Margaret. 2000. *Understanding Early Christian Art*. New York: Routledge.

Johnson, Richard F. 2005. *Saint Michael the Archangel in Medieval English Legend*. Woodbridge: Boydell Press.

Kantorowicz, Ernst H. 1958. *Laudes Regiae: A Study of Liturgical Acclamations and Mediaeval Ruler Worship.* Berkeley: University of California Press.

Landon, Richard. 1990. "The Stillman Drake Galileo Collection." In *Nature, Experiment, and the Sciences: Essays on Galileo and the History of Science*, edited by Trevor H. Levere and William R. Shea, 321–37. Dordrecht, the Netherlands: Kluwer Academic.

Leung Lai, Barbara M. 2008. "Ancient Sage or Dysfunctional Seer? Cognitive Dissonance and Pastoral Vulnerability in the Profile of Daniel." *Pastoral Psychology* 57:199–210.

Macintosh, Andrew. 1997. *Hosea*. ICC. Edinburgh: T&T Clark.

Madden, Ed. 2000. "Gospels of Inversion: Literature, Scripture, Sexology." In *Divine Aporia: Postmodern Conversations about the Other*, edited by John C. Hawley, 123–52. London: Associated University Presses.

Makdisi, Saree. 2003. *William Blake and the Impossible History of the 1790s*. Chicago: University of Chicago Press.

Mills, Mary. 2006. "Household and Table: Diasporic Boundaries in Daniel and Esther." *CBQ* 68, no. 3:408–20.

Newport, Kenneth G. C. 2000. *Apocalypse and Millennium: Studies in Biblical Eisegesis*. Cambridge: Cambridge University Press.

Nickelsburg, George W. E. 2006. *Resurrection, Immortality, and Eternal Life in Intertestamental Judaism and Early Christianity*. Cambridge, MA: Harvard University Press.

Nickelsburg, George W. E., and James C. VanderKam. 2004. *1 Enoch: A New Translation*. Minneapolis: Fortress Press.

Pace, Sharon. 2008. *Daniel*. Smyth and Helwys Bible Commentary. Macon, GA: Smyth and Helwys.

Portier-Young, Anathea. 2010. "Languages of Identity and Obligation: Daniel as Bilingual Book," *VT* 60:1–18.

———. 2011. *Apocalypse against Empire: Theologies of Resistance in Early Judaism*. Grand Rapids: Eerdmans.

Reeves, Eileen. 1991. "Daniel 5 and the *Assayer*: Galileo Reads the Handwriting on the Wall." *Journal of Medieval and Renaissance Studies* 21, no. 1:1–27.

Rochberg, Francesca. 1988. *Aspects of Babylonian Celestial Divination: The Lunar Eclipse Tablets of Enūma Anu Enlil*. Horn, Austria: Ferdinand Berger & Söhne.

———. 2004. *The Heavenly Writing: Divination, Horoscopy, and Astronomy in Mesopotamian Culture*. Cambridge: Cambridge University Press.

Rowland, Christopher, with Patricia Gibbons and Vicente Dobroruka. 2006. "Visionary Experience in Ancient Judaism and Christianity." In *Paradise Now: Essays on Early Jewish and Christian Mysticism*, edited by April D. DeConick, 41–56. Atlanta: Society of Biblical Literature.

Runions, Erin. 2008. "Queering the Beast: The Antichrists' Gay Wedding." In *Queering the Non/Human*, edited by Noreen Giffney and Myra J. Hird, 79–110 Aldershot: Ashgate.

Sack, Ronald. 2004. *Images of Nebuchadnezzar: The Emergence of a Legend*. Selinsgrove, PA: Susquehanna University Press.

Sörries, Reiner. 2006. *Daniel in der Löwengrube. Zur Gesetzmäßigkeit frühchristlicher Ikonographie*. Wiesbaden: Reichert.

Stone, Michael. 2003. "A Reconsideration of Apocalyptic Visions." *HTR* 96, no. 2:167–80.

Theodoret of Cyrus. 2006. *Commentary on Daniel*. Translated and edited by Robert C. Hill. Atlanta: Society of Biblical Literature.

Toorn, Karel van der. 1998. "In the Lions' Den: The Babylonian Background of a Biblical Motif." *CBQ* 64:626–40.

Tracy, S. J., P. Lutgen-Sandvik, and J. K. Alberts. 2006. "Nightmares, Demons, and Slaves: Exploring the Painful Metaphors of Workplace Bullying." *Management Communication Quarterly* 20, no. 2:148–85.

Valdez, Maria Ana Travassos. 2011. *Historical Interpretations of the "Fifth Empire": The Dynamics of Periodization from Daniel to António Vieira, S.J.* Leiden: Brill.

Valeta, David. 2008. *Lions, Ovens, and Visions: A Satirical Reading of Daniel 1–6*. Sheffield: Sheffield Phoenix.

HOSEA

Alice A. Keefe

Introduction

The book of Hosea is the first of the twelve books of the Minor Prophets scroll, composed of collected oracles attributed to the eighth-century-BCE prophet Hosea. The collection originated in the northern kingdom of Israel and was transmitted to Judah after the Assyrian conquest, where it helped to shape—and was shaped by—the emerging Deuteronomistic school. The collection most likely underwent further redaction during the Babylonian exile—a time when Hosea's prophecies resonated with the experiences of a new generation.

Hosea son of Beeri was most likely a native of Ephraim, the name he favored for the northern kingdom of Israel. His oracles evidence extensive knowledge of the kingdom's history, its current domestic and foreign politics, and the duplicitous conduct of its priestly and political leaders. The prophet Hosea situates himself within a lineage of prophets going back to Moses (Hosea 6:5; 9:8; 12:13), and grounds his message in recollection of the sacred traditions of the exodus from Egypt, the forging of the covenant at Sinai, and YHWH's providential care for Israel in the wilderness. As part of his prophetic mission, he marries a woman named Gomer, characterized as a "woman of promiscuity," and gives bizarre and ominous names to their children. This symbolic action points to Hosea's core concern: the failure of the nation to live up to the terms of the Sinai covenant.

According to the book's superscription, Hosea's prophetic activity began sometime in the middle of the eighth century BCE, during the last years of King Jeroboam II of Israel, and continued through the troubled years leading up to the Assyrian conquest in 722 BCE. This was a politically turbulent era in the northern kingdom, marked by palace coups and multiple regicides, war with Judah, and a vacillating foreign policy, all of which opened the way for Assyria's invasion. Meanwhile, the cult of sacrifice at the national shrines functioned as an arm of the royal administration, lending divine sanction to the monarchy and its policies. As a prophetic witness to the era, Hosea denounced the duplicity, faithlessness, and foolishness of Israel's elite establishment. In his eyes, the nation had violated the nation's covenant with YHWH, and divine punishment in the form of historical disaster would soon ensue. While the book includes several oracles offering hope of reconciliation and redemption, the overall tone is dark with warnings of impending national catastrophe.

Hosea 1–3: YHWH's Wife of Promiscuity

▌ THE TEXT IN ITS ANCIENT CONTEXT

The book of Hosea is best known for the marriage metaphor of Hosea 1–3. This trope was a rhetorical innovation that deployed an image of something familiar to Hosea's ancient audience—the structure of Israelite marriage—to evoke a renewed understanding of something less familiar or perhaps forgotten, that is, the requirements of the covenant relationship between YHWH and the nation. Hosea 1:2 reports that the inspiration for this metaphor came in a divine revelation, whereby the prophet was instructed to take "a wife of promiscuity" and have "children of promiscuity." In following this command, Hosea acted out on the stage of his own life a message concerning Israel's covenant with YHWH (portrayed as marriage) and "her" neglect/violation of that covenant (portrayed as wifely infidelity).

Hosea's original audience would have received and understood his marriage metaphor in relation to the meanings that marriage and sexual transgression carried in the ancient world. In modern culture, we tend to think of marriage as being primarily a romantic or personal relationship, and value mutual and equal relations between husband and wife. In Hosea's world, the primary aim of marriage was reproduction and the continuation of the patrilineage, and the relationship between husband and wife was hierarchical and asymmetrical. A wife in ancient Israel was under the authority of her husband, was dependent on him for her subsistence, and owed him exclusive sexual rights so that the paternity of his children could be assured. A wife who strayed sexually was subject to divorce and even death (Num. 5:11-31; Deut. 22:22-24). Her obligation of fidelity, however, was not reciprocal; a husband could enjoy sexual relations with other women, such as prostitutes or concubines, so long as no other man's "rights" over "his" women were violated. Codes of honor and shame provided indispensable support for this social system. A man's honor depended on his ability to maintain sexual control over his wife/wives and daughters. A woman who had illicit sexual relations—even if it was forced on her through rape—brought shame on the men in her family (Gen. 34:31; Lev. 21:9). Hosea's metaphor draws on these social codes, comparing the nation to an adulterous wife giving birth to children of uncertain paternity (powerful symbols of transgression and shame in his world) in order to awaken his audience to the gravity of their own transgression of their covenant obligations to YHWH.

Hosea's marriage metaphor is deployed in different configurations in each of the book's first three chapters. In the third-person narrative of Hosea 1:2-3, the prophet is instructed to marry a woman named Gomer, who is characterized as a woman or wife of *zĕnûnîm*. *Zĕnûnîm* carries the meaning of repeated or habitual sexual transgression, and is best translated as "whoredom(s)" or "promiscuity" (Bird 1989, 80). (Although some older translations render "whore" or "harlot," the term for a

professional prostitute, zônâ, is not used.) When Gomer gives birth, the children are likewise characterized as children of zĕnûnim, and Hosea gives them ominous names that signal God's displeasure.
The name of the firstborn, Jezreel (Hosea 1:4-5), evokes memories of the blood spilled at the town of
Jezreel by the usurper Jehu in his bloody coup against the house of Ahab (2 Kings 9–10) and invites
comparison between that era and the violent politics of Hosea's own time. The names of the second
and third children—"Not Pitied" and "Not My People" (Hosea 1:6-8)—effect ironic reversals of the
Mosaic traditions of election and covenant, in which YHWH had pity on the enslaved Israelites
and announced they would be his people (Exod. 3:7-9; 19:5). Hosea 1 concludes with the hope for
future restoration, figured poetically through a lifting of the curses implied in these names (1:10-11).

In Hosea 2, YHWH accuses his wife, the nation Israel, of chasing after other lovers, believing that it is they, and not her "first husband," who provide her with the gifts of the land's bounty
(Hosea 2:5). Outraged, the husband, YHWH, threatens to exercise his legal rights to violently
punish and/or divorce her; he promises that he will strip her naked "in the sight of her lovers" (2:10),
put an end to "all her appointed festivals" (2:11), and "lay waste" her vineyards and orchards (2:12).
Abruptly, these divine threats shift to a promise of reconciliation in the wilderness, a kind of second
honeymoon that revives the original intimacy that existed between YHWH and Israel in the years
of wandering in the wilderness (Hosea 2:14-15). The chapter ends with YHWH's promise of a new
covenant/betrothal that includes the whole of creation and is founded on the virtues of righteousness, justice, ḥesed ("steadfast love" or "covenant fidelity"), and mercy (Hosea 2:16-23).

Hosea 3 offers a first-person account of YHWH's command to the prophet to love an adulterous woman. Hosea tells the woman that she must refrain from sexual pleasures for a time, even
with her husband; the point being that Israel itself must dwell for a time in a state of separation (or
exile), without political leaders or its sacrificial cult. The brief chapter ends with the prospect of the
reunification of Israel under a Davidic king. A similar promise of Israel and Judah being "gathered
together" under "one head" also is found at the conclusion of Hosea 1 (1:10-11).

While the metaphor of female sexual transgression dominates and unites these chapters, the
referent of the metaphor—the actual sins being condemned—is not clear. The motif of the wife
chasing after "her lovers" in conjunction with reference to the "feast days of the ba'alim" suggests
that Israel's sin is pursuit of other gods. Many have understood these "lovers" or ba'alim as the fertility gods of ancient Canaan. In this view, Hosea objects to popular participation in a syncretistic
fertility cult in which the people sought assurance of agricultural fertility through rituals of worship
and sacrifice to the rain god Baal and other deities connected with the powers of nature.

▮ THE TEXT IN THE INTERPRETIVE TRADITION

Hosea's marriage metaphor made a lasting impact on the religious language of subsequent generations. In Christianity, marital imagery shaped both ecclesiology, where the church is envisioned as
the bride of Christ, and mystical theology, in which the soul unites with the divine. And within
both Christianity and Judaism, female sexual transgression, or "whoring," has had a long history as
a primary trope for sin.

Perhaps because of the marriage metaphor's influence in Western religious thought, it has
attracted considerable attention over the centuries. Much of this commentary has been focused

on efforts to reconstruct the biographical facts concerning the relationship between Hosea and Gomer (Sherwood, 40–54). Many premodern commentators were so offended by the thought of Hosea, God's righteous prophet, being sullied by marriage to an "impure" woman that they interpreted Hosea's marriage as occurring only in a dream, as the Jewish exegete Abraham Ibn Ezra suggested (Lipschitz, 20), or as a visionary experience, as the Protestant Reformer John Calvin maintained (43–44). Twentieth-century biblical scholars have generally assumed the literal intent of the marriage, but have filled in the gaps to create a romanticized narrative of Hosea's unrequited love for Gomer, his personal pain at her betrayal, and his heroic forgiveness of her. This preoccupation with the details of Hosea's personal life has been motivated by the premise that the prophet's own emotional turmoil served as his inspiration for understanding YHWH's experience with Israel, suffering from their rejection, but forgiving them and loving them in the end (e.g., Rowley, 97).

The details of Gomer's sexual life have also been the topic of much speculation. Many twentieth-century commentators, building on the thesis that rituals of sacred prostitution were part of the fertility cult Hosea condemns, have argued that Gomer's infidelity involved the performance of ritual sex acts within the fertility cult. She might have been a sacred prostitute who had sex with men at the shrines (e.g., Mays, 25–26), or alternatively, a virgin who had been ritually "deflowered" in bridal rites at the shrines (e.g., Wolff, 14–15).

The view that Hosea opposed a popular fertility cult, in which the worship of nature deities was accompanied by sexual rituals, has served to articulate and reinforce a theological opposition between pagan nature worship and ethical monotheism. Evidence supporting the scenario of a sexualized fertility cult in ancient Israel is slim. In response, some have sought an alternative approach to reconstructing Hosea's religious contexts by attending to the interrelationships between religion, politics, and economics in ancient Israel (Keefe; Yee 2001; Kelle). These interpreters highlight the political and cultural connotations of Baal and the Baalim in Hosea's world, and suggest that Israel's "lovers" are not fertility gods but foreign gods, that is, the state deities of other nations— Israel's allies, trading partners, and/or overlords. From this perspective, the nation's "promiscuity" is a symbol for its deepening investments in international "liaisons" and cosmopolitan orientations (see also Hosea 8:9), and those whom Hosea accuses as "whoring" are not the people in general, but Israel's elite power brokers.

In the twentieth century, many biblical scholars argued that rituals of sacred prostitution were included in Baalim fertility cult under the theory that human sex acts performed in imitation of the sacred marriage of the gods helped to secure the fertility of the land. In recent years, however, this reconstruction of the religious contexts behind Hosea's rhetoric has been challenged. Scholars who have revisited the "sacred prostitution" hypothesis have found no compelling evidence for ritual sex in ancient Israel or neighboring cultures in this era (Toorn; Oden). The existence of a popular fertility cult or widespread Baal worship in Hosea's Israel, as are presupposed by most interpreters, also is uncertain (Kelle, 137–52). Further, the cult practices that Hosea explicitly attacks—rites of sacrifice at the high places and the presence of the bull icon at Bethel—were not foreign accretions, but accepted features of Yahwism in his day (Yee 2001, 351).

█ THE TEXT IN CONTEMPORARY DISCUSSION

Contemporary theological reflection on Hosea 1–3 demands attention to issues of gender and the problematic legacy of patriarchal symbols within Western religious traditions. Feminist readers contend that Hosea's marriage metaphor reinforces patriarchal social structures, silences woman's voice, legitimates violence against her, and identifies women with sin and evil. The metaphor presupposes and legitimates a patriarchal social system in which husbands have a unilateral right to control their wives' sexuality and the legal authority to inflict physical punishment on her if she violates that right. Furthermore, YHWH's threats of violence against the metaphorical woman—threatening to strip her naked in the sight of her lovers, presumably so they can rape her (2:10)—is a highly disturbing motif, and one that some find to be almost pornographic in its conjunction of voyeurism and violence (e.g., Setel). How does a woman who has been battered relate to the image of God as a wife batterer (Weems, 8)? Can this text function as sacred Scripture for her, or for anyone who seeks liberation from the violence that sustains patriarchy?

Another problem with this metaphor is its gender assignments, which link maleness with the divine and femaleness with sinful humanity. Although metaphors posit an "as-if" relation between vehicle and tenor, readers tend to devolve into literalism. Thus the metaphorical comparison of God with a man (a husband) has supported the belief that males have a closer resemblance to the divine than do females. Such is the case, for example, among those Catholic theologians who justify the exclusion of women from the priesthood in part with reference to the Bible's "nuptial mystery" in which God is the husband of Israel (as in Hosea), or Christ is the bridegroom of the church, as in the New Testament. Because God is metaphorically a bridegroom, those who represent him in the church—the priests—must also be male (Sacred Congregation, section 5; Yee 1996, 227–28). Ironically, a metaphor that in its ancient context was intended to critique men of power becomes a tool for the maintenance of male power over women.

Hosea 4:1—5:7: The Land Mourns

█ THE TEXT IN ITS ANCIENT CONTEXT

Hosea 4 opens with an announcement of YHWH's "indictments against the inhabitants of the land" and specifies its cause. Absent are faithfulness, loving-kindness (ḥesed), and knowledge of God (Hosea 4:1); these are among the virtues that should bind Israel and YHWH together (Hosea 2:19-20). Instead, there is cursing, lying, killing, stealing, adultery, and bloody murder (Hosea 4:2): sins that closely correspond to the ethical prohibitions of the Decalogue (Exodus 20). As a result of this proliferation of sin, the land will "mourn" and all the animal life that dwells in it will die (Hosea 4:3).

Hosea then turns his attention to Israel's religious leadership and the rituals over which they preside. A certain priest is singled out (Hosea 4:4); he might have been an important official within the royal cult, or perhaps he represents the institution of the priesthood as a whole. This priest is charged with forgetting YHWH's tôrah ("law/teaching") and rejecting knowledge (Hosea 4:6). The priests were responsible not only for presiding over sacrifices but also for teaching knowledge of the covenant and its obligations to the people (Deut. 33:10). But the religious leaders have failed in this mission, and as a result, the people "are destroyed for lack of knowledge" (Hosea 4:6). The venerable shrines where the priests officiate are also condemned. Hosea admonishes the people not to "go up" to Gilgal or Beth-aven (literally "house of iniquity"), the latter being Hosea's pejorative term for the national shrine at Bethel (Hosea 4:15).

Throughout this section, Hosea communicates his judgments through further metaphors of sexual transgression. The nation has been led astray by a "spirit of whoredom" (Hosea 4:12; 5:3-4), and consequently the people "play the whore" and "devote themselves to whoredom" (Hosea 4:10, 15). Also, the high places are depicted as places of orgiastic promiscuity where male worshipers consort with prostitutes and dependent females brazenly commit adultery (Hosea 4:13-14).

■ THE TEXT IN THE INTERPRETIVE TRADITION

Those commentators who believe that rituals of sacred prostitution were part of Canaanite religion find support for this theory in Hosea 4:13-14, reading these verses as literal descriptions of ritual sex taking place at or near the high places (e.g., Mays, 73–75; Wolff, 86–87). Reference to men consorting with whores and qĕdēshôt, a term usually translated as "sacred prostitute," along with depictions of fornicating daughters and daughters-in-law, have led commentators to envision a scenario of orgiastic revelry at the shrines. However, in a society in which female sexual transgression was a grievous crime (see Deut. 22:13-27), it is unlikely that any women other than prostitutes would engage in illicit sex in public locations (Christl, 266; Keefe, 100–101); if read figuratively, these references to public sex appear to be rhetoric designed to provoke shock and shame in its male audience. Worse than the worst imaginable crime—subordinate women in sexual rebellion—is the behavior of Israel's men. Though their crimes are not clearly specified, their participation in the cult is likened to having sex with prostitutes and qĕdēshôt (Hosea 4:14b), terms that pejoratively refer perhaps to the male priests themselves (Keefe, 101–2) or to female cult personnel serving at the shrines (Bird, 87; Wacker, 233–34).

Another approach has been to envision the high places as sites of goddess worship, a view supported by Hosea's sarcastic remarks about the sacred trees standing in the vicinity of Israel's open-air altars (Hosea 4:13b). The tree of life was a well-known symbol for the goddess Asherah, a point that leads to the suggestion that Hosea objects to the worship of Asherah at the high places (Christl; Wacker). Also, some have found hints of goddess worship in Hosea 4:19, emending the text to read "a wind has wrapped her up in her skirts," that is, the skirts of a goddess (Emmerson; Wacker, 221–23).

■ THE TEXT IN CONTEMPORARY DISCUSSION

This section opens with a disturbing prediction of the withering of the land and all that lives in it. The beasts of the field, the birds of the air, and the fish of the sea that God created at the beginning (Gen. 1:20-31) will be taken away, and as a result, the land will "mourn" (Hosea 4:1-3). Noting the connection with the creation story, DeRoche argues that the text portends a "reversal of creation" in which all life is undone. The root cause of this ecological collapse, says Hosea, is human greed, violence, and perfidy, which poison the land. His prophecy of a world stripped of its animal life is particularly relevant today as disruptions in our global ecosystems threaten the extinction of many species. Heeding Hosea, we might attend to the interconnections between human beings and nature, and consider the role of human sin in the deterioration of the environment, on which we and future generations depend.

Also relevant today is Hosea's scathing criticism of the failures of Israel's religious leadership, who pursue "a spirit of harlotry" rather than teaching knowledge of God and modeling right action. In Hosea's eyes, the self-serving, short-sighted behavior of Israel's priesthood was a significant contributing factor leading toward national catastrophe. Reflecting on these points in relation to our own perilous situation in the modern world, the text invites reflection on the crucial responsibilities of religious leaders today and the far-reaching consequences of failure to uphold those responsibilities.

Hosea 5:8—10:15: They Shall Return to Egypt

▋ The Text in Its Ancient Context

The oracles in this section address a range of issues relating to warfare, Assyrian tribute demands, and the politics of regicide, along with further attacks on the high places and shrines. Although no certain correlations can be made between particular passages and specific historical events, the oracles reflect the chaotic politics and ill-advised foreign policies of the years leading up to Assyrian conquest.

The historical context for Hosea 5:8-14 is probably the Syro-Ephraimitic War (734–733 BCE). The looming threat of invasion is evoked twice by Hosea's prophetic commands to "blow the horn" in warning of danger (Hosea 5:8; 8:1). The prophet mocks Israel and Judah's feeble attempts to find safety in alliances or the paying of tribute to Assyria or seeking alliance with Egypt (Hosea 5:13; 7:11; 8:9). Ephraim "mixes himself with the peoples," says the prophet, and therefore "foreigners devour his strength" (Hosea 7:8-9).

Hosea 7 comments on the endemic violence swirling around the royal house as one regicide followed another (Hosea 7:2-7; cf. 2 Kgs. 15:8—17:23). In Hosea's eyes, Israel's present monarchy—established by bloodshed and not by divine authorization—has become illegitimate and shall fall (Hosea 8:4; 10:7). The fate of the monarchy is interdependent with that of its premier symbol, the "calf of Samaria" (that is, the calf image at Bethel that authorized the power of the state based in Samaria); it will be carried off as tribute to Assyria (Hosea 8:5; 10:6). Both the monarchy and the calf image are illegitimate human creations (Hosea 8:4) that provide no protection from foreign incursions or divine wrath.

Hosea 9 opens with an oracle of judgment delivered to participants in a harvest festival, most likely the seven-day festival of Sukkot. The celebrants are accused of having loved a "prostitute's pay" on their threshing floors (Hosea 9:1), suggesting, as in Hosea 2, that their sin is a failure to acknowledge YHWH as the source of the land's fertility. Dire prophecies follow concerning the failure of human fertility. The prophet prays for YHWH to give them "a miscarrying womb and dry breasts," and predicts that Ephraim, the fruitful one, shall "bear no fruit," thus negating all hope for the future (Hosea 9:14, 16).

Hosea speaks of the sins of the present through allusions to the primordial sins of Israel's past. Twice he speaks of the nation's guilt with reference to "the days of Gibeah" (Hosea 9:9; 10:9), alluding perhaps to the horrific rape and murder of a woman at Gibeah and the bloody, pointless civil war that ensued (Judges 19–21). Hosea also recalls the sin of Baal Peor (Hosea 9:10), Israel's first "intercourse" with the nations where shared worship and interethnic marriage compromised Israel's identity as God's chosen one (Numbers 25). The shrine of Gilgal is also evoked as the place where YHWH "first began to hate them" (Hosea 9:15), perhaps referencing the "original sin" of the establishment of the monarchy under Saul at Gilgal, an event that Samuel saw as a rejection of YHWH (1 Sam. 8:7-8).

Bitter tropes of reversal unify this section. Those who celebrate the harvest with wine and rejoicing will go hungry and will eat "unclean" bread in Assyria (Hosea 9:1-4). YHWH's promise that Abraham's descendants will be "exceedingly fruitful" (Gen. 17:6) becomes a prophetic "prayer" for sterility and a nation bereft of children (Hosea 9:11-14, 15-17). And for the people who were brought forth out of slavery in Egypt, the trope of a return to Egypt vividly figures the destruction and exile to come (Hosea 7:16; 8:13; 9:6; 11:5).

■ THE TEXT IN THE INTERPRETIVE TRADITION

Although the bulk of the oracles in this section concerns political issues, theologically oriented commentary has focused on particular passages that contain hope for the future or guidance as to what YHWH requires. It is instructive to note how Jewish and Christian commentators have interpreted the same passages in different ways.

Hosea 6:1-3 places a liturgical prayer for collective restoration in the mouth of the people, expressing hopes of salvation through the metaphor of healing and the image of being raised up by YHWH "on the third day" (Hosea 6:2). The apostle Paul probably had this verse in mind when he wrote that Jesus was raised on the "third day" in accordance with the Scriptures (1 Cor. 15:4), but Tertullian was the first to refer explicitly to this verse as a prophecy of Jesus' resurrection (*Adversus Marcionem* 4.43; *Adversus Judaeos* 13.23). Rabbinic tradition, on the other hand, cites this passage as a proof text for the teaching concerning the resurrection of the dead at the end of time (McArthur).

Hosea 6:6 has been an important text over the centuries for discussions about the role of sacrifice and ritual observance in biblical religions. Here, Hosea announces that YHWH desires "steadfast love" (*ḥesed*), not sacrifice, and knowledge of God, not burnt offerings. Similar views are found in 1 Sam. 15:22 and the oracles of other eighth-century prophets (Isa. 1:10-17; Amos 4:4-5; 5:21-27; Mic. 6:6-8). In Christian contexts, Hosea 6:6 is sometimes taken in support of the view that Jesus' sacrifice replaced the ritual requirements of the Torah. Jesus quotes Hosea 6:6 twice in the book of Matthew in answer to objections from the Pharisees concerning the lax ritual observance of his disciples (Matt. 12:6) and to explain his practice of eating with "unclean" sinners (Matt. 9:9-13). Subsequently, many Christian theologians have read Hosea 6:6 as proving that after Jesus, the ritual requirements of the Torah are nullified.

Rabbinic tradition, however, interpreted Hosea 6:6 as indicating YHWH's progressive revelation to the Jewish people, as the center of Judaism shifted from temple to Torah. Rabbi Yohanan ben Zakkai cited this passage to console a disciple who was grieving over the loss of the Jerusalem temple, fearing that without the cult of sacrifice there was no way to atone for sin. Rabbi Yohanan explained that YHWH had removed the temple to make way for another, and perhaps higher, form of atonement: moral action and covenant fidelity (*Avot D'Rabbi Natan* 9). The rabbinic tradition is clear, however, that the ritual requirements of the Torah, other than those that require a temple, still stand.

◼ THE TEXT IN CONTEMPORARY DISCUSSION

This section directs our attention to sins relating to the political realm, inviting us to observe the militarism, duplicitous politics, and realpolitik diplomacy of our own time in a more critical light. Hosea condemns Israel's princes and collaborators who "burn with intrigue and "devour their rulers" (Hosea 7:6-7, RSV), using their power to fight and kill for more power. He mocks their efforts to find security through building strongholds and fortified cities (Hosea 8:14) or by making alliances with the region's strong man, Assyria (Hosea 8:9). Trust in militarism, announces Hosea, leads not to security but to devastation (Hosea 8:14, 10:13-15). And against those who glorify the male "sport" of waging war, Hosea depicts war as bitter carnage in which mothers are gratuitously slaughtered along with their children and pregnant women are ripped open for fun (Hosea 10:14; see also 13:16).

Today nations still go to war proudly proclaiming that God is on "our side." But what if the Almighty is not with "our" nation, but against it? Hosea asks us to imagine that unthinkable scenario through intense metaphors of divine wrath. YHWH will be like dry rot or the maggots that feed on dead bodies (Hosea 5:12), like a lion ripping his prey to shreds (Hosea 5:14), or like a fowler who catches hapless birds in his snares (Hosea 7:12). There is no domestication of the deity here, but multiple revelations of YHWH's absolute power over life and death (Yee 1996, 250). These disquieting depictions of YHWH are a powerful counterpoint to any religious nationalism that complacently assumes God will always be on our side.

Perhaps most disturbing of all are Hosea's images of female sterility and the death of children. The parallel between Hosea's dark prayer that YHWH give them dry breasts and miscarrying wombs and the ancient prayer beseeching the "blessings of the breasts and of the womb" (Gen. 49:25) suggests that Hosea has reversed the ancient blessing formula and transformed it into a curse (Krause, 197). Like his warning prophecy of ecological collapse in which all animal life perishes (Hosea 4:3), Hosea's evocation of universal sterility and a world without children is an intentionally disturbing sign for the approaching annihilation. Today these images appear as more than just prophetic hyperbole. Given the threats to human flourishing and even human survival posed by our modern weapons of mass destruction and our destabilization of the ecosystem, Hosea's prophecies of a lifeless world can remind us of what is at stake in the decisions we, as individuals and as nations, make today.

Hosea 11–14: Divine Pathos and Human Repentance

▊ THE TEXT IN ITS ANCIENT CONTEXT

In these final chapters, the major themes of Hosea's book are reiterated: Israel's election and redemption out of Egypt, Israel's rebellion and sin, the pending punishment, the call for repentance, and the hope for covenant renewal.

Hosea 11 reviews the story of Israel through the metaphor of Israel as YHWH's adopted child. Called forth from Egypt, and held tenderly within the "bonds of love," they nevertheless soon turned to idolatry and now deserve punishment. As with Hosea's marriage metaphor, this metaphor presupposes the family structures of ancient Israel, in which power relations were asymmetrical and the disobedience of the subordinate family member (wife or child) could be a capital offense (Deut. 21:18-21). But at the same time, family relations may be characterized by love and intimacy, and the pain that comes from discord can be mutual. The parental metaphor makes way for depiction of YHWH as a god of compassion as well as justice; in the midst of announcements of punishment to come, the compassion of YHWH for his child wells up, and the deity recoils from his wrathful intention, proclaiming, "I am God and not man" (Hosea 11:9). In contrast to Samuel, who says that YHWH "is not a man" and therefore will not reverse his judgment on Saul (1 Sam. 15:29), Hosea asserts that YHWH's divinity means he is not bound by his anger, and can choose forgiveness.

In Hosea 12, the story of the grasping and duplicitous Jacob serves as the paradigm for Israel's present sinful condition (Hosea 12:2-4, 12). Israel is also pejoratively termed "a Canaanite" or "a trader" who brags over his ill-gotten wealth (Hosea 12:7). The term "Canaanite" had become a synonym for "trader" in Hosea's time, due to the association of Canaanites with mercantile activities, but the suggestion of Israel becoming like foreign "others" (the Canaanites) is also present.

Hosea 13 opens with a pointed invective against the idolatry practiced within the national cult. Hosea again echoes Samuel's objection to the establishment of the monarchy (13:10) and suggests that trust in the power of their kings is part and parcel of Israel's sin. The coming wrath of YHWH is compared to a wild beast—a leopard, a lion, or a bear—that will rip them to shreds (Hosea 13:7-8), or to the east wind, the sirocco, which will dry up all sources of life-giving water (Hosea 13:15).

As in Hosea 1–3, where threats of punishment and divorce give way to the promise of reconciliation, Hosea 14 closes the book on a note of hope and promise that is set through images of abundant fertility. Hosea 14 begins with a call for Israel to return to YHWH, and gives instructions for true repentance (14:2-4). This is followed by a promise of redemption, figured in images of abundant fertility. YHWH pictures himself as the moisture providing dew, or as a tree under whose shade the people shall flourish like a garden (14:5-8).

▊ THE TEXT IN THE INTERPRETIVE TRADITION

Many interpreters have taken Hosea 11 to be the climax or turning point of the book of Hosea. Through the metaphor of YHWH's prodigal son, the story of Israel's election and rebellion is retold, and the audience is prepared to hear yet another oracle of divine rejection and punishment. Instead, the love YHWH bears for his adopted child causes his heart to turn from its wrathful intentions.

Numerous Christian commentators read Hosea's depiction of YHWH's anguished love for Israel, despite its sins, as anticipating the Christian concept of God as love. The doctrine of retributive justice is here "transcended by Hosea's conception of God's holiness as redemptive love" (Ward, 204). For Abraham Heschel, a Jewish theologian, the "divine pathos" so powerfully communicated in Hosea 11 teaches that not only is YHWH a God who demands justice, but "He is also a God Who is in love with His people" (44).

Hosea's references to the Jacob traditions in Hosea 12 are opaque and difficult to interpret. The motif of Jacob weeping and seeking "his" favor may refer to Jacob weeping and pleading with the angel after a night of struggle in Genesis 32 (although this motif is not preserved in the canonical version of the story), or to Jacob's weeping for forgiveness when he encounters Esau the next day (Gen. 33:4). In either case, Jacob's journey, from being a deceiver to a weeping penitent, models the transformation from sin to repentance that the nation must make (Yee 1996, 284).

In Hosea 14:1-3, the prophet instructs the people on the correct attitude of repentance, which will restore divine favor. For this reason, this passage serves as the prophetic reading that follows the Torah reading on the Sabbath between Rosh Hashanah and Yom Kippur, the holy days focusing on repentance for sin.

The use of tree imagery to depict YHWH's providential care (14:5-8) has intrigued many commentators, given that the tree of life was a common iconographic image of the goddess Asherah. This connection has prompted suggestions that Hosea has here appropriated goddess symbolism and applied it to YHWH. Julius Wellhausen's proposed emendation of Hosea 14:8b to read "I am your Anat and your Asherah" (134) has continued to fuel discussion about whether Hosea here is displacing goddess worship by attributing the powers of fertility to YHWH alone (e.g., Wacker).

▮ THE TEXT IN CONTEMPORARY DISCUSSION

In this section, Hosea offers a rich array of divine imagery that can expand our repertoire of metaphors for God. Of special note is the image of YHWH as Israel's parent in Hosea 11:1-4. While most commentators have taken this as a metaphor of YHWH as a father, the depiction of YHWH's parental care for the infant Israel may better describe the activity of a mother. Schüngel-Straumann argues for this point by translating the very difficult text of Hosea 11:4b as a description of YHWH breastfeeding "her" son: "I was for them like those who take a nursling to the breast ... in order to give him suck" (4–5). Feminine divine imagery is also suggested by the depiction of YHWH as a fruitful tree in Hosea 14:7-8. For Gale Yee, this image of YHWH's providential care resonates with the figure of Woman Wisdom from Proverbs, who is also described as a life-giving tree (Prov. 3:18; Yee 1996, 297). The presence of these female metaphors for the divine in Hosea is somewhat surprising, given that in the history of the biblical traditions, Hosea's influential image of YHWH as a divine husband helped to foreclose on the possibility of imagining "him" as female. Hosea's theological imagination, however, was not so constricted, and his use of feminine and fertility imagery for YHWH contribute to today's quest for a more holistic and inclusive vision of the divine reality.

The incorporation of Greek philosophical ideas (in which the divine is defined as unchangeable perfection) into Christian thought in late antiquity has also made it difficult to imagine God as passionate and capable of changing his mind. But Hosea's YHWH expresses great passion as he wavers between implacable anger and inconsolable love for his people. Such representations of the divine pathos of YHWH underscore his freedom to change his mind and to choose to redeem rather than to destroy. This divine openness to change reminds us of our own human capacity for remorse and repentance; if YHWH can change his mind, so perhaps we humans can change our ways before we, like Ephraim, must "reap the whirlwind" (Hosea 8:7) and suffer the consequences of our present follies.

Works Cited

Bird, Phyllis. 1989. "'To Play the Harlot': An Inquiry into an Old Testament Metaphor." In *Gender and Difference in Ancient Israel*, edited by Peggy L. Day, 75–94. Minneapolis: Fortress Press.

Calvin, John. 1984. *Commentaries on the Twelve Minor Prophets*. Translated by John Owen. Reprint, Grand Rapids: Baker.

Christl, Maier. 2009. "Myth and Truth in Socio-Historical Reconstruction of Ancient Societies, Hosea 4:11-14 as a Test Case." In *Thus Says the Lord*, edited by John J. Ahn and Steven L. Cook, 256–72. New York: T&T Clark.

DeRoche, D. 1981. "The Reversal of Creation in Hosea." *VT* 31:400–409.

Emmerson, Grace. 1974. "A Fertility Goddess in Hos IV 17-19?" *VT* 24:492–97.

Heschel, Abraham J. 1962. *The Prophets*. New York: Jewish Publication Society.

Keefe, Alice A. 2001. *Woman's Body as the Social Body in Hosea*. Sheffield: Sheffield Academic Press.

Kelle, Brad E. 2005. *Hosea 2: Metaphor and Rhetoric in Historical Perspective*. Leiden: Brill.

Krause, Deborah. 1992. "A Blessing Cursed: The Prophet's Prayer for Barren Womb and Dry Breasts in Hosea 9." In *Reading Between Texts: Intertextuality and the Hebrew Bible*, edited by Danna Nolan Fewell, 191–202. Louisville: Westminster John Knox.

Lipschitz, Abe, ed. and trans. 1988. *The Commentary of Rabbi Abraham Ibn Ezra on Hosea*. New York: Sepher-Hermon Press.

McArthur, Harvey K. 1971. "On the Third Day." *NTS* 18:81–86.

Mays, James L. 1969. *Hosea: A Commentary*. Philadelphia: Westminster.

Oden, Robert A., Jr. 1987. "Religious Identity and the Sacred Prostitution Accusation." In *The Bible Without Theology: The Theological Tradition and Alternatives to It*, 131–53. San Francisco: Harper & Row.

Rowley, H. H. 1963. "The Marriage of Hosea." In *Men and God: Studies in Old Testament History of Prophecy*. London: Nelson.

Sacred Congregation for the Doctrine of the Faith. 15 October 1976. "Declaration *Inter Insigniores* on the Question of the Admission of Women to the Ministerial Priesthood." http://www.vatican.va/roman_curia/congregations/cfaith/documents/rc_con_cfaith_doc_19761015_inter-insigniores_en.html (accessed April 3, 2014).

Schüngel-Straumann, Helen. 1987. "God as Mother in Hosea 11." *TD* 34, no. 1:3–8.

Setel, T. Drorah. 1985. "Prophets and Pornography: Female Sexual Imagery in Hosea." In *Feminist Interpretation of the Bible*, edited by Letty Russell, 86–95. Philadelphia: Westminster.

Sherwood, Yvonne. 1996. *The Prostitute and the Prophet: Hosea's Marriage in Literary-Theoretical Perspective*. Sheffield: Sheffield Academic Press.

Toorn, Karel van der. 1992. "Prostitution, Cultic." In *ABD* 5:510–13.

Wacker, Marie-Theres. 1995. "Traces of the Goddess in the Book of Hosea." In *A Feminist Companion to the Latter Prophets*, edited by Athalya Brenner, 219–41. Sheffield: Sheffield Academic Press.

Ward, James M. 1966. *Hosea: A Theological Commentary*. New York: Harper & Row.

Weems, Renita. 1995. *Battered Love: Marriage, Sex, and Violence in the Hebrew Prophets*. Minneapolis: Fortress Press.

Wellhausen, Julius. 1963. *Die Kleine Propheten.* Skizzen und Vorarbeiten 5. 4th ed. Berlin: Reimer.

Wolff, Hans Walter. 1974. *Hosea: A Commentary on the Book of the Prophet Hosea*. Philadelphia: Fortress Press.

Yee, Gale A. 1996. "The Book of Hosea." In *The New Interpreter's Bible*. Vol. 7, *Introduction to Apocalyptic Literature, Daniel, The Twelve Prophets*, edited by Leander E. Keck, 197–297. Nashville: Abingdon.

———. 2001. "'She Is Not My Wife and I Am Not Her Husband': A Materialist Reading of Hosea 1–2." *BibInt* 9, no. 4:345–83.

JOEL

Ronald A. Simkins

Introduction

Nothing is known about the prophet Joel or his father Pethuel, and little is known about the historical context of the book that bears his name. On this all scholars agree; on other interpretive issues regarding the book of Joel, there is little unanimity. The date of the book has been assigned to a range from as early as the ninth century BCE to as late as the Maccabean period for its final compilation. A fifth-century-BCE date, putting it in the mid-Persian period, has attracted many scholars due to the vocabulary and expressions that Joel shares with other late books, such as its emphasis on the role of the temple and cult, and the scribal activity evident from Joel's citation of other biblical texts and references to biblical ideas.

The composition and structure of the book of Joel are also unsettled, though the dividing lines are much clearer. Following Bernhard Duhm, most scholars before the middle of the twentieth century argued that the book was composed in two distinct parts or with multiple layers: 1:1—2:27 represent the oracles of the prophet Joel in response to a past and present catastrophe, and 2:28—3:21 are later apocalyptic oracles addressing a future eschatological hope. The day of the LORD passages in the first part of the book were also interpreted by some as later editorial additions to connect the two parts of the book. Most recent commentators, however, have argued for the unity of the book, noting the symmetry between the two parts (e.g., Wolff), or emphasizing repetition and development of themes, such as the day of the LORD, between the two parts (e.g., Simkins). John Barton continues to support Duhm's division of the book. Regardless of how the composition of the book is understood, the two parts of the book demonstrate a shift in tense and tone. Joel 1:1—2:17 is written in the past and present tenses and is descriptive and prophetic in tone. Beginning in 2:18, the book shifts to the future tense, and by 2:28 the tone becomes eschatological.

The book has an anthological character, with the prophet drawing on numerous prophetic themes. Moreover, the prophet cites many other prophetic texts or traditions, suggesting that Joel was perhaps a learned scribe and an interpreter of the prophetic tradition (see Crenshaw, 26–28, 35–39).

The book of Joel appears to have been occasioned by an unprecedented catastrophe, which is described in 1:1—2:11, and the meaning of the book is shaped by the interpretation of the nature of the catastrophe, the role of the cult in response to the catastrophe, and the relationship of the catastrophe to the proclamation of the day of the LORD.

Joel 1:1-20: Locust Plague and Lamentation

■ THE TEXT IN ITS ANCIENT CONTEXT

The book of Joel begins with the proclamation of an unprecedented catastrophe: locusts have devoured everything in the land (1:2-4). How this locust plague differs from previous plagues is not stated; the text only emphasizes the locusts' voracious appetite. The four terms for locusts in verse 4 have often been interpreted as denoting developmental stages of the common desert locust (*Schistocerca gregaria*)—though only three distinct stages of the locust's metamorphosis are apparent to the casual observer—but the terms elsewhere are used interchangeably. Here the terms are used rhetorically to emphasize the complete destruction caused by the locusts.

Scholars debate the nature of the catastrophe. The references to locusts and their destruction may describe a literal plague, or they may be interpreted metaphorically, referring to an invading enemy army. A few passages (1:12, 19-20) elicit images of drought, which is generally incompatible with locust infestations. Although multiple interpretations are possible, it is unlikely that the locusts are metaphors for an invading army when they are *compared to* an invading nation (1:6) or an army (2:6-9). The drought imagery may refer to the normal dry conditions of summer, whose effects are intensified by the locusts' devastation, or it may be stock poetic imagery used to emphasize the totality of the natural catastrophe.

The remainder of chapter 1 can be divided into a call to lamentation (vv. 5-14) delivered by the prophet to the people, and the lament (vv. 15-20) that the people should cry to God. The call to lamentation can be divided into four strophes (vv. 5-7, 8-10, 11-12, and 13-14), each beginning with an imperative call (v. 5: "wake up," "wail"), followed by a vocative designating those addressed (v. 5: "drunkards," "wine-drinkers"), and then a substantiation clause giving the reason for lamentation (v. 5: "for [the sweet wine] is cut off from your mouth"). The first three strophes then continue with additional lines describing the devastation, but the final strophe concludes with a series of imperatives directed to the temple priests.

The first strophe (vv. 5-7), which begins by calling for drunkards to awake, perhaps suggests for many that Joel's audience has been complacent or foolish in not giving attention to the significance of the locust plague. Other scholars simply note that drunkards, coupled with wine-drinkers, are those who have experienced the consequences of the locusts' devastation firsthand. Similarly, in the third strophe (vv. 11-12), the farmers and vinedressers are called to lament. Both the first and the third strophes emphasize the agricultural devastation caused by the locusts. The second strophe

(vv. 8-10) lacks an explicit addressee in the vocative, but the feminine singular imperative and the reference to the temple in verse 9 perhaps implies a personified Jerusalem. The call to lamentation reaches its climax in the fourth strophe (vv. 13-14), where the priests, the ministers of the altar, are addressed. In both the second and fourth strophes, emphasis is placed on the consequences of the agricultural devastation for the temple liturgy: namely, that the grain and drinking offerings to God at the temple have come to an end.

Joel's call to lamentation demands a liturgical response to the catastrophe. The priests should summon all the people to fast and to assemble at the temple to cry out to God. Verses 15-20 are perhaps the words of the lament that the people should cry. They should bewail that "the day of the Lord is near," or better, that it is "now at hand." The lament identifies the devastation of the locust plague with the day of the Lord, which since the time of Amos has been associated with YHWH's judgment, both on Israel and on the nations. Although in 2:31 and 3:14 Joel perhaps refers to *the final* day of the Lord, in which YHWH will bring an end to human history, inaugurating the eschatological era, in 1:15 (and also 2:1, 11), Joel is only referring to *a* day of the Lord—a present but limited day of God's judgment. As a day of the Lord, the locust plague has not only destroyed the agriculture but also threatens the community of living creatures. Thus the people should cry out to God as even the cattle and wild animals do (vv. 18, 20).

▉ The Text in the Interpretive Tradition

Although the four terms used for locusts in Joel 1:4 refer to a literal locust plague, the interpretive tradition has generally understood the terms metaphorically. One Greek translation, for example, renders them as Egyptians, Babylonians, Assyrians, and Greeks. The Targum interprets the terms to be peoples, tongues, governments, and kingdoms. Ephrem the Syrian (d. 373) and Isho'dad of Merv (c. 850) take the locust terms as metaphors for Tiglath Pileser III, Shalmaneser V, Sennacherib, and Nebuchadnezzar.

▉ The Text in Contemporary Discussion

By identifying the locust plague with the day of the Lord, the book of Joel raises questions of theodicy and the role of God in natural disasters, even today. Can God's activity or will be discerned in such catastrophes? Many today seem to be willing to identify natural disasters as God's judgment on one corporate sin or another, but such diagnoses demonstrate little more than the prejudices of the interpreters. Joel too thought a natural catastrophe signaled God's activity, the day of the Lord, but his reasoning and response are instructive to us. Joel's diagnosis is not simply based on the destruction caused by the locust plague, but on its effect on the temple: the grain and drink offerings, the daily sacrifices, were brought to an end. In a world in which such events were not explained scientifically (or through natural causality), such a calamitous event was surely an act of God. Joel does not, however, respond with a moral diagnosis to explain God's actions; he does not blame the catastrophe on the people's sins. He calls instead for a fast and the self-abasement of lamentation. As Joel will articulate in the next chapter, God is merciful and gracious (2:13) and will hear the humble cry of his people.

Joel 2:1-11: Invasion by the Army of YHWH

■ THE TEXT IN ITS ANCIENT CONTEXT

Although the first chapter presents the catastrophic locust plague as a past event, a present and ongoing catastrophe is heralded in chapter 2. Through multiple metaphors, Joel 2 describes the invasion of YHWH's army on a city, presumably Jerusalem and its environs. Scholars disagree on the nature of this second catastrophe and on its relationship with the locust plague lamented in chapter 1. This catastrophe has been understood in three different ways: (1) the invasion of a historical enemy of Judah, such as the Babylonians; (2) the invasion of an apocalyptic army; and (3) a locust plague that is compared to an invading army. Joel's use of metaphor makes option 1 the least likely interpretation; the catastrophe is *compared to* an invading army rather than being a historical army. According to the second option, the locust plague of chapter 1 becomes a metaphor for an eschatological enemy from the north on the day of the LORD. The enemy army would thus be compared to locust-like apocalyptic creatures (compare the apocalyptic army in Rev. 9:1-11). The difficulty with this interpretation is that the description of the invasion in verses 3-9 has a this-worldly orientation and reflects the activity of *real* locusts; apocalyptic language is not otherwise evident in the first part of the book. (Whether it is characteristic of the second part of Joel is debated.) Thus most scholars interpret Joel 2:1-11 as referring to a locust plague that was presently "assaulting" the environs of Jerusalem.

The relationship between this locust plague and the plague whose destruction was lamented in chapter 1 is uncertain. The use of perfect verbs in chapter 1 and primarily imperfect verbs in chapter 2 indicates only the temporal orientation of the oracle in relation to the speaker, not the temporal relationship between the oracles. The locust plague in chapter 2 may thus refer to the same event that is lamented in chapter 1. Nevertheless, because locust plagues in the Middle East often occurred over several years (such as the 1915 plague documented by John Whiting) and because Joel 2:25 refers to the "the years that the swarming locust has eaten" (NRSV), the locust invasion described in chapter 2 may also be interpreted as a continuation of the previous year's infestation.

Verses 3-9 describe the onslaught of a locust plague consisting of innumerable hoppers marching in array. Their destruction is compared to that of fire; their appearance, to that of horses. Their assault on the people is likened to an army attacking a city whose defenses are ineffectual. Although these metaphors present a realistic portrait of a locust plague, verses 1-2 and 10-11 signal the uniqueness of this plague because of its supranaturalistic qualities. The locust infestation is YHWH's own army, whose march heralds the day of the LORD. Using traditional theophanic language, the prophet describes the cosmic convulsions that accompany the locust plague as YHWH the divine warrior marches to battle.

■ THE TEXT IN THE INTERPRETIVE TRADITION

The Christian tradition has generally interpreted 2:1-11 to be referring to the future, to the second coming of Jesus, when he will come on the day of the LORD to judge the world. This understanding is already apparent in the book of Revelation, where Joel 2 appears to be the inspiration, based on numerous similarities, for the apocalyptic locust army unleashed by the fifth angel (9:1-11). The differences are striking, however. Whereas Joel's locusts act like typical locusts, the locusts of Revelation do not consume the vegetation, as would be expected, but rather torture humans with their scorpion-like tails.

▌THE TEXT IN CONTEMPORARY DISCUSSION

Joel sees in the locust plague a theophany of YHWH—a visible intensification of God's presence. Biblical theologians have often noted that the Bible portrays God to be actively involved in human affairs, and the prophets discern God's activity in relation to human conduct (most often in terms of the covenant). But this is not the whole story. As Joel makes clear, God's activity and presence are discernible also in the natural world. Indeed, most biblical descriptions of God's theophany emphasize the natural forms of God's appearance. Although God is transcendent, God does not remain outside of the natural world, and it is through creation that God is known. For Joel, the locust plague was as revelatory of God as a divinely spoken oracle.

Joel 2:12-27: Appeal to and Response from YHWH

▌THE TEXT IN ITS ANCIENT CONTEXT

This unit consists of two parts: an appeal to YHWH, which consists of a call for the people to return to YHWH (vv. 12-14) followed by a call to lamentation (vv. 15-17) and YHWH's response to the people's appeal (vv. 18-27). The transition between the two parts in verses 18-19a, using converted imperfect verbs, presumes that some time has elapsed since Joel's appeal and that the people heeded his call to return to YHWH and to lament.

The prophetic call to return in verse 12 is presented as an oracle of YHWH, and so YHWH addresses the people in the first person ("return to me"), but by verse 13 Joel is again the speaker and YHWH is addressed in the third person. "Return to YHWH" is often interpreted as a call to repent from sin, but Joel enumerates no such sins. Joel's emphasis is not to blame the people (and perhaps no blame could be assessed), but to simply to call the people to turn to "the national God in the hope that YHWH would save the people" (Barton, 77). Joel's confidence that "even now" YHWH can save his people is expressed through Joel's use of a well-known creedal confession in verse 13. Found elsewhere, in Exod. 34:6-7; Num. 14:18; Neh. 9:17; Pss. 103:8; 145:8; Nah. 1:3; and Jonah 4:2, Joel cites a version, also found in Jonah, that underscores YHWH's mercy and eliminates the reference to God's justice or judgment (see Crenshaw, 136–37).

The call to lamentation (vv. 15-17) explains how the people should return to YHWH—through a national assembly of mourning. All should attend, from children to the elderly, even those who would otherwise be celebrating. The people should rend their hearts, and not only their garments (v. 13)—the ritual lamentation should also have an inward motivation. And the priests should bring the people's case to YHWH: YHWH should deliver his people for the sake of his own reputation (v. 17).

YHWH's response to the people's lamentation is a salvation oracle that is characterized by both YHWH's jealousy and compassion. YHWH's jealousy on behalf of the people is an expression of YHWH's passionate commitment to them. No longer will God allow the people to become a mockery to the nations; no longer will the people be put to shame. Compassion is YHWH's response to the people's suffering as a result of the locust plague. Thus YHWH will destroy the locust plague—called the "northerner" in reference to the "enemy from the north" tradition—and YHWH will restore the land from all the devastation caused by the locusts. Similarly, in response to the drought lamented in 1:19-20, YHWH promises to bring the rains in their seasons.

▮ THE TEXT IN THE INTERPRETIVE TRADITION

In part because Joel does not enumerate the sins of the people or otherwise denounce their behavior, Joel 2:11-17 plays a prominent role in the Christian liturgies of Ash Wednesday at the beginning of Lent. The general nature of Joel's call to return to YHWH enables the text to be used as a generalized invitation to enter into the period of contrition that prepares Christians for celebrating Christ's redemption.

▮ THE TEXT IN CONTEMPORARY DISCUSSION

It is significant that in the face of the devastating locust plague, Joel does not enumerate the sins of the people. He does not blame the people for the catastrophe nor, in Deuteronomic fashion, link the catastrophe to the people's infidelity to the covenant. Joel is also not interested in the question of theodicy; he seeks neither to explain nor justify God in the presence of the destructive plague. Instead, Joel simply asks the people to turn to God in supplication. Openness to lamentation with God is the proper response to such catastrophes. In the shame of their suffering, the people had turned away from YHWH. Joel's call to return is not to indict the people for their sins but to renew their faith in God through visible acts of devotion.

Joel 2:28—3:21: The Coming Day of the Lord

▮ THE TEXT IN ITS ANCIENT CONTEXT

The final unit of the book consists of five oracles (2:28-32; 3:1-3, 4-8, 9-17, and 18-21), which take on a future-oriented, eschatological tone that has occasioned many early twentieth-century interpreters to conclude that these final oracles are later additions to the book. Following in this tradition, Barton characterizes this unit as a collection of miscellaneous oracles whose predictions do not amount to a coherent set of expectations (2001, 92). Most recent scholars, however, continue to attribute these oracles to Joel, even though the focus of their utterance no longer seems to be the locust plague. The literary style and scribal character of these oracles is similar throughout the book. What unite these oracles thematically to the first part of the book are references to the day of the Lord. Indeed, in the first part of the book, Joel sees in the unprecedented locust plague the advent of the day of the Lord. In these final oracles, Joel explains in scribal fashion how the day of the Lord will unfold.

"Then afterward" (NRSV), which begins the first oracle in 2:28-32, connects the final oracles temporally to what precedes them. "These things" may refer to YHWH's restoration of the locust devastation described in 2:18-27, or to Joel's call for the people to assemble and lament in 2:12-17. If the latter is the case, then the events predicted in the oracles of this unit are amplification on the events of YHWH's salvation oracle in 2:18-27.

The first oracle, Joel 2:28-32, envisions the outpouring of YHWH's spirit and the cosmic convulsions that will take place on the day of the LORD. In this context, the spirit is associated with prophecy and divine communication (see Num. 11:29), and hence the emphasis on dreams and visions, rather than on empowerment (cf. Judg. 6:34). YHWH will pour out his spirit on "all flesh," which generally refers to everyone, irrespective of gender or ethnicity, but the context limits it to the people of Judah and Jerusalem. In the prophetic tradition, the democratization of YHWH's spirit is characteristic of the coming period of salvation, when God's people will be free from oppression, the righteous will live in peace, and justice will reign on the earth. It is also accompanied by the regeneration of the natural world (see Isa. 32:9-14; 44:1-5; Ezek. 39:25-29), and so corresponds with the agricultural bounty promised in 2:18-27. Although the day of the LORD will bring cosmic upheavals (vv. 30-31) and destruction of the nations (3:1-17), Joel echoes the royal or Zion theology when he declares that YHWH's people—those who call on his name (v. 32)—will remain safe in Jerusalem (see Psalms 46; 48).

As Joel 2:18-27 promised the restoration of the land destroyed by the locusts, 2:28-32 promises salvation for the people who "return to YHWH." Similarly, just as YHWH will destroy the locust army (2:20), so also will YHWH punish the nations who have oppressed his people (3:1-17). In chapter 3, Joel develops the consequences of the day of the LORD for the nations, connecting them to the salvation of God's people in the preceding oracles with the adverbial phrase, "in those days and at that time." The oracles in chapter 3 may be interpreted in reference to the divine warrior hymns, which are attested in early Israelite and royal hymns (Exod. 15:1-18; Judges 5; Psalms 2; 24; 29; 68; 89; 97) but are revived in a number of late eschatological prophecies (Isa. 59:15b-20; 66:14b-16, 22-23; Ezekiel 38–39; Habakkuk 3; Zechariah 14). Based on a mythic pattern of divine conflict, such as found in the *Enuma Elish*, the divine warrior hymns celebrate YHWH's battle and victory over Israel's enemies (see Hiebert, 875–76). In Joel 3, the first two oracles (vv. 1-3, 4-8) describe how the nations have challenged YHWH's sovereignty by oppressing his people. In the third oracle (vv. 9-17), YHWH declares war on the nations, and the natural world convulses as YHWH marches out to battle. No actual battle is described; YHWH's victory is assured. Then YHWH is enthroned in Zion, which becomes an eternal sanctuary for his people. The fourth oracle (vv. 18-21) concludes the hymn with a description of the rejuvenation of the natural world and a reaffirmation that YHWH will indeed render justice on behalf of his people (see further, Simkins, 219–41).

Although the oracles in Joel 3 in their final form correspond to the structure and themes of the divine warrior hymns, this is probably a consequence of Joel's scribal activity. Joel drew on common prophetic traditions to interpret the coming day of the LORD. Scholars have usually noted that verses 4-8 are different in style from what precedes and follows it, they disrupt the flow from verse 3 to verse 9, and thus should be viewed as a later addition. However, if chapter 3 is viewed as a scribal composition, nothing precludes verses 4-8 from being added by Joel as an amplification of the crimes spelled out in verse 3.

▌ THE TEXT IN THE INTERPRETIVE TRADITION

Because this unit relies so heavily on existing prophetic traditions for defining the day of the LORD, it is not surprising that later writers drew on Joel for interpreting eschatological events. As Joel interpreted the events of his day in light of known traditions, so also later prophets and writers interpreted their current events in light of Joel's prophecies. Thus, on Pentecost, Peter quotes Joel 2:28-32 to explain the outpouring of the Spirit on the followers of Jesus (Acts 2:17-21). According to Peter's speech in Acts, this happened in the "last days," and rather than YHWH, it is Jesus of Nazareth who pours out the spirit. Although Joel seems to limit the outpouring of the spirit to those in Judah, and indeed Peter addresses the men of Judea, perhaps following the text of Joel, the context of Peter's speech extends the outpouring of the Spirit to the Diaspora, all of whom hear the followers of Jesus speaking in their own languages. The tendency to universalize Joel's "all flesh" is complete in Paul, who quotes Joel 3:5, "Everyone who calls on the name of the Lord will be saved," to emphasize that there is no distinction between Jew and gentile (Rom. 10:12-13).

▌ THE TEXT IN CONTEMPORARY DISCUSSION

This unit presents two conflicting voices. On the one hand, Joel 2:28-32 speaks with an inclusive voice, as Paul recognized in Romans. Even though the context of Joel might limit the scope of "all flesh" (v. 28) and "everyone" (v. 32), the reappropriation of the text in new contexts cannot ignore its inclusive tendencies. The mercy of God is available to the one who calls on the name of the LORD. On the other hand, Joel 3:1-21 speaks with an exclusive voice. The inhabitants of Judah and Jerusalem stand in opposition to all the nations, whom YHWH will judge through war. The justice of God is not itself the difficult issue, for YHWH applies the *lex talionis* as the justification for the nations' punishment: The nations will be treated in the same way that they have treated God's people. What is missing, however, at least from our perspective, is the role of the individual. Both Judah (God's people) and the nations are treated as singular collectives; there is no exception for individual choices. The conflicting inclusive and exclusive voices of the text can only be resolved when both voices are heard in tension, giving due weight to both God's mercy and justice, individual and collective.

Works Cited

Barton, John. 2001. *Joel and Obadiah*. OTL. Louisville: Westminster John Knox.

Crenshaw, James L. 1995. *Joel: A New Translation with Introduction and Commentary*. AB 24C. New York: Doubleday.

Duhm, Bernhard. 1911. "Anmerkungen zu den Zwölf Propheten." *ZAW* 31:184–88.

Hiebert, Theodore. 1992. "Joel, Book of." In *ABD* 3:873–80.

Simkins, Ronald A. 1991. *Yahweh's Activity in History and Nature in the Book of Joel*. Lewiston, NY: Edwin Mellen.

Whiting, John D. 1915. "Jerusalem's Locust Plague." *National Geographic* 28:511–50.

Wolff, Hans Walter. 1977. *Joel and Amos*. Hermeneia. Philadelphia: Fortress Press.

AMOS

M. Daniel Carroll R.

Introduction

The superscription (Amos 1:1; cf. 7:9-11) sets the historical context of the prophet's ministry in the early to mid-eighth century BCE, during the reigns of Jeroboam II of Israel and Uzziah/Azariah of Judah. Amos is said to come from Tekoa in Judah, modern Khirbet Tequ'a, about ten kilometers southeast of Jerusalem. The opening verse mentions an earthquake (see also 6:9-11; 8:8; 9:1, 5; cf. Zech. 14:5), which seismic studies locate between 760 and 750 BCE.

International circumstances had allowed Israel to attain prominence (2 Kgs. 14:25). Aram/Syria, Israel's northern neighbor and principal foe in the second half of the ninth century, was in decline. Assyria was weakened after the death of Adad Nirari III in 783 and would not influence the region again until Tiglath Pileser III assumed the throne in 745. The oracles in Amos 1 and in 4:10; 6:3, 13, if they reflect this setting, suggest that Israel was not as strong as the national ideology pretended. In addition to recent defeats by bordering countries, in the future an unnamed enemy would invade the land (3:11; 6:14). These words would be fulfilled by Assyria.

The book accuses the powerful of oppression, even as they enjoyed a comfortable lifestyle (Amos 3:15; 4:1; 5:10-11; 6:1, 4-6). The judicial system was compromised (5:12, 15), and many had fallen into debt slavery (2:6-8; 8:4-6). Sociological approaches try to reconstruct these mechanisms of exploitation (see surveys in Houston; Coomber). Some argue that the text attacks a form of rent capitalism, others an inequitable tributary mode of production under the monarchy's control. Another possibility is that the mutual obligations of the patron-client relationship had been violated. A cultural-evolutionary perspective suggests that environmental factors, changes in traditional sociocultural roles, asymmetric economic relationships, and the actions of religious elites all played a part. Each option alerts readers to the concreteness of the prophetic message.

Composition, Structure, Literary Elements

From the late nineteenth and into the twentieth century, scholarship attempted to distinguish the *ipsissima verba* ("actual words") of the prophet from later additions. Subsequently, form and tradition critics claimed to identify editorial stages connected to specific historical settings (e.g., Wolff). Several hypotheses about the redactional history have been put forward in the last two decades (see the surveys in Carroll R.; Barton). Some recent scholars contend that the book is a postexilic creation of a scribal class in the Persian province of Yehud in the fifth to fourth centuries BCE. There have also been efforts to correlate the production of Amos with the process of compiling the Book of the Twelve. Similar wording might imply mutual influence between books. For example, Joel 3:16a is repeated in Amos 1:2a, and the mention of Edom at 9:12 anticipates Obadiah.

A second group of scholars defends the authenticity of all or most of the book. Some connect the diverse emphases in the book to different times in Amos's ministry (e.g., Andersen and Freedman). Others look to comparative ancient Near Eastern linguistic and archaeological data as the basis for an eighth-century date (e.g., Paul). New archaeological discoveries, such as the excavations at Tell es-Safi (referred to as Gath in Amos 6:2) and the discovery of extensive copper smelting in the Arabah of Edom (1:11-12), suggest a stronger historical basis than many have considered viable. Evidence from Mesopotamia reveals that prophecies could have been recorded soon after the delivery of oracles. This contradicts the common view that prophetic oracles circulated orally for a long time before being written down.

Literary studies are yet another kind of approach. They presuppose the unity of the book. Its artistry of form and language and intricate theological argument suggest a consistent authorial or editorial hand. Critical scholars increasingly recognize the book's literary features and incorporate them into their redaction studies (e.g., Jeremias). Those who conceive of Amos as part of the Scripture of the church also champion the canonical form. This is the text that Christians read and use for worship and the practice of their faith. The new field of the theological interpretation of the Bible seeks to nurture skills for such readings and values precritical interpretations.

Literary features of Amos include many metaphors and similes, wordplays, rhetorical questions, chiasms, and merism. Recognizable form-critical categories are the messenger formula ("thus says the LORD"), judgment speeches, the proclamation formula ("Hear this"), and the woe-cry. The oracles against the nations (Amos 1:3—2:16) use the $n/n + 1$ graded numerical saying ("For three transgressions of . . . , and for four"). The book has a penchant for series of five and seven items, which will be pointed out in the commentary. Finally, some believe that the entire book exhibits a chiasm with 5:7-8 at its center. A chiasm is a concentric structure, which repeats similar ideas or terminology in a reverse matching sequence. Its climax is in the middle, not at the end of the pattern.

Key Themes

The most important theme is the person of YHWH. This is the battleground of the prophet's ministry. The people celebrate a deity of blessing and victory (Amos 5:18-20), although the recent past had been characterized by disaster (1:3-15; 4:6-11). The book predicts more catastrophes. The deity of the national ideology did not question the exploitation of the poor. Appropriately, the prophetic message denounces Israel's religiosity and announces the destruction of the sanctuaries (3:14; 4:4-5; 5:4-6; 7:9; 8:3; 9:1).

Instead of this YHWH, the book presents a God who is sovereign over all nations (1:3—2:3; 9:7) and manifests power in the natural order (1:2; 4:7-13; 5:7-9; 7:1-6; 8:8-9; 9:5-6). This YHWH of Hosts mandates social justice and will punish Israel for the exploitation of the vulnerable. Other themes include the exodus (2:10; 3:1-2; 9:7), the remnant (3:12; 5:3; 6:9-10; 9:8), and the hope of a restored creation under a Davidic king (9:11-15). The presence of a formal idea of covenant is debated (for the covenant idea, see Stuart).

Amos 1:1—2:16: Preface (1:1-2) and Oracles against the Nations (1:3—2:16)

▌ THE TEXT IN ITS ANCIENT CONTEXT

Amos 1:1 combines "words" with "he saw," thereby connecting the prophet's spoken message with the visions (chapters 7–9). Verse 2 is a fitting foreword to the themes of the book: YHWH's roar (3:8; see also 3:4, 12), distressed fields (4:7-9), mourning (NRSV "wither"; 5:16; 8:8, 10; 9:5), Zion (6:1; 9:11), and Carmel (9:3). The force of the message is communicated through the metaphor of a devouring lion. YHWH appears as a lion in several prophets (Isa. 31:4; Jer. 25:38; Lam. 3:10-11; Hosea 5:14; 13:8; Mic. 5:8). The lion conveys power and fear. Importantly, the voice of YHWH comes from Jerusalem and Zion, not Samaria and Bethel. From the beginning, the book discredits the northern kingdom's government and religious system. The future beyond the judgment lay with the southern monarchy (9:11). The Judean Amos probably was a man of means, not a simple shepherd. He is called a *noqed* in 1:1, a term used elsewhere only of a king with huge flocks (2 Kgs. 3:4). According to 7:14-15, Amos was a herdsman, which could suggest that he also owned cattle. Sycamore trees do not grow in the region of Tekoa, so he may have owned other properties. Amos is knowledgeable of international affairs, and, if these messages do come from him, he was quite the poet. No poor shepherd here!

The oracles against the nations in 1:3—2:16 constitute the first of three major sections in Amos. These oracles set the tone of judgment for the rest of the book. These two chapters begin by condemning the transgressions of surrounding peoples before turning their gaze to Judah and Israel. Oracles against the nations is a common genre in the prophetic literature (see Isaiah 13–23; Jeremiah 46–51; Zephaniah 2). These oracles use what is called the *n/n* + 1 formula, where *n* is the number three, but do not list the four transgressions. The purpose may be to convey the habit of wrongdoing or to single out the worst behavior. Some believe that the numbers three and four should be added together, with seven symbolizing the fullness of sin. The repetitious language, with slight variations, interconnects the series (Paul, 7–15).

It is difficult to identify the events that lie behind these indictments, as no specifics are given. Some of these nations were long-standing enemies, so various settings are possible. Perhaps these oracles refer to ongoing skirmishes along national boundaries (see Amos 4:10). The constant thread throughout is cruelty in warfare. "Threshing sledges of iron" in Amos 1:3 might refer to physical torture or could be a figurative expression for ruthlessness (cf. 2 Kgs. 13:7; Isa. 41:15), while 1:11 reveals uncontrolled bloodlust in battle. Philistia and Tyre are denounced for human trafficking, probably of captives taken in war (1:6-10). Ripping open pregnant women bespeaks unbelievable barbarity (1:13; cf. 2 Kgs. 8:12; 15:16), and the desecration of a tomb violated ancient respect for the dead (2:1; cf. 2 Kgs. 23:16).

Amos 1:3—2:3 announces judgment on these other nations for their atrocities; fires will consume the fortresses of their capital cities, symbols of military strength. Several oracles target the leadership, decreeing either death or exile (1:5, 8, 15; 2:3). These persons were most responsible for instigating armed conflicts and the suffering of the casualties. All but the last oracle may allude to Israel's defeats. If so, they put the lie to the boasting of 6:13 and the nation's patriotic theology about the day of the LORD (5:18-20).

The formulaic introduction and endings to the Judah and Israel oracles (Amos 2:4-6, 6-16) echo those of 1:3—2:3. That is, they are transgressors like the other nations and will suffer a similar fate. Their sin, though, is directed inward: violation of the law's demands (Judah) and the socioeconomic exploitation of the poor (Israel). It is difficult to specify with confidence the nature of the abuse. For instance, does 2:6 refer to bribery of judges or to unpaid debts, however small, that lead to debt slavery (see 8:6)? Is the young woman of 2:8 a relative with whom father and son commit sexual impropriety or a debt slave abused by the men of the house? Whatever their exact meanings, all options are unacceptable. Israel also ignored the gracious acts of God in their past and compromised his representatives (2:9-12). Note that the seven transgressions of 2:6-8 are matched by seven kinds of soldiers in 2:14-16. Perfect sin merits complete defeat.

▌ THE TEXT IN THE INTERPRETIVE TRADITION

War was a constant reality in Old Testament times. The prophetic literature does not shy away from describing its horrors or denouncing religious ideologies that legitimated war. These oracles declare that cruelty in war will not go unpunished, as human life is precious in the sight of God. History is not purposeless; it has a moral framework and direction. This section teaches that God judges by turning warlike peoples over to the violence they perpetrate. In the Old Testament, this judgment takes the form of *lex talionis*: punishment corresponds to the crime. Here, to instigate war will mean experiencing the same at the hand of another people (cf. Isa. 10:5-19; Hab. 2:4-17).

Interpreting the oracles of 1:3—2:3 as attacks on Israel, rabbinic commentators emphasized the cruelty of the Gentiles and their punishment as an indication of God's favor (Neusner, 16–17, 63; Sweeney et al., 1036–37). Some church fathers allegorized certain lines. Gregory the Great held that 1:13 referred to the enemies of the gospel. To enhance their reputation (borders), they twist the truth about God in those whose full understanding of the gospel has not yet matured. Tertullian believed that 2:6 predicted the selling of Jesus by Judas (Ferreiro, 86, 88). The Reformers Martin Luther and John Calvin connected the censure of 2:8 with the greed of the priests and monks of their day (Luther, 141; Calvin, 187). For Calvin, the stubborn distortion of the Word of God by the Jews (cf. Acts 7:51) and the lies of the Catholic Church are manifest in 2:4; appeal to tradition (their "fathers") is no excuse (Calvin, 178).

▮ THE TEXT IN CONTEMPORARY DISCUSSION

This last century and a half has been the bloodiest in history. The realism of this section of Amos stands as a warning to our society, with its multibillion-dollar military budget and involvements in wars around the world, the ownership of millions of firearms in homes, the violence in our neighborhoods, and our fascination with violence in media. What future might these political policies and lifestyle choices portend?

The assertion that the LORD judges through war does not mean that every war comes from God's hand. To say as much would be to blame God for the evils wrought by human arrogance and greed. What is certain is that God will eventually call human violence to account. History is not a senseless trajectory across the centuries; the prospect of judgment should give us pause about our complicity—personally, socially, and politically—in violence of any kind.

For those who champion social justice, such as liberation theologians, Amos 2:6-8 and its condemnation of oppression is a foundational passage. The anonymity of the exploiters and their victims and the vagueness of the accusations allow for wide appropriation of these verses. Modern oppressors and workers of injustice embody these descriptions in today's societies, and these wrongs demand denunciation by new prophetic voices. These realities, however, cannot be oversimplified. Lai Lung Elizabeth Ngan warns Asian Americans, who can enjoy a privileged status vis-à-vis other minorities, about imitating the actions Amos condemns. Exploitation crosses all classes and ethnicities. Some feminist scholars wonder if the prophet is aware of the disproportionate burdens that poor women bear (such as low salaries, poor nutrition, the care of children), but are appreciative of his recognition of the terrible abuse of women in war (1:13). If the maiden of 2:8 is a debt slave, there may be greater attentiveness to destitute women than some believe.

Amos 3:1—6:14: The Words of God and the Prophet

▮ THE TEXT IN ITS ANCIENT CONTEXT

These four chapters provide details that substantiate the condemnation of Israel's social and religious transgressions and the announcement of divine judgment. Chapters 5 and 6 also weave in laments for the losses that this punishment will bring.

"Hear this," declares the prophet in Amos 3:1-2. These lines communicate that to be the chosen people of God carries special responsibility. Israel could not claim ignorance of the ways of YHWH. A series of seven rhetorical questions follows (3:3-6), progressing from an undefined meeting in 3:3 through to encounters that all lead to death and culminating in the disaster God brings to the city—in context, Samaria the capital. YHWH the lion (cf. 1:2; 3:12) has roared this decree through his prophet (3:7-8). The rest of the chapter reveals its sense: an enemy will destroy Samaria's defenses, Bethel's altars, and the extravagant homes of the well-to-do. Oppression reigns, and its fruits sustain the sociopolitical system—practices that would shock even Israel's enemies (3:9-10). Amos 4:1-3 announces the fate of the self-indulgent wives of the powerful, whom he mocks as "cows of Bashan" (a fertile area famous for its cattle; Jer. 50:19; Mic. 7:14). In a change of metaphor, the text says that they will be taken far away to exile, like hooked fish, through breaches in the walls of the defeated city.

A new subsection begins at Amos 4:4. Surprising irony gives bite to the prophetic word. Israel is beckoned to worship at the historic shrines of Bethel and Gilgal, but the people's worship is sin. The sacrifices mentioned in 4:4-5 do not deal with transgression; this is a religion of celebration and gratitude to the national deity. These activities satiate their religious impulses (4:5), but they are disconnected from the recent tragedies of hunger, drought, crop failure, and war (4:6-11). The refrain "yet you did not return to me" is repeated five times, emphasizing their estrangement from God. All their religious fervor was for naught and misplaced. Now they must prepare for a terrifying meeting with YHWH, not at those sanctuaries but face-to-face. Amos 4:13 is the first of three hymns that highlight the power of the sovereign God to judge (cf. 5:8-9; 9:5-6). He is YHWH God of Hosts, a name that includes a foreboding military epithet.

Like Amos 3:1 and 4:1, 5:1 begins with "Hear this word." Amos 5:1-3, following as it does the announcement of 4:12-13, reveals that the encounter with God will mean decimation of the towns in war, surely the conflict foretold in 3:6—4:3. Israel is compared to a young woman dying before reaching her potential in maturity. This oracle opens a chiasm that extends through 5:17. The deaths of 5:1-3 are matched by the ubiquitous laments in 5:16-17. The call to seek God and not the sanctuaries is echoed in 5:14-15 by the exhortation to seek and love the good, which is justice under YHWH God of Hosts. The distortion of justice and righteousness in 5:7 is fleshed out in 5:10-13 as the exploitation of the poor through taxes, bribery in the courts, and the silencing of those who would stand up to defend them. At the heart of this chiasm is the book's second hymn, in 5:8-9. The powerful creator God, who made the stars and controls the daily rhythms of nature, tears down the strong and their fortresses. In this hymn is found the climax of the chiasm and perhaps of the entire book: "YHWH is his name." Once again, as in 4:4-13, the person of God is at stake for the prophet. The YHWH perpetrated and praised at Bethel and Gilgal does not question injustice and in the end cannot save them. The true God indeed would be with them (5:14), but not in the way they had imagined. The prophet's YHWH will punish Israel's perverse theology and the society that it legitimated.

Amos 5:18-27 continues the themes of unacceptable civil religion and defeat. It begins with "woe!" connecting these verses back to the wailing of 5:16-17. This passage can be appreciated as a conceptual chiasm that again announces defeat. The negation of the mistaken common belief in future victory (5:18-20) will be confirmed by a future exile, when Israel will carry with them the foreign gods who were supposed to protect them (5:26-27). The many unacceptable practices of Israel's worship (5:21-23) stand in contrast to an earlier, purer faith (5:25). At the center of this structure is the demand to have justice and righteousness flow—not as intermittent water in the wadis of that dry land, but as a never-ending stream. Once more, religion and ethics are portrayed as inseparable. How different this mandate for justice and righteousness is from the nation's values (cf. 5:7)!

Several literary features highlight the message of divine rejection. Amos 5:20 emphatically repeats the notion of darkness in 5:18, while 5:19 conveys the inescapability of painful judgment. In other words, the triumphal day of the LORD (its earliest mention in the prophetic literature) anticipated by the national ideology will be turned on its head. Defeat not victory is in the offing, and that by God's hand. The emotive verbs with which 5:21 begins demonstrate how visceral is the rejection of Israel's religious practices. Note that 5:21-23 lists seven religious practices, expanding on those mentioned in 4:4-5. Amos 5:26 is a disputed verse in terms of the tense of the verb (past or future) and the apparent reference to astral deities (for a survey of opinions, see Paul, 194–98).

Amos 6 opens with another woe (6:1-7). The first target of the prophetic invective is the powerful, who feel confident in comparing the nation to surrounding peoples. They selfishly enjoy in abundance the finest meat, wine, and oils, while the rest of the population suffers want (cf. 4:6-10). The scene described in these verses could be a *marzeah* feast, apparently a banquet celebrated by the wealthy that might have been connected to funerary rights (cf. Jer. 16:5). This fete is known from different parts of the ancient world, so there may have been influence from other cultures that made the activity even more unacceptable. The fate of this uncaring elite repeats that of the women of 4:1-3.

The second half of Amos 6 broadens the judgment to include all Israel (6:8-14). Here the transgression is national arrogance. Its military is ridiculed in 6:13. The people rejoice in having taken *lo' davar*, literally "no-thing." A great victory indeed! Their fortresses and armies, supposedly the proof of Israel's power, will not be able to shield it from the death and border-to-border destruction of the coming invasion. The foolish confidence of Israel—from the wealthy to the masses—is as incomprehensible as plowing the sea, as imprudent as the manipulation of justice (cf. 5:7).

▌THE TEXT IN THE INTERPRETIVE TRADITION

Not many lines of Amos are cited in the literature of Qumran and the New Testament. The Damascus Document, however, reinterprets Amos 5:25-26 as a word of encouragement for the Essene community, who successfully took the true Word of God into exile—that is, away from the evil city of Jerusalem. Stephen quotes the Septuagint translation of 5:25-27 in his speech before the Sanhedrin to demonstrate Israel's historic rebellion and idolatry (Acts 7:42-43). This is the first of only two occasions where the words of Amos appear explicitly in the New Testament. The other passage is 9:11, to which James appeals at the Council of Jerusalem in Acts 15 (for other possible allusions, see Sweeney et al., 1038–39).

Rabbi Simla in the third century suggested that Amos 5:4 ("Seek me and live") was a précis of the 613 commandments (*b. Mak.* 23b–24a). Though appreciative of Amos's moral focus, rabbinic commentators were reluctant to accept the comprehensive destruction of the people of God predicted in the book. Some limited the judgment of 5:18-19, for example, to the gentiles and believed that the light of the day of the LORD referred to the redemption of Messiah. Others explained the wounding by various animals in 5:19 as that done to the Jews by the sequence of empires, beginning with Babylon (Neusner, 67–68).

Alberto Ferreiro (95–96) reports that based on the Septuagint's mistranslation, Tertullian, Cyril of Jerusalem, Ambrose, and Augustine saw in Amos 4:13 a prediction of the coming of Jesus ("he makes known to humanity his Messiah"). Further, Athanasius and Ambrose argued against those who said that the creation of the wind in this verse referred to the creation of the Spirit (the word for both is the same in Hebrew). Other passages the church fathers employed in contending with others include Tertullian's interpretation of 5:10 as a general negative description of the Jewish people; John Chrysostom's belief that 5:21-24 substantiated the worthlessness of Jewish rituals;

and Jerome's connection of the boast of 6:13 with the arrogance of heretics. In his comments on 6:1, Tertullian pointed to the conversation with the Samaritan woman at the well (John 4) and the healing of the Samaritan leper (Luke 17:17) as Jesus reversing the condemnation of 6:1 for those responding to him. Chrysostom and Basil the Great warned Christians not to fall into the fleeting and self-destructive excesses of 6:4-6 (Ferreiro, 100, 102, 104–6).

The Reformers also applied the prophetic oracles of Amos 4–6 to their context. Luther, for instance, preached that the victories of the Turks were God's chastisement of Europe to help bring them to faith, just like what had been preached to Israel in 4:6-10 (Luther, 153). He related 5:10 to Germany's political and religious leaders; and Calvin perceived the evils of 5:10-13 as present in his day too (Calvin, 265). Both read their doctrinal frameworks back into Amos's words. In 5:4-6, Luther (158–59) finds the distinction between true faith accepted in grace and the empty religious works of the Catholic Church. Calvin (252–55) uses these verses to teach that the wider preaching of repentance does not contradict the salvation of only the predestined elect; public proclamation renders all beyond excuse and confirms them in their sin.

An outstanding case of the appropriation of Amos's message is the Dominican friar Girolamo Savonarola (1452–1498). In a series of sermons on Amos and Zechariah preached in Florence during Lent of 1496, Savonarola railed against the civil and ecclesiastical authorities of the city for their corruption and for the emptiness of the rituals of the Catholic Church. For this boldness, he was jailed and executed (Barton, 172–74).

THE TEXT IN CONTEMPORARY DISCUSSION

Liberation theologians find prophetic support in Amos 5:7, 10-13, to condemn structural evil. Amos 3–6 also provides material for denouncing religious stances that support oppressive and nationalistic ideologies of the status quo. Some Latin American liberationists developed new liturgies and structures of Christian life (base ecclesial communities) as alternatives to the historic ecclesiastical institutions, which did not condemn oppression and had provided religious backing for unjust ideologies. These theologians utilized a measure of the Marxist critiques of religion against the blessings of dictatorships by many Catholic and Protestant churches (or at least their passive acceptance) and their promotion of a fatalistic, otherworldly religion that did not respond to the needs of the people. The goal of these liberationists was the creation of fresh expressions of the faith that would partner in social transformation (Carroll R. 1992, 91–122, 289–306).

The most well-known verse in the book is Amos 5:24: "But let justice roll down like waters, and righteousness like an ever-flowing stream." Martin Luther King Jr. quoted it in his famous speech on the Washington mall in August 1963. From an African American perspective, this line is also a rebuke of Southern evangelicalism's past support of slavery and segregation. The resiliency of African American Christian faith is evident in its songs, so the hymns of Amos resonate too (see Robertson). Some feminists dislike 4:1, believing it to be a distasteful characterization of women, though it may be more of a mockery of the excesses of a small wealthy elite than of women in general. They do point out, however, that Amos does not use the harlot metaphor prominent in other prophetic books.

The issue of the historical judgments of God was touched on earlier, but a particular dimension of the means of judgment surfaces conspicuously in these chapters: the role of the created order. The power of God in nature appears in the hymns of Amos 4:13 and 5:8-9 (cf. 9:5-6); 4:6-10 cites ecological disasters as divine judgments (cf. 1:2; 8:8-9); and the rhetorical questions of 3:4-5 and 6:12 appeal to the animal world. These passages suggest nature's cooperation with YHWH in judgment, even as human transgressions have ecological impact (cf. Hosea 4:1-3). The future flourishing of the community is also defined by natural bounty (9:11-15). These observations do not mean that the book is concerned directly with ecological matters, nor does it mean that all natural disasters should be identified as divine judgments. At the very least, however, the prophetic message should stimulate reflection on the interconnectedness of human communities and their ethical behavior with the nonhuman world, for good or for ill (Marlow, 120–57 and passim).

Amos 7:1—9:15: Visions of Israel's Future

▋ THE TEXT IN ITS ANCIENT CONTEXT

The last three chapters of Amos contain five visions, three of which are followed by material that illustrates and expands their themes (Amos 7:10-17; 8:4-14; 9:5-10). The book closes with a brief description of a glorious restoration after the judgment of God.

The first two visions describe devastating judgments (Amos 7:1-6). The first is a locust plague (cf. Exod. 10:12-15; Deut. 28:42; Joel 1), which occurs after the second crop (vegetables and legumes) was sprouting and while the grain would be maturing in the fields. The timing could not be worse, as this represented complete agricultural loss. The second vision is more mythological in its mention of the cosmic deep (Gen. 7:11; Isa. 51:10), but the message is similar: complete destruction. The prophet intercedes, pleading for YHWH to forgive and stop. Note the contrast between the nation's delusional hubris and Amos's clear appreciation of Israel's standing before God and in the world ("How can Jacob stand? / He is so small")!

With the third vision, intercession ends. Any hope for reprieve is dashed (Amos 7:7-9). The usual translation of 'anak (this word appears only in this passage in the entire Old Testament) is "plumb line." This has led to the interpretation that the people, represented by the wall, have not lived in conformity to YHWH's standards. This Akkadian loanword, however, means "tin" (Andersen and Freedman, 757–59; Paul, 233–35). This translation fits well in context and reinforces the declaration about the weakness of Israel. In this vision, the mighty fortresses of Israel are made of tin. While at a distance, the impression might be that they are of iron, in truth they are feeble. Once again, the nation is deceived, its boasting empty (cf. 6:13). God rips out a piece of this pathetic wall and throws it in their midst. It follows, then, that the defenses of Israel can protect its illegitimate worship places or the monarchy (7:9).

The narrative of Amos 7:10-17 carries on the thread of the destruction of the religious and political institutions. Bethel was Israel's most important sanctuary, where the civil religion of Israel was celebrated and promoted (7:13). Amaziah, the chief priest, recognizes the threat of Amos's words to that social construction of reality and demands that he return to his own country and earn his keep as a prophet there. Amos's response is to declare that he is not a prophet by trade or descent, but rather by the calling of God. As explained earlier, 7:14 and 1:1 suggest that he was a man of some status. Amos's standing probably gave weight to his words, enough so that his audience would pay attention and the king and his priest worry about his impact. The fate of the priest, along with his family's, encapsulates the coming national experience of judgment (7:17).

The meaning of the fourth vision (Amos 8:1-3) is based on a wordplay: *qayits* ("summer fruit") and *qēts* ("end"). The basket of ripe fruit symbolizes that Israel's end has come. With that will come wailing in the temple (or palace; the Hebrew term is the same for both). Either place was appropriate, as each was central to how the nation had devolved. There would be mourning, not celebratory songs (cf. 8:10; 5:16-17). The text returns to the economic exploitation of the poor and exposes from another angle the elite's perverse view of religion (8:4-6). Once again, the text emphasizes the power of the Creator in judgment (8:7-9). Soon the prophetic word would end, and lack of food (4:6) would be superseded by the absence of a word from God (8:11-13). Amos 8:14 may refer to foreign gods or different appellations of YHWH at various cultic sites (Paul, 268–72). Either option merited censure, as both exhibited syncretistic tendencies.

The final vision pictures the destruction of the temple at Bethel (Amos 9:1-4). Previous passages foretold the breaking of its altars (3:14) and its burning (5:6), but here its demolition is definitive. This was where the false YHWH of the national ideology was constructed and worshiped; this was where everything that was wrong with the nation—socially, economically, politically, militarily— received religious sanction. Here the judgment must begin. The punishment's comprehensiveness here is communicated by merisms—that is, the mention of two extremes with the idea that everything in between is meant.

Like previously, the incomparable sovereignty of the God who will judge Israel is celebrated in a hymn (cf. Amos 4:13; 5:8-9). The nation, although chosen of YHWH, is not exempt from judgment (9:7; cf. 3:1-2). YHWH was involved in the history of its neighbors too (cf. 1:3—2:3). Amos 9:8-10 clarifies that comprehensive punishment did not mean the eradication of Israel. A remnant would be left, even if in exile. This glimpse of hope is expanded in 9:11-15. After the devastation of judgment would come a new government, not of the misdirected northern regime but of the Davidic line (cf. 1:2). From the rubble would rise a people restored to the land, secure and prosperous, no longer attacked by other nations but sharing with them a relationship with YHWH. This time would be the reversal of the want and war of their present condition. This stark contrast has long led many scholars to argue that 9:11-15 is an exilic or postexilic addition, inserted to give hope after the fulfillment of the predicted judgments.

▌ THE TEXT IN THE INTERPRETIVE TRADITION

Some church fathers believed that Amos came from humble beginnings. Thus Gregory the Great pointed out how the Spirit can raise the humble to do great things for God (Ferreiro, 109–10). Irenaeus, Tertullian, Lactantius, and Cyprian believed that Amos 8:9-10 predicted the signs accompanying the crucifixion of Jesus (Ferreiro, 112). The warning of the famine of the word of God in 8:11-13 was taken by both the rabbis and the Reformers as an alert to heed the teaching of the Torah and correct doctrine, respectively (Sweeney et al., 1036; Luther, 182–84; Calvin, 376–80).

Among the Qumran materials, Amos 9:11 is listed in the collection of texts of the Florilegium (4QFlor 1:1-13). Apart from 5:5-26, this is the only passage cited and expounded in that community's literature. Rabbinic commentators understood 9:11-15 eschatologically as descriptions of the messianic era (Neusner, 103; Sweeney et al., 1037). In the New Testament, James quotes Amos 9:11-12 at the Council in Jerusalem (Acts 15:12-21). He grounds his argument for the inclusion of the gentiles on the Septuagint of 9:12 ("so that the rest of humankind may seek the Lord").

In the Christian tradition, Amos 9:11 has been interpreted christologically. Augustine and Chrysostom believed that the raising of the fallen tabernacle of David was a reference to the resurrection of Jesus (Ferreiro, 116). Luther says that the tabernacle of David is his descendants, out of whom Christ would arise, who would build the church (Luther, 189). Likewise, Calvin sees here a reference to the first advent (Calvin, 404–7). Both equate 9:12-15 to the spiritual blessings that accompany Christ's kingdom (Luther, 189–90; Calvin, 407–13).

▌ THE TEXT IN CONTEMPORARY DISCUSSION

What has been said earlier about the modern appropriation of Amos holds true in this final section. Here, too, are found the critique of the false consciousness of civil religion, the denunciation of socioeconomic oppression, and the connection between nature and the acts of God. Here also is a model of performing the prophetic office despite official opposition. The narrative of Amos 7:10-17 has empowered advocates of the marginalized in their struggle to proclaim and work for social transformation in YHWH's name. That courageous stance for justice, come what may, is one of this book's enduring legacies. Martin Luther King Jr. said that Christians should be as "maladjusted" as Amos to their context and speak out against injustice (Carroll R. 2002, 57–58).

Finally, Amos 9:11-15 teaches that the oppressions of today and the judgments of those wrongs are not the final word of God (Carroll R. 2002, 70–72). Beyond the losses inherent in those two realities and as a reversal of what we now endure will come the rebuilding, the raising, and the repairing of the ruins, abundance instead of want, and secure roots instead of displacement. We may live now in the place and hour of oppression as we await divine validation, or perhaps in that in-between time after what we believe is God's judgment and as we await God's new tomorrow. This prophetic hope can sustain the weary and encourage perseverance in the march toward justice.

Works Cited

Andersen, Francis I., and David Noel Freedman. 1989. *Amos: A New Translation with Notes and Commentary*. AB 24A. New York: Doubleday.

Barton, John. 2012. *The Theology of the Book of Amos*. Old Testament Theology. Cambridge: Cambridge University Press.

Calvin, John. 1986. *Joel, Amos and Obadiah. A Commentary on the Minor Prophets*. Vol. 2. Edinburgh: Banner of Truth Trust.

Carroll R., M. Daniel. 1992. *Contexts for Amos: Prophetic Poetics in Latin American Perspective*. JSOTSup 132. Sheffield: Sheffield Academic Press.

————. 2002. *Amos—The Prophet and His Oracles: Research on the Book of Amos*. Louisville: Westminster John Knox.

Coomber, Matthew J. M. 2010. *Re-Reading the Prophets through Corporate Globalization*. Biblical Intersections. Piscataway, NJ: Gorgias.

Ferreiro, Alberto, ed. 2003. *The Twelve Prophets*. Ancient Christian Commentary on Scripture, Old Testament 14. Downers Grove, IL: InterVarsity Press.

Houston, Walter J. 2009. *Contending for Justice: Ideologies and Theologies of Social Justice in the Old Testament*. Rev. ed. London: T&T Clark.

Jeremias, Jörg. 1995. *The Book of Amos: A Commentary*. Translated by D. W. Stott. OTL. Louisville: Westminster John Knox.

Lessing, R. Reed. 2009. *Amos*. Concordia Commentary. St. Louis: Concordia.

Luther, Martin. 1975. *Luther's Works*. Vol. 18, *Minor Prophets I: Hosea–Malachi*. Translated by R. J. Dinda. Saint Louis: Concordia.

Marlow, Hilary. 2009. *Biblical Prophets and Contemporary Environmental Ethics*. Oxford: Oxford University Press.

Neusner, Jacob. 2006. *Amos in Talmud and Midrash: A Source Book*. Studies in Judaism. Lanham, MD: University Press of America.

Ngan, Lai Lung Elizabeth. 2004. "Amos." In *Global Bible Commentary*, edited by Daniel Patte, 277–85. Nashville: Abingdon.

Paul, Shalom M. 1991. *Amos: A Commentary on the Book of Amos*. Hermeneia. Minneapolis: Fortress Press.

Robertson, Cleotha. 2010. "Amos." In *The Africana Bible: Reading Israel's Scriptures from African and the African Diaspora*, edited by Hugh R. Page Jr., 172–79. Minneapolis: Fortress Press.

Stuart, Douglas. 1987. *Hosea-Jonah*. WBC 31. Waco, TX: Word.

Sweeney, Marvin A., et al. 2009. "Amos (Book and Person)." In *Encyclopedia of the Bible and Its Reception*, edited by Hans-Josef Klauck et al., 1028–44. Berlin: de Gruyter.

Wacker, Marie-Theres. 2012. "Amos." In *Feminist Biblical Interpretation: A Compendium of Critical Commentary on the Books of the Bible and Related Literature*, edited by Luise Schottroff and Marie-Theres Wacker, 397–405. Grand Rapids: Eerdmans.

Wolff, Hans Walter. 1979. *Joel and Amos: A Commentary on the Books of the Prophets Joel and Amos*. Hermeneia. Translated by Waldemar Janzen, S. Dean McBride Jr., and C. A. Muenchow. Philadelphia: Fortress.

OBADIAH

Joseph F. Scrivner

Introduction

This prophecy of twenty-one verses is the shortest book in the Old Testament. The prophet's name means "servant of YHWH." Outside the book, this name is given for eleven individuals (1 Kgs. 18:3-16; 1 Chron. 3:21; 7:3; 8:38 [9:44]; 9:16; 12:9; 27:19; 2 Chron. 17:7-9; 34:12; Ezra 8:9; Neh. 10:5 [Neh. 10:6]; Neh. 12:25). Yet, none of these fits Obadiah's prophecy. This prophecy is a judgment oracle against the nation of Edom, because it exploited Judah while it was under attack by another, more powerful nation. In fact, Obadiah's language fits the time of Babylon's destruction of Judah in 586 BCE. Yet the prediction of restoration for the dispersed in the book's conclusion likely indicates a final form composed during the exile (586–539 BCE). Produced in this provenance, Obadiah's proclamations provoke reflection on the appropriate response to violent violation.

Obadiah 1:1-21: Speaking Judgment and Restoration

▌ THE TEXT IN ITS ANCIENT CONTEXT

Obadiah can be divided into two uneven sections, with the first focused on God's judgment on Edom (vv. 1-16), prosecuting its case with varying metaphors in the course of three subsections (vv. 1-4, 5-7, 8-16). The second section predicts Judah's restoration, when its exiles will possess its enemies' land (vv. 17-21). These two sections are united by their emphasis on a time of righteous reckoning: judgment on Edom but restoration for Judah.

The first section begins with the use of first-person plural verbs, which convey a decree by YHWH and the divine council. The council has dispatched a messenger with a charge of attack (v. 1). Yet Edom is self-deceived, believing it is protected by its location in the hills (v. 3). Regardless, God promises to bring Edom low (vv. 2, 4).

857

Obadiah continues by employing "the prophetic perfect" to predict divine judgment on Edom's excessive exploitation (Pagán). Even thieves, plunderers, and grape-gatherers know when enough is enough, but not so for Edom (v. 5). They did not exercise any restraint with Judah. In return, God will repay their voracious violence. Indeed, as Edom turned on Judah, so God will use Edom's allies against it (vv. 6-7).

Obadiah's message of divine retribution progresses in verses 8-16, as this subsection is framed by the motifs of the Day of the Lord and *lex talionis* (vv. 8, 15). God has set an appointed time when divine judgment will be relentless (vv. 8-9). Moreover, since Edom and Judah are "brothers" (vv. 10, 12), Edom should have shown Judah mercy, not enabled and extended its destruction. Indeed, verses 10-14 repeat the phrase "you should not have . . ." in its list of grievances detailing how Edom took advantage of Judah at every turn. Now, the prophet reports,

> As you have done, it shall be done to you;
>   your deeds shall return on your own head. (v. 15)

God will employ the nations as vehicles of vengeance to accomplish this judgment (v. 16).

In the book's final section (vv. 17-21), Obadiah foretells restoration for Judah. In contrast to Edom drinking on God's holy mountain (v. 16), days are coming when Mount Zion will once again be a place of holy refuge and God will give Judah's enemies into its hands (v. 17). These enemies include Edom, who will burn as stubble in Judah's fire (v. 18). Yet God's restoration will not be limited to Edom's destruction. Rather, the formerly dispossessed in Judah will possess the surrounding nations: the Philistines to the west, Ephraim to the north, and the towns of the Negev to the south (vv. 19-20). In addition, the rescued will return to Mount Zion and rule over Edom. Then the kingdom will belong to YHWH (v. 21).

▌ THE TEXT IN THE INTERPRETIVE TRADITION

Two themes from Obadiah's oracle can be highlighted in light of their significant role in the larger biblical tradition. First, an important literary motif is Obadiah's use of hierarchical imagery to denounce Edom's haughtiness. This is a recurrent device in prophetic judgment speeches. The prophets repeatedly condemn the surrounding nations for arrogantly exalting themselves in their abuse of other nations. Accordingly, God will respond in due time, showing them that only YHWH is worthy of exaltation (Isa. 2:11; 3:16; 5:15; 10:12; 37:23; Jer. 13:15; 48:29; Ezek. 16:50; Mic. 2:3; Zeph. 3:11). This applies even in cases when God has used the nation as an instrument of judgment (Isa. 47:1-15).

Another important topic is Israel and Judah's generational conflict with Edom. Of course, this relationship is portrayed as a sibling rivalry in the eponymous narratives about Jacob and Esau (Gen. 25:19-34; 27:1-28:22; 32:3-33:17). Conflict is described again when Edom does not allow Moses and Israel to pass through its land (Num. 20:14-21; see also Deut. 2:2-13). In addition, Edom was sacked by King David and served as Judah's vassal until it successfully revolted (2 Sam. 8:13-14; 1 Kgs. 22:47; 2 Kgs. 8:20-22). This historical relationship should inform one's interpretation of Obadiah and other biblical condemnations of Edom (Ps. 137:7; Isa. 34:5; Jer. 49:7-22; Lam. 4:21-22; Ezek. 25:12-14; Joel 3:19; Amos 1:6; Mal. 1:4-5). Obviously, Edom likely viewed its plunder of Judah in the sixth century as overdue justice. In Judah, however, the perception of Edom's role during the Babylonian campaign only worsened, so much so that one writer in the second century accused Edom of participating in Babylon's destruction of the temple (1 Esd. 4:45).

THE TEXT IN CONTEMPORARY DISCUSSION

The issues involved in the specific conflict between Judah and Edom can be extended to tensions within groups as well as between groups. In the early church, for instance, Luke portrays a relatively minor clash between Jewish Palestinians, on the one hand, and Hellenistic Jews, on the other (Acts 6:1-6). A more significant division is that between Jews and gentiles in the early church. The seeds of this struggle are planted in the arguments about Jewish identity for early believers as witnessed in our early writings from Paul in Galatians and Romans. Later, Luke in Acts 15 also portrays this fight, so too with the polemical depictions of Jews in the Gospels of Matthew and John.

Accordingly, an important question for modern readers of Obadiah in particular and the Bible in general is how one can facilitate mutual respect and reconciliation between warring parties. How does one examine deeply rooted distrust with empathy and compassion? Can one find constructive alternatives to cynical accusations and recriminations? Two scholars reflecting recently on Obadiah lament their ability to cite contemporary analogies, one from Korea (Ahn) and another from Africa (Farisani).

In the United States, numerous analogies can also be cited, such as continued obfuscation about slavery and the Civil War (Levine), and disingenuous forgetfulness regarding the role of persistent racial bias in the creation and reproduction of urban decay, poverty, and violence (Sugrue). In each case, few participants and parties want to engage in the necessary spadework found in various attempts at "Truth and Reconciliation" (Hayner). Yet this is likely the only way one can address past wounds and pursue authentic, healing communities. Such should be the charge of those who claim to hear and obey the biblical call for reconciliation.

Works Cited

Ahn, John J. 2009. "Obadiah." In *The Peoples' Bible*, edited by Curtiss Paul Deyoung, Wilda C. Gafney, Leticia Guardiola-Saenz, George E. Tinker, and Frank M. Yamada, 1063–64. Minneapolis: Fortress Press.

Farisani, Elelwani B. 2010. "Obadiah." In *The Africana Bible: Reading Israel's Scriptures from Africa and the African Diaspora*, edited by Hugh R. Page Jr., Randall C. Bailey, Valerie Bridgeman, Stacy Davis, Cheryl Kirk-Duggan, Madipoane Masenya, Nathaniel Samuel Murrell, and Rodney S. Sadler Jr., 181. Minneapolis: Fortress Press.

Hayner, Priscilla B. 2011. *Unspeakable Truths: Transitional Justice and the Challenge of Truth Commissions.* New York: Routledge.

Levine, Bruce. 2007. *Confederate Emancipation: Southern Plans to Free and Arm Slaves during the Civil War.* New York: Oxford University Press.

Pagán, Samuel. 1996. "Obadiah." In *The New Interpreter's Bible*. Vol. 7, *Introduction to Apocalyptic Literature, Daniel, the Twelve Prophets*, edited by Leander E. Keck, 447–49. Nashville: Abingdon.

Sugrue, T. 1996. *The Origins of the Urban Crisis: Race and Inequality in Postwar Detroit.* Princeton Studies in American Politics. Princeton: Princeton University Press.

JONAH

Matthew J. M. Coomber

Introduction

The book of Jonah, the fifth book of the Minor Prophets, is one of the most popular stories of the Hebrew Bible/Old Testament. In addition to being read as the prophetic portion of the afternoon service on Yom Kippur, Jonah's story has been popularized in art, theater, and children's stories.

In the Hebrew Bible, the book of Jonah stands in stark contrast to other prophetic writings, in that it only contains five Hebrew words of actual prophecy. Instead, the book follows the absurdist and wayward journey of a prophet who is called to preach to a sinful enemy city so as to save its inhabitants from YHWH's wrath. Rather than piously following this divine command, the prophet flees from YHWH's will, only to be forced to carry out his mission and to struggle with God's compassion for Jonah's oppressors. While the meaning behind Jonah's reluctance to help his oppressors is clear, the authors' intent in transmitting the story has been interpreted in a number of ways. Many interpreters have received the story as a tale of God's acceptance for the outsider, conveying an idea of God's universal love. More recent interpretations, especially those from a postcolonial perspective, view the story as sharing in the frustrations that are experienced by those who suffer foreign oppression.

The book's protagonist, an eighth-century prophet named Jonah ben Amittai, is said to have been active during the time of King Jeroboam II (786–746 BCE). He foretells Jeroboam II's expansion of Israel's borders "from Lebo-hamath as far as the sea of the Arabah" in 2 Kgs. 14:25. In 1 Esdr. 9:23 (Greek), Jonah is listed among the Levites who divorced their foreign wives during Ezra's religious reforms. The Hebrew account, found in Ezra 10:23, lists Eliezer instead of Jonah. Jonah is the only one of the twelve Minor Prophets mentioned by name in the Qur'an (10:98). While the book of Jonah is set in the eighth century, the story's emphasis on God's sovereignty over all nations and themes of forgiveness for the penitent suggests a postexilic composition, with the earlier prophet's name borrowed for storytelling purposes.

The historicity of the book, and its fantastical narrative involving a man who is swallowed by a great fish ("sea monster" or "large sea creature" in the Septuagint) as a means of rescue, has long been a source of controversy among Christian readers. The controversy stems not so much from post-Reformation literalism, but Jesus' references to the story in both Matt. 12:39-41 and Luke 11:29-32, leading some to assert its historical accuracy. This, however, disregards Jesus' frequent use of parables, suggesting that his teachings were not bound to historical accuracy. Modern scholarship widely receives the book of Jonah as a parable or a work of religious fiction to teach a lesson or transmit wisdom.

Jonah 1:1-17: Rebellion against a Divine Command

THE TEXT IN ITS ANCIENT CONTEXT

The book opens with a common prophetic call, "the word of the LORD came to Jonah," but is followed by a command that not only takes Jonah by surprise but would have also seemed surprising to the ancient audience. YHWH commands his servant to go straight to the Assyrian capital of Nineveh, "that great city," as described in Gen. 10:11-12, because "their wickedness has come up before me" (Jon. 1:2). But whereas YHWH's taking notice of a people's "wickedness" tends to be a harbinger of doom (Gen. 6:5; Deut. 9:5; Jer. 23:11; Hosea 9:15), and the words "come up before me" reflect YHWH's words prior to Sodom's destruction (Gen. 18:11)—a sentence that Jonah would have been happy to deliver—in this story, YHWH's command leads to a chance for repentance. Rather than heed this most offensive command, Jonah chooses to flee.

In the context of the prophetic genre, Jonah's decision to abandon God and his prophetic call so resolutely is shocking; his reaction stands in contrast to the eagerness of most prophets to heed YHWH's call. This prophet's decision to flee YHWH was intended to startle, and the fact that the "wickedness" of Nineveh is not specified leads the reader to focus on Jonah's struggle with his deity's will. From a sociohistorical standpoint, however, Jonah's reaction is most understandable. The Assyrians whom Jonah was called to warn were notorious for their use of physical and psychological terror tactics to subdue weaker states, including Israel. During their eighth-century campaigns into the Levant, the Assyrians inflicted punishments of disfigurement and/or death on regional leaders and resisters, while leaving many areas in economic ruin (Coomber, 103–5). The thought of bringing YHWH's mercy to Nineveh would have been repugnant, and is in juxtaposition to the xenophobic sentiment of Jonah's contemporary books, Ezra and Nehemiah. But despite Jonah's best efforts, his plan to escape YHWH's call ends in spectacular failure.

Jonah's flight emphasizes his desire to challenge YHWH's command in most every way. Whereas YHWH commands Jonah to "arise" (*qôm*) and go eastward to Nineveh, the prophet goes "down" (*yārad*) to the port city of Joppa, "down" into a ship that was headed to Tarshish in southern Spain, which was considered to be the western edge of the world. Jonah then continues his descent by going "down" into the ship's hold, where he lies "down" and falls into a deep sleep.

In response to Jonah's flight, YHWH sends a violent wind that puts the ship and its sailors in mortal danger. The sailors' inability to save the ship by jettisoning cargo and praying to their gods leads the ship's captain to demand that Jonah pray to his god (Jon. 1:5-6), rebuking the prophet who will not rebuke the Ninevites. After successfully prophesying that Jonah's presence caused the storm (1:7), the prophet who refuses to prophesy demands to be thrown into the sea, rather than simply turning the ship back toward Nineveh. After a failed attempt for shore and praying to Jonah's god for forgiveness for killing his prophet, the sailors throw Jonah overboard (1:15). While Jonah's preference for death over heeding YHWH's call further emphasizes the prophet's resolve to avoid his mission in Nineveh, the prophet will not be released so easily. Before Jonah can drown, YHWH sends a "great fish" to swallow him, and he dwells in its belly for three days and three nights (1:17 [16:1 MT]).

This scene in which pagan sailors pray to YHWH, while Jonah refuses to talk to his God, highlights both the prophet's anger and the deity's universal nature. Not only is mercy shown to the sailors by calming the sea, but they also go on to make a sacrifice and vows to YHWH (1:16), perhaps suggesting that further sacrifices would be offered onshore. In a polytheistic world, the sailors' willingness to offer sacrifices to YHWH makes sense, and a total religious conversion should not be assumed. What is emphasized is their acknowledgment of YHWH's place as a major deity among the nations, as found in 1 Kgs. 17:24 and 2 Kgs. 5:15-18.

▌ THE TEXT IN THE INTERPRETIVE TRADITION

The dramatic imagery and supernatural events of Jonah 1 have inspired a variety of receptions over the millennia. Jonah's anger at YHWH has been used to address the problems of nationalism, xenophobia, and also particularism and exceptionalism: the latter two being ideas of superiority for one particular group, setting them apart and above all others. Uriel Simon notes that the introduction of the protagonist reveals that his loyalties rest not in obedience to the "Lord of the universe," but with his people, the nation of Israel (Simon, viii). This interpretation of Jonah reflects a midrash composed by first-century teacher Rabbi Ishmael that admonishes a particularism that understood the welfare of Israel to be the supreme value and considers Jonah's disobedience in contrast to the prophets Elijah and Jeremiah. Jeremiah is represented as asserting the dignity of the father (God) and the son (Israel), and thus his prophecy is repeated. Elijah asserted the dignity of the father but not the son, and thus was replaced with Elisha. Jonah, however, asserted the dignity of the son but not the father, and thus God's voice leaves him after two chances (Simon, viii).

Whereas Rabbi Ishmael's midrash—adopted by Rashi, Joseph Kara, David Kimḥi, and Abraham Ibn Ezra—was intended to discourage an exceptionalism that places the state above the divine, Jonah 1 has also been used to promote exceptionalism and empire. English cartographer John Speed's use of Jonah and the fish in his late sixteenth-century map titled *Canaan* (raremaps.com) reflects an English imperialist interpretation of the prophet Jonah as the *sinful* subversive peoples whom the English controlled. The British Empire, however, is seen through the lens of the great city and repentant city of Nineveh, which represented both power and, as unfolds in Jon. 3:5-9, perfect piety (Staffell, 489–92).

From earliest Christianity, as seen in Matthew 12 and Luke 11, theologians have placed importance on the messages of the book of Jonah. Early interpretations often focused on the allegorical, sometimes using Jonah's rebellion as a vehicle for anti-Jewish sentiment. Rather than finding messages of God's universal love, St. Jerome connected Jonah's name—Hebrew for "dove" and a reference to Israel—to read Jonah's rebellion as allegorical to Israel's rejection of the salvation of the gentiles (Pyper, 352). John Chrysostom interpreted Jonah's rejection of God as allegorical to the Jewish people's rejection of Jesus, writing, "It is because you killed Christ . . . that there is no restoration, no mercy anymore and no defense . . . you have eclipsed everything in the past and through your madness against Christ, you have committed the ultimate transgression" (Holmgren, 128). These anti-Jewish interpretations, in contrast with those of Rabbi Ishmael, highlight the cultural subjectivity of biblical interpretation.

During the Reformation, many turned from allegorical interpretations to focus on the story as the human drama of Jonah's disobedience. Contemporary readings commonly view Jonah's rebellion as a satirical work against the intolerance of the postexilic era to promote a more universal view of God, while postcolonial interpretations have been effective in wrestling with the questions that arise when a God of the oppressed takes the side of the oppressors, as addressed in the third section of Jonah, 3:1—4:11, below.

THE TEXT IN CONTEMPORARY DISCUSSION

Rabbi Ishmael's use of Jonah's flight as an admonishment of first-century-CE particularism is relevant to the modern world, in which an us-versus-them mentality is used to attack the other, whether due to religious affiliation, political beliefs, or sexual preference. The questions raised by Jonah 1 lead the reader to acknowledge, through the person of Jonah, that our own ideologies should not be assumed to be those of God. The problem of projecting one's ideology onto respected figures is also common in the secular realm, as often happens with the invocation of influential thinkers from "the Founding Fathers" to Karl Marx. The narrative behind the so-called War on Terror, for example, is commonly framed as a clash of civilizations, with Christianity and Islam on opposing sides. Those who engage in Islamophobia—such as Pastor Terry Jones, who engaged in burning the Qur'an, new atheist author Sam Harris, who has claimed that Muslims are intellectually inferior (Crossley, 82–84), or Ann Coulter, who has asserted that the United States "should invade their [referring to Muslim] countries, kill their leaders, and convert them to Christianity" (Crossley, 69)—dehumanize people in ways that make it easier to engage in and accept such atrocities as the Haditha massacre, in which US soldiers killed twenty-four unarmed Iraqi civilians; after six years of court proceedings, no jail time was sentenced.

Chen Nan Jou finds modern value in YHWH's compassion toward the Ninevites. Addressing Christians who see all other religions as incapable of good and who disparage attempts to discern the theological relevance of non-Christian cultures, Chen notes that it is not God's prophet Jonah who is depicted as devout and religious in Jonah 1, but the pagan sailors on the boat. Considering this, and Jesus' willingness to break social boundaries and commune with the others of his time, Chen promotes Jonah as a vehicle for overcoming Christian attitudes of exceptionalism that have impeded interreligious dialogue (Chen, 292–94).

Jonah 2:1-10: Submission in the Face of Divine Will

▌ THE TEXT IN ITS ANCIENT CONTEXT

The second chapter of Jonah, thought by some to be a later addition (e.g., Benckhuysen, 6–9), contains a psalm of thanksgiving. Jonah's psalm can be divided into five parts. The first section, 2:2-3 (2:3-4 MT), recalls the prophet's call for help, suggesting that Jonah's preference for drowning was changed when faced with death. Interestingly, in 2:3 (2:4 MT), Jonah asserts that it was YHWH who cast him into the waters, rather than the sailors, at Jonah's behest (1:12-15). The second section, 2:4-6a (2:5-7a MT), likens Jonah's descent into the sea and the fish's belly as being cut off from God. The psalm's third section, 2:6b-7 (2:7b-8 MT), recalls how YHWH, in his temple, heard Jonah's prayer from the sea's depths and concludes with a thanksgiving prayer and sacrifices. But unlike other psalms of thanksgiving, which offer a means of meditation on the goodness of God, Jonah's psalm continues Jonah 1's absurdist narrative.

The first oddity of Jonah's prayer is that it is composed from the belly of a fish, which is an unlikely location from which to give thanks for salvation; most who venture through a fish's mouth consider themselves anything but saved. Second, Jonah only opens his mouth to give his psalm—his first utterance in the book—after sitting mute for three days in the fish's belly. Third, while thanking God for saving him from death, the prophet appears to assume that he will be exiting the fish from the same direction he entered. Jonah does not repent for the disobedience that led him into his present predicament. Thus the reader is presented with the absurd situation in which an unrepentant prophet reluctantly agrees to seek repentance from a foreign people who tormented Israel.

▌ THE TEXT IN THE INTERPRETIVE TRADITION

The image of Jonah being swallowed by a great fish has ignited the imaginations of artists and theologians alike, leading to interpretations through various mediums. Jewish midrashim have used Jonah's seventy-two hours of silence inside of the fish to offer additional meanings and interpretations to the story. Casting the fish as an ancient beast—supported by the adjective for the fish in the Septuagint, *megalos*, which can mean "ancient"—Rabbi Eliezer writes how entering into the fish was like walking into a synagogue. Jonah and the fish then confront and chase away the sea monster Leviathan (Isa. 27:1; Pss. 74:14; 104:26; Job 3:8; 40:25) before miraculously arriving under the foundations of the temple of Jerusalem, where God listens to Jonah's prayer (Green, 128).

Among early Christians, Augustine of Hippo reflected on Ps. 130:1, celebrating Jonah's time in the fish as a reassurance that no matter how deeply a person might fall into sin, God can always hear their repentance and deliver them (Green, 16–18). In addition to themes of repentance and forgiveness, Jonah's journey in and out of the fish has been interpreted as a promise of resurrection.

In entering into the sea and then being swallowed by a great fish, Jonah became dead to the world, or at least to the sailors who threw him out of their boat. But the certainty of Jonah's demise was wrong. Despite all evidence to the contrary, Jonah was not truly dead, and early Christians used this illusion of death to promote hope in the afterlife. Jesus used Jon. 1:17—2:10 to explain that despite the apparent finality of his demise he would only remain in the tomb for three days

(Matt. 12:40). In the same way, Christians turned to Jonah 2 to convey their hope in life after death, despite the apparent finality seen in a corpse. This message of resurrection is reflected in the carvings on several early-Christian sarcophagi, which reassured loved ones that their deceased's life only appeared to be over (see Lawrence; Britishmuseum.org; livius.org; rome101.com).

▌ THE TEXT IN CONTEMPORARY DISCUSSION

Themes of repentance and deliverance in Jonah 2, highlighted by Augustine, can be beneficial to both those within and outside of Abrahamic faith communities. For those who derive religious significance from Jonah, the idea of a God who listens and gives aid, regardless of how far one has fallen, can be a great source of comfort. In both religious or secular contexts—for example, dealing with a breakdown in international relations or coping with a personal addiction—the idea that people cannot fall so low that they cannot stand back up is powerful.

Jonah 3:1—4:11: Struggling with the Consequences of Divine Mercy

▌ THE TEXT IN ITS ANCIENT CONTEXT

After Jonah's flight from YHWH's command and vow to fulfill the deity's will, the story reopens with the "word of the LORD" once again commanding Jonah to go up to Nineveh to proclaim God's message. This time the prophet heeds (Jon. 3:1-3a). Juxtaposed, the parallelism used in Jon. 1:1-3 and 3:1-3a becomes apparent. While YHWH's call to action is essentially the same, Jonah's response is the opposite. Rather than attempting to flee from God and his mission, Jonah's voiceless response is to do exactly what is asked of him. However, YHWH does not repeat the rationale that is given in 1:2, "for their wickedness has come up before me," but simply relies on Jonah's sense of duty to obey, which Simon reads as a hint that the prophet's external compliance was accompanied by internal opposition (Simon, 25–26).

Upon his arrival at the enemy city of Nineveh, described as a three-days' walk across (Jonah 3:3b), Jonah walks for a day before proclaiming the only words of prophecy in the book: "Forty days more and Nineveh shall be overthrown" (3:4)! To Jonah's great dismay, his few words of prophecy are received with astounding effect. Highlighting the power of an utterance from YHWH and this foreigner's God's identity, the people of Nineveh are instantly moved to repent from their undefined sin (3:5). In hopes that YHWH's anger can be appeased, their king orders not only his people to submit to total repentance but also the city's animals, who are commanded to fast, put on sackcloth, and cry "mightily to God" (3:7-8). The ironic contrast between the Ninevites' and Jonah's reaction to impending doom should not be overlooked: while YHWH's prophet refuses to repent for rebelling against God while in the fish, the nonbelieving inhabitants of Nineveh fully repent for whatever wrong they have committed. And just as the Ninevites are swift to atone for their evil (ra'), YHWH is also swift to repent from the evil (ra') that he had planned for them.

Considering that YHWH destroyed Sodom despite Abraham's intercessions in Gen. 18:16-33, a peaceful outcome for Nineveh may not have been a foregone conclusion. But now that Jonah's work has proved successful and the people have repented, Jonah ironically appears to have lost all optimism. Jonah 4 opens with what is commonly considered to be Jonah's second rebellion: the prophet's anger toward God. Whereas the people and the animals of Nineveh have everything to celebrate, a distraught Jonah confesses that his unsuccessful run to Tarshish was an attempt to subvert what he now fears will happen: YHWH will hear to the Ninevites' repentance and give them his mercy (4:1-2). Joseph Blenkinsopp argues that YHWH's merciful nature not only offended the prophet by aiding his enemies but also discredited Jonah's powers of prophecy, as there was apparently a tradition of Jonah predicting Nineveh's demise, as found in Tob. 14:4 and 14:8 (Blenkinsopp, 242).

In Jonah 4:2, the reader is presented with yet another ironic twist. Jonah quotes Exod. 34:6-7, which extols YHWH's attributes of mercy and forgiveness, not as a form of praise, for which they are so often used, but as a protest. That God is indeed merciful and slow to anger has become loathsome to him under his current circumstances. Having played a role in the fruition of God's mercy toward the Ninevites gives him such great despair that Jonah again seeks out death in 4:3, claiming that "it is better for me to die than to live." But rather than granting his servant's request, YHWH questions Jonah's right to be angry in 4:4; in the Septuagint, YHWH asks if Jonah is really that angry. Without a word of response, Jonah leaves to the east of Nineveh and makes a booth for himself, where he sits and waits to see what will become of the city.

Despite Jonah's anger and his desire to die, God does not abandon Jonah, but follows and engages him through three supernatural events. God causes a plant to shoot up and provide Jonah with shelter from the hot desert sun (4:6), sends a worm to attack the plant and cause it to wither (4:7), and finally sends a scorching wind from the east, which combined with the heat of the sun rekindles the prophet's death wish. Yet again, rather than heeding Jonah's desire to be put out of his misery by death, God admonishes the prophet for exercising compassion on behalf of the shade-giving bush, but withholding it for the hundreds of thousands of Ninevites who "do not know their right hand from their left."

▌ THE TEXT IN THE INTERPRETIVE TRADITION

Whereas the contents of Jonah 3:1—4:11 do not contain the vivid and miraculous imagery of the book's first two chapters, the story's conclusion demands much reflection on the part of the reader. Blenkinsopp interprets both YHWH's decision to retract the evil he planned for Nineveh and Jonah's despair at his God's mercy as a wisdom critique of Hebrew prophecy that attempted to wrestle with the sorts of theological problems that accompany prophecy, such as nationalism (Blenkinsopp, 242). By pitting a nationalist prophet against his own god's willingness to extend mercy to an enemy nation, the authors worked to promote a YHWH who was free from the sociopolitical constraints of the prophetic word. Such an interpretation can be taken in a couple of ways. One interpretation is to take the book of Jonah as a rejection of the exceptionalism that is promoted in much of Hebrew prophecy, encouraging readers to abandon their nationalist views.

While traditional interpretations of Jonah's fourth chapter have read YHWH's rebuttal of Jonah as a statement against Hebrew particularism, pitting Jonah's sense of exceptionalism against the more universal outlook of the divine, as discussed above of Jon. 1:1-17, another way of reading

Jonah is found in recent postcolonial interpretations of the prophet's reaction to the forgiveness of his nation's imperial tormenters, shedding new light on the text.

■ The Text in Contemporary Discussion

Jonah's disapproval of God's mercy toward the Ninevites has traditionally been treated as an indefensible position. However, when viewed from the colonized perspective of the protagonist and the book's original audience, new levels of meaning are uncovered. From the perspective of a people who have suffered brutal colonization, the Koreans, Chesung Justin Ryu finds it difficult to condemn Jonah's anger: "As long as the oppression or colonization and its painful memories are ongoing, how can the oppressed hide their anger in learning that their oppressors and colonizers are saved by their God—the God of the oppressed?" (2009, 198). Considering the colonized perspective of Jonah's postexilic authors and audience, Chesung does not believe that the story was intended to mock an angry prophet's particularism, but to share in the silence of an oppressed people (Chesung, 202, 218). In this light, Jonah's anger is not narrow-minded and stubborn, but a legitimate grievance to which the prophet responds with silent resistance.

In her Africana reading of Jonah, Valerie Bridgeman takes issue with YHWH's questioning of Jonah's anger (Jon. 4:4, 9-11), claiming that this storyline can have the negative outcome by demanding silence from those who face oppression and stifling revolution (Bridgeman 2010, 186). To simply assume that the pious answer to YHWH's question concerning Jonah's right to be angry is "no" disregards the context surrounding the text, in which Jonah is asked to aid and abet an enemy in the destruction of his own culture and people; despite any repentance against evil in Nineveh, the Assyrians went on to destroy the northern kingdom of Israel in 722 BCE, some forty years after the story of Jonah's journey is to have taken place. Rather, Bridgeman sees YHWH's question as an invitation for the reader to consider how anger can factor into "justice making, evangelization, and reconciliation" (Bridgeman 2010, 186). In confronting this problem, Bridgeman notes that some black preachers have read Jonah as a message about the dangers of going against God's will, or as a springboard for conversations on releasing hatred for a greater good, even when the hatred may be deserved (Bridgeman 2013).

Chen's postcolonial reception of Jonah finds a message of God's universal love that calls on Christian readers to consider the "undesirables" to whom Jesus preached, and to foster openness and camaraderie with peoples of other faiths so as to bring an end to religious bigotry in our time (Chen, 293–94).

Works Cited

Benckhuysen, Amanda W. 2012. "Revisiting the Psalm of Jonah." *Calvin Theological Journal* 47, no. 1:5–31.

Blenkinsopp, Joseph. 1996. *A History of Prophecy in Israel: Revised and Enlarged.* Louisville: Westminster John Knox, 1996.

Bridgeman, Valerie. 2010. "Jonah." In *The Africana Bible: Reading Israel's Scriptures from Africa and the African Diaspora*, edited by Hugh R. Page Jr., R. C. Bailey, V. Bridgeman, and Stacy Davis, 183–88. Minneapolis: Fortress Press.

Britishmuseum.org.www.britishmuseum.org/explore/highlights/highlight_objects/pe_mla/m/marble_sar-cophagus_carved_with.aspx

Chen Nan Jou. 2004. "Jonah." In *Global Bible Commentary*, edited by Daniel Patte, J. S. Croatto, N. W. Duran, T. Okure, and A. Chi Chung Lee, 291–94. Nashville: Abingdon.

Chesung Justin Ryu. 2009. "Silence as Resistance: A Postcolonial Reading of the Silence of Jonah in Jonah 4.1-11. *JSOT* 34, no. 2:195–218.

Coomber, Matthew J. M. 2010. *Re-Reading the Prophets through Corporate Globalization: A Cultural-Evolutionary Approach to Economic Injustice in the Hebrew Bible*. Piscataway, NJ: Gorgias.

Crossley, James G. 2008. *Jesus in an Age of Terror: Scholarly Projects for the New American Century*. London: Equinox.

Gaines, Janet Howe. 2003. *Forgiveness in a Wounded World: Jonah's Dilemma*. Studies in Biblical Literature 5. Atlanta: Society of Biblical Literature, 2003.

Green, Barbara. 2005. *Jonah's Journeys*. Collegeville, MN: Liturgical Press.

Holmgren, Fredrick C. 1994. "Israel, the Prophets, and the Book of Jonah." *CurTM* 21:127–32.

Lawrence, Marion. 1962. "Ships, Monsters and Jonah." *AJA* 66, no. 3:289–96.

Livius.org. www.livius.org/jo-jz/jonah/jonah-sarcophagus.html

Pyper, Hugh S. 2000. "Jonah." In *The Oxford Companion to Christian Thought*, edited by Adrian Hastings, Alistair Mason, and Hugh Pyper, 352–53. New York: Oxford University Press.

Raremaps.com. www.raremaps.com/gallery/archivedetail/15530/Canaan/Speed.html

Rome101. www.rome101.com/Topics/Christian/Magician/pages/Vat31496_0609_0680WS.htm

Simon, Uriel. 1999. *Jonah*. JPS Bible Commentary. Philadelphia: Jewish Publication Society.

Staffell, Simon. 2008. "The Mappe and the Bible: Nation, Empire and the Collective Memory of Jonah." *BibInt* 16:476–500.

MICAH

Matthew J. M. Coomber

Introduction

The book of Micah is attributed to the work of Micah of Moresheth, an eighth-century-BCE Judean prophet whose prophecies were directed toward both Samaria and Jerusalem in the latter half of the eighth century. The book represents the sixth scroll of the twelve Minor Prophets in the Masoretic Text and is placed between Jonah and Nahum. In the Septuagint, it is the third scroll of the Minor Prophets and is placed between Amos and Joel. According to Mic. 1:1, the prophet Micah's work extended from the reigns of King Jotham (742–735) to King Hezekiah (715–687), making him a contemporary of Isaiah. In the book of Jeremiah, Micah of Moresheth is celebrated as a bold prophet who was not afraid to speak to power during Hezekiah's reign (26:18). He is also listed among the great leaders in 2 Esd. 1:38.

While the book of Micah may be short in length, it is long on scathing attacks against those who use political, religious, or economic power to exploit their neighbors for personal gain. But despite its numerous threats of YHWH's wrath and prophecies of doom, Micah also expresses God's eagerness to maintain relations with God's people.

Considering the book of Micah's ability to address a variety of religious and societal issues, its use within popular religion has probably been less frequent than it deserves. Unlike the book of Exodus, which enjoys an easy-to-follow narrative, Micah's poor preservation, its large number of authors and redactors, and an irregular timeline pose a number of hermeneutical challenges. Additionally, there are disagreements as to Judah's sociopolitical situation at the turn of the seventh century BCE. While Micah's hermeneutical issues will be explored in the following sense units, issues surrounding Judah's historicity should first be addressed.

Traditional views on Judah's history find a thriving, centuries-old kingdom by the late eighth century, the time to which the book of Micah is attributed. However, recent archaeological discoveries indicate that Judah was a largely undeveloped region until Israel's destruction in 721, during Assyria's expansion into the Levant. While the debate over Judah's historicity has been limited almost entirely to academic circles, a later dating of Judah's rise to prominence has very real implications for those who wish to use the Bible in struggles against modern political, religious, and economic injustice, as will be explored below. Regardless of Judah's historicity, and while much of Micah was likely written during the postexilic period, the fact that the book is set in a time of economic development and imperial incursion, rather than within an already well-established state, opens the book to new interpretations.

Another challenge to interpreting Micah has been the book's contextual ambiguity. The transgressions condemned by the prophet are often presented without any information as to who was abusing whom or how these abuses occurred. While the lack of clarity regarding the book's historic context have frustrated attempts to understand the book in its original settings, this ambiguity can also allow the text to step outside of its origins and speak more fluently across culture and time, as discussed in the following sense units.

For the purposes of this commentary, the book of Micah's lack of overarching narrative makes it difficult to divide into clearly defined units. Many ideas and themes within the book are repeated and revisited, leading to a certain amount of repetition from one sense unit to the next.

Micah 1:1—3:12: Attacks against Political and Religious Abuses of Power

▌ THE TEXT IN ITS ANCIENT CONTEXT

The authors of Micah waste little time in laying out the sense of doom and destruction that they want to convey. After a brief biography of the prophet in Mic. 1:1, the text launches into a series of oracles that convey YHWH's rage against both Israel and Judah, foretelling severe punishments for their transgressions. The contextual ambiguity, addressed above, is prevalent here; negligible information is offered as to the nature of Israel and Judah's sins or the identities of their perpetrators and of their victims. But while the details may be understated, a sense of looming doom is not.

Following Micah's biography in 1:1, the book immediately proceeds to a prophecy that foretells the impending arrival of YHWH, who will judge Israel—for the acts of idolatry and corruption that it used to procure its wealth—and Judah for unspecified crimes (1:5-7). In return for their sins, both kingdoms will be laid to ruin at the hands of invading forces (1:15). The impact of YHWH's justice is to be swift and, despite Micah's proclamation, unexpected; in an ironic twist of fate, the inhabitants of the Judean town of Maroth will suffer YHWH's wrath while eagerly awaiting the fruits of its favor (1:12).

Chapter 2 offers more specifics about the nature of the transgressions for which God's people are to be punished. Micah lashes out at those who use their power to steal land from others (Mic. 2:1-2, 9). There are many Hebrew words for oppress, but 'ashaq, which is used in 2:2, refers to violence, robbery, and poverty, and conveys well the serious consequences of land seizures in agrarian societies.

The sociological field of cultural-evolutionary theory reveals that as agrarian societies are absorbed into world systems of trade, a series of societal patterns tends to unfold, regardless of culture or time. As administrative elites are enticed by the earning potential of newly available trade routes, they coerce subsistence farmers into abandoning traditional risk-reducing strategies for the high-risk, specialized cultivation of exportable crops. As heightened risk translates into crop failure, producers are forced to take out survival loans at exorbitant rates, which ultimately leads to default and foreclosure. Administrators then consolidate these lands into huge estates that can be effectively managed for the large-scale cultivation of export goods. In the end, these rulers hoard the benefits of trade as previously self-sufficient subsistence farmers are either forced into wage labor or become displaced (Coomber 2011, 217–19). To combat such suffering, agrarian societies often establish prohibitions against the permanent sale of farmland, as found in biblical texts (Lev. 25:10, 23-28; Num. 27:1-11; Ruth 4:3-6; and 1 Kgs. 21:1-4), Sumerian and Babylonians laws, and in former colonies of the Ottoman Empire (Coomber 2010, 109, 197). In response to their crimes, the Judean landgrabbers would have to watch as foreign armies divided the very estates they had stolen from their neighbors (2:4).

The only hopeful message in Micah 1–3 is found in 2:12-13, which provides assurance that the survivors of YHWH's wrath will be gathered back together like a flock in pasture. The origins and meaning of this passage are much disputed. Whereas Francis Andersen and David Friedman interpret 2:12-13 as a later, postexilic addition (Andersen and Friedman, 32–34), others read these words of hope as mocking the lies of Judah's false prophets who cry peace when there is war (Ben Zvi, 67). Whether taken as original text, postexilic redaction, or example of false prophetic assurances, the "comfort" tone found in 2:12-13 does not last.

Chapter 3 continues with oracles of doom, targeting corrupt politicos and religious leaders who, like the landgrabbers of Micah 2, will be punished by foreign invasion. Without listing their crimes, the authors of 3:1-3 launch a salvo against Judah and Israel's political elites, likening them to cannibals who devour the flesh from people's bones. This imagery, which is graphic to the extreme, would have resonated with the prophets' intended audience. While the Hebrew word *pashat*, commonly translated as "flay," refers to a specific method of butchering that was used in cultic sacrifice (Lev. 1:6), the authors' audience would have also recognized *pashat* as a common Assyrian terror tactic that was widely advertised to discourage rebellion in occupied areas (Andersen and Friedman, 353). At the time of the resulting invasion, YHWH would answer the ruling elites' cries with the same silence with which they had responded to their subjects' cries for justice (3:4).

In Mic. 3:5-8, YHWH's anger focuses on the prophets, who are condemned for neglecting the people by crying "peace" for those who fill their mouths and declaring "war" against those who do not or cannot offer food (3:5). YHWH's anger at the religious establishment, however, appears to pit divine expectations against the religious norms of the time. Most prophets, such as Ezekiel, Jeremiah, and Isaiah, were professionals who expected to be compensated for their craft; this is found in Saul's concern over not being able to offer Samuel food in return for a prophetic request (1 Sam. 9:6-8). Whether or not the prophets of Mic. 3:5-8 were aware that their expectations of payment had offended their God, 3:5-7 proclaims that YHWH will cut them off by removing their ability to practice their craft. It appears that the transgression of the priests and prophets in 3:11 is rooted in willingness to perform their rites for money, but not as YHWH's earthly representatives.

As with the use of *pashat* in Mic. 3:3, the threats leveled against Israel's and Judah's religious and political leaders in this passage were rooted in the geopolitical events of the late eighth century. The threat of Assyrian aggression was realized in Israel's destruction in 721 and during Judah's invasion and near annihilation in 701, and the punishments would have been read in light of these foreign invasions.

▪ THE TEXT IN THE INTERPRETIVE TRADITION

While the greater geopolitical context of the late eighth century is largely known, the book of Micah offers very little information regarding the nature of the particular transgressions that it condemns; it is possible that those who contributed to the book at later dates were also unaware of the exact nature of these misdeeds. Other than general accusations of corruption and idolatry, Micah's first chapter gives little information as to the crimes that were to bring Israel and Judah's destruction, which led the Presbyterian English commentator Matthew Henry (d. 1714) to focus on more general meanings of the text in his commentary. He warns of "spiritual diseases" to which those who are given great power are exposed, setting a negative example for their subjects (Henry, on Mic. 1:1-7).

The ambiguity of Mic. 2:1-4, which informs the reader only that one anonymous group took land from another anonymous group through unspecified means, lends itself to varied interpretations, mostly involving the sin of coveting another's land. John Calvin, for example, interpreted this passage as a reminder of God's disdain for frauds and plunderers, encouraging the reader to channel his or her desires toward what is right and just (Calvin, 175).

Reading Mic. 2:1-4 through the lens of international capitalism, twentieth-century interpretations have largely read the text as an admonishment of greedy merchants or businessmen who seized land from poor farmers. Such commentators as James Mays and Ralph Smith have framed the contents of Mic. 2:1-2 as a struggle between the interests of Judah's wealthy and poor. Both Mays and Smith view the passage as condemning a small group of merchants who used corrupt government officials to steal arable land from poor farmers (Mays, 64; Smith, 24). Neither merchants nor poor farmers are mentioned in the text, but since the perpetrators and victims are not identified, such speculations are understandable, if not useful. Juan Alfaro takes even greater interpretive license, suggesting that the *mishpakhah* ("family") mentioned in 2:4 refers to a "mafia family" of organized criminals that profited through stealing poor farmers' lands (Alfaro, 25).

The condemnation of corruption among religious elites caught the attention of early Christian commentators who were dealing with corruption in their own times. Jerome drew on the corruption of priests and prophets in Mic. 3:11 to limit the pay of clergy in order to prevent them from chasing the purse rather than the Spirit (Arelatensis, 76:456). Cyril of Alexandria (253–54) referenced Mic. 3:9 to address the problem of those who would "pervert what is right" by corrupting holy texts to suit their own needs. Despite the aforementioned troubles in transmitting the book of Micah, the contents of 1:1—3:12 have resonated with interpreters through the centuries and remain highly relevant in the early twenty-first century.

■ THE TEXT IN CONTEMPORARY DISCUSSION

Despite the fact that the first three chapters of Micah focus on issues that are prevalent in almost any society—problems of political and religious corruption—they are rarely used to confront modern injustices. Perhaps this is due to a lack of an overarching narrative or the cumbersome nature of the book. However, recent archaeological and sociological research has uncovered previously unrecognized levels of relevance that these texts have in addressing modern-day imperialism and economic exploitation.

Considering the vast societal transformations that Judah experienced in the late eighth century as the region was absorbed into Assyria's trade nexus, it is plausible that the land seizures of Mic. 2:1-2 did not represent a few venal individuals who subverted an otherwise just system, as Mays, Smith, and Alfaro suggest, but were the result of a pan-Judean shift in economic policy. Marvin Chaney argues that as Judah was presented with new opportunities to trade wine, olive oil, and cereals with Assyria and its trade partners, Judah's rulers coerced previously autonomous farm families into abandoning their traditional risk-reducing subsistence practices for the specialized, trade-focused cultivation of these crops. As increased risk led to crop failure, survival loans resulted in the foreclosure of family-held lands, allowing ruling elites to consolidate and control the productive efforts of the region. Such forms of exploitation are found in our modern economic context.

Building on Chaney's work, Coomber has used examples of these patterns in agrarian societies that have been absorbed by global capitalism to shed light on Mic. 2:1-4's hidden contexts and consider the relevance of such prophetic complaints in the modern world (Coomber 2010, 2011, 2013). Uncovering connections between trade exploitation in the ancient and modern world not only offers a voice for agrarian workers displaced by market forces, whether Tunisian peasants or Iowan farmers who must to compete against heavy subsidies for corporations (Levins and Galbraith), but can also provide a powerful critique of those who benefit from such injustices today.

Micah 4:1—5:15: Hope for a Restored Relationship with YHWH

■ THE TEXT IN ITS ANCIENT CONTEXT

Commonly considered a postexilic addition, Micah 4 makes for an abrupt transition from the foreboding mood of Micah 1–3. The prophecy of chapter 4 moves the reader forward in time, envisioning a day when YHWH's house not only will be reestablished but also will become the center of worship for the peoples of many nations. While God's role as judge is foretold to be both active and present, YHWH will serve as a vehicle for peace by arbitrating between powerful nations, which will beat their swords into plowshares and spears into pruning hooks as war is rendered a thing of the past (Mic. 4:3-4).

It should be noted that Mic. 4:1-3 is nearly identical to Isa. 2:2-4, raising questions as to which passage was the original. While it has traditionally been thought to have originated with Micah, recent scholarship suggests that the oracle was borrowed from the Isaianic tradition and given greater power through extending God's reign over nations that were far away (Mic. 4:3; cf. Isa. 2:4). This more powerful rendering places Jerusalem not only at the center of Israel but also at the center of YHWH's reign in history.

Immediately following Mic. 3:12, which proclaims Jerusalem would be reduced to "a heap of ruins," Mic. 4:1-8 reverses the city's destruction to make it more powerful than it had ever been. Ben Zvi suggests that this reversal was created to assure postexilic audiences that YHWH's power had not been diminished by Jerusalem's fall, but would be expanded to ensure that the city remained at the center of God's power (Ben Zvi, 104–5, 111–13). By connecting the past of King David's reign to a Jerusalem that would serve as a harbinger of peace to the nations of the world, 5:1-5a would have offered its ancient audience encouragement and pride as they awaited Israel's coming glory.

Connections between Israel's past and future continue into Micah 5, where a ruler from Bethlehem is prophesied to bring peace and security to the land (5:2-6). The placement of this great monarch's origins in Bethlehem, the city of King David's birth, gave ancient audiences a sense of continuity after the interruption in rule of Israel's and Judah's defeats and exile. The power of this coming king, and his mandate by YHWH, is revealed through the grand shift in power that is prophesied in 5:5-6; if the once-great Assyrian Empire decides to invade the once-weaker state of Israel, the Assyrians will be routed and conquered under the promised Bethlehemite ruler. Such words would have bolstered the wounded pride of postexilic audiences.

The greatness of this new era is further emphasized in Mic. 5:10-15, which promotes Israel's dominance into the future and YHWH's ongoing role in human history. The passage depicts YHWH as playing an active role in Israel's affairs, cleansing Israel of military and cultic objects and destroying disobedient nations who stand in the way of God's plans.

▌ THE TEXT IN THE INTERPRETIVE TRADITION

While both Judaism and Christianity have received Micah 4–5 as a portrayal of Zion's coming restoration, there has been significant divergence between Jewish and Christian interpretation. Many of these differences rest in the fact that the fourth and fifth chapters feed into the Christian narrative of Jesus' birth in Bethlehem and also the evangelical image of all nations coming together under God's reign, as described in the New Testament.

The promise of peace found in the imagery of turning weapons of war into tools of farm production, as found in Mic. 4:3 (and also in Isa. 2:4 and Joel 3:10), has captured the hopes and imaginations of its audiences. Rather than an event pertaining to the second coming of Jesus of Nazareth, Maimonides, a twelfth-century-CE rabbinic scholar, interpreted the prophecy of Micah 4 as pertaining to a bright future on earth during the time of the Messiah. In addition to reading 4:1 as a glorious period in which rule would return to Israel and subjugation to wicked kingdoms would become a thing of the past (Maimonides 1975, 171), he interpreted the words of Mic. 4:3, "nation shall not lift up sword against nation," as heralding a virtuous time in which people would "attain much perfection and be elevated to the life of the world-to-come" (Maimonides, 166–67). This passage invited audiences not only to hear the warnings against corruption in the book of Micah, but it also offered the promise of a brighter future.

Many Christian interpretations have taken Micah 4 out of its ancient Hebrew context to address their own religious systems. In *The City of God*, Augustine (18.30) claimed that Micah used the mountain imagery in 4:2 to describe a gathering of nations under Christ. Justin Martyr read Mic. 4:1-3 as a foretelling of Christ's coming and that the beating of swords into plowshares happened when the twelve disciples came together with Christ to "teach to all the Word of God" (Justin Martyr, Mic. 4:1-3). Later, Matthew Henry interpreted Mic. 4:1-8 as a promise to the Christian church of a time in which "the reign of Christ shall continue till succeeded by the everlasting kingdom of heaven" (Henry, on Micah 4). Each of these interpreters reshaped the passage's message to relate to their own religious beliefs and spiritual needs.

The imagery of Mic. 4:3 has also appeared in recent popular culture. The imagery of turning weapons into farm tools has also been used in such popular songs as "Down by the Riverside" and Don Henley's hit single "The End of the Innocence."

▌THE TEXT IN CONTEMPORARY DISCUSSION

Beyond hopes for peace in a distant future, the fourth chapter's powerful and hope-filled imagery of turning weapons of war into tools for peacetime productivity can be an effective tool for promoting nonviolence today. There are many recent examples of Mic. 4:3 being used to address war, from its domestic economic impact to the threat of nuclear annihilation. American president and former general Dwight Eisenhower used a reversal of the peaceful imagery in 4:3 to warn of the rise of a military industrial complex, which he feared would bring about a time in which plowshares would be turned into swords.

The imagery of Mic. 4:3 has also been adopted by a number of antiwar organizations that have taken it upon themselves to help fulfill Micah's prophecy. Operation Plowshares, a Christian antinuclear-weapons group, became famous in 1980 when eight of its members broke into a Pennsylvania nuclear-missile site and successfully damaged warhead nose cones and engaged in other acts of civil disobedience. Another group called Silo Pruning Hooks entered a Missouri Air Force base in 1984, where they used a jackhammer to damage the lid of a nuclear silo. Eight members of the Catholic Worker Movement, who called themselves Pitstop Ploughshares, broke into Shannon Airport in Ireland in 2003, where they caused £80,000 of damage to United States bombers that had been awaiting sorties during the second Gulf War. Many of the aforementioned activists served prison sentences for their faith-based acts of nonviolent resistance to war.

In addition to the above examples of how Mic. 4:3 has been used to address violence in the modern world, the imagery of this verse can also speak to how nations use their money. For example, the fact that the United States allocates vast amounts of national wealth toward its military says a great deal about its fiscal priorities. In the 2013 budget, the US defense department was allocated $525 billion in discretionary spending, as compared to $23 billion for agriculture and $70 billion for education (United States Government, 2013). Whether or not these priorities are in order, the vision found in Mic. 4:3 has the potential to play a powerful role in the conversation.

Micah 6:1-8: The Trial of the Accused

▌ The Text in Its Ancient Context

From the early twentieth century, scholars have dated this section of Micah to the postexilic period. But regardless of its time of origin, Mic. 6:1-8 presents audiences with a court setting in which Judah's injustices are placed on trial. The passage opens with a demand that the accused people plead their case before the judgment of YHWH and the whole earth (6:1-2), and concludes with a correctional instruction in 6:8 that was considered by Northrop Frye (206) to be one of history's greatest moral breakthroughs. This trial scene, however, breaks from some of the standard conventions of its time.

Whereas court cases traditionally start with a leveling of charges against the accused, here the deity opens the proceedings in the defendant's box, raising concerns about YHWH's own possible shortcomings and giving the accused a chance to voice any complaints that they may have (6:3-5). Through YHWH's line of questioning, which suggests a sense of confusion and betrayal as YHWH works to understand how it might have offended the people and caused them to go astray, YHWH highlights all that has been done for the people (6:3-5). The accused does not appear to take the opportunity to lodge any complaints, but responds in 6:6-7 with a series of questions as to how the accused might appease YHWH's anger, offering a crescendo of cultic sacrifices from burnt calves to the climax of child sacrifice. Thomas Römer (21) argues that the accused were not referring to some ancient practice that had been replaced by animal sacrifice, but an institution of child sacrifice that coexisted alongside animal sacrifice. The reference to child sacrifice in 6:7, and its rejection in 6:8, is commonly thought to have marked a break from the practice.

Whereas Mic. 6:6-7 is often received as an earnest attempt to make amends with God, Ben Zvi (147) argues that the dialogue's conclusion in instruction, rather than an announcement of salvation, may indicate that 6:6-7 represents a defense against YHWH's charges. Using an intertextual approach, Mignon Jacobs reads 6:6-7 as a complaint against the deity, in which Israel refutes its God for wearying its people by offering a sarcastic list of outlandish sacrificial demands (Jacobs, 177–78).

In the pinnacle of the unit (Mic. 6:8), the voice of the prophet summarizes the Torah, laying out what it means to live well under YHWH: "to do justice, and to love kindness, / and to walk humbly with your God." Whereas the accused party's response to YHWH's anger is cultic sacrifice (6:6-7), 6:8 moves their religious practice beyond temple ritual and into the way they conduct their daily lives. This message is congruent with Isa. 1:11-17, where cultic offerings are also rejected in favor of a lifestyle that promotes the peace and justice of God. In so doing, Mic. 6:8 works to replace the notion that justice is YHWH's job, and places its responsibility on the shoulders of the people.

◼ THE TEXT IN THE INTERPRETIVE TRADITION

The futility of the people's offerings in Mic. 6:6-7 has been received as a push for right living. Ambrose (306–7) looked to cultic offerings of 6:6-7 as a call to turn away from ritual appeasement and concentrate on living "a good life."

One of the most shocking aspects of Mic. 6:1-8 is the suggestion of child sacrifice in 6:7. Clement of Alexandria asserted that the suggestion of child sacrifice spoke out against "those human impulses that are unhelpful in gaining knowledge of God" (Ferreiro, 171).

Calvin read 6:6-7 as the prophet's voice, mocking his audiences' futile remedies for atonement. He relates this to those of his own time who devise means to alleviate their guilt before God. Using the Catholic Church's leadership as an example, Calvin relates the extreme remedy of child sacrifice (6:7) to the mentality of papacy, which will "toil in ceremonies, and if they pour forth some portion of their money, if they sometimes deprive nature of its support, if with fastings and by other things, they afflict themselves, they think that by these means they have fully performed their duties" (328).

◼ THE TEXT IN CONTEMPORARY DISCUSSION

The powerful messages and thought-provoking problems that the authors of Mic. 6:1-8 posed to their audiences can provide modern readers with ample material for discussion. From a faith perspective, the passage raises questions about what it means to live a life of faith under a God who seeks justice, kindness, and humility.

The people's response to the court proceedings of Mic. 6:1-5 is to shield themselves with ritual piety and prescribed laws. The prophet's rejection of these means of atonement can speak to modern "holier-than-thou" attitudes toward spiritual purity, suggesting that piety comes not simply through ritual observance but in how the faithful conduct themselves toward their neighbor and also God. This passage can serve to encourage faith practitioners and communities to move beyond traditional ritual practice and into engaged spiritual practice that centers itself on kindness, justice, and humility, as had been displayed in Pope Francis I's calls to view service to the poor as service to God. He exemplified this sentiment by taking the unprecedented step of washing the feet of prisoners during his first Maundy Thursday service as pontiff. Included in the foot-washing were people of other faiths and women, the latter of whom may have broken liturgical law.

What it means to live in justice, kindness, and humility is left open to interpretation, enabling the text to flow into the varied cultural contexts into which it is received. This ambiguity not only lends the passage an ongoing relevancy but also demands reflection on the part of the reader and encourages conversation with others. The powerful messages of 6:8 can also serve as a rallying cry, tempered with humility, for such justice struggles as the Catholic Worker Movement, School of the Americas Watch, Christian Peacemaker Teams, and the work of liberation theologians from Latin America to India.

The humility aspect of Mic. 6:8 also speaks to the tendency to resolve tensions by blaming an other (see Gen. 3:12-13), which can cause harm to innocent parties and also deny oneself the benefits of self-reflection. An extreme example of blaming the other is found in the followers of

Pastor Fred Phelps, who view the September 11, 2001, attacks as a direct outcome of God's anger against homosexuality, leading them to celebrate at the funerals of fallen service members and the victims of LGBT violence. Pastors Pat Robertson and the late Jerry Falwell also asserted that the 9/11 attacks were a product of God's wrath against "homosexual culture," while adding feminists, supporters of legalized abortion, and the American Civil Liberties Union to their list of scapegoats. While several passages within the Old Testament do promote corporate punishment for perceived sins—recently addressed by Hugh Pyper and Philip Davies—Mic. 6:6-8 presents an opportunity to focus on one's own conduct rather than on the conduct of the "other." Within the context of theologies that perceive God as punishing sin through historic events, Phelps, Falwell, and Robertson laid blame at the feet of those with whom they disagreed, but did not consider how their own failings may have brought about such wrath. The instruction of 6:8 can encourage a spirituality that searches for kindness, justice, and humility within oneself rather than finding fault in others.

Micah 6:9—7:7: Accusations and Verdicts against Corruption, Revisited

▌ THE TEXT IN ITS ANCIENT CONTEXT

Following the instruction of Mic. 6:8, the text returns to the problems of corruption that were addressed in Micah 1–3. Addressing "the city," its assembly, and the tribe, YHWH's anger is directed against their "treasures of wickedness" and the wickedness of the temple that houses them. In 6:10-12, the city—commonly thought to be Jerusalem though it could also be Samaria—is presented with a list of crimes, including financial inequity, general violence, and deceit, which will lead to its destruction by foreign invaders, as laid out in 6:13-16.

The accusations of Mic. 6:9-12 reflect those found in Micah 1–3, but offer a wider focus by denouncing the people alongside of their leaders. In 6:11, YHWH condemns an economic practice that was used by merchants and is also supported by the archaeological record: using different weights for the selling and purchases of goods in the temple market (Yeivin, 64–68). What is often lost in English translations, and may give insight into the urgency with which the authors addressed economic injustice in a religious context, is a suggestion that these corrupt activities affected YHWH's well-being. The NRSV translation of 6:11 reads, "Can I tolerate wicked scales / and a bag of dishonest weights?" However, "tolerate" comes from the Hebrew word *zakah*, which means "to be clean" or "pure." In its first-person singular interrogative form in 6:11, the meaning conveyed is "Can I be made pure/clean/innocent by these wicked scales and a bag of dishonest weights?" Arnold Ehrlich (287) and William McKane (195) argue that this is an error in the Masoretic Text, based on the Septuagint's third-person presentation of the verb *dikaiōthēsetai*, which means "shall they be justified?" However, there is precedent to consider that the authors were concerned that YHWH could be tainted by human injustice. If this is the case, 6:11 offers a greater sense of urgency in rooting out injustices pertaining to religious economic practice.

The passage's focus on the violence and deceit of the wealthy and city dwellers in Mic. 6:12 reflects common connotations of monarchic Jerusalem in the postexilic era (Ben Zvi, 164). Whether the text's origins are in the eighth century or after the Babylonian exile, the authors and audience were able to draw on the accusations and curses of 6:13-15, and again in 7:2-3 to help explain the destruction of the unnamed city.

■ THE TEXT IN THE INTERPRETIVE TRADITION

John Calvin and Matthew Henry both interpreted Mic. 6:9-16 as a warning against trapping oneself through fraudulent acts. Calvin saw the individuals in the city as more wicked than the other inhabitants because they not only robbed their neighbors but also set up a system in which the victims were forced to become perpetrators; the general inhabitants were not engaged in sin with the intent of doing harm, but forced to cheat in order to avoid poverty (Calvin, 336). Matthew Henry's commentary adds that for the whole of the city, "what is got by fraud and oppression, cannot be kept or enjoyed with satisfaction" (Henry, on Micah 6).

Early Christian theologians used the agrarian analogy of the harvest in 7:1 as an opportunity to reflect on the works of those who align themselves with the church, writing that not only pagan nations but also those of the church must consider what they are cultivating within themselves. Origen proclaimed, "Let each of us scrutinize himself. Is he an ear of corn? Will the Son of God discover something in him to pick or harvest?" This call for introspection dovetails with the call for humility in 6:8.

■ THE TEXT IN CONTEMPORARY DISCUSSION

In the wake of the financial collapse of 2008, caused largely by the world's most powerful financial institutions' dishonest investments and lending schemes, Mic. 6:9-16 remains pertinent in our time. The passage promotes the idea that God pays attention to financial conduct, suggesting that marketplace dealings are not to be viewed as separate from religious practice. The phrase "that's business," often used to justify questionable financial dealings, did not appear to absolve YHWH's targets in Micah.

The imagery of people using wicked scales and dishonest weights in 6:11, the violence and deceit of 6:12, and the imagery of hunting each other in nets in 7:2 dovetail with the Ponzi schemes of Bernard Madoff and Alan Stanford, as well as recent cases of mutual-fund fraud, misleading mortgage practices, and illegal foreclosures that have left so many in ruin. These biblical images can also speak to prosperity theologians who promise congregants God-given monetary wealth if they donate their money into these pastors' vast coffers.

Whether from a faith or secular perspective, Calvin's aforementioned interpretation of Mic. 6:9—7:7, which considers the inhabitants of the city as unwilling perpetrators of injustice, raises questions about the inherent injustice in our global economy. Many poorer and middle-class citizens in the world's wealthiest nations cannot afford to purchase goods that are not produced by sweatshop labor. In our current economic system, it is difficult for people to prepare for retirement or their children's college education without investing in corporations that are involved in unethical practices. Micah 6:9—7:7 raises a lot of uncomfortable questions that serve as a starting place for conversations on how economics might move beyond bottom-line motivations to consider more equitable approaches to prosperity and growth.

Micah 7:8-20: Hope in a Restoration, Yet to Come

▌ THE TEXT IN ITS ANCIENT CONTEXT

The closing verses of Micah return to the themes of hope that are found in Micah 4–5. The passage opens with the city's voice expressing a steadfast faith in YHWH and the idea that even when the prophet falls (7:8) YHWH will execute judgment on the city's behalf. While Mic. 7:9 promotes the idea that Jerusalem's fall was the work of God—an indignity that the city endured for its sins—it will be the enemies of Judah who will suffer the final downfall (7:10).

With a promise of restoration, found in Micah 4–5, the prophet foresees a time when the city's walls will be rebuilt (7:11) and the people of the great empires will come to its gates (7:12). Only this time, the Assyrians and Egyptians will not approach as conquerors seeking the spoils of war, but in shame and with fear as they stand in dread of YHWH's power (7:16-17). The passage offered its ancient readers hope in the face of overwhelming adversity, whether a looming Assyrian invasion or the humiliation of exile. Other renderings of 7:12 view those approaching the city from Assyria and Egypt not as foreigners but as the returning Hebrews who are coming home after the exile, highlighting their penitence and willingness to adhere to YHWH's will.

In the form of a praise offering, the book of Micah concludes with an idyllic picture of a God of justice and mercy. With great hope, the prophet asks what other gods can be compared to YHWH, a God who forgives sins, lets anger abate, and will cast out the people's sins to offer compassion (7:18-20). This closing praise promoted the idea that despite the iniquities of the people, YHWH's covenant had not been broken, but would continue, stronger than ever.

▌ THE TEXT IN THE INTERPRETIVE TRADITION

The messages of hope and divine forgiveness in Mic. 7:8-20 have been a focus of interpreters throughout the centuries, and are reflected in the Jewish practice of *tashlik*, which comes from the verb *shlk*, or "to throw," in 7:19. Performed on Rosh Hashanah (the Jewish New Year), the practice consists of participants casting rocks that represent their sins into a body of water. It has been thought to be a good omen to see a fish during this ritual, which can serve to take away the participants' guilt. The sixteenth-century Jewish mystic Moshe Cordovero also drew on Mic. 7:18-20; he viewed this passage as an embodiment of the Jewish ethic of forgiveness (Schimmel, 85–88).

Origen referenced God's forgiveness in Mic. 7:19 as an example of mortal charity. Referencing Micah, he wrote, "The prophet in Scripture says, 'We should cast our sins into the depths of the sea.' John continues, 'He who has food should do likewise.' Whoever has food should give some to one who has none" (94.99). Basil the Great offered another interpretation of this verse, likening the waters in 7:19 to the Christian baptismal waters that wash away the baptized person's sins (Ferreiro, 177). Calvin interpreted this passage as a testament to the power of God's promises, remaining loyal to the covenant made with Abraham, despite Israel's sins (389–90).

▌ THE TEXT IN CONTEMPORARY DISCUSSION

The themes drawn from Mic. 7:8-20 in Jewish and Christian interpretive tradition continue to find relevance in the modern world. Calls to trust in God and the levels of compassion the passage promotes are applicable in a number of ways. As addressed in Cordovero's interpretation, this passage could serve as a force for reconciliation. Various religious debates generate anger and hurt within their communities, leading to both violence and schism. A reminder of God's willingness to pardon wrongdoing, slowness to anger, and delight in pity (7:18) can serve as a starting place for healing.

Furthermore, whether in one's spiritual or secular life, the message of hope in the face of overwhelming adversity, as found in 7:8-17, can address such seemingly hopeless cases as healing fractured relations, bringing about peace where there is little cooperation or willingness to work through the aftermath of a tragedy.

Works Cited

Alfaro, Juan I. 1989. *Justice and Loyalty: A Commentary on the Book of Micah*. Grand Rapids: Eerdmans.

Ambrose of Milan. 1972. *Seven Exegetical Works*. Translated by Michael P. McHugh. FC 65. Washington, DC: Catholic University of America Press.

Andersen, Francis I., and David Noel Freedman. 2000. *Micah*. Edited by William Foxwell Albright and David Noel Freedman. AB 24E. New York: Doubleday.

Arelatensis, Caesarivs, ed. 1953. *Corpus Christianorum Series Latina*. Turnhout, Belgium: Brepols.

Augustine. 1954. *The City of God: Books XVII–XXII*. Translated by Gerald Walsh and Daniel Honan. FC 24. New York: Fathers of the Church.

Ben Zvi, Ehud. 2000. *Micah*. Edited by Gene M. Tucker, Rolf P. Knierim, and Marvin A. Sweeney. FOTL 21B. Grand Rapids: Eerdmans.

Calvin, John. 2010. *Commentary on Jonah, Micah, Nahum*. Christian Classics Ethereal Library. http://www.ccel.org/ccel/calvin/calcom28.html.

Chaney, Marvin, L. 1989. "Bitter Bounty: The Dynamics of Political Economy Critiqued by the Eighth-Century Prophets." In *Reformed Faith and Economics*, edited by Robert L. Stivers, 15–30. Lanham, MD: University Press of America.

Coomber, Matthew J. M. 2010. *Re-Reading the Prophets through Corporate Globalization: A Cultural-Evolutionary Approach to Understanding Economic Injustice in the Hebrew Bible*. Biblical Intersections 4. Piscataway, NJ: Gorgias.

———. 2011. "Prophets to Profits: Ancient Judah and Corporate Globalization." In *Bible and Justice: Ancient Texts, Modern Challenges*, edited by Matthew J. M. Coomber, 212–37. BibleWorld. London: Equinox.

———. 2013. "Debt as Weapon: Manufacturing Poverty from Judah to Today." *Diaconia: Journal for the Study of Christian Social Practice* 4, no. 2:143–58.

Cyril of Alexandria. 2008. *Commentary on the Twelve Prophets*. Vol. 2. Translated by Robert C. Hill. FC 116. Washington, DC: Catholic University of America Press.

Davies, Philip. 2011. "Rough Justice?" In *Bible and Justice: Ancient Texts, Modern Challenges*, edited by Matthew J. M. Coomber, 43–55. BibleWorld. London: Equinox.

Ehrlich, Arnold B. 1968. *Randglossen zur Hebräischen Bible: Textkritisches, Prachliches und Sachliches*. Vol. 5, *Ezechiel und die Kleinen Propheten*. Hildesheim: Georg Olms.

Ferreiro, Alberto, ed. 2003. *The Twelve Prophets*. Ancient Christian Commentary on Scripture, Old Testament 14. Downers Grove, IL: InterVarsity Press.

Frye, Northrop. 2006. *The Collected Works of Northrop Frye*. Vol. 19, *The Great Code: The Bible and Literature*. Edited by Alvan Lee. Toronto: University of Toronto Press.

Henry, Matthew. 1935. *Matthew Henry's Commentary on the Whole Bible in Six Volumes*. Vol. 4, *Jeremiah to Malachi*. New York: Fleming H. Revell.

Jacobs, Mignon R. 2001. *Conceptual Coherence of the Book of Micah*. Sheffield: Sheffield Academic Press.

Levins, Richard A., and John K. Galbraith. 2003. *Willard Cochrane and the American Family Farm*. Lincoln: University of Nebraska Press.

Maimonides, Mosheh. 1975. *Ethical Writings of Maimonides*. Ed. Raymond L. Weiss and Charles E. Butterworth. New York: Dover Publications.

Martyr, Justin. 1948. *Saint Justin Martyr: The First Apology, The Second Apology, Dialogue with Trypho, Exhortation to the Greeks, Discourse to the Greeks, The Monarchy; or the Rule of God*. Trans. Thomas B. Falls. The Fathers of the Church 6. New York: Christian Heritage.

Mays, James L. 1976. *Micah: A Commentary*. London: SCM.

McKane, William. 2000. *The Book of Micah: Introduction and Commentary*. New York: T&T Clark.

Pyper, Hugh S. 2010. "Rough Justice: Lars von Trier's *Dogville* and *Manderlay* and the Book of Amos." *Political Theology* 11, no. 3:321–34.

Römer, Thomas. 2010. "Le Sacrifice Humain en Juda et Israël au premier millenaire avant notre ére." In *Archiv für Religionsgeschichte* 1:17–26.

Schimmel, Solomon. 2002. *Wounds Not Healed by Time: The Power of Repentance and Forgiveness*. New York: Oxford University Press.

Smith, Ralph L. 1984. *Micah–Malachi*. Edited by David A. Hubbard, Glenn W. Barker, John D. W. Watts, and Ralph P. Martin. WBC 32. Waco, TX: Word.

United States Government. 2013. *Fiscal Year 2013 Budget of the U.S. Government*. Washington, DC: US Government Printing Office, 2013.

Yeivin, Shmuel. 1969. "Weights and Measures of Varying Standards in the Bible." *PEQ* 101:63–68.

NAHUM

Wilhelm J. Wessels

Introduction

Nahum is a short prophetic book specified in verse 1 as an oracle (*maśśā'*) from YHWH. This short book is a display of YHWH's power over the Assyrians, the enemy of Judah. With impressive rhetoric, a dismayed Judah is challenged to imagine YHWH's victory over their powerful oppressor (Wessels, 55–73). Very little is known about the author and his origin. Although Elkosh is designated as his town of origin, this place is unknown. Some regard Nahum as a cultic prophet or even a scribe, while still others focus on his poetic abilities. The prophet acted in the seventh century, but that is not necessarily the date of the completion of Nahum as a literary work. Very little detail is available from the book itself to determine a date. In Nahum 3:8-9, Thebes is mentioned, a city that was ransacked by Assyrian forces in 667 BCE. The other historical reference is the fall of Nineveh in 612 BCE. The book should most probably be dated after the fall of Nineveh in 612 BCE. The composition and unity of Nahum is also a contentious issue and has implications for the dating of the final text of the book (see Mason, 63, 74–75). Those who believe the book evolved over a long period of time would opt for a postexilic date for the final version of the document (see Roberts, 38–39; Schulz; O'Brien 2002, 14–15).

There are several views on the genre of Nahum. It has been treated, for example, as a prophetic liturgy (Coggins, 9–10), a prophetic refutation speech, a prophetic historical exemplum (Floyd, 18), a propagandistic anti-Assyrian tract, nonviolent resistance literature, a collection of songs of soldiers, and a type of city lament (see Huddlestun). A key characteristic that should be considered when analyzing Nahum is the poetic nature of the book with its use of rhetorical devices and imaginative language and images. The following literary units have been proposed for the discussion of the Nahum's content: 1:1-15 [Heb. 1:9-2:1]; 2:1-13 [2:2-14]; 3:1-17; 18-19.

Nahum 1:1-15: YHWH and the Fate of Judah and Their Enemies

■ THE TEXT IN ITS ANCIENT CONTEXT

The oracles in Nahum concern Nineveh, symbol of power to the Assyrians. The dominance of Assyria forms the background of the discussion. Nineveh was situated on the eastern bank of the Tigris River near Mosul. Sennacherib (705–681 BCE) made Nineveh his capital, and it remained the capital under his successors Esarhaddon (680–669) and Ashurbanipal (668–627) (see Baker, 560–61). Nineveh was finally destroyed in 621 BCE by the Medes. As the enemy of Judah and Israel, Nineveh was also the enemy of YHWH.

Nahum 1:2-8 is a hymn about YHWH in the form of an incomplete acrostic. David Petersen (198) regards Nahum 1 as "a theological prolegomenon" to the book as a whole. The pericope concerns the nature and power of YHWH as the sovereign power. Three aspects of YHWH are highlighted in this short poem: First, his nature is described as jealous, avenging, slow to anger, and great in power (vv. 2-3a); second, his actions are emphasized (vv. 3b-6). His theophanic appearance affects nature and depicts his power. It is stated that his mighty presence will affect the wind, clouds, sea, rivers, and mountains. His enemies should take note of his sovereign power over nature and people. In the third instance, YHWH is presented as both protector of his people and destroyer of his enemies (vv. 7-8). On the one hand, he is described as good: a stronghold in times of trouble who knows the people who seek shelter in him. On the other hand, verse 8 states that he will annihilate his enemies and pursue them into darkness.

This poem serves the purpose of fostering trust in YHWH on the part of the people of Judah. The very nature of YHWH testifies to Judah that YHWH will counter the force of their powerful enemy Assyria. Nahum 1:9-15 reveals an alternating pattern of doom for Nineveh (1:9-11, 14; 2:1) and deliverance for Judah (1:12-13, 15 [Heb. 2:1]; 2:2). In verses 9-11, the people of Judah are assured that the unknown enemy's plans will not succeed. Like fire devours thickets and stubble, so will the enemy be devoured. Nahum 1:12-13 confirms that YHWH's acts will favor his people. The strong enemy will be destroyed. Images of a yoke being broken and a band snapped are used to depict the destruction of the enemy. The doom proclamation directed against the enemy in 1:14 entails a threat of total extinction: their name will be wiped out, images of their gods destroyed, and their death a sure reality. Verse 15 [Heb. 2:1] is an appeal to Judah to celebrate YHWH's victory over the enemy and to show their loyalty to YHWH by keeping their vows.

■ THE TEXT IN THE INTERPRETIVE TRADITION

The book of Nahum was interpreted and applied through the centuries by biblical authors and by proponents from the Jewish and Christian traditions. Scholars have referred to the relationship between the books of Jonah and Nahum. Both concern Nineveh and it inhabitants, but Klaas Spronk (16–17) is convinced that Jonah is a reaction to the uncompromising condemnation of the Assyrians in Nahum, leaving room for the possibility that the nations can also enjoy YHWH's grace. There is also a correspondence between Nah. 1:15 and Isa. 52:7, both referring to the messenger motif, but there is no consensus among scholars on this literary correspondence.

It should be noted that the book of Nahum played an important role in the Qumran community. Fragments as well as interpretations of passages from Nahum testify to this (see 4QpNah [4Q169]). Some of the words from Nahum were regarded as relevant and therefore applied to the context within which this community lived (Coggins, 14). One example mentioned by Jin H. Han (20) is Nah. 1:4, which refers to YHWH's power over the waters of the sea. According to the Qumran commentator, YHWH will release the same power against his enemies (4QpNah, fragments 1 and 2 cited in Berrin, 77). Furthermore, it seems that Nahum 1 had influence on some psalms of thanksgiving (Spronk, 16–17).

When it comes to the use of the book of Nahum in the Christian tradition, several of the church fathers applied aspects of it to their context and experiences. It is clear that Nineveh had become a symbol of all that is evil. Most of these fathers also interpreted the text of Nahum christologically. Huddlestun (106–7) refers to several such persons including Julian of Toledo, Haimo of Auxerre (Nahum 2—judgment of the devil and associates), Athanasius of Alexandria, and Tertullian (Nah. 1:4—referring to the calming of the sea by Jesus). Cyril of Alexandria (c. 375–444) should also be mentioned in this regard. He wrote a commentary on several of the prophets in which he tried to do justice to the historical setting of the text. In his commentary, he easily engages the society of Jesus' time and speaks of Satan, the unholy scribes and Pharisees, and how Christ will crush rulers and authorities as is mentioned in Nahum 1 (Cyril of Alexandria, 292). There are several more such examples from Cyril's commentary on Nahum, where he applies the text in similar fashion. An interesting example of the interpretive tradition of Nahum 1 is Origen's interpretation of the phrase in Nah. 1:9, "no adversary will rise up twice." According to Han (23), "Origen declares that the death penalty resolves guilt. For God does not exact justice from offenders twice" (*Homilies on Leviticus* 11.5). Nahum 2:15 has in particular attracted the attention of Christian interpreters because of the association of the "good news" with the gospel of Jesus Christ in the New Testament (see Rom. 10:15). For a detailed discussion of the interpretive tradition of Nahum, Han (6–30) has much more to offer than space allows here.

▌THE TEXT IN CONTEMPORARY DISCUSSION

The book of Nahum concerns the destruction of the enemy Assyria, emphasizing the sovereignty of YHWH as supreme power. Despite the criticism leveled against the book (see Mason, 57–58), most scholars have high regard for its literary quality and poetic brilliance. It employs metaphors, similes, rhetorical questions, repetitions, and numerous other stylistic devices to highlight the themes it wishes to convey. However, one can also appreciate the problems people experience when reading the book of Nahum. The content of the book raises serious theological issues, not the least of which are the following: How can such brutal and disturbing deeds, portrayed in the book of Nahum with regard to the fate of Nineveh, be ascribed to YHWH? Can YHWH be associated with such atrocious deeds? Nahum should be read as coming from a prophet/poet who has related his experience of oppression at the hands of the Assyrians to his understanding of YHWH. The poet/prophet is clear on this: YHWH alone possesses sovereign power and in exercising this power will counter and surpass the brutal force of the Assyrians. Contemporary interpreters should be careful to avoid a narrow "God is for us alone" theology and therefore should not lose sight of a more inclusive message of "God is for people."

Nahum 2:1-13: The Downfall of Nineveh

▮ THE TEXT IN ITS ANCIENT CONTEXT

In Nahum 2:1-13 (Heb. 2:2-14), the focus is on the downfall of Nineveh. Although the city is not named in the early verses, it later becomes clear that the proclamation is aimed at the city. Verse 1 alerts Judah's enemy of a scatterer that will pose a threat to them. This is followed in 2:1 by a word of encouragement that YHWH will restore his people. In the following verses, a scene is painted of a battlefield of which Judah is the spectator observing the downfall of the powerful Assyrian enemy. This is done in poetic style with skillful application of imagery and rhetoric. In 2:3-5, the siege of Nineveh is described, followed in 2:6-8 with scenes portraying the emotional impact of the carnage on the citizens in the city. The image of a flooded city is presented in verse 6. Verse 7 is difficult, but it seems that the Hebrew word *huzzab* should be understood as "it is decreed" that the inhabitants of the city will be carried away, slave girls lamenting the state of affairs of an empty city (Coggins, 41–42; Roberts, 65–66). According to verse 8, Nineveh is like a dam leaking water, a metaphor for power dwindling. In staccato style, the prophet describes the plundering of the wealth of the city (v. 9) and also the tragic consequences of defeat.

> Devastation, desolation, and destruction!
> Hearts faint and knees tremble,
> all loins quake,
> all faces grow pale! (Nah. 2:10)

Nahum 2:11-12 makes use of a lion metaphor to taunt the king of Assyria and the nobles because of their diminishing power. The chapter ends with a declaration that YHWH will totally destroy Nineveh and its leaders in war and leave Assyria powerless.

▮ THE TEXT IN THE INTERPRETIVE TRADITION

As already noted, the book of Nahum played an important role in the Qumran community (see 4QpNah). A Dead Sea fragment of Nah. 2:11-13 testifies to this. This passage refers to lions, interpreted by the Qumran commentary, according to some, as referring to Antiochus IV Epiphanes (175–163) and probably Demetrius III (died in 88 BCE; Coggins, 15). Others seem to see in the reference to the lion an allusion to Alexander Janneus, who reigned from 103 to 27 BCE (Huddlestun, 106). The Nahum pesher is an invaluable source of information on the Maccabean period. The midrash associates the lion with Nebuchadnezzar, the monarch responsible for the exile (*Exod. Rab.* 29.9; Han, 29).

An interesting example of how some readers interpreted Nahum involves the issue of the "scatterer" mentioned in 2:1. The Septuagint offers the reading "one who breathes on your face." In light of this translation, the church father Cyril of Jerusalem (c. 315–387) relates this to John 20:22-23, where Jesus breathes on the apostles to receive the Holy Spirit. This action according to Cyril represents the restoration of creation after the fall of Adam, when the first breathing of the Holy Spirit took place (see Han, 27). Later in history, there are examples others who made the Nahum text relevant to their time. Luther, for example, says that the "Assyrians perished because they were unable to use their prosperity moderately" (Spronk, 17), and arrives at the conclusion that the pope will similarly be destroyed (see Huddlestun, 107, for more on Luther's interpretation of aspects of the Nahum text). Many interpreters regard Nineveh as synonymous with evil, and its defeat as the demise of evil itself.

■ THE TEXT IN CONTEMPORARY DISCUSSION

As mentioned above, the issue of violence rears its head particularly in chapter 2. The people of Judah are invited to observe how YHWH destroys their enemy. One possible way to approach the theological dilemma of YHWH's involvement in violence is to regard Nahum as similar to "resistance poetry." In this way, Nahum can be approached with a focus on societal issues and as a reflection of anti-Assyrian sentiments. The issue here is the poetic "overstatement" of expression. Not only is the sovereignty of YHWH stated in awesome overtones and theophanic imagery, creating an atmosphere of awe and reverence, but it also concerns Nineveh. The city and king's destiny is described in language and pictures that are disturbing and even repulsive in nature. By means of these excessive overtones, an atmosphere of emotional tension is created for a functional purpose. This resistance poetry, born out of rage and frustration, depicts the defeat of the enemy in the strongest possible language as an outlet of suppressed or heightened emotions. At the same time, faith is expressed in the supremacy of YHWH, who represents real power. However, it is one thing for the contemporary interpreter to read the book of Nahum with an understanding of its historical context, but it is quite another matter to use it to condone violence in the name of YHWH. Perhaps the book of Nahum should be read for the repulsive effect it can have on the reader or audience when confronted with such brutal and violent scenes and to encourage contemporary readers to search for other nonviolent ways of addressing oppression.

Nahum 3:1-19: Demise and Downfall of Nineveh

■ THE TEXT IN ITS ANCIENT CONTEXT

Nahum 3 is subdivided between verses 1-17 and 18-19. Verses 1-17 can be further subdivided into two units: 1-7 and 8-17. This chapter describes the demise and downfall of Nineveh. Nahum 3:1-7 is a threat against Nineveh described as an evil city. Again, a scene of war and carnage is depicted showing the literary skill of the poet. What is striking is that YHWH is the antagonist of the adulterous city, announcing that Nineveh will be humiliated as a female. In verses 8-17, the defenselessness of Nineveh is the subject. The city Thebes was found not to be invincible; on what grounds, then, can Nineveh claim to be better than Thebes? Verse 12 employs the simile of a ripe fig to refer to Nineveh, shaken from a tree and falling into the mouth of an eater, meaning her enemy. The powerlessness of Nineveh's army is again depicted by comparing its troops to women.

In the next verses, three media are mentioned that will cause Nineveh's destruction: fire will devour the city, a sword will cut her off, and an enemy will invade the city as young locusts consume a field. The inhabitants of Nineveh can multiply like locusts, but this will still not prevent YHWH from destroying them. The last two verses of chapter 3 are addressed to the king of Assyria, informing him that he cannot rely on his officials to save the day. His situation is to be compared to an incurable wound; he can expect hardship in the future. This news will bring joy to people he had oppressed and who suffered as a result of his unceasingly evil actions.

■ THE TEXT IN THE INTERPRETIVE TRADITION

It is worth mentioning that there is possible influence of Nah. 3:8 on Rev. 17:2, which describes the whore of Babylon (Coggins, 14). There are also other instances of influence of Nahum 3 one can see in Rev. 18:3, 22, with its mention of sorcery (see Nah. 3:4); and in Rev. 17:6, with its allusion to Babylon as "drunken with blood" (see Nah. 3:1, 11). Both Nah. 3:1, 7, and Rev. 18:9-19 lament the burning of the city (Spronk, 113). The commentary on Nahum from Qumran regards the "city of blood" in Nah. 3:1 as "the city of Ephraim," meaning "Jerusalem filled with treachery and lies by the Pharisees" and "Amon is Manasseh, that is, the Sadducees" (Spronk, 114). Jerome regards No-of-Amon (Nah. 3:8) as Alexandria, and Cyril interprets the "eater" of 3:13 as Satan. Even more extreme is Luther's interpretation of Nah. 3:5 ("I will lift up your skirts over your face") as the gospel revealing the prostitution of the pope (see Spronk, 114).

■ THE TEXT IN CONTEMPORARY DISCUSSION

A major issue that confronts readers is the stereotyping and humiliation of females. It was argued above that metaphors are keys for interpreting the book of Nahum. However, the metaphors used in Nahum 3 need careful attention since they are offensive to women. Julia O'Brien (2004, 29–30) has rightly argued that the issues addressed here should be understood in terms of the larger underlying gender concern, that of male honor. An understanding of this underlying issue should sensitize contemporary readers of the text to discern and address such issues in their own societies. The text of Nahum should in no way be used to justify unsavory prejudices and ideologies (see also Han, 31–32).

The book of Nahum poses many interpretive challenges. One thing, however, is clear: this short book demands that its readers confront their own beliefs and prejudices.

Works Cited

Baker, David W. 2012. "Book of Nahum." In *Dictionary of the Old Testament Prophets*, edited by Mark J. Boda and J. Gordon McConville, 560–63. Downers Grove, IL: InterVarsity Press.

Berrin, Shani L. 2004. *The Pesher Nahum Scroll from Qumran: An Exegetical Study of 4Q169*. Studies on the Texts of the Desert of Judah 53. Leiden and Boston: Brill.

Coggins, Richard J. 1985. *Nahum, Obadiah, Esther: Israel among the Nations*. Grand Rapids: Eerdmans.

Cyril of Alexandria. 2008. *Commentary on The Twelve Prophets*. Vol. 2. Translated by Robert C. Hill. FC. Washington, DC: Catholic University of America Press.

Floyd, Michael H. 2000. *Minor Prophets*. Part 2. Grand Rapids: Eerdmans.

Han, Jin H. 2011. "Nahum." In *Six Minor Prophets through the Centuries: Nahum, Habakkuk, Zephaniah, Haggai, Zechariah, and Malachi*, by Richard Coggins and Jin H. Han, 7–35. West Sussex: Wiley-Blackwell.

Huddlestun, John R. 2011. "Nahum." In *The Oxford Encyclopedia of the Books of the Bible*, edited by Michael D. Coogan, 100–119. Oxford: Oxford University Press.

Mason, Rex 1991. *Micah, Nahum, Obadiah*. Sheffield: Sheffield Academic.

O'Brien, Julia M. 2002. *Nahum*. Sheffield: Sheffield Academic.

———. 2004. *Nahum, Habakkuk, Zephaniah, Haggai, Zechariah, Malachi*. Nashville: Abingdon.

Petersen, David L. 2002. *The Prophetic Literature: An Introduction*. Louisville: Westminster John Knox.

Roberts, J. J. M. 1991. *Nahum, Habakkuk and Zephaniah*. Louisville: Westminster John Knox.

Schulz, H. 1973. *Das Buch Nahum. Eine redaktionskritische Untersuchung*. Berlin: de Gruyter.

Spronk, Klaas. 1997. *Nahum*. Kampen, the Netherlands: Kok Pharos.

Wessels, Wilhelm J. 2005. "Yahweh, the Awesome God: Perspectives from Nahum 1." *JSem* 14, no. 1:55–73.

HABAKKUK

Hugh R. Page Jr.

Introduction

A work incorporating first-person narrative, oracles, prudential wisdom, liturgical doxologies (2:14, 20), and an ancient (or perhaps archaizing) Hebrew poem, Habakkuk is best understood as a prophetic pastiche presenting the prophetic insights of an impatient sentinel who bravely takes Israel's deity to task for inaction in the face of injustice. Structurally, this seer's complaint is followed by a vision ensuring recompense—one that he is commanded to record (2:2); a doxology (2:20); and a prayer filled with reminiscences of God's power and exploits as Divine Warrior. It concludes with a reaffirmation of trust in YHWH from this emotionally shaken, though confident, visionary. Habakkuk offers an evocative model for context-specific theological reflection and social activism in the twenty-first century, that is, one that in no way limits the agency of those who identify and seek redress for injustice. The book takes seriously the role of the sacred in reform initiatives and allows for the deployment and rearticulation of ancestral traditions as points of reference in fashioning spiritualities of resistance that eschew facile hopes for immediate earthly intervention by a divine patron. It presents readers with, in the words of Cheryl Kirk-Duggan, "a matrix of injustice, theodicy, and triumph" (197).

The date and life setting for the book of Habakkuk are difficult to establish with any degree of certainty. The prophet's name, derived from a Hebrew root meaning "to embrace" or "clasp," suggests that perhaps the one delivering the prophecy has either seized or been emotionally taken by the message relayed in the book. It has been proposed that the oracles in Habakkuk were delivered between 609 and 597 BCE (Roberts, 82–83). Reference to the "raising up" of "the Chaldeans" (1:6), along with the eschatological thrust of its oracles, suggest a sixth-century-BCE origin for this prophetic anthology. The presence of ancient mythological motifs akin to those in Ugaritic and Sumero-Akkadian lore have suggested to some scholars a much earlier date for Hab. 3:1-15 (e.g.,

Hiebert; and Roberts, 84, 151–57). Insofar as the reappropriation of traditions focusing on creation and cosmic warfare is common to biblical literature produced in the exilic period, especially in Isaiah 40–66, this poem may serve as the interpretive fulcrum for the entirety of the book.

Habakkuk 1:1—2:1: An Impatient Seer Calls God to Task

THE TEXT IN ITS ANCIENT CONTEXT

In the popular imagination, prophets, seers, and visionaries are viewed as enjoying a particular closeness to God. For some, that unique connection suggests an implicit harmony, an ongoing meeting of the minds, between the source and recipient of a revelatory experience. However, the Hebrew Bible reveals a far more complex reality. We see evidence of prophets struggling with and seeking to make sense of their vocation and instructions (e.g., Isa. 6:1-13; Jer. 11:18-23; Ezek. 4:9-14; 11:13; 37:3). In Jonah, perhaps the theological linchpin of the Book of the Twelve Minor Prophets, we even have a parody focusing on the fraught relationship between God, seer, and mission. At times, the adversarial relationship between prophet and God is central to the rhetoric and structure of Habakkuk.

The book, which is identified as an oracular record of a vision (i.e., "The oracle that the prophet Habakkuk saw"), opens with the prophet registering a complaint to YHWH, the essence of which can be summed up in a single question: Why in the face of pervasive and enduring "wrongdoing" (1:3) and injustice (1:4) has the LORD failed to act? Operating from the presupposition that the righteous should always triumph over the wicked, a concept echoed in both Deuteronomic (e.g., Deut. 7:12-15) and sapiential traditions (e.g., Prov. 11:8; 12:7), Habakkuk calls Israel's God to task for failing to function as either loving patriarch or omnipotent suzerain.

THE TEXT IN THE INTERPRETIVE TRADITION

Habakkuk has a fascinating interpretive history. Jewish and Christian readers have pondered its more opaque passages and sought to mine its oracles for gems of wisdom to sustain people of faith in times of crisis. The book is a point of reference for several New Testament writers (see the indexes in Aland et al., 888, 900). The Old Greek/Septuagint version of Hab. 1:5 is quoted directly in Acts 13:41 at the conclusion of Paul's homily on salvation history in the synagogue of Antioch. Hebrews 10:37-38 quotes and offers an eschatological interpretation of Hab. 2:3-4. In the Pauline corpus, we find two additional quotations of Hab. 2:4 in Rom. 1:17 and 3:11 respectively. Passages alluding to Habakkuk are found in 2 Pet. 3:9 (Hab. 2:3); 1 Cor. 12:2 (Hab. 2:18-19); and Luke 13:6 (Hab. 3:17).

Biblical manuscripts and a detailed commentary (Hebrew—pesher) exploring the eschatological implications of Habakkuk are extant in the Dead Sea Scrolls corpus. Such indicate the esteem in which the book was held among those for whom the sectarian community founded at Qumran was a spiritual sanctuary. In the Habakkuk pesher (1QpHab), "the wicked," "righteous," and "Chaldeans," referenced in Hab. 1:4, 6, are understood to be the opponents of the community, those aligning themselves with the mysterious "upright teacher," and—perhaps—the armies of the Roman

Empire respectively (Graham, 475; Reventlow, 31–32). Engagement of the book by a vast array of Jewish and Christian interpreters from late antiquity to the modern era illustrates its broad applicability in a variety of life settings (see Graham).

THE TEXT IN CONTEMPORARY DISCUSSION

Habakkuk reminds those in all generations to stand at their "watchpost"; speak truth to power, whether spiritual, temporal, or—in some cases—ultimate; and await appropriate responses to any "complaint" made on behalf of those without agency (Hab. 2:1). In our own world, application of the laws maintaining our social fabric all too often appear "slack" (1:4), and justice, it seems, at least for those radically "othered" or at the bottom of our social or economic hierarchies, "never prevails" (1:4). The deaths of Trayvon Martin (Sanford, FL, 2012), Jonathan Ferrell (Charlotte, NC, 2013), and Renisha McBride (Dearborn, MI, 2013); the disproportionate impact that stop-and-frisk practices by the New York City Police Department have on people of color living in the city's boroughs (on which see http://www.nyclu.org/issues/racial-justice/stop-and-frisk-practices, accessed January 27, 2014); and the insensitive representations of Asian peoples and cultures in cinema (e.g., the 2012 movie *Cloud Atlas*) and television (e.g., season 9, episode 14 of the CBS serial *How I Met Your Mother*) raise major concerns about the ways in which negative racial stereotypes influence public perceptions of African Americans and Latino/a cultures in the United States. The marginalization and mistreatment of the LGBTQ community by several mainstream Christian denominations raises comparable concerns. The same can be said regarding policies governing colonization and ideologies (e.g., that of Manifest Destiny) promoting territorial expansion that resulted in the genocide of native peoples here and in others parts of the world. Habakkuk issues a clarion call to those who would assume the prophetic mantle to speak evocatively about what needs to be done to address injustice and set things right.

Habakkuk 2:2-20: The Divine Sovereign Responds— Words to Ponder

THE TEXT IN ITS ANCIENT CONTEXT

The LORD provides an intriguing answer to Habakkuk's query, instructing him to record clearly what he is told. Patience is counseled (2:2-3) and a reminder given that the upright should rely on faithfulness to sustain them (2:4). Warnings are given against pride (2:4), wealth, and arrogance (2:5), those who exploit and despoil (2:6-8), those profiting from ill-gotten gain (2:9-11), the bloodthirsty (2:12-13), the wrathful (2:15-17), and idol makers (2:18-19). Two remarkable doxologies are strategically placed in this extensive collection of "Woe" admonitions. The first affirms the pervasive influence of YHWH's presence (2:14). The second demands silence in light of the LORD's presence in the sacred precinct (2.20). The rhetoric of the speech seems intended to elicit awe and reverence rather than directly to address Habakkuk's primary concerns. Sapiential musings that reduce the complexities of human behavior to moral binaries (2:4) offer little solace when injustice is rampant and political upheaval is about to consume one's homeland (1:6).

■ THE TEXT IN THE INTERPRETIVE TRADITION

Habakkuk 2 has given rise to considerable theological, musical, and esoteric musings. In the Qumran community, Hab. 2:4 is seen as a reference to the upright adherents of Torah teaching (Reventlow, 31). Pauline thought owes undeniable indebtedness to Hab. 2:4. Along with Gen. 15:6, it is certainly one of the texts that inspired the itinerant apostle from Tarsus. M. Patrick Graham has noted fascination with this chapter among Christian apologists ranging from antiquity to the Protestant Reformation, among whom he numbers Cyril of Alexandria, Martin Luther, and John Calvin. He notes that both Luther and Calvin affirmed the christological import of Hab. 2:4 (see Graham, 475–76). Arthur Ainger's nineteenth-century hymn "God Is Working His Purpose Out" is an extended reflection on Hab. 2:14. George Root's hymn "The Lord Is in His Holy Temple" builds a theme expressed in Hab. 2:20 (Carpenter and Williams, 627). In recent years, Hab. 2:2 has been popularized as a mantra for focused pursuit of one's vision by musical artist and preacher the Rev. Joseph Simmons, also known as "DJ Run" of the pioneering rap group Run-D.M.C. (see http://www.youtube.com/watch?v=SC2oh6s6d7o). These passages are likely to continue firing the imaginations of future interpreters.

■ THE TEXT IN CONTEMPORARY DISCUSSION

In the worldview of the Bible, the God of Israel sheds light on elements of the divine plan to selected women and men from time to time. On some occasions, those celestial communiqués are straightforward responses to queries (Exod. 3:13-15). On others, they are either voluntary disclosures accompanying theophanies (Gen. 12:1-3), or tantalizing clues that have to be either wrestled from mysterious envoys (Gen. 32:22-32), or secured through deft negotiation (Gen. 18:16-33). In a few very special cases, such as Job 38–41 or Hab. 2:2-20, a revelatory experience with the ineffable confronts a seeker with oblique advice shrouded in unfathomable mystery. Many members of today's Jewish and Christian communities would no doubt speak of their relationship with God in similar terms. A stern rebuke like that in Job 38:2—"Who is this that darkens counsel by words without knowledge?"—might cower an anguished soul into accepting its place in the cosmos. A firm admonition like that of Hab. 2:20—"The Lord is in his holy temple; let all the earth keep silence before him!"—might well have the same impact. However, the literary texture of Habakkuk allows for a more nuanced encounter with God and lived experience. Habakkuk, after all, ignores the divine "gag order." He speaks, as should all people of conscience.

Habakkuk 3:1-19: The Prophet Prays with Steely Resolve

■ THE TEXT IN ITS ANCIENT CONTEXT

In what appears to be an inversion of the pattern encountered in Job 38–41, it is Habakkuk—not YHWH—who has the final word in this high-stakes verbal game of challenge and riposte. It is the prophet who recounts the cosmogonic march from Teman (Hab. 3:3) to rescue the faithful (3:13), acknowledges the devastating realization that disaster in his own world is imminent (3:16), refuses to embrace despair (3:18), and affirms his fidelity to the one who is his "salvation" and "strength" (3:18-19). Inclusion of this ancient poem and the prophet's admonitions to his God makes Habakkuk an instructional manual for those who would make themselves open to the incursions of the spirit without succumbing to the strictures of Deuteronomic thought, the narrow binaries of the sages, the eschatological musings of apocalyptic separatists, or the fatalistic strains expressed in Qohelet (Eccles. 1:1-11).

▮ THE TEXT IN THE INTERPRETIVE TRADITION

Habakkuk is an enigmatic figure who—like Enoch, Elijah, Joseph of Arimathea, and Mary Magdalene—spawned fanciful speculation in antiquity, some of which is retained in apocryphal and pseudepigraphic sources (see Bel 33–39; and the *Martyrdom of Isaiah* 2:9). Habakkuk 3, one of the most intriguing chapters of this prophetic anthology, has also received considerable attention. The Septuagint deploys Egyptian solar imagery to make sense of 3:5 (Reventlow, 23). Augustine views the entire poem as discourse between Habakkuk and Jesus (Graham, 475). William Hayes Ward long ago posited that the poem was likely part of liturgical worship in the Jerusalem temple (Ward, 6). Among more recent commentators, Roberts (84) and Anderson (260) argue convincingly that this poem has an ancient pedigree. Many of its interpretive cruxes are intractable and unlikely to be resolved in the near future. Whatever its age or original provenance, it is integral to the canonical form of the book and confronts all readers with the question: Why did Habakkuk lift up this *tefilla* ("prayer"); and why should every subsequent generation of readers follow his example?

▮ THE TEXT IN CONTEMPORARY DISCUSSION

In the presence of inexplicable tragedy, few options are left to those who trust that the universe is governed by a compassionate and all-knowing divine sovereign, and yet feel exposed, unprotected, and abandoned. One option is the modification or rejection of one's core beliefs. Another option is to seek communion with—and answers from—that celestial monarch through prayer. Yet a third choice is to reaffirm one's allegiance to and faith in that deity: even in that God's apparent absence. In Habakkuk, we have a model, indeed a *prophetic paradigm*, for seeking connection with, challenging, and asserting continuing fidelity to YHWH. Its main features are steely resolve and a commitment to healing and personal empowerment through "talking back" to—*signifying on* (in *Africana* parlance) as it were—God.

The book of Habakkuk affirms that the one thing of which we are never deprived is our voice, our ability to affirm the painful particularities of our circumstances, and to demand that God hear and respond. As S. D. Snyman has noted, prophets such as Jeremiah and Habakkuk acknowledge that "struggle" is part of the spirituality articulated in Scripture; that there are occasions when God's responses to us "remain incomprehensible"; and that there are those instances when, in confronting ambiguity or apparent divine absence, "conversation with God is in itself enough" (see the summary of Snyman's position in Lombaard, 43). For Kent Keith, author of ten maxims for leadership known as the "Paradoxical Commandments," Habakkuk offers an eleventh adage by which to live: "The world is full of violence, injustice, starvation, disease, and environmental destruction, *Have faith anyway*" (Keith, xiv–xv). The reader can take these proposals an additional step further and suggest that in Habakkuk we are reminded that when confronting despair, the one thing we should *never* do is to remain silent.

Works Cited

Aland, Barbara, Kurt Aland, Johannes Karavidopoulos, Carlo M. Martini, and Bruce M. Metzger, eds. 2005. *The Greek New Testament*. 4th rev. ed. (9th printing). Stuttgart: Deutsche Bibelgesellschaft / United Bible Societies.

Anderson, Francis I. 2001. *Habakkuk*. AB. New York: Doubleday.

Carpenter, Delores, and Nolan Williams, eds. 2001. *African American Heritage Hymnal*. Chicago: GIA.

Graham, M. Patrick. 1999. "Habakkuk, Book of." In *Dictionary of Biblical Interpretation*, edited by John H. Hayes, 475–78. Nashville: Abingdon.

Hiebert, Theodore. 1986. *God of My Victory: The Ancient Hymn in Habakkuk 3*. HSM 38. Atlanta: Scholars Press.

Keith, Kent M. 2008. *Have Faith Anyway: The Vision of Habakkuk for Our Times*. San Francisco: Jossey-Bass.

Kirk-Duggan, Cheryl. 2010. "Habakkuk." In *The Africana Bible: Reading Israel's Scriptures from Africa and the African Diaspora*, edited by Hugh R. Page Jr., 197–201. Minneapolis: Fortress Press.

Lombaard, Christo. 2012. *The Old Testament and Christian Spirituality*. International Voices in Biblical Studies. Atlanta: Society of Biblical Literature.

Reventlow, Henning Graf. 2009. *History of Biblical Interpretation*. Vol. 1, *From the Old Testament to Origen*. Translated by Leo G. Perdue. Resources for Biblical Study. Atlanta: Society of Biblical Literature.

Roberts, J. J. M. 1991. *Nahum, Habakkuk, and Zephaniah*. OTL. Louisville: Westminster John Knox.

Ward, William Hayes. 1911. "A Critical and Exegetical Commentary on Habakkuk." In John Merlin Powis Smith, William Hayes Ward, and Julius August Bewer, *A Critical and Exegetical Commentary on Micah, Zephaniah, Nahum, Habakkuk, Obadiah, and Joel*. New York: Charles Scribner's Sons.

ZEPHANIAH

Jin Hee Han

Introduction

The book of Zephaniah introduces the prophet as the son of Cushi, suggesting an African connection (Bennett 1996, 659), whose lineage includes King Hezekiah of Judah (Zeph. 1:1). The historical background is set in the late seventh century, probably before Josiah's Deuteronomic reform, which removed the kind of religious practices that Zephaniah berated. One of the twelve Minor Prophets, Zephaniah follows Nahum and Habakkuk. The rationale behind the order of the Twelve is not transparent, but Nahum's condemnation of Nineveh and Habakkuk's search for God's justice and grace form a suggestive backdrop to the prophecy of Zephaniah, who announces divine judgment for all nations and salvation for the faithful remnant of Israel. The book is made of the following sections: oracles of doom and destruction (1:2-13); the great day of YHWH (1:14-18); repentance and redemption (2:1-3); oracles against the nations (2:4-15); the remnant of Israel (3:1-13); and the celebration of YHWH rejoicing over the divine work of salvation (3:14-20).

Zephaniah 1:2-13: Doom and Destruction

■ THE TEXT IN ITS ANCIENT CONTEXT

The prophet sounds an alarm setting forth God's announcement of the total devastation of the world in Zeph. 1:2. The catastrophe will clear away both humans and animals, for corruption has become so extensive as to leave no living thing untouched (1:3). It is going to be even more sweeping than Noah's flood, which did not include the fish of the sea (see Gen. 6:7). The prophet identifies the primary basis of judgment as Judah's worship of other gods. The NRSV translates Zeph. 1:3 as God causing the wicked to stumble, but the original Hebrew actually envisions divine judgment removing "the stumbling blocks along with the wicked" (author's own translation). The prophetic catalog of venerated objects that incurred God's wrath in Judah and Jerusalem includes the Canaanite god Baal, idols, the host of the heaven (referring to the stars), and the Ammonite god Milcom (1:4-5). Zephaniah 1:5b adds another offense: the duplicity of conflating the worship of God with that of Milcom, which may be another name of the deity Molech, who is associated with child sacrifice (see Lev. 18:21; 20:2-5). The honoring of Milcom, whose Hebrew (*malkām* in Zeph. 1:5) can be translated "their king," may also suggest idolatrous worship of human kings (1:5). These wrongful worshipers have committed the offense of abandoning God (1:6).

In Zeph. 1:7, the prophet proclaims the sobering day of YHWH (1:7), anticipating the forthcoming poem "The Great Day of YHWH" (1:14-18). To deal with the rampant corruption that has contaminated the universe, God institutes a sacrificial meal for consecrated guests (1:7). The meaningful worship is set in contrast with the ruinous cult of Judah and Jerusalem. The latter half of 1:7 contains a humorous play on words, making it ambiguous as to whether the guests are to partake of the feast or to be slaughtered as ritual sacrifice. The faithful remnant of Zeph. 3:12-13 would constitute the former kind of guests, while the powerful officials and princes of 1:8 would be the latter.

On the anticipated day of YHWH, God is expected to punish the noble and the royal (1:8b); those dressed in foreign attire (1:8c); those who leap over the thresholds, an imitation of a practice of Canaanite priests (1:9a; see also 1 Sam. 5:4-5); and those who participate in treacherous economic exploitation in the name of loyalty to their master, whether they are serving their king or another god (Zeph. 1:9b). Wailing will be heard throughout Jerusalem in the Fish Gate and the Second Quarter and in the Mortar, which all have been associated with the bustling of profit-seeking commerce (1:10-11a). On the day of God's judgment, both traders and trading will be finished (1:11b). The prophet imagines God searching through Jerusalem with lamps to seek out those who are complacent while denying God's relevance in human affairs (1:12). The prophet predicts the catastrophic collapse of the rich who trust in their wealth more than God (1:13), recalling the curses compiled in Deuteronomy 27–28.

▐ THE TEXT IN THE INTERPRETIVE TRADITION

The prophetic oracle of doom in Zeph. 1:2-13 is marked by the vision of God's exhaustive judgment. Judah and Jerusalem are clearly the offenders, but animals are also included in the cosmic carnage. The midrash compares God's action to destroy the whole creation to that of a king who punishes his prince and the teacher who led him astray (*Gen. Rab.* 28.6; cf. *b. Sanh.* 108a). Citing Hosea 4:1-4a and Isa. 59:1-4, Cyprian (546) argues that the thoroughgoing destruction is necessary to purify the polluted creation.

The comprehensive list of offenses that focus on idolatrous worship combines cultic aberrations with economic exploitation and complacency (Zeph. 1:4-8). The internal social ills are linked with the issue of foreign clothing, whose offensive nature may have to do with foreign influence that promotes corruption (Theodore of Mopsuestia, 291). Martin Luther (327) ridicules the donning of foreign clothes in 1:8 as an act of abandoning one's own religion and culture. The rich who profit from godless pursuits will be exposed by God's search through Jerusalem with lamps, which the Jerusalem Talmud imagines as a picture of the Lord, who examines the heart of the people (*y. Pesah.* 27a).

▌ THE TEXT IN CONTEMPORARY DISCUSSION

Zephaniah's depiction of cosmic upheaval fuels the modern discussion on faith and ecology. Due to their sins of idolatry and predatory exploitation of nature, human beings risk losing the privileged status described in Gen. 1:28 when they fail to live up to the creator's charge (Kay, 226). The prophetic word threatens to cancel even the covenant of Noah in Genesis 9, which is supposed to be eternal (Berlin, 82). The prophet's critique of a corrupt cult that causes the cosmic catastrophe is in consonance with the idea of faithful worship that enables the worshiper to endure evil and experience order, as Jon D. Levenson charts in *Creation and the Persistence of Evil.*

Zephaniah 1:14-18: The Day of YHWH

▌ THE TEXT IN ITS ANCIENT CONTEXT

In Zeph. 1:14-18, the prophet offers a full description of the consequences of the day of YHWH that he mentioned in 1:7 (see also Isa. 13:6, 9, 13; Jer. 30:7; 46:10; Ezek. 30:2-3; Joel 1:15; 2:1-2, 11; Amos 5:18-20; 8:9-14; Mal. 4:5). Following Amos, Zephaniah treats it as a day of disaster for Judah, who may have thought that it was set aside for her enemy nations. The scope of destruction on the day includes the whole earth (echoing Zeph. 1:2), providing a dramatic backdrop to God's salvation of the remnant of Israel in 3:8-20. However, the oracle maintains its focus on those who "have sinned against YHWH" (1:17; see Sweeney 2003, 97).

The day is approaching fast and accompanies ominous cries (1:14). Zephaniah delineates the day as a time of divine wrath and assembles no less than eight words to depict a hopeless situation (1:15). This day of despair reveals enemy forces attacking Judah and Jerusalem (1:16), and the prophet explains the havoc as YHWH's punishment against the sinners (1:17). No treasure will shield them from the attackers when YHWH unleashes sweeping destruction that the prophet hyperbolically presents as the end of "the whole earth" (1:18).

▌ THE TEXT IN THE INTERPRETIVE TRADITION

Zephaniah 1:14-18 has been interpreted in a number of ways. Origen (107–13) cites the passage as the source of inspiration for Paul's language in Rom. 2:5-6, which announces the day of God's final judgment and whose darkness is contrasted with God, the light of the spiritual world. Theodore of Mopsuestia (292) interprets the day of YHWH as a specific time in history when God's decrees are fulfilled. Gregory the Great expects the day of YHWH to open up minds that are closed to truth; and for the church, it will be like the day of a wedding marked by "the happiness of the elect, those who will be found worthy to rejoice" (1990, 72). Luther (334–35) calls the day of YHWH a day of Babylonian captivity rather than the final day of history. According to Calvin (226), the oracle of the day of YHWH confirms that there is no salvation apart from God.

■ THE TEXT IN CONTEMPORARY DISCUSSION

Zephaniah's eschatological expectation of a day when God would restore justice is far from a defeatist's delayed wish fulfillment. It challenges worshipers to seek the redress of contemporary social ills in light of God's concern for the oppressed and sovereignty over history. The prophet's call for justice reverberates in Jürgen Moltmann's theology of hope, which inspires mission in service of justice. The prophet's perspective on the day of YHWH anticipates Wolfhart Pannenberg's eschatology, in which the future facilitates the construction of peace in this world in light of the eschatological kingdom of God.

Zephaniah 2:1-3: Repentance and Protection

■ THE TEXT IN ITS ANCIENT CONTEXT

In Zeph. 2:1, the prophet calls on the people of Judah, the "shameless nation," to gather together. This imperative of assembly serves as a pun. On the one hand, it summons them to communal repentance; on the other hand, it threatens to dispose of the people like stubbles of grain gathered to be thrown away. The prophet emphasizes that time is running out; each of the three lines of 2:2 begins with the sentence-starter "before." As the doom brewing for the whole world (1:14-18) is about to unleash its destructive forces against the nations (2:4-15), the prophetic word offers the last chance for the humble who have kept the law of the Lord to find the path of salvation, which is to be accomplished through seeking out YHWH and doing God's demands for justice and humility (2:3a). To the urgent exhortation the prophet adds the cautious qualifier "perhaps" (2:3b; see also Amos 5:15), underscoring that deliverance is purely YHWH's doing. It is not the prophet's to guarantee it, much less the outcome of the works of righteousness by the pious. God has set aside the humble among God's people (see also Zeph. 3:12-13), who will be instrumental in Judah's possible salvation (2:3). By contrast, the nations that lack humility and willingness to seek YHWH will meet destruction (2:4-15).

■ THE TEXT IN THE INTERPRETIVE TRADITION

The midrash finds in Zeph. 2:1 a mandate of self-correction before correcting others, for Judah cannot criticize the sins of other nations or exhort them to follow her example until she first heeds God's call to repentance and is found worthy for God's salvation (*Lam. Rab.* 3:50). Zephaniah's words cause the monastic church father Pachomius (36) to grieve over the imminent end of the age with no adequate instruction in faith available; he attributes the egregious situation to the lack of mortification as a pious practice.

■ THE TEXT IN CONTEMPORARY DISCUSSION

In his book *Option for the Poor*, Norbert Lohfink observes that Zephaniah displays a distinctive interest in the poor, while most prophets direct their oracles against the kings and the nobles. Lohfink's insight exerts important influence on liberation theology, which observes the link between poverty and spirituality. While the world faces extinction, the poor and the humble on the margin have the possibility of salvation by God (see Sobrino). Through "the orthopraxis of the marginalized," God's peace and justice come true (Bail, 456).

Zephaniah 2:4-15: Against the Nations

■ THE TEXT IN ITS ANCIENT CONTEXT

Oracles against the nations (Philistines, Moabites, Ammonites, Ethiopians, and Assyrians) underscore God's sovereignty over the world. These declarations contain puns in Hebrew whose sound effects are left out in English versions. For example, one could paraphrase the translation as follows: "Gaza shall be zapped; Ashkelon, shattered; Ashdod, pushed away; and Ekron, eradicated" (Zeph. 2:4). The seacoast of Canaan, where Philistines and Cherethites dwell, will be devastated and repopulated by the remnants of Judah (2:5-7). Moab and Ammon will become like Sodom and Gomorrah (Gen. 19:24-38) as a punishment of the offense of humiliating the people who belong to the Lord of Hosts (Zeph. 2:8-10). God's wrath will destroy other gods, and the world will worship God alone (2:11). The Ethiopians, who represent the farthest corner of the world, will also be under God's judgment (2:12). The oracles against the nations conclude with Assyria, for whom these other nations have been vassals. God will annihilate Assyria, the enemy from the north, and its capital city Nineveh for their arrogance (2:13), and their lair will be inhabited by wild animals (2:14-15). The hubris of Nineveh and her dilapidation serve as a lesson of history that promises no eternal glory—no matter how powerful and proud she may be. The tale serves as a comfort for those who have been hurt by her aggression (2:15).

■ THE TEXT IN THE INTERPRETIVE TRADITION

Early church fathers find the spread of the gospel alluded to in the prophet's vision of God whom each will worship in his or her own place. John Chrysostom (2:69–70) regards Zeph. 2:11 and 3:9 as comments on the actualization of Isaiah's peaceable kingdom (Isa. 11:1-9), which will come true when all nations serve God under one yoke in their own place. Based on Zephaniah's vision, Augustine reflects on God who gathers the predestined believers into one body of Christ (2004, 248). In his homily on Psalm 97, Jerome (192) imagines churches secure with Christ as their foundation, although they are like islands beaten by the waves of the ocean. Whereas Luther (340–42) maintains that Judah would also be destroyed, leaving only the faithful remnant to be saved, Calvin (240) acquires a message of hope for Judah, in that divine retribution is moved to other nations.

■ THE TEXT IN CONTEMPORARY DISCUSSION

The prophet underscores God's central role in the course of the history of the nations and their international affairs. Their offenses include worshiping other gods, menacing God's people, and boasting that their power will be eternally secured as exemplified in the pride of Assyria. The prophet's critical assessment of proud nations lends a theological corrective to political powers that seek their glory and preservation by imperial militarism that threatens the livelihood of other nations, and also by exploitative colonialism that leaves other peoples impoverished. This theme provides biblical support for postcolonial interpreters and those who combat ills of imperialism in the contemporary world.

Zephaniah 3:1-13: The Remnant of Israel

▌ THE TEXT IN ITS ANCIENT CONTEXT

Commentators debate over whether one should read Zeph. 3:1-13 as condemning Judah or other nations. The identity of the city denounced in 3:1 is ambiguous. Does "the oppressing city" refer to Nineveh or Jerusalem? The immediately preceding passage may invite one to posit that the verse is a continuation of the oracle against Assyria in 2:13-15; however, the ensuing verses reveal that Judah is being depicted in 3:1 as the place of the impurity and oppression.

The first offense of the city is the rejection of instructive correction and trust in God (3:2). Its evil outcome manifests itself in the societal ills marked by rampages of rapacious political leaders and irresponsible religious leaders (3:3-4). The main offenders are leaders: officials, judges, prophets, and priests, all of whom the prophet casts with beastly images. The inclusion of judges among the culprits may represent the collapse of the system of justice. By contrast, YHWH's rule is marked by justice (3:5). God expects the judgment against the nations to be a good lesson for the oppressing city that needs cleansing, but the city compounds her guilt by rejecting correction and exacerbating corruption (3:6-7).

Recalling the day of YHWH in Zephaniah 1, the prophet announces that God will initiate legal proceedings against the oppressing city, render a verdict, and execute her punishment, which will affect the whole world (3:8). The time of judgment will be followed by a new era, when the pure community emerges, transformed to worship God in unity (3:9-10). The day will reveal that, whereas the proud who have rebelled against God will be removed (3:11), the humble remnant will find security in God's presence, empowering them to do right (3:12-13).

▌ THE TEXT IN THE INTERPRETIVE TRADITION

The Hebrew homonym *yônâ* in 3:1 could mean either "oppressing" or "dove." The Septuagint construes it as "dove," and the midrash adds another pun by scathing the city for acting like a dove and ignoring the lesson from Nineveh the city of Jonah (*yônâ; Lam. Rab.*, proem 31). Theodore of Mopsuestia (299) regards the dove as signifying Israel, which is charming but refuses to trust in YHWH. Luther (349) suspects that by the "dove" the prophet secretively refers to the Holy Spirit present in Jerusalem.

Cyprian (555) construes the prophet's call for patience (3:8) as a charge to wait for the day when God avenges the wrongs that the faithful go through during the time of persecution. The prophet's vision of "pure speech" (3:9) leads the medieval Jewish philosopher Ibn Ezra to argue that it means the universal use of Hebrew (*Commentary on Ecclesiastes* 5.1). The image of the pure speech and one accord (3:9) provides Gregory the Great (1844–1850, 2:541–42) with the vision of the universal worship of God. Augustine (1998, 868–69) concludes that the prophet speaks of the day when the world will worship God.

▌THE TEXT IN CONTEMPORARY DISCUSSION

The prophet's criticism of leadership portrays how the people suffer when leaders fail to do what they are called to do and, more seriously, when they do the opposite, as Sweeney observes with the prophets and priests (2000, 520). Civil rights activist Howard Thurman (1028–29) charges modern religious workers to pay attention to Zephaniah's criticism of prophets and priests so that they may not fall into the pit of professional banality and the loss of moral sensitivity. Christian Marxist writer José Miranda (120) finds God waging a war of liberation against the powerful oppressors in Zeph. 3:1-13. God places the oppressors under judgment, and Israel's humble remnant will see God's salvation.

Zephaniah 3:14-20: The Jubilation of YHWH

▌THE TEXT IN ITS ANCIENT CONTEXT

The book ends with an uplifting message of hope that dwells on the glorious prospect of the salvation of Israel. Jerusalem, the "daughter Zion" that represents Israel, is exhorted to sing a song of jubilation (3:14), for Judah has been saved by YHWH, the king of Israel, who now fills Jerusalem with courage (3:15-16). The book reaches its climax in the portrayal of the divine warrior (see also Exod. 15:3), who fights on behalf of God's people and takes delight in the people who have been saved (Zeph. 3:17). The NRSV's rendering of God, who "will renew you in his love" (3:17), is based on the Greek and the Syriac. The Hebrew says, "He will be silent in his love" (author's own translation), which ironically juxtaposes the scene of God engaged in loud jubilation in the same verse. The Hebrew could be translated alternatively as "[God] will bring you to silence," creating a picture of God soothing the people (Roberts, 220, 222). God is restoring the joy of feast, taking away guilt and disaster (3:18). In the reversal of fortunes, God who expels Jerusalem's internal oppressors and external aggressors will heal the poor who have suffered at their hands (3:19). God will bring those who were dispersed in humiliation, and their restoration will be a theme of praise for the whole world (3:20).

▌THE TEXT IN THE INTERPRETIVE TRADITION

The Targum finds in the "Song of Zephaniah" (3:14-20) a depiction of the Lord dwelling among the people through Shekinah (the manifestation of God's presence among the people). The Talmud depicts the messianic end time as "when the highhanded disappear from Israel" (*b. Sanh.* 98a). The coming of the Messiah and the restoration of Israel based on Zeph. 3:20 is reflected in the traditional Jewish liturgy.

Cyril of Jerusalem (117–18) derives the blessing for candidates of baptism from the exhortation to sing and rejoice over God's deliverance. Zephaniah's vision of God's joy inspires Theodoret of

Cyrus (218) to dwell on the love of God in Christ, who gives his life. Theodore of Mopsuestia (304) constructs a scene in which God the king removes troubles and restores Zion out of divine love. The reversal of fortunes reminds Luther (364) of the early martyrs who were despised like refuse, but are now signs of blessings. Now God's song causes the redeemed to give thanks to the Lord, for in this unusual passage God sets aside divine majesty to show love for the redeemed (Calvin, 304). The Baptist preacher Charles Haddon Spurgeon (271) lifts up the unique nature of this scene of divine jubilation, recalling that God did not sing at the creation and simply rated it as "very good" (Gen. 1:31), but redemption gives joy to the Trinity.

■ THE TEXT IN CONTEMPORARY DISCUSSION

Zephaniah portrays God as the divine warrior, a depiction deeply rooted in the ancient conceptual world of Old Testament times (see Miller). The militaristic overtone of this portrayal of God is troublesome for contemporary sensitivities that value peace, and some interpreters warn against the danger of using divine violence to legitimate individual and nationalistic pursuits as God's will (Heffelfinger, 341). Most significantly, the divine warrior in Zeph. 3:14-20, and elsewhere in the Bible, exerts divine power on behalf of the people who have no one else to whom they can turn. The book that began with the prospect of the world's annihilation caused by the people and their leaders—along with their national self-aggrandizement—then concludes with God's exuberance over the divine work of salvation. The prophet calls on the redeemed to join with the song of joy and thanksgiving for God, who alone can save.

Works Cited

Augustine of Hippo. 1998. *The City of God against the Pagans*. Cambridge Texts in the History of Political Thought. Cambridge: Cambridge University Press.

———. 2004. *Letters 156–210*. WSA II/3. Hyde Park, NY: New City Press.

Bail, Ulrike. 2012. "Zephaniah; or The Threefold Jerusalem." In *Feminist Biblical Interpretation: A Compendium of Critical Commentary on the Books of the Bible and Related Literature*, edited by Luise Schottroff and Marie-Theres Wacker, 450–59. Grand Rapids: Eerdmans.

Bennett, R. A. 1996. "Zephaniah." In *The New Interpreter's Bible*. Vol. 7, *Introduction to Apocalyptic Literature, Daniel, and the Minor Prophets*, edited by Leander E. Keck, 657–704. Nashville: Abingdon.

Berlin, Adele. 1994. *Zephaniah: A New Translation with Introduction and Commentary*. AB 25A. New York: Doubleday.

Calvin, John. 1984. *A Commentary on the Twelve Minor Prophets*. Vol. 4. Translated by John Owen. Geneva Series Commentary. Edinburgh: Banner of Truth Trust.

Chrysostom, John. 1998. *Commentary on the Psalms*. 2 vols. Translated by Robert C. Hill. Brookline, MA: Holy Cross Orthodox Press.

Coggins, Richard, and Jin H. Han. 2011. *Six Minor Prophets through the Centuries*. Blackwell Bible Commentaries. Chichester, UK: Wiley-Blackwell.

Cyprian. 1978. "The Treatises." In *ANF* 5:421–564.

Cyril of Jerusalem. 1969. *The Works of Saint Cyril of Jerusalem*. Vol. 1. Translated by Leo P. McCauley, SJ, and Anthony A. Stephenson. FC 61. Washington, DC: Catholic University of America Press.

Ferreiro, Alberto, ed. 2003. *The Twelve Prophets*. Ancient Christian Commentary on Scripture, Old Testament 14. Downers Grove, IL: InterVarsity Press.

Gregory the Great. 1844–1850. *Morals on the Book of Job*. Vol. 2. Library of Fathers of the Holy Catholic Church 21. Oxford: Parker.

———. 1990. *Forty Gospel Homilies*. Translated by David Hurst. CS 123. Kalamazoo, MI: Cistercian.

Heffelfinger, Katie M. 2012. "Zephaniah." In *Women's Bible Commentary*, edited by Carol A. Newsom, Sharon H. Ringe, and Jacqueline E. Lapsley, 339–42. 3rd ed. Louisville: Westminster John Knox.

Jerome. 1964. *The Homilies of Saint Jerome*. Vol. 1. Translated by Sister Marie Liguori Ewald, IHM. FC. 48. Washington, DC: Catholic University of America Press.

Kay, Jeanne. 1989. "Human Dominion over Nature in the Hebrew Bible." *Annals of the Association of American Geographers* 79:214–32.

Levenson, Jon D. 1988. *Creation and the Persistence of Evil: The Jewish Drama of Divine Omnipotence*. San Francisco: Harper & Row.

Lohfink, Norbert F. 1987. *Option for the Poor: The Basic Principle of Liberation Theology in the Light of the Bible*. Translated by Linda Maloney. Berkeley, CA: Bibal.

Luther, Martin. 1975. *Luther's Works*. Vol. 18, *Lectures on the Minor Prophets I*. Edited by Hilton C. Oswald. St. Louis: Concordia.

Miller, Patrick D. 1973. *The Divine Warrior in Early Israel*. HSM 5. Cambridge, MA: Harvard University Press.

Miranda, José Porfirio. 1974. *Marx and the Bible: A Critique of the Philosophy of Oppression*. Maryknoll, NY: Orbis.

Moltmann, Jürgen. 1967. *Theology of Hope: On the Ground and the Implications of a Christian Eschatology*. New York: Harper & Row.

Origen of Alexandria. 2001. *Commentaries on the Epistle to the Romans: Books 1–5*. Translated by Thomas P. Scheck. FC 103. Washington, DC: Catholic University of America Press.

Pachomian Koinonia: Instructions, Letters, and Other Writings of Saint Pachomius and His Disciples. 1982. Vol. 3. CS 47. Kalamazoo, MI: Cistercian.

Pannenberg, Wolfhart. 1984. "Constructive and Critical Functions of Christian Eschatology." *HTR* 77:119–39.

Roberts, J. J. M. 1991. *Nahum, Habakkuk, and Zephaniah: A Commentary*. OTL. Louisville: Westminster John Knox.

Sobrino, Jon. 1984. *The True Church and the Poor*. Maryknoll, NY: Orbis.

Spurgeon, C. H. 1992. *Faith's Checkbook: A Devotional*. New Kensington, PA: Whitaker House.

Sweeney, Marvin A. 2000. *The Twelve Prophets*. Vol. 2. Berit Olam. Collegeville, MN: Liturgical Press.

———. 2003. *Zephaniah: A Commentary*. Hermeneia. Minneapolis: Fortress Press.

Theodore of Mopsuestia. 2004. *Commentary on the Twelve Prophets*. Translated by Robert C. Hill. FC 108. Washington, DC: Catholic University of America Press.

Theodoret of Cyrus. 2006. *Commentary on the Prophets*. Vol. 3. Translated by Robert C. Hill. Brookline, MA: Holy Cross Orthodox Press.

Thurman, Howard. 1956. "The Book of Zephaniah: Exposition." In *The Interpreter's Bible*. Vol. 6, *Lamentations; Ezekiel; Daniel; Hosea; Joel; Amos; Obadiah; Jonah; Micah; Nahum; Habakkuk; Zephaniah; Haggai; Zechariah; Malachi*, edited by George A. Buttrick, 1007–36. New York: Abingdon-Cokesbury.

HAGGAI

J. Blake Couey

Introduction

The book of Haggai contains one of the Bible's clearest pictures of early postexilic Jerusalem. Its four units mix prophetic speeches with brief narrative segments. Each unit has a specific date, together covering a period of four months in 520 BCE. It describes the work of the prophet Haggai, whose name is fittingly related to the Hebrew word for "festival." Haggai encourages his community to rebuild and rededicate the temple of YHWH in Jerusalem, which had been destroyed by the Babylonians in 587 BCE (Hag. 1:1—2:19). He also makes bold but cryptic promises concerning Zerubbabel, the governor of Judah and a descendant of King David (2:20-23). Haggai's vision of postexilic Jerusalem is thus thoroughly traditionalist, seeking some degree of restoration for the two most important institutions of the preexilic period—the temple, and the monarchy.

In its final form, the book celebrates Haggai's success as a prophet—an unusual phenomenon in the Hebrew Bible, as other prophets typically face great opposition (e.g., Jer. 26:7-11; Amos 7:10-13)—and reaffirms the centrality of the second temple in postexilic Judaism (Petersen, 36). The prophecies in Zechariah 1–8 concern similar issues and are dated around the same time; consequently, some commentators have proposed that the two books are an editorial unity (e.g., Meyers and Meyers, xliv-xlviii), but others disagree. Haggai and Zechariah were remembered for their roles in the reconstruction of the temple in Ezra 5:1; 6:14.

Haggai has received minimal attention from later interpreters. Selected texts appear in discussions of ritual purity or the character of God in rabbinic Jewish sources, and a few verses have attracted notice in Christianity for their perceived christological significance. The book may likewise seem to hold little significance for contemporary readers; however, it is a helpful model for encouraging a hurting, disillusioned community, and it offers profound reflections on the connections between past, present, and future during times of rapid change. Its ambivalent attitude toward the Persian Empire also deserves attention in a global, postcolonial age.

Haggai 1:1-15: Rebuilding the Temple

■ THE TEXT IN ITS ANCIENT CONTEXT

This unit opens with a prophetic speech criticizing the postexilic community for their hesitancy to rebuild the temple (Hag. 1:1-11). Although it concerns the larger community, it is addressed to "Zerubbabel . . . governor of Judah" and "Joshua . . . the high priest" (1:1), who are also remembered for their leadership in Ezra and Zechariah. The term "governor" refers to a position of political authority in the Persian administrative system, although it is unclear precisely how much power the governor of Judah would have held at this time. The position of high priest gained increased power in the postexilic period in the absence of the monarchy.

Ezra 3 suggests that the foundations of the new temple had been laid when the first Judean exiles returned from Babylon in 538 BCE. Haggai 1 is set eighteen years later (1:1), and the temple remained unfinished. For Haggai, this is an affront to YHWH's honor (1:8). In ancient Near Eastern religion, temples were understood as the locus of divine presence on earth. The concern for building a "house" for Baal in Ugaritic myths suggests that the lack of a temple diminished a deity's status. According to Ezra 4:4-5, the delay in rebuilding the temple resulted from conflict between the returning exiles and local populations, but Haggai blames it solely on the indolence of the people, who are more concerned with the state of their own homes (Hag. 1:4, 9). Scholars disagree over the translation of the Hebrew *sapun* (NRSV "paneled") in verse 4. In other biblical texts, it refers to fine cedar paneling (e.g., 1 Kgs. 7:3; Jer. 22:14). Some commentators suggest that, by itself, the word simply means "covered" or "roofed," and that the postexilic Jewish community would not have been able to afford such luxurious homes (e.g., O'Brien, 142–43). Haggai's description, however, may be rhetorically exaggerated to heighten the contrast between the people's houses and YHWH's house (Petersen, 48–49). The community's attitude contrasts sharply with David's anxiety in 2 Sam. 7:2 that he lives in a palace while the deity lacks a temple. The prophet does acknowledge the difficulties faced by the postexilic community in Hag. 1:5-11, but he explains their lack of prosperity as the result of YHWH's anger. The language of these verses echoes biblical and ancient Near Eastern futility curses associated with broken treaties or covenants (Kessler, 130–33; cf., e.g., Lev. 26:26; Deut. 28:38, 48). Other prophets similarly understand drought and other natural disasters as divine punishments (e.g., Hosea 2:9, 12; Amos 4:7-10).

Haggai 1:12-15 is a narrative recounting the community's response to Haggai's speech (1:12-15). Resumption of work on the temple is attributed simultaneously to multiple causes: the leadership of Zerubbabel and Joshua, the initiative of the community, the prophetic encouragement of Haggai, and the empowerment of YHWH's spirit. Even before the work has resumed, God already promises to be "with" the people in Hag. 1:13, echoing similar promises from other prophetic books (e.g., Isa. 7:14; 43:2). It is this promise that motivates them to rebuild the temple. Some commentators treat these verses as a separate unit from the rest of the chapter, due to the parallel date formulas in verses 1 and 15 (e.g., Petersen, 55–60). Rather than marking a separate pericope, however, the second formula underscores Haggai's success as a prophet by quantifying the speediness with which the people responded to his message.

Haggai supported Persia's imperial agenda, although perhaps unintentionally, through his passionate advocacy for rebuilding the temple. Local temples were an integral part of the Persian administrative system, which explains their financial support for temple construction (see Ezra 6:8-9). The references to Darius and the use of Persian regnal years in dating formulas further reinforce the validity of their rule. Although the construction of the second temple served Persian interests, it also played an indispensable role in the survival of the postexilic community. The temple would become the chief symbol of their identity and the center of their religious activity, as seen in later texts, such as 1–2 Chronicles and Malachi.

THE TEXT IN THE INTERPRETIVE TRADITION

The single-minded focus on the temple in this unit has been a problem for many Christian readers; Augustine, John Calvin, and the editors of the Geneva Bible, among others, understood the text to refer to the "spiritual" temple composed of believers, with reference to 1 Cor. 3:16-17 (Ferreiro, 22; Coggins, 137). Nonetheless, interpreters have been able to connect individual verses to particular Christian beliefs or practices; for instance, Calvin saw in Hag. 1:13 a proof text for election through divine grace. A lack of sympathy for Haggai's project persists among some modern commentators, who dismiss the prophet's concerns as excessively nationalistic. The potentially anti-Judaic overtones of such readings have been noted by more recent interpreters (Kessler, 2–4; O'Brien, 137–38).

THE TEXT IN CONTEMPORARY DISCUSSION

In today's world, many disenfranchised persons find themselves in situations like that described in Haggai 1, such as residents of distressed neighborhoods or refugee and migrant communities. This unit demonstrates the difficult balance that must be maintained when challenging such groups to action. Haggai's explanation of the people's hardships may come across as victim blaming, yet his words helped counteract their feeling of powerlessness. How does one honor the agency of persons in distress without reductively attributing their complex situations to their own choices? The prophet's demand that the people rebuild the temple before repairing their own homes also raises questions. While it may be appropriate to expect individuals to make economic sacrifices for the good of their communities, at what point does it become unjust to ask persons who are already economically distressed to ignore their own well-being?

It is difficult for contemporary readers to appreciate fully the tremendous importance of the temple for the postexilic Jewish community. Nonetheless, Christian readers should avoid using this unit to caricature Second Temple Judaism as materialistic or nationalistic, as some interpreters have done. The temple functioned as a tangible symbol of God's presence with the community and their continued status as God's people. To understand the concerns of the text more sympathetically, one might think of the trauma experienced by congregations whose places of worship have been vandalized or destroyed.

Haggai 2:1-9: Disappointment and Hope

▮ THE TEXT IN ITS ANCIENT CONTEXT

Nearly one month after the previous episode (Hag. 2:1), some members of the postexilic Jewish community were disappointed by the edifice that they had begun rebuilding. Over sixty-five years after the first temple was destroyed, it is doubtful that many in Haggai's audience could actually remember it (but see Ezra 3:12), yet it looms in their collective memory as a sign of a better past. Other prophetic texts portray preexilic Judah as a nation plagued by inequality (e.g., Isa. 1:10-17), however, suggesting that the temple's "former glory" resulted in part from oppressive policies toward the poor and vulnerable. Haggai agrees that the second temple cannot compare to its predecessor, but he minimizes that difference by referring to the two structures as if they were the same building (Kessler, 165–67).

In Hag. 2:4-5, the prophet encourages the people using language that occurs throughout the Hebrew Bible. These references to familiar traditions subtly but powerfully reestablish the community's connection to their history (Kessler, 170–71). The admonition "take courage" (Heb. *hazaq*, literally "be strong") is especially associated with Joshua, the successor to Moses (Deut. 31:7; Josh. 1:6), and it may be used here to connect the postexilic high priest with his earlier namesake. The command "do not fear" is a staple of salvation oracles in Isaiah (e.g., Isa. 35:4; 41:10). Verse 5 evokes the exodus traditions, situating the current community in their ongoing covenantal relationship with YHWH.

The focus shifts to the future in Hag. 2:6-9, which announces imminent divine activity. Again, the prophet relies on traditional themes. The verb "shake" (Hebrew *ra'ash*) in verses 6-7 occurs frequently in descriptions of cosmic upheaval accompanying YHWH's appearance (e.g., Judg. 5:4; Ps. 18:7). Verse 7 evokes another familiar motif, the pilgrimage of foreign nations to Jerusalem (e.g., Isa. 2:2). As in other exilic and postexilic texts, these nations financially support the community in Jerusalem (Isa. 45:14; 61:6). Here, their support does not appear to be offered willingly, and it is only their wealth—not the nations themselves—that comes to Jerusalem. The suggestion that the temple's construction would be funded by foreign wealth obliquely acknowledges its funding by the Persians. By reframing this support as the result of divine activity rather than an imperial handout, however, Haggai undercuts claims of Persian supremacy. In verse 9, YHWH promises to bless the temple with *shalom*; in this instance, "prosperity" is an appropriate translation of the Hebrew term, but its range of meanings also includes "peace" and "wholeness."

▮ THE TEXT IN THE INTERPRETIVE TRADITION

Haggai 2:6-9 has received more interpretive attention than other parts of the book. The phrase "treasure of all nations" in verse 7, which could also be translated "desire of all nations" (e.g., Vulgate; KJV), has traditionally been taken as a reference to Christ. Allusions appear in music for Advent and Christmas, such as Handel's *Messiah* or the hymn "O Come, O Come, Emmanuel." Other interpreters, including Augustine, associated it with Christ's second coming (Ferreiro, 226). Similarly, verse 6 is quoted in Heb. 12:26-27—the only unmistakable quotation from Haggai in the

New Testament—with eschatological overtones. For many Christian readers, the promised "splendor" in Hag. 2:9 is also fulfilled by Christ. In rabbinic Jewish texts, it is taken as a prediction of the greater size of the second temple (Coggins, 147; Neusner, 67–68), which Calvin accepts as a valid but partial fulfillment of the prophecy.

▉ THE TEXT IN CONTEMPORARY DISCUSSION

During times of rapid change, it can be tempting to look back wistfully on a selectively remembered past. While space should be allowed for appropriate grief, this sense unit cautions us that excessive indulgence in nostalgia may hinder a community from living wholeheartedly into its future. Moreover, the text encourages us to be sensitive to persons with very different experiences of the past. Some white Americans, for example, have positive memories of the 1950s, while many African Americans remember the same period as a time of institutionalized segregation and racial injustice. The "good old days" were not equally good for everyone.

The denigration of foreign nations in verses 7-8 might make contemporary readers uncomfortable, especially in contexts in which hypernationalism poses problems. One should remember that these words were written for a community adjusting to imperial subjugation. It may be unrealistic and even unfair to expect victims of recent injustice to forswear resentment against their oppressors—especially when one's instinctive sympathies lie with the oppressors. Most contemporary American readers of Haggai, after all, have far more in common with citizens of the Persian Empire than the postexilic Jewish community.

Haggai 2:10-19: Ritual Questions

▉ THE TEXT IN ITS ANCIENT CONTEXT

In Hag. 2:11-13, the prophet asks the priests for a "ruling" on two scenarios concerning "holy" and "unclean" objects. As understood in the ancient world, uncleanness is a state of ritual impurity that impedes contact with the deity. It is not the same thing as sinfulness, although there is overlap between the categories. The transmission of uncleanness via dead bodies, which is the premise for Haggai's second scenario, is discussed in Num. 19:11-22.

The priests' rulings indicate that uncleanness can be easily transmitted, but ritual holiness cannot. Based on these rulings, Haggai declares the people's "work" unclean in verse 14. It is not clear to whom he refers. Some commentators have argued that he means the Samaritans, whom the returned exiles would have regarded suspiciously. Although Ezra 4 describes tension between the two groups at the time of the temple's reconstruction, the book of Haggai shows no awareness of such conflict. Recent scholarship generally assumes that the verse refers to the entire postexilic community. Apparently, they had begun to make offerings again, but the temple structure had not been sufficiently consecrated. As a result, their offerings became unclean through contact with the impure altar, and that uncleanness was transmitted to all of their agricultural produce ("work of their hands," Hag. 2:14).

Nonetheless, the tone of verses 15-19 is largely positive. The prophet promises that their fortunes will change dramatically once some task related to the temple's reconstruction is completed (2:15, 18). Verse 18 implies that this task would be completed on the same day as the proclamation of the oracle. It cannot simply be the rebuilding of the temple, which the previous units indicate had been going on for two months. The reference to the "foundation" in verse 17 probably indicates the formal dedication of the temple, involving a ceremonial foundation stone (see Ezra 3:10-11; Zech. 4:9); ancient evidence confirms the existence of a similar ritual in Babylon (Petersen, 88–90). As a result of this ceremony, the community would be able to offer acceptable sacrifices again, restoring their contact with the deity and making future blessings possible (2:19).

■ THE TEXT IN THE INTERPRETIVE TRADITION

Not surprisingly, given its concerns with purity issues, this unit has been more significant in Jewish interpretation than in Christian interpretation. The Jerusalem Talmud, for instance, depicts a spirited rabbinic debate over whether the priests answered Haggai's questions correctly and suggests that Haggai cursed the people by declaring their offerings unclean (Coggins, 148; Neusner, 49–51).

■ THE TEXT IN CONTEMPORARY DISCUSSION

For the same reasons that traditional Christian interpretation has largely ignored this unit, some contemporary readers may have difficulty sympathizing with its concerns—particularly readers from Protestant traditions that place little value on ritual. Nonetheless, these verses encourage reflection upon the character of God and the nature of worship.

For Haggai, ritual is only effective when specific expectations are met. Other prophetic texts famously condemn thoughtless or hypocritical worship, such as Amos 5:21-24, yet Haggai cautions that good intentions do not always make worship acceptable to God. Ritual actions belong to complex symbolic systems informed by rich traditions, apart from which their meaning may be compromised. At the same time, the people are not without recourse. God communicates to them through priests and prophets, making it clear how divine demands can be satisfied so that God may bless the people.

Haggai 2:20-23: A Promise to Zerubbabel

■ THE TEXT IN ITS ANCIENT CONTEXT

The speech in Hag. 2:20-23 has the same date as the previous unit. Directed to Zerubbabel, it is the only speech in the book addressed to a single individual. Verse 21 repeats language from Hag. 2:6 to announce future divine activity, although without the same sense of imminence. In verse 23, the phrase "that day" resonates with "this day" in Hag. 2:18, placing the temple dedication on the same trajectory as these future events. The climax of these events is the divine election of Zerubbabel, a descendant of King David (1 Chron. 3:19). Appropriately, Hag. 2:23 uses language associated with David, including the term "servant" (2 Sam. 7:5; Ps. 132:10) and the verbs "take" (2 Sam. 7:8) and "choose" (Ps. 78:70). The promise to "make [Zerubbabel] like a signet ring" alludes to Jer.

21:24-25, in which the exiled King Jehoiachin/Jeconiah—Zerubbabel's grandfather—is compared to a signet ring removed from YHWH's finger. The reversal of that image may imply the restoration of the Davidic monarchy, especially if Persia is imagined as one of the "kingdoms" overthrown in Hag. 2:22. Such hopes are only given restrained expression, though, and even that is deferred to the future. While the oracle stops short of advocating rebellion against Persia, it is surely no accident that the first verse in the book acknowledges Darius's kingship, but the final verse announces Zerubbabel's election.

This oracle might seem out of place following units that focused on the temple. Temple building and repair, however, were chiefly royal prerogatives in the ancient world. The Davidic monarchy and the Jerusalem temple were closely connected institutions in preexilic Judah (2 Samuel 7; 1 Kings 8). It would only have been natural, then, for Zerubbabel's role in the reconstruction of the temple to have forced the question of his royal status, and this connection is even clearer in Zech. 6:11-13.

THE TEXT IN THE INTERPRETIVE TRADITION

The messianic implications of these verses were not lost on early Christian interpreters, who regarded Zerubbabel as a prototype of Christ. For example, Ambrose connected the signet ring language in Hag. 2:23 with that in Song 8:6, which was also interpreted christologically (Ferreiro, 229). Rabbinic Jewish interpreters noted the connection between Jer. 21:24 and Hag. 2:23, which they harmonized by supposing that Jehoiachin must have repented, causing God to rescind the oath that Jehoiachin's line would cease (Neusner, 55–56).

THE TEXT IN CONTEMPORARY DISCUSSION

Despite its cautious depiction of the future, this text almost certainly raised expectations that were disappointed. We do not know what happened to Zerubbabel. Persian rule persisted for another two centuries, only to be replaced by Greek and then Roman rule, and the Davidic family seems to have faded in prominence. We should recognize that this text contains a failed promise, a problem that is only partially mitigated by its association with Christ in the Christian tradition. How does one navigate the theological questions raised by this claim? At the very least, we should remember that speaking about God's future activity remains incredibly risky, even when undertaken with great care. Persons of faith might even find it reassuring that God is not limited by our hopes for the future but remains free to act in new and surprising ways.

Works Cited

Calvin, John. 1950. *Commentaries on the Twelve Minor Prophets.* Translated by John Owen. Grand Rapids: Eerdmans.

Coggins, Richard, and Jin H. Han. 2011. *Six Minor Prophets through the Centuries.* Blackwell Bible Commentaries. Malden, MA: Wiley-Blackwell. [Cited as Coggins]

Ferreiro, Alberto, ed. 2003. *The Twelve Prophets.* Ancient Christian Commentary on Scripture, Old Testament 14. Downers Grove, IL: InterVarsity Press.

Kessler, John. 2002. *The Book of Haggai: Prophecy and Society in Early Persian Yehud.* VTSup 91. Leiden: Brill.

Meyers, Carol L., and Eric M. Meyers. 1987. *Haggai, Zechariah 1–8*. AB 25B. New York: Doubleday.

Neusner, Jacob. 2007. *Zephaniah, Haggai, Zechariah, and Malachi in Talmud and Midrash: A Source Book.* Lanham, MD: University Press of America.

O'Brien, Julia M. 2004. *Nahum, Habakkuk, Zephaniah, Haggai, Zechariah, Malachi.* AbOTC. Nashville: Abingdon.

Petersen, David L. 1984. *Haggai and Zechariah 1–8.* OTL. Philadelphia: Westminster.

ZECHARIAH

Amy Erickson

Introduction

The superscriptions in Zechariah 1–8 (Zech. 1:1, 7; 7:1) locate Zechariah's prophetic activity in the early reign of the Persian king Darius (520–518 BCE), prior to the completion of the Second Temple (dedicated in 515 BCE). Haggai's prophetic activity dates roughly to the same period (see Ezra 5:1; 6:14), and for both prophets, the rebuilding of the temple is an essential precursor to the realization of the postexilic community's future prosperity and well-being. Zechariah 1–8 consists of a series of vision reports framed by hortatory speeches. The apocalyptic prophecies in Zechariah 9–14, while difficult to situate historically with any precision, reflect a later time period, perhaps the mid-fifth century BCE. At that time, Greece's program of military expansion led the Persians to fortify the empire's western borders, resulting in an increased military presence in the province of Yehud (Petersen 1995; Cook 2011). Given these differences, the majority of scholars divide Zechariah into two (Zechariah 1–8; 9–14) or even three (Zechariah 1–8; 9–11; 12–14) discrete collections.

While readers will appreciate the different themes and literary styles in the two parts of the book, there is continuity across the material as well. The book as a whole expresses a priestly theology, similar to that reflected in Ezekiel and the Holiness strands of the Pentateuch (Leviticus 17–26). Also evident in both parts of the book is an apocalyptic worldview. While the apocalyptic literary features in Zechariah 1–8 appear in a more nascent form ("proto-apocalyptic"), they are evident in the prophet's radical eschatology and in the sharp distinctions Zechariah makes between the present time and the coming age, heaven and earth, and the faithful and the wicked (Cook 1995, 125–33). Although Zechariah 9–14 is not a full-blown apocalypse, many of the hallmarks of apocalyptic thought take clearer form in the second part of the book (Collins). This material details not only God's disruptive entrance into the earthly plane at the start of the coming new age and a final battle waged in Jerusalem, but also the tribulation and suffering that a portion of humanity must endure prior to the divine implementation of a new age.

Both parts of the book arise from experience of life in Yehud (formerly Judah), a colony in the Persian Empire. The population of Yehud consists of returnees from exile in Babylon, the nondeported population of the land, inhabitants of Samaria, and officials from the Persian Empire (who may also be returnees). That there were tensions among these groups is evident in the books of Ezra and Nehemiah. For its part, the book of Zechariah refers to these groups, but the distinctions between them figure minimally in his visions of restoration.

The nature of prophetic books produced during the Persian period reflects changes in practices of reading, writing, preaching, and teaching. In contrast to prophets from earlier periods who were depicted as preaching God's word channeled through them to a "live audience" (e.g., Jeremiah 7), after the exile, the locus of revelation begins to shift from the mouth of the prophet to the word on the scroll (Sommer). While the prophet's oral performance of his message provides the book with its starting point, the scroll of Zechariah was shaped by producers who were interacting more and more with religiously significant written texts (Mason). Consistently engaging earlier prophetic literature, Zechariah advocates for Israel to view its present and future both in light of its past failures, captured in the prophets' words of judgment, and its testimonies to YHWH's desire to bless Israel and the world.

Zechariah 1:1-6: "Do Not Be Like Your Ancestors"

▋ THE TEXT IN ITS ANCIENT CONTEXT

Zechariah begins with a sermonic address that implores the audience to depart from the ways of their ancestors. Memories of exile and Jerusalem's destruction are marshaled to encourage the people to embrace a new way of being. Zechariah's rhetoric seeks to form a community whose memory of the past runs deep but does not predetermine its future. Restored to Jerusalem and awaiting the return of YHWH, Zechariah conditions the final restoration and reconciliation with YHWH on the people's return to YHWH (1:3). The report in Zech. 1:6 indicates that the people do indeed repent, which sets the stage for the visions that follow to imagine YHWH's return to the temple in Jerusalem.

▋ THE TEXT IN THE INTERPRETIVE TRADITION

The early church fathers highlighted the tension between divine grace and human free will in this passage. Augustine's interpretation of this passage is strongly shaped by his debate with Pelagius, who taught that humans could achieve moral perfection on their own and thus earn God's grace. Augustine argued that while Zechariah "simultaneously commends" divine grace and human free will, ultimately it is God who extends grace to the people and enables them to repent and return (Ferreiro).

▋ THE TEXT IN CONTEMPORARY DISCUSSION

Zechariah 1:1-6 raises fundamental questions about identity. To what extent are peoples' lives shaped by the behavior of our ancestors? How might communities negotiate the intersections

between their memories of the past and their vision of the future? In the opening verses of Zechariah, the prophet does not palliate or deny the community's history of pain, rebellion, and alienation from God. Nor does he encourage Israel to reinvent its identity apart from its past. Indeed,
through allusion and image, the book of Zechariah weaves together language from Israel's prophetic traditions and stories of its past to address the community's present concerns and anxieties.
And yet, the book's warnings and exhortations, formulated out of prophetic messages of judgment,
lead the people to make a choice for a fundamentally different future. Zechariah's way of interacting with authoritative texts may offer a model for contemporary communities to engage Scripture,
balancing the voices of the tradition with the context and needs of later readers in complex and
creative ways.

Zechariah 1:7—2:13: Visions of God's Return to Jerusalem

■ THE TEXT IN ITS ANCIENT CONTEXT

Zechariah 1:7—2:13 contains the first three of Zechariah's eight visions. In form, these visions have
much in common with prophetic symbolic visions (Jer. 1:11-12, 13-14; 24; Amos 7:7-9; 8:1-3; see
Niditch). However, different from most of the visions in Amos and Jeremiah, Zechariah's visions
aim to express hope rather than judgment and introduce of a new figure: the interpreting angel.
The angel, who translates the meaning of the obscure visions to the prophet, becomes a hallmark
of apocalyptic literature (Daniel 7–12). Scholars often characterize Zechariah's visions as proto-
apocalyptic; as such, the material evinces an apocalyptic perspective but lacks the formal features of
later apocalyptic texts. This perspective is evident in the idea that a divine plan is unfolding in the
heavens that will have radical repercussions for earth in the near future, but the divine program is
hidden from most of God's people. Even the prophet, with his privileged view of events unfolding
on a transcendent plane, needs an angel to explain the significance of his visions.

The movement of Zechariah's eight visions can be seen to reflect a move from the periphery
of the world to its center, the temple (the fifth vision), and back out to the periphery (Stead).
These first three visions communicate God's intention to return to Jerusalem, which is not only
the center of commercial and political activity but also the site of the temple. In the ancient
world, temples marked the apex of heaven and earth. As such, Jerusalem is the place where Israel
encounters God and the taproot from which God's blessings grow. Zechariah's visions, as they
move toward the mythological center of the world and back out into the wider world, track the
restoration of sacred space.

A close examination of the first vision of the horsemen in the glen (1:7-17) raises more questions than answers, but in general, it communicates that the apparent peace that dominates the
Persian Empire (1:11) will now begin to permeate Jerusalem and the cities of Judah and will find
its ultimate expression in the rebuilding of the temple ("my house," 1:16), where God will again be
present to God's people. YHWH's anger will be redirected from the people of Judah to the nations.
The time of suffering and punishment for Judah—seventy years, which accords with Jeremiah's

prophecy (Jer. 25:9-12; 29:10)—is over, and it is time now for a message of comfort (1:14-17) (cf. Isa. 40:1-2).

That God is enacting a reversal of fortune on behalf of Judah is also evident in the second vision of the horns and the smiths (1:18-21). The angel identifies the four horns as the nations that scattered Judah and explains that these horns will be cut off by four heavenly blacksmiths, suggesting that God's agent will overthrow those who oppress Judah and that those nations will lose their power to dominate. Evident in this vision are features of proto-apocalyptic literature, including imagery of a final battle between God's agents (the smiths) and God's enemies (the horns) as well as the prophet's conviction that only direct divine intervention will allow for change to take place on earth. For Zechariah, Judah's restoration will only come about when the transcendent breaks into the ordinary realm of history.

The third vision of the surveyor (2:1-5) reveals that the population of Jerusalem will explode beyond the confines of the city walls. The absence of walls in the vision is not a sign of the city's vulnerability and of God's abandonment, as in Lam. 2:3, 7-9. Rather, Jerusalem's safety will be ensured by the abiding presence of God in the city and not by its defenses and walls. In the exposition that follows the vision (2:6-13), YHWH will reverse the circumstances of Zion and the nations (2:8-9), but YHWH's choice to dwell in Zion once again also has implications for "many nations," who will "join themselves to the Lord on that day, and shall be my people" (2:11).

■ THE TEXT IN THE INTERPRETIVE TRADITION

Revelation's "four horsemen of the Apocalypse" (Rev. 6:1-8) likely takes its cue from the image of the four horses of different colors (1:7-10), and the figure of the interpreting angel features prominently in the New Testament (i.e., Luke 1:26-38) as well as in some contemporaneous Jewish traditions (1 Macc. 7:41; 2 Macc. 15:22; *2 Baruch (Syriac Apocalypse)* 63:7; *Jub.* 42:11; 27:21).

In some evangelical traditions, the image of "a brand plucked from the fire" (3:2) has become a powerful symbol to express the individual's struggle with evil and sin. The image is featured in the legends of John Wesley and in the so-called "Wesleys' Conversion Hymn," by Charles Wesley, which refers to "A slave redeemed from death and sin, / A brand plucked from eternal fire" (Coggins, 158–59).

■ THE TEXT IN CONTEMPORARY DISCUSSION

Zechariah offers a radical vision of hope to communities in despair. For those who no longer believe that life can change, he renders the present temporary and relative in light of a divinely ordained future that is not structured according to any earthly form of logic. In calling for the people to repent (1:1-7), Zechariah provides his audience with a way to participate in and commit to God's unfolding future plans. Then as a witness to the secret designs of God in heaven, he unfolds a series of obscure but compelling visions. As he dramatizes God's moves to bring about the community's full restoration to God and to safety and prosperity, he shapes a countercultural community of hope. At the same time, precise timelines for God's intervention—the hallmark of many modern millennialist groups—are notably absent.

Zechariah 3:1—4:14: Visions of Leadership

▌ THE TEXT IN ITS ANCIENT CONTEXT

The fourth and fifth visions (3:1-10; 4:1-14) suggest the restoration of Israel's central institutions: the priesthood and the monarchy.

In the fourth vision, Zechariah witnesses the accusation and cleansing of Joshua the high priest (Jeshua in Ezra and Nehemiah). The satan, a member of God's council who accuses Joshua, may represent Joshua's critics in the postexilic community. Alternatively, the vision of Joshua's cleansing may seek to alleviate anxiety about the guilt and worthiness of the community as a whole. The vision concludes on a note of uncertainty as the angel of YHWH issues a conditional promise that alludes to the failings of Judah's former leaders: "if you will walk in my ways and keep my statutes, then you shall rule my house and have charge of my courts" (3:7).

In the fifth vision, YHWH's presence is encoded in the specific modes and symbols of the temple, culminating with the image of the lampstand. The two olive trees that flank the lampstand likely represent the diarchy of priest and king. The remainder of the vision consists of the word of YHWH to Zerubbabel, governor of Yehud, promising that he will rebuild the temple, not by might but by God's spirit.

In the ancient Near Eastern world, temple building was a task for kings; therefore, images of Zerubbabel as the one who lays the foundation of the temple (4:9) activate messianic expectations. Many scholars have assumed that Zechariah views Zerubbabel as the Messiah based, in part, on the designation of him as "the Branch" (3:8), a term that refers to an ideal future ruler (Jer. 23:5; 33:15). However, Zerubbabel fades from the book without explanation. Perhaps the Persians removed him from power, or he was confined to a merely ceremonial role in the temple's rebuilding and founding ceremonies (Redditt). Or if Zechariah looked initially to Zerubbabel with messianic expectations, later his anticipation may have shifted toward an ideal Davidic leader (an unnamed Branch), who would implement justice on earth (Cook 1995).

▌ THE TEXT IN THE INTERPRETIVE TRADITION

In the Targum of Jonathan, the account of Joshua's dirty clothes and their replacement sparks a haggadic treatment that draws on Ezra 10:18 to explain that Joshua's offense had to do with unacceptable marriages: "And Joshua had sons who had married wives who were not permitted for the priesthood" (*Tg. Zech.* 3:3; see also *Sanh.* 93a; see Coggins).

Fathers of the early church understood Joshua's cleansing in light of Christian doctrines of baptism, sin, and incarnation. For Gregory of Nyssa, the high priest Joshua is Jesus Christ (LXX renders the high priest's name as *Iēsous*, which is *Yeshua* in the MT), and the replacement of dirty garments with clean ones is a figure of the regeneration of the person that happens in and through baptism. Jerome connects the filthy garments with the sin that Jesus voluntarily takes on when he becomes human (Ferreiro).

■ THE TEXT IN CONTEMPORARY DISCUSSION

This text provides an opportunity to discuss and challenge the common assumption that a prophecy is only "true" if it is later proven to have accurately predicted the future. Zechariah's prophecy imagines specific historical people, Zerubbabel and Joshua, in ideal leadership roles. Because these figures fade from history, should Zechariah's prophecy be viewed as a failure? Or is such particularity a risk all prophets must take lest Scripture be removed from the real world and become a "disembodied word" (Ollenburger)? While at times Zechariah surely supports particular "candidates" for office, in other instances, his imagination surpasses endorsement for particular human leaders. In the final form of the book, ideas about Zerubbabel stand in tension with references to the "Branch"; the messianic ideal both informs and serves to critique and challenge human leaders. The notion that prophecy is merely predictive limits the ways we might appreciate how the prophet's visions serve to restructure a community's worldview and revive its imagination about the ways God may be at work in their midst.

Zechariah 5:1—6:15: Visions of Purification

■ THE TEXT IN ITS ANCIENT CONTEXT

Whereas the earlier visions are focused on YHWH's return to Jerusalem, Zechariah's final three visions are concerned with the elimination of impurity and reflect a movement outward from the temple, which stands at the center of Zechariah's world. The verb "to go out" appears thirteen times in this unit (Floyd; Stead). The presence of God's holiness requires the removal of corruption and, as such, reflects a priestly concern for purity in Zechariah. In order for Jerusalem to accommodate the presence of the returning holy God (8:3), the land itself must be become holy (2:16).

The vision of the flying scroll (5:1-4) addresses the threat of internal corruption and the perversion of justice ("false swearing" and "stealing"). The scroll continually monitors practices that threaten not only the health and security of the community but also God's willingness to be present in their midst. As the scroll flies about, it is able to detect potential threats to the people's well-being and immediately issue curses against thieves and liars that will remove them from the land.

The vision of the woman in the basket (5:5-11) features a woman called "Wickedness" who is carried off to Shinar (Babylon) in some sort of container (an *ephah*) by winged women. Precisely what sort of iniquity the woman represents is not clear. However, the image has a cultic dimension and implies the veneration of foreign, feminine deities (e.g., the Queen of Heaven, Jer. 7:18; 44:17-25; O'Brien). *Ephah* may refer to woven baskets as houses for deities, used in household shrines. However, as a unit of measurement, *ephah* also has an economic dimension and recalls the Persian king Darius's creation of standard weights as a means to collect taxes more efficiently. The concern behind the vision is to rid the land not only of individual sinners but also of communal practices Zechariah considers "wicked" in a cultic as well as an economic sense (Ollenburger).

The last of Zechariah's eight night visions is of four chariots (6:1-8). This final vision parallels the first of the four horsemen (1:7-11) and structurally returns back to the periphery of the world from the center. However, in the first vision, the horsemen have completed their patrol and the announcement of peace on earth prompts a lament related to the exile's continuation (1:12). By contrast, in the last vision, four chariots burst out from between two mountains of bronze (6:1), ready to patrol in the four compass directions (6:7). The chariots, associated with military armament, are identified as "the four winds of heaven" and indicate God's military omnipotence and readiness to engage all the nations in battle. With sacred space restored and the cosmic army marshaled, YHWH's spirit is set at rest in the north (6:8), alluding perhaps to the restoration of the exiles still in exile there (Petersen 1984).

Actions imagined as taking place on earth and in the present link the visions of the future with the here-and-now (6:9-15). Moving from vision to word, God commands Zechariah to collect silver and gold from the exiles (6:9) to make crown(s) for Joshua (6:11). Scholars debate whether the one who is called the Branch (6:12) refers to Joshua as the one charged to build the temple (Floyd, 405) or if the less specific designation "Branch" refers to a future ideal ruler (see 3:8; Cook 1995). The report implies a complementary, though perhaps subordinate, role for the priesthood ("a priest by his throne," 6:13). The chapter concludes with a vision of a harmonious, inclusive temple-building project (6:15) that contrasts with Ezra's account of the temple's construction as beset by conflict and delay.

▌THE TEXT IN THE INTERPRETIVE TRADITION

In Martin Luther's treatment of the sixth (flying scroll) and seventh (woman in the ephah) visions in his lectures on Zechariah, he claims Zechariah predicts the "treachery of the Jews" and details their punishment for failing to accept Jesus as "King and Savior." His shockingly negative characterization of the Jewish people and use of the Bible to condemn Judaism exemplifies the Christian anti-Jewish polemics common for at least a thousand years prior to his teaching (Schramm and Stjerna). Anti-Jewish sentiment continued to inform the interpretive rubrics of historical-critical biblical scholarship into the late nineteenth and twentieth centuries, when Protestant scholars tended to view priestly concerns about purity and impurity as a sign of the degeneration of Israelite religion. In the wake of the Shoah (Holocaust), Protestant biblical scholarship has become increasingly self-critical and self-reflective about the biases inherent in such readings.

▌THE TEXT IN CONTEMPORARY DISCUSSION

That Zechariah's vivid and evocative images are particularly open-ended has enabled centuries of their creative, often historically specific appropriation. The same creative potentiality in Zechariah's visions that enabled Christian readers to see Jesus in the Branch also led them to equate the Jews with a woman called Wickedness. Literature in the vein of Zechariah is a double-edged sword.

In the interpretive tradition, there has been a tendency to equate the woman in the ephah with contemporary "others" (e.g., Jews and women) and to use the text to justify the expulsion of that other from the community that sees itself as positioned to inherit the blessings promised in the book. The revulsion prompted by these interpretations could provide an opportunity for contemporary communities not to judge such readings, but to consider how their own assumptions about otherness function to structure the boundaries of their communities.

Zechariah 7:1—8:23: A Homily Contrasting the Past and the Present

∎ THE TEXT IN ITS ANCIENT CONTEXT

The superscription in Zech. 7:1 situates the oracles that follow in the fourth year of the Persian king Darius's reign (518 BCE), two years after Zechariah received his visions. The reference to the completion of the laying of the temple's foundations (8:9) suggests that while the temple-building project is underway, it is not yet complete (completion dates to 515 BCE). The style of Zechariah 7–8 is comparable to that of Zech. 1:1-6 and has been linked to the "sermons" in Chronicles (e.g., 2 Chron. 30:6-9) and the teaching and preaching associated with the personnel of the Second Temple.

In general, this material is concerned to create a contrast between previous generations and the new community now living in Jerusalem. The ancestors' state of disobedience and punishment (7:7-12a) is contrasted to the peace-filled situation of the new community (8:4-8), which pivots on the announcement of YHWH's return to Jerusalem (8:3). YHWH's presence in Zion will lead to the reestablishment of a rich communal life, characterized by children playing and the elderly imparting wisdom (8:4-5). This vision of life restored is connected to the hortatory elements of the sermon (8:9-10, 16-17), which emphasize "neighborly" values (speaking truthfully, rendering right judgments, showing kindness and mercy, caring for the vulnerable, and not devising evil "in your hearts against one another").

The sermon's teachings on fasting (7:4-6; 8:18-19) can also be understood in light of the text's rhetorical creation of a contrast between the past and the present on the verge of the future. Fasts previously linked to mourning (7:3) "shall become seasons of joy and gladness, and cheerful festivals for the house of Judah" (8:19).

Although Zechariah does not refer directly to the visions that precede this sermon, his preaching reflects similar concerns and themes, including the return of YHWH to Jerusalem (cf. 1:16; 2:10-11 with 8:3, 8, 15), and a concern for the nations (cf. 2:11 with 8:20-23). But whereas the nations came to Jerusalem to be subjugated in 2:10-11, they come now to worship God.

∎ THE TEXT IN THE INTERPRETIVE TRADITION

The images of a restored humanity in this material may have influenced Paul's understanding of Israel's relationship to the nations. In Paul's eschatology, the reunification of Israel and the nations, such as Zechariah imagines in 8:20-23, is a key feature of the new creation, marked by God's cosmic reign and Jews and gentiles worshiping God together (Gal. 3:26-29; Rom. 15:7-13; Sherwood). The ultimate restoration of humanity begins with Israel, but Israel's redemption cannot be realized apart from that of the gentiles.

∎ THE TEXT IN CONTEMPORARY DISCUSSION

The way Zechariah configures the concept of universalism, with its resonances in Paul's thought, has implications for contemporary interreligious dialogue. The universalism in Zechariah is not unqualified; rather, it is rooted in the particular practices of the Jews (8:20-23). While the salvation of all people is essential for Zechariah's vision of the future reign of YHWH, the text does not depict humanity as an undifferentiated mass. Indeed, as in Paul, Israel's distinct theological heritage figures prominently in Zechariah's visions featuring the shalom of all.

Zechariah 9–11: War and Peace

▌THE TEXT IN ITS ANCIENT CONTEXT

Zechariah 9 makes use of and transforms the ancient ritual pattern of the Divine Warrior's "victory enthronement" (Hanson). In this pattern, YHWH as a Divine Warrior marches forth into battle against his enemies (9:1-7, 14). Elsewhere in the Hebrew Bible, these enemies represent the forces of chaos and take the form of monsters like the sea or Leviathan, human enemy armies, and even those perpetrating injustice within Israel. Following YHWH's victory over his foes, he enters his palace/temple where he takes his throne (9:8). YHWH's success in battle and subsequent enthronement are commemorated with victory shouts (9:9a), a procession (9:9b), sacrifices, and a banquet (9:15). The victory and enthronement of the Divine Warrior translates to the implementation of order, justice, and peace for his people.

When Zechariah 9 transposes and reimagines this pattern, God as Divine Warrior marches to Zion and reverses the current political realities for Israel. After routing the nations in battle, instead of taking his throne, YHWH encamps at his house as a guard (9:8). A human, rather than YHWH, is declared king, and while he is triumphant and victorious, he is also humble (9:9; cf. Ps. 72:2). Ringing with traditions of the ideal messiah, this king will end war for all time and in all places (9:10).

Symbols of blood play a role in the prophet's vision of restoration. The blood of the covenant in 9:11 sets apart Israel from the mass destruction of the nations (cf. Exodus 12, in which the blood on the Israelites' doorposts deters the angel of death during the plague of the firstborn). The blood that protects YHWH's people also serves to draw the people into ritual intimacy with God. As God and Israel partake of blood together in a banquet (9:15; cf. Exodus 24), the distance between Israel and God is bridged. Blood here evokes a rich and multivalent network of symbols to point to radical communion with God (Niditch).

Images of reversal dominate the next chapter (Zechariah 10). God indicts and vows to punish the leaders of Israel ("shepherds," 10:3), who have abdicated their responsibility to care for the people ("his flock, the house of Judah," 10:3); in turn, YHWH transforms the lowly into "the proud war-horse" (10:3), so that they may fight with God to scatter those who have persecuted them (10:4-5). God promises to gather, redeem, and strengthen the people whom God punished and scattered (10:6). Their restoration to God and to their land will represent an overwhelming reversal of the punishment of exile (10:8-12). This victory for Israel and the implementation of peace for the world has ecological consequences as well: the rain falls and vegetation flourishes (10:1).

The precise meaning of the narrative of the two shepherds (Zech. 11:4-17) is debated. The story appears to reverse the hopeful promises in Zechariah 9–10. God commands the prophet (?) to play the role of the unjust, greedy shepherd doomed to slaughter (11:4), and then vows that this shepherd will devastate the land. God then has the prophet symbolically break the covenant that God made with all the peoples (11:10). Although scholars have offered a number of different proposals with regard to the precise identity of these shepherds, generally speaking, "shepherds" are leaders; and as a Persian-period composition, it is likely that Zechariah is referring to Yehud's political leadership—governors who, though appointed by the Persian Empire, were Israelite.

■ THE TEXT IN THE INTERPRETIVE TRADITION

The Gospel writers in the New Testament draw on Zechariah's image of the king riding on a donkey (9:9) to describe Jesus entering Jerusalem (Matt. 21:4-5; John 12:14-15). For them, the juxtaposition of power and humility captured in Zechariah's imagery is embodied in the person of Jesus Christ (Matt. 21:9; Mark 11:9-10; Luke 19:38; John 12:13). Zechariah's visions of peace (9:10), enabled by God's radical in-breaking to the world, resonate with the New Testament's understandings of the kingdom of God, made possible because of the incarnation, a particularly embodied instance of God's transcendence breaking in and becoming immanent on earth.

■ THE TEXT IN CONTEMPORARY DISCUSSION

Contemporary readers are invited to grapple with Zechariah's suggestion that God approves of, and even participates in, acts of violence and aggression. While such theological claims may at first seem primitive to contemporary communities, the daily news continually reminds us that human beings are capable of great brutality and of justifying their acts of violence with "divine approval."

And yet, while glorified visions of God's violence are difficult to contend with, the text makes plain that it is God, not human beings, who will make war in order to end war. Zechariah does not encourage human beings to take up arms in order to initiate or enact the envisioned process of reversal. The Divine Warrior motif in (proto-)apocalyptic literature asserts that God as a warrior will break into history to deal personally with overwhelming evil and defend God's people against such evil. In this worldview, God is so infuriated by the presence of injustice and oppression that God physically appears to set things right and destroy evil once and for all.

The claim that God is more powerful than nations and empires and acts to temper their hubris and aggression flies in the face of the reality on the ground, and as such constitutes a powerful act of resistance. Nations and empires assert control over those they dominate by attempting to define the parameters of reality. One way of implementing such hegemonic control is to reshape myths to justify subtly the current reign as preordained, part of the structures of the cosmos. Proto-apocalyptic texts, such as Zechariah 9–11, present a counter-reality. The world may think the powerful nations are in control, but Zechariah asserts that their rule is temporary, even fragile. YHWH will appear with a vengeance to turn the current structures of power upside down, so that compassion, humility, and justice will reign in the lives of people who are currently suffering.

Zechariah 12–14: A Final Battle and a New Creation

■ THE TEXT IN ITS ANCIENT CONTEXT

The superscription, "an oracle" (12:1), sets off this block of material (Zechariah 12–14) from that which precedes it. The repeated formula "on that day" (and its variant, "it will be on that day") introduces a variety of eschatological scenarios and also serves to structure the disparate material in these two chapters (Clark).

In 12:2-8, Jerusalem is at the center of the end-time battle waged by God against the nations. Zechariah uses a variety of metaphors to express the ways YHWH will use Jerusalem to execute YHWH's wrath and punishment against "the surrounding peoples." Jerusalem will be a "cup of reeling" (12:2), "a heavy stone" (12:3), and "a blazing pot" (12:6). God's promise to punish the nations physically and brutally does not lead immediately to Judah's restoration and safety. God's plan is to bring people hostile to Judah into the city to start a war there (12:3b) so that the nations will acknowledge that Jerusalem's strength comes from YHWH (12:5). God promises victory to Judah and Jerusalem (12:7).

Texts and traditions about David provide the comparisons for the "shield" God will provide for the inhabitants of Jerusalem (12:8) when God induces the nations to come against the city so that God can destroy them (12:9). The house of David also features prominently in the section on mourning that follows (12:10-14), but the thematic connections between these two halves of the chapter are difficult to discern as Zech. 12:10-14 is concerned that "the house of David" look on and mourn "the one whom they have pierced" (12:10). Some scholars argue that "the pierced one" is a royal figure, perhaps invoking the memory of Gedaliah's assassination (Jer. 41:1-3; Meyers and Meyers). However, the text provides few clues as to the precise identity of this one; rather, it focuses on eliciting feelings and actions of deep mourning from the people. Perhaps as a means of preparation for the new age, Zechariah calls the community to recognize and grieve for the one(s) on whom they have inflicted violence. It may be that "the spirit of compassion and supplication" God pours out on them enables them to view in a new light not only their own persecution but also their past involvement in the oppression of others. Alternatively, it may seek to present a particular manifestation of the suffering and mourning to be endured by the remnant as they await the coming reign of God.

As part of Zechariah's program of renewal, the city will be cleansed of its impurity with a salvation-flowing fountain (13:1-2). While this is a comforting image, the majority of the material in chapter 13 emphasizes a theme that will become a hallmark for apocalyptic literature, namely, the idea that a time of great suffering and testing for the faithful will precede the arrival of God's reign (Collins).

Zechariah's views of prophecy recall condemnations of false prophecy (Jer. 14:14; 23:16; 27:15; Ezek. 13:6-8) but go far beyond them to declare all prophecy to be deception (13:3-4). The order for parents to pierce their children who prophesy (13:3) recalls the physical afflictions of the one pierced (12:10), but it rings of brutality in the absence of mourning rituals to mark the violence. The preparation for God's new order entails a complete change in the religious order of business. In particular, the enforced censure of prophets entails a suspension of all attempts to discern God's will. The faithful will be utterly in the dark as to when the suffering will end, and they will be without divine reassurance about their fate.

In Zech. 13:7-9, the prophet returns to the theme that the coming ruler will suffer a sacrificial death (12:10—13:1). God calls on a sword to strike "my shepherd" and "the man who is my associate" (13:7) in order that the leaders' people (the sheep) will be scattered. Only a remnant will survive (a third of the population, 13:8) to be refined and tested (13:9). Religious leaders of all stripes, royal and prophetic, will be cleared away to make space for God alone to rule over the new order.

The book's drama culminates in Zechariah 14. The final battle in which all the nations will come against Jerusalem recalls chapter 12. However, in this final scene, there are no human leaders in view. The lack of references to the house of David, shepherds, royal figures, and prophets indicates that all leadership positions have been washed away. Chapter 14 exalts YHWH *alone* as king.

The chapter begins with, and intersperses throughout, graphic images of the intense suffering of the people in the city of Jerusalem (14:1-2, 12). As in 12:2-8, God enters the fray of battle, this time in giant human form, standing on the Mount of Olives, dividing the land (14:4) and shaking the earth with the force of an earthquake (14:5). In 14:10, the whole land will be turned into a plain so that the mountain of Zion will tower over all, aligning its physical prominence with its status as the holy mountain and the center of the world. The result will be the perpetual shalom and security of its inhabitants (14:11).

This radical act of divine intervention results in a radical reordering of creation. Polarities, like day and night (14:7) and holy and profane (14:21), are eliminated, while other divisions are implemented in the land itself (14:4) and in the course of the living waters flowing from Jerusalem (14:8; see also 14:13, 17). The book concludes with the temple's holiness extending beyond the temple altar to the courts and out into Jerusalem. Even everyday cooking pots become as holy as temple vessels (14:21).

Zechariah's radical eschatological vision of a new creation, which bridges priestly and apocalyptic modes of thinking, stipulates an equally radical program for cleansing the people and the land after generations of evil deeds (1:4; Cook 1995). Instead of human agents acting on God's behalf to govern all creation (e.g., Gen. 1:26-27), in Zechariah, it is God who will assume the duties of earthly governance (14:9). As a result, transcendence will no longer be an experience limited to the temple; rather, that transcendence will flow out from the temple and pervade the earthly realm. In Zechariah's imagination, this paradox of immanence and transcendence requires dramatic acts of purification.

▌THE TEXT IN THE INTERPRETIVE TRADITION

Several allusions to Zechariah 12–14 appear in the Gospels to emphasize the belief that the Hebrew Scriptures foretold and prefigured Jesus' death and crucifixion. The pierced one in 12:10 is equated with Jesus in John 19:37. The striking down of the shepherd (13:7-9) figures in the story of the passion, in particular in the accounts of Jesus' abandonment by his followers at the time of his death (Matt. 26:31; Mark 14:27).

Allusions to the paired themes of messianic suffering and the redemption of Israel in Zech. 12:10 are also evident in rabbinic texts about Messiah ben Joseph, including *Aggadat Mashiah* and *Sefer Zerubbabel*. Expanding on Zech. 12:10, the targumic Tosefta to Zechariah identifies the one pierced as Messiah bar Ephraim, likely the same figure whom the Talmud later identifies as Messiah ben Joseph, said to die in an eschatological battle ("And they will look to me and inquire of me why the nations pierced Messiah bar Ephraim, and they will mourn for him"; Mitchell 2006, 223).

Images of the end times and the last battle in Zechariah 9–14, along with those in Revelation, figure prominently in the theologies of dispensationalism and millennialism. Martin Luther also believed that the events of Zechariah 14 applied to a future as yet unrealized and provided an account of the period of history beginning with the New Testament era and ending in the second coming of Christ. By contrast, John Calvin saw the promises of chapter 14 as fulfilled in the past through God's restoration of Israel to the land in the wake of the exile (Wolters).

■ THE TEXT IN CONTEMPORARY DISCUSSION

In a world saturated with religious violence, it is difficult to imagine how Zechariah might function in a theologically constructive way. And yet, the text might function positively if readers approach it, not as a model for how the world ought to be, but rather as a means to examine deeply held assumptions about the ways violence figures into rubrics of salvation. In the Bible, acts of brutality frequently precede redemption. Indeed, the crucifixion of Jesus himself, which is linked to an ultimate act of salvation, testifies to the pervasiveness of the biblical connection between destruction and renewal. Honestly confronting and grappling with the disturbing aspects of one's religious tradition can positively inform, even transform, the faith and practice of religious communities.

What disgusts many contemporary readers about biblical texts like this one is the graphic imagery used to depict the consequences of violence. The realities of war are not hidden or sanitized or explained in rational terms: women are raped (14:2), live human bodies rot like corpses (14:12), and neighbors will kill each other to survive (14:13). While Zechariah views violence and suffering as precursors to salvation, he does not gloss over the impact of war or rush to the happy ending. By contrast, modern warfare allows most of the United States' upper classes to ignore the cost to human bodies, which are regularly mutilated, broken, and blown to pieces. While we may be tempted to condemn Zechariah for being too violent, it is significant that the prophet makes us look when we would prefer to look away. Perhaps it is in the act of seeing suffering that we might find our way to redemption.

Works Cited

Clark, David. 1988. "Discourse Structure in Zech 9-14: Skeleton or Phantom?" in *Issues in Bible Translation*, edited by P. Steine, 64–80. UBS Monograph Series 3. London: United Bible Societies.

Coggins, R. J., and Jin Hee Han. 2011. *Six Minor Prophets through the Centuries*. Malden, MA: Wiley-Blackwell.

Collins, John J. 1998. *The Apocalyptic Imagination: An Introduction to Jewish Apocalyptic Literature*. Grand Rapids: Eerdmans.

Cook, Stephen L. 1995. *Prophecy and Apocalypticism: The Postexilic Social Setting*. Minneapolis: Fortress Press.

———. 2011. "Zechariah." In *The Oxford Encyclopedia of the Books of the Bible*, edited by Michael Coogan. New York: Oxford University Press. www.oxfordreference.com/view/10.1093/acref:o bso/9780195377378.001.0001/acref-9780195377378-e-57.

Ferreiro, Alberto, ed. 2003. *The Twelve Prophets*. Ancient Christian Commentary on Scripture, Old Testament 14. Downers Grove, IL: InterVarsity Press.

Floyd, Michael H. 2000. *Minor Prophets*. Vol. 2. Grand Rapids: Eerdmans.

Hanson, Paul. 1973. "Zechariah 9 and the Recapitulation of an Ancient Ritual Pattern." *JBL* 92:37–59.

Mason, Rex. 2003. "The Use of Earlier Biblical Material in Zechariah 9–14: A Study in Inner Biblical Exegesis." In *Bringing Out the Treasure: Inner Biblical Allusion in Zechariah 9–14*, edited by Mark J. Boda, and Michael H. Floyd, 1-208. London: Sheffield Academic.

Meyers, Carol L., and Eric M. Meyers. 1993. *Zechariah 9–14: A New Translation with Introduction and Commentary*. AB. New York: Doubleday.

Mitchell, David C. 2006. "Messiah bar Ephraim in the Targums," Aramaic Studies 4.2:211–28.

Niditch, Susan. 1983. *The Symbolic Vision in Biblical Tradition*. Chico, CA: Scholars Press.

———. 2011. "Good Blood, Bad Blood: Multivocality, Metonymy, and Mediation in Zechariah 9." *VT* 61:629–45.

Ollenburger, Ben C. 1996. "The Book of Zechariah." In *New Interpreter's Bible*. Vol. 7, *Introduction to Apocalyptic Literature, Daniel, the Twelve Prophets*, edited by Leander E. Keck, 733–840. Nashville: Abingdon.

Petersen, David L. 1984. *Haggai and Zechariah 1–8: A Commentary*. Philadelphia: Westminster Press.

———. 1995. *Zechariah 9–14 and Malachi: A Commentary*. Louisville: Westminster John Knox.

Redditt, Paul L. 2008. *Introduction to the Prophets*. Grand Rapids: Eerdmans.

Schramm, Brooks, and Kirsi Irmeli Stjerna. 2012. *Martin Luther, the Bible, and the Jewish People: A Reader*. Minneapolis: Fortress Press.

Sherwood, Aaron. 2012. *Paul and the Restoration of Humanity in Light of Ancient Jewish Traditions*. Leiden: Brill.

Sommer, Benjamin D. 1998. *A Prophet Reads Scripture: Allusion in Isaiah 40–66*. Stanford: Stanford University Press.

Stead, Michael R. 2009. *The Intertextuality of Zechariah 1–8*. New York: T&T Clark.

Wolters, A. 2002. "Zechariah 14: A Dialogue with the History of Interpretation." *Mid-America Journal of Theology* 13:42–55.

MALACHI

Richard J. Coggins and
Jin Hee Han

Introduction

It is universally agreed that Malachi is to be dated within what is often referred to as the "postexilic" period of Israel's history. It is perhaps better to think of this as the Persian or Second Temple period; "postexilic" seems to imply a universal exile of the community, whereas the great majority of the population remained in Palestine through the political turmoil of the sixth century BCE. By the time of Malachi's writing, however, this turmoil had died down; the book refers to a "governor" (*peḥâ* 1:8) whose position seems to be taken for granted as that of the established ruler. Since the governor is not named, one cannot establish a more precise date—attempts to date Malachi by reference to the various reforms described in Ezra and Nehemiah (see *b. Meg.* 15a) have largely been abandoned because of uncertainties relating to those books. The earliest reference to "the Twelve" as a collection is found in a deuterocanonical book (Sir. 49:10), so by then it seems that Malachi was established as part of a larger collection. It is widely held that the fifth century BCE is the most likely date, but any time during the period of Persian rule—that is, from the sixth century down to the conquests of Alexander the Great (c. 330 BCE)—is possible.

The uncertainty with regard to a precise historical setting has been one of the causes of a different approach to Malachi (and other prophetic collections) in recent study. The twelve Minor Prophets have usually been treated entirely independently of each other, implying that the "eighth-century prophets" such as Amos or Hosea would have had no connection with much later works such as Malachi. Even when historical approaches were still the norm, links were noted between Malachi and what immediately precedes it: Zech. 9:1 and 12:1, as well as Mal. 1:1, are all introduced by the word *maśśā'*, usually translated "oracle," though there was no suggestion of identical authorship. A number of recent studies have maintained that one should take more seriously the idea of a "Book of the Twelve," noting links between the different components (see Nogalski 1993a; 1993b). On such a literary reading, Malachi is to be seen as the end point of a coherent literary collection rather than as an isolated unit. It is too early to say whether this approach will become more general; it should certainly be borne in mind as an alternative to more customary readings.

In any case, the fact that virtually all the collections of the twelve Minor Prophets place Malachi at the end has been important in traditional Christian interpretation. In Judaism, the Prophets are followed by the Writings, so that the overall structure is different. Protestant Christians, reading through their Bible, found Malachi immediately followed by the Gospel of Matthew, and it was natural to conclude that such passages as the hoped-for return of Elijah (4:5) were prefiguring the world of the New Testament.

It may be helpful to note that, whereas historical-critical scholarship has claimed to identify later additions to many prophetic collections, it is usually held that virtually the whole of Malachi is likely to come from one period. Malachi 4:4-6 to some extent stands apart as a kind of appendix, either to the book or to the Book of the Twelve as a whole, and there are a few breaks in the flow that will be noted below; otherwise, whereas some prophetic books can readily be divided into different "sense units," that is scarcely possible here. One possible way of dividing the book is offered below, but the book exists more naturally as a whole.

Malachi 1:1-5: God Loves Israel

■ THE TEXT IN ITS ANCIENT CONTEXT

Is "Malachi" a personal name (1:1)? Many have supposed that the word (which does not occur as a personal name elsewhere in the Hebrew Bible) is best understood as "my messenger" (as in 3:1) and only came to be understood as a personal name when these oracles were taken to be a distinct collection (see 2 Esd. 1:40). Certainty is impossible; what is clear is that there is no basis for developing a "personality" approach such as used to be popular with many prophetic figures. However that may be, it is noteworthy that the message is addressed to "Israel." This is clearly no longer a reference to the northern kingdom of Israel and its inhabitants; Malachi is in the middle of the process that led to Israel being characteristically the name of a religious grouping. One feature of that process is brought out well in 1:2-5. Part of the language is appropriate for a political entity, with the reference to the futile rebuilding of ruins of Edom and "the borders of Israel" (1:4-5).

■ THE TEXT IN THE INTERPRETIVE TRADITION

The Septuagint construes "Malachi" as a common noun and translates "his messenger," forming a link between 1:1 and 3:1 ("my messenger"). Most versions regard it as a personal name, and some suspect that the idea of his anonymity led to an unfortunate situation in which "these chapters have been taken less seriously than they deserve" (Baldwin, 221).

Malachi 1:2-3 makes a clear allusion to the stories in Genesis that set out the basis of the hostility between Jacob and Esau, the latter seen as the ancestor of Edom (Gen. 25:19—28:9). Whereas at an earlier period the main concerns of biblical scholarship were historical, and diligent efforts were made to find a plausible historical context involving a dispute between Israel and Edom in the Persian period, recent scholarship has to a much greater extent been concerned with drawing out literary linkages. In Jewish liturgy, the Torah lesson from Gen. 25:19—28:9 (*parashat toledoth*) is paired with Mal. 1:1—2:7 as the *haftarah* (reading from the Prophets) that connects God's election of Israel with the divine demand of faithfulness.

▌THE TEXT IN CONTEMPORARY DISCUSSION

It is likely that a major concern for the modern audience is the assertion put into God's mouth: "I have loved Jacob but I have hated Esau" (1:2-3), a judgment whose difficulty is made even more acute by Paul's use of this passage for an elaborate theological reflection (Rom. 9:13). Those without any personal religious commitment may be content simply to observe that strong nationalistic feelings can be attributed to gods as much as to humans; religious believers will be more reluctant to think in this way of the one whom they worship. It has been proposed that "hate" here can be understood as "love less" (Kaiser 1984, 27), but there are no clear grounds for understanding the Hebrew verb (*sānā'*, "hate") in this sense. It may be relevant that the strong covenantal language found later in the book (Mal. 2:4-11) implies not only the election of Israel but also the implicit rejection of other communities. By contrast, in one popular introduction to Judaism, Malachi is cited for contending that "all nations have a share in God's goodness" based on the theology of "God as the One Father, the Creator of all" (Levine, 49).

Malachi 1:6—2:9: God's Demand of Proper Worship

▌THE TEXT IN ITS ANCIENT CONTEXT

The prophetic charge of Israel's dishonoring of God (1:6a) unveils aberrations in the practice of worship (1:7-9). Their heinous offense is compounded by the priests' failure or refusal to recognize the wrong (1:6b-7) even as they sacrifice blemished animals (1:8). Although prophetic condemnations of the sacrificial cult are well known (e.g., Isa. 1:11; Amos 5:21-24), Mal. 1:6-10 differs from the others in that what is here condemned is the unacceptable quality of the offerings being made (see Lev. 1:3, 10). The prophet compares the unacceptable worship to the unlikely scenario of gifting the governor with a damaged good (Mal. 1:8), although there is no obvious parallel elsewhere in the Hebrew Bible to the presentation here of offerings to God and to the secular authorities being set out as matters of comparison. God demands penitence (1:9) and the cessation of the corrupt cult (1:10).

Malachi 1:11 seems to have been the subject of greater attention than any other in this prophetic book, and there is still no agreement as to how its implications are to be understood. What is clear is that a sweeping claim is being made as to the power and extent of the rule of YHWH of hosts. It may also be relevant to note the similarity between Ps. 50:1 and the beginning of Mal. 1:11. There, too, the universality of the rule of YHWH and its implications are set out; the claims of the Jerusalem cult and its priests to be the sole means of access to God's favor cannot be upheld. One may note also that three times in the verse stress is laid on the "name" of God; increasingly in

Jewish practice, any direct reference to God——or usage of the divine name itself—was avoided, and circumlocutions such as that found here became customary.

It is clear from Mal. 1:12 that a contrast with contemporary Jerusalem practice is intended. The remainder of the chapter continues the condemnation of the current worship being offered (1:12-14; see also 1:6-10). It is striking that both the quality of the offerings and the attitude of those making the offerings are strongly condemned. As noted above, whereas in other prophetic condemnations of the worship being offered it seems as if no form of sacrifice could be acceptable to God, here the implication is that better-quality offerings and a different mental attitude would be acceptable.

In 2:1-2, God gives a stern warning to the priests, who assumed an increasingly important and often contested role in the Judaism of the last centuries BCE. That there were divisions within the community as to the proper exercise of the priestly role is evident both from 2:1-9 and other writings of the period. The distinction between priests and Levites is not always clear in much of the Hebrew Bible. Although the reference to "the covenant with Levi" (2:4; "the covenant of Levi," 2:8) has no obvious parallel elsewhere, this is one of a number of passages in Malachi that suggest links with the Deuteronomic tradition rather than with the Priestly code. It may well be, though it cannot be proved, that the idea of what should be called "Scripture" was becoming established, and part of Malachi's concern was to draw out for the community of his own time the implications of earlier texts. This may also help to account for an unusual feature of the book—the prominence of the series of questions and answers, expressed as if the audience should know how to behave but are neglecting to apply that knowledge. In general, the themes tie in with the emphases of Deuteronomy, though it will be shown below that the view of divorce set out here is at odds with that found in Deut. 24:1-4.

▮ The Text in the Interpretive Tradition

One widely held approach has been to interpret Mal. 1:11 in a Christian context and to see it as prefiguring the Catholic Mass; it was much used in the sixteenth century CE at the time of the Protestant Reformation in controversies relating to proper forms of worship. Much Old Testament (and here that expression is more appropriate than "Hebrew Bible") material has been understood as relating to events from a completely different period. This may be acceptable if one's approach is purely literary, although it is clearly far from historical-critical approaches.

Other interpretations of this verse may be more plausible if the aim is to discover a possible "original" intention. It could be understood as setting out a surely rather overstated view of what came to be known as the Diaspora; Jewish communities came to be established all round the Mediterranean world, though the evidence for this is later than any plausible date for Malachi. It is also worth bearing in mind that there are other texts which imply that pagan worship may be better than the state to which the Jerusalem temple had descended. Jonah's view of the sailors and the people of Nineveh would be an obvious example (Rudolph 1975, 263).

▮ The Text in Contemporary Discussion

Malachi's vision has also been construed as the worship of God worldwide (Kaiser 1996, 348). One modern scholar has called this "an instance of religious liberalism unparalleled in the Old

Testament," and adds that "the author would have undoubtedly repudiated the implications of this utterance in a calmer and more reflective mood" (Pfeiffer, 613). The thought, at one time quite widely maintained, that Mal. 1:11 is suggesting that all forms of worship are acceptable, has not found any recent advocates among critical scholars, but may provide a basis for common ground among those religious groups who are in the midst of schism and intra- or interconflict.

Malachi 2:10-16: Fidelity in Marriage

▌ THE TEXT IN ITS ANCIENT CONTEXT

After the rather generalized condemnations of Mal. 2:1-9, matters become much more explicit in 2:10-16. The reference to the "daughter of a foreign god" (2:11) has elicited a wide variety of interpretations. One possibility is that in some quarters YHWH was thought to have a female consort, but this would have been a quite unacceptable view for Malachi. There is some evidence from earlier times to suggest such an understanding of YHWH (see Meshel), but none from this period, and the more usual view among commentators has been that the reference is either to marriage with foreign wives or the (perhaps surreptitious) worship of foreign deities. Certainty is impossible, and the extremely cryptic form of 2:12 does not help. There are not many major problems with the Hebrew text of Malachi, but this verse presents one such. Two words in Hebrew (ʿēr and ʿōneh) are translated by NRSV as "any to witness or answer," and a glance at different translations will show how uncertain the meaning is (for example, "the master and the scholar" in the KJV based on the Vulgate).

The terms of the rejection of divorce in 2:16 as something that YHWH detests are somewhat unexpected. The prophet condemns divorce in that it "serves to veil something that is amiss" (Petersen, 205). As noted above, some of the concerns link Malachi with Deuteronomy; here it seems as if there is a sharp disagreement with Deut. 24:1-4. There it appears that the possibility of divorce is taken for granted and the procedure for carrying it out is laid down; here (whether the third person of the Hebrew text or the first person favored by many translations including the NRSV is followed) it seems clear that the very possibility of divorce is rejected.

▌ THE TEXT IN THE INTERPRETIVE TRADITION

In ancient versions, Mal. 2:16 is mostly interpreted as a concession of divorce. The Septuagint translates, "If you hate, send away." The Targum says, "If you hate her, divorce her." The text in a Qumran scroll (4Q82) is close to the Targum. Jewish scholars have been much exercised about the appropriate understanding of 2:16, but have mostly concluded that it is important that the woman so rejected should receive compassionate treatment. On the Christian side, the great seventeenth-century poet John Milton claimed to follow other contemporary interpreters in reading "he who hates let him divorce" (11), and justified this on the grounds that it was better for the woman to be spared any hard-heartedness (or worse) that might occur if she were in unwilling servitude.

■ THE TEXT IN CONTEMPORARY DISCUSSION

Some refer to the apparent condemnation of divorce in Mal. 2:16 as a biblical teaching that prohibits divorce (see Sassoon, 25); it has even been called "a cosmic argument against divorce" (Lilly, 351), but it is not clear whether the denunciation is about cruelty (Hill, 258), intermarriage (Sweeney, 738), or breach of covenant in divorce (Block, 51). Some argue that this condemns divorce without justification prompted by dislike (Collins, 125). It may also be "the combination of . . . marriage to foreign women who worship 'foreign' gods and . . . 'faithlessness' toward one's own wife" (Wacker, 477).

Malachi 2:17—3:18 God of Covenantal Faithfulness

■ THE TEXT IN ITS ANCIENT CONTEXT

The paragraph divisions in the Masoretic text suggest that Mal. 2:17 should be read along with 3:1-12. The combined section of Mal. 2:17—3:12 is marked by the question-and-answer form typical of Malachi, that much of the people's behavior remains unacceptable (2:17; see also 3:7-9). In English Bibles, Malachi 3 ends with a characteristic warning to the audience (3:13-18).

Whereas the last section of the book is divided into Malachi 3 and 4 in English Bibles, it is one chapter in the Hebrew, and thus forms the conclusion to the middle section of the Hebrew Bible, the *nĕbî'îm*, or Prophets. In English versions, this means that these chapters form the conclusion to the "Old Testament," and this may partly explain that they played a significant part in biblical studies before historical criticism became more or less the only approved approach. It is now almost universally accepted that the book of Daniel only reached its present form in the second century BCE, but when Daniel was taken as a sixth-century creation, Malachi was accepted as the last product of Judaism before what used to be described as the "intertestamental period."

"My messenger" in 3:1 translates "Malachi," and as is shown above it is likely that it was only at a later stage that this was taken to be a proper name (see 2 Esd. 1:40). The identity of this messenger is not revealed until Mal. 4:5, which is perhaps an explanatory gloss on 3:1. The figure expected is no mere bringer of a message (3:2-4). The prophet's words in 3:5 are typical of many prophetic condemnations of false practice, especially in religious matters. It may be that one can establish from 3:5 the particular problems affecting the community in Malachi's time, but to do this may be too specific—each of the evils condemned here could have been found at many different times in the people's history.

Following the affirmation of YHWH's continuing relationship with "the children of Jacob" (3:6), two rather divergent lines are pursued in 3:7-10. Malachi uses language typical of the Deuteronomistic tradition to warn the people against long-established practices regarded as sinful; they are to "return" to the requirements of the statutes laid down from of old (3:7). The verb *šûb*, here translated "return," is common throughout the prophetic collection (e.g., Isa. 1:27; Jer. 3:12; Hosea 6:1), and has been seen by some as supplying a connecting thread binding together the Book of the Twelve as a single coherent collection. It is much disputed whether it implies that at some point in the past the people really had been loyal and obedient, or whether a better translation would be "turn," implying something of a new start. In any case, following the promise of blessing for those who offer tithes and offerings (LXX "tithes and firstfruits," 3:8-10), the next verses have a rather different emphasis, expressing the hope of a universal affirmation of Israel in a way uncommon in the Old Testament prophetic speeches with their overwhelming message of doom (3:11-12).

In Mal. 3:13-15, the prophet returns to the more characteristic note of warning. The values espoused by at least some in the community are to be reversed. The idea of a book (or scroll) of remembrance in 3:16-18 is a new development as far as the Hebrew Bible is concerned, though it is not difficult to envisage how it emerged from such origins as the scroll found in Josiah's time (2 Kings 22).

▌ THE TEXT IN THE INTERPRETIVE TRADITION

Malachi 3:1 has been very important in Christian tradition. Each of the Synoptic Gospels uses this passage to bring out their understanding of the figure of Jesus; the messenger is John the Baptizer, seen here as a precursor of Jesus. Mark, usually taken to be the earliest of the Gospels, attributes the passage to Isaiah (Mark 1:2). Whether this is a simple error or it reflects the way in which "Isaiah" came to be regarded as *the* typical prophet cannot be decided here. In any case, the later Gospels strengthen the association with the prophetic tradition by attributing the citation to Jesus himself (Matt. 11:10; Luke 7:27).

The early Christian writers, except Theodore of Mopsuestia (d. 428) (415), were confident that in Mal. 3:2-4 the reference was to Jesus, but this vivid language was scarcely borne out by what was known of his earthly ministry. From an early stage, therefore, they came to be associated with an anticipated second coming of Jesus, and an understanding of this kind was common through much of Christian history, as is illustrated by the use of this passage in Handel's oratorio *Messiah*, which combines Mal. 3:1-3 with Hag. 2:6-7. This type of usage tended to play down the implications of Mal. 3:4, with its suggestion that the devastation would be followed by a speedy restoration of divine favor.

In later times, such a theme as "a book of remembrance" found in 3:16-18 became prominent, in the Dead Sea scrolls and the New Testament (Rev. 3:5), and of course through much of both Jewish and Christian history (see Daniélou, 198). Another matter that came to be of major significance in many religious traditions has been the distinction between the loyal members of the community ("the righteous"—those who serve God) and the rest ("the wicked"—those who do not). One is not far here from the themes of heresy and schism, which have occupied religious believers down the ages.

▌ THE TEXT IN CONTEMPORARY DISCUSSION

Malachi 3:6 found an unexpected contemporary application when the cricket World Cup played in India in 2011, with vast crowds gathering in Mumbai. Many religions were of course represented, and apparently a large Christian church near the ground had a big neon sign using this verse proclaiming "I am the LORD; I change not" (*Wisden Cricketers' Almanack* 2012, 791, has the reference;

it is not clear whether the sign had any effect!). More conventionally, this stress on the unchange-ability of the God worshiped by Jews and Christians has been used by apologists for those faiths, contrasting them with the fickleness of other forms of belief.

It is noteworthy that those condemned in 3:13-15 raise a question that has constantly arisen in philosophical and theological discussion to this day: Is there any point in following the words of a demanding God when those who are described as evildoers "not only prosper" but are also able to put God to the test with impunity? The claim is that it would be better to recognize that those who take matters into their own hands ("the arrogant") are really the blessed ones.

Malachi 4:1-6: The Day of Healing and Reconciliation

▌ THE TEXT IN ITS ANCIENT CONTEXT

The theme of a day of judgment characterized by the burning of the wicked (Mal. 4:1-3) may be a development of the "day of YHWH" referred to in Amos 5:18; Zeph. 1:14-17; and elsewhere. The final verses of the book (Mal. 4:4-6) are widely regarded as a kind of appendix, perhaps by the same author as the main part of the book, but more probably by a later editor. In any case, it functions as an appendix not just to the book of Malachi, but probably to the Twelve Minor Prophets as a whole, or even to the whole of the prophetic collection, which might include the "Former Prophets" (Joshua–2 Kings), as well as the material that has been customarily considered as "prophetic." The likelihood of its being the whole collection as the appropriate unit has been strengthened by the literary approach to this collection mentioned several times above.

Whereas in Mal. 4:4 the hearers or readers had been instructed to cast their mind back to God's past dealings with the people, in 4:5-6 the emphasis is clearly on the future. It becomes clear in 4:5 why there has been reference to the sending of Elijah, for this was a topic that became prominent later. It may be that he is singled out, not only because of the prominent role he played in the books of Kings, resisting the temptation of alien worship, but also because he is said not to have died but to have been "[taken] up to heaven by a whirlwind" (2 Kgs. 2:1), the obvious implication being that God had some further purpose in mind for him. One needs to bear in mind that to the best of the currently available knowledge there was no established belief in a future life for all at this period.

The final verse (4:6) is distinctly and surely deliberately ambiguous. Many modern translations, including the NRSV, have "children" here, in accordance with twenty-first-century expectations, but the Hebrew speaks of "sons"; in antiquity, the male members of the community were those who spelled out the demands of obedience to the torah. So the book, and the whole prophetic collection (covering from the Former Prophets of Joshua–2 Kings to the Latter Prophets of Isaiah, Jeremiah, Ezekiel, and the Twelve Minor Prophets) ends with the threat of a drastic curse.

▌ THE TEXT IN THE INTERPRETIVE TRADITION

The majority of Christian interpreters down the centuries have understood Mal. 4:1 as a reference to an anticipated time of final judgment. John Calvin took it to mean the first coming, and others regard it as the second coming (see Verhoef, 32). The KJV rendering of the end of 4:1 ("neither root nor branch") has become a standard way of describing the totality of judgment. The seventeenth-century English Long Parliament used the phrase "root and branch" to describe their desire to abolish episcopacy completely, and the situation eventually escalated to civil war.

The fate of the wicked is again the theme of 4:3, but the intervening, much more optimistic, verse (4:2) has been the source of a good deal of later reflection. In particular, the Gospels give no indication of the time of year at which Jesus was born, but his birth has come to be celebrated on December 25, following the winter solstice, and seen as the rising of a new sun of righteousness. Milton took up the theme in his *Ode on the Morning of Christ's Nativity*, and it is also found in the well-known Christmas hymn "Hark, the Herald Angels Sing," with its reference to Christ as "the sun of righteousness."

Malachi 4:5 offers the clearest reference within the Hebrew Bible itself to "the law of Moses." This may be a reference to the whole of the Pentateuch, but the most direct links are with Deuteronomy. As in Deuteronomy, "Horeb" is the name given to the holy mountain, rather than the more familiar "Sinai," and it was of course to Horeb that Elijah fled in 1 Kings 19 from the threat of revenge from Jezebel.

The New Testament Gospels clearly have in mind the expectation of a return of Elijah in Mal. 4:5-6; it is not clear whether the figure of the returning Elijah should be seen as John the Baptizer. Matthew 11:14 appears to accept this identification, and John 1:21 to deny it. In any case, it is noteworthy that in the account of what is usually termed the "transfiguration" of Jesus, Elijah is actually named before Moses (Mark 9:4). In Jewish tradition also, Elijah became important, with particular emphasis on his role in sustaining family life (*m. 'Ed.* 8:7; Danby 1933, 436–37); it is still a widespread custom to lay an extra place for Elijah at the Passover-tide meal.

The book (and the whole prophetic collection) ends with the threat of a drastic curse. Already by the time of the Greek translation (LXX), this was found unacceptable, and it was indicated that 4:4 should be read again after 4:6, to mitigate this threat. Some Jewish Bibles repeat 4:5 again in small print after 4:6, so that the book may end in the note of hope.

▌THE TEXT IN CONTEMPORARY DISCUSSION

Depressingly familiar is the projected fate of those who are regarded as arrogant and evildoers in 4:1-3. By contrast, those who will fear the Lord are expected to experience healing with the return of Elijah. In light of 4:6, it is to be hoped that strong family traditions will ensure that Elijah's warnings will be taken to heart, so that the people may be proactive in seeking reconciliation and healing in broken relationships.

Works Cited

Baldwin, Joyce G. 1972. *Haggai, Zechariah, Malachi: An Introduction and Commentary*. TOTC. London: Tyndale Press.

Block, Daniel I. 2003. "Marriage and Family in Ancient Israel." *Marriage and Family in the Biblical World*, edited by Ken M. Campbell, 53–102. Downers Grove, IL: InterVarsity Press.

Coggins, Richard, and Jin H. Han. 2011. *Six Minor Prophets through the Centuries*. Blackwell Bible Commentaries. Chichester, UK: Wiley-Blackwell.

Collins, John J. 1997. "Marriage, Divorce, and Family in Second Temple Judaism." *Families in Ancient Israel*, by Leo G. Perdue, Joseph Blenkinsopp, John J. Collins, and Carol L. Meyers, 105–62. Louisville: Westminster John Knox.

Danby, Herbert, trans. 1933. *The Mishnah*. Oxford: Oxford University Press.

Daniélou, Jean. 1964. *The Theology of Jewish Christianity*. Vol. 1. London: Darton, Longman & Todd.

Hill, Andrew H. 1998. *Malachi: A New Translation with Introduction and Commentary*. AB 25D. New York: Doubleday.

Kaiser, Walter C., Jr. 1984. *Malachi: God's Unchanging Love*. Grand Rapids: Baker Books.

Kaiser, Walter C., Jr., Peter H. Davids, F. F. Bruce, and Manfred T. Brauch. 1996. *Hard Sayings of the Bible*. Downers Grove, IL: InterVarsity Press.

Levine, Ephraim. 1913. *Judaism*. People's Books 75. London: T. C. and E. C. Jack.

Lilly, Ingrid E. 2012. "Malachi." In *Women's Bible Commentary*, edited by Carol A. Newsom, Sharon H. Ringe, and Jacqueline E. Lapsley, 350–53. Rev. ed. Louisville: Westminster John Knox.

Meshel, Zeev. 1979. "Did Yahweh Have a Consort?" *BAR* 5:24–35.

Milton, John. 1645. *The Doctrine and Discipline of Divorce*. London: n.p.

Nogalski, James D. 1993a. *Literary Precursors to the Book of the Twelve*. BZAW 217. Berlin: de Gruyter.

———. 1993b. *Redactional Processes in the Book of the Twelve*. BZAW 218. Berlin: de Gruyter.

Petersen, David L. 1995. *Zechariah 9–14 and Malachi: A Commentary*. OTL. Louisville: Westminster John Knox.

Pfeiffer, Robert H. 1948. *Introduction to the Old Testament*. New York: Harper & Bros.

Rudolph, Wilhelm. 1975. *Micha, Nahum, Habakuk, Zephanja*. KAT 13/3. Gütersloh: Gütersloher Gerd Mohn.

Sassoon, Isaac. 2011. *The Status of Women in Jewish Tradition*. Cambridge: Cambridge University Press.

Schuller, Eileen M. 1996. "Malachi." *The New Interpreter's Bible*. Vol. 7, *Introduction to Apocalyptic Literature, Daniel, the Twelve Prophets*, edited by Leander E. Keck, 841–77. Nashville: Abingdon.

Sweeney, Marvin A. 2000. *The Twelve Prophets*. Vol. 2, *Micah, Nahum, Habakkuk, Zephaniah, Haggai, Zechariah, Malachi*. Berit Olam. Collegeville, MN: Liturgical Press.

Theodore of Mopsuestia. 2004. *Commentary on the Twelve Minor Prophets*. FC 108. Washington, DC: Catholic University of America Press.

Verhoef, Pieter A. 1987. *The Books of Haggai and Malachi*. NICOT. Grand Rapids: Eerdmans.

Wacker, Marie-Theres. 2012. "Malachi: To the Glory of God, the Father?" In *Feminist Biblical Interpretation: A Compendium of Critical Commentary on the Books of the Bible and Related Literature*, edited by Luise Schottroff and Marie-Theres Wacker, 473–82. Grand Rapids: Eerdmans.